lonely planet

Tahiti & French Polynesia

Hilary Rogers
Jean-Bernard Carillet
Tony Wheeler

LONELY PLANET PUBLICATIONS
Melbourne • Oakland • London • Paris

FRENCH POLYNESIA

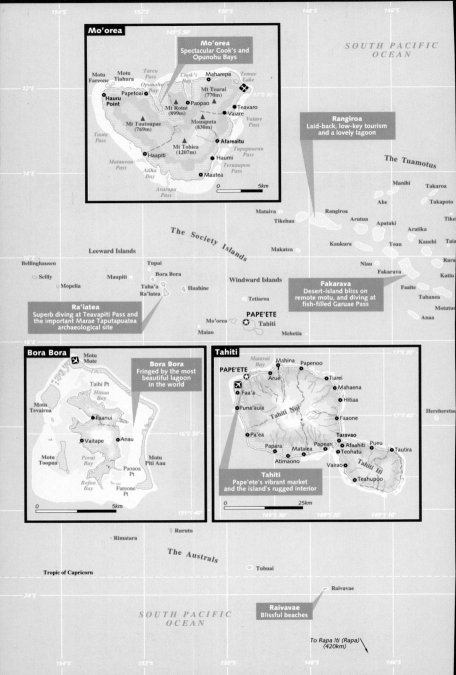

Mo'orea

Mo'orea
Spectacular Cook's and Opunohu Bays

SOUTH PACIFIC OCEAN

Motu Fareone · Motu Tiahura · *Tareu Pass* · *Opunohu Bay* · Cook's Bay · Maharepa · *Temae Lake*

Papetoai
Hauru Point
Mt Tearai (770m)
Paopao · Teavaro
Mt Rotui (899m) · Vaiare
Mt Tautuapae (769m) · Mouaputa (830m) · *Vaiare Pass*
Taota Pass · Afareaitu · *Tupapaurau Pass*
Mt Tohiea (1207m) · Haumi · *Temaupou Pass*
Matauvau Pass · Haapiti · *Atiha Bay* · Maatea
Avarapa Pass

0 — 5km

Rangiroa
Laid-back, low-key tourism and a lovely lagoon

The Tuamotus

Manihi · Takaroa
Mataiva · Rangiroa · Ahe · Takapoto
Tikehau · Arutua · Apataki · Tike
Makatea · Kaukura · Toau · Aratika · Kauehi · Taia

The Society Islands

Leeward Islands

Bellinghausen · Tupai · Niau · Rara
Scilly · Bora Bora · Fakarava · Katiu
Mopelia · Maupiti · Huahine · Windward Islands · Faaite · Faite · Tahanea
Taha'a · Ra'iatea · **Fakarava** · Motutu
Tetiaroa · Anaa

Ra'iatea
Superb diving at Teavapiti Pass and the important Marae Taputapuatea archaeological site

Fakarava
Desert-island bliss on remote motu, and diving at fish-filled Garuae Pass

Mo'orea · **PAPE'ETE** · Tahiti
Maiao · Mehetia

Bora Bora

Motu Mute
Taihi Pt
Hitiaa Bay
Motu Tevairoa
Faanui
Vaitape · Anau
Povai Bay
Motu Toopua
Motu Piti Aau
Paoaoa Pt
Rofau Bay · Fareone Pt

Bora Bora
Fringed by the most beautiful lagoon in the world

0 — 5km

Tahiti

Matavai Bay · Mahina · Papenoo
PAPE'ETE · Arue · Tiarei
Faa'a · Mahaena
Puna'auia · Hitiaa
Faaone
Tahiti Nui
Pa'ea · Taravao
Papara · Papeari · Pueu
Mataiea · Afaahiti · Tautira
Atimaono · Teohatu
Vairao · *Tahiti Iti*
Teahupoo

Hereheretue

Tahiti
Pape'ete's vibrant market and the island's rugged interior

0 — 25km

Rurutu
Rimatara

The Australs

Tropic of Capricorn · Tubuai

SOUTH PACIFIC OCEAN

Raivavae

Raivavae
Blissful beaches

To Rapa Iti (Rapa) (420km)

Tahiti & French Polynesia
6th edition – May 2003
First published – October 1985

Published by
Lonely Planet Publications Pty Ltd ABN 36 005 607 983
90 Maribyrnong St, Footscray, Victoria 3011, Australia

Lonely Planet Offices
Australia Locked Bag 1, Footscray, Victoria 3011
USA 150 Linden St, Oakland, CA 94607
UK 10a Spring Place, London NW5 3BH
France 1 rue du Dahomey, 75011 Paris

Photographs
Many of the images in this guide are available for licensing from
Lonely Planet Images.
W www.lonelyplanetimages.com

Front cover photograph
Pontoon over the lagoon, Rangiroa in the Tuamotus (Jean-Bernard
Carillet)

ISBN 1 74059 229 8

Contents – Text

Contents – Maps

The Authors

Hilary Rogers
Hilary delights in the details of travelling: murky coffees, feisty taxi drivers, magical carpets. She has spent much of her life gallivanting around the world seeking such experiences. She has lived in the UK, studied in France, traipsed through much of Asia, been fascinated by the Middle East, blown away by the Indian subcontinent and seduced by the Pacific. Travel continues to entice Hilary from her base in Melbourne, Australia, where she works at Lonely Planet as a commissioning editor.

Jean-Bernard Carillet
Jean-Bernard joined Lonely Planet's French office in 1995 as an editor and is now a full-time author. A diving instructor and incorrigible traveller, he will decamp at the slightest opportunity to travel round the world but always returns to his native Lorraine in the east of France. He has also contributed to Lonely Planet's *South Pacific*, *Corsica*, diving & snorkelling guides to French Polynesia and the Red Sea, and several French-language guides.

Tony Wheeler
Tony was born in England but grew up in Pakistan, the Bahamas and the USA. He returned to England to study engineering, worked as an automotive design engineer, completed an MBA then set out with his wife, Maureen, on an Asian overland trip that ultimately led to them founding Lonely Planet in Australia in 1973. They have been travelling, writing and publishing guidebooks ever since.

A long-time Pacific traveller, Tony has contributed to almost every one of Lonely Planet's Pacific guides at one stage or another.

FROM THE AUTHORS

Hilary Rogers

Many thanks to everyone at LP, in particular Errol Hunt, Helen Papadimitriou, Nikki Anderson, Leonie Mugavin (who waved her magic wand over the Getting There & Away chapter), and Virginia Maxwell and Robert Reid (who let me leave Africa in the lurch in the first place). Thanks also to Jean-Bernard Carillet for his suggestions and guidance. In French Polynesia, thanks to the impeccably well organised Tahiti Tourisme, in particular Torea, who was ever cheerful and helpful; François 'la bonne' guide, who stepped in just when I needed help; the women at Manava Visitors Bureau; and to Chloé, *compagnon* extraordinaire. Finally, thanks to Nick, dedicated proofer and delightful partner.

Jean-Bernard Carillet

A heartfelt *mauruuru roa* to Yan, my *faaamu* brother, and to Vaianu, for help and support. I am also indebted to Hubert and Majo and all the *fetii*, including Sean, Maryvonne and Alain, Christian and Bella, and the grandmother. I would also like to thank Yves Lefèvre, Patrick Marinthe and Maud, Moearii Darius, Marie-Claude Rajaud, Simone Chan, Sandrine Dupain, Laetitia Scuiller, Christian Vagman, Herenui, Eric Heranval, Jacques Mendiola and Patricia Ehl, among others, together with Tepupu, Valerie and Reata. I also want to express my sincere admiration to Rodrigue Ah-Min, Louise Kimitete and Fabien Dinard, the fabulous dancers. Thanks also to Frederique, Sophie, Geraldine, Thomas, Sandrine, Zahia, Caroline, Arno, Soph, Valerie, and fabulous Cecile for her dedication.

This Book

This 6th edition of *Tahiti & French Polynesia* was updated by Hilary Rogers and Jean-Bernard Carillet. Hilary updated the Facts about French Polynesia, Facts for the Visitor, Tahiti, Mo'orea, Bora Bora and the Rangiroa section of the Tuamotus chapter; Jean-Bernard updated the rest. Jenny Mullaly translated Jean-Bernard's updates into English. Tony Wheeler, coauthor of the 4th edition, contributed supplementary material.

FROM THE PUBLISHER

This book was produced in Lonely Planet's Melbourne office. Brigitte Barta coordinated the editing, Kusnandar coordinated the mapping and Nick Stebbing coordinated layout. The book was commissioned by Errol Hunt. Isabelle Young was the managing editor and Huw Fowles was the project manager. Margaret Toohey and Cherry Prior lent a hand with editing the book, and Kim Hutchins, Jocelyn Harewood, Rebecca Chau and Bruce Evans proofed it. Brigitte did the index. Cameron Duncan helped with layout, and Maria Vallianos designed the cover. Climate charts were produced by Kusnandar, with some assistance from Chris Lee Ack. The managing cartographer was Corie Waddell, who also assisted in commissioning the book. Kate Mc-Donald, Isabelle Young, Darren O'Connell and Huw Fowles did the layout checks. Quentin Frayne provided the language chapter. Thanks also to Jacqui Saunders and Sally Morgan, who helped with last-minute layout corrections.

THANKS

Ted Baglin, David & Mary Bargman, Peggy Bendall, Suzanne Bermingham, Bev Blythe, Monica Breitenstein, Shyrel Burt, Ann Cabot, Edmur Caniato Arantes, Joesph Chong, Daniel Christen, Cis Cis, Liliane Roy Condron, Christopher Cooper, Claude Corneglia, Luis Costa, Charlotte Cotton, Ted Davis, Allison Dobbie, Graham Dowden, Rueben Driedger, J Edwards, Ken E Edwards, Dirk Elaut, Dr Tony Feeney, Mitt German, David Gidmark, Cathy Gray, Eva Hampel, Geoff Hawthorn, Keith Hetherington, Gavin Hirst, Melissa Hockey, Tim Hogard, Julie Horn, Bill Hoskins, Brian Jackson, Ann Jeffrey, Daniel Joli, Wayne Jordan, Martha Kernohan, Vicky Lamb, Patricia Laporte, Manfred Lenzen, Milton Lever, Karen Levine, Kathryn Lewis, Lorraine Little, Magnus Lofgvist, Laura Losee, Ian Mackersey, Diana Maestre, William P Main, Vainui Marakai, Michael Marquardt, Allegra Marshall, Nick Martin, Pat Mathews, Peter Mayes, R E McGeorge, Jerry Muller, Maite Navarrete, Tony O'Toole, Steen Overballe, Bill Owens, Patrik Persson, Werner Platner, Chris Pouney, Lawrence Powell, Vendula Ralkova, Sofia Rehn, Laura Reyno, Joanna Rischitelli, Jean-Francois Sauvage, Christian Schober, Prof Gour C Sen, Peter Skinner, Rob Smallwood, Erin Smith, Federica Spagni, M A Stewart, Neil Thistle, Béatrice Trombetta, Rhonda & Peter Turner, Erwin van Engelen, Gavin Vessey, Peter Wakeman, Bonnie & John Williams, Maurice Wilson, Judi Wolford, Kathleen Yasuda

Foreword

ABOUT LONELY PLANET GUIDEBOOKS

The story begins with a classic travel adventure: Tony and Maureen Wheeler's 1972 journey across Europe and Asia to Australia. There was no useful information about the overland trail then, so Tony and Maureen published the first Lonely Planet guidebook to meet a growing need.

From a kitchen table, Lonely Planet has grown to become the largest independent travel publisher in the world, with offices in Melbourne (Australia), Oakland (USA), London (UK) and Paris (France).

Today Lonely Planet guidebooks cover the globe. There is an ever-growing list of books and information in a variety of media. Some things haven't changed. The main aim is still to make it possible for adventurous travellers to get out there – to explore and better understand the world.

At Lonely Planet we believe travellers can make a positive contribution to the countries they visit – if they respect their host communities and spend their money wisely. Since 1986 a percentage of the income from each book has been donated to aid projects and human rights campaigns, and, more recently, to wildlife conservation.

Although inclusion in a guidebook usually implies a recommendation we cannot list every good place. Exclusion does not necessarily imply criticism. In fact there are a number of reasons why we might exclude a place – sometimes it is simply inappropriate to encourage an influx of travellers.

UPDATES & READER FEEDBACK

Things change – prices go up, schedules change, good places go bad and bad places go bankrupt. Nothing stays the same. So, if you find things better or worse, recently opened or long-since closed, please tell us and help make the next edition even more accurate and useful.

Lonely Planet thoroughly updates each guidebook as often as possible – usually every two years, although for some destinations the gap can be longer. Between editions, up-to-date information is available in our free, monthly email bulletin *Comet* (w www.lonelyplanet.com/newsletters). You can also check out the *Thorn Tree* bulletin board and *Postcards* section of our website, which carry unverified, but fascinating, reports from travellers.

Tell us about it! We genuinely value your feedback. A well-travelled team at Lonely Planet reads and acknowledges every email and letter we receive and ensures that every morsel of information finds its way to the relevant authors, editors and cartographers.

Everyone who writes to us will find their name listed in the next edition of the appropriate guidebook. The very best contributions will be rewarded with a free guidebook.

We may edit, reproduce and incorporate your comments in Lonely Planet products such as guidebooks, websites and digital products, so let us know if you don't want your comments reproduced or your name acknowledged.

How to contact Lonely Planet:
Online: e talk2us@lonelyplanet.com.au, w www.lonelyplanet.com
Australia: Locked Bag 1, Footscray, Victoria 3011
UK: 10a Spring Place, London NW5 3BH
USA: 150 Linden St, Oakland, CA 94607

Introduction

It's hard to believe that places like French Polynesia actually exist. Pin cushions of land, dotted with palm trees, in an impossibly clear, aqua lagoon? Tropical fruit dripping from the trees? Butterscotch limbs stretched out in the sun? Only in your fantasies, you may think.

French Polynesia is like a choose-your-own adventure. You can paint the town red in the glamorous restaurants and seedy bars of the cacophonous capital Pape'ete, whittle away lazy days on a remote atoll, or splash around ogling big, bright fish. No matter where you go, the air is heavy with not only tropical humidity but also romance and history.

The ancient sacred sites and marae will give would-be historians plenty to ponder; dazzling accommodation options will keep honeymooners indoors (despite the perfect weather outside); and the lack of nasty beasts will reassure parents while the kids splash around in the saltwater heaven of alluring lagoons.

Although 'French Polynesia' may draw a blank, 'Tahiti' gets the mind wandering, as it has done for centuries. Tahiti captured the imaginations of repressed 19th-century Europeans when explorers began returning home with vivid depictions of a paradise on earth where life was simple, the water was aqua, and sex was plentiful and guilt-free. Ever since, artists and travellers have flocked to Polynesia, escaping the constraints of 'civilised' society, to paint the tableau of a career or pen the novel of a lifetime.

Famous for luring painters such as Paul Gauguin and writers such as Herman Melville and Robert Louis Stevenson, and inciting uprisings such as the famous mutiny on the *Bounty*, French Polynesia has also been heaped with layer upon layer of colonialisation – territorial, political, religious, moral, financial – during centuries spent as a pawn on the European colonial chessboard. Just as Gauguin presented Europe with a romanticised version of an exotic and erotic paradise, the brochures of

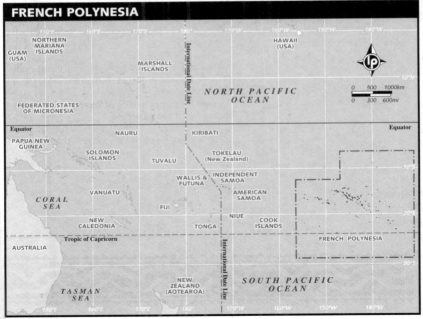

today continue to promise an unblemished region. Beneath this surface, however (if you wish to look), lie more complex economic and social undercurrents.

It's no wonder the colonial world vied to gain control of this area. Its incredible, wildly varying beauty ranges from the postcard greens and blues of the Society Islands to the transparent lagoons and white-sand motu (islets) in the low-lying atolls of the Tuamotus. Further northeast lie the remote and mysterious Marquesas, and to the south, on the other-worldly Austral Islands and in the Gambier Archipelago, time ticks slowly by.

Tourism is a particularly luxurious affair in French Polynesia, allowing new heights of decadence: days spent on uninhabited islands, afternoons spent sipping umbrella-shaded drinks, and evenings spent drinking French wines and gorging on freshly caught seafood. If you're penny counting, you can stay in quaint bungalows on the beach and whip up your own feasts every night from the lagoon's fruits of the sea.

Pack your bags today, but before you go beware: you may feel like mounting your own mutiny instead of returning home at the end of your stay.

Facts about French Polynesia

HISTORY

The idyllic, isolated islands of Polynesia form a triangle from Hawaii in the north, Aotearoa (New Zealand) in the west and Rapanui (Easter Island) in the east. These islands were among the last places on earth to be settled by humans and, a thousand or so years later, were also some of the last places to be colonised by Europeans.

Within this immense area, Polynesians – Samoans, Tongans, Tahitians, Marquesans, Hawaiians, and Cook Island and New Zealand Maori – all come from common ancestors, and all speak related languages.

The Polynesians

Archaeologists, linguists and anthropologists have argued for years about where the ancestors of today's Polynesians came from; *why* they came to the area is an even more intriguing question. Whether motivated by territorial conflict, overpopulation or mere curiosity, these waves of migration were proof of a remarkable maritime prowess, only matched by the Europeans more than a thousand years later.

Conjecture that these first migrations originated in South America has long been discredited, and it's generally agreed that the Polynesians' ancestors came from present-day Indonesia and the Philippines. These long voyages were phenomenal feats of navigation and endurance, and were no haphazard affair: the coconuts, *uru* (breadfruit), taro, sugar cane, dogs, pigs and chickens that remain an integral part of life in Polynesia today were all carried on the pirogues, and all originated in Southeast Asia. Polynesia's westernmost islands – Samoa and Tonga – were populated around 1500 BC, via Melanesia (modern Papua New Guinea, the Solomon Islands and Vanuatu) and Fiji. The eastern islands, including the Society Islands, Marquesas, Hawaii and Easter Island, were then populated between 200 BC and AD 400. Although we'll never know, the massive expanses of ocean and the tiny patches of land that characterise the region must have meant these migrations sometimes failed, ending in starvation and shipwreck.

Without a written Polynesian language to provide a record, historians struggle to understand what kind of life these early settlers led. Most sources stem from European exploration over a thousand years later, sources that are necessarily clouded by the preoccupations and prejudices of 18th-century Europe.

Contact with Europeans

It was around 1500 years later that European explorers first ventured into the region. Lacking the navigation methods that Polynesians had developed over millennia of Pacific travel, the Europeans searched for islands in the Pacific by means of a rather random needle-in-a-haystack method. The navigational instruments of the day were such that, having chanced upon an island, it was equally problematic to locate it on a return trip.

Contact with the Europeans was highly destructive for traditional Polynesian life. The Europeans, on the other hand, celebrated the discovery of a Pacific utopia, and raced back to Europe with reports of sublime women and a harmonious society. Although the Europeans had largely peaceful intentions, these first interactions were often bloody and short; fear of the 'other' and a lack of mutual language brought out the worst in both parties, and the Polynesians didn't stand a chance against European weaponry.

The Spanish The first Europeans to arrive on the scene were Spanish. In 1520, Ferdinand Magellan (who was actually Portuguese, but in the service of the Spanish) sailed across the vast island-dotted ocean. He managed to miss most of the islands in Polynesia, but he did sight Puka Puka in the remote northeast of the Tuamotus.

Magellan was followed by Alvaro de Mendaña y Neira, who sighted the Solomons and, later, the most northeasterly of the Polynesian island groups, which he named Las Marquesas de Mendoza after the Viceroy of Peru. Mendaña's visit was a bloody one: he was of the 'shoot first and ask questions later' school.

In 1606, Mendaña's chief pilot, Quirós, sighted a number of the Tuamotus and the Cooks.

Polynesian Migration

Two factors were crucial to the success of the mass migrations of the Polynesians: the boats themselves and the art of navigation. Ancient Polynesians had a very detailed knowledge of the paths of heavenly bodies, wind direction, and sea and current movement.

Nothing remains of the boats used to make these fascinating voyages. We have to make do with descriptions given by 18th-century Europeans of *va'a* (canoes) that were in use at the time of their arrival. During the Cook period, three types of boats were used: simple monohulls, monohulls with outrigger (float), and double canoes (two canoes firmly joined by a large platform). Monohulls were always paddled, while pirogues (outrigger canoes) and double canoes could be driven by sail or paddle, or both. All materials in the canoes and woven sails were of plant origin, and construction tools were of stone, shell or bone.

Each type of canoe had a precise role. The smallest monohulls (5m to 10m long), either with or without an outrigger, were paddled over short journeys and used for lagoon fishing. Somewhat larger pirogues (10m to 15m) were sailed on short inter-island trips. The longest paddle-driven single canoes (often 30m long) could carry well over 100 people and were used in battle or for ceremonies. Double canoes, forerunners of the catamaran, had two parallel hulls fused together by cross beams or platforms into an integral structure. They could carry up to 70 people and were used for long journeys – on the connecting platform could be carried the plants, seeds and animals (chickens, pigs and dogs) needed to colonise the new land.

Nowadays the canoe is still highly valued symbolically even though it is often made of synthetic materials. It naturally appears as the centrepiece of the French Polynesian flag with five figurines on board, each one representing one of the archipelagos. A major yearly sporting event in French Polynesia is the Hawaiki Nui canoe race, at the beginning of November, in which there are several hundred participants (see the boxed text 'Hawaiki Nui Canoe Race' in the Facts for the Visitor chapter).

The Dutch Already firmly established in the Dutch East Indies (now Indonesia), the Dutch soon took up the banner. In 1615–16, Jacques Le Maire sailed through the Tuamotus. Other Dutch explorers started to trace in the boundaries of Australia, New Zealand and other islands of the western Pacific, but it was not until 1722 that the first of what is now known as the Society Islands was sighted.

Jacob Roggeveen came to Easter Island during Easter of that year and continued west through the Tuamotus, passing the island of Makatea on his way to the Society Islands, where he came across Maupiti, the most westerly of the group's high islands. Other islands of the group are clearly visible from Maupiti, so it's a mystery why Roggeveen did not 'discover' other islands as well.

The British After the Dutch, the British came, led in 1765 by John Byron, who was an English admiral and the grandfather of the poet. Byron 'found' more of the Tuamotus.

In 1767, Philip Carteret, in command of HMS *Swallow*, and Samuel Wallis, on HMS *Dolphin*, rounded Cape Horn, but they lost contact with one another. The small fleet became two separate expeditions, both searching for the mythical Great Southern Continent. Carteret found Pitcairn Island, later to be the refuge of the *Bounty* mutineers, and went on to rediscover Mendaña's long-lost Solomons. But Wallis was to carry the real prize home when he became the first European to visit Tahiti.

The *Dolphin* anchored at Matavai Bay (Baie de Matavai) in Tahiti's lagoon in late June. A quarter of the crew was down with scurvy (this was before Cook's ingenious introduction of sauerkraut into crews' diets), and Wallis himself was incapacitated during most of his visit. Initially, the arrival was greeted with fascination as hundreds of canoes surrounded the ship, including canoes carrying young women 'who played a great many droll wanton tricks'. When the locals' fascination turned to fear an attack was launched on the *Dolphin*. British cannons, loaded with deadly grapeshot, were turned upon the Tahitians, and after a second attack on the British, a raiding party went ashore and destroyed houses and canoes.

According to British reports, the Tahitians didn't resent the killing of some of their people, and from then on a friendly trade relationship developed. The crew was desperate for fresh supplies and the Tahitians, who had not yet discovered metals, were delighted to receive knives, hatchets and nails in exchange. The crew also discovered that a single nail could buy sex – the mind boggles at how an 18th-century British man would have behaved in such an environment (indeed, reports of men pulling nails from the *Dolphin* itself gives an idea of their enthusiasm; see the boxed text 'The Island of Lust' on the following page). Wallis only stayed in Matavai Bay for a few weeks, just long enough to name the island King George's Land and to claim it for Britain.

The French With his ships *La Boudeuse* and *L'Etoile*, Louis-Antoine de Bougainville, the first great French Pacific explorer, arrived on Tahiti in April 1768, less than a year after Wallis. At this time Wallis was still homeward bound, so Bougainville was completely unaware that he was not the first European to set eyes on the island. His visit only lasted nine days, but Bougainville was a more cultured, considered man than Wallis and had no unfriendly clashes with the Tahitians.

Supporting earlier reports of a utopian sexual playground, Bougainville explained that the Tahitians 'pressed us to choose a woman and come on shore with her; and their gestures, which were not ambiguous, denoted in what manner we should form an acquaintance with her'. Bougainville's reports of Venus-like women with 'the celestial form of that goddess', and of the people's uninhibited attitude towards matters sexual, swept through Paris like wildfire.

According to Bougainville, the Tahitians were expert thieves (a year later, James Cook's expedition was to concur; see the boxed text 'An Earful of Cook' later in this chapter). In fact, this supposed proclivity for theft reflected the absence of any notion of private property – theft would have been an oxymoron in a world where everyone had the necessities. And when the Europeans helped themselves to all they could find in the way of fresh food and other supplies on the islands, it's no wonder the islanders felt they could do the same with the strange objects possessed by the strange white men.

Unaware that the Union Jack had already flown over the island, Bougainville took time out to claim Tahiti for France but, like Wallis, he was soon overshadowed when the greatest Pacific explorer of them all arrived on the scene.

The Tahitian's attack the *Dolphin* (engraving 1786)

NATIONAL LIBRARY OF AUSTRALIA

The Island of Lust

When the *Dolphin* returned to Europe, Wallis, a rather unimaginative man, wrote his official report describing Tahiti. This earnest, dull report, which focused on the geographical beauty of the region, was soon overshadowed by gleeful rumours of uninhibited and beautiful women greeting the sailors with 'lascivious gestures'.

If Wallis was uncommunicative, the cultured Bougainville compensated for this with his tales of a new Cythera and his companion Dr Commerçon's gushing avowals that the Tahitians knew 'no other god than love'. Cook in turn was less florid, but his prosaic reports confirmed the view that Tahitian women would 'dance a very indecent dance' while 'singing most indecent songs'.

In reality, Polynesian women were not hanging around waiting to seduce a shipload of uncouth and strange white men. Sex was simply a natural part of everyday life, so it's hardly surprising that Polynesian women wanted to check whether these white men had all the right bits and pieces. This uninhibited approach to sex was soon exploited by sex-starved sailors, whalers and traders, who began buying sex with nails (coveted by the locals for making fish hooks), clothes and alcohol, creating a demand for prostitution, spreading European diseases and palpably contributing to the rapid decline of the Polynesian culture.

The British Return In three great expeditions between 1769 and 1779, James Cook filled out the map of the Pacific so comprehensively that future expeditions were reduced to joining the dots. Cook had been sent to the Pacific with two ambitious tasks. One, which was for the Royal Society, was to observe the transit of Venus as it passed across the face of the sun. By timing the transit from three very distant places it was hoped that the distance from the earth to the sun could be calculated. Tahiti was selected as one of the three measuring points (the other two were in Norway and Canada). Cook's second objective was to hunt for the mythical great continent of the south.

The instruments of the time proved to be insufficiently accurate to achieve Cook's first objective, but Cook's expeditions did yield impressive scientific work. Cook was the perfect man for the task: an expert seaman, a brilliant navigator, a keen observer, an inspiring leader and an indefatigable explorer. Furthermore, he was ably supported by endlessly enthusiastic and inquisitive associates, most notably the wealthy young Joseph Banks. As a result Cook's voyages communicated the wonders of not only Tahiti but also New Zealand and Australia to an appreciative European audience.

In April 1769 Cook and the *Endeavour* arrived at Tahiti, where he stayed for three months before sailing south to New Zealand and Australia. While Bougainville brought back a poet's view of paradise, the pragmatic Cook, with his scientists and artists, surveyed the flora and fauna and described traditional society and Polynesian customs in words and pictures.

Cook took as a hitchhiker from Tahiti a remarkable navigator-priest, Tupaia, who led him to various islands across the South Pacific and successfully translated for Cook when he met the New Zealand Maori. Cook's comprehensive survey of the Australian east coast ended in a disastrous encounter with the Great Barrier Reef. After emergency repairs, the *Endeavour* limped into Batavia (now Jakarta), the capital of the Dutch East Indies. The enforced stop for repairs in the desperately unhealthy city was a disaster – dysentery and malaria killed seven of the crew, including Tupaia, during the three-month stop and 23 more died on the way home. Nevertheless the voyage was considered a resounding success and Cook returned to Tahiti in 1772–75 and again in 1776–80. Cook was killed during a clash with Hawaiians in early 1779.

The Spanish Return The Spanish, who were firmly established in South America, looked upon the Pacific as their backyard and were less than happy to hear of the visits to Tahiti by other European navigators. In 1772 Don Domingo de Boenechea sailed the *Aguilla* from Peru and anchored in the lagoon off Tautira on Tahiti Iti. For the third time, the island was claimed by a European nation. Boenechea took four Tahitians back with him to Lima, returning in 1774 with two of the four Tahitians (two had died in Lima). Boenechea installed two inept missionaries and established Tautira as the first long-term European settlement on the island.

In 1775 the *Aguilla* again returned from Peru. The two Spanish missionaries, who had been spectacularly unsuccessful at converting 'the heathen', and who from all reports were terrified of the islanders, were more than happy to scuttle back to Peru. Boenechea died on Tahiti during this visit, and thus ended the Spanish role on Tahiti.

Cook had the last word when he found a Spanish cross in front of the abandoned mission house in 1777. It was carved with the year 1774, the date of the mission house's establishment. On the back of the cross Cook added the far more impressive list of Tahitian visits by British expeditions.

There was a pause of nearly 10 years before Europeans returned to Tahiti. It was an important break because it marked the transition from exploration to exploitation.

The Mutiny on the Bounty

There had been some colourful chapters in the history of European exploration in the Pacific, but none captured the imagination like the mutiny on the *Bounty*. This most talked-about event made HMS *Bounty* one of the most famous ships in history and William Bligh's name a byword for bad-tempered cruelty. It also inspired three Hollywood extravaganzas, almost the sum total of cinematic interest in Tahiti (see the boxed text 'Mutiny in the Cinema' in the Facts for the Visitor chapter).

Bligh, an expert navigator who had learnt his trade under James Cook and who had already visited Tahiti, was sent off to convey breadfruit from Tahiti to the Caribbean after someone had the bright idea that breadfruit would make a fine food source for enslaved Africans in the Caribbean. Sir Joseph Banks, botanist on Cook's first expedition and then Britain's top man of science, agreed that breadfruit was the ideal plant.

Bligh's expedition started late in 1787. He found it impossible to round stormy Cape Horn and had to double back and sail right around the world eastbound to Tahiti. As a result, the *Bounty* arrived at Tahiti, after an arduous 10-month voyage, at a time

An Earful of Cook

History depicts Captain James Cook as one of the greatest explorers of all time. Indeed, Cook's navigational and surveying skills, his ability to control unruly crews and keep them healthy and, above all, his cultural understanding, did set him apart. He is generally described as having been a dispassionate and tolerant man; it's often claimed he did not want to harm or offend the islanders, and that he made concerted efforts to befriend them. He ordered the humane treatment of the Polynesians and on the whole embraced such an attitude himself. But Cook's composure was far from impenetrable.

All European explorers observed that the Polynesians were somewhat light-fingered. Having no concept of property or wealth – or the inextricable link European society had constructed between the two – the islanders would help themselves to the white men's odd and plentiful possessions. In the beginning at least, this was probably more a game than any real coveting of European possessions.

According to diary entries, by Cook's third and final voyage in the late 1770s some of the crew were feeling uncomfortable with Cook's treatment of those locals caught stealing. There are stories of an irate Cook wreaking havoc, burning houses and smashing canoes, in anger at having had something stolen. David Howarth, a respected historian and author of *Tahiti: A Paradise Lost*, recounts the time when a Polynesian took a sextant. When the culprit confessed and the instrument was returned, Cook had the man's ears cut off.

when breadfruit-tree saplings could not be transplanted. The crew remained on Tahiti for six long, languorous months. Eventually, with the breadfruit trees loaded on board, the *Bounty* set sail, westbound, for the Caribbean. Three weeks later, on 28 April 1789, when passing by Tonga, the crew, led by the mate, Fletcher Christian, mutinied and took over the ship. From all reports, it appears that Bligh had no idea of what had been brewing under his leadership.

Bligh was pushed onto the *Bounty's* launch with 18 faithful crew members and set adrift. That might have been the end of Bligh, but whatever the controversy about his management style, nobody has ever denied that he was a champion navigator and sailor. With consummate skill he sailed his overloaded little boat across the Pacific and past islands inhabited by hostile cannibals, threaded it through the dangerous complexities of the Great Barrier Reef and through Torres Strait, rounded the northeast coast of Australia and eventually made landfall in Dutch-controlled Timor after a 41-day, 5823km voyage that was promptly written into the record books. By early 1790 Bligh was back in England; an inquiry quickly cleared him of negligence and a ship was dispatched to carry British naval vengeance to Tahiti.

Christian and his mutineers had not meekly waited for naval justice to catch up. After dispatching Bligh in late April, the *Bounty* returned to Tahiti before sailing off to find a more remote hideaway. Two attempts were made to settle on Tubuai in the Australs. After the second Tubuai interlude had ended without success, Christian returned briefly to Tahiti, where the mutineers split into two groups. A larger group remained there while a smaller group left with Christian and the *Bounty* in late September.

The 16 mutineers who remained on Tahiti met exactly the fate Christian had predicted. Vengeance arrived in 1791 in the shape of HMS *Pandora*. Captain Edward Edwards, who made Bligh look like a thoroughly nice guy, quickly rounded up the 14 surviving mutineers (two had already been killed in disputes) and informed the men's new Tahitian wives that the men were going back to Britain to get their just desserts. The mutineers were then stuffed into a cage on deck to travel home in considerable discomfort. When Edwards' ship ran aground on Pandora's Reef, Edwards refused to open the cage holding the mutineers. At the last moment the cage was opened, but four of the mutineers had already drowned. Back in Britain, the surviving 10 mutineers were put on trial. Six of them were eventually sentenced to death but three were pardoned; the other three were hung. It's possible that some of the mutineers were unwilling participants: with 18 crew Bligh's overloaded launch was close to foundering, and others who might have followed their captain were possibly not able to do so.

As for Christian, he led the remaining eight British seamen, together with a group of Tahitians, to uninhabited Pitcairn Island, where a settlement was successfully established. Many years later, reports trickled back of a strange English-Tahitian colony, where half the residents bore the surname Christian. Today, thanks to Fletcher Christian's mutiny, Pitcairn Island is one of the last vestiges of the British Empire.

Bligh himself was back on Tahiti in 1792, this time in command of HMS *Providence* and with 19 marines to ensure there was no repeat performance. Bligh duly picked up his breadfruit saplings and transported them in record time to the Caribbean. As it turned out, the slaves never developed a taste for the fruit.

Bligh's voyages successfully transferred two other plants to a much more appreciative audience. On his first voyage he introduced pineapples from Rio de Janeiro to Polynesia, where they remain popular to this day; on his second voyage he brought the apple to Tasmania, which even today is known as Australia's 'Apple Isle'.

The Rise of the Pomares

Before the arrival of Europeans, no one Polynesian ruler was strong enough to extend control very far, although the war-like rulers of Bora Bora, propelled by their lack of arable land, frequently sailed off to wreak havoc on neighbouring islands. It was a considerable feat for an *ari'i* (chief) to control a whole island, and power on Tahiti was divided among a number of squabbling groups. European arms soon changed these traditional power structures.

The Tahitians quickly realised the importance of European weaponry and pressed the early explorers to take sides in local conflicts. Most explorers had strenuously resisted this, but the *Bounty* mutineers were happy to offer themselves as mercenaries to the highest bidder. The highest bidders were the Pomares, one of a number of important families, but by no means the most important at that time.

And so the mutineers and their weapons helped create the political environment where one group could feasibly control all of Tahiti. The Pomares became the most important rulers of Tahiti. Pomare I, the nephew of Obarea, the 'fat, bouncing, good looking dame' who befriended Wallis et al, already controlled most of Tahiti when he died in 1803. His son, Pomare II, took over.

The Missionaries
The early explorers were portents of the dangers to come, and the mutineers played a clumsy part in the introduction of European weaponry. But the real disaster arrived in the late 18th century in the form of the missionaries. The arrival of the missionaries saw the censorship of many important cultural and religious practices.

Descriptions of Tahiti and its people had European intellectuals developing theories about the 'noble savage', but before long the devout were planning to do something about the savages, noble or not. Thirty members of the London Missionary Society (LMS) set out on the *Duff* to bring Christianity to the Pacific. In March 1797, 25 of them landed at Point Venus and set to work.

Their success is evident in the Protestant churches – bursting with devout locals on Sunday mornings – that today still dot the islands throughout the Society group, the Tuamotus and the Australs. Success, however, was not immediate and within a few years most of the original missionaries had drifted off. Pomare II fell from power in 1808 and the remaining Tahitian missionaries, too closely associated with him to be safe, also had to flee the island. Pomare II took refuge on Mo'orea and when he returned to power on Tahiti in 1815, he established Christianity as the dominant religion.

The missionaries were an unyielding bunch, and although they had the best intentions, they made no attempt to combine the best elements of traditional Polynesian beliefs with Christianity, but rather smothered many important, ancient customs with a rigid interpretation of Protestantism. Soon dancing was forbidden, cover-all clothing was decreed, tattoos were banned and silence on Sunday was enforced. More difficult to understand and suppress were the practices of infanticide, human sacrifices, polygamy and indiscriminate sex, but these too were added to the list. A century later, the English writer Robert Keable, who had been a vicar with the Church of England, commented about the pioneering missionary William Ellis that 'it was a thousand pities that the Tahitians did not convert Mr Ellis'.

Whalers & Traders
The advent of whalers and traders added another layer to the insidious affront to Polynesian life. Whalers started to appear in Polynesian waters in the 1790s. Sailing from England, and later from the New England region of the newly independent USA, they hunted whales in southern waters during the summer months and then retreated to islands such as Tahiti during the winter, escaping their harsh shipboard life, buying supplies, introducing alcohol and spreading diseases. These men were rough, hard-drinking and looking for sex (see the boxed text 'The Island of Lust' earlier in this chapter). Traders also started to appear from the convict colonies in Australia; they exchanged

NATIONAL LIBRARY OF AUSTRALIA

Pomare I

weapons for food supplies, encouraged prostitution and established stills to produce alcohol.

Listless, disinterested and plagued by diseases against which it had no natural immunity, the Polynesian population continued to plummet. It's estimated that the population of Tahiti in the late 1760s was around 40,000; in 1800 another estimate put the population at less than 20,000; and by the 1820s it was down to around 6000. In the Marquesas the situation was even worse: it has been estimated the population dropped from 80,000 to 2000 in one century.

Consolidation of Power

After 1815 the Pomares ruled Tahiti, but the English Protestant missionaries were the power behind the throne, advising on government and laws and doing their best to keep unsavoury influences, such as whalers and traders, at arm's length. Pomare II soon extended his power over the Leeward Islands, when he forced the traditionally hostile chiefs to form a Christian alliance. The Code of Pomare was instituted in 1819, but Pomare II had adopted Christianity more as a convenience than because of any profound faith. He died in 1821, probably after drinking himself to death. In 1827 his successor Pomare III also died and was succeeded by the young Queen Pomare IV.

The new queen's missionary advisers saw her as an interim ruler until the next king and as a result they turned a blind eye to some of the queen's youthful excesses. The queen was not averse to a little traditional 'indecent' singing and dancing, and 'visiting' passing ships was not unknown. But Queen Pomare was no passing fancy, and she actually ruled over Tahiti for 50 years. She skilfully extended her control to islands in the Austral group and forged strategic alliances with other islands in the Society group. Unhappily, she also lived to see her islands fall into the hands of the French.

The French Takeover

The missionaries were effectively a colonial power. Although the LMS missions reigned supreme in the Society Islands, the Australs and the Tuamotus, the French Catholic missionaries were in firm control in the Gambier Archipelago from 1834 and the Marquesas from 1838. In 1836, Father Honoré Laval and François Caret, French missionaries from the Gambier Archipelago, were quietly dropped off near Tautira at the eastern extremity of Tahiti Iti. When the Catholics arrived in Pape'ete they were arrested and deported by the British.

France was already effectively in control of the Marquesas, and the deportation of the two French missionaries from Tahiti was considered a national insult. Demands, claims, counterclaims, payments and apologies shuttled back and forth until 1842, when Rear Admiral Dupetit-Thouars arrived in *La Reine Blanche*, pointed his guns at Pape'ete and took power. Queen Pomare was forced to yield to the French, and soldiers and Catholic missionaries were promptly landed.

The French moved quickly and arrested George Pritchard, a British missionary, consul and unofficial chief adviser to Queen Pomare; Pritchard was then forced to leave the islands. The queen, still hoping for British intervention, fled to Ra'iatea in 1844 and a guerrilla rebellion against the French broke out on Tahiti and other islands. The presence of French forts around Tahiti confirms that it was a fierce struggle, but eventually the rebels were subdued, and by 1846 France had control over Tahiti and Mo'orea. In 1847 Queen Pomare IV was persuaded to return to Tahiti, but she was now merely a figurehead.

Queen Pomare died in 1877 and was succeeded by her son, Pomare V. He had little interest in the position and effectively abdicated power in 1881; in true Pomare fashion he drank himself to death in 1891. French power did not initially extend to all the Society Islands, which remained with local rulers and their mission advisers. Most islands had come under French control by 1888, although rebellions rumbled on in Ra'iatea until almost the end of the century. The Gambier Archipelago was annexed in 1881 and the Australs in 1900–01. In 1903 the five archipelagos officially took the name Établissements Français d'Océanie (EFO).

Nonetheless, Catholicism has never made serious inroads on the islands originally converted by Protestants.

The 20th Century

The foundations of the colonial system, laid down during the 19th century, were consolidated at the turn of the 20th century. At the outbreak of WWI, the economy was flourishing and local products such as vanilla, cotton, copra, mother-of-pearl and fruit were exported in exchange for manufactured goods. In 1911 there were about 3500 Europeans living in the EFO. Chinese immigration, which had begun in 1864 with the production of cotton at Atimaono on Tahiti, continued during this time.

Although a long way from the centre stage, Polynesia was directly involved in both world wars. In WWI, almost 1000 Tahitian soldiers fought in Europe, and in September 1914 two German cruisers sank the French cruiser *Zélée* and shelled the Marché de Pape'ete (Pape'ete Market). Polynesia gained strategic significance during WWII with the entry of the USA into the war in December 1941. To thwart the Japanese advance in the Pacific, the Americans used Bora Bora as a supply base. Five thousand soldiers were posted on the island in February 1942 and a 2000m-long runway was completed in April 1943. From April 1941 young Polynesian volunteers fought with the forces of the Free French in North Africa, Italy and France.

In 1946 the EFO became an overseas territory within the French Republic, inciting the first rumblings of a push for independence from France. The Rassemblement Démocratique des Populations Tahitiennes

French Nuclear Testing

French nuclear testing started in the Sahara, but Algerian independence forced France to look for a new testing site. In 1963 it was announced that Moruroa and Fangataufa, atolls in the Tuamotus, were the 'lucky winners', and testing began with atmospheric nuclear explosions in 1966. The Centre d'Expérimentation du Pacifique (CEP; Pacific Experimentation Centre), the euphemistic name for the nuclear-testing programme, soon became a major component of the French Polynesian economy.

In 1963 the USA, the USSR and Britain agreed to stop patently unsafe atmospheric testing (although they continued testing underground), but in 1973 France refused an International Court of Justice request to halt above-ground testing. In that eventful year, the New Zealand government sent a naval ship to Moruroa in protest, the first Greenpeace protest vessels were boarded by French forces, and Peru broke off diplomatic relations with France.

In 1981, in the face of continuing international opposition to all forms of nuclear testing, the French drilled bomb shafts under the central lagoon and moved the tests underground.

International and local opposition to nuclear testing in the Pacific grew stronger and stronger over the years. In 1985, French secret-service agents bombed and sank the Greenpeace ship *Rainbow Warrior* in Auckland Harbour, New Zealand, killing a crew member, Fernando Pereira. Captain Dominique Prieur and Major Alain Mafart, the only two of the French team that the New Zealand police were able to capture, were tried, found guilty (on reduced charges of manslaughter) and sentenced to 10 years' imprisonment. The French government then pressured New Zealand to allow Prieur and Mafart to be transferred to serve reduced sentences on Hao in the Tuamotus. France soon reneged on the agreement, the Club Med–style prison sentence was ended, and the two agents were returned to France to be rewarded for their parts in the fiasco.

In 1995 French president Jacques Chirac announced a new series of underground tests, and a storm of protest broke out worldwide. Pacific and Pacific Rim nations uniformly condemned the announcement and Greenpeace vessels were once again sent into the fray. The first test was conducted in September, and in another round of international protests, Chile and New Zealand recalled their ambassadors from Paris. Severe rioting broke out in Pape'ete but fell on deaf ears in France, far from the strong antinuclear sentiment in the Pacific and around the Pacific Rim. The tests were finally concluded in early 1996, and it was announced there would be no further testing in the Pacific.

For many years, the French government denied that the tests posed any ecological threat to the region. Finally, in 1999 a French study reported that there had been radioactive leakage into underground water, and later that same year the existence of cracks in the coral cones of Moruroa and Fangataufa were also acknowledged. These cracks could cause leakage into the ocean, so, while the issue may be off the international stage, it is an ongoing debacle for those living in the region.

(RDPT; Democratic Assembly of Tahitian Populations), a party founded in 1949 by nationalist Pouvana'a a Oopa, dominated the political scene for about 10 years (see the boxed text 'Pouvana'a a Oopa – A Tahitian Leader' in the Huahine chapter).

The 1960s were a real turning point. Three events in quick succession had a considerable impact on Polynesian society. On 22 July 1957, the EFO officially became French Polynesia. In a September 1958 referendum, 65% of Polynesians demonstrated their wish to remain linked to France. In 1961, the construction of Faa'a international airport opened up Polynesia to the world. Shortly after, filming of the blockbuster *Mutiny on the Bounty* starring Marlon Brando began, requiring thousands of extras and pouring millions of dollars into the island's economy. The establishment of the Centre d'Expérimentation du Pacifique (CEP; Pacific Experimentation Centre) in 1963 at Moruroa and Fangataufa propelled Polynesia into the nuclear age (see the boxed text 'French Nuclear Testing' on the previous page).

Violent antinuclear protests took place in Pape'ete in the 1980s and '90s, and worldwide condemnation of the French government resounded. France agreed to continue its aid until 2005, but the end to nuclear testing in February 1996 was the death knell for the French-funded prosperity of the previous 30 years.

French Polynesia Today

Over the last few decades, French Polynesia's control over internal management has been widened and reinforced (see Government & Politics, later in this chapter). Although independence remains a possibility in the future, ongoing economic dependence on France renders this unlikely in the foreseeable future. The standard of living in the region is relatively high, and access to adequate health care and fresh water is improving, but French Polynesia is in a vulnerable economic situation, with very few natural resources to draw upon and a system based on imports. The impact of El Niño, felt strongly in French Polynesia as in other parts of the Pacific in 2000–01, serves as a reminder of how small Pacific nations are at the mercy of the large industrialised and polluting nations. The refusal of the USA and Australia to ratify the Kyoto protocol on greenhouse gas emissions demonstrates a continued lack of global cooperation on environmental issues.

GEOGRAPHY

French Polynesia is 6000km west of Chile, 5200km east of Australia and 15,700km from Paris, and east of the International Date Line. The nearest islands to the west are the Cook Islands, which are 900km away; the nearest land to the east is solitary Easter Island (Rapanui). French Polynesia is made up of 118 islands – only six of which are larger than 100 sq km and only 76 of which are inhabited – scattered over a vast expanse of ocean stretching more than 2000km from Hatutu in the north to Rapa Iti in the south. In Europe, the islands of French Polynesia would occupy a quadrilateral marked by Stockholm, London, Madrid and Bucharest.

French Polynesia is divided into five archipelagos with a total land area of barely 3500 sq km.

The Society Islands, the westernmost archipelago, is subdivided into the Windward Islands (Tahiti and Mo'orea) and the Leeward Islands (Huahine, Taha'a, Bora Bora and Maupiti) and is home to over three-quarters of the population.

The Tuamotu archipelago, to the east of the Society Islands, consists of 77 atolls. The Marquesas, north of the Tuamotus and not far from the equator, comprises about 15 islands and islets, six of which are inhabited. The Australs, south of the Societies, consists of five high islands and an atoll, straddling the Tropic of Capricorn and lying between 575km and 1275km south of Tahiti. The tiny Gambier Archipelago, southeast of the Tuamotus, is 1600km from Tahiti and is the most remote part of French Polynesia.

Pape'ete, on Tahiti, is the capital of French Polynesia.

GEOLOGY

The islands of French Polynesia are all the result of volcanic activity, but can be subdivided into high islands and atolls.

High Islands

High islands are mainly found in the Society Islands, the Marquesas and the Australs. They are essentially mountains rising above the surface of the ocean, often surrounded by a coral ring that forms a barrier reef.

Between the barrier reef and the island proper is the lagoon, a sort of shallow buffer zone with a gentle aquatic environment where the calm turquoise waters contrast with the darker blue of the ocean. The Marquesas group is a consistent exception – the islands have no barrier reef and no lagoon.

The reefs are often pierced by passes (openings that allow water to flow between the lagoon and ocean) that, if they are wide and deep enough, permit boats to go back and forth. The high islands often have impressive calderas (volcano craters), sharp peaks, knife-edged ridges, and even plateaus. Some coastlines are smooth and regular; some are cut by deep and magnificent bays.

Atolls

An atoll is a circular coral reef, or string of coral islands, emerging above the surface of the water and surrounding a lagoon. Atolls are particularly common in the Tuamotus, where they vary from 75km in length to just 4km across.

The strips of land formed around the reef, made of coral debris and calcareous substances, can reach a height of 6m, and are usually covered in bushes and coconut palms. The ring is generally, but not always, broken by passes. Smaller, shallower *hoa* (channels) only connect the lagoon and the ocean at high tide. The lagoon is often shallow, rarely exceeding 40m in depth. On the ocean side the reefs often fall directly to great depths.

CLIMATE

French Polynesia is between the tropic of Capricorn and the Equator and so enjoys a humid and tropical climate. Although it is warm in most areas year-round, contrary to received notions the weather is not always beautiful in French Polynesia – there can be a large variation from year to year.

There are two (fairly similar) seasons. The summer rainy season runs from November to April, with maximum temperatures in February–March. It's humid, cloudy and *very* rainy. Three-quarters of the annual rainfall occurs during this period, generally in the form of brief, violent storms, although torrential rains lasting several days are not uncommon. The winter dry season lasts from May to October. This is the ideal time to visit: rain is less frequent, the air is dry and temperatures are slightly cooler.

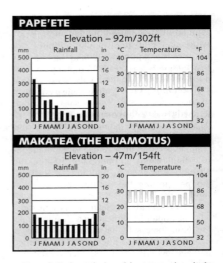

French Polynesia is subject to trade winds that blow from the northeast. The *maraamu* (southeast trade wind) is common throughout the dry season and can bring lower temperatures and rain. The *toerau* (north-northeast wind) is often followed by rain and blows occasionally during the wet season. On the high islands, a pleasant morning breeze, the *hupe*, relieves the sometimes suffocating heat of the coastal plain.

Cyclones are an ever-present threat to South Pacific nations. French Polynesia is generally spared, but on rare occasions has suffered major damage.

For local weather reports phone ☎ 36 65 08.

ECOLOGY & ENVIRONMENT

The environmental repercussions of French nuclear testing are still hotly debated. The view that Moruroa and Fangataufa were fissured by tests and that radioactivity has been allowed to escape was confirmed in 1999 when the French government admitted, for the first time, the existence of cracks in the atolls' coral cones (see the boxed text 'French Nuclear Testing' earlier in this chapter).

Atolls and high islands are ecologically fragile and easily susceptible to damage, but French Polynesia has been slow to implement policies for environmental protection. Tourism is the region's main resource and focuses almost entirely on the natural heritage of the region, so French Polynesia has a strong incentive to protect its environment.

Despite a limited number of 'green' establishments that are springing up, and the rigorous requirements of public buildings and hotels to blend in with the landscape, pollution is nonetheless steadily chipping away at the picture of paradise (see also Responsible Tourism in the Facts for the Visitor chapter).

Rubbish & Wastewater Treatment

Rubbish is perhaps the most visible environmental problem. While inhabitants of larger landmasses send their refuse to remote landfills, that's rarely an option on small Pacific islands. It's not unusual to see garbage dumps spoiling the natural setting, often right by the lagoon. But it's also not unusual to see school kids on cleaning bees on some islands, hopefully indicating a shift in thinking. Nonetheless, the issues are much bigger than a propensity to litter: carefully planned garbage disposal projects, such as the one planned for the Taravao area, have met with local opposition. Rubbish pollutes watercourses, which in turn pollute the lagoons. After heavy rain the forceful run-offs on the high islands certainly don't help.

Only Bora Bora has a state-of-the-art sewerage plant. On other islands, private septic tanks and small sewerage stations are often badly maintained and unreliable, and inevitably the poorly treated outflow ends up in the lagoon. A 1996 survey of swimming areas found that 45% of the places checked on Mo'orea and 40% of the places on Tahiti were polluted. Coral reefs are especially vulnerable, and the situation is a particular concern in urban areas of Tahiti and the other Leeward islands. The tourist infrastructure is strictly controlled and has generally not been a contributor to this problem. Big hotels are built to very strict standards, and their sanitary facilities are part of the basic architectural plan.

Protection of Fauna

With the exception of Scilly there are no marine or terrestrial reserves in French Polynesia, although several species are protected, notably rays and turtles. There are limits placed on the fishing of some fish and crustaceans, particularly lobsters, but fish continue to be caught indiscriminately and shells are still collected for decorative purposes. Although turtles are highly protected, they continue to be poached for their flesh and their shells, which are used as ornaments. Visitors should not encourage this practice in any way (see also Responsible Tourism in the Facts for the Visitor chapter).

FLORA & FAUNA

The bulk of the Pacific's flora and fauna originated in Asia/Melanesia and spread east; the further east you travel, the less varied it becomes. Numerous plant and animal species have been introduced by humans at different times, with varying degrees of success.

Flora

The luxuriant flora of Polynesia, particularly that of the high islands, is recent and introduced. In the course of their migrations to the east, Polynesian navigators brought plants and fruits that easily acclimatised. In the 19th century, missionaries and settlers imported other plants of ornamental and commercial value.

Vegetation varies significantly from one archipelago to another. On the atolls, where the soil is poor and the winds are constant, bushy vegetation and coconut palms prevail. On the high islands, plant cover is more diverse.

Along the paths of French Polynesia you will encounter sumptuous porcelain roses, heliconias, ginger and birds of paradise. Among the fruit trees, you are bound to find soursops, pineapples, guavas, avocados, tamarind, lemons, limes, grapefruits, pacayers, cashews, papayas and custard apples. Melons and watermelons are also grown. *Mati* (the berries of which provide a red colouring), acacia and kapok trees are also fairly common.

At higher altitudes, in addition to *puarata* (which has red flowers), there are several types of fern. The *Albizia falcata* has been introduced to counteract the effects of erosion, particularly in the Marquesas.

Motoi (ylang-ylang), which has strongly scented flowers, also grows in Polynesia, as does *pitate* (jasmine) and bougainvillea.

Other commonly seen plants include the following:

Ahi (sandalwood) – Sandalwood was systematically plundered in the 19th century by Westerners. The sawdust from its wood, renowned for its subtle fragrance, is sometimes used to make Marquesan monoi (fragrant coconut oil; see Arts later in this chapter).

Aute (hibiscus) – Very widespread, this plant has strongly scented flowers of varying colours, generally orange-yellow.

Fara (pandanus) – This tree has a span of 5m to 7m and is easily recognised by its aerial roots, which grow obliquely from the trunk and look like arches. The strong leaves are dried to make traditional roofing, wickerwork and woven articles.

Flamboyant – The majestic, umbrella-shaped flamboyant has vivid crimson flowers at the beginning of the wet season in December. It originated in Madagascar, off the east coast of Africa.

Meia (banana) – Banana leaves are used in traditional Tahitian ovens to wrap food for cooking. One variety is the fei, similar in appearance to the plantain, the fruit of which grows upwards and can only be eaten when cooked.

Noni or nono – The yellowish fruit of this tree looks like a bloated soft potato. It is edible, but its nauseating smell (which resembles goat's cheese) and its acidic taste are certainly not very appealing for the uninitiated. It has medicinal properties (see the boxed text 'Nuts about Noni' on the following page).

Ora (banyan) – This Indian fig tree has numerous aerial roots that form a dense tangle. A sacred tree, its ghostly silhouette is often seen near traditional religious buildings. It was an ancient Marquesan custom to put the long bones and the skull of a deceased person in among the banyan roots along with a conch shell.

Tamanu or ati – The reddish-brown wood of this tree is very strong and rot-resistant. It is used for carving and to make canoes.

Taro – The purplish-red rhizome of this plant is commonly eaten in Polynesia.

Tiare – The tiare is the emblem of French Polynesia. Snow-white in colour, it gives off a subtle fragrance and is used to make garlands or is woven into the hair.

Tiare apetahi – Found only on Mt Temehani on Ra'iatea, this rare and protected white flower is shaped like a half-corolla and has five petals on one side only.

Tipanie (frangipani) – The frangipani bush has very strongly scented white flowers with yellow or pink shading and is used to make crowns and flower lei (wreaths).

Tumu haari (coconut palm) – Found all over the Pacific islands, the coconut palm is the Pacific's most important tree. It is thought to have been introduced by the first Polynesians, and then cultivated by the missionaries in the 19th century. Its uses are many. The water inside the coconut is sterile and a popular drink, and young coconut flesh is squeezed to produce coconut milk. When mature and dried, the coconut produces copra. Coconut oil is the basis of monoi (perfumed beauty oil). Coconut wood is used to make containers, and the palm fibres make rope, *niau* (plaited palm) for roof coverings and *peue* (braided palm) for basketwork.

Uru or maiore (breadfruit) – This impressive grey-trunked tree, of which there are several dozen varieties in Polynesia, has a large grainy fruit that forms the basis of local cuisine. Its whitish fibrous flesh is rich in starch and can be eaten cooked or as a fermented paste. The bark is used to make *tapa* (paper-like cloth; see Arts later in this chapter).

Vanira (vanilla) – This orchid produces a 20cm pod used in cooking. It is cultivated particularly on Taha'a, Huahine and Ra'iatea and has to be hand-fertilised because the insects that do the job elsewhere are not found in French Polynesia.

Fauna

French Polynesia's fauna, like its flora is rather limited compared with regions in the west Pacific, due to the region's great distance from the origin of the fauna.

The first Polynesians, knowing they would be settling new lands, deliberately brought pigs, chickens and dogs in their canoes. They also brought geckos and the small Polynesian rat, probably as stowaways. (The modern rat arrived with European explorers after stowing away on their ships.) The gecko remains Polynesia's most visible reptile – it's a small, harmless lizard with a translucent colour. You'll often see it hovering just above the bed. There are no snakes in French Polynesia.

There are few insect species. You are certain to meet with wasps, cockroaches and their predators, centipedes. The latter can be up to 20cm long and the spikes at the front of the head inject venom that causes inflammation in humans. Mosquitoes are omnipresent, and can transmit dengue fever and filariasis. The *nono* (black flies) are particularly problematic on the Marquesan coasts, where eradication campaigns are being carried out (see the boxed text 'Nono a Gogo' in the Marquesas chapter). *Nono* are not a disease carrier, but their bite causes itching and inflammation.

French Polynesia's horses, which originated in Chile, were introduced on Tahuata in 1842 and are bred in the Marquesas. Goats are also a familiar part of the landscape in this archipelago, where they roam around unchecked.

Nuts about Noni

The best-known fruit in Polynesia is the *noni* (sometimes called *nono* – not to be confused with the insect common in the Marquesas). It has long been used in traditional medicine to boost the immune system, to aid digestion, to add lustre to skin and hair and to increase mental clarity, and since the mid-1990s it has enjoyed enormous success in the American market.

Following work done by an American researcher, who is reported to have highlighted its anti-ageing virtues, a network has been rapidly put in place to supply the American market with *noni* juice. Large numbers of Polynesians, especially in the Marquesas, are abandoning traditional agricultural activities to devote themselves to the much more lucrative activity of growing *noni*, which thrives in the wild. The crop is puréed on Tahiti and then shipped off to the USA, where it is processed by the Morinda company, which also holds exclusive marketing rights. Due to the distribution system known as pyramid selling, the price of the product may be increased 100-fold.

The risk for Polynesian farmers is that this craze might die as quickly as it started, although most people are aware that *noni* may be little more than a passing fad. But the West being as obsessed by ageing as it is, this seems increasingly unlikely.

The waterways are home to eels and freshwater shrimps, which are both highly valued in local cuisine.

Bird Life There are about 100 species of birds *(manu)* in French Polynesia. On the low islands, many nest on the ground or in the bushes. The feathers of certain birds were once much sought-after as costume accessories (such as for headdresses and chieftains' belts).

Sea birds, which live on fish, include terns, petrels, noddies, frigatebirds, boobies and the superb tropicbirds, which have long red or white feathers in their tails. The sheltered Tetiaroa atoll is home to several species of sea birds. The number of *kaveka* (sooty terns) nesting on 'Ua Huka has been estimated at nearly one million. In the Tuamotus there are numerous 'bird islands'.

The pigeon and the buzzard were introduced, as was the chicken, which was brought at the time of the first migrations and has now partly reverted back to its wild state.

Lagoon, Reef & Ocean Fauna The coral reefs of the high islands and atolls provide a rich environment for diverse fauna.

Shellfish Most shellfish are edible. They have diverse habitats, ranging from reef crevices, coral pinnacles and the sandy bottom of lagoons. The most numerous are gastropods and bivalves, including the pearl oyster and the *pahua* (giant clam). Pearl shells were once used to make fish hooks, lures, utensils, tools and, during the 19th century, buttons. *Pahua* have brightly coloured, velvety-looking mantles, which they draw in when threatened. The outer edges of the shells are crinkled.

Greatly prized for their flesh, lobsters and other shellfish live on the outer slopes of reefs (in the Tuamotus) or carpet the bottom of caves in cliffs (in the Marquesas). Hermit crabs, which are common on reefs, wedge their abdomens inside the empty shells of gastropods. In the Tuamotus, the *kaveu* (coconut crab), which feeds at night, can reach an impressive size. The *tupa* (land crab) infests coconut plantations, where it digs a network of tunnels.

Cone shells can be dangerously venomous; the beautiful porcelain cones are particularly valued by collectors. The conch shell is often used as a wind instrument in traditional ceremonies.

Fish The grey shark is very common in the Tuamotus. It is found in abundance near channels and shelves, and is a powerful, streamlined shark that reaches about 2m in length. The lemon shark has a slightly yellowish skin and can reach 3m in length. It can be aggressive. The white-tip reef shark can be recognised by the white mark at the tip of its dorsal fin. It frequents the shelves around the Tuamotus at greater depths than the grey shark, but will come into the shallows if enticed by food. It can reach more than 3m in length. The black-tip reef shark and the white-tip lagoon shark are small, harmless and found primarily in lagoons and channels. Tiger, hammerhead and sleeper sharks are also occasionally seen.

The *ono* (barracuda), with its tapering profile and metallic sheen, is also a predator, and swims close to the channels.

Three types of *fafa piti* (rays) are found in Polynesian waters: manta rays, which are easily recognised by the horns on either side of the mouth and can reach 4m across; leopard rays, which are smaller and have dark spots; and whip-tailed stingrays, which live on the sandy sea floor, where they partially bury themselves.

Among the hundreds of species of smaller fish in French Polynesia, the moray eel is the most impressive. Hidden in the coral crevices of the shelf, only its half-open mouth, edged with sharp fangs, can be seen. The good-natured *mara* (napoleon wrasse), with its blue-green livery, thick-lipped mouth and bump on its forehead, often reaches more than one metre in length. The loach and *roi* (grouper) families are well represented, as are *maito* (surgeonfish), especially the black and convict varieties.

Mahi mahi (dorado), bonito, wahoo and tuna, all greatly prized for their meat, are generally found in the open sea.

Reptiles Sea snakes are very rare in French Polynesia. *Honu* (turtles) are an endangered species but are often encountered around the reefs.

Mammals Dolphins are encountered in all the archipelagos, particularly around the reef passes. Electra dolphins, also known as pygmy orcas or melon-headed whales, are a major attraction of Nuku Hiva in the Marquesas. They gather in groups of several hundred, a phenomenon found nowhere else in the world. In the Australs, whales are the stars – you can even swim with them.

GOVERNMENT & POLITICS

French Polynesia is not an independent state, but a Territoire d'Outre-Mer (TOM; Overseas Territory), with autonomous status within the French Republic.

French Polynesia was given internal management autonomy in 1977, with further powers added in 1984, 1990 and 1996. The Territory itself looks after territorial administration, education (elementary, primary and secondary), taxation, prices, foreign trade and the regulation of maritime resource exploration and exploitation. The French state remains in control of territorial defence, law and order, foreign affairs, citizenship and immigration, justice, higher education and research, audiovisual communications and currency.

The Territory's main institutions are the Gouvernement de la Polynésie Française (Government of French Polynesia), the Assemblée de Polynésie Française (Assembly of French Polynesia) and the Conseil Économique, Social et Culturel (CESC; the Economic and Social Committee). The Republic of France is represented in the Territory by a high commissioner, appointed by the French government, who controls the authorities of the Territory and who can submit matters to the administrative court.

The Assemblée de Polynésie Française is composed of 41 councillors from the five archipelagos, elected by direct universal suffrage every five years. The assembly elects the president of the Government of French Polynesia, the head of the Territorial administration, who in turn appoints a council of ministers. The president represents the authorities of the Republic of France before regional Pacific organisations, and negotiates and signs agreements with Pacific states on matters for which the Territory has responsibility. The assembly sits in Pape'ete, the capital.

French Polynesians participate in all French national elections, and elect two deputies and a senator to represent them in the French parliament. Proposed constitutional changes, with France retaining control of foreign affairs, defence and justice but French Polynesia being able to sign its own international treaties and having the capacity to negotiate with other Pacific nations, have been approved by the National Assembly, but are awaiting final ratification. Other constitutional amendments, such as the creation of French Polynesian citizenship, and the move towards the status of Pays d'Outre-Mer (POM; Overseas Country) rather than an overseas territory, are also on the table but remain unratified.

The reign of Gaston Flosse, a *demi* (literally 'half'; half-Polynesian, half-French) who has been in power since 1991, has been peppered with corruption allegations. In 1999 Flosse was actually found guilty of corruption, on charges of accepting almost three million French francs from the owner of an illegal casino. Although some charges have since been overturned by the Appeals Court in Paris, which ruled there was insufficient evidence against the president, Flosse still faces fraud charges.

Political Parties

Political life in French Polynesia concentrates on two principal parties. On one side is the autonomist but loyalist Tahoeraa Huiraatira (Gathering of the People) party, which is currently in power and led by Gaston Flosse, the president of the government of French Polynesia. On the other side is Tavini Huiraatira (To Serve the People), the pro-independence party led by Oscar Temaru, mayor of Faa'a, who argues for the breaking of all ties with France, and who extols a return to traditional Polynesian principles. Between these two heavyweights smaller parties attempt to make themselves heard – without much success. Only the autonomist Fetia Api (New Star), which is ˙ opposed to the Tahoeraa party and was created in 1995 by Boris Léontieff, the mayor of Arue, has had any success in proposing a third way.

Local political practices are often disconcerting for foreign observers. Political meetings start with a prayer, speeches are dotted with biblical quotes, U-turns are frequent and fail to shock anybody, and cronyism – which sometimes drifts towards corruption – is everyday currency. The numerous corruption charges that have been laid against Gaston Flosse in the last decade are a case in point.

ECONOMY

Far from the myths of a carefree paradise, French Polynesia faces many economic challenges. During the nuclear testing era, the region became financially dependent upon France, although this dependence is gradually being reduced as the local government modernises and embraces autonomy.

Economic Indicators

French Polynesia is one of the richest countries in the South Pacific with a per-capita GNP comparable to that of Australia. This elevated standard of living is, of course, somewhat artificial since it depends on lots of input from France. Exports may be increasing, but they still don't amount to one-

fifth of the imports. The main trading partners are France (37% of imports and 21% of exports), the USA, Japan, Australia and New Zealand. Exports include pearl products (pearls, mother-of-pearl), fishing boats and agricultural and food products (vanilla, *noni*, flowers, fruits, monoi, copra oil, fish). Imports include consumer durables, equipment and food.

Unemployment is officially 13.2% of the active population and is a particular problem for women and young people without qualifications. Of course, this figure is virtually meaningless in the local context. On some atolls there is really no job market at all and the population is primarily self-sufficient. Combine that with the *fetii* (extended family) concept, and employment levels don't have the same impact as they do in the industrialised nations of the West (in fact, many people will tell you anecdotally that there is no unemployment in French Polynesia). Pape'ete is the one exception, where unemployment has brought the same social problems experienced in other urban centres worldwide.

The End of the CEP Era

The establishment of the euphemistically named Centre d'Expérimentation du Pacifique (CEP) in 1963, and the subsequent flood of finance into the Territory, artificially inflated the standard of living. The change encouraged many outer-islanders to leave their traditional livelihoods behind and migrate en masse to Pape'ete. This well-known pattern of urbanisation created pockets of poor communities who were unable to support themselves in the city as they had on the islands, and the standard of living plummeted as never before. Understandably, support for political parties pressing for independence swelled. For many Polynesians who have been thrust into the alluring modern world of consumerism, the traditional way of life is no longer viable.

The close of the CEP has meant a return to economic reality and the announcement of a pending end to the financial assistance. France has undertaken to compensate the loss of financial resources linked to the cessation of CEP activities during a transition period, and continues to provide assistance in the fields of education, training, research, health and transport infrastructure, agriculture, tourism and housing. Financial transfers to the Territory will amount to 18 billion CFP (US$150 million) a year until the end of 2005.

Areas of Productivity

Agriculture The spectacular boom in the services sector and the public service during the CEP period caused a huge rural exodus and a marked decline in agricultural output. The agricultural sector is vital for the Territory's social and economic stability given that French Polynesia is not self-sufficient in food production. However, the development of the agricultural sector is handicapped by some fundamental problems including small plot sizes, difficult climatic conditions and poor distribution. The effects of El Niño, felt in 1998 and again in 2002–03, have wreaked havoc on agriculture, in particular the production of copra and vanilla.

Copra production is the main source of income for nearly 12,000 people, particularly in the Tuamotus (where it amounts to 50% of production) and the Marquesas. The Territory guarantees a price per kilogram that is considerably higher than that found on world markets. Market gardening and vegetable production is concentrated in the Leeward Islands and the Australs. Vanilla is grown on Taha'a, Ra'iatea and Huahine and is considered to be the best in the world. Production is increasing, reaching 30 tonnes in 2001, but this is still far below the pre-CEP annual level of 150 tonnes a year. Fruit production is mainly bananas, pineapples, coconuts and citrus fruit, but only Mo'orea's intensively grown pineapples are exported. Staples – taro, sweet potatoes, and cooking bananas – are grown entirely for local consumption. Flower exports, mainly to Europe, have been recording good results. The production of *noni* has also become an important export (see the boxed text 'Nuts about Noni' earlier in this chapter).

Chicken, pork and beef production (at Taravao on Tahiti and Nuku Hiva in the Marquesas) cannot meet local demand; there are extensive imports from Australia, New Zealand and France.

Fishing Polynesia's huge marine areas remained underexploited until the mid-1990s. Small-scale fishing in lagoons and offshore using small boats, fish traps and spear fishing has always been important for meeting local demand but the development of a fishing fleet for exports is also now achieving good results. The Territory is aiming to increase fishing production to 11,000 tonnes by 2003, with 7000 tonnes to be exported.

Pearl Culture The real locomotive of the French Polynesian economy, the pearl business, is booming. Second only to tourism, French Polynesia's pearl exports amounted to US$117 million in 2000, which was actually less than in previous years. Production is mainly concentrated in the atolls of the Tuamotus and the Gambier Archipelago, where it plays an important part in local life. Pearl culture is also being developed in the Leeward Islands, particularly Huahine, Ra'iatea, Taha'a and Maupiti.

The apparent buoyancy of this sector does not, however, conceal certain basic weaknesses. There's little organised merchandising despite a professional union overseeing the business. The many small pearl cultivators' professional practices are sometimes naive: selling pearls too cheaply drives prices downwards and tarnishes the image of black pearls. Overproduction is another consequence of this relative anarchy, and again depresses prices. Between 1994 and 2001, the per gram price of black pearls fell 57%. Prices have since stabilised, and it is hoped that increased regulation of the business, introduced in the late 1990s, will control the peaks and troughs.

Tourism As the main source of income in the Territory, tourism is the principal lever by which the government intends to achieve its objectives of economic independence. The number of tourist arrivals had been increasing regularly up until 2000 (which was a huge year for tourism, with 252,000 visitors recorded), after which there was a slump, perhaps as a result of the September 11 attacks in the USA in 2001. The long distance from principal markets, the cost of living on the islands, competition from other tropical destinations and perhaps a lack of professionalism in some areas all combined to restrain demand.

In 2001, French Polynesia welcomed around 228,000 visitors, with Americans

(42.5%) easily outnumbering the French (22%). In that rather troubling year for international tourism, only the number of Japanese tourists to the region increased (over 19,000 arrivals in 2001 compared with 14,300 in 1999).

Thanks to some attractive tax breaks there's been a boom in luxury hotel construction in Pape'ete and on Bora Bora. Small hotels and *pensions* (guesthouses) have also been developing in more remote locations, opening up the region to budget travellers.

The most visited islands are Tahiti, Mo'orea, Bora Bora and Rangiroa, but recently there has been increased promotion for the other islands. Cruise ships, honeymoons, aquatic activities (sailing, scuba diving, boat tours of the lagoons) and local art and culture (handicrafts, traditional dances and feasts) are all growth areas. The region has great possibilities for tourism focused on archaeology, hiking, horse riding and whale watching, but these are as yet largely underdeveloped.

Industry The industrial sector is understandably little developed in French Polynesia. The region's geographical isolation, the lack of primary materials and the elevated cost of labour combine to make it a difficult sector to develop; there are just some small-scale agro-food businesses and specialised clothing and textile operations.

Taxation

The taxation system is skewed in favour of indirect taxes, particularly import taxes. All goods entering the Territory are weighed down with import duties. At the other end of the spectrum, income taxes are derisory. In short, the fiscal system is the main reason for the elevated prices in French Polynesia and is often on the receiving end of many a grumpy retort.

French Polynesia is heavily dependent on imports, and even locally manufactured goods do not escape hefty taxation, as they invariably include imported components.

Reforms introduced in 1998 brought in a *taxe sur la valeur ajoutée* (TVA; value-added tax), intended to balance the system and progressively replace customs duties, which it is slowly doing. This TVA is now a big part of the tax you'll be paying every night you stay in French Polynesia (for more details, see Costs under Money in the Facts for the Visitor chapter).

POPULATION & PEOPLE

The population of French Polynesia is estimated to be about 239,500 and is characterised by its youth – half the population is under 25 years of age – and its uneven geographic distribution. Although the birth rate has dropped markedly over the last two censuses, it is still relatively high at 21 per 1000 (it's around 13 per 1000 in Australia and France).

The Society Islands are home to more than 86% of the total population, the Tuamotus 7%, the Marquesas 4% and the Australs less than 3%.

Paralleling worldwide patterns of urbanisation, the isolated Marquesas and Australs have lost large parts of their populations to Pape'ete, although the boom in cultured pearls lured many back to the Tuamotu-Gambier region in the 1980s and '90s.

On all the islands, the majority of the population lives in coastal zones. The rugged interiors are rarely populated nowadays, but archaeological evidence indicates that this was not always the case.

Ethnicity

French Polynesia is a multiethnic society of four major groups: Polynesians (65%), *demis* (people of Polynesian-European or Polynesian-Chinese descent; 16%), *popaa* (Europeans; 12%) and Chinese (or French of Chinese origin; 5%). These distinctions are becoming less and less relevant as the groups continue to intermarry.

Polynesians tend to make up the least privileged part of society. They are generally engaged in the fishing, agriculture, building and construction industries, and mostly live in the outlying districts and on the islands.

Demis are mainly the descendants of marriages between colonial administrators and traders and the women of important Polynesian families that began to take place around the turn of the 19th century. Today *demis* appear to have comfortably integrated the two cultures, and navigate both with relative ease. *Demis* occupy some of the most important positions in public life and dominate the political sphere. They are concentrated in Pape'ete.

The first Chinese were shipped in during the 19th century as cheap labour for the cotton plantations. Since then, they have excelled in the trade and business sectors and, unlike ethnic Chinese communities in some other parts of the world, are relatively well integrated into French Polynesian life.

The *popaa* are essentially French who have made a life in French Polynesia and work as teachers, military or medical personnel, civil servants, restaurateurs and the like.

The Polynesians have demonstrated an extraordinary generosity and ability to assimilate the people that have arrived, always uninvited and often armed, on their shores. Nevertheless, racial tensions have developed in the face of the increasingly stark inequalities among the different community groups. In broad terms, a gulf has come about between the French, Chinese and *demis* – the power-wielders in modern French Polynesia – and the Polynesians, who have struggled to find their place in the process of Westernisation.

EDUCATION

The education system in French Polynesia is identical to that of France. School is compulsory between the ages of five and 16. Teaching is in French; only a few hours of Tahitian a week are offered in primary and secondary schools. This tends to disadvantage Polynesian children, who have greater difficulty working in French and following the French education system than *demi*, *popaa* and Chinese children.

There are primary schools in each community, but the six high schools (of which two are private and one an agricultural school) are all in the Society Islands, which means many students have to go to boarding school or stay with relatives in order to continue their studies.

School holidays are for one month from mid-December to mid-January, seven weeks in July and August, two weeks in March and one week for La Toussaint (All Saints' Day; 1 November).

The Université de Polynésie française (UPF; University of French Polynesia) has about 1660 students. It has not been an outstanding success: many students drop out at the end of the first year, and those that pursue their studies often head overseas to France, New Zealand, Australia or the USA.

ARTS

The zealous missionaries endeavoured to wipe out all forms of 'primitive' Polynesian art and culture. They destroyed temples and carvings, banned tattooing and dancing, and generally took a lot of the joy out of life. Fortunately some traditions survived this period of cultural censorship, and in recent years there has been a revival of Polynesian culture, particularly in music, dance and tattooing (which has been appropriated worldwide as a fashionable form of bodily adornment). See Shopping in the Facts for the Visitor chapter for more information on crafts.

Dance

The early explorers didn't know what had hit them when they first caught sight of Polynesian dancing. These men, whose lives were governed by the rigid social order of 18th- and 19th-century Europe, all commented on the erotic explicitness of Polynesian dancing. Naturally, it was one of the first things the missionaries banned when they arrived, although it continued clandestinely. Since the 1950s, dance has been revived and is now one of the best ambassadors for Polynesian culture. See the special section 'Tahitian Dance' later in this book for more information.

Music

Traditional Polynesian music, usually performed as an accompaniment to dance, can still be heard reverberating through the islands. Ukuleles and percussion instruments dominate this style of music, which is structured by a hypnotic and often complex drum beat (see the special section 'Tahitian Dance' later in this book for more information). Song, both secular and religious, is also popular and important. Sunday *himene* (hymns) feature wonderful harmonies.

Modern Polynesian music by local artists is the blaring soundtrack to everyday life, whether it's in a le truck (bus), at a café or on the radio, and some groups also perform in hotels and bars. The high-pitched voice and political lyrics of Angelo Ariitai Neuffer will quickly become familiar; other well-known local names include Andy Tupaia, Gabilou, Esther Tefana, Michel Poroi, Maruia, Barthélémy, Bobby, Te Ava Piti, le

Royal Band and the Trio Kikiriri (which plays at the Royal Kikiriri in Pape'ete). Marquesan groups include Rataro and the Kanahau Trio. The group Fenua fuses traditional and electronic music forms.

Literature

Polynesia has been getting the European pen flowing since the first European explorers returned with accounts of paradise islands and beautiful people (see Books in the Facts for the Visitor chapter for more information on books about the region). But oral recitation was the fountain pen of the Pacific, and the written word only came into being after the missionaries began producing texts in Tahitian in the 19th century. This dependence on the spoken word has meant that Polynesia's history has been recreated out of European observations, and the Polynesian experience constructed out of European suppositions. It also means that literature written by Polynesians has only started to grace the bookshelves relatively recently.

There are a number of interesting Polynesian writers who are slowly changing the literary landscape, but few have been translated into English. If you read French, writers such as Henri Hiro, Turo Raapoto, Hubert Bremond, Charles Manutahi, Michou Chaze, Chanter Spitz and Louise Peltzer are all of interest. A search on the Internet or, when in Pape'ete, asking at one of the many good bookshops, will yield information about these authors and their works.

Breadfruit by Celestine Hitiura Vaite (2000), a Tahitian living in Australia, is a novel set in contemporary Tahiti. The poverty and social problems facing many Tahitians are not glossed over, and the dialogue is evocatively garnished with Tahitian and French (don't worry, a glossary is provided).

Architecture

Traditional Polynesian architecture has always blurred the line between indoors and outdoors, and buildings are rarely entirely closed from the elements, even today. The *fare* (house) is the traditional Polynesian dwelling and is constructed entirely from plant materials. It is built directly on the ground, without foundations. The framework is made of coconut wood and the roof of woven coconut palms or pandanus leaves, which are waterproof. New construction techniques and designs, which are more practical but less aesthetically appealing, are supplanting traditional methods of construction: *fare* are often now made of plywood or cement and have corrugated iron roofs, which better withstand cyclones.

The average *fare* is fairly utilitarian; beautiful Polynesian homes are predominantly found among the wealthy. Paradoxically it's at modern luxury hotels that you are most likely to be able to admire ornate traditional architecture with frames and rafters in ironwood, roofs thatched with *niau* (plaited coconut palm) and walls covered in plaited bamboo. Thanks to the ravages of storms, colonial-era buildings are now fairly rare, although Christian religious architecture can still be found at almost every turn.

Painting

Even today, well over a hundred years after his arrival on Tahiti, painting in the South Pacific is synonymous with Paul Gauguin, the French postimpressionist painter. Gauguin spent much of his later life in Polynesia, and presented Europe with images of the islands that moulded the way Europeans viewed (and, arguably, continue to view) Polynesia. In his wake a number of predominantly European artists – working in media ranging from watercolour to line drawing – have also sought inspiration in the region. These artists have contributed to the very characteristic painting style of the region, which is largely representational. The shops and galleries in Pape'ete and on the more touristy islands are groaning under the weight of reproductions and more recent originals.

Matisse made a short visit to Tahiti, but his work on Polynesia is eclipsed by Jacques Boullaire's. Boullaire, a French artist who first travelled to Tahiti in the 1930s, produced magnificent watercolours; reproductions of his work are readily available today.

Other artists of French and Polynesian descent who have influenced the art scene locally and internationally include Christian Deloffre, François Ravello, Michèle Dallet, Bobby (also a singer and musician; he died in 1991), André Marere, Jean Masson, Yrondi, Noguier and Erhart Lux.

Sculpture & Woodcarving

Traditionally the best sculpture and wood-carvings have come out of the Marquesas, where fine tiki, bowls, mortars and pestles, spears and clubs are carved from rosewood, *tou* wood or in stone. The best-known contemporary sculptor is the potter Peter Owen, who lives on Huahine, but the work of the appropriately named Woody on Mo'orea is also well known.

Unfortunately, some of the woodwork sold in French Polynesia is actually made elsewhere (much of it is from Indonesia), so if you feel strongly about authenticity and supporting Polynesian artists, ask around to ensure you are getting the real thing.

Clothing & Decoration

Dress in French Polynesia is an odd combination of the very dowdy, inspired by the missionaries, and the very sexy, inspired by the traditional, scant clothing to be expected in the tropics, and Western fashion.

The former is embodied in the Mother Hubbard or mission dress, which is a long floral dress, often trimmed with lace that is today really only worn by older women.

Younger Polynesians tend to wear Western clothes and pareu. Like the Southeast Asian sarong, the pareu is a cool, comfortable, all-purpose piece of fabric. A modern pareu is usually about 180cm by 90cm (about 6ft by 3ft) and is often imported from Asia. Hand-painted Polynesian pareu are also popular (but more expensive), and are readily available on the more touristy islands. Hibiscus flowers, *uru* (breadfruit) leaves and Gauguin-esque prints are the most popular designs, but motifs vary from island to island. Men usually wear the pareu like a wrap-around skirt for casual wear or around the house. Tucked up like shorts it becomes workwear. Women have a variety of ways of wearing a pareu. It can be worn as a wrap-around skirt or tied above the breasts or worn with two corners tied behind the neck as a halterneck.

Monoi The local fragrant oil, made from coconut oil and perfumed with flowers (*tiare*, jasmine and so on) and sandalwood, is known as monoi. It's used as hair oil, ointment, sunscreen and even mosquito repellent. What can't it do? It costs from 400 CFP to 600 CFP a bottle, and is great on the skin after a day of sizzling in the sun. A bottle of monoi makes a great gift (although it does solidify in cooler climates).

Tifaifai Brilliantly coloured *tifaifai* (appliquéd or patchwork blankets) are produced on a number of islands, in particular Rurutu in the Australs. The craft was introduced by the missionaries, and a *tifaifai* now has several important uses. Wrapping someone in a *tifaifai* is a sign of welcome, and traditionally it's an important wedding gift. A *tifaifai* may also be used to cover a coffin. Flowers or fruit are often used in *tifaifai* patterns.

Tapa Traditionally made throughout the Pacific, *tapa* (paper-like cloth) is a nonwoven fabric made from the bark of *uru*, banyan or *aute* (paper mulberry) trees. The colour depends upon the wood used, and so varies from white to chestnut. Collecting the bark is the men's job, while the preparation of the *tapa* falls to the women. The bark of young trunks or branches is slit and removed from the wood using a sharpened stick. It is then soaked in water to soften. The outer layer is scraped away with a shell, leaving just the sapwood. The sheets of bark, about 15cm wide, are spread out on a flat, elongated stone anvil. Using a square-shaped ironwood beater, the bark sheets are then pounded repeatedly for several hours, during which time the bark becomes thinner and gradually stretches.

When the piece is finished, it is dried and then dyed with the sap of various plants or decorated with traditional designs.

The making of *tapa* rapidly declined when European cloth became available in the region, but it is still produced, particularly on Fatu Hiva in the Marquesas, for ceremonial use and for collectors.

Plaiting & Basketwork Baskets, hats and the panels used for roofing and the walls of houses are all made by women. Coconut-palm leaves are used for the more rough-and-ready woven work, while pandanus leaves or thin strips of bamboo are used for finer hats, bags and mats, which are often decorated with flowers or shells.

Some of the finest work comes from Rurutu in the Australs, where hillside pandanus (rather than common lagoonside pandanus) is used.

Flowers & Shells Flowers are omnipresent in French Polynesia. From the moment you arrive at the airport, where you'll be presented with a *tiare* (a fragrant white flower) to sniff as you brave the customs queues, to hotel rooms and even public toilets, flowers are displayed, offered and worn. The Annual Flower Show, held in Pape'ete in September, is an olfactory and visual delight. *Tiare*, jasmine, hibiscus and frangipani are the flowers most often used for necklaces and crowns.

Engraved mother-of-pearl is another favourite and is often used to decorate dance costumes. Shells are used to make necklaces, and it's an ongoing tradition to garland people with them when they arrive and depart the islands.

Tattoos The practice of tattooing traditionally signified social status, with more tattoos gradually being added over a lifetime. Paradoxically, tattoos increased an individual's desirability on the one hand and were seen as a way of intimidating the enemy on the other hand. See the special section 'Tattooing' later in this book for more information.

RELIGION

The arrival of Protestant missionaries at the end of the 18th century, followed soon after by the Catholics, marked the suppression of traditional religious beliefs and practices (see the special section 'Civilisation & Archaeology' later in this book for more information). Although the missionaries were not immediately successful, over time Christianity gained dominance, helped in a large part by the Pomares, the ruling family who befriended the missionaries. The missionaries involved themselves in all aspects of life, and even dictated that women wear tent-like Mother Hubbards, those all-enveloping mission dresses, once they reached maturity.

The missionaries changed the religious and cultural landscape forever, and even today French Polynesia has a surprising number and variety of churches relative to its population. Around half of the population follows the Église évangélique de Polynésie (Evangelical Church of Polynesia), which is Protestant and particularly strong in the Society Islands and the Australs. Catholics make up around 30% of the population and live mostly in the Marquesas, the eastern Tuamotus and the Gambier Archipelago, but also on Tahiti (many of the *demis* and Chinese are Catholic). The balance is made up of Mormons, Seventh-Day Adventists, Sanitos (the local name for the reorganised Church of Jesus Christ of the Latter Day Saints, a dissident branch of the Mormons), Jehovah's Witnesses and Jews (Pape'ete has a synagogue). Most Chinese converted to Catholicism in the 1950s and '60s, although there is a Chinese temple in Pape'ete.

The churches wield strong financial power and play a major role in the social life, politics and culture of the islands. The division between church and state sometimes seems tenuous, and biblical references pepper political speeches. Most religious figures play an important part in public life, and the Protestant church took a strong position against nuclear testing. Curiously, the churches today actively promote the Polynesian traditions that the missionaries set out to quell, and Tahitian and Marquesan are the languages of church services.

A few pre-Christian rituals and superstitions still survive alongside Christianity. In some dwellings a light is always left on overnight for fear that *tupapau* (irritating spirits of dead people) or a *varua ino* (malevolent spirit) might be on the prowl. Christian Polynesians continue to respect and fear ancient *tapu* (taboo) sites, and nothing would persuade a Polynesian to move a tiki or *marae* stone; on occasion, a *tahua,* or faith healer, is still consulted.

OLIVER STREWE

TONY WHEELER

PAUL KENNEDY

The people of French Polynesia

Woodcarving, the Marquesas

Painting on bus, Pape'ete

Silk-screened pareu (sarong)

Hat-making, Rurutu

Fabrics, Marché de Pape'ete

CIVILISATION & ARCHAEOLOGY

Ancient Polynesian civilisation almost disappeared with the arrival of Christianity and the first Europeans. Nowadays, it is given the consideration it deserves and is back in the limelight. Polynesian culture was essentially based on oral traditions, and the only written records of it are the accounts of the first Westerners to arrive in French Polynesia. It is mainly through archaeological heritage that visitors are able to discover the different facets that made up this culture.

The pleasures of the lagoons are enough to occupy most tourists, and it is often by chance that they become aware of the wealth of Polynesian heritage. The sites possess nothing like the imposing character of the *moai* (sacred statues) of Easter Island, and their development has, to date, been limited to restoration works. However, they present a unique opportunity to discover another aspect of Polynesia.

Polynesian Myths

The Polynesians were polytheistic, worshipping various important *atua* (guardian divinities) surrounded by a pantheon of secondary gods. The main gods were Ta'aroa (God of Creation), Tu (Man God), Tane (God of Craftsmen), 'Oro (God of War) and Hiro (God of Thieves and Sailors). Gods competed with each other and could be ousted. Moreover, their power was geographically limited – they were not recognised in all the archipelagos. Tane, for instance, was ousted by Ta'aroa who was in turn replaced by his son 'Oro, whose cult never extended beyond the limits of the Society Islands. Hiro was worshipped on Ra'iatea and Huahine – his finger (or his phallus) can be admired as a backdrop to Maroe Bay at Huahine. All these legends were handed down via spoken legends relating the exploits and adventures of the gods.

The image of the gods was symbolised by the *to'o*, a wooden stick wrapped in plaited coconut fibres and decorated with red feathers.

Social Organisation

Ancient Polynesian society was far removed from the sweet and naive description given by the French explorer Bougainville. It was fundamentally aristocratic: an extremely hierarchical and structured caste system governed relationships between members of the communities, which were feudal in nature and organised around chieftaincies. In this heavily ritualised society, the practice of human sacrifice, as offerings to the gods, was commonplace.

Political Authority: The Ari'i The high chiefs who held sway over a portion of an island were known as the *ari'i*. The rank was hereditary and was passed to the eldest son. Their supremacy and legitimacy were sanctioned by the recital of their genealogy (which could be traced back to the illustrious godlike ancestor who founded the clan) on festival days by the *'orero* (orators).

Inset: Carved tiki (Photograph by John Borthwick)

The status and dignity of the *ari'i* were represented by an adornment comprising the *maro ura* (belt of red feathers), a headdress, a ceremonial stick and a fan. Deemed to be holy people, they possessed *mana* (supernatural power). The *ari'i* controlled the major activities connected with the life of the clan: fishing, harvesting and warfare. Sometimes an island was governed by an *ari'i rahi* (supreme chief), usually from the dominant clan, who had succeeded in imposing his authority upon the other *ari'i*.

Spiritual Authority: The Tahua Also belonging to the aristocracy, the *tahua* (priests) were allied to the *ari'i*. In charge of liturgy and the marae (traditional temples), these priestly dignitaries were assisted by a host of officiating priests including the *haere po* (reciters of oral traditions) and the *'orero*. As trustees of *mana*, they consulted and invoked the gods, practised divination, attended to the observance of rites, pronounced *rahui* (temporary restrictions affecting the consumption of farm produce) and presided over ceremonies.

Pleasures & Festivals: The Ario'i Joined in brotherhood, the *ario'i* enjoyed a very special status. They too were holy figures descended from the god 'Oro, and were connected with the itinerant artist-troubadours whose role it was to entertain Polynesian society with dancing and theatrical shows, sometimes with erotic overtones. Selected for their physique and talent for dancing, *ario'i* went through a long initiation period. They were not allowed to have children; infanticide was practised if their wives gave birth, but children who managed to utter a shout before being killed were spared.

The Landowners: The Ra'atira The middle caste, comparable to the European bourgeoisie at the close of the Middle Ages, was known as the *ra'atira*. Their status was derived from the ownership of land.

The Common People: The Manahune The lowest rank in the social pyramid was the *manahune*, which grouped together the lower classes. It comprised various subclasses, among them fishermen, servants, farmers, slaves and prisoners of war. The only social advancement possible was to become an *ario'i*. For the benefit of the *ari'i* they had to carry out menial duties and produce offerings. It was from this caste that human sacrifices were drawn.

Daily Life

See Polynesian Myths, earlier, and Archaeological Remains, later, for information about religion, ceremonies and places of worship.

Provisions & Diet The livelihood of the ancient Polynesians was based on fishing, animal husbandry, farming and fruit picking. *Uru* (breadfruit), which was eaten fermented, was a staple food, together with taro and sweet potato. Turtle was reserved for members of the higher castes. Dog was eaten in the Tuamotus.

Rahui, temporary bans on eating specific products, were issued by the priests or *ari'i* in order to regulate the supply of food.

Arts & Crafts Little remains of traditional Polynesian art, which was created exclusively for religious and utilitarian purposes.

Before the arrival of Europeans, metal was unknown. Craftsmen worked with stone, coral, bone, wood, shells, mother-of-pearl and plant matter. They made weapons, utensils and tools (dishes, pestles, adzes, paddles, fish-hooks), tapa, ceremonial costumes (of animal fur and feathers) and tiki. Petroglyphs (patterns engraved on stones) are another Polynesian form of artistic expression.

Music & Dance Singing, music and dance were inextricably linked. Many different forms of *heiva* (celebration) featured in the life of the community, and many celebrations would last several days. The instruments played were *pahu* (drums) and *vivo* (nasal flute).

Sports Polynesians traditionally engaged in many games of skill and strength. Archery was a form of aristocratic entertainment, practised on specially constructed platforms – there are some on Mo'orea, in the Opunohu Valley. Surfing, which was also highly popular, is a sport of Polynesian origin. Javelin throwing (in the Tuamotus), dugout-canoe racing, stone lifting and wrestling were equally commonplace.

War Battles between clans were frequent. When unable to extend their kingdoms by virtue of an alliance by marriage, the various *ari'i* of an island would resort to military conquest. There would be ceremonies on the marae, after which the chief and his warriors would go off to fight on land or sea. The defeated were often massacred and their marae destroyed. The victors would take possession of the defeated clan's land, and new investiture ceremonies would take place.

The weapons used included clubs, lances, whips and slings. At sea, the warriors would travel in dugout canoes.

Mana & Tapu The essential ingredients of holiness are *mana* and *tapu*. The term *mana* is difficult to translate: it may be defined as a supernatural power, force or aura surrounding a person or object. The priests and the *ari'i* possessed *mana*, as do some tiki.

Tapu (taboo) is a word that has entered many Western languages in various forms, and signifies that something has a complete ban on it. Anyone who transgresses incurs a curse and consequent punishment. Places and things can be *tapu*. Anything to do with the *ari'i* was *tapu*.

The Marquesas Although belonging to the same melting pot as other Polynesians, the Marquesans have, over the centuries, developed their own distinct culture. The practice of cannibalism, officially outlawed in 1867, was concealed for many years since it was, to Western thinking, considered repulsive. The victims were warriors who were captured or killed in battle. Only chiefs and warriors were allowed to seize the *mana* of the enemy in this way.

Social organisation also differed from the Polynesian model. Every *huaka* (clan) lived in a valley considered to be exclusive territory and which was jealously defended. Fighting between clans was frequent and bloody.

A *hakaiki* (chief), either male or female, exerted authority and enforced the clan's social and religious laws.

Ta'u'a (high priests), endowed with powerful *mana*, acted as intermediaries between the tribe and the gods. The role of the *toa* (chief warrior) was to lead the soldiers. Finally there were the *meie* (common people).

Art and craft reached a very high degree of perfection, especially tattooing. Warriors' bodies were tattooed more extensively as they performed ever-increasing acts of bravery.

It was in the Marquesas that sculpture took on its most accomplished form, with the most imposing tiki in French Polynesia.

Musical instruments were similar to those used in the other archipelagos. However, dances and traditional singing were different from those on Tahiti.

Archaeological Remains

Evangelism resulted in the complete loss of the ancient religion and abandonment of places of worship. Fortunately, excavations have unearthed many sites that had been completely forgotten and overgrown. These are mainly places of worship built out of stone, sometimes with patterns carved in stone and statues. All evidence of plant matter – dugout canoes, dwellings, clothes and woodcarvings – has disappeared.

The state of preservation of the sites varies. In some places there are piles of stones, completely surrounded by vegetation, which have little meaning for visitors. Other sites are well looked after and regularly visited. Unfortunately, they almost always lack explanatory signs. On the plus side, you will be able to enjoy these sites in peace, far from the crowds and souvenir vendors. However, in order to appreciate their full historical and cultural significance, you will need the services of a competent local guide who will make the site 'come to life' and explain it all within its context.

There are remains in every archipelago. On the Leeward Islands the sites are well cared for and easy to reach. The Tuamotus' heritage is more restricted, while on the Marquesas every island is an open-air archaeological museum containing several sites. In the Marquesas, the emergence of small-scale 'archaeological tourism' in the medium term would not be beyond the bounds of possibility.

Marae These were places of worship, cloaked in *tapu*, built in the open air for the purpose of celebrating the religious and social life of the clan. Within their confines, the gods were honoured and invoked, the chiefs formally installed, wars prepared, rituals performed and offerings and human sacrifices made. Marae were set up either along the coast or on the sides of mountains. Usually the trees surrounding them, especially the banyan, were considered holy.

There were several types of marae, of varying importance. The simplest type of marae were the family ones, where events affecting the life of the entire clan, such as births and deaths, were celebrated. The most complex were the royal marae, such as Marae Taputapuatea on Ra'iatea, which had worldwide influence, attracting Maohi chiefs from several islands of Polynesia, who would come to pledge allegiance to the *ari'i*. The most important religious symbols and objects, such as the *too*, were placed out of sight in a tabernacle-like recess.

Marae are like large paved rectangular platforms, sometimes more than 50m long. They were built of blocks of basalt and slabs of coral. The smaller stones or pebbles were coarsely shaped and assembled. Their design varies from island to island but there are certain common architectural features, namely a paved level space, a sort of open rectangular platform, surrounded by a wall. At one end is the *ahu*, an altar and the most holy place, which was reserved for the priest and the *ari'i*. Depending on the type of marae, the *ahu* may have several levels. Some contain three or four tiers like a stepped pyramid, while others are on one level only. The latter consists of a simple facing of coral slabs placed vertically, the inside of which is filled with broken stones.

On the front of the *ahu* facing the platform there are three vertical slabs of coral known as 'upright stones'. The centre of the platform is adorned with several 'sitting stones', intended for the chiefs and priests, symbolising their social rank. The design of the family marae is simpler: they only have one upright stone and three sitting stones. Various adjoining wooden structures, such as the *fare tupapau*, where the dead were laid out, were built around the marae. None has survived to this day.

Petroglyphs These are designs carved on stones; their significance has not yet been clearly established. The pictures feature octopuses, turtles, dugout canoes, suns, geometric designs, anthropomorphic figures and extremely schematic facial features. The best known are those on Tahiti and in the Marquesas.

Tiki At the meeting point of art and religion, tiki are humanlike statues, of enigmatic appearance, carved in basalt or *keetu* (volcanic tuff), or in wood, though the wooden ones have not withstood the ravages of time.

They nearly all conform to the same model: the legs are short and bent and the elbows held close to the sides. Some have been only very roughly carved out, making it very difficult to identify them. Others have a head that is quite visible but the upper and lower limbs are hardly discernible. The head is a direct extension of the trunk. The highly stylised mouth and eyes are the most striking features. The disproportionate mouth is represented by an extremely long but narrow rectangle, and the eyes are large concentric circles.

Tiki vary in size considerably. The tallest, located in the Marquesas, stands 2.7m high. Since they were generally erected on or near a holy place, experts believe tiki had a religious and symbolic function, representing deified ancestors or protective power. Providing an interface between men and gods, they also marked the boundaries of properties or places that were *tapu*. Sculpted in the form of statues, tiki can also be carved in bas-relief, on weapons (clubs), paddles, dugout canoes, and utensils. The most significant remains are found on the Marquesas.

Shrouded in *mana*, the ancient tiki continue to instil some degree of fear among Polynesians, who believe that tiki have a potential for evil that can manifest itself if they are moved or handled.

The Marquesas The *tohua* is a paved rectangular level space with stepped rows of stone seats on either side. Festivals were held here and public events such as dancing took place. They can be up to 100m long. At one end is a platform reserved for sacrifices and offerings. Flat boulders form a sort of stage on which one-man dances took place, and which was also used by young chiefs to show off their tattoos.

Pae pae are platforms of stone blocks, on which *ha'e* or *fae* (dwellings) were built of plant matter. The *pae pae* is divided into two parts. The front part forms a level that was reserved for daily activities. The back section, which was covered and slightly raised, served as a sleeping area. The roof was constructed of leaves from the *uru* tree and coconut palm. The front portion was also made from leaves and the whole structure was held up by several wooden stakes.

Only the stone foundations have survived. The covered areas, which contained plant matter, have been destroyed. You will find models of reconstructed *ha'e* on Nuku Hiva, Hiva Oa and 'Ua Pou.

On the Marquesas the term used is not marae, but *me'ae* (the difference in names is largely one of dialect). *Me'ae* are religious sites built from basalt blocks placed side by side and piled up. Generally found in the valleys and away from secular places, the *me'ae* was the sacred precinct *par excellence*. It was a place of worship, burial and offerings, and was strictly *tapu*. Access was restricted to a few initiated individuals endowed with *mana*, such as the priest or chief. Cannibalistic rites, restricted to chiefs, priests and warriors, also took place there when human sacrifices were made. *Me'ae* were generally built near a banyan, the sacred tree.

Facts for the Visitor

HIGHLIGHTS

Landscapes

If you have time to archipelago-hop, you will enjoy the widely varying landscapes of the Society Islands, where bold and angular tropical plants line the roads, and mountains leap out of valleys. Contrasting with the landscape of the Society Islands is the flat, rocky terrain of the Tuamotus – a moonscape in paradise – and the gloomy cliffs and rugged contours of the Marquesas. Sweat it out on a bicycle, meander around on foot or hire a pea-sized French car and explore the magic on wheels.

Activities

Surfers and body (boogie) boarders will find their wave in the region, particularly on Tahiti, Mo'orea and Huahine, which are home to internationally renowned sites.

Exhilarating hikes through the dense, tropical vegetation and up to the volcanic peaks of Tahiti, Mo'orea, Ra'iatea, Bora Bora and Maupiti are worthwhile, and good local guides are available. On Tahiti, put exploring the verdant Fautaua Valley or conquering the impressive Mt Aorai on the list, as well as braving the wild and remote Te Pari on Tahiti Iti. On Mo'orea, the walk from Vaiare to Paopao makes for a nice change from splashing around in the lagoon, and the Three Coconut Trees Pass will get that heart-rate up. See the Outdoor Activities chapter for details on these and other walks in the region.

You can dive to your heart's content in French Polynesia, and most dives are only a few minutes away by boat. Ra'iatea and Tahiti have shipwreck dives so you can act out your *Titanic* fantasies, and almost every other island will have a dive or two (if not 20) to keep you in the blue depths.

Yachts can be chartered from Ra'iatea, the yachting centre of French Polynesia, and you can explore many of the lagoons with smaller pirogues or outboard-powered dinghies. Or you could just play Robinson Crusoe on a deserted motu (small islet).

Culture

Nowhere else in the world will you find the delightful melange of Polynesian, French

and, to a lesser degree, Chinese influences. Fascinating and evocative archaeological sites are as common as imposing churches, and most Polynesians manage to practise Christianity while at the same time respecting their ancient marae (sacred sites). Tiki, *tohua* (esplanades of stone) and petroglyphs (pictograms incised into stone) adorn many islands, particularly in the Marquesas.

Getting your head around the basics of Tahitian, the colourful and expressive language spoken throughout French Polynesia, can be fun, but understanding how to combine it with Pacific-flavoured French phrases and words takes years!

Polynesia has long been a source of inspiration for artists, and you'll be tripping over galleries and interesting handicrafts, including wood and stone Marquesan sculptures, shell work, flower necklaces, *tapa* (bark-cloth), hand-painted pareu (sarongs), basketwork and *tifaifai* (appliqué blankets).

The Heiva festival, held throughout the month of July, celebrates Maohi (Polynesian) culture with awe-inspiring displays of agility. Dance groups gyrate, music resonates through the streets, and all sorts of sporting and cultural events take place.

Food

Foodies, gluttons and hedonists rejoice! You'll dine in style in French Polynesia. You can ease your way into the day with a perfect croissant and coffee, escape the heat of the day with a cold beer and a grilled tuna salad, and top it all off with a traditional meal of *poisson cru* (raw fish) served with lime and coconut milk, freshly caught *mahi mahi* (dorado), a local fish, and some fresh fruit for dessert. The food is always fresh, and is a unique mix of Polynesian, French and Chinese influences.

Pearl Farms

You can explore French Polynesia's famed black-pearl farms on Manihi, Rangiroa, Fakarava and Taha'a, or at the Musée de la Perle (Pearl Museum) in Pape'ete. Innumerable jewellery shops sell mounted and unmounted pearls all through the region. If you like pearls, it will take some willpower to go home empty-handed.

Off the Beaten Track

Yes, you can definitely get off the beaten track in French Polynesia, particularly if you are happy to travel the old-fashioned way – by boat. Voyage to the Tuamotus, the Marquesas or even the Australs or the Gambier Archipelago on a cargo ship and you'll feel a million miles away from the glamour and bustle of the Society Islands. There's no public transport; hotels and restaurants are few and far between; and time ticks slowly by.

SUGGESTED ITINERARIES

When you arrive in French Polynesia you may decide to ditch your action-packed itinerary in favour of Pacific-paced languor, but here are some suggestions anyway. Don't expect to see everything, unless you want to come back exhausted from your trip. Getting around the islands can take time, and there's nothing worse than being in a hurry in the Pacific – the locals will think you are mad. That said, try to visit a few different islands so you can get a feel for the variations in culture, climate and geology.

One Week

Even with only one week to spare, you could still visit Tahiti, Mo'orea and Bora Bora; depending on how hard you want to travel, you could also squeeze in a quick visit to Rangiroa (or Tikehau) in the Tuamotus, thanks to direct flights from Bora Bora to Rangiroa.

Two Weeks

With two weeks up your sleeve, you can really get a feel for the various islands of the Society group, and also continue to an atoll in the Tuamotus. Allow two days for Tahiti, two for Mo'orea, two for Huahine, three for Ra'iatea and Taha'a, two for Bora Bora, one for Maupiti and, if you're a scuba-diving or lazing-about enthusiast, two to three for Rangiroa in the Tuamotus.

Three Weeks

A three-week visit will allow you to explore several islands and archipelagos in depth. You could visit all the main islands of the Society group, by air or sea, and continue on to the Tuamotus (Rangiroa, Tikehau and Manihi) or the Australs (Rurutu and Tubuai) by air. Another possibility is to allow a week and a bit for the Society Islands and then take a cruise to the Marquesas.

Four Weeks

A whole month will give you time to see the Society Islands, two or three atolls in the Tuamotus and several islands in the Marquesas, if you use flights from Bora Bora to Rangiroa and from Rangiroa to Nuku Hiva in the Marquesas. You can even maintain the languid Pacific pace!

PLANNING
When to Go

French Polynesia is an outdoor destination, so the timing of your trip will probably be influenced by the weather. The dry winter period from May to October is the best time to go; the weather is cooler and there is much less rainfall during this time.

French Polynesia is south of the equator, but school holidays still fall in line with those of the northern hemisphere. This means that the peak season is July and August, and during this period it's no mean feat getting flights and accommodation. Christmas to early January, late February and early March, the Easter period, early May and early October are also quite busy times (which almost covers the entire year!). The peak July–August season coincides with the Heiva festival, held throughout July, when the region comes to life. Unfortunately this is no secret, so plan ahead if July interests you.

Diving is popular year-round, and each season brings its share of discoveries (see the special section 'Diving' following the Outdoor Activities chapter for more details). Surfing is also a year-round activity, but if you are sailing, it's best if you avoid the November to March tropical depressions – they can be depressing! Walking is best in the dry season, as some of the trails are simply impassable when it's wet.

Maps

The map *Tahiti Archipel de la Société* (IGN No 3615) at 1:100,000 is readily available in Pape'ete and at map specialists abroad. It covers the Society Archipelago and is the one really useful map for travellers. You'll find this map in Pape'ete on the ground floor of the **Prince Hinoi Centre** *(Av du Prince Hinoi; open 7.30am-6pm Mon-Fri, 8am-5pm Sat)* and in the **Librarie du Vaima** *(Vaima Centre; open 8.30am-6pm Mon-Fri, 8am-5pm Sat)*. IGN also publishes maps at 1:50,000 for each island in the archipelago, although these are harder to track down. The SHOM navy maps are the best available of the Tuamotus; for the Marquesas, there are SHOM maps and IGN maps at 1:50,000 for Hiva Oa, Nuku Hiva and 'Ua Pou.

What to Bring

When packing, bear in mind that all imported goods are expensive in French Polynesia, and that most goods are imported. So, bring sunscreen, film and toiletries with you from home, where they are sure to be cheaper.

The climate is mild, and shorts, dresses, skirts and sandals reign supreme, so you don't need to bring many clothes, even in the cooler months (jackets and ties are not required except on the most formal business occasions). Shorts, swimsuits and lightweight cotton clothes are the order of the day. Plastic shoes or waterproof sandals are also vital for wading in the shallows.

Small *pensions* (guesthouses) often don't supply towels or soap, so be sure to bring both. Laundrettes are rare outside Pape'ete, where they're very expensive, so come prepared to wash your own clothes.

Also be prepared for the intense sun (bring sunscreen, sunglasses and a hat), which can disappear and be replaced by heavy downpours (consider bringing a raincoat). Insect repellent is almost as important as your passport, and a small first-aid kit (see Health later in this chapter) is always wise. To keep your camera gear protected from water and humidity, bring a plastic bag and desiccating sachets.

If you're going hiking, bring good shoes and a light jacket or sweater: it can get surprisingly cool up in the mountains. Don't forget your mask, snorkel and flippers for exploring the lagoons, and your dive card if you're a certified diver.

RESPONSIBLE TOURISM

Brochures may continue to paint French Polynesia as an unspoilt destination, but the environmental impact of some 230,000 visitors a year – a similar figure to the entire population of French Polynesia – cannot be swept under the carpet forever.

Although much of the development is low rise and local style – thus avoiding the concrete and glass horrors of Hawaii – safe waste disposal, the recycling of materials and the use of solar power have until recently been the concern of the minority. 'Green' hotels are still fairly rare but are slowly emerging. Among the more conventional places to stay, consider staying in a locally owned hotel or guesthouse rather than a foreign-owned one. Although the foreign-owned companies provide valuable employment opportunities for locals, the profits do not stay on local shores.

Water activities in French Polynesia sometimes take on a fairly irresponsible hue. Controversial practices such as the feeding of rays and sharks – so that tourists can touch the beasts as they scramble for food – and even pulling sharks on board to be stroked, is a far from natural or necessary experience (see the boxed text 'All Aboard' under Rangiroa in the Tuamotus chapter), and is an obvious disruption to the food chain. Expressing your distaste for these practices should help discourage them. A quick list of 'shoulds': avoid collecting shells and buying turtle shell; take care when diving or swimming to avoid damaging the fragile coral; if you are yachting, ensure that the anchor does not drag on the coral.

Prostitution is really only evident within Pape'ete, where sex workers can sometimes be seen walking the streets, wandering around the hotels and drinking at the bars. Needless to say, travellers are cautioned against engaging with the sex industry. Prostitution only emerged in the region when philandering Europeans created a demand for it in the 18th and 19th centuries (see the boxed text 'The Island of Lust' in the Facts about French Polynesia chapter). You can't take responsibility for past wrongs, but you can avoid perpetuating them.

TOURIST OFFICES
Local Tourist Offices
The main tourist office is the **Manava Visitors Bureau** (☎ 50 57 10, fax 43 16 78; e tahiti-manava@mail.microtech.pf; Fare Manihini, Blvd Pomare; open 7.30am-5pm Mon-Fri, 8am-noon Sat & public holidays) in the centre of Pape'ete. This office has information about the whole of French Polynesia, and the staff are very helpful. The more touristy islands generally have some sort of tourist office or counter, but they vary widely in usefulness and dependability.

For information before you leave home, contact **Tahiti Tourisme** (☎ 50 57 00, fax 43 66 19; e tahiti-tourisme@mail.pf; w www .tahiti-tourisme.com; Immeuble Paofai, Batiment D, Blvd Pomare, Pape'ete).

Tourist Offices Abroad
Overseas representatives of Tahiti Tourisme include:

Australia (☎ 02-9281 6020, fax 9211 6589, e info@traveltotahiti.com.au; w www.travelto tahiti.com.au) 12 Ann St, Surry Hills, NSW 2010
Chile (☎ 02-251 2826, fax 233 1787, e tahiti@cmet.net) Av 11 de Septiembre 2214, OF-116, Casilla 16057, Santiago
France (☎ 01 55 42 64 34, fax 01 55 42 61 20, e tahititourisme@voyagetahiti.com) 28 Blvd Saint-Germain, 75005 Paris
Germany (☎ 69-9714 84, fax 7292 75) Bockenheimer Landstr 45, 60325 Frankfurt/Main
Italy (☎ 02-66 980317, fax 66 92648) Piazza Caiazzo 3, 20 124 Milan
New Zealand (☎ 09-368 5362, fax 368 5263, e info@tahiti-tourisme.co.nz, w www.tahiti-tourisme.co.nz) Level 1, Studio 2A, 200 Victoria St West, Auckland
Singapore (☎ 6733 4295, fax 6732 3205, e pl_holdings@pacific.net.sg) c/- Pacific Leisure Holdings Pte Ltd, 321 Orchard Rd, 09-01 Orchard Shopping Centre, Singapore 238 866
USA (☎ 310-414 8484, fax 414 8490, e tahiti lax@earthlink.net) 300 Continental Blvd, Suite 160, El Segundo, CA 90 245

VISAS & DOCUMENTS
Passport & Visas
Everyone needs a passport to visit French Polynesia. The regulations are much the same as for France: if you need a visa to visit France then you'll need one to visit French Polynesia. Anyone from a European Union (EU) country can stay for up to three months without a visa, as can Australians and citizens of a number of other European countries, including Switzerland.

Citizens of Argentina, Canada, Chile, Japan, Mexico, New Zealand, the USA and some other European countries can stay for up to one month without a visa. Other nationalities need a visa, which can be applied for at French diplomatic missions. Visa regulations for French Polynesia can change at short notice, so check with a travel agent shortly before departing.

Apart from permanent residents and French citizens, all visitors to French Polynesia need to have an onward or return ticket.

Visa Extensions Travellers who must have a visa, or those who have a one-month exemption and wish to extend their stay, should contact the **Police aux Frontières** (Frontier Police; ☎/fax 42 40 74; e pafport@ mail.pf; airport office open 8am-noon & 2pm-5pm Mon-Fri, Pape'ete office open 7.30am-noon & 2pm-5pm Mon-Fri), at Faa'a airport and next to the Manava Visitors Bureau in Pape'ete, at least one week before the visa or exemption expires. An extension is for a maximum of two months, and incurs a fee of 3000 CFP.

Stays by foreign visitors may not exceed three months. For longer periods, you must apply to the French consular authorities in your own country for a residence permit; you cannot lodge your application from French Polynesia (see Work later in this chapter for information on work permits).

Formalities for Yachts In addition to presenting the certificate of ownership of the vessel, sailors are subject to the same passport and visa requirements as travellers arriving by air or by cruise ship. Unless you have a return air ticket, you are required to provide a banking guarantee of repatriation equivalent to the price of an airline ticket to your country of origin.

Yachties must advise the **Police aux Frontières** (*Frontier Police; open 7.30am-noon & 2pm-5pm Mon-Fri*), next to the tourist office in Pape'ete, of their final departure. If your first port of call is not Pape'ete, it must be a port with a *gendarmerie*: Afareaitu (Mo'orea), Uturoa (Ra'iatea), Fare (Huahine), Vaitape (Bora Bora), Taiohae (Nuku Hiva, Marquesas), Hakahau ('Ua Pou, Marquesas), Atuona (Hiva Oa, Marquesas), Mataura (Tubuai, Australs), Moerai (Rurutu, Australs), Rairua (Raivavae, Australs), Avatoru (Rangiroa, Tuamotus) or Rikitea (Mangareva, Gambiers). The *gendarmerie* must be advised of each arrival and departure, and of any change of crew.

Before arriving at the port of Pape'ete, announce your arrival on channel 12. You can anchor at the quay or the beach, but there are no reserved places. Report to the **Capitainerie** (*Harbour Master's Office; open 7am-11.30am & 1pm-4pm Mon-Thur, 7am-11.30am & 1pm-3pm Fri*) in the same building as the Police aux Frontières to complete an arrival declaration.

Travel Insurance

A travel insurance policy, to cover theft, loss and medical problems, is vital. There are a wide variety of policies available and your travel agent will have recommendations. The policies offered by STA or other student-travel organisations are usually good value. Some policies offer different medical-expense options, but the higher ones are chiefly for countries such as the USA, which has extremely high medical costs.

Some policies specifically exclude 'dangerous activities', which can include scuba diving, motorcycling and even trekking. If such activities are on your agenda, you obviously don't want that sort of policy.

You may prefer a policy that pays doctors or hospitals directly rather than you having to pay on the spot and claim later. If you have to claim later, make sure you keep all documentation. Some policies ask you to call (reverse charges) a centre in your home country where an immediate assessment of your problem is made.

Check the small print: for example, does the policy cover ambulances or an emergency flight home? If you have to stretch out you will need two seats and somebody has to pay for them!

Other Documents

Car rental agencies in French Polynesia only ask to see your national driving licence, so an international driving licence is unnecessary. Bring your dive certification card if you plan to do any scuba diving in French Polynesia.

Copies

All important documents (passport data page and visa page, credit cards, travel insurance policy, tickets, driving licence etc) should be photocopied before you leave home. Leave one copy with someone at home for safekeeping and keep another with you, separate from the originals.

You can also store details of your vital travel documents in Lonely Planet's free online Travel Vault, in case you lose the photocopies or can't be bothered with them. Your password-protected Travel Vault is accessible online anywhere in the world – create it at w www.ekno.lonelyplanet.com.

EMBASSIES & CONSULATES
French Embassies & Consulates

You will find French diplomatic representation in:

Australia (☎ 02-6216 0100, fax 6216 0127, w www.ambafrance-au.org) 6 Perth Ave, Yarralumla, ACT 2600

Belgium (☎ 02-548 8711, fax 513 6871, w www.ambafrance-be.org) 65 rue Ducale, 1000 Brussels

Canada (☎ 613-789 1795, fax 562 3735, w www.ambafrance-ca.org) 42 Sussex Dr, Ottawa, ON K1M 2C9

Chile (☎ 02-470 80 00, fax 470 80 50, w www.france.cl) Av Condell 65, Casilla 38-D, Providencia, Santiago

Fiji (☎ 331 22 33, fax 330 18 94) Dominion House, Scott St, Suva

Germany (☎ 69-2063 9000, fax 2063 9010) An der Kochstrasse 6/7, D-10969 Berlin

Ireland (☎ 01-260 16 66, fax 283 01 78, w www.ambafrance-ie.org) 36 Ailesbury Rd, Ballsbridge, Dublin 4

Israel (☎ 03-520 8300, fax 520 8340, w www.ambafrance-il.org) 112 Promenade Herbert-Samuel, 61033 Tel Aviv

New Zealand (☎ 04-384 2555, fax 384 2577, w www.ambafrance-nz.org) Rural Bank Bldg, 13th floor, 34-42 Manners St, PO Box 11-343, Wellington

Singapore (☎ 6880 7800, fax 6880 7801, w www.france.org.sg) 101-103 Cluny Park Rd, Singapore 259595

Switzerland (☎ 031-359 2111, fax 352 2191, Ⓦ www.ambafrance-ch.org) Schosshalden-strasse 46, 3006 Berne
UK (☎ 020 7073 1200, fax 020 7073 1201, Ⓦ www.ambafrance-uk.org) 21 Cromwell Rd, London SW7 2EN
USA (☎ 202-944 6000, fax 944 6166, Ⓦ www .ambafrance-us.org) 4101 Reservoir Rd NW, Washington, DC 20007

Consulates in French Polynesia

Given that French Polynesia is not an independent country, there are no foreign embassies, only consulates, and many countries are represented in Pape'ete by honorary consuls. Canada, the USA and Japan are without diplomatic representation in French Polynesia. If you need a US visa the nearest place to inquire about it is Fiji. If you're a Canadian and you lose your passport, the Australian consulate may be able to help.

The following consulates and diplomatic representatives are all on Tahiti.

Australia (☎ 43 88 38, fax 41 05 19) c/- Qantas Airways, Vaima Centre, Pape'ete BP 1695, Pape'ete
Austria (also represents Swiss and Liechtensteiner residents; ☎ 43 91 14, fax 43 21 22) Rue Cannonière Zélée, Pape'ete BP 4560, Pape'ete
Belgium (☎ 82 54 44, 83 75 09, fax 83 55 34) École Notre-Dame des Anges, Faa'a BP 6003, Faa'a
Chile (☎ 43 89 19, fax 43 61 62) Passage Cardella, Pape'ete BP 952, Pape'ete
Germany (☎ 42 99 94, 42 80 84, fax 42 96 89) Rue Gadiot, Pira'e BP 452, Pira'e
Italy (☎ 43 45 01, fax 43 45 07) Puna'auia, Punaruu Valley BP 380 412, Tamanu
Netherlands (☎ 42 49 37, 43 06 86, fax 43 56 92) Mobil Bldg, Fare Ute, Pape'ete BP 2804, Pape'ete
New Zealand (☎ 54 07 47/40, fax 42 45 44) c/- Air New Zealand, Vaima Centre, Pape'ete BP 73, Pape'ete

CUSTOMS

The duty-free allowance for visitors entering French Polynesia includes 200 cigarettes or 50 cigars, 2L of spirits or wine, two cameras and 10 rolls of unexposed film, one video camera and 50g of perfume. No live animals can be imported (if they're on a yacht they must stay on board) and certification is required for plants. For information on customs regulations for yachts, see Formalities for Yachts earlier in this chapter.

MONEY
Currency & Exchange Rates

The unit of currency in French Polynesia is the *franc cours pacifique* (CFP), referred to simply as 'the franc'. There are coins of 1, 2, 5, 10, 20, 50 and 100 CFP, and notes of 500, 1000, 5000 and 10,000 CFP. The CFP was pegged to the French franc, and so is now pegged to the euro.

country	unit		franc cours pacifique
Australia	A$1	=	67 CFP
Canada	C$1	=	80 CFP
euro zone	€1	=	119 CFP
Japan	¥100	=	103 CFP
New Zealand	NZ$1	=	57 CFP
UK	UK£1	=	186 CFP
USA	US$1	=	123 CFP

Exchanging Money

There are fairly hefty bank charges for changing money and travellers cheques in French Polynesia. You generally pay at least 450 CFP commission on travellers cheques and to exchange cash, although exchange rates do vary from bank to bank, so if you have time, shop around to find the best rate. Given the cost of living in French Polynesia, and the low crime rate, you are better off exchanging larger sums of money (ie, fewer transactions) than smaller amounts. Rates offered on Tahiti tend to be better than those offered on the other islands.

Banks There are three major banks operating in French Polynesia: Banque de Tahiti, Banque de Polynésie and Banque Socredo.

Most banks are concentrated in Pape'ete and the more populous islands of Mo'orea, Ra'iatea and Bora Bora. All the main islands in the Society group, apart from Maupiti, have at least a banking agency. In the Tuamotus, only Rangiroa has a permanent banking service. In the Marquesas there are Socredo agencies on 'Ua Pou, Nuku Hiva and Hiva Oa. In the Australs group, Rurutu and Tubuai have some banking services.

Banking hours vary from branch to branch but are typically from 8am to noon and 1pm to 4pm Monday to Thursday, and 8am to noon and 1pm to 3pm on Friday. Some branches in Pape'ete do not close for the traditional Polynesian lunch break, and a handful of Tahiti branches open on Saturday morning. The Banque de Polynésie has banking facilities at Pape'ete's Faa'a airport for flight arrivals.

ATMs Known as *distributeurs automatiques de billets* or DABs in French, ATMs will give you cash advances on your Visa or MasterCard or, if linked to the international Cirrus or Maestro networks, will let you withdraw money straight from your home bank account. In the past the system has worked perfectly for some travellers and yet posed inexplicable problems for others, so make sure you have a back-up plan on the off-chance your card doesn't work every time.

The exchange rate on these transactions is usually better than you get with travellers cheques, and the charge your own bank makes on these withdrawals (typically about US$5) is far less than you'll be charged by banks in French Polynesia.

ATMs can be found dotted around Tahiti, but they're less common on other islands. Mo'orea, Huahine, Ra'iatea, Bora Bora and Rangiroa have ATMs (Rangiroa has the only ATM in the Tuamotus). On Nuku Hiva and Hiva Oa in the Marquesas and on Rurutu and Tubuai in the Australs there are ATMs inside the Socredo agencies.

Credit Cards All top-end and mid-range hotels, restaurants, jewellery shops, dive centres and bigger supermarkets accept credit cards, preferably Visa or MasterCard. You can also pay for Air Tahiti flights with a card. Most budget guesthouses and many tour operators don't accept credit cards, so you can get caught out on the weekends if there's no ATM on the island.

Costs

French Polynesia is expensive by anyone's standards. Flights tend to be a substantial cost, and once in French Polynesia, food and accommodation loom large in the financial foreground. Taxation is the bugbear here: a TVA (*taxe sur la valeur ajoutée*; value-added tax), which was introduced in 1998, currently adds 6% to your hotel bill (and that's not including the 5% government tax and the *taxe de séjour*, accommodation tax or daily tax, which top off the bill). See the boxed text 'Cheap Thrills' for more information about prices in French Polynesia,

---

Cheap Thrills

Forewarned is forearmed: you can do French Polynesia on a shoestring budget, but it's a real challenge.

The cost of activities can quickly add up, the glamorous hotels charge an arm and a leg, and the restaurant prices rival those in Paris. If you are surrounded by travellers who appear to have heavier wallets than you do, it can all feel a bit disheartening.

Do not despair! A fresh baguette (around 50 CFP) is never far away, the cheapest dish on almost any menu is the wonderful and filling *poisson cru* (raw fish), and the warm weather means camping or rudimentary accommodation is far from unpleasant. A batch of quaint and affordable little *pensions* (guesthouses) is springing up to help you in your budgeting endeavours. This is a magnificent part of the world to explore, and once on an island, distances are generally 'cycle-able', which makes for a jolly old way of getting around. Bicycles can be hired on most islands. If you bring a mask and snorkel, the joys of pottering about the aqua shallows of a lagoon are priceless.

French Polynesia can be the playground of mere mortals, as well as the rich and famous. It just takes a bit of creativity.

---

and Economy in the Facts about French Polynesia chapter for more information about the taxation system.

Tipping & Bargaining

Tipping and bargaining are not a part of life in French Polynesia. The price quoted is the price you are expected to pay, which certainly simplifies things and goes in some way to recompense the extraordinary expense of the region. The only exception to this is for black pearls, where some discounts may be offered; you may also be able to bargain when buying craftwork directly from an artist (Marquesan sculptures, for example).

POST & COMMUNICATIONS
Post

The postal system in French Polynesia is generally quite efficient, and there are modern post offices on all the main islands. Mail to Europe, the USA and Australia takes about a week. Postcards or letters weighing up to 20g cost 85 CFP to France, 120 CFP to anywhere else.

French Polynesian stamps are often beautiful, but even more often they're massive. Put the stamps on your postcard first so you know how much space is left to squeeze the address in. If you're lucky there may still be room for a message.

Post offices are generally open from around 7.30am to 3pm Monday to Friday, although the main post office in Pape'ete has longer opening hours and the post office at Faa'a airport is also open from 6.30am to 10am Saturday and Sunday.

There is no door-to-door mail delivery in French Polynesia, so mail is usually addressed to a *boîte postale* (BP; post office box). If you want to receive mail, ask for it to be addressed to you care of poste restante at the appropriate place (eg, James Cook, c/- Poste Restante, Vaitape, Bora Bora, French Polynesia).

Telephone

The public telephone system is modern, easy to use, widespread and, when it comes to international calls, rather expensive. Public phone boxes are found even in surprisingly remote locations, and all use the same phonecards. Phonecards can be bought from post offices, newsagencies, shops and some supermarkets. They're even available from vending machines at Faa'a airport. Phonecards are available in 1000, 2000 and 5000 CFP denominations.

There are no area codes in French Polynesia. Local phone calls cost 33 CFP for four minutes at normal tariff rates. The rates for inter-island or inter-archipelago calls are more expensive (33 CFP a minute inter-archipelago).

To call a number in French Polynesia from overseas, dial the international access number, then ☎ 689 (Tahiti's international dialling code), then the local number.

To call overseas from French Polynesia dial ☎ 00, then your country code, the area code (dropping any leading 0) and the local number. Most phone boxes have an information panel that explains, in French and English, how to make overseas calls. If you have any difficulty, call **information** (☎ 3612).

If you want to make a reverse-charge call, ask for *un appel payable a l'arrivée*.

Fax

You can send faxes from post offices, but this is no cheap exercise. It usually costs around 1300 CFP for the first page. Some of the bigger hotels have fax machines for their guests' use.

Email & Internet Access

Surfing in Polynesia has always been something you do with a surfboard, but the Internet is finally starting to take hold of French Polynesia. Internet cafés are still fairly few and far between, although most top-end hotels offer Internet access to their guests, and access is fairly straightforward on Tahiti, Mo'orea, Bora Bora, Rangiroa and Ra'iatea. You'll generally pay around 500 CFP per half-hour.

DIGITAL RESOURCES

The Web is a rich resource for travellers. You can research your trip, hunt down bargain air fares, book hotels, check on weather conditions or chat with locals and other travellers about the best places to visit (or avoid!).

There's no better place to start your Web explorations than at the **Lonely Planet** website (W *www.lonelyplanet.com*). Here you'll find succinct summaries on travelling to most places on earth, as well as postcards from other travellers and the Thorn Tree bulletin board, where you can ask questions before you go or dispense advice when you get back. You can also find travel news and updates to many of our most popular guidebooks, and the subwwway section links you to the most useful travel resources elsewhere on the Web.

There are heaps of websites with good information about travelling to French Polynesia, but make sure your boss is out of earshot if you are researching your tropical holiday at work (many of the sites have sound effects of swishing waves and local music – a dead giveaway that your mind is elsewhere). The majority of sites are still in French, but practical English-language websites for French Polynesia include the following: **Tahiti Tourisme** (W *www.tahiti-tourism.com*), **Tahiti Nui Travel** (W *www.tahiti-nui .com*), **Tahiti Communications** (W *www.ta hiti.com*), **Tahiti Explorer** (W *www.tahiti-explo rer.com*) and **PolynesianIslands.com** (W *www .polynesianislands.com*).

BOOKS

There is a smorgasbord of literature about French Polynesia, but most of it is in French, and much of it is only available in French Polynesia. Although the suggestions that follow are predominantly for books available in English, there are a few French titles that may be of interest even if your French is poor (or nonexistent).

Most books are published in different editions by different publishers in different countries. As a result, a book might be a hardcover rarity in one country while it's readily available in paperback in another. Fortunately, bookshops and libraries search by title or author, so your local bookshop or library is best placed to advise you on the availability of the following recommendations. See Literature in the Facts about French Polynesia chapter for texts written by French Polynesians.

Lonely Planet

If French Polynesia is just one stop on your Pacific travels, look for Lonely Planet's *South Pacific* guidebook, which is packed with information on nations dotted across the great South Seas.

The extensively illustrated Lonely Planet Pisces guide *Diving & Snorkeling French Polynesia* covers 40 popular dive sites in the Society Islands, the Tuamotus and the Marquesas.

To come to grips with the Tahitian tongue, look for Lonely Planet's *South Pacific phrasebook*, which also covers 12 other Pacific languages.

Guidebooks

Mave Mai: The Marquesas Islands, by Chester, Baumgartner, Frechoso & Oetzel (1998), is a travel guide that focuses on archaeology and natural history. The nuts and bolts of travel in the region are not covered.

Even if you don't read French, keen walkers will enjoy the invaluable *Randonnées en Montagne* by Paule Laudon. It grades by difficulty all the best walks on Tahiti and Mo'orea.

Visiting yachties will probably carry a copy of *Landfalls of Paradise: a Cruising Guide to the Pacific Islands* by Earl R Hinz. This title gives a thorough coverage of Pacific cruising, including a number of islands in French Polynesia.

Travel

In *Blue Latitudes: Boldly Going Where Captain Cook Has Gone Before* (2002), Pulitzer-winning writer Tony Horwitz follows the voyages of Captain Cook with his beer-swilling friend Williamson. It's a frustrating, funny and insightful read.

Art of Travel by Alain de Botton (2002) is a philosophical text examining why we travel and is rich food for thought for the compulsive traveller.

Sultry Climates: Travel and Sex Since the Grand Tour by Ian Littlewood (2001) takes an unabashed look at the history of travel and sex, a particularly pertinent topic given the attitude of many early explorers towards Tahitian women. The lure of Tahiti for the European was, arguably, inextricably linked with the lure of uninhibited sex.

The congenitally acerbic Paul Theroux was at his sourest when he visited *The Happy Isles of Oceania* (1992), describing Tahiti as 'a paradise of fruit trees, brown tits and kiddie porn'. Crossing the South Pacific from Australia and New Zealand to Hawaii, he didn't find much of it to be very happy, but the insights are up to his usual high standards. As usual, his fellow passengers are prodded unmercifully with his sharpest pen and the beautiful, gloomy Marquesas are the perfect site for a Theroux visit. The French don't come out of it very well, but nor do the Polynesians, who are presented as eagerly embracing their own decline.

Much more upbeat is Gavin Bell's award-winning *In Search of Tusitala* (1994), which traces the Pacific wanderings of Robert Louis Stevenson. Like a number of other writers, Bell finds the Marquesas fascinating, beautiful and deeply depressing. 'How long has it been raining?' Bell asks the first Marquesan he meets. 'About one year,' comes the reply.

History

One of the few Polynesian accounts of pre-European Tahiti is Teuira Henry's *Ancient Tahiti,* published in 1928, which focuses on the ancient religion of the islands.

The Word, the Pen, and the Pistol by Robert Nicole (2000) is a detailed examination of the mythical values attributed to the Polynesians, as well as a look at the more recent history of French control, nuclear testing and local oscillation between collaboration with and resistance to the French.

Tahiti by George Calderon, who travelled around the Pacific in 1906, has recently been reprinted (2002). Calderon's drawings and elegant prose are captivating.

David Howarth's *Tahiti: a Paradise Lost* maps the rapid destruction of traditional Polynesian life as a result of contact with Europeans. This is an insightful and concise text if you can find a copy (it is out of print). *The Fatal Impact,* by Alan Moorehead, is also out of print but is a riveting account of the impact of European contact.

The most thorough version of Captain James Cook's logbooks is Professor John C Beaglehole's four-volume, 3000-page *The Voyages of the Endeavour, 1768-1771,* which has been reprinted by Boydell & Brewer, and now fetches a mean US$1070. Beaglehole edited Sir Joseph Banks' account in the two-volume *The Endeavour Journal of Joseph Banks,* and has also written *The Exploration of the Pacific* and *The Life of Captain James Cook.*

Briefer accounts of Cook's voyages include *The Explorations of Captain James Cook in the Pacific,* a collection of annotated extracts from Cook's logs, and *The Voyage of the Endeavour: Captain Cook and the Discovery of the Pacific,* by Alan Frost.

Joseph Banks: A Life by Patrick O'Brian traces the life of the young scientist on Cook's first expedition.

The American duo Nordhoff and Hall wrote three books in the 1930s on the *Bounty* mutiny and its aftermath. *Mutiny on the Bounty* recounts the famous mutiny; *Men Against the Sea* follows Bligh's epic open-boat voyage; and *Pitcairn Island,* which is partly fiction because so little is known about the facts, follows Fletcher Christian and his band of mutineers and Tahitians to their Pitcairn hideaway. Greg Dening's *Mr Bligh's Bad Language* is an excellent and insightful book about the man history loves to hate and the mutiny that history loves.

In *Kon-Tiki: Across the Pacific by Raft,* Norwegian explorer Thor Heyerdahl recounts his epic voyage to prove his (now discounted) theory that Polynesia had been populated by Incas from South America.

Gauguin's Skirt by Stephen F Eisenman (1999) examines the gulf between Gauguin's dream of an exotic paradise and the fraught reality of the French colony he found. This publication wins the best title award.

If you read French, *Pouvana'a A Oopa: Père de la culture politique tahitienne* by Bruno Saura (1999) is a meaty, satisfying look at Tahiti's political father, Pouvana'a, who was exiled in the 1960s by the French administration. Pouvana'a was exonerated in the late 1960s and was elected as French Polynesia's senator to Paris. He advocated autonomy and the recognition of Tahitian as the official language, and gave many a provocative speech before his death in 1977.

The Radiological Situation at the Atolls of Moruroa and Fangataufa (2001), published by the International Atomic Energy Agency (IAEA), is a dry but revealing look at the history and politics of French nuclear testing in the Pacific. This report was commissioned by the French government, and what it omits is as revealing as what it says.

Natural History

A variety of small books are available on the flora and fauna of Polynesia, although nothing new has been published in quite some time. Two worth looking at are *Birds of Tahiti,* by Jean-Claude Thibault & Claude Rivers (Les Éditions du Pacifique), and *Sharks of Polynesia,* by RH Johnson (Les Éditions du Pacifique).

Fiction & Autobiography

For 150 years, European writers have flocked to Polynesia like bees to honey. French Polynesia's remarkable magnetism has produced some impressive literary works, as well as its share of duds.

Melville was the first of the important literary visitors. His experiences in the 'cannibal' valley, where he made his Marquesan escape, resulted in his first novel, *Typee – A Peep at Polynesian Life,* published in 1846. This rather idealistic travelogue was an instant success and was followed by *Omoo* (1847).

French literature's primary addition to the Tahiti bookshelves was Pierre Loti's 1876 classic *Le Mariage de Loti* (The Marriage of Loti), which made a strong contribution to the myth of a Pacific paradise full of beguiling young women.

Robert Louis Stevenson's trip through Polynesia yielded *In the South Seas* (1900), not the author's best work.

Carved tiki, Pape'ete

Marae Umarea, Mo'orea

Tiki from Raivavae, Musée Gauguin, Tahiti

Marae Taputapuatea, Ra'iatea

Diving and snorkelling

Jack London also cruised the Pacific but, again, *South Sea Tales* (1911) is not the writer at his best. The greedy pearl buyer portrayed in 'The House of Mapuhi' successfully took London to court.

Noa Noa: The Tahiti Journal of Paul Gauguin is Gauguin's troubled account of his life on Tahiti, in which he describes what he sees as a grotesque imitation of European 'customs, fashions, vices, and absurdities of civilisation'. It is an easy and interesting read, and contains some of Gauguin's sketches.

W Somerset Maugham's *The Moon & Sixpence*, published in 1919, portrays the mildly absurd and overtly misogynist character of Strickland, a fictional Gauguin.

In 1947, James A Michener launched his prodigious career of writing populist, popular novels with *Tales of the South Pacific*. Based on the author's experiences in the region during WWII, this novel was adapted for the stage and was also made into a film. Michener returned to this happy hunting ground with *Return to Paradise* (1951) and *Rascals in Paradise* (1957).

Henderson's Spear by Ronald Wright (2002) is a poly-plotted novel about a woman's search for the truth about her father's disappearance while an RAF pilot, which leads her to Tahiti.

Art & Culture

The Art of Tahiti, by Terence Barrow, is a succinct and colourfully illustrated introduction to the art of the Society, Austral and Cook islands. Unfortunately, it does not extend to the Marquesas, and it's out of print.

You'll be tripping over the countless books that have been written about Gauguin and his works. Some of the most recent publications on the artist include John Borthwick's *Chasing Gauguin's Ghost: Tales of a Professional Tourist* (2002) and Eckhard Hollmann's *Paul Gauguin: Images from the South Seas* (2002), a close and illustrated look at Gauguin's work and life with some excellent reproductions of the artists' work.

Tatau – Maohi Tattoo, by Dominique Morvan, with photographs by Claude Corault and Marie-Hélène Villierme (1993, Tupuna Productions), is an interesting account of the resurgence of traditional tattooing in French Polynesia (see also Coffee-Table Books, following).

Hiva Oa – Glimpses of an Oceanic Memory, by Pierre Ottino & Marie-Noëlle de Bergh-Ottino, is a locally produced book on the archaeology and art of the Marquesan island of Hiva Oa.

Publisher Le Motu has launched a series on local artists with a short introductory text in English and French. These include *Dubois, Deloffre* and *Boullaire*.

Coffee-Table Books

French Polynesia incites camera-happy behaviour and so lends itself beautifully to glossy coffee-table books.

Fabled Isles of the South Seas, by Winston Stuart Conrad, makes an erratic swing through the islands of Polynesia and has images of remote and rarely visited areas. Conrad contrasts contemporary images with historical photos and old illustrations.

Photographer Marie-Helen Villierme's *Visages de Polynésie* (Faces of Polynesia) contains more than 100 black-and-white photographs of Polynesians, from cargo-ship mechanics to village tradesmen, together with brief conversations in both French and English.

Tahiti Tattoos, by the Italian fashion photographer Gian Paolo Barbieri, is a great-looking book, bordering on the homoerotic, which features the human canvases of some of Tahiti's best-known tattooists.

Tahiti from the Air, by Erwin Christian & Emmanuel Vigneron, has interesting aerial photographs of French Polynesia. It's almost 20 years old, and it's interesting to note how the area has changed since then. Other books on the Polynesian islands by the same photographer include *Marquesas, Images from the Land of Men* and, in French, *Bora Bora: Impressions d'une Île* and *Lumières du Lagon*.

Islands of Tahiti, by Raymond Bagnis with photographs by Erwin Christian, is out of print but has good photos and some interesting text if you can find a copy.

James Sears' *Tahiti – Romance & Reality* is an odd mix of contemporary photos and excerpts from early visitors' journals, but it does make for a good read.

The History of Aviation in French Polynesia/L'Aviation a Tahiti, by Jean-Louis Saquet, uses photographs and illustrations to tell the story of aviation in the region (just as well because the translation is appalling).

FILMS

There's a dearth of films made about or set in French Polynesia. Tahiti's role as a movie backdrop is almost exclusively tied up with the *Bounty* (see the boxed text 'Mutiny in the Cinema'). James Michener's *South Pacific* may have been about Polynesia, but it certainly wasn't filmed there. Oddly enough, the film world has turned a blind cinematographic eye to the great Polynesian migration voyages, European exploration, French colonialism and (apart from *The Thin Red Line*) to the world wars in the Pacific. Perhaps Tom Hanks will play Captain Cook in a Hollywood extravaganza sometime soon.

Tabu, released in 1931, was filmed in Bora Bora. This work of fiction explores the notions of *tapu* (taboo), and when one of the directors was killed in an accident shortly after finishing filming, there was plenty of speculation that his death may have been the result of including taboo parts of the island in the film.

In 1979, a big-budget remake of *Hurricane*, the 1937 classic based on a Nordhoff & Hall novel, was filmed on Bora Bora. The film was a major flop, despite an all-star cast; for TV it was retitled *Forbidden Paradise*.

NEWSPAPERS & MAGAZINES

Most newspapers and magazines available in French Polynesia are in French, although you can usually find an English-language newspaper from a few days ago for a hefty sum. Good international magazines, such as the *Economist*, are sometimes available at the better newsagencies and bookshops.

In Pape'ete, **Maison de la Presse** *(Blvd Pomare)* has a good selection of newspapers and magazines, as does **Le Kiosque** *(Blvd Pomare)*, **Librarie du Vaima** *(☎ 45 57 57; Vaima Centre)*, the bookshop in the **Prince Hinoi Centre** *(Av du Prince Hinoi)* and **Librarie Archipels** *(☎ 42 47 30; 68 Rue des Remparts)*.

If you read French, there are two Tahitian dailies, *Les Nouvelles de Tahiti* and *La Dépêche de Tahiti*, although they are not easy to find away from Tahiti and Mo'orea. Both papers are part of the local Hersant empire and are strong supporters of the loyalist Tahoera Huiraatira political party. *Tahiti Pacifique* is a monthly news magazine covering political, economic, social and cultural life in French Polynesia. It doesn't shirk controversial issues and could be considered an opposition newspaper.

Mutiny in the Cinema

Everybody loves a filmic mutiny, and nobody loves an excuse for a good-guy-versus-bad-guy flick more than Hollywood. The story of the famous uprising aboard the *Bounty* has been embellished by big-budget film-makers three times in 50 years. If another version is ever made, audiences could be forgiven for having a mutiny of their own.

The original *Mutiny on the Bounty* epic was made in 1935. It was directed by Frank Lloyd and starred Charles Laughton as Bligh and Clark Gable as Fletcher Christian (Gable's last moustache-less film). Although critics insist that this is the classic *Bounty* film, it certainly played fast and loose with history. Bligh flogs, keelhauls, lies and cheats his way through the entire film, while Christian is a charming, brave, purposeful, rather American aristocrat. Poetic licence has Bligh storming back to Tahiti to round up the mutineers, while Christian et al dutifully wait for British naval justice. Very little of the film was actually shot on Tahiti.

The lavish three-hour 1962 remake *Mutiny on the Bounty* was directed by Lewis Milestone, and stars Trevor Howard as Bligh and Marlon Brando as Christian. This film is a much more extravagant affair than the black-and-white original and was filmed on Tahiti and Bora Bora, to the great benefit of the local economy. Bligh is again portrayed as a monster, while Christian is a sort of simpering fop who clearly would have driven any captain nuts.

The third and final remake of the now-familiar tale, *Bounty*, produced by Dino de Laurentis and directed by Roger Donaldson, is surprisingly respectable. Most of the location filming was done on Mo'orea, and 1980s cinematic freedom meant that Polynesian nudity, and those goddess-like 'celestial forms' Bougainville so enthusiastically described, finally made it on to the screen. Anthony Hopkins plays the not-quite-so-bad-and-mad Bligh and Mel Gibson is the more-handsome-than-ever Christian. The scenery on Mo'orea looks fantastic.

Tahiti Beach Press is a weekly English-language tourist paper that has some local news coverage.

RADIO & TV

There are about 10 independent radio stations that broadcast music programmes with news flashes in French and Tahitian and the occasional interview. Most broadcasting is from Tahiti and Mo'orea. Among the best-known stations are Tiare FM (the pioneer nongovernmental radio station), Radio Bleue, Radio Maohi, Te Reo o Tefana (a pro-independence station), Radio 1, NRJ and RFO-Radio Polynésie. RFO-Radio Polynésie is received everywhere and broadcasts many local programmes in Tahitian as well as the news from France Inter live every hour.

Radio France Outremer (RFO) has two television channels: Télépolynésie and Tempo. The local news (Vea Tahiti) is broadcast in Tahitian at 6.45pm and in French at 7.05pm. On Tahiti, Mo'orea, Huahine, Ra'iatea and Bora Bora there's Canal +, and on Tahiti and Mo'orea there's Téléfenua, a cable package that includes CNN, Canal J, Planète, Eurosport and Ciné Cinéma. For the time being, the Australs, Tuamotus and Marquesas have to make do with Télépolynésie.

VIDEO SYSTEMS

The video format in French Polynesia is Secam, but videos made for tourists are generally also available in PAL and NTSC.

PHOTOGRAPHY

The tropical light is very intense in French Polynesia, so it's better to take photographs in the early morning or the late afternoon. Take slow film (100 or 50 ISO), as well as more sensitive film (200 or 400 ISO) and a flash for dance performances or archaeological sites hidden in the vegetation, particularly on the Marquesas. A 28-80mm lens, or even a 35-80mm lens will meet most of your needs, and don't forget a sunshade or a polarising filter. You'll need a macro lens if you want to take photographs of flowers.

The sand, heat, salinity and air humidity are very tough on camera equipment, so bring desiccating sachets. Take a waterproof bag or even a bin liner, and clean your lenses regularly. The humidity can also be tough on video cameras.

No cultural restrictions apply to photography, but as a courtesy you should always ask permission before taking any photographs of people.

Film is expensive in French Polynesia, and gets more difficult to find and more expensive the further you travel from Pape'ete. Fast film developing and printing is easy to find on Tahiti and other touristy islands but is ridiculously expensive.

Underwater Photography

The lack of plankton in the region guarantees maximum water clarity for underwater shots. For beginners, a disposable camera will do, but these are waterproof only to 3m or 4m.

Divers with high-performance equipment should check that the charger and pins are compatible before plugging in the flash.

TIME

French Polynesia is 10 hours behind GMT, and is just two hours east of the International Date Line. The Marquesas are a half-hour ahead of the rest of French Polynesia (noon on Tahiti is 12.30pm in the Marquesas). Check flight schedules carefully: Air Tahiti departures and arrivals in the Marquesas may run on Tahiti time.

ELECTRICITY

Electric current is generally 220V, 60Hz, although some deluxe hotels may have 110V supply for electric shavers. Sockets are French-style, requiring a plug with two round pins.

WEIGHTS & MEASURES

French Polynesia uses the metric system; see the inside back cover of this book for a conversion chart.

LAUNDRY

The big hotels can wash clothes, but the price almost makes it feasible to throw your things away and buy clean clothes. Laundrettes are just about unknown outside Pape'ete, where the prices are very high. You may need to reconcile yourself to hand-washing while in French Polynesia, which is actually not such a hassle given how quickly everything dries.

HEALTH

Travel health depends on your predeparture preparations, your daily health care while travelling and how you handle any medical problem that does develop. While the potential dangers can seem quite frightening, in reality few travellers experience anything more than an upset stomach.

French Polynesia is a wonderfully healthy, outdoorsy destination – you'll probably come back healthier than when you left! There are few endemic diseases, and the most serious health problem visitors are likely to experience is sunburn.

If you do need medical care, the facilities in French Polynesia are generally of a high standard, and although the number of medical practitioners is limited on the outer islands, there are hospitals or dispensaries even out there.

Predeparture Planning

Immunisations No vaccinations are required for entry into French Polynesia unless you are arriving from an area infected with yellow fever. Most travellers from Western countries will have been immunised against various diseases during childhood, but your doctor may still recommend booster shots against measles or polio, diseases still prevalent in many developing countries. Plan your vaccinations ahead: some of them require more than one injection, and some should not be given together. It is recommended that you seek medical advice at least six weeks before travel. Record all vaccinations on an International Health Certificate, available from your doctor or government health department.

Discuss your requirements with your doctor, but vaccinations you might consider for French Polynesia include diphtheria, tetanus, hepatitis A, hepatitis B, polio and typhoid.

Health Insurance Make sure that you have adequate health insurance. See Travel Insurance under Visas & Documents earlier in this chapter for details.

Travel Health Guides Lonely Planet's *Healthy Travel: Australia, New Zealand & the Pacific* is a handy pocket-sized guide packed with useful information including pretrip planning, emergency first aid, im-

---

Medical Kit Check List

Following is a list of items you should consider including in your medical kit – consult your pharmacist for brands available in your country.

- ☐ **Aspirin or paracetamol (acetaminophen in the USA)** – for pain or fever
- ☐ **Antihistamine** – for allergies, eg, hay fever; to ease the itch from insect bites or stings; and to prevent motion sickness
- ☐ **Cold and flu tablets, throat lozenges and nasal decongestant**
- ☐ **Multivitamins** – consider for long trips, when dietary vitamin intake may be inadequate
- ☐ **Antibiotics** – consider including these if you're travelling well off the beaten track; see your doctor, as they must be prescribed, and carry the prescription with you
- ☐ **Loperamide or diphenoxylate** – 'blockers' for diarrhoea
- ☐ **Prochlorperazine or metaclopramide** – for nausea and vomiting
- ☐ **Rehydration mixture** – to prevent dehydration, which may occur, for example, during bouts of diarrhoea; particularly important when travelling with children
- ☐ **Insect repellent, sunscreen, lip balm and eye drops**
- ☐ **Calamine lotion, sting relief spray or aloe vera** – to ease irritation from sunburn and insect bites or stings
- ☐ **Antifungal cream or powder** – for fungal skin infections and thrush
- ☐ **Antiseptic (such as povidone-iodine)** – for cuts and grazes
- ☐ **Bandages, Band-Aids (plasters) and other wound dressings**
- ☐ **Water purification tablets or iodine**
- ☐ **Scissors, tweezers and a thermometer** – note that mercury thermometers are prohibited by airlines

---

munisation and disease information and what to do if you get sick on the road. Lonely Planet's *Travel with Children* includes advice on travel health for younger children.

There are also a number of excellent travel health sites on the Internet. The Lonely Planet website has links to the World Health Organization (WHO) and the US Centers for Disease Control & Prevention at www.lonelyplanet.com/subwwway/.

Other Preparations Make sure you're healthy before you start travelling, and if you're going on a long trip make sure your teeth are OK. If you wear glasses take a spare pair and your prescription.

If you require a particular medication take an adequate supply because it may not be available locally. Take part of the packaging showing the generic name rather than the brand, as this will make getting replacements easier. It's also a good idea to have a legible prescription or a letter from your doctor to show that you legally use the medication.

Basic Rules

Food This is where we normally wheel out that old adage about avoiding raw or 'unpeelable' food. But raw fish is French Polynesia's favourite (and most delicious) dish, and the fruit of the region, peelable and otherwise, is a sheer delight. If you have a delicate stomach or are feeling uncertain about the food, obviously exercise caution, but you are unlikely to have any problems with the food in French Polynesia. Be careful with fish sold along the side of the road. Usually this is a great way to eat freshly caught fish, but just make sure you are getting that day's catch (yesterday's will have sunstroke after all that time dangling by the road in the afternoon sun).

Water Tap water is only completely safe in Pape'ete, on Bora Bora and on Tubuai, but depending on your constitution, you may find the water is drinkable on other islands too (for example, on Mo'orea) – if in doubt, ask a local. On some islands, particularly low-lying atolls, rainwater is collected and stored separately from well water, which can be tainted by sea water. If you are concerned about water purity stick to bottled water, which is readily available, or boil water for at least five minutes (or use iodine water-purification tablets – follow the directions carefully and remember that too much iodine can be harmful).

In hot climates you should always make sure you drink enough – don't rely on feeling thirsty to indicate when you should drink. Not needing to urinate or very dark yellow urine is a danger sign. Excessive sweating is another problem and can lead to loss of salt and muscle cramping.

Medical Problems & Treatment

Self-diagnosis and treatment can be risky, so you should always seek medical help if you're feeling unwell. An embassy, consulate or good hotel can usually recommend a local doctor or clinic.

Medical facilities in French Polynesia are of an equivalent standard to those in the West. Pape'ete has a public hospital, two private clinics and numerous excellent pharmacies. On all touristy islands you will find at least a medical clinic with one or more physicians, and on Mo'orea, Ra'iatea, Bora Bora, Rangiroa, Nuku Hiva and Hiva Oa there are small medical centres. Even the most remote islands have a clinic.

A consultation with a doctor costs about 3300 CFP. French visitors can get the fee refunded when they return home; citizens of the EU should obtain a form E 111 before leaving home.

Environmental Hazards

Although the northern islands in French Polynesia can get much hotter and more humid than the islands to the south, the climate does not suffer from major extremes.

External Ear Infections This condition can affect divers and swimmers in tropical waters. Warm water, microorganisms in coral, and humidity in the external ear ducts can encourage the proliferation of germs, leading to a very painful ear some hours after swimming or diving. Consult a physician if you are affected. To prevent the condition, rinse your ears thoroughly with fresh water after each immersion, and use drops of alcohol to disinfect the duct.

Fungal Infections Hot-weather fungal infections are most likely to occur on the scalp, between the toes or fingers, in the groin and on the body. You can get ringworm (which is a fungal infection, not a worm) from infected animals or other people. Moisture encourages these infections.

To prevent fungal infections wear loose, comfortable clothes, avoid artificial fibres, wash frequently and dry carefully. If you do get an infection, wash the infected area daily with a disinfectant or medicated soap and water, and rinse and dry well. Apply an antifungal powder such as the widely available Tinaderm. Try to expose the infected area to air or sunlight as much as possible, wash all towels and underwear in hot water and change them frequently.

Heat Exhaustion Dehydration and salt deficiency can cause heat exhaustion. Take time to acclimatise to high temperatures, drink sufficient liquids and do not do anything too physically demanding.

Salt deficiency is characterised by fatigue, lethargy, headaches, giddiness and muscle cramps; salt tablets may help, but adding extra salt to your food is better.

Anhidrotic heat exhaustion is a rare form of heat exhaustion caused by an inability to sweat. It affects people who have been in a hot climate for some time, rather than newcomers. It can progress to heatstroke. Treatment involves removal to a cooler climate.

Heatstroke This serious, occasionally fatal, condition can occur if the body's heat-regulating mechanism breaks down and the body temperature rises to dangerous levels. Insufficient fluids and long, continuous periods of exposure to high temperatures can leave you vulnerable to heatstroke.

Symptoms include feeling unwell, not sweating very much (or at all) and a high body temperature (39° to 41°C, or 102° to 106°F). Where sweating has ceased, the skin becomes flushed and red. Severe, throbbing headaches and lack of coordination will also occur, and the sufferer may be confused or aggressive. Eventually the victim will become delirious or may convulse. Hospitalisation is essential, but in the interim get victims out of the sun, remove their clothing, cover them with a wet sheet or towel, and then fan continually. Give fluids if they are conscious.

Sunburn You can get sunburnt surprisingly quickly in the tropics, even through cloud. Use a sunscreen and take extra care to cover areas that don't normally see the sun, such as your feet. A hat provides added protection and you can use zinc cream or some other barrier cream for your nose and lips. Take special care in situations where a cool breeze may disguise the power of the sun, such as when riding around in an open 4WD vehicle or travelling in an open boat. Calamine lotion is good for mild sunburn; most locals use the ubiquitous *monoi* (perfumed coconut oil) to treat sunburn.

Infectious Diseases

Diarrhoea Simple things such as a change of water, food or climate can all cause a mild bout of diarrhoea, but a few rushed toilet trips with no other symptoms is not indicative of a major problem.

Dehydration is the main danger with any case of diarrhoea, particularly for children or the elderly, who can dehydrate quite quickly. Under all circumstances fluid replacement (at least equal to the volume being lost) is the most important thing to remember.

Ciguatera This is a form of food poisoning that comes from eating infected reef fish. Reefs that have been disturbed, for example by urban development, are particularly prone to develop the microorganism, which becomes present in small reef fish and passes up the food chain until a human eats it. The symptoms of ciguatera poisoning include nausea, vomiting, diarrhoea and stomach cramps, alternating fevers and chills, and tingling in the skin and mouth. A feeling of weak muscles and joints and aching pain in the fingers and feet may last weeks or even months. Hot may feel cold and vice versa. Seek medical advice. It's always wise to seek local advice before eating reef fish (open-water fish are perfectly safe), as any ciguatera outbreak will be well known. It's also wise to avoid eating fish heads or organs.

Typhoid This is a dangerous gut infection caused by contaminated water and food. Medical help must be sought.

In its early stages sufferers may feel they have a bad cold or flu on the way, as early symptoms are a headache, body aches and a fever which rises a little each day until it is around 40°C (104°F) or more. The victim's pulse is often slow relative to the degree of fever present – unlike a normal fever where the pulse increases. There may also be vomiting, abdominal pain, diarrhoea or constipation.

Insect-Borne Diseases

Malaria does not exist in French Polynesia.

Dengue Fever This viral disease is transmitted by mosquitoes and is fast becoming one of the top public health problems in the tropical world. Unlike the malaria mosquito, the mosquito which transmits dengue is most active during the day and is found mainly in urban areas, in and around human dwellings.

Signs and symptoms of dengue fever include a sudden onset of high fever, headache, joint and muscle pains (hence its old name, 'breakbone fever') and nausea and vomiting. A rash of small red spots sometimes appears three to four days after the onset of fever. In the early phase of illness, dengue may be mistaken for other infectious diseases, including malaria and influenza.

You should seek medical attention as soon as possible if you think you may have been infected. Aspirin should be avoided, as it increases the risk of haemorrhaging.

There is no vaccine against dengue fever. The best prevention is to avoid mosquito bites at all times by covering up, using insect repellents containing the compound DEET and using mosquito nets.

Filariasis Although not uncommon among French Polynesians, especially in rural areas, this disease poses no risk to travellers.

Cuts, Bites & Stings
Cuts & Scratches Any puncture of the skin can easily become infected in the tropics and may heal slowly. Treat any cut with an antiseptic solution and Mercurochrome or protective antiseptic cream. Where possible avoid bandages and plasters, which can keep wounds wet; if you have to keep a bandage on during the day to protect the wound from dirt or flies, take it off at night while you sleep to let it get air.

Coral cuts are notoriously problematic – they seem to be particularly susceptible to infection, can take a long time to heal and can be quite painful. If you do get cut by coral, clean the wound thoroughly, get all the coral out and keep the wound clean and disinfected until it heals. You can treat it with Mercurochrome or another protective antiseptic cream or try the local cure – fresh lime juice. Avoid coral cuts by trying not to touch coral when swimming.

Any cut or puncture to the skin can turn septic in a humid, tropical climate, so don't hesitate to visit a doctor if you notice any sign of infection.

Bites & Stings French Polynesia's mosquitoes can be bad, but they have nothing on the *nono* (black flies) of the Marquesas, which, at

their worst, make life a misery. Unfortunately, *nono* are found on beaches. In his book *In Search of Tusitala*, Gavin Bell describes the problem with these creatures, for while mosquitoes are 'like flying hypodermic needles, inserting suckers and withdrawing blood with surgical precision, the latter chew and tear at flesh to drink the blood, leaving ragged wounds susceptible to infection'.

Mosquitos and *nono* are at their most ferocious during the wet season from November to March. There are a number of ways to fight insect bites:

- Wear light-coloured clothing
- Wear long trousers and long-sleeved shirts
- Use mosquito repellents containing the compound DEET on exposed areas (prolonged overuse of DEET may be harmful, especially to children, but its use is considered preferable to being bitten by disease-transmitting mosquitoes)
- Avoid perfume and aftershave
- Use a mosquito net (often provided) and burn mosquito coils, which are readily available in French Polynesia

Other insect stings are usually painful rather than dangerous. Take care on some walking routes, where wasp nests sometimes overhang the path. Large centipedes can give a painful or irritating bite but it's no more dangerous than a bee or wasp sting (despite the strange dread Polynesians have of these creatures).

If you are bitten, using calamine lotion, ammonia, antihistamine skin cream or ice packs to reduce the pain, swelling and itching will help. Or you can try the local remedy: pick a frangipani leaf and rub the white liquid that oozes from the stem onto the bite. If you are allergic to bee or wasp stings, be sure to carry your medication with you.

Marine Creatures Jellyfish are not a big problem in French Polynesia because people mostly swim in protected lagoons, and jellyfish are rarely washed in from the open sea. Stings from most jellyfish are simply rather painful. Dousing in vinegar will deactivate any stingers that have not 'fired'. Ammonia is also effective, but the folk remedy, used all over the world, is to apply fresh urine to the sting as soon as possible – this also neutralises the venom. Calamine lotion, antihistamines and analgesics may reduce the reaction and relieve the pain.

Poisonous stonefish are rare, but are extremely painful and potentially fatal to those unfortunate enough to step on one. These ugly and well-disguised creatures lurk on the sea floor, and if stepped on, force poison into the victim's foot. Heeding local advice about areas that may harbour stonefish, and wearing shoes or thongs (flip-flops) when walking in the lagoon, is the best protection. If you do step on a stonefish, bind the affected limb tightly to slow circulation and then seek medical attention, because there is an antidote available.

Stingrays have sharp tails that can lash up, causing a nasty cut that is slow to heal. Rays usually zip away as they sense your approach.

Sea urchins are another unpleasant thing to step upon. The spines break off in your foot and can be difficult to remove. The wound can become easily infected.

You'll sometimes encounter stinging coral or fire coral (usually brown or yellow and branched). The simple solution is to avoid touching all coral. If you are stung, it's more bothersome than dangerous, and the wound can be treated like a jellyfish sting.

Some cone shells can fire a dangerous, potentially fatal, dart if picked up. Treat any cone shell with caution.

Shark bites are a very unlikely occurrence – the sharks regularly encountered around the reefs in French Polynesia are impressive to look at but are generally quite innocuous.

Women's Health

Tampons and pads are available in the bigger supermarkets around French Polynesia, but are remarkably expensive (800 CFP for 16 tampons; 400 CFP for 16 pads), so stock up before you leave home.

In the tropical climate, antibiotic use, synthetic underwear, sweating and contraceptive pills can lead to uncomfortable fungal vaginal infections. Thrush or vaginal candidiasis is characterised by a rash, itch and discharge. Nystatin, miconazole or clotrimazole pessaries are the usual treatment, but some people use more traditional remedies involving vinegar or lemon juice douches, or yogurt. Maintaining good personal hygiene and wearing loose-fitting clothes and cotton underwear may help prevent these infections.

SOCIAL GRACES

French Polynesians are generally very easy-going and there are few social pitfalls for the unwary visitor. Nonetheless, it's worth remembering that religion permeates everyday life. Grace often precedes a meal and the churches are jammed on Sunday mornings. Given how religious the Polynesians are, it's wise to avoid criticism of the missionaries. Attending church on a Sunday is interesting, but dress and behave politely.

Locals embrace an intriguing blend of Polynesian and French customs – you'll see Polynesian friends greeting one another with a kiss on both cheeks, and a 'ia ora na' being followed by a stream of French, or a 'bonjour' being followed by Tahitian. These sorts of greetings are not to be confused with public displays of intimacy, which are unusual in Polynesia. You won't see local couples kissing or embracing in public, so this behaviour is best avoided.

When visiting archaeological sites, don't move stones or tiki. For many Polynesians, the marae are important spiritual sites, and such actions are taboo and offensive. Respect private-property signs, which often indicate that entry is *tapu* (taboo). Although all beaches are public property, most waterfront land is privately owned, so before trying to make your way down to the water, ask permission. Fruit trees are almost always private property, so never pick fruit without asking first.

If visiting a Polynesian home, take your shoes off at the front door. Your hosts may claim that it's unnecessary, but you'll win friends if you refuse their entreaties and insist that you would be more comfortable shoeless. At the table, helping others before yourself and watching what others do will usually cover you from making any terrible faux pas. Some Tahitian foods are eaten with fingers, so don't always expect utensils.

Shorts and T-shirts are ubiquitous: coats and ties are not necessary at even the swankiest restaurants in Pape'ete. On the more remote islands, local women usually wear shorts and T-shirts in the water, although the bikini is unlikely to shock. Nudity on the beach is not really *de rigueur*, but unlike other more straight-laced Pacific islands, women sometimes go topless, particularly at hotel beaches and swimming pools. Elsewhere, use your common sense: if you are the only person on the beach over 12 baring your breasts, best to cover up.

Note that tipping is not expected in French Polynesia and also that bargaining (except for pearls) is not practised.

WOMEN TRAVELLERS

French Polynesia is a great place for solo women to explore. Local women are very much a part of public life in the region, and it's not unusual to see Polynesian women out drinking beer together, or walking alone, so you will probably feel pretty comfortable following suit. The author of this edition travelled alone through French Polynesia while researching this book, and never felt threatened by the lack of a burly companion. It's a sad reality that women are still required to exercise care, particularly at night, but this is the case worldwide. Some women have commented on being the object of unwanted interest in parts of French Polynesia, but this attention is on the whole harmless, although annoying. As anywhere in the world, give drunks and their beer breath a wide berth.

Perhaps it's the locals' way of getting their own back after centuries of leering European men ogling Polynesian women, but there is reportedly a 'tradition' of Peeping Toms in Polynesia, particularly in the outer islands. Take special care in establishments that seem to offer opportunities for spying on guests, particularly in the showers, and make sure your room can be securely locked.

GAY & LESBIAN TRAVELLERS

French laws concerning homosexuality prevail in French Polynesia, which means there is no legal discrimination against homosexual activity. Homophobia in French Polynesia is uncommon, although open displays of affection in public should be avoided. French Polynesia does feel remarkably heterosexual, given the preponderance of honeymooning couples, but you will meet lots of very camp *mahu* (men living as women) working in restaurants and hotels.

The **Tiki Soft C@fé** in Pape'ete is a popular and hip spot for popaa (Western) gays, as well as those on the straight and narrow.

Te Anuanua o Te Fenua (*Gay, Lesbian & Bisexual Association of French Polynesia;* ☎ *77 31 11*) was formed in 1997, and is based on Tahiti.

Gender Bender

The whitewashing of traditional – 'uncivilised' – aspects of Polynesian society by Christian missionaries saw the abandonment of many ancient customs. But not all customs met this sticky end.

In their writings, the missionaries described 'unnatural crimes', referring to the traditional Polynesian practice whereby the eldest son is raised by his parents as a girl, and goes on to live life as a woman. The missionaries observed that the Tahitians seemed to have no problems with these *mahu* (men living as women), and that *mahu* were perfectly acceptable members of society.

According to François Bauer, author of *Raerae de Tahiti*, popular belief has it that among a family with eight children, one will inevitably be a *mahu*. It remains unclear, however, whether this practice has a sexual or a social origin, but it is generally assumed to be the latter as *mahu* don't necessarily have sex with men.

DISABLED TRAVELLERS

Travellers with restricted mobility will find French Polynesia full of hindrances. With narrow flights of steps on boats, high steps on le trucks (public buses) and difficult boarding on Air Tahiti aircraft, French Polynesia resembles a tropical obstacle course. What is more, hotels and guesthouses are not used to receiving disabled guests, and nautical and open-air activities are geared for the 'able-bodied'. However, all new hotels and public buildings must conform to certain standards, and so a gradual change can be expected.

Those who are not put off by these obstacles can contact **Te Nui o Te Huma, La Fédération des Handicapés de Polynésie** (*Polynesian Federation for the Handicapped;* ☎ *43 30 62*) for more information.

SENIOR TRAVELLERS

Older travellers will have no problems travelling in French Polynesia. If you are over 60, Air Tahiti offers a Carte Marama (Third Age Card), which costs 1000 CFP and allows you substantial reductions on Air Tahiti flights (see the Getting Around chapter for details).

TRAVEL WITH CHILDREN

Fire the babysitter and bring the kids: French Polynesia is a great destination to explore with children. There are no major health concerns, the climate is good and the food is easy to navigate. Most locals have a number of children themselves and will not be troubled by a screaming child at the next table, should the treasure be throwing a tantrum over dinner. Children are very much a part of public life in Polynesia.

Nonetheless, ensure that vaccinations are up-to-date, and that you have health records with you. Make sure that your repatriation insurance also covers your child. Consider bringing a baby carrier, and pack light clothes that cover the whole body. Total-block sunscreen is almost as important as your passport and tickets (it is readily available in French Polynesia, but is very expensive); nappies (diapers) are also available but pricey (1700 CFP for 38 nappies!). The water is completely safe in Pape'ete, on Bora Bora and on Tubuai, but you may like to buy bottled water anyway, particularly if your child has a delicate stomach – on the other islands you will all be dependent on bottled water. Remember to encourage your child to drink frequently.

There are medical facilities everywhere in Polynesia. Mamao Hospital in Pape'ete has a modern paediatric department.

You will have priority when boarding Air Tahiti aircraft. A Carte Famille (Family Card), which costs 2000 CFP, entitles you to significant reductions on some flights (see the Getting Around chapter for details). At hotels and guesthouses, children under 12 generally pay only 50% of the adult rate; very young children usually stay for free.

Some dive centres, such as **Tahiti Plongée** (☎ 41 00 62) on Tahiti, take children aged eight and over on dives.

USEFUL ORGANISATIONS

Te Fare Tauhiti Nui (☎ 54 45 44, 54 45 40; 646 Blvd Pomare, Pape'ete; open 8am-noon & 1pm-5pm Mon-Thur, 8am-noon & 1pm-4pm Fri), the Maison de la Culture (Cultural Centre), is to the west of Pape'ete. This is where you come to buy tickets for Heiva (see Heiva in the special section 'Tahitian Dance' later in this book) performances. The centre also organises concerts and craft exhibits, and stages plays. Cultural activities and gatherings are held here regularly. Tahitian language courses are also available, and there is a library.

DANGERS & ANNOYANCES

French Polynesia is not a particularly dangerous or annoying destination, which is all the more reason to go there.

Although it's rarely a problem for travellers, Polynesian men like their beer, particularly at festivals and feasts, in which case there are two points to remember: some Polynesians are not good drunks and most Polynesians are probably bigger than you. There is a locally grown marijuana known as *pakalolo*; the local police can be extremely unpleasant if they catch you using it.

You're unlikely to be kept awake by late-night revelry anywhere except in the heart of Pape'ete, but the roosters are another matter. A non-stop symphony can 'entertain' you until the early hours (when roosters are supposed to make a racket) and then some of them duly begin all over again. Dogs can also be an annoyance, and although they are generally too lethargic to be bothered with travellers, a few travellers have been bitten (see the boxed text 'Doleful Dogs').

French Polynesia may not have malaria, but the mosquitoes are hell-bent on sucking

Doleful Dogs

French Polynesia is riddled with dogs. These aren't cute, pampered doggies but rather the mangy, stray variety. They rarely have the energy to be aggressive, and simply potter around, lazing in the shade by the side of the road and sniffing at your heels as you try to eat.

The first wave of immigrants to present-day French Polynesia brought dogs with them in their pirogues. Dogs featured in Polynesian cuisine and in ritual sacrifices until the missionaries put an end to these practices during the 19th century.

Dogs certainly found a lucky reprieve in the rectitude of the missionaries, but canine history also serves as another example of the unforeseen impact of stymied practices, with stray, neglected dogs now posing a significant problem in the region.

blood anyway. They are tolerable during the cooler season from May to October but can be a real bother in the hotter, wetter months. For some reason, marae (sacred sites) seem to attract them in swarms, and standing to read an explanatory noticeboard at a historic marae can be a real test of any visitor's enthusiasm. If anything, the tiny *nono* (black flies) of the Marquesas are even worse (see under Health earlier).

Swimming in French Polynesia usually means staying within the calm, protected waters of a lagoon, but swimmers should always be aware of tides and currents, and particularly of the swift movement of water out of a lagoon and through a pass into the open sea.

Although early explorers all complained about the Polynesian propensity for theft, it is not a problem today. This is not to say that your camera won't disappear if you leave it lying around on the beach. Even busy Pape'ete is relatively safe compared with cities in the USA and Europe, although there is the odd pickpocket and occasional robberies do occur. If you have valuables and you are staying in a more expensive hotel, it's probably wise to use the hotel safe. Don't leave anything of value in a rental car.

Violence is also rarely a problem in French Polynesia. Intoxicated youths are the most likely troublemakers – they might address you as a *titoi* (wanker), but this is unlikely to ruin your holiday!

BUSINESS HOURS

Shops and offices are normally open from around 7.30am to 5pm Monday to Thursday and from 7.30am to 4pm Friday, although a long lunch break is still common. Shops are generally open Saturday morning, but almost all are closed that afternoon, and most are closed on Sunday. Some supermarkets open on Sunday, but don't bank on it.

PUBLIC HOLIDAYS & SPECIAL EVENTS

Public holidays, when businesses and government offices close, include the following:

New Year's Day 1 January
Arrival of the First Missionaries 5 March
Easter March/April
May Day 1 May
VE Day 8 May

Ascension Late May
Pentecost & Pentecost Monday Early June
Internal Autonomy Day 29 June
Bastille Day 14 July
Assumption 15 August
All Saints' Day 1 November
Armistice Day 11 November
Christmas Day 25 December

Festivals

French Polynesia's festivals are made up of an eclectic mix of reasons to celebrate.

The **Chinese New Year**, which usually falls between late January and mid-February, is ushered in with dancing, martial-arts displays and fireworks.

If you're keen to run around most of the island (or watch others while they do), the **Mo'orea Marathon** is held in February.

The **arrival of the first missionaries** is commemorated on 5 March. The landing is re-enacted at Point Venus on Tahiti, and there are celebrations on Tahiti and Mo'orea. The missionaries actually arrived on 4 March but didn't know about the International Date Line.

The Tahitians love a **beauty contest**, and there are lots of them held in April and May leading up to the Miss Tahiti and Miss Heiva i Tahiti contests in June. There are also Mr Tahiti contests.

The **Tahiti International Golf Open** is a four-day championship held in late June and early July at the Olivier Bréaud Golf Course on Tahiti.

The cream of the festival crop, the **Heiva i Tahiti** (*heiva* means 'festival') is the major French Polynesian festival. Held in Pape'ete each July, the festival lasts throughout the month and is so impressive it's almost worth timing your trip around it. Mini-Heiva events take place on other islands in August. See the special section 'Tahitian Dance' later in this book for details.

The **Annual Flower Show** normally kicks off in September in the Bougainville Park in Pape'ete, but this area was under construction at the time of writing, so check what the plans are with the tourist office. Also in September, a major **surfing competition** is held at Puna'auia on Tahiti.

A traditional **stone-fishing contest** takes place on Bora Bora during the first half of October. During **Carnival** at the end of October in Pape'ete there are parades of floats decked with flowers.

The **Hawaiki Nui Canoe Race** is held in late October or November. French Polynesia's major sporting event of the year, this is a three-day pirogue race from Huahine to Ra'iatea, Taha'a and Bora Bora. See the boxed text 'Hawaiki Nui Canoe Race' later in this chapter.

The national flower, the ubiquitous but delightful *tiare*, is celebrated with **Tiare Tahiti Days** on 1 and 2 December.

The **Marquesas Festival** is held at least every four years in December, and is an arts festival celebrating Marquesan identity.

ACTIVITIES

See also the Outdoor Activities chapter and the special section 'Diving' later in this book.

Diving & Snorkelling

French Polynesia is a diver's wet dream. The warm, bright waters, the lack of plankton (which ensures water clarity) and the myriad tropical fish will entice you from the shore.

All dive certifications are recognised, including CMAS, PADI and NAUI, and there are professional dive centres on Tahiti, Mo'orea, Ra'iatea, Huahine, Bora Bora, Rangiroa, Tikehau, Manihi, Ahe, Nuku Hiva and, from July to September, Rurutu. Bring your certification card and dive log.

The coral reefs and coral outcrops that are dotted around the lagoons are perfect sites for snorkelling. You can join a lagoon tour by boat, rent an outboard-powered boat or just grab your gear and head out to explore the lagoon yourself.

Surfing

Polynesia was the birthplace of *horue* (surfing), and in recent years there has been a major resurgence of local interest. Tahiti in particular has surf shops, board shapers and a local surfing scene. Tahiti, Mo'orea and Huahine are the three main islands for surfing, but Rangiroa and Tikehau in the Tuamotus also have good surfing spots.

Yachting

Ra'iatea is the main yachting base in French Polynesia, although there are a number of yacht charter operations around the islands, with a flotilla of modern monohulls and catamarans.

Hiking

The high islands offer superb walks, but the tracks are sometimes unmarked and are hard to follow: a guide is often necessary. Tahiti and Mo'orea are the main islands for walking, but there are also good walks on Ra'iatea, Bora Bora and Maupiti. The Marquesas has huge untapped potential; currently the only popular walking trail is on Nuku Hiva.

Cycling

On many islands it is possible to rent bicycles, which is the perfect way to get around. The rough roads leading into the interior are great for mountain-biking, should you decide to bring one with you from home.

Horse Riding

There are equestrian centres on Tahiti, Mo'orea, Ra'iatea, Huahine and Bora Bora in the Society Islands. Most places offer short jaunts and longer excursions that explore the island interiors. Horses are an important part of life in the Marquesas, and there are various places to rent them, with or without a guide; you can also horse ride on Rurutu in the Australs.

Other Activities

For all other activities, contact the **Manava Visitors Bureau** (*☎ 50 57 10, fax 43 16 78; e tahiti-manava@mail.microtech.pf; open 7.30am-5pm Mon-Fri, 8am-noon Sat & public holidays*), the tourist office in Pape'ete, for details.

There are squash and tennis courts on Tahiti, and tennis courts can sometimes be found at the larger hotels and resorts on the other islands.

Tahiti has the only golf course in French Polynesia, although there are controversial plans to build another on Mo'orea.

Tahiti's soaring mountains make for spectacular opportunities for parapente (parasailing). There is also a parasailing centre on Nuku Hiva in the Marquesas.

Windsurfing is popular and many resorts offer instruction and use of equipment. Unfortunately, jet skis, those noisy and antisocial devices, are also popular on some islands. You can rent small boats for exploring the lagoons on a number of islands. Further afield, game-fishing boats can be chartered.

COURSES

Tahitian language can be studied at **Asfor** (☎ 41 33 89; Immeuble Fara, Rue Nansouty, Pape'ete, Tahiti); the **Chambre de Commerce** (Chamber of Commerce; ☎ 47 27 00; Rue du Dr Cassiau, BP 118, Pape'ete, Tahiti); and **Te Fare Tauhiti Nui** (Maison de la Culture; ☎ 54 45 44; 646 Blvd Pomare, Pape'ete, Tahiti).

There are dance schools dotted around, particularly in Pape'ete, where you can learn to move those hips like the Polynesians; ask at the tourist office for recommendations.

WORK

French citizens are not required to complete any formalities but for everyone else, even other EU citizens (with the exception of those with very specialised skills), it is difficult to work in French Polynesia. Unless you are a Japanese pearl grafter, a tourist guide, a Chinese chef or a banking executive, you stand little chance. Authorisation to take up paid employment is subject to the granting of a temporary-residence permit, issued by the French state, and a work permit, issued by the territory.

ACCOMMODATION

Glossy brochures may focus on the idyllic over-water bungalows, but French Polynesia actually has a pretty wide range of accommodation options, from camping to extreme luxury. Whatever the category, the price-to-quality ratio is invariably discouraging. It's not that standards are necessarily low, it's just that at the prices charged visitors have a right to expect more. There's not much you can do about the prices, so stop fingering the worry-beads and deal with the credit-card bill when you get home.

Even some quite expensive places may not have air-con, but this is generally not a problem. Even at the hottest times of year, a cool breeze seems to blow at night and a fan is all that's needed.

The overwhelming majority of accommodation is in bungalows. Unless otherwise stated, bungalows sleep two, although young children are usually allowed to stay with their parents for free or at reduced rates.

All accommodation prices quoted in this book include the relevant taxes, but be aware that many places will quote you before-tax prices, only to surprise you with a rather hefty list of add-ons at the end of your stay. We have rounded prices to the nearest 100 CFP as appropriate, so use quoted prices as a guide only and be ready for an increase in taxes (which seems to happen every few years). The most frustrating aspect of the taxation system is the *taxe de séjour* (accommodation tax), which is charged per person per night: if you are travelling as a family, this can really add up.

Camping & Dorm Beds

There are camping options springing up around French Polynesia, but generally it's a matter of guesthouses having areas where you can pitch your tent and allowing use of the facilities; you'll pay anywhere from around 1000 CFP to 2500 CFP per person. Camping is possible on Tahiti, Mo'orea, Huahine, Ra'iatea, Bora Bora, Maupiti, Rangiroa, Tikehau and Mataiva. You may need to rethink camping if the rain is too hard; and make sure your tent is mosquito-proof or lather yourself in repellent.

Some guesthouses have dorm beds ranging from 1500 CFP to 3500 CFP per person per night.

Pensions

Pensions (guesthouses) are a godsend for travellers who baulk at the prices (and gloss) of the big hotels. These little establishments, which are generally family affairs, are a great way to meet locals and other travellers. Brace yourself for cold showers, lumpy pillows and thin walls, but lap up the charm, interesting discussions and artistic touches that are often part and parcel of the *pension* experience. Many *pensions* have local-style bungalows, which usually have a quaint homemade feel to them (generally because they are homemade!); some of the more up-market *pensions* have very comfortable versions of the bungalow.

Many *pensions* offer (and sometimes insist upon) half-board (or *demi-pension*), which usually means breakfast and dinner. It can cost anything from 4500 CFP to 9000 CFP per person per day, although prices vary widely from island to island. Young children are often allowed to stay for free, and children up to about 12 usually pay half-price.

Think ahead in terms of money, as most *pensions* do not take credit cards.

Hotels

There is a glut of mid-range hotels on the more touristy islands, but on the more remote islands it's sometimes all (five-star glamour) or nothing (rudimentary *pensions*). Most mid-range places are well situated and more comfortable than the *pensions*, and there's usually a restaurant on site. You'll typically pay from around 10,000 CFP to 40,000 CFP per night for a bungalow; almost all places in this category accept credit cards.

If you are ever going to pamper yourself silly, French Polynesia is a great place to do it. The sumptuous luxury hotels often manage to blend their opulent bungalows into the natural setting. Some of the top hotels are on isolated motu (islets), and can only be reached by boat. Four- and five-star hotels are found on Tahiti, Mo'orea, Bora Bora, Huahine, Ra'iatea, Taha'a, Rangiroa, Hiva Oa Manihi and Nuku Hiva. You can expect restaurants, bars, a swimming pool, a shop or two and a well-organised activities desk. Most of the bigger hotels put on a Polynesian dance performance, often with buffet meal, a few times a week. Glass-bottomed coffee tables, which look straight down into the lagoon, have become standard features of the over-water bungalows. The prices are just as dazzling: expect to pay from 35,000 CFP to 100,000 CFP a night, not including meals.

FOOD

For those who like to experience other places and cultures through their bellies, French Polynesia is for you. Fish and seafood lovers may well mistake French Polynesia for nirvana; vegetarians can happily pick their way through the available produce; and even carnivores hunting down a good steak can come away satiated.

Traditional Polynesian cuisine is called *maa'a tahiti* in the Society Islands and the Tuamotus, and *kaikai enana* in the Marquesas; it is traditionally eaten with the fingers. A traditional *ahimaa* (Polynesian oven) is dug into the ground. Branches and stones are arranged at the bottom of the hole; the branches are then kindled and heat the stones. A layer of banana leaves is placed on top of the stones, and the food (usually a suckling pig, fish and vegetables) is placed on this. The whole thing is covered with leaves and canvas and then sand to make it

perfectly airtight. Cooking takes several hours. The *ahimaa* is nowadays often replaced by a barbecue.

There is a wondrous array of restaurants in and around Pape'ete. The rest of French Polynesia simply can't compete with the capital, but on the more touristy islands you'll still be able to enjoy excellent French, Polynesian and Chinese food. The prices are fairly intimidating – expect to pay about 1500 CFP to 2500 CFP for a main – but the food is very good. Funnily enough, the prices in the swank hotel restaurants are often comparable to restaurants elsewhere. Most of the hotel restaurants host buffet and dance performances a few times a week, which usually cost around 6000 CFP. This may seem steep, but the dancers are generally of a very high standard, and the buffets are usually excellent.

Snacks

A *snack* in French Polynesia is actually a little snack-bar-cum-café. These places are usually pretty simple and cheap, and serve everything from sandwiches, often made from wonderful French-style baguettes, and salads to *poisson cru* (raw fish) and burgers (meat and fish). Sandwiches, known locally as *casse-croûte*, are a delicious and cheap way of refuelling; meat, cheese and tuna feature heavily.

The other bargain-priced dining possibility is the roulottes (mobile food vans or diners). These vans have a kitchen inside and a fold-down counter along each side. The inventive use of eskies (coolers) allows the roulottes to whip up surprisingly good food in a flash. The nightly gathering of roulottes near the tourist office in Pape'ete is a real institution.

Most restaurants are happy to have weary travellers popping in for a coffee and/or quick snack. Their appetizers are often substantial and reasonably priced, particularly with all that good French bread you can use to wipe the plate clean (fresh bread will magically appear, free of charge, no matter what you have ordered). Count on paying about 800 CFP to 1500 CFP for an appetizer.

Main Dishes

Open-sea fish (tuna, bonito, wahoo, scad and *mahi mahi*) and lagoon fish (parrotfish, perch and mullet) feature prominently in traditional cuisine and will make regular appearances on your plate. *Poisson cru*, raw fish in coconut milk, is the most popular local dish (see the boxed text 'Raw Pleasure'), though fish is also served grilled or poached with lime, coconut milk or vanilla sauce. *Fafaru*, a traditional dish of raw fish soaked in seawater, is renowned for its strong smell and hangover-easing properties. *Ina'a* (young fish), mixed with fried dough, is enjoyed in various ways. Lobster, crayfish, sea urchin and *chevrette* (freshwater shrimp), often served in curry, are highly prized but fairly limited in supply. Salmon and trout generally come from Australia or New Zealand, and lobsters and prawns may also be imported.

Pua (suckling pig) is the preferred meat for the traditional underground oven, and chicken is also common. Lamb and beef from New Zealand also often feature in dishes. On the Marquesas, goat meat takes pride of place, and dog is still eaten on the remote atolls of the Tuamotus. Although it is protected, turtle is still eaten in French Polynesia. Categorically refuse to eat this endangered animal.

The most common accompaniments are coconut milk, which is obtained by grating the white flesh inside the nut and wringing it in a cloth; *miti hue*, a fermented sauce based on coconut flesh mixed with shrimphead juice and salt water; and *taioro*, another variety of fermented sauce.

Among the Chinese specialities, chow mein is the most common. This fried noodle dish usually has pork and/or chicken in it, but vegetarians can always order a meat-less version. Pizza and pasta are also very popular on the touristy islands.

Fruit & Vegetables

In the right season, French Polynesia is dripping with tropical fruit, including mangoes, grapefruits, green lemons, watermelons and melons (grown on the motu of Maupiti and Huahine), pineapples (from Mo'orea) and bananas. *Pamplemousses* (grapefruits) are the large, thick-skinned Southeast Asian variety. The rambutan, another Southeast Asian introduction, is a red spiny-skinned cousin of the lychee. If you go in the cooler, winter season (May to October), you may find it difficult to find much fresh produce, particularly in the atolls (though Pape'ete is always brimming with fresh fruit and vegies).

Raw Pleasure

Raw fish in coconut milk (*i'a ota* in Tahitian, *poisson cru* in French) has pride of place on almost every menu. Quantities and vegetables can be altered. Throw caution to the wind and be adventurous with this recipe.

If you are cooking for four, use:

2 cloves garlic, crushed
2 tomatoes, roughly chopped
1 cucumber, thinly sliced
2 carrots, grated
1 green onion
juice of 2 or 3 limes
grated coconut (or packaged coconut milk)
1kg of red or white tuna, cubed

Rinse the cubed tuna in sea (or salt) water, and leave to soak for half an hour in salt water and crushed garlic.

Drain the fish and place in a large bowl. Add lime juice, and leave fish to stand for at least five minutes (longer if you want the fish to 'cook' in the lime juice; up to an hour is fine).

If using grated coconut, wrap the grated coconut in a cloth and wring it to extract the milk (if using packaged coconut milk, simply pour over fish). Season to taste and add tomatoes, cucumber and carrot. Mix and garnish with green onion. Serve with white rice or fresh bread, and feast away.

Vegetables do not feature prominently in Polynesian cuisine. *Uru* or *maiore*, breadfruit, is a staple, and is usually eaten roasted or fried as chips. In the Marquesas, the basic dish is *popoi*, a sweet-and-sour dish that looks like a yellow paste. It consists of cooked *uru*, crushed in a mortar, mixed with *uru* pulp and left to ferment; coconut milk is added. The whole thing is covered with a *purau* leaf. *Fei*, a sort of plantain banana, is only eaten cooked and has a bittersweet taste. Taro root is eaten cooked, as are sweet potato and manioc (cassava). *Fafa* (*taro* leaves) are often served with chicken.

Desserts

Faraoa coco (coconut bread) is a tasty cake, and comes in many different forms. Sometimes it's quite dry and bread-like, while other times it's flourless and very moist. Devote yourself to trying its various forms as you travel around.

Firifiri (donuts) are generally shaped like a figure eight or a plait and are a popular Sunday-morning treat dipped in coffee *à la française*.

Ipo, a heavy Tuamotuan bread, is made from flour mixed with coconut juice, sugar and grated coconut.

Pai are little pastries filled with coconut or banana.

Baked papaya is a succulent dish, as is *poe*, small pieces of crushed fruit (papaya or banana) mixed with starch, wrapped in a banana leaf and baked in the oven with a vanilla pod split down the middle. The whole thing is then sprinkled with coconut milk.

Self-Catering

Self-catering can be quite fun in French Polynesia and will save you a lot of money; many budget and mid-range places to stay have well-equipped kitchens. The Marché de Pape'ete, in the centre of Pape'ete, is the heart and belly of French Polynesia. It opens at 5am and is laden with food from all the archipelagos. Consider stocking up while you are here, as the range on the other islands – where you'll often be limited to little stalls along the side of the road – doesn't come close. The market in Pira'e, east of Pape'ete, also deserves a detour.

Supermarkets of varying sizes are dotted around the islands. Some have dusty little collections of tins and packaged goods, while others, particularly those on Tahiti, Mo'orea and Ra'iatea, are very well equipped. The best supermarkets on Tahiti are the Carrefour chains (in Arue and Puna'auia), Hyper U in Pira'e and Cash & Carry in Faa'a. On other islands you're at the mercy of cargo-ship schedules.

European imports are heavily taxed (at 1000 CFP for a camembert, you'd have to really want that cheese fix!), but a fresh baguette only costs around 50 CFP and a *pain au chocolat* (chocolate croissant) costs about 120 CFP.

DRINKS
Nonalcoholic Drinks

Several delicious fruit juices are made locally, notably the Rotui brand. Freshly squeezed juices are sometimes available but are incredibly expensive (it's not uncommon to see a fresh juice on the menu for 500 CFP and a glass of French wine for 300 CFP). *Pape haari* (coconut juice) is the healthiest, cheapest, most natural and thirst-quenching drink around. It is totally free of microbes and bacteria. After the fibre surrounding the coconut is removed, the top of the nut is taken off with a machete. You can drink directly from the nut or through a straw.

The big international soft-drink brands are distributed in French Polynesia: you'll often see a Coca-Cola sign before you see the café. Several brands of mineral water are available, the main ones being French (Volvic, Vittel). The cheapest is the local spring water, Eau Royale or Vaimato.

If you want a real coffee, order a *café express* (espresso coffee), otherwise you'll probably be served instant Nescafé. The further you get from the tourist hubs the further you get from the espresso machines, so if you're an addict heading to the more isolated islands, prepare yourself for some instant coffees or some mid-morning headaches (your best bet for an espresso is the bar of a top-end hotel). A coffee in a Pape'ete bar or café costs around 250 CFP to 300 CFP.

Alcoholic Drinks

The local brand of *pia* (beer), Hinano, is sold everywhere and is available in glass 500ml bottles, 330ml and 500ml cans, and on tap. It is a fairly light, very drinkable beer. Foreign beers, notably Heineken, are also available. Allow at least 350 CFP for a beer in a bar or restaurant.

Most supermarkets stock red and white wines, imported from France. When the wine is imported in properly refrigerated containers it can be excellent. But the tropical heat is a good wine's worst enemy, and you sometimes happen upon a crate of bottles that has spent time sitting in the sun at the port. Urgh! The cheapest (and nastiest) bottles cost around 800 CFP. Restaurants enjoy a tax reduction on alcohol sold at 'agreed prices', which makes it affordable (allow 1500 CFP to 3000 CFP for a bottle).

You must try a *maitai*, a local cocktail similar to a punch, made with brown and white rums, pineapple, grenadine and lime juices, coconut liqueur and, in some cases, Grand Marnier or Cointreau. Go easy on it if you've had a long day in the sun.

ENTERTAINMENT

Leave your dancing shoes at home: this is a place to catch up on early nights.

Entertainment Polynesian-style tends to be a quiet drink in a bar, or perhaps dinner and a local dance performance in a big hotel. Either way, you'll still be tucked up in bed by 11pm (which is fine because you'll be wide awake at 7am the next morning). Pape'ete is the only place with a thumping nightlife.

Bringues (small parties) are an interesting slice of life. If there's a guitar around, the singing can go late into the night (the standard invariably plummets as the singers get more and more drunk and tired).

Pape'ete is the only place with cinemas. You'll generally be limited to Hollywood blockbusters.

SPECTATOR SPORTS

The national sport is, without dispute, *va'a* (pirogue racing). You can admire the pirogue teams training on the lagoon, and if you are on Tahiti in late October or early November, you might catch the Hawaiki Nui canoe race (see the boxed text 'Hawaiki Nui Canoe Race'). Tahiti has hosted events in the world surfing championship, and French Polynesia participates in the annual South Pacific Games.

SHOPPING

There are plenty of art-and-craft shops waiting to lure you in. Beware of local souvenirs that aren't local at all – many colourful wood carvings, even those with Bora Bora neatly painted on them, come from Bali or Colombia. Nevertheless, French Polynesia does have some excellent local crafts, many of which can be found on Tahiti, especially in the Marché de Pape'ete. When shopping remember that bargaining is rarely appropriate (see Tipping & Bargaining, earlier in this chapter).

There are duty-free shopping facilities in Pape'ete and at Faa'a airport with the usual liquor, tobacco and perfume discounts, but the prices are not very exciting by international standards.

Stamp collectors will get excited at the interesting and very colourful stamps on sale. The Centre Philatélique is next door to the main post office in Pape'ete.

Clothing & Decoration

Hats, bags and mats of woven pandanus are among the best examples of a true local craft. The best work is said to come from the Australs.

Tapa is a traditional nonwoven fabric made from the bark of *uru*, banyan or paper mulberry trees. Nowadays the craft is gradually being superseded by fabric from Europe, but it is still made on Fatu Hiva in the Marquesas and can be bought in Pape'ete.

Tifaifai are large, brilliantly coloured patchwork cloths, usually decorated with stylised flower or fruit designs. Produced on a number of islands, including Rurutu, *tifaifai* are often sold as tablecloths, bedspreads and curtains.

The pareu is a single piece of cloth, colourfully decorated and usually worn by

Hawaiki Nui Canoe Race

In Europe it's lithe lads in shiny shorts, in the USA it's men in shoulder pads and in Australia it's burly boys with an oval ball. In French Polynesia it's muscle-bound men in canoes.

The sporting spectacular that has French Polynesians glued to their TV sets and talking passionately about favourites and challengers is indeed a canoe race. The three-day, four-island, Hawaiki Nui Va'a race pits around 60 of the islands' best six-man pirogues against each other and against anyone who is brave enough to turn up from overseas.

The 116km race, held in November, starts on Huahine. The brawny paddlers, who often sport vivid Tahitian tattoos, head across the open sea to Ra'iatea, from there to Taha'a, and then finally on to Bora Bora. The canoes are a superb sight, with men paddling three on each side for about 10 strokes before switching sides with precise timing and lightning speed.

There's also a women's Hawaiki Nui race, known as the Va'a Hine, a play on words (*va'a* is Tahitian for 'canoe', and *vahine* is Tahitian for 'woman'). The Va'a Hine is usually held in October.

Check out [w] www.tahitivaa.com for more details.

women – although it's equally appropriate for men. They cost about 1500 CFP to 2500 CFP, but be aware that many of them are imported from Asia.

French Polynesia's favourite beauty product, *monoi* (coconut oil), is used as moisturising oil, soap, shampoo, sunscreen and perfume. You'll pay around 600 CFP for a bottle, and this blend of coconut oil perfumed with flowers makes for a great present.

Painting & Sculpture

A number of interesting Polynesian and European artists work in French Polynesia, and their work is on display in galleries and little studios on Tahiti, Mo'orea and Bora Bora. Originals and high-quality prints and posters are available.

Sculpture and woodcarving, done in fine wood and in stone or bone, are particularly renowned in the Marquesas. Many settlements in that archipelago have craft centres where you can see local artists' work, although you can also approach the artists directly. Tiki, *umete* (traditional wooden bowls), trunks, spears, hair pins and other personal adornments are the most popular items.

Specialist galleries in Pape'ete also sell sculptors' work, but at higher prices. Twice a year Marquesan sculptors have an exhibition and sale in the Territorial Assembly in Pape'ete, usually in June and November.

Music

Polynesian song has developed into a sort of island country-and-western music, with melancholic tales of lost love and day-to-day life set to the accompaniment of guitar and ukulele. It's easy on the ear and is very catchy. If you happen to be trying to sleep near a *bringue* (see Entertainment earlier in this chapter), drunken renditions of these songs will lull you to sleep (or keep you awake). Traditional dance music, based around drums, has strong, complex rhythms. There are a number of music shops in and around Pape'ete where you can find local and international music.

Tattoos

Tattooed flesh abounds in French Polynesia, on locals and travellers alike. Given that everyone is so tanned, and nobody wears many clothes, they usually look great. Before you launch in and get one though, have a think about how it will look in 20 years' time, in winter. If you're still keen, there are plenty of places to choose from. See the special section 'Tattooing' later in this book for more information.

Black Pearls

Black pearls – surely a gal's second-best friend – are cultivated in the Tuamotus and are an important industry in French Polynesia. You can visit the pearl farms in the Tuamotus, particularly on Rangiroa, and there are jewellery shops and black-pearl specialists all over Pape'ete and on other touristy islands. The pearls can be bought both mounted and unmounted. In Pape'ete, allow anywhere from 5000 CFP to 200,000 CFP and more for a single pearl.

Getting There & Away

French Polynesia is a long way from anywhere: it's roughly halfway between South America and Australia. So, unless you have access to a high-speed magic carpet, prepare yourself for a bit of travelling.

AIR

Most visitors to French Polynesia arrive by air. Faa'a airport, on Tahiti, is the only international airport in French Polynesia.

There is no departure tax within French Polynesia.

Airports & Airlines

Faa'a airport is on the outskirts of Pape'ete, about five kilometres west of the capital. International check-in desks are at the east end of the terminal.

A number of international airlines serve French Polynesia from different parts of the world. Airline offices in Pape'ete include the following:

Aircalin (Air Caledonie International; ☎ 85 09 04, Ⓦ www.aircalin.nc) Faa'a airport
Air France (☎ 47 47 47, Ⓦ www.airfrance.com) Rue Georges Largarde
Air New Zealand (☎ 54 07 47, Ⓦ www.airnz .com) Vaima Centre, Blvd Pomare
Air Tahiti Nui (☎ 45 55 55, Ⓦ www. airtahiti.com) Immeuble Dexter, Rue Paul Gauguin
Corsair (☎ 42 28 28, Ⓦ www.corsair.fr) Cnr Blvd Pomare & Rue Clappier
Hawaiian Airlines (☎ 42 15 00, Ⓦ www.hawaiian air.com) Vaima Centre, Blvd Pomare
LanChile (☎ 42 64 55, Ⓦ www.lanchile.com) Vaima Centre, Blvd Pomare
Qantas Airways (☎ 43 06 65, Ⓦ www.qantas .com) Vaima Centre, Blvd Pomare

In addition to the following information about country-specific flights, see Organised Tours at the end of this chapter for information on package tours.

Other Pacific Islands

There are regular connections between French Polynesia and New Zealand, Fiji, New Caledonia, the Cook Islands, Wallis and Fortuna, and Hawaii. Island-hopping around the Pacific is not difficult, but because some flights only operate once a week

Warning

The information in this chapter is particularly vulnerable to change: prices for international travel are volatile, routes are introduced and cancelled, schedules change, special deals come and go, and rules and visa requirements are amended. You should check directly with the airline or a travel agent to make sure you understand how a fare (and ticket you may buy) works and be aware of the security requirements for international travel.

The upshot of this is that you should get opinions, quotes and advice from as many airlines and travel agents as possible before you part with your hard-earned cash. The details given in this chapter should be regarded as pointers and are not a substitute for your own careful, up-to-date research.

or every few days you may be faced with some scheduling problems if your time in the Pacific is limited. Contact a travel agent with a good knowledge of the vagaries of travel in the region, such as **Hideaway Holidays** (in Australia ☎ 02-9743 0253, fax 02-9743 3568; in the USA ☎ 530-352-4069; Ⓔ sales@hideawayholidays.com.au).

The USA & Canada

Coming from the USA, you can either fly direct from Los Angeles to Pape'ete, or go via Honolulu (there's no difference in the fare). Air New Zealand and Air Tahiti Nui serve this route, and Air France and Corsair flights from Paris to Pape'ete go via Los Angeles (Corsair flights are also available via San Francisco). Return fares from Los Angeles to Pape'ete range from around US$866 to US$990. If you are starting your trip in Honolulu, return fares from Honolulu to Pape'ete start from US$690 in the low season (January to May) and US$880 in the high season (November to December).

If you are interested in exploring other parts of the Pacific, Air New Zealand also offers an excellent deal that allows four stopovers – Honolulu, Nadi (Fiji), Pape'ete and Rarotonga – en route to Auckland. Check with Air New Zealand or your travel agent for ticket options and fares.

There are no direct flights from Canada, so you will need to go via Honolulu or the West Coast of the US. Return fares from Vancouver via Los Angeles start from C$2017 in the low season.

Australia & New Zealand

All flights from Australia to Pape'ete are via Auckland. In Auckland, Qantas Airways flights connect with either Air Tahiti Nui or Polynesian Airlines for the Auckland–Pape'ete leg. Fares increase considerably in the high season (July to September and over Christmas). From Sydney, expect to pay around A$1100/1530 for a return trip in the low/high season with either Qantas Airways or Air New Zealand.

As in Australia, fares from New Zealand increase during the high season. From Auckland, return fares start at NZ$900/1280 in the low/high season. Both Air New Zealand and Qantas/Air Tahiti Nui offer connecting flights from Pape'ete to Los Angeles.

The UK & Continental Europe

Air New Zealand (from London and Frankfurt) and Air France, Air Tahiti Nui and Corsair (all from Paris) have flights to Pape'ete via Los Angeles. Return fares from Paris and Frankfurt start at around €1450; return fares from London start at around £1120 in the low season.

From other destinations in Europe the easiest option is to travel to one of these cities and connect with flights to Pape'ete.

Asia

Air Tahiti Nui operates flights between Japan (Tokyo and Osaka) and Pape'ete. Return flights from Tokyo start at ¥177,516 (US$1495). From other parts of Asia, the simplest connection is via Australia or New Zealand.

South America

LanChile operates flights between Santiago and Pape'ete; one flight a week has a stopover on Easter Island. Return fares cost around US$1500.

Special Fares

A Round-the-World (RTW) ticket that takes in French Polynesia costs about £1045, A$2300 or US$2140, depending on where you start. RTW tickets are usually excellent value, particularly given the high price of return flights to French Polynesia.

A Circle Pacific ticket is similar to a RTW ticket but is cheaper and covers a more limited region. This ticket uses a combination of airlines to connect Australia, New Zealand, North America and Asia, with a variety of stopover options in the Pacific islands. Generally, Circle Pacific fares are a better deal from the USA and Asia than from Australia.

SEA
Cruise Boat

Getting to French Polynesia by sea can be a real challenge, although cruise ships from the USA and Australia do occasionally pass through for a day or so. Another possibility by sea is to travel with the US-based **Society Expeditions** (☎ 206-728 9400, 1800 548 8669, fax 728 2301; W www.societyexpeditions.com), which has regular sailings aboard the *World Discoverer* between Tahiti, Pitcairn and Easter Islands. Departures are from Los Angeles and fares start at US$6515 per person.

Yacht

Travelling to French Polynesia by yacht is eminently feasible. Yachts heading across the Pacific from North America, Australia or New Zealand are often looking for crew and, if you're in the right place at the right time, it's often possible to pick up a ride. It's also possible to pick up crewing positions once in French Polynesia. Sailing experience will definitely score extra points, but so will the ability to cook soup when the boat's heeled over and waves are crashing through the hatch.

On the eastern side of the Pacific, try the yacht clubs in San Diego, Los Angeles, San Francisco or Honolulu. On the western side, Auckland, Sydney and Cairns are good places to try. Look for notices pinned to bulletin boards in yacht clubs and yachting-equipment shops, and post your own notice offering to crew.

Ideally do some sailing with the boat before you actually set off. A month from the next landfall is not the time to discover that you can't bear the crew or that the ogre of seasickness is always by your side.

It takes about a month to sail from the US West Coast to Hawaii and another month south from there to the Marquesas; with stops, another month takes you west to Tahiti and the Society Islands. Then it's another long leg southwest to Australia or New Zealand.

There are distinct seasons for sailing across the Pacific so as to avoid cyclones. Late September to October and January to March are the usual departure times from the USA. Yachts tend to set off from Australia and New Zealand after the cyclone season, around March and April.

ORGANISED TOURS

French Polynesia lends itself to the package tour. Given the high price of flights to the region, and the often astronomical price of accommodation once there, a package tour can work out to be a financial godsend.

There is a variety of tour packages available from travel agents in all Western countries. If you want more than just a straightforward cheap fare, a general travel agent can be an excellent first stop. A good travel agent can negotiate better prices at the larger hotels, can handle Air Tahiti bookings for your domestic flights once in French Polynesia, and have your schedule finalised before you arrive. In addition to the traditional travel operators, there are agencies that specialise in diving tours. Their packages typically include flights, accommodation, diving fees and diving tours.

Tahiti specialists in the USA include **Tahiti Legends** (☎ 800-200-1213; W *www.tahitilegends.com*) and **Tahiti Vacations** (☎ 800-553-3477; W *www.tahitivacation.com*). Packages for seven nights start at US$1090 on Mo'orea and US$1750 on Bora Bora.

In Australia, **Hideaway Holidays** (☎ 02-9743 0253; W *www.hideawayholidays.com.au*) is a South Pacific specialist that offers heaps of flight and accommodation deals to Tahiti. Seven-night packages from Sydney to Tahiti start at A$1675.

In the UK, **Sunset Faraway Holidays** (☎ 020 7498 9922; W *www.sunsetfaraway.com*) arranges packages to French Polynesia. Ten-night packages start at £1819 to Tahiti and £2278 to Bora Bora.

Getting Around

Getting around French Polynesia is half the fun. There are regular and affordable connections between the larger islands by boat (wonderfully languorous) and aeroplane (dramatic and scenic). Getting to the remote islands can be time-consuming and difficult, but it's never boring.

On some islands there are paved roads, le truck (bus) services and myriad car-rental companies; on others there are rough dirt tracks, and public transport is unheard of. Generally, your best bet is to rent a car or, even better, a bicycle and to be the master of your own destiny.

Island to Island

AIR

There are some (expensive) charter operators with small aircraft and helicopters, but, essentially, flying within French Polynesia means Air Tahiti and its associate, Air Moorea. Air Tahiti flies to 38 islands in all five of the major island groups. Window seats on its modern fleet of high-wing turboprop aircraft offer great views, but for the nervous flyer these flights can be rather hair-raising. Air Moorea is the secondary airline, operating smaller aircraft between Tahiti and Mo'orea and Tetiaroa. Note that Pape'ete is very much the hub for flights within French Polynesia and, with a few exceptions, you will generally have to pass through Pape'ete between island groups.

The cheapest way to visit a number of islands by air is to buy one of the air passes that Air Tahiti offers.

Domestic Air Services

All Air Tahiti flights are nonsmoking. You can take up to 32kg of luggage on board (there is a left-luggage facility at Faa'a airport in Pape'ete).

Flight frequencies ebb and flow with the seasons, and in the July–August peak season, extra flights are scheduled. Air Tahiti publishes a useful flight schedule booklet, which is essential reading for anyone planning a complex trip around the islands. If you are making reservations from afar, you can email or call **Air Tahiti** (☎ 86 42 42, fax 86 40 99; e reservation@airtahiti.pf); see the individual island chapters for Air Tahiti's island-specific phone numbers.

The Society Islands From Pape'ete, there are direct flights every half-hour or so to Mo'orea and several times a day to other major islands in the group, except for Maupiti, where connections are less frequent (about four a week). There are daily connections on most routes between Mo'orea, Huahine, Ra'iatea and Bora Bora. On some routes, such as the busy Pape'ete–Bora Bora connection, there are up to eight flights a day in the high season. The Society Islands are quite close together, and the longest nonstop flight (between Pape'ete and Bora Bora) takes only 45 minutes. Other flights, such as the speedy trip between Pape'ete and Mo'orea, may be as short as seven minutes.

The Tuamotus Air Tahiti divides the Tuamotus into the busier and more touristy northern Tuamotus (Ahe, Apataki, Arutua, Faaite, Fakarava, Kauehi, Manihi, Mataiva, Napuka, Rangiroa, Tikehau, Takapoto, Takaroa) and the much less frequented eastern Tuamotus (Anaa, Fakahina, Fangatau, Hao, Makemo, Nukutavake, Puka Puka, Pukarua, Reao, Takume, Tatakoto, Tureia, Vahitahi). The Gambier Archipelago is reached via the eastern Tuamotus.

Rangiroa is the main flight centre in the Tuamotus, with between one and five flights to/from Pape'ete daily (one hour). On most days, at least one flight continues on to Manihi. Other flights from Pape'ete, either direct or via Rangiroa, include Apataki, Arutua, Faaite, Fakarava, Ahe, Kaukura, Mataiva, Takaroa and Takapoto and Tikehau.

Apart from Tahiti, the only Society Island with a direct connection to the Tuamotus is Bora Bora. There's one daily Bora Bora–Rangiroa flight and a weekly flight from Rangiroa to Nuku Hiva (and on to Atuona on Hiva Oa) in the Marquesas.

There are connections to Anaa, Fakahina, Fangatau, Hao, Makemo, Napuka, Nukutavake, Puka Puka, Pukarua, Reao, Takume, Tatakoto, Tureia and Vahitahi in the eastern

Tuamotus. Some of these connections are very infrequent, so check a current Air Tahiti timetable.

The Marquesas Flights to the Marquesas are usually direct from Pape'ete (about three hours), but some are via Rangiroa, and a few are via Bora Bora. There are seven or eight flights weekly to Nuku Hiva, some of which continue on to Hiva Oa. From Nuku Hiva there are three flights weekly to 'Ua Pou, and one flight weekly to 'Ua Huka.

The Australs Air Tahiti has five flights weekly from Pape'ete to Rurutu (1½ hours) and Tubuai. One flight travels Pape'ete–Rurutu–Tubuai–Pape'ete, the other one travels Pape'ete–Tubuai–Rurutu–Pape'ete. There are also flights to Raivavae.

The Gambier Archipelago There is one flight weekly to Mangareva from Pape'ete (about 3½ hours with a half-hour stop at Hao).

Charter Flights Both based at Faa'a airport, **Wan Air** (☎ 86 61 63, fax 86 61 72) and **Air Archipels** (☎ 81 30 30, fax 86 42 69) can arrange charter flights with small aircraft to any destination in French Polynesia. **Héli-Inter Polynésie** (☎ 81 99 00, Bora Bora 67 62 59; e helico-tahiti@mail.pf) and **Héli Pacific** (☎ 85 68 00, fax 85 68 08) are also at the airport and organise helicopter charters (around 15,500 CFP for 20 minutes; minimum of four people required). In the Marquesas, **Héli-Inter Marquises** (☎/fax 92 02 17) operates regular shuttle services (see the Marquesas chapter).

Buying Tickets

You can pay for flights by credit card at all Air Tahiti offices or agencies.

Reservations If your travel agent tells you that Air Tahiti flights are fully booked, do not despair. It seems to be fairly common for people to reserve seats and then change their mind at the last moment. Seats may therefore become available right up to the last minute. Reapply frequently.

You can make reservations at a travel agency or by phone and be issued with a purchase date; if you haven't paid for the flight by that date the reservation is auto-matically cancelled. If, however, you buy the ticket and don't show up for the flight you'll be penalised 25% of the ticket price.

Remember to reconfirm your Air Tahiti flights, as flight changes and overbooking are certainly not unheard of. Note that if you fail to fly on a confirmed flight, all your subsequent reservations may be cancelled. So if you decide to get from one island to an-other by some different means, make sure you reconfirm the rest of your flights.

In French Polynesia call the central book-ing number for **Air Tahiti** (☎ 86 42 42, 86 41 84 Sat, Sun & public holidays, fax 86 40 99; e reservation@airtahiti.pf; w www.airtahiti.pf) to reconfirm, book or change a booking.

Fares See the Domestic Air Fares map on the following page for fares between the various islands of French Polynesia. Be-cause distances to the remote islands are so great, some of the full fares are quite high. However, Air Tahiti has been reviewing its prices and, in some cases, lowering them. There are a number of air passes that bring prices down to more acceptable levels, and there's also a system of reduced-fare cards (see later in this section).

Another cost-saving option is a flight-and-accommodation package. For some is-lands there are even weekend packages. Contact **Séjours dans les Îles** (☎ 86 43 43, fax 86 40 99).

Children from age two to 11 pay roughly 50% of the adult fare. Infants under two years of age pay 10%. If you buy tickets overseas they may work out about 5% more expensive due to travel agency commissions.

Flights are classified (in ascending order of demand) as blue, white or red. If you have an air pass, there may be restrictions on the flights you can use, particularly the popular peak-period red flights.

Reduced-Fare Cards Air Tahiti has several cards available that let you buy tickets at re-duced prices, depending on whether the flight is blue, white or red. If you're under 25, the Carte Jeune (Youth Card) gives you a 50% reduction on blue flights and 30% on white flights. If you're over 60, a Carte Marama (Third Age Card) gives you 50% and 30% re-ductions respectively. A Carte Famille (Fam-ily Card) provides family members with a 50% (adults) and 75% (children) discount

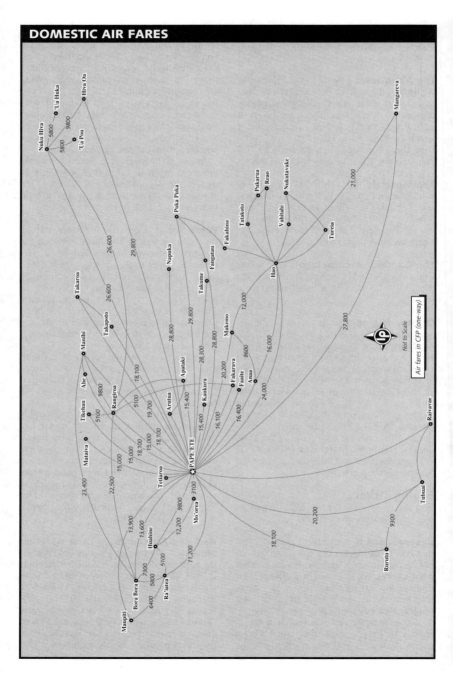

on blue flights, 30% and 50% on white flights and 10% and 50% on red flights.

The Carte Jeune and Carte Marama cost 1000 CFP and require a passport-type photo and your passport or other form of identification; the Carte Famille costs 2000 CFP and requires photos of the parents and birth certificates or equivalent for the children – just having them listed in your passport isn't enough.

These cards are issued on the spot, but are available only in French Polynesia.

Air Passes

There are five island-hopping air passes offering inclusive fares to a number of islands.

Travel must commence in Pape'ete and there are restrictions on the number of transits allowed through Pape'ete. You are only allowed one stopover on each island, but you can transit an island if the flight number does not change. If you stop at an island to change flights, it counts as a stopover.

Passes are valid for a maximum of 28 days and all flights (except Pape'ete–Mo'orea or Mo'orea–Pape'ete) must be booked when you buy your pass, though dates can be changed at any time. You can use either Air Tahiti or Air Moorea on the Pape'ete–Mo'orea sector. Once you have taken the first flight on the pass, the routing cannot be changed, and the fare is nonrefundable.

You can extend any of the following passes to include the Marquesas (Nuku Hiva and Hiva Oa) for 45,000/23,400 CFP adults/children. An extension to the Australs (Rurutu and Tubuai) costs 20,000/10,900 CFP. A Marquesas and Australs extension to cover all four islands costs 65,000/34,300 CFP.

Passe Decouverte The Passe Decouverte *(Discovery Pass; adults/children 23,000/ 13,000 CFP)* is the most basic pass and allows visits to Mo'orea, Ra'iatea and Huahine from Pape'ete.

Passe Bora Bora The Passe Bora Bora *(Bora Bora Pass; adults/children 32,500/ 17,800 CFP)* allows you to visit the six main islands in the Society group: Tahiti, Mo'orea, Huahine, Ra'iatea, Bora Bora and Maupiti.

Passe Bleu Decouverte & Passe Bleu The Passe Bleu Decouverte (Blue Discovery Pass) covers travel to Mo'orea, Huahine and Ra'iatea for 16,000 CFP; the Passe Bleu (Blue Pass) adds Bora Bora and costs 22,000 CFP (there are no children's fares offered). You must leave Pape'ete on a blue flight, you can only use blue or white flights on subsequent sectors, and Mo'orea must be your last visit.

Passe Lagons The Passe Lagons *(Lagoons Pass; adults/children 37,000/20,000 CFP)* allows you to visit Mo'orea, Rangiroa, Tikehau, Manihi and Fakarava.

Passe Bora-Tuamotu This pass *(adults/ children 47,500/25,300 CFP)* allows you to visit Mo'orea, Huahine, Ra'iatea, Bora Bora, Maupiti, Rangiroa, Tikehau, Manihi and Fakarava.

BOAT

Within the Society group, boat travel is a delight. Between Tahiti and Mo'orea, a number of companies shuttle back and forth daily; other routes between the islands are served at least twice a week.

In the other archipelagos, travel by boat is more difficult. If you are short on time and keen to travel beyond the Society Islands, you may need to consider flying at least some of the way.

Cargo ships, known as *goélettes*, or schooners, are principally involved in freight transport. They do take passengers, however, and for those who want to get off the beaten trail such a voyage can, depending on the circumstances, be anything from a memorable experience to an outright nightmare. The level of comfort is rudimentary: some ships don't have passenger cabins and you have to travel 'deck class', providing your own bedding to unroll on the deck, and all your own meals. You will get wet and cold. And then there's seasickness.

A notice posted at Chez Guynette in Huahine sums up the cargo ship schedules: 'The boats arrive when they are here and leave when they are ready'.

Ferry & Cargo Ship

The Society Islands It takes between half an hour and an hour to travel between Tahiti and Mo'orea, depending on which company you go with. The car ferries, such as those run by Moorea Ferry, are slower than the high-speed ferries which take only passengers, motorcycles and bicycles. The **Ono-Ono** (☎ 45 35 35 in Pape'ete; one-way/return 1050/2200 CFP) has at least four crossings daily and docks at Cook's Bay rather than Vaiare, which is handy if you are staying nearby. See the Mo'orea chapter for more information about ferries to/from Mo'orea.

Vaeanu (☎ 41 25 35, fax 41 24 34) operates the Pape'ete–Huahine–Ra'iatea–Taha'a–Bora Bora round trip, leaving Pape'ete on Monday, Wednesday and Friday at 5pm (the Wednesday trip does not stop at Taha'a). It sets out from Bora Bora on Tuesday, Thursday and Sunday. The Huahine and Ra'iatea arrivals are in the middle of the night (most guesthouse owners will not pick you up). Reservations are advisable. The office is at Motu Uta, near the *Aranui* office. Take le truck No 3 from the *mairie* (town hall).

Hawaiki Nui (☎ 45 23 24) also travels the Society Islands circuit, and has two departures a week (Tuesday and Thursday at 4pm; per person deck/cabin 1700/4850 CFP); **Aremiti 3** (☎ 74 39 40, 74 39 41) sails from Pape'ete on Monday and Friday for Huahine and Ra'iatea (one-way/return 5500/11,000 CFP; between the islands 1500 CFP). The *Taporo VII* also travels to Huahine.

The **Maupiti Express** (☎ 67 66 69 on Bora Bora) makes regular trips between Bora Bora, Maupiti, Taha'a and Ra'iatea.

Jet France (☎/fax 56 15 62) and **L'Escapade** (☎ 72 85 31) both travel from Pape'ete to Tetiaroa (for more information see the Other Windward Islands chapter).

The small cargo ship **Maupiti Tou Ai'a** (☎ 50 66 71, fax 43 32 69) goes to Maupiti from Pape'ete once a week, with an occasional stop at Ra'iatea and Mopelia. The ship leaves on Wednesday evening, arrives at Maupiti the following morning, and returns to Pape'ete two days later. The one-way fare is 2400 CFP.

The Tuamotus The small cargo vessels that serve the Tuamotus, *goélettes,* are true lifelines between Tahiti and the atolls of the archipelago. They can and do take passengers, but their main purpose is to transport freight and the standard of comfort is generally basic.

The routes and fares mentioned are purely an indication and are subject to change. It's best to check with the shipowners in the Motu Uta port area in Pape'ete (take le truck

No 3 from the *mairie*). The offices are generally open Monday to Friday from 7.30am to 11am and from 1.30pm to 5pm. Some also open on Saturday morning.

The **Dory** (☎ 42 30 55; office open 7.30am-noon & 1.30pm-4.30pm Mon-Thur) runs the Pape'ete–Tikehau–Rangiroa–Ahe–Manihi–Apataki–Arutua–Kaukura–Pape'ete route, departing Pape'ete on Monday and returning on Friday.

There's deck and berth accommodation available, but no meals for passengers, so you must buy food at each stop. A single trip, deck/cabin class, costs around 3700/5500 CFP (children travel half-price).

The **Corbia** (☎ 43 36 43; office open 7.30am-3.30pm Mon-Fri, 8am-11am Sat) travels Pape'ete–Kaukura–Arutua–Apataki–Aratika–Toau–Pape'ete once a week; there are no cabins and no meals are served. The fare is about 3150 CFP.

Rairoa Nui (☎ 48 35 78, fax 48 22 86) runs the Pape'ete–Rangiroa–Arutua–Apataki–Kaukura–Pape'ete loop once a week. There are no cabins and no meals are available; the cost is around 3000 CFP.

The **Saint-Xavier Maris-Stella** (☎ 42 23 58; office open 7.30am-11am & 1.30pm-4pm Mon- Fri) travels Pape'ete–Mataiva–Tikehau–Rangiroa–Ahe–Manihi–Takaroa–Takapoto–Arutua–Apataki–Kaukura–Toau–Fakarava–Kauehi–Raraka–Niau–Pape'ete every 15 days. Departing from Pape'ete, allow 5050 CFP to Rangiroa, 6060 CFP to Manihi and 7575 CFP to Fakarava. Prices are for deck class, but meals are included.

The **Nuku Hau** (☎ 45 23 24, fax 45 24 44; office open 7.30am-4pm Mon-Fri) travels around Pape'ete–Hao–Nego Nego–Tureia–Vanavana–Marutea–Rikitea–Tematangi–Aruanuraro–Nukitepipi–Hereheretue–Pape'ete every 25 days. It costs around 7800 CFP on the deck; it's an extra 2000 CFP per person per day for meals.

The **Mareva Nui** (☎ 42 25 53; office open 7.30am-11.30am & 1.30pm-5pm Mon-Thur) follows a Pape'ete–Makatea–Mataiva–Tikehau–Rangiroa–Ahe–Manihi–Takaroa–Takapoto–Raraka–Kauehi–Aratika–Taiaro–Fakarava–Arutua–Apataki–Niau–Toau–Kaukura–Pape'ete route. Fares vary from 2750 CFP to 5800 CFP for a part-journey (add 2200 CFP per person per day for meals) on deck and from 3850 CFP to 8200 CFP in a sleeper; the complete trip takes eight days.

The **Vai-Aito** (☎ 43 99 96; office open 8am-4pm Mon-Fri) does a Pape'ete–Tikehau–Rangiroa–Ahe–Manihi–Aratika–Kauehi–Toau–Fakarava–Pape'ete trip two or three times a month. From Pape'ete it's 5400 CFP to Rangiroa, 8080 CFP to Manihi and 18,800 CFP to Fakarava on deck, meals included; the trip takes seven to eight days.

The **Kura Ora II** and **Kura Ora III** (☎ 45 55 45; office open 7.30am-3pm Mon-Thur) do a trip every 15 days to the remote atolls of the central and eastern Tuamotus, including Anaa, Hao and Makemo. Deck-class prices cost from around 6000 CFP, depending on the distance travelled, plus around 2300 CFP per person per day for meals. The complete trip takes about three weeks. To get to the office, take the same road as for the *Saint-Xavier Maris-Stella* office.

The *Hotu Maru*, *Taporo V* and *Taporo VI* also visit the Tuamotus. The *Taporo IV* and *Aranui* serve certain atolls in the Tuamotus en route to the Marquesas, as does the *Nuku Hau* on its way to the Gambier Archipelago.

The Marquesas The *Aranui* and the *Taporo IV* both go to the Marquesas. The **Aranui** (☎ 42 62 40, fax 43 48 89; [w] www.aranui.com) is a veritable institution. It takes freight and passengers on 16 trips a year from Pape'ete (see the boxed text 'The Aranui' in the Marquesas chapter for details). The **Taporo IV** (☎ 42 63 93, fax 42 06 17) takes a maximum of 12 passengers on its 10-day trip around the Marquesas; the boat runs every 15 days. The shipowner, **Compagnie Française Maritime de Tahiti** (☎ 43 89 66) has its office at Fare Ute, just before the entrance to the Motu Uta port area.

The Australs Services between the Society Islands and the Australs are limited, so make sure you plan ahead.

The 60m *Tuhaa Pae II* leaves Pape'ete for the Australs three times a month. It stops at Rurutu and Tubuai on every trip, Rimatara and Raivavae twice a month, Rapa once every two months and Maria Island in the Gambiers very occasionally.

You can choose between deck class, berths and air-con cabins. From Pape'ete to Rurutu, Rimatara or Tubuai a deck/berth/air-con cabin costs 4046/5664/7789 CFP; to Raivavae it costs 5832/8164/11,226 CFP. Three meals adds another 2800 CFP a day.

The **Tuhaa Pae II office** (☎ 50 96 09, 50 96 06, fax 42 06 09; [e] snathp@mail.pf) is in Motu Uta, between the *Kura Ora* and *Mareva Nui* offices.

The Gambier Archipelago Every three weeks, the *Nuku Hau* does a 15-day circuit to Rikitea on Mangareva in the Gambier Archipelago via several remote atolls in the eastern Tuamotus. One-way places on the deck cost 7900 CFP, plus 2100 CFP per day for meals. The **Nuku Hau office** (☎ 45 23 24) is in the Motu Uta port area, close to the warehouses of the other ship operators.

Once or twice a month, the *Taporo V* does a 16-day trip through the eastern Tuamotus and the Gambier Archipelago. One-way places on the deck to Rikitea cost around 33,500 CFP, meals included. The **Taporo V office** (☎ 42 63 93) is at Fare Ute, in the same building as the *Taporo VI* office.

Tuhaa Pae II occasionally stops at Maria Island (see The Australs, earlier in this chapter).

Cruise Ship

At the other end of the spectrum from rudimentary cargo ships are the luxury cruise ships that operate in the Society Islands. These cruise ships are incredibly stylish and comfortable and offer shore excursions at each stop – this is a long way from the leaky copra boats of traditional inter-island travel.

Managed by **Bora Bora Pearl Cruises** (☎ 43 43 03, fax 45 10 65; [e] haumana@mail.pf; [w] www.boraborapearlcruises.com), the *Haumana* is a magnificent 36m catamaran that accommodates up to 60 people and does three- or four-day cruises between Bora Bora, Ra'iatea, and Taha'a. The *Tia Moana* and the *Tu Moana*, both also managed by Bora Bora cruises, offer seven-day cruises in the Society Islands.

You may see the enormous *Paul Gauguin*, a 320-passenger ship, anchored in Pape'ete. It departs Pape'ete every week for a one-week cruise that includes Ra'iatea, Taha'a, Bora Bora and Mo'orea. Contact **Tahiti Nui Travel** (☎ 54 02 00, fax 42 74 35; [e] sales@tahitinuitravel.pf; [w] www.tahitinuitravel.pf) for information.

The *Renaissance* cruise ships, the *R3* and *R4*, have had a rather tumultuous history. Owned by the company American Renaissance Cruises, these two monsters can each accommodate 684 passengers but have been out of action for some time. Contact **Tahiti Tourisme** (☎ *50 57 00, fax 43 66 19;* ⓔ *tahiti -tourisme@mail.pf;* ⓦ *www.tahiti-tourisme .com)* for an update.

Yacht
French Polynesia is an enormously popular yachting destination, as the international line-up of yachts along the Pape'ete waterfront testifies. It's also possible to rent a yacht in French Polynesia (see the Outdoor Activities chapter). See Formalities for Yachts in the Facts for the Visitor chapter for information about bringing your own boat into French Polynesian waters.

On the Islands

In the Society group, most islands have one road that hugs the coast all the way around. Tahiti (where there is even a stretch of freeway), Mo'orea and Bora Bora have paved and reasonably well-maintained roads. On Ra'iatea and Huahine the coast roads are mostly sealed, though there are occasional stretches of ground coral. On Taha'a and Maupiti there are only limited stretches of sealed road. On all of these islands, tracks leading inland are often rough-and-ready and almost always require a 4WD.

There are far more boats than land vehicles in the Tuamotus, although there is a sealed road running the length of Rangiroa's major island – all 10km of it!

Except in towns, there are hardly any sealed roads in the Marquesas. Tracks, suitable for 4WDs only, connect the villages.

Sealed roads encircle both Tubuai and Raivavae in the Australs, and there are reasonable stretches of sealed road on Rurutu. Otherwise, roads in this archipelago are fairly limited and little transport is available.

LE TRUCK
Le trucks are French Polynesia's public bus system, and are just what the name indicates: trucks. Along each side in the back is a bench seat for passengers.

Only Tahiti has a reasonably comprehensive and regular system of le trucks. Although there are official le truck stops, complete with blue signs, they are rather difficult to spot, and le trucks will generally stop anywhere

sensible for anybody who hails them. Note that you pay at the end of your trip and that for many routes there is a set fare, irrespective of distance.

Le trucks are gradually being replaced by air-con buses that, in theory, will only stop at designated stops and will run to a timetable.

CAR & SCOOTER
If you want to explore the larger islands of the Society group at your own pace, it may be worth renting a car or scooter, particularly given the price of taxis and the dismal state of public transport outside Pape'ete.

Road Rules
Driving is on the right-hand side in French Polynesia. Although the accident statistics are pretty grim, driving in French Polynesia is not difficult, and the traffic is light almost everywhere apart from the busy coastal strip around Pape'ete on Tahiti. However, the overtaking habits of locals can sometimes get the heart rate up. Beware of drunk drivers at night, and of pedestrians and children who may not be used to traffic, particularly in more remote locations.

Rental
There are many different car rental agencies on the more touristy islands, but the prices really don't vary much: compared with rental costs in the rest of the world, prices are high. For a small car expect to pay from 2000 CFP a day, plus 40 CFP per kilometre and 1400 CFP a day for a collision-damage waiver – and that's not even including petrol! A daily rate with unlimited mileage will probably work out cheaper (from around 8350 CFP a day, including insurance). Rates drop slightly from the third day onwards, and 10% reductions are often offered.

Fortunately the cars available are pretty economical and you won't cover too many kilometres, no matter how hard you try. Off-road excursions into the interior are usually off limits to anything other than a 4WD.

Most places offer four-, eight- and 24-hour rates, as well as two- and three-day rentals. At certain times of year (July, August and New Year's Eve), it's wise to book vehicles a few days in advance. An international driving permit is useful, but your national driving licence is usually enough. You'll need a credit card, of course.

On Tahiti you will find the major international car rental agencies such as Avis, Budget, Europcar and Hertz. On other islands such as Mo'orea, Huahine, Ra'iatea and Bora Bora, as well as on Rangiroa in the Tuamotus, the market is divided up between Avis and Europcar. Smaller local agencies exist on some islands, but the rates are almost as high.

You can hire a car on Rurutu in the Australs, but on the Marquesas, rental vehicles are mainly 4WDs complete with a driver. Rental without a driver is possible only on Atuona (Hiva Oa) and Taiohae (Nuku Hiva).

Avis and Europcar rent scooters on a number of islands. It's a good way of getting around the small islands, but bear in mind you won't be wearing protective gear, so this is probably not the place to learn to drive a scooter. You'll pay around 5000 CFP a day. After numerous accidents there are no rental scooters on Tahiti.

TAXI

Tahiti, Mo'orea, Huahine, Ra'iatea and Bora Bora have taxis, but the prices are so prohibitive that taxis should be avoided where possible. You'll pay US$15 to US$20 for the 6km trip between Faa'a airport and Pape'ete. Thankfully, taxi drivers in French Polynesia do not expect a tip.

On other islands, official taxis do not exist, but if there's a car and a customer, arrangements can usually be made. As there are no taxis on the Marquesas, you have to hire a 4WD vehicle and a driver.

If you've booked accommodation, hotels and *pensions* (guesthouses) will generally pick up guests from the airport or ferry quay, which is something you should jump at (although you may be charged for this service; clarify this when you book).

BICYCLE

Cycling around the islands of French Polynesia is a sheer delight. The distances are rarely great, the traffic is rarely heavy (except in Tahiti) and the roads are rarely hilly. Bikes can be rented on many of the islands for about 1500 CFP a day, but you may find yourself riding an antique. Consider bringing your own bike if you are a really keen cyclist. Bicycles are accepted on all the inter-island boats.

HITCHING

Hitching (*auto-stop* in French) is a widely accepted way of getting around the islands in French Polynesia, although it's not really a part of life on Tahiti any more. However, hitching is never entirely safe, and on principle we don't recommend it. Travellers who decide to hitch are always taking a risk, even though French Polynesia is generally a safe location. Hitching in pairs, and letting someone know where you are planning to go, reduces the risks. Women should avoid hitching alone.

BOAT

On some islands, such as Mo'orea, Bora Bora and Ra'iatea, it's possible to rent small outboard-powered boats. No permit is necessary, and if you can get a few people together, this can be a great and economical way to explore the lagoons.

If you need to get across a lagoon, there will generally be somebody available with the appropriate boat. Just ask.

ORGANISED TOURS

Even those who normally shun organised tours may find themselves enjoying one in French Polynesia. Given that transport can be difficult and expensive, organised tours are often a great way of seeing parts of the islands you wouldn't otherwise get to. Everything from half-day, around-the-island trips to sun-soaked days of snorkelling, shark-feeding and picnics on remote motu are available. You can generally organise these trips through your hotel or *pension;* see individual chapters for details.

Outdoor Activities

French Polynesia's exceptional natural heritage lends itself to a range of leisure activities. Scuba diving (see the special section 'Diving' later in this book) is the main activity, but sailing is also very popular. Increasing numbers of surfers are sampling the islands' excellent reef breaks, while the jagged relief of the high islands makes for some superb walking.

Hiking

A single glance at the mountains of Tahiti and Mo'orea hints at the opportunities available to walking enthusiasts (or anyone keen to find an alternative to the lagoons). Unfortunately, the trails are rarely well kept and are poorly marked. A local guide is often essential.

Tahiti and Mo'orea are the only islands offering serious walking options. Walks on the other islands are usually simple, short jaunts; these are covered in the relevant island chapters. The walks described here are only a selection; local guides will probably have other suggestions.

The ideal time for hiking is April to October. During the rainy season (November to April), the paths can be dangerous and even impassable.

EQUIPMENT

Sunglasses, sunscreen, a hat, mosquito repellent, something to keep the rain off and, if you're climbing the high peaks, something to keep you warm are all essential. You'll need good walking shoes, and plastic sandals for crossing rivers. Also bring plenty of drinking water, and a plastic bag or something similar to keep your camera equipment dry.

GUIDES
Tahiti & Mo'orea

Tiare Mato (☎/fax 43 92 76, 77 48 11; e tiaremat@mail.pf) offers walking guides for all the Tahiti and Mo'orea walks, from 6500 CFP to 15,000 CFP per person. This operation also offers canyoning trips to lava tubes, to the waterfalls of Tiki (Papenoo) and to Tahiti Iti.

On Tahiti, **Polynesian Adventure** (☎ 77 24 37, ☎/fax 43 25 95; W www.polynesianadv .com) charges 5800 CFP to 7700 CFP for a one-day walk, depending on the itinerary, and 14,500 CFP for two-day walks to Pito Iti, Te Pari, Mt Aorai, Pihaiateta and the Diadème.

Le Circuit Vert (☎ 57 22 67) is run by Zéna Angélien and specialises in walks on Tahiti Iti.

On Mo'orea, contact **Tahiti Évasion** (☎/fax 56 48 77; e tahitievasion@mail.pf), which offers day walks from 3500 CFP to 6000 CFP, depending on the itinerary. **Hiro Damide** (☎ 56 16 48, 79 41 54) offers walks for between 2750 CFP and 8250 CFP. Also contact Bernard Genton at the **Ferme Agricole du Mou'a Roa** (☎ 56 58 62).

Derek Grell of **Tefaarahi Safari Tours** (☎/fax 56 41 24, 78 82 61) can take you to Three Coconut Trees Pass or Mt Rotui for about 1000 CFP per hour.

For most trips a minimum number of participants, from two to five people, is required. Contact the operators well in advance.

Ra'iatea

As there are no marked paths, a guide is highly desirable for walks to Temehani Plateau. Contact Patrick Marinthe, owner of **Kaoha Nui Ranch** (☎ 66 25 46). His speciality is botany and he can take you to Temehani Plateau, the Three Waterfalls and Marae Taputapuatea.

TAHITI
Fautaua Valley

This is one of the most pleasant and accessible walks on Tahiti. It is also one of the rare walks for which you don't need a guide. On the other hand, you'll need an access permit, which you can get at the Pape'ete *mairie* (town hall) at the **Service des Régies des Recettes** (☎ 41 58 36, 41 58 34; *adult/child 600/150 CFP*); enter from Rue des Écoles.

To get to Fautaua Valley, follow Av du Prince Hinoi from the Pape'ete seafront for about 2km. At the third set of traffic lights, at the Total petrol station, turn right towards the mountains. You will pass in front of the Bain Loti (Loti Bath). Go straight ahead, as far as the Service de l'Hydraulique, where you hand in your access permit. The easy 4km walk to the Fachoda (Tearape) Bridge takes about an hour. After the bridge there's a rather steep climb; after about 45 minutes you reach a superb viewpoint over Fautaua Waterfall. Another half an hour and you reach the summit of the waterfall, where you can swim in the basin. Along the way you can see the ruins of Fort Fachoda where, in 1846, French soldiers climbed ropes up a cliff face to overpower a Tahitian position.

Mt Aorai

Mt Aorai (2066m) is the third-highest peak on Tahiti and only about a dozen kilometres as the crow flies from Pape'ete. The ascent is one of the island's classic climbs. The path is clearly visible and well maintained by the Centre d'Instruction Militaire (CIM), so you don't need a guide. There are signposts at trail junctions to prevent confusion. It takes at least 4½ hours of steady walking to reach the top.

Two refuges break up the route. They each accommodate about 20 walkers and have electricity. They are equipped with aluminium cisterns that are usually filled with drinkable rainwater.

The climb is feasible for anyone in good physical condition who has experience walking in the mountains. There are, however, several difficult sections at about the mid-point and near the summit; people who suffer from vertigo should stop at the first refuge. Hardier walkers can make the return trip in a day, but start at dawn because the summit tends to be covered in cloud after 11am. All in all, it makes more sense to allow a day and a half. By spending a night in the second shelter you can be on the summit to see the sunrise and enjoy the view across the neighbouring valleys.

Before starting an assault on Aorai, make sure you have warm clothing and a change of clothes, at least 2L of water (in the dry season the water cisterns may be empty) and good walking shoes. Never go alone.

The starting point is at Le Belvédère restaurant, at 600m altitude and accessible by car. From central Pape'ete take Av Georges Clémenceau and turn right at the intersection 200m after the Total petrol station. Turn right again at the sign for Le Belvédère, which is 7km from the coast road.

From the restaurant it's an hour's walk to get to Hamuta Pass (900m), the easiest part of the walk. From the CIM, you reach the ridge via a reasonably wide track that winds up the flank of the mountain. From the pass you can see all of the Fautaua Valley, the ghostly and disjointed silhouette of the Diadème, Mt Marau (preceded by its TV-transmission aerial to the south) and the walls of the ravines of the Pic Vert massif to the west.

It's then 1¼ hours' walk to the first refuge, Fare Mato, perched on a rocky promontory at 1400m. The route this far isn't difficult except for a steep section before the refuge. Mo'orea stands on the horizon to the northwest, while to the east the Pira'e Valley forms a breach in the massif.

The path continues to the ridge and about 10 minutes later reaches a difficult passage, Devil's Rock (Mato Mati), which is probably the toughest part of the climb. The path passes along a flank of the ridge, where you'll have to keep a tight grip on the judiciously placed cables and cords. It's about an hour's steep climb to the second refuge, which you'll see high up on the ridge.

At 1800m, Fare Ata, the second refuge, has two units. An open-sided *fare potee* on the promontory functions as the open-air 'dining room'. The water in the cistern is not drinkable, but there are two cisterns of drinking water outside the actual refuge, 50m away and slightly below.

The summit is less than an hour from here. The path continues along a jagged ridge, like a flight of steps, very narrow on this section and bearing off to the south. The vegetation is more sparse as this is the upper limit for the *puarata* bushes. The view from the top is definitely worth the effort: to the east is Mt Orohena, Pito Iti and the Pira'e Valley. To the northwest lies Mo'orea, Pape'eté is to the north, and beyond is the line of the reef.

Don't relax on the way down, as the rock can easily crumble.

Mt Orohena

The ascent of Mt Orohena (2241m) is a tough two-day mission. You'll have to contend with dense undergrowth, a crumbling ridgeline and often fierce winds. Despite numerous earlier attempts, the first European ascent of the mountain did not take place until 1953. This walk definitely requires the assistance of local experts.

From the Thousand Springs, the route climbs to the ridgeline at Moto Fefe (1142m; about 1½ hours) and follows the ridge from there to the summit. It's a further 1½ hours to Pihaiateta (1742m), two hours more to Pito Iti (2110m) and another two hours to the summit. There are some extremely narrow ridgelines on the ascent but fixed cables on certain tricky sections make the climb a little easier.

Hitiaa Lava Tubes

Lava tubes are the result of the cooling and more rapid hardening of the surface of lava flows. As they solidified, the deepest layers of lava contracted, creating tubular spaces between the layers closest to the surface and the deeper ones.

It's possible to walk through the Hitiaa Lava Tubes, but this fascinating walk can only be attempted when there is no danger of a sudden downpour.

From the turn-off at PK39.9, a 4WD track runs 6km inland past a dam at 500m altitude, 1km before the start of the walk at 630m. A powerful and (most importantly) reliable torch (flashlight) is essential for investigating the lava tubes. A walk through all three takes about three hours.

It's less than 15 minutes' walk to the first tube, at 750m. It's about 100m long and only about 200m from the second tube (300m long), with two waterfalls just before the entry. Between the second and third tube, the trail goes under a stone bridge, which is the remains of a collapsed lava tube. The third tube is longer, darker and more complex. About 100m in, it divides: the left fork continues about 300m to an exit and the right fork leads to a large cave, complete with lake and waterfall.

Te Pari

Te Pari means 'The Cliffs' in Tahitian; it's the name applied to the stretch of the Tahiti Iti coast from Tautira in the north to Vaipoiri Cave in the south. It's practically uninhabited, a wild and desolate area light years from the noise and confusion of Pape'ete. You will definitely need a guide, as some parts can be dangerous. Since you will often have to wade through water, bring a change of clothes, plastic shoes and a waterproof bag to protect your camera equipment. If your guide does not provide a mask and fins, bring your own.

From Tautira you usually go directly to the mouth of the Vaiote River by speedboat (about 25 minutes). This saves three hours of dull walking along the coast. The boat is moored over the coral near a small motu in the lagoon; you'll find petroglyphs facing the motu, 30m back from the beach, to the right of a banyan tree. One of these petroglyphs is of a solar disk with its rays surmounting a pirogue. The second illustrates the same motif but with hands around it. Apparently the chiefs of neighbouring tribes met here to hold councils of war and to plan attacks on the rival tribes of Teahupoo. A god answered their incantations and left his imprints on the stones.

The Honoura Drums (Te Pahu O Honoura) are a 15-minute walk inland, after crossing the Vaiote River. These are rocks with cavities about 20cm in diameter that resonate when struck with a coconut-tree branch. According to legend, the hero Honoura tapped on the first rock (the one with two holes) to warn the inhabitants of Tautira of an impending attack by their enemies from Teahupoo.

Back on the track, follow the Vaiote for about 15 minutes; on the left is a *pae pae* (traditional meeting platform) hidden in a tangle of ferns and *mape* (chestnut) and *purau* (hibiscus) trees. This valley's rich archaeological remains speak of a significant pre-European population.

Continuing south along the coast, 10 minutes by boat brings you to Vaitomoana Cave, partially invaded by the sea. The guide will lend you a mask and snorkel to collect sea urchins, which cling to the bottom of the cliff, 5m below.

A further five minutes by boat, or 1½ hours on foot along a ledge overhanging the ocean, brings you to Devil's Passage (Vahi Hororaa; literally, 'Place Where One Must Run'). It's a narrow passage on the side of the rock that you must cross over quickly as the waves retreat. You're helped by the ropes attached to the cliff.

Anaihe Cave is 20 minutes' walk from Devil's Passage. Well known to fishers from the Tahiti Iti peninsula, it serves as a shelter during bad weather. It is fitted out with a basic table and benches of coconut wood and is a popular place for visitors to picnic. The coral formations a few metres from the shore make a great snorkelling site.

There's a waterfall not far from here. You emerge in a narrow and slippery horseshoe-shaped passage about 20m long, which brings you out 5m above the waves. There are good handholds on the rocks, and ropes attached to the sides with pitons help you. Your efforts are rewarded by the view of Queen's Cave, about 10 minutes from here. According to legend, the queen who lived in the Taapeha Valley was accustomed to bathing in the small water hole in the interior of the cave and sitting on the nearby rock to be tended to by her servants. If the sea is calm you can dive in the turquoise water a few metres below. Watch for the returning waves.

The very deep Taapeha Valley is 10 minutes' walk from here. About 100m back, where the stream threads its way through the huge stone blocks, you'll find on the right the giant *umete* of Taapeha. An *umete* is a Tahitian wooden dish or bowl, and erosion has given this rock that characteristic shape. This rock makes multiple appearances in legends and was used to make traditional medications. It was a traditional birthing site – its shape follows the body's contours perfectly and newborn children were washed in the stream and coated with *monoi* (fragrant coconut oil).

The Faaroa refuge is the next stopping point. It's on the banks of the river of the same name, which marks the Tautira-Teahupoo district boundary. If you are on a two-day walk, this is where you spend the night. The walk can continue the next day to Vaipoiri Cave, where you can go swimming. The return to Tautira is by boat, with a possible picnic stop on Motu Fenua Ino.

It's also possible to follow the trail from Teahupoo to the Vaipoiri Cave.

Other Walks

Other walks on Tahiti include Faananu Valley (Tiarei), Vaipohe Valley (Pa'ea), Tuauru Valley (Mahina), Vaihi Valley (Hitiaa), Orofero Plateau (Pa'ea), the Diadème and Pito Iti.

MO'OREA
Vaiare to Paopao

This interesting and reasonably easy walk takes about two hours, starting from Vaiare and climbing to the ridge between Mt Tearai (770m) and Mt Mouaputa (830m) before dropping down into the valley and emerging at Paopao on Cook's Bay. There are great views, and dense vegetation cloaks the steep mountains.

From the ferry quay in the centre of Vaiare, walk south across the first bridge and turn inland along the road beside the Chez Méno store. There are two intersections; take the right fork on both occasions. Don't take the next turn right but keep following the road, which deteriorates to a muddy track as it passes through plantations of pineapples, taro, papaya and bananas and climbs up above the south bank of the river. Do not follow the track right to the end; it follows the river to an eventual dead end. Instead, look for a walking track, which turns sharply off the vehicle track just before it becomes too narrow for a 4WD.

Finding the start of the track is the most difficult part of this walk. There may be a red arrow painted on a pole on the opposite (river) side of the vehicle track, or you may just have to cast around until you find the trail markers (splashes of red paint on trees).

The walking track climbs steeply uphill and can be slippery after rain; but once you've found it it's easy to follow. Eventually the track emerges on the ridge between the two peaks. Follow the ridge uphill a short way to a rock with a wonderful view of Tahiti and of the pineapple plantations in the valley below. Towering above is the spectacular peak of Mt Mouaputa, the mountain with the 'hole' through it.

The track drops very steeply, but handy vines and creepers make the descent fairly simple. The track passes through a thicket of bamboo and crosses a river before emerging on the flat valley floor.

It's much easier to do this walk in the direction Vaiare to Paopao.

Three Coconut Trees Pass

This is an exhilarating climb. It's hard, sweaty work but the payoff is superb views from the ridge separating Mt Mouaroa (880m) from Mt Tohiea (1207m). There are not, however, three coconut trees – two were blown down in an early-1980s cyclone.

Start by taking the inland road from the top of Opunohu Bay towards Marae Titiroa and the *belvédère* (lookout). Shortly after the Cook's Bay road joins the route, and before the agricultural college, another road turns to the right. There's a sign pointing the way to the 'Vue de Roto Nui et du Marae' and a much smaller and rather obscure pictogram of three coconut trees. Follow the turnoff road a couple of hundred metres to its end and park just before the pig farm.

The walking path, with red trail-markers, continues straight on from the road; it drops down to a small stream then climbs up the other side, through ferns, with the ridge and the coconut tree clearly visible to the right.

The route takes a sharp turn and drops steeply down to a wider river. Cross this river but don't go straight up the other side. The path now follows the river, crossing it half-a-dozen times as it tumbles down through a dark and magnificent *mape* forest. Eventually the walking trail diverges from the river and heads up the hill. If you're uncertain whether you're still on the correct route, search for the red markers. If you go far without them, you're lost.

Higher up the hill the markers seem to fade but bits of plastic tied to branches help. Clearings are the easiest places to get lost; each time you exit one, make sure you're on the right trail. A clearing closer to the top can cause confusion, but there's a marker on a big, mossy rock off to the right of the clearing.

The final climb to the top of the knife-edge ridge is a real root-hanger, but you emerge from the undergrowth to unobstructed views on the way up.

Trodden-down barbed wire along the ridgeline shows where a fence once ran. Follow the ridge to the right (west) for the best views over the bays (and all the way to Tetiaroa on a clear day).

Keep an eye out for the route markers on your way down. It's even easier to lose them when you're walking fast and possibly paying less attention.

Opunohu Valley Loop

This relatively easy one-day walk starts at the agricultural college. After climbing up to Three Coconut Trees Pass, follow the ridgeline through undergrowth of *mape* and *purau* until you get to the *belvédère* (about 1½ hours). From there, it's about 45 minutes to Three Firs Pass, from where there are superb views of Cook's Bay and Opunohu Bay, facing the ridge of Mt Rotui. This section presents no particular difficulties, apart from a short, steep rise just before the pass.

The last stage is the return to the agricultural college, about 1¾ hours. After a steep descent you come to the basin of the caldera (volcano crater). As you approach the college you pass through banana plantations, a pine forest and coffee trees.

Mt Mouaputa

The ascent of Mt Mouaputa (Pierced Mountain; 830m) is challenging, but you'll be amply rewarded for your efforts. Starting at Afareaitu, it's an easy 30-minute walk along the Vairo River to a stream (you'll pass the Afareaitu Waterfall). From there, it's just under an hour to a thalweg (outline of a river). The path is shaded and the first 20 minutes are steep.

You'll come to a little valley. Continue for about another hour, following the watercourse (which runs into the waterfall below). At the end, leave the thalweg and climb up onto a small platform where there is a coconut palm (15 minutes' climb).

The last stage (about 1½ hours) takes you up to the summit. This is the most difficult and testing part; it's steep and the ridge is exposed. Eight times you'll have to help yourself with the fixed ropes. Crowning your efforts is the arrival on a small lookout at the summit, from where you can take in the 360° view.

Mt Rotui by the North Ridge

More than a mere walk, this ascent is akin to a real mountain climb. Mt Rotui (899m) is oriented north–south, parallel to Opunohu and Cook's Bays, which lie on either side. The height isn't that spectacular but the panoramic view over the two bays makes the effort worthwhile. It takes a minimum of four hours to do the exhausting climb and about two hours to come down.

It is definitely not a good idea to attempt this walk without a local guide. The route is used infrequently and a machete is often necessary to cut through the dense vegetation. There are dangerous drops where you need to hang onto the bushes and on both sides of the ridge there are vertical drops. In case of an injury – a simple sprain, for example – you would not be able to descend to get help. Don't undertake the walk if there has been rain in the past few days. This is not a good walk for anyone who suffers from vertigo. You need to be in good physical condition and, at the risk of being repetitive, there are many passages that are more like rock climbing than walking. You have been warned!

It's vitally important to take plenty of drinking water because once you're on the ridge there is no shade. A hat or cap, sunscreen and sunglasses are also necessary. Wear walking shoes with good grip, and trousers to protect your legs from scratches.

The departure point is near the Village Faimano hotel. The first part of the climb is the most testing. You have to climb up to the clump of *aito* (flame trees) perched on a rocky spur, which you can see from the road, in order to get to the ridge. You will have to hack a way through the bushes covering the path with a machete (watch out for wasps' nests in the guava trees). There are particularly steep rocky boulders just before the *aito* trees. The route continues along the ridge, unprotected from the sun, through *puarata* and ferns. Take great care on this stretch – the path is narrow and there are sheer drops on each side. It's like walking up a series of stairways, with relatively flat passages followed by steep slopes where you will need to hang on with your hands. The views of Cook's Bay to the left and Opunohu Bay to the right defy all superlatives; when it's clear you can see the foothills of Tahiti to the southeast.

At the summit you can see the volcano crater and, to the south, Mt Tohiea (1207m) and Mt Mouaputa (830m). The descent should be made with the maximum of care, particularly near the *aito*, where it is necessary to go round to the right. It's easy to miss the trail among the piles of rocks. Take care, as there are cliff faces nearby.

RA'IATEA
Mt Tapioi
Between the post office and *gendarmerie* (police station) in Uturoa, take the road inland towards Mt Tapioi (294m). A short distance along this road a sign indicates 'Mt Tapioi' off to the right, followed by another sign proclaiming (in French): 'Private road, beware of dog, no entry', but there are no physical barriers to stop you driving up. There are several more Tapioi signs as the slightly rough road switchbacks up. Unhappily, the next 'no' sign means it; there's a chain across the track, backed up by several

padlocks. From here it's a half-hour uphill stroll past some surprised cows to the TV masts and superb views.

Temehani Plateau
Tracks suitable for 4WD vehicles climb to the 800m Temehani Plateau at the northern end of the island. There are also some interesting walks. The plateau is home to the *tiare apetahi*, a white gardenia endemic to Ra'iatea (see the boxed text 'Ra'iatea's Emblem' in the Ra'iatea & Taha'a chapter). You'll need a guide for this walk.

Three Waterfalls
This beautiful walk, departing from Kaoha Nui Ranch at PK6 on the east coast, lasts about four hours.

It's an easy walk to the first waterfall, the smallest, in which you can bathe. The walk then becomes steeper, and some sections have ropes to help you. Passing the second waterfall, higher up, you cross a forest of bamboo along the river bed. Some parts are roped. Reaching the third waterfall is a real reward: the waterfall, in two parts, is 60m long, and you can bathe in the basin.

BORA BORA
The views from **Mt Pahia** are superb but it's no easy climb; allow five hours for the return trip – if you're fit.

A track behind Banque Socredo in the centre of Vaitape leads towards the mountain. At the start the path is not easy to follow. There's a trail to the left, but it soon peters out; another trail leads off slightly to the right (south). Keep to the east while going up, to avoid getting lost. It's often very steep (though not as steep as it looks from sea level) and involves hauling yourself from one tree root to another. The trail is not marked, but it's pretty easy to see where it goes.

The climb reaches the rocky band around the top of the peak and then traverses the mountain northwards. It sticks closely to the rock face at first, but eventually diverges from the face and climbs steeply up the narrow, rocky course of a stream (dangerously slippery when wet).

This difficult climb takes you back to the rock face, where there's another clamber up a rocky course, although not so steep or difficult. That brings you out to a point overlooking Faanui and the track across the island. Another steep and rather loose climb brings you to the bushy top of the peak, from where it's a short and easy climb to the summit of Mt Hue (619m). The top is marked by a flagpole and there are superb views of the motu encircling Bora Bora.

A short descent and another climb along the knife-edge ridge takes you from Mt Hue to the summit of Mt Pahia (661m) and more superb views.

Surfing

French Polynesia is a paradise for surfing and body (boogie) boarding; some of the breaks are internationally known. Expert or beginner, there's a site to suit. The main islands for surfing are Tahiti, Mo'orea and Huahine.

In general, there are good conditions on the north and east coasts from November to April and on the west and south coasts for the other half of the year – but these distinctions are really theoretical. In practice it is the direction of the swells that makes a spot good at any given time.

Access to the shore breaks is generally easy from the coast roads. You may need to find a boat to take you out to the reef breaks, or resign yourself to a lot of paddling. There's no problem taking a surfboard on le trucks.

For more information on surfing in French Polynesia, check out the website ⓦ www .surfingtahiti.com.

Always check the weather reports and ask the locals about the conditions. Like surfers anywhere else, French Polynesians can be very possessive of *their* waves. If you want to enjoy the surf, observe all the usual surfing etiquette and give way to local surfers.

The sites in this section are marked on the relevant island maps.

EQUIPMENT

There are several surf shops in Pape'ete. You certainly don't need a wetsuit in the warm waters of French Polynesia, but a T-shirt or Lycra vest will protect you from the sun. The local surf shops all have boogie-board equipment as well as shortboards and traditional surfboards.

LESSONS

On Tahiti the **Surf School** (☎ 45 44 00, 41 91 37; ⓔ surfschool@mail.pf) offers 10 half-day lessons for 26,500 CFP. The courses are run by a qualified instructor and include equipment, transport to the different surfing spots and insurance.

TAHITI
East Coast

Tahiti's east coast offers many great surfing spots:

Lafayette Beach PK7. Shore break – November to April. Easy access from the coast road. A fairly radical shore break with powerful waves and a shallow bottom. The best spot is towards the river mouth.

Matavai Bay (Baie de Matavai) & Point Vénus PK10 (access from coast road). Shore break – November to April. Reef break – year-round depending on the swell. The right-hand reef break at Point Vénus reef is one of the most spectacular on the island.

Ahonu – Orofara PK12.5-13. Shore break – November to April. These spots are good when there's a northern swell and the waves are rather easy. There's access from the coast road.

The Right Line at Papenoo: La Source (The Spring) – Les Sapins (The Firs) – Rocky Point PK13-14. Shore break – November to April. The waves here are more hollow and more powerful. Beware of occasional strong currents. Easy access.

Papenoo: The Bay PK14.5. Shore break – November to April. An ideal spot for beginners, with long and not very hollow waves.

Papenoo: L'Embouchure (The Mouth) PK15.5. Shore break – November to April. The waves here are difficult and are best in the early morning.

Faaone: Mouth of the Mahaena & Mouth of the Vaiiha PK33.5 & PK44.5. Shore break – November to April. Fairly difficult waves at the mouth of the river.

West Coast

There are several surfing opportunities on Tahiti's west coast:

Papara PK38.7. Shore break – May to October. A very popular spot with easy access from the coast road, and moderately challenging waves. Beware of strong currents if there's a heavy swell.

Pa'ea PK21.5. Shore break – May to October. In front of the Pa'ea *mairie*, this spot is rarely good, but when it is the waves are powerful.

Sapinus – Pointe des Pêcheurs (Fisherman's Point) PK15. Shore break – May to October. A fairly radical shore break with fast hollow waves.

Taapuna PK12. Reef break – all year. A classic, with a very beautiful left that attracts lots of surfers.

Tahiti Iti
For experienced surfers, Tahiti Iti offers some prime surfing spots:

Big & Small Vairao Passes Reef break – all year. Magnificent lefts and rights for experienced surfers. Ask the locals for the best way to get to these breaks.

Teahupoo Reef break – April to October. At the end of the coast road. The Tahiti Billabong Pro takes place here around May each year. The prime spot is the tremendous left, reserved strictly for the best surfers. A guaranteed rush.

MO'OREA
Temae Reef break – year-round, depending on the winds. Not far from the airport, this spot is unusual in that it isn't at a pass. The break is a right and appears where a recess and the curvature of the reef combine perfectly. A wave for experienced surfers.

Paopao (Cook's Bay) & Opunohu Bay Reef break – mainly from November to April. A magnificent setting. Look for the left at Paopao and the right and left at Opunohu.

Moorea Beachcomber Intercontinental Resort Reef break – June to October. Not far from the hotel's beach. A difficult left which can be dangerous if there is a big swell because of the narrowness of the pass and the strong currents that run through it.

Haapiti PK30. Reef break – May to October. The left at Haapiti is a must. It combines the regularity and strength of the reef waves with the security of the beach waves. There's a reasonable depth at the take-off point.

HUAHINE
Fare Reef break – year-round. The left here attracts the big names of world surfing. The right is also pretty good.

Fitii Reef break – year-round. As with the left at Fare, this one is best when a southwest swell is running.

Parea Reef break – year-round. Beautiful waves as long as the trade winds aren't blowing.

THE TUAMOTUS
The locals speak highly of Tuheiava Pass at Tikehau and Avatoru Pass at Rangiroa.

PLACES TO STAY
Tahiti
Moana Surf Tours (☎/fax 43 70 70; e moana surftours@mail.pf; half-board 12,000 CFP per person), on the inland side of the road at PK8.3 in Puna'auia, is run by Moana David, the brother of Vetea David, a world-class Tahitian surfer. Accommodation is in a five-bed dorm and the price includes airport transfers and transfers (if necessary by boat) to the best surfing spots. Book well in advance.

Pension Te Miti (☎/fax 58 46 61) in Pa'ea is another good place.

Pension Bonjour (☎ 57 02 15, ☎/fax 43 69 10) looks straight out onto the famous and fabulous break at Teahupoo.

Huahine
Surfers on Huahine usually head for Chez Lovina (☎/fax 68 88 06) in Fare, or Vaihonu Océan (☎ 68 87 33, fax 68 77 57), near Fare.

Ariiura Camping Écologie (☎ 68 85 20), in the south of the island, is also a good place close to the surfing spots.

Sailing

See Formalities for Yachts under Visas & Documents in the Facts for the Visitor chapter for important information on the legalities of entering French Polynesian waters.

SEASONS & CONDITIONS
The dominant winds are the easterly trade winds. In the dry season (May to October) the southeasterly *maraamu* sometimes blows. It's best to avoid the November to March cyclone season.

Anchorages are described later in this section. Crews should take precautions against theft at popular tourist centres such as Bora Bora and in the Marquesas. Never leave cash, travellers cheques, passports or other documents on board. Always lock up the boat when you go ashore and take special care of any outboards and tenders. A runabout tied up beside a yacht at night can quite easily sail away before dawn.

CREWING POSITIONS
It's often possible to pick up crewing positions on yachts, particularly if you have had some relevant sailing experience. Check notice boards in popular restaurants and at

the yacht clubs on Tahiti, Ra'iatea, Bora Bora and other popular yachting stops. Yacht owners have to put up with some complex paperwork when making crew changes, so make sure your own papers are in order.

The yacht owner will want to vet potential crew members, but it's equally important to check the boat and crew you are considering joining. Make sure the boat is safe and the crew are compatible. Readers have suggested that the Marquesas is probably not the ideal place to join a boat; as the first arrival point for yachts from North America it makes little sense for a crew member to leave his or her boat there – unless there is something seriously wrong with it!

ANCHORAGES
The Society Islands
Only enter lagoons through passes with navigation markers. Navigation inside the lagoon is relatively simple, but beware of coral outcrops and avoid shallow water; if the water looks clear, it's shallow.

On Tahiti you can anchor at the yachting quay along the Pape'ete waterfront, at the marina at Taina and at the Arue Yacht Club.

On Mo'orea the most beautiful anchorages are in Cook's and Opunohu Bays, each accessible by a pass. There is a yacht marina at Vaiare.

Huahine has Maroe, Bourayne, Haapu and Avea Bays. The area around Fare, the main town, is not ideal because it's simply too busy.

Ra'iatea is an ideal stopover, with all the services a visiting crew could ask for. The Apooiti Marina has mooring buoys, as does the Stardust Marina . It's also possible to tie up at the Uturoa quay, although it's busy. There's also a magnificent anchorage at Motu Nao Nao, to the south.

On Taha'a you can stop at Haapu Bay or Haamene Bay, off Motu Tuuvahine (where the Vahine Island resort is) and in Tapuamu Bay. **Hôtel Hibiscus** (☎ 65 61 06, fax 65 65 65), **Hôtel Marina Iti** (☎ 65 61 01) and **Vahine Island** (☎ 65 67 38, fax 65 67 70) all have mooring buoys and offer an excellent welcome to yachties.

On Bora Bora, it's not possible to moor at Vaitape itself, but many boats anchor at Raititi Point, near the Hotel Bora Bora.

The Tuamotus
Yachts crossing the Pacific from east to west appreciate the lagoons of Takaroa, Manihi, Ahe, Rangiroa and, to a lesser extent, Toau, Fakarava, Arutua, Apataki and Aratika.

The most direct route to Pape'ete makes a stop at Takaroa then runs slightly southeast via the channel separating Rangiroa and Arutua. It's also possible to leave Takaroa to the north and cross the channel between Fakarava and Toau.

Caution is required with these low-lying islands because they do not come into view until you are very close. Also, most of the lagoons are sprinkled with coral outcrops that are rarely marked; these areas can be real labyrinths. If possible, take along a fisherman who knows the lagoon.

Restrictions apply to atolls where there are pearl farms – the lagoons here are dotted with numerous platforms imperfectly marked by buoys. At Takaroa, a sign beside the pass states that you are not allowed to anchor in the lagoon. Ask a local to guide you to a safe anchorage spot.

Getting in and out of the passes can also be dangerous, so it's wise to avoid the countervailing currents on entry and departure.

The Marquesas
The Marquesas is an important stop for yachts crossing the Pacific, and is usually the first point of entry for those westbound.

At Nuku Hiva, as well as the Taiohae's port, you will find excellent anchorages in Hakatea and Hakaui Bays to the southwest, Hatiheu and Anaho Bays to the northeast and Taipivai Bay to the east. At Taiohae, contact Rose Corser at **Nuku Hiva Keikahanui Pearl Lodge** (☎ 92 07 10, fax 92 07 11) for laundry and poste-restante services.

At 'Ua Huka, you can stop in Haavei, Vaipaee and Hane Bays.

Hakahau Bay at 'Ua Pou has a marina. **Restaurant-Pension Pukuéé** (☎/fax 92 50 83) offers laundry and poste-restante services. Other anchorages are found on the west coast at Hakamaii, Hakahetau and Vaiehu Bay. At Hakahetau, ask for Étienne Hokaupoko, the multilingual *tavana* (mayor).

At Hiva Oa, the serrated coastline near Tahauku is well sheltered and has a marina with moorings close to the yacht club. On the north coast of the island it is possible to make stops at Hanapaaoa or Hanamenu.

Tahuata has several idyllic creeks, especially at Hanahevane and Hanamoenoa Bays; Hapatoni is also beautiful. At Fatu Hiva, the mythical Bay of Virgins (Baie des Vierges; Hanavave) is a stopover well-known in the yachting world.

BAREBOAT CHARTERS & CRUISES

Renting a yacht is a fine way to explore French Polynesia, whether it's a bareboat charter (which you sail yourself) or a cabin on a fully crewed yacht. It's not even necessary to be an experienced sailor as there are options for a variety of experience levels – see the boxed text 'Hiring a Yacht'.

Ra'iatea, centrally positioned in the Society Islands and with a fine lagoon, has become the yacht-charter centre of French Polynesia. Most operations will offer whatever a customer demands and prepare fully stocked and equipped boats. Bareboat charter rates vary seasonally (July to August is the high season).

Cruises on a crewed yacht will usually include tour programmes at the stops en route. Dive cruises are also possible. It takes eight to 10 days to explore the Leeward Islands from Ra'iatea.

Aqua Polynésie (π/fax 73 47 31, e aquapol@club-internet.fr) Luxurious 14m catamarans with crewed cruises around the Leeward Islands and the Tuamotus. Boat specially equipped for dive cruises. Departures are from Bora Bora or Huahine or Fakarava (Tuamotus).

Archipels Croisières (π 56 36 39, fax 56 35 87, w archipels.com) Luxurious 18m catamarans with crewed cruises to the Leeward Islands and the Tuamotus. Departures are from Rangiroa (Tuamotus) or Pape'ete. It also has day cruises aboard a 32m schooner departing from Mo'orea.

Bisou Futé (π 65 64 97, fax 65 69 08, w www.multimania.com/tahiticharter) The name means 'Crafty Kiss'. This Taha'a-based operation charters boats by the day and offers cruises.

Blue Lagoon Charter (π/fax 67 73 48, e bluelagoonchart@mail.pf) Based on Bora Bora, this operation offers cruises in the Leeward Islands and the Tuamotus.

Catamaran Tane Charter (π/fax 66 16 87, w www.raiatea.com/tane/) Based at Ra'iatea, this operation offers catamaran cruises in the Leeward Islands.

Hiring a Yacht

There are four basic ways to rent a yacht:

Bareboat Hire You charter the boat without crew or skipper and it's up to you to organise supplies and sail it. The chartering operations can often arrange to provision the boat for you.

Hire with a Skipper You rent the yacht with a skipper; it's a good way to go if you're uncertain of your own abilities or have limited knowledge of the islands. A host can also be provided.

Charter You rent the yacht with skipper, host and crew so you don't have to do a thing, unless you want to, of course.

Cabin Charter Similar to a charter except you only rent one cabin; it's ideal if you do not have a big enough group for a whole boat.

Croisières Danae (π 66 12 50, fax 66 39 37, w www.raiatea.com/danaefishing/) This operation offers a variety of crewed cruises, from one to seven days, departing from Ra'iatea.

Faimanu (π 65 62 52, fax 65 69 08, w www.multimania.com/tahitivoile) Based on Ra'iatea, this operation organises cruises by the day.

The Moorings (π 66 35 93, 66 26 26, fax 66 20 94, w www.moorings.com) About 20 boats of a variety of types – bareboat charters, hire with skipper and host, or cabin charter. It's based at Apooiti Marina at Ra'iatea and offers cruises to the Leeward Islands.

Pacific Dream Charter (π/fax 43 23 12) Catamarans based at the Taina Marina at Puna'auia on Tahiti. All destinations on request.

Sailing Huahine Voile (π 68 72 49, w sailing-huahine.com) This operation, based at Huahine, has monohulls and offers cruises in the Leeward Islands and the Tuamotus.

Stardust Marine (π 60 04 85, fax 66 23 19, w www.sunsail.com) Based at the Stardust Marina at Ra'iatea, this operation offers bareboat charters, hire with skipper and/or host, and cabin charter. About 20 boats of a variety of types are available for hire. Cruises in the Leeward Islands and the Tuamotus.

Tahiti Yacht Charter (π 45 04 00, fax 42 76 00, w www.vpm.fr) Catamarans and monohulls; bareboat charter, or hire with skipper and host. Cruises are possible in all the archipelagos. Departures from Ra'iatea or Tahiti.

Titaina (π/fax 67 11 75, e cruisepolynesia@mail.pf) Based at Ra'iatea, this operation offers cruises in the Leeward Islands and the Tuamotus.

DIVING

Translucent lagoons, a deep, blue ocean, warm water year-round and exceptional marine life make French Polynesia a dream destination for scuba divers.

There is also a variety of dive cruises; for more details on these, see Bareboat Charters & Cruises in the Outdoor Activities chapter.

Dive Centres

There are about 25 professional dive centres in French Polynesia. They're open year-round, most of them every day. They typically offer two to four dives a day, generally at 8am or 9am and around 2pm. Most centres don't have a definite schedule for dives but decide each day which sites are most suitable for the weather conditions and the divers who have signed up. It's a good idea to reserve at least a day in advance.

Many of the centres' offices close during dives, so contact them before or after the morning or afternoon dives. The centres are affiliated with a number of diving associations. Some are attached to the FFESSM (the French diving federation), others are also PADI or SSI centres. All are at least Level 1 on the French CMAS scale. There are personnel who speak English at all the tourist-oriented dive operations.

Costs & Services The dive centres in French Polynesia offer beginners dives for children and adults, exploration dives, night dives, multi-dive packages and dive courses. Dive courses are generally only offered for the most frequently requested French Level 1 and the basic PADI course (Open Water, or OW) and typically cost 40,000 CFP to as much as 51,000 CFP.

A single dive typically costs 5500 to 6500 CFP (more for beginners), usually including equipment rental but not necessarily the 8% TVA. At some centres you get a reduction after five dives, or five- and 10-dive packages are offered. International visitors get a 20kg baggage allowance on Air Tahiti flights but on inter-island flights the limit is just 10kg, so don't bring more equipment than necessary (though some dive operators' equipment may be rather old and worn).

Many centres have arrangements with hotels offering reduced-price accommodation for divers, or accommodation-and-dive packages. Most dive centres (except for those on Tahiti) offer free pick-ups from your accommodation to dives within a certain area.

Almost all dive centres accept credit cards and many video-record dives; cassettes typically cost 8000 to 12,000 CFP.

Inset: Aquarium fish at Le Méridien Bora Bora (Photograph by Tom Cockrem)

Documents If you are a certified diver you will need your dive card; it's a good idea to have your dive logbook with you as well. Centres accept any dive-association accreditation (PADI, CMAS, NAUI etc), but may ask you to do a preliminary dive to check your expertise and make sure you're not too rusty. A medical certificate is necessary if you're doing

ADRIANA MAMMARELLA

a dive course, and some operators may require one for general dives. No certification is required for beginners dives – *baptêmes* or baptisms, as they're known – although parental authorisation is required for minors.

All operators have professional insurance for their local liabilities, but it's a good idea to obtain supplementary insurance from your own country. Check that your travel insurance covers scuba diving and that you're covered for repatriation in case of an accident. The Diver Alert Network (DAN) is a popular worldwide association for divers, and membership covers air evacuation for dive-related illness or injury. Some of the Tahiti operators, who principally cater to local French residents, require divers to have an FFESSM licence that includes insurance.

Choosing a Centre Each dive centre has its own personality and style. At one extreme there are small family-run centres, and at the other, highly professional, technical centres. On islands with several centres, it's worth paying a visit to each one to check the welcome, the dive masters, the organisation, the equipment and the general feel and ambience. Talk to other divers, although almost every centre has its critics and fans.

Tahiti At the Arue Marina is **Scuba Tek Tahiti** (☎/fax 42 23 55; e plc.scubatek@mail.pf; closed Sun afternoon & Mon) at the Arue Yacht Club. This centre covers dive sites along the east coast, including Les Failles (The Falls) and Le Banc du Dolphin (The Dolphin Bank).

Aquatica Dive Center (☎ 53 34 96, mobile 77 60 01, fax 53 34 74; w www.aquatica-dive.com) is based at the Tahiti Beachcomber Intercontinental Resort. Nitrox diving is offered (7000 CFP).

Eleuthera Plongée (☎ 42 49 29, fax 43 66 22; e eleut@tahiti-dive .com) is at the Taina Marina in Puna'auia, just south of the Carrefour supermarket. Monthly trips are made to Mo'orea, 55 minutes away by boat, and sometimes to Tetiaroa.

A Beginners Dive in the Lagoon

French Polynesia is a great place for your first scuba dive. The water is warm and clear and the lagoon is like a giant swimming pool, secure and not too deep. All the main dive centres offer beginners dives *(baptêmes* in French scuba-diving jargon). These typically take place in relatively shallow (3m to 4m) and calm water and last about 30 minutes. No formalities are required unless there are serious medical contraindications, and parental permission is required for minors. The cost of a first dive is usually about US$50.

The dive master takes only one or two pupils and, before entering the water, briefly explains the elementary rules and the equipment (mask, fins, regulator, air tank, buoyancy compensator and weight belt).

The big moment comes with that first immersion in the lagoon. On the surface you test the regulator and then descend, with the dive master keeping an eye on you all the way. All you have to do is breathe and experience that firost sensation of weightlessness! If it appeals, you can sign up for a course to obtain a dive card that will let you dive anywhere in the world.

Tahiti Plongée *(☎ 41 00 62, 43 62 51, fax 42 26 06; ⓔ plongee .tahiti@mail.pf; closed Mon)*, beside the lagoon at PK7.5, is a local institution. Its director, Henri Pouliquen, pioneered scuba diving in French Polynesia. He's renowned for teaching very young children to dive. There are several dive boats and various sites from Arue to Pa'ea are regularly visited. Local residents, the main clientele, come to Tahiti Plongée for the relaxed family atmosphere.

Iti Diving International *(☎/fax 57 77 93; ⓦ www.itidiving.pf)* is the only centre on Tahiti Iti. It's at the Puunui Marina in Vairao at PK6. Gilles Jugel offers some little-known dives to drop-offs rich with gorgonia corals and a more varied marine life than at Tahiti Nui sites, including the Marado, Trou du Lagon (Hole in the Lagoon), La Grotte de Tetopa (Tetopa Cave) and Les Gorgones (the Gorgonias). The atmosphere is friendly and family oriented.

Mo'orea In the Moorea Beachcomber Intercontintental Resort, **Bathy's Club** *(☎ 56 31 44, 56 38 10; ⓔ bathys@mail.pf)* is a well-equipped PADI centre. The centre hosts shark-feeding dives and is the only centre offering dives with the rays at the Stingray World lagoon.

Moorea Fun Dive *(☎ 56 40 38, ☎/fax 56 40 74; ⓦ www.dive moorea.com)* is a pleasant centre next to Mo'orea Camping at Hauru Point. It also has a base at the Sofitel Ia Ora.

Scubapiti *(☎ 56 20 38, 56 47 79; ⓦ www.scubapiti.com)*, a small and friendly centre on the beach at Les Tipaniers Hotel Restaurant doesn't believe in fish feeding. It covers the same sites as other centres but also, for experienced divers, some less well known sites on the western side of the island, such as the Canyons de Taota (Taota Canyons) or the Grande Passe de Haapiti (Big Haapiti Pass).

Topdive – MUST *(☎ 56 17 32, ☎/fax 56 15 83; ⓔ mustdive@ mail.pf)* is run by Philippe Molle, a pioneer of scuba diving in France. The centre is beside the lagoon on Cook's Bay, a stone's throw from Kaveka Hotel. Shark feeding is on the menu at the morning dive.

Huahine Right on the quay at Fare, **Pacific Blue Adventure** *(☎ 68 87 21, fax 68 80 71; ⓦ www.divehuahine .com)* is a friendly centre that offers dives at the Avapeihi Pass, Fa'a Miti, La Cité de Corail (Coral City) and the Vallée Jaune (Yellow Valley).

Ra'iatea Based at Apooiti Marina, **Hémisphère Sub** *(☎ 66 12 49, fax 66 28 63; ⓔ hemis -subdiving@mail.pf)* offers dives on the east and west coasts as well as around Taha'a. Snorkelling trips to the Teavapiti Pass are also possible. This centre also has a base at Raiatea Pearl Resort Hawaiki Nui.

Te Mara Nui *(☎ 72 60 19, ☎/fax 66 11 88; ⓔ temaranui@mail.pf)* is a small centre based at the Uturoa Marina. It accepts cash payments only.

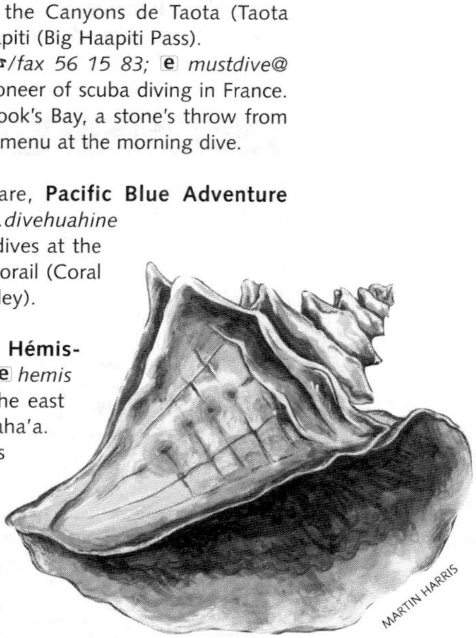
MARTIN HARRIS

Taha'a Based at the Taha'a Pearl Beach Resort & Spa, one of the most luxurious establishments in French Polynesia, **Taha'a Blue Nui** (W www .bluenui.com) was due to commence operations when we visited. It is part of the Blue Nui chain, which has centres on four islands in French Polynesia.

Bora Bora Right next to Hotel Bora Bora at Matira Point is **Bora Diving Center** (☎ 67 71 84, ☎/fax 67 74 83; e boradiving@mail.pf). It's managed by Anne and Michel Condesse.

Nemo World (☎ 67 63 00, 67 77 85; e divebora@ mail.pf) is opposite Hotel Sofitel Marara. Transfers from hotels to the centre are free.

Topdive Bora Bora (☎ 60 50 50, fax 60 50 51; W www .topdive.com) is a luxurious and very high-tech centre in the accommodation complex of the same name on the northern edge of Vaitape. There's a swimming pool for dive training.

Bora Bora Blue Nui (☎/fax 67 79 07; W www.bluenui.com) is based on the grounds of Bora Bora Pearl Beach Resort on Motu Teivairoa.

Diveasy (☎ 79 22 55, ☎/fax 67 69 36), at Matira Point, offers dives for one (12,000 CFP) or two people (8000 CFP per person) accompanied by a dive master. During the dive you are equipped with a communication system that allows the dive master to provide a commentary on what you are seeing.

Rangiroa At the eastern end of the string of islets, near Chez Glorine, and operated by Bernard White, is **Paradive** (☎ 96 05 55, fax 96 05 50; e paradive@mail.pf).

Raie Manta Club (☎ 96 84 80, fax 96 85 60; e raiemantaclub@ mail.pf; W http://raiemantaclub.free.fr) is beside the lagoon at the entrance to Avatoru village, between Pension Herenui and Rangiroa Lodge. The centre has a second office near the Tiputa Pass, next to Pension Teina & Marie. The director Yves Lefèvre played a major part in the growth of diving in the Tuamotus, and the centre has a strong reputation.

Six Passengers (☎ /fax 96 02 60; e the6passengers@mail.pf) is a small, simple and relaxed operation in an airy *fare* beside the lagoon, about 500m east of Hotel Kia Ora. It specialises in small groups. It also organises safari trips in sailing boats to little-frequented sites such as Motu Paio and Les Failles (the Falls).

Dream Dive (☎ 79 24 53, ☎/fax 96 03 72; e hubertyann@dream dive.pf) is a convivial centre located between the college and Pension Tuanake. Trips to Motu Paio and Maherehonae Point are also offered.

Topdive (☎/fax 96 05 60; W www.topdive.com), 300m from the Hotel Kia Ora, is the newest dive centre on Rangiroa.

Blue Dolphins (☎/fax 96 03 01; e bluedolphins@mail.pf) is a high-tech centre located on the beach at Hotel Kia Ora. It offers Nitrox diving (9350 CFP), as well as diving with rebreathers, and provides training in both techniques.

Manihi At Manihi Pearl Beach Resort, **Manihi Blue Nui** (☎ 96 42 17, fax 96 42 72; W www.bluenui.com) is, like the hotel, luxurious and immaculate.

Tikehau Rangiroa's **Raie Manta Club** (☎/fax 96 22 53; e *raieman taclub@mail.pf*) has a small operation at the Tikehau Village offering dives in Tuheiava Pass.

   Tikehau Blue Nui (☎/fax 96 22 40; ☎ 96 23 00; e *tikehaublue nui@mail.pf*), based at the luxurious Tikehau Pearl Beach Resort, belongs to the Blue Nui chain.

Fakarava Offering dives mainly in the Garuae Pass, and in Tumako-hua Pass on request, is **Te Ava Nui** (☎/fax 98 42 50; e *jcla peyre@net courrier.com*).

Ahe At the Coco Perles *pension*, **Ahe Plongée** (☎/fax 96 44 08; e *ahe.plongee@mail.pf*) is run by two dive masters from Rangiroa. Dives take place in the pass, about 20 minutes away by boat; you get to do two dives.

Makemo Opened in April 2002, **Scubamakemo** (☎/fax 98 03 08; e *makemodive@hotmail.com*) is run by a dive master who knows the Tuamotus very well, offering dives in little-frequented sites near Ariki-tamiro Pass. It offers some of the best rates in French Polynesia and can also organise accommodation.

The Marquesas On the Taiohae marina embankment on Nuku Hiva, **Centre Plongée Marquises** (☎/fax 92 00 88; e *marquises dives@mail.pf*) is a pleasant and well-run operation. Day excursions are sometimes offered.

The Australs The **Raie Manta Club** (☎ 96 84 80, fax 96 85 60) of Rangiroa sends a dive master to Rurutu for the July to October whale-watching season. The cost is 10,000 CFP per person for a half-day trip, including transfers and equipment.

Dive Sites

Diving conditions in French Polynesia are exceptional. The water temperature varies from 26° to 29°C, reaching a peak during summer (November to March). Each location and season has its particular attraction, and visibility is excellent, often reaching 40m, apart from during rainy periods, when sediment is carried into the lagoon. The exception is the Marquesas, where visibility rarely exceeds 20m.

   The dive sites are wonderfully situated. On most islands the sites are very accessible, typically just a five- to 15-minute boat ride away, except for the Marquesas, where it is sometimes necessary to travel for 30 to 40 minutes by boat, in which case a trip will usually include two dives. Only Tahiti and Ra'iatea have shipwreck dives. See the boxed text 'Spectacular Dives' later for more information on the types of dives available.

ADRIANA MAMMARELLA

The site reports that follow are only a sample. For more information see Lonely Planet's *Diving & Snorkeling Tahiti & French Polynesia*, which fully describes around 50 dive sites.

The region's marine life is varied. Sharks and rays are the main attraction, but there are other interesting species as well. Corals and invertebrates are not the region's strong point and do not rival those found in the Indian Ocean.

The positions of the dive sites in this section are shown on the relevant island maps in each chapter.

Tahiti There are about 20 lagoon and ocean sites between Arue and Puna'auia.

The best-known site on the east coast is **Les Failles d'Arue** (Cliffs of Arue), in Matavai Bay (Baie de Matavai). On the outside of the reef a plateau of coral emerges at 5m depth – ideal for beginners – and is situated above a steep drop-off. Less than 100m from here, between 10m and 30m depth, two narrow rifts shelter an abundance of marine life, including a variety of corals, nudibranchs (sea slugs), alcyonaires, coral polyps, anemones and crabs.

The **Aquarium** is a delight for beginners. With dozens of fish species, it is indeed an aquarium, part-natural, part-artificial, created using air bags to assemble hundreds of tons of coral in the lagoon not far from Faa'a airport's runway. They also tossed in an old Cessna aircraft and the wreckage of a cargo boat at about 7m depth.

La Source (the Spring), in front of La Pointe des Pêcheurs (Fisherman's Point) at Puna'auia on the west coast, is a freshwater spring that looks like frosted glass as it merges with the salt water. Coral pinnacles shelter dense marine life at a depth of 15m to 20m.

The south coast of Tahiti Iti offers several excellent dive sites. **Trou du Lagon** (Hole in the Lagoon) is a vast depression in the lagoon bottom where numerous rays are found at around 25m depth. Beside the Tetopa Pass, on the ocean side, lobsters and shellfish abound in the **Grotte de Tetopa** (Tetopa Cave), a cavity hollowed out of the coral reef in barely 8m of water.

Mo'orea The sites of Mo'orea are mainly along the north coast.

The water clarity is usually superb at the **Tiki**, off the extreme northwestern corner of the island, close to Motu Fareone. The exceptional density of marine life includes perch, surgeon fish, triggerfish, snapper, butterfly fish, groupers and wrasse. This is a popular site for shark feeding; black-tip reef sharks and grey sharks usually join the divers, while large lemon sharks sometimes make a fleeting appearance.

Squadrons of leopard rays regularly keep an appointment in the 20m-deep **Couloir des Raies** (Ray Passage), on the west side of Tareu Pass. Currents often limit the visibility but they also bring in greater numbers of rays. The drop-off, in just 6m of water, shelters all sorts of reef life and the shallow upper part of the drop-off is ideal for beginners.

Between the Tareu and Teavaroa Passes, the **Jardin des Roses** (Rose Garden) is for experienced divers only; the descent is made through open water to a depth of 50m. The coral 'roses' open out to 3m across, catching maximum light on the ocean side of the reef.

Stingray World, a stone's throw from the Moorea Beachcomber Intercontinental Resort, is a site exclusive to Bathy's Club. The stingrays here are almost tame and you are able to gently stroke them as they brush past.

Huahine The **Avapeihi Pass**, near Fare, is the leading site in the north of the island. Divers encounter many barracudas, jackfish and grey sharks (they don't even expect to be fed!), as well as rays. The current can be strong. Other popular sites include **Fa'a Miti**, northwest of the island near the airport, where moray eels, stingrays and a wide variety of small fish can be seen around the coral outcrops.

South of the island is **Parea Pass**, close to the village of the same name. There is also the **Canyon**, which forms a large rift in the Tiare Pass.

Ra'iatea & Taha'a Close to Raiatea Pearl Resort Hawaiki Nui on the east coast of Ra'iatea is one of French Polynesia's rare shipwrecks, the relatively well-preserved *Nordby*, which lies in 18m to 29m of water. The 50m-long three-master, launched in 1900, lies on its side. Further to the south, the superb **Teavapiti Pass** has many fish and beautiful coral massifs. The local club feeds grey sharks at this site.

On the other side of the island is **Miri Miri Pass**, where purple coral can be seen on the drop-off. **Les Roses** (the Roses), a little further north, has a vast field of coral roses at 40m depth.

At Taha'a, peaks vary the relief in the **Céran Pass**, a superb untouched site with yellow coral, barracudas, grey sharks and white-tip reef sharks at about 35m.

Bora Bora There are magnificent lagoon dives at Bora Bora, including **Toopua** and **Toopua Iti** to the southwest. The drop-off, at 3m to 34m, is frequented by leopard rays, moray eels and abundant reef life. **Toopua Iti** has an interesting relief with many small canyons and tunnels.

Anau, in front of the Méridien resort on the eastern side of the island, is a popular spot for manta rays and black-tip reef sharks. The visibility can be limited because of the sandy bottom, but that's what rays like.

North of the island, outside the reef but close to the airport, **Muri Muri** (also known as La Vallée Blanche or the White Valley) is a magnificent site. Sharks are the main attraction; accustomed to being fed, they converge on the site as soon as the boat stops. **Tapu**, to the west of the island by the large motu of the same name, is a site for more experienced divers. Canyons and crevasses vary the relief and lemon sharks are encountered at 15m to 40m depth.

Tupitipiti is a magnificent but little-frequented dive site, as it's a long way to go – out the Teavanui Pass and right round the island to the southern tip of Motu Piti Aau.

Rangiroa Although Rangiroa is one of the best-known dive areas in the Pacific, in fact just five or six sites are regularly dived and the coral is relatively poor. The powerful currents running through the passes, and the density of sharks that those currents attract, account for Rangiroa's fame. Divers enter on the ocean side with the current flowing into the lagoon; a Zodiac inflatable follows the divers and recovers them at the end of the dive. This type of dive is strictly for the experienced.

Tiputa Pass is the most famous site and the dive usually starts outside the pass with a visit to **Shark Cave** (Grotte aux Requins) at 35m, where there are usually about a dozen grey sharks. From November to February enormous hammerhead sharks can be seen sticking close to the bottom. Napoleon wrasses, barracudas, manta and leopard rays are also encountered. The dive ends at **Motu Nuhi Nuhi**, a calm and sheltered reserve popular with beginners and snorkellers, where there is a great density of small marine life around the coral and the depth doesn't exceed 10m.

Avatoru Pass, 10km to the west, also offers plenty of interest. Manta rays appear in the pass and the Raie Manta Club feeds whitetip reef sharks, which approach divers as soon as they appear. Inside the lagoon, **Mahuta** is a magnificent and calm site with channels of sand between pretty coral massifs that attract an abundant reef life. On the axis of the Avatoru Pass, it also attracts larger fish species.

Spectacular Dives

Shark feeding, diving with rays, whale watching, drift diving – French Polynesia provides superb dive sites and close encounters that will seduce even the most blasé diver. All these dives are accessible to divers with a simple Level 1 or PADI OW dive card.

Shark feeding is a popular activity at Mo'orea, Ra'iatea and sometimes at Bora Bora and Manihi. The dive master drops down to the bottom at around 15m to 20m, signals to the divers to form a semicircle, and produces a large hunk of fish from a feedbag. The dive master is enveloped in a cloud of fish, and soon black-tip reef sharks, grey sharks and even lemon sharks appear. After 15 minutes of intense activity, the remains are tossed aside and the dive continues at a calmer pace.

Feeding any fish, let alone sharks, is a controversial practice and not all dive centres approve. It clearly disrupts natural behaviour patterns, and encouraging sharks to associate divers with a free feed is not a good idea.

Diving with rays is less thrilling than mingling with sharks but just as spectacular. You may see manta and leopard rays at a number of sites, but Mo'orea and Bora Bora have shallow waters where you'll encounter stingrays so accustomed to divers that they will dance around and gently brush against them.

A drift-dive through a pass is the major speciality in the Tuamotus. On the rising tide, as ocean water flows into the lagoon, the narrow passes create powerful currents surging through at 3 to 6 knots. Outside the pass, divers drop into the flow and are swept through into the calm waters of the lagoon. It's an indescribable sensation.

Diving with whales takes place at Rurutu in the Austral Islands when the humpback whales stage their annual migration (July to October). Having found the whales it's simply a matter of donning snorkelling equipment and jumping in with them – they're unconcerned about being approached.

Diving with Electra dolphins is the speciality of the Marquesas. On the east side of Nuku Hiva, hundreds of these white-lipped dolphins gather daily; again, a mask, snorkel and fins are all that's necessary to join in.

Manihi At **Le Tombant** (Drop-off), on the ocean side of Tairapa Pass, a dizzy wall topples towards an abyss. Grey sharks, Napoleon wrasses, jackfish, barracudas and banks of perch appear regularly. Every year in July, impressive formations of marbled groupers hang out there.

Tairapa Pass forms a passageway about 70m wide and 20m deep; you simply let yourself get sucked into the lagoon by the current and observe the amazing density of marine life as you slip past. There are banks of barracudas and unicorn fish, sharks sleeping in cavities in the pass wall, and white-tip reef sharks and triggerfish. This dive ends at **Le Cirque** (the Circus), inside the lagoon, where there's an entanglement of pinnacles from 20m right up to the surface, peppered with coral fish. Eagle rays often hunt around this area, but the visibility may not be the best.

La Faille (the Cliff) is another ocean dive at a fracture in the reef, where dive masters feed grey sharks and black-tip reef sharks.

Tikehau Dives generally take place in **Tuheiava Pass**, 30 minutes by boat from Tuherahera. A site somewhat like the passes at Rangiroa, it can offer magnificent surprises. Manta rays, grey sharks, jackfish, barracudas and white-tip reef sharks all make regular appearances.

Fakarava There are a dozen untouched sites on this atoll. The huge **Garuae Pass** measures nearly 800m across and offers divers a fantastic spectacle of sharks, dolphins, rays, barracudas and enormous banks of fish. It makes the Avatoru and Tiputa Passes in Rangiroa seem like timid little playgrounds in comparison.

Ahe The local dive centre runs dives in the pass, which has a beautiful topography. On the ocean side the depth is to 30m, climbing progressively to 10m before descending as far as 35m on the lagoon side. The bottom of the pass features small corridors and faults. There are sharks, rays and turtles.

Diving Terms

You'll find that most dive centres are used to dealing with English speakers but the following French terms may be useful.

air tanks	*des bouteilles de plongée*
beginners dive or first dive	*un baptême*
dive	*une plongée*dive
centre	*un centre de plongée*
diving licence	*un brevet de plongée*
drift dive	*une plongée à la dérive*
fins	*des palmes*
mask	*un masque*
regulator	*un détendeur*
snorkel	*un tuba*
weight belt	*une ceinture de plomb*
wetsuit	*une combinaison de plongée*

Makemo In the heart of the Tuamotus, Makemo guarantees dives with a wild edge. The local centre takes divers to **Arikitamiro Pass**, rich in sharks, Napoleon wrasses, barracudas, tuna and groupers.

The Marquesas The diving conditions in the Marquesas are completely different. The dives take place in water saturated with plankton and close to cliffs battered by surge. As a result, visibility is generally only 10m to 20m, but these waters support a most unusual abundance of species. The cliffs are honeycombed with cavities and there are some superb cave dives. Diving trips here are dependent upon weather conditions, since the swell can make manoeuvring and anchoring very difficult.

There are about 10 sites that are regularly dived on the south and west coasts of Nuku Hiva. On the eastern side of the island, **Orques Pygmées** (Pygmy Orcas) is an exceptional site where you can snorkel among the group of Electra dolphins (*Peponocephala electra*, also known as pygmy orcas or melon-headed whales) that assembles there every morning.

At the entrance to Taiohae Bay is the **Sentinelle aux Marteaux** (Sentry of the Hammerheads) where, at between 10m and 40m depth, there are hammerhead sharks with curious wavy protuberances (known as festoons) close to their mouths, as well as manta and leopard rays, moray eels, sea urchins and beautiful shells.

Grotte Ekamako (Ekamako Cave), to the east of Taiohae Bay, is a submarine cavity about 10m in diameter, penetrating more than 100m into the cliff at a depth of about 15m. The main attraction is the stingrays that bury themselves in the sand and enormous lobsters that crouch in the rocky debris.

Tikapo is the name of the headland at the southeastern corner of Nuku Hiva. Facing this point, surrounded by the sea, a rock emerges from the ocean; circling around it is abundant fauna including sharks, jackfish, leopard rays, barracudas and perch. This dive can only be made in calm sea conditions.

The rocky **Motumano Point** advances onto a sandy plateau to the southwest of the island. It's a good site for manta rays and sharks. At the other end of the island, on the west coast, **Matateiko Point** is a rocky pinnacle frequented by manta and leopard rays, jackfish and sharks.

The Australs The Raie Manta Club of Rangiroa stations a dive master on **Rurutu** from July to October and organises whale watching and swimming with the whales that congregate around the island at that time.

The Society Islands

The Society Islands form the most important archipelago of French Polynesia. They include the largest islands and are home to most of French Polynesia's population. Most of the group are 'high islands', as opposed to the low-lying coral atolls of the Tuamotus. Captain Cook dreamed up the name Society Islands in 1769 because the islands were close to each other, or 'in close society'.

The Society Islands are subdivided into the eastward Windward Islands (Îles du Vent) and the westward Leeward Islands (Îles Sous le Vent). The Windward Islands are made up of two major islands (Tahiti and Mo'orea) and three smaller islands (Tetiaroa, Maiao and the unpopulated Mehetia). The Leeward Islands are made up of Huahine, the twin islands of Ra'iatea and Taha'a, Bora Bora, Maupiti and the four smaller islands of Tupai, Mopelia, Scilly and Bellinghausen.

Tahiti is the largest island in French Polynesia. This is where you'll find French Polynesia's vibrant capital, Pape'ete, and the only international airport, Faa'a.

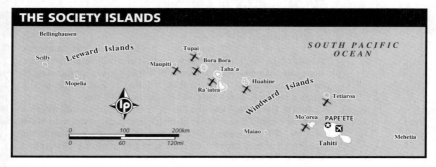

Tahiti

pop 169,700 • area 1045 sq km

Upon arriving on Tahiti you may not feel inspired to dash off a few masterpieces as did Gauguin all those years ago. This Pacific 'Garden of Eden' is actually a very busy, industrialised island; its capital, Pape'ete, is a throbbing and polluted city. But after a few fabulous meals in Pape'ete, an evening stroll along the waterfront, a visit to one of the island's museums and a rewarding interaction with some locals, you may find it hard not to feel a certain fondness for this isle.

The disparity between the alluring hype and the dusty reality of Tahiti can be troubling. Many visitors head straight for other islands, giving Tahiti no more than a cursory glance. But in doing so, you'll miss out on some interesting museums, ancient marae, and the wild and uninhabited interior of the island, with its secret valleys and impressive peaks. So if you can pack away received notions of a tranquil and idyllic life and reconcile yourself to the fact that Tahiti is no paradise, you'll probably have a ball.

History

Like other islands in the Society group, Tahiti is the creation of volcanic eruptions. The larger circle of Tahiti, Tahiti Nui, came into existence around two-and-a-half to three million years ago; the smaller circle, Tahiti Iti, was created less than a million years ago.

Tahiti was not the first of the Society group to be populated in the great Polynesian migrations. Legends relate that the first settlers came to Tahiti from Ra'iatea, which was the most politically important island despite being much smaller than Tahiti.

Tahiti's importance grew as it increasingly became the preferred base for European visitors. The island soon developed into a minor pawn in the European colonial quest.

Tahiti's population is currently about 150,700, which constitutes more than 60% of French Polynesia's entire population. Tahiti is the economic, cultural and political centre of French Polynesia. The capital, Pape'ete, has become the region's Big Smoke, the place of bright lights and fragile

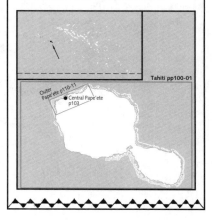
prospects that attracts the hopeful and the helpless from all over French Polynesia. See also History in the Facts about French Polynesia chapter, and History under Pape'ete, later in this chapter.

Geography & Geology

Tahiti divides neatly into two circles: the larger and more populated Tahiti Nui (literally 'Big Tahiti') to the northwest is connected by an isthmus to the smaller Tahiti Iti (literally 'Little Tahiti') to the southeast. The narrow coastal fringe of Tahiti Nui, where the vast majority of the population is concentrated, sweeps rapidly inwards and upwards to a jumble of soaring, green-clad mountain peaks.

A fringing reef encloses a narrow lagoon around much of the island, but parts of the

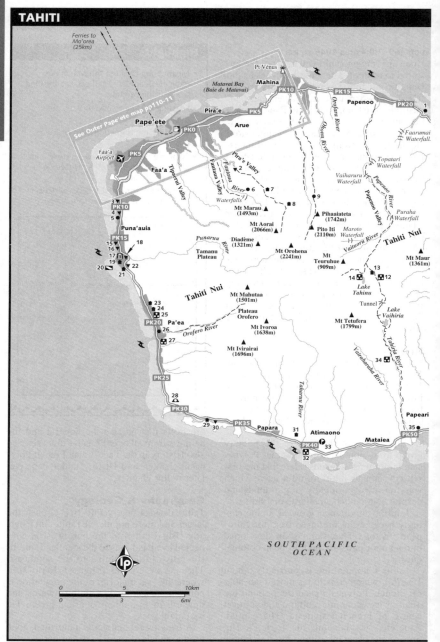

TAHITI

Ferries to
Mo'orea
(25km)

Pt Vénus

Mahina

Matavai Bay
(Baie de Matavai)

PK10

Orofara River

PK15

Papenoo

PK20

1

Pira'e

PK5

Faarumai
Waterfall

Pape'ete

PK0

Arue

Ohoni River

See Outer Pape'ete map pp110–11

Faa'a
Airport

PK5

Faa'a

Pira'e Valley

Topatari
Waterfall

Fautaua Valley

2

Fautaua River

Vaiharuru
Waterfall

Thaerui Valley

Waterfalls

6

7

Papenoo River

Puraha
Waterfall

PK10

3
4
5

8

9

Mt Marau
(1493m)

Pihaaiateta
(1742m)

Maroto
Waterfall

Tahiti Nui

Puna'auia

Mt Aorai
(2066m)

Pito Iti
(2110m)

Vaituoru River

Papenoo Valley

PK15

18

Punaruu River

Diadème
(1321m)

Mt Maur
(1361m)

15
16
17
19

22

Tamanu
Plateau

Mt Orohena
(2241m)

Mt Teuruhue
(909m)

13

20

21

Tahiti Nui

Mt Mahutaa
(1501m)

14

12

Lake
Tahinu

23
24
25

Plateau
Orofero

Tunnel

Lake
Vaihiria

PK20

Pa'ea

26

Orofero River

Mt Ivoroa
(1638m)

Mt Tetufera
(1799m)

27

Mt Ivirairai
(1696m)

34

PK25

Vairaharudua River

Tahiria River

28

PK30

Tahurnu River

29

30

PK35

Papara

31

Atimaono

35

PK50

PK40

Mataiea

32

33

Papeari

SOUTH PACIFIC
OCEAN

0   5   10km
0   3   6mi

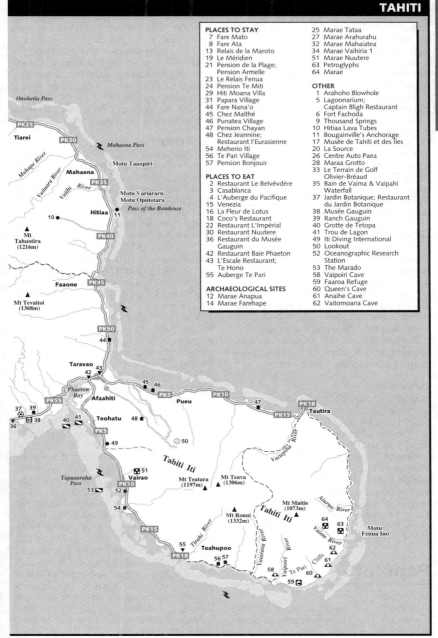

PLACES TO STAY
7 Fare Mato
8 Fare Ata
13 Relais de la Maroto
19 Le Méridien
21 Pension de la Plage;
   Pension Armelle
23 Le Relais Fenua
24 Pension Te Miti
29 Hiti Moana Villa
31 Papara Village
44 Fare Nana'o
45 Chez Maïthé
46 Punatea Village
47 Pension Chayan
48 Chez Jeannine;
   Restaurant l'Eurasienne
54 Meherio Iti
56 Te Pari Village
57 Pension Bonjouir

PLACES TO EAT
2 Restaurant Le Belvévdère
3 Casablanca
4 L'Auberge du Pacifique
15 Venezia
16 La Fleur de Lotus
18 Coco's Restaurant
22 Restaurant L'Impérial
30 Restaurant Nuutere
36 Restaurant du Musée
   Gauguin
42 Restaurant Baie Phaeton
43 L'Escale Restaurant;
   Te Hono
55 Auberge Te Pari

ARCHAEOLOGICAL SITES
12 Marae Anapua
14 Marae Farehape

25 Marae Tataa
27 Marae Arahurahu
32 Marae Mahaiatea
34 Marae Vaihiria 1
51 Marae Nuutere
63 Petroglyphs
64 Marae

OTHER
1 Arahoho Blowhole
5 Lagoonarium;
   Captain Bligh Restaurant
6 Fort Fachoda
9 Thousand Springs
10 Hitiaa Lava Tubes
11 Bougainville's Anchorage
17 Musée de Tahiti et des Îles
20 La Source
26 Centre Auto Paea
28 Maraa Grotto
33 Le Terrain de Golf
   Olivier-Bréaud
35 Bain de Vaima & Vaipahi
   Waterfall
37 Jardin Botanique; Restaurant
   du Jardin Botanique
38 Musée Gauguin
39 Ranch Gauguin
40 Grotte de Tetopa
41 Trou de Lagon
49 Iti Diving International
50 Lookout
52 Oceanographic Research
   Station
53 The Marado
58 Vaipoiri Cave
59 Faaroa Refuge
60 Queen's Cave
61 Anaihe Cave
62 Vaitomoana Cave

coast, particularly along the north coast from Mahina through Papenoo to Tiarei, are unprotected. There are 33 passes through the reef, the most important of which is the Pape'ete Pass in to Pape'ete's harbour. Less than 10km east is Matavai Bay (Baie de Matavai), the favourite anchorage point of many early explorers.

The mountainous centre of Tahiti Nui is effectively one huge crater, with the highest peak being Mt Orohena (2241m). A ridge runs northwest from the summit to Mt Aorai (2066m), and continues south to the spectacular rocky Diadème (1321m) and north to Mt Marau (1493m). A number of valleys run down to the coast from the mountains, the most impressive being the wide Papenoo Valley to the north. Tahiti Iti has its highest point at Mt Ronui (1332m).

Orientation

The *pointe kilométrique* (PK; kilometre point) markers start at zero in Pape'ete and increase in both a clockwise and an anticlockwise direction around Tahiti Nui; the counting starts again on Tahiti Iti, where the markers only go as far as the sealed road.

Pape'ete and the surrounding suburbs dominate the northwestern coast of the island.

Remarkably, you still cannot drive the entire way around Tahiti, as the easternmost coast of Tahiti Iti has no sealed road.

Activities

Walking, surfing, diving and sailing are the most popular activities on Tahiti. The tourist office is a good place to start your research; see also the Outdoor Activities chapter and the special section 'Diving'.

Ranch Gauguin (☎ 57 51 00; PK53.1), half a kilometre inland from the coastal road, organises horse rides for 3000 CFP an hour in the Papeari area. **Deep-sea fishing** can be organised through the tourist office, and many of the luxury hotels have **tennis** courts. You can play **golf** at Le Terrain de Golf Olivier-Bréaud (☎ 57 40 32; PK42).

Pape'ete

pop 26,180

Pape'ete divides its guests – you either love it or hate it. Don't expect a gentle paradise: Pape'ete is a vibrant, concrete-dominated city, and has been dubbed the 'Las Vegas of the Pacific', although this is possibly going a bit far. Nonetheless, you'll need to look elsewhere for your Pacific paradise. But Pape'ete's charm asserts itself if you relish the ebullience of a big city and surrender yourself to great dining, excellent dance and music performances, funky bars and a bustling waterfront.

All roads in French Polynesia lead here, so you might as well enjoy it.

HISTORY

Pape'ete means 'basket of water', probably referring to the springs where water was once collected.

In 1769, when Cook anchored in Matavai Bay (Baie de Matavai), there was no settlement in Pape'ete. Towards the end of the century European visitors realised the value of its sheltered bay and easy access through the reef. London Missionary Society (LMS) missionaries arrived in Pape'ete in 1824 and the young Queen Pomare became a regular visitor to the growing town, which gradually swelled to a religious and political centre.

Visiting whaling ships made Pape'ete an increasingly important port, and it was selected as the administrative headquarters for the new French protectorate in 1843. By 1860 the town had taken its present form, with a straggling European settlement between the waterfront and the street known as the Broom (now Rue du Commandant Destremeau, Rue du Général de Gaulle and Rue du Maréchal Foch).

Chinese merchants and shopkeepers also started to trickle in to Pape'ete, but at the beginning of the 20th century the population was still less than 5000. A disastrous cyclone in 1906 and a German naval bombardment in 1914 took a toll, but during WWII the population reached 10,000 and by the early 1960s it was over 20,000.

The opening of Faa'a airport in the 1960s kick-started the tourist industry, while French nuclear testing brought in basketfuls of money. The huge expansion of administrative and government jobs lured a flood of people from other islands. This type of rapid expansion usually has its flipside, and the last few decades have seen the almost total destruction of the charming old colonial heart of Pape'ete.

CENTRAL PAPE'ETE

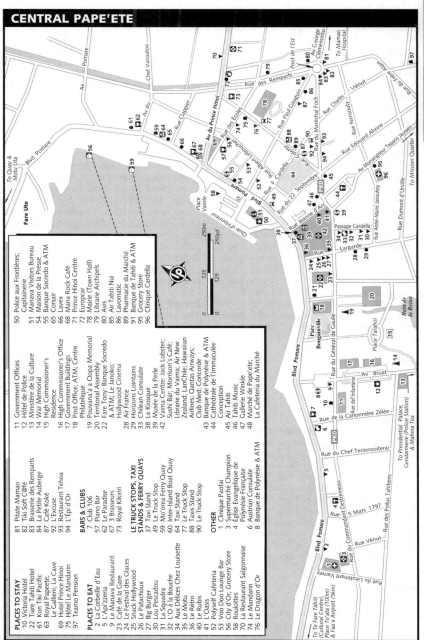

PLACES TO STAY
10 Victoria Hotel
22 Tiare Tahiti Hotel
61 Kon Tiki Pacific
63 Royal Papeete;
   Le Gallieni; La Cave
69 Hotel Prince Hinoi
75 Hôtel Le Mandarin
97 Teamo Pension

PLACES TO EAT
2 La Corbeille d'Eau
9 L'Api'zzeria
9 Le Manava Restaurant
23 Café de la Gare
24 Le Festival des Glaces
25 Snack Hollywood
26 Le Patachoux
27 Big Burger
30 Lou Pescadou
31 La Squadra
32 L'O à la Bouche
34 Aux Délices Chez Louisette
35 Le Motu
36 Le Rétro
40 Le Rubis
41 L'Oasis
52 Polyself Cafeteria
53 Voo Doo Lounge Bar
53 City d'Or; Grocery Store
58 Roulottes
70 La Restaurant Saïgonnaise
76 Le Mandarin
76 Le Dragon d'Or

81 Pitate Mamao
82 Tiki Soft Cōfé
83 Brasserie des Remparts
84 La Petite Auberge
87 Café Kōké
92 L'Excuse
93 Restaurant Tehoa
94 L'Épi d'Or

BARS & CLUBS
7 Club 106
57 Piano Bar
62 Le Paradise
67 3 Brasseurs
73 Royal Kikiriri

**LE TRUCK STOPS, TAXI
STANDS & FERRY QUAYS**
37 Taxi Stand
49 Le Truck Stop
59 Mo'orea Ferry Quay
64 Inter-Island Boat Quay
64 Taxi Stand
77 Le Truck Stop
88 Taxis Stand
90 Le Truck Stop

OTHER
1 Clinique Paofai
3 Supermarché Champion
4 Église Evangélique de
   Polynésie Française
6 Austrian Consulate
8 Banque de Polynésie & ATM

11 Government Offices
12 Hôtel de Police
13 Ministère de la Culture
14 War Memorial
15 High Commissioner's
   Residence
16 High Commissioner's Office
17 Government Buildings
18 Post Office; ATM; Centre
   Philatélique
19 Pouvana'a a Oopa Memorial
20 Territorial Assembly
22 Fare Tony; Banque Socredo
   & ATM; Le Janoko;
   Hollywood Cinema
28 Air France
33 Chilean Consulate
38 Le Kiosque
39 Musée de la Perle
42 Vaima Centre: Jack Lobster;
   Sushi Bar; Morrison's Café;
   Librarie du Vaima; Air New
   Zealand; LanChile; Hawaiian
   Airlines; Qantas Airways;
   Club Med; Concorde
43 Banque de Polynésie & ATM
44 Cathédrale de l'Immaculée
   Conception
45 Air Tahiti
46 Tahiti Music
47 Gallerie Winkle
48 Marché de Pape'ete;
   La Cafeteria du Marché

50 Police aux Frontières;
   Capitainerie
51 Manava Visitors Bureau
54 Maison de la Presse
55 Banque Socredo & ATM
65 Corsair
66 Lavex
68 Mana Rock Café
71 Prince Hinoi Centre
72 Europcar
78 Mairie (Town Hall)
79 Librairie Archipels
80 Avis
85 Air Tahiti Nui
86 Lavomatic
89 Pharmacie du Marché
91 Banque de Tahiti & ATM
95 Grocery Store
96 Clinique Cardella

ORIENTATION

The backbone (albeit a bent one) of central Pape'ete is Blvd Pomare, which curves around an almost enclosed bay. This central district is easily covered on foot. Clustered around here and on the blocks back from Blvd Pomare are most of the central businesses, banks and restaurants, and some hotels. The Vaima Centre marks the centre of Pape'ete, but it's along the waterfront that the city throbs with life. The port zone, comprising Fare Ute and Motu Uta, is easily visible across the harbour to the north.

Greater Pape'ete forms a vast conurbation, squeezed between the mountains and the lagoon along the north coast of Tahiti. The westward sprawl of Pape'ete extends beyond the airport in the drab suburb of Faa'a (yes that *is* three consecutive vowels) and on to Puna'auia. The coastal road westwards is complemented by the Route de Dégagement Ouest (RDO) freeway, which runs slightly inland, starting on the western edge of central Pape'ete and extending to just beyond Faa'a airport before rejoining the coastal road.

On the other side of Pape'ete, Av du Prince Hinoi and Av Georges Clémenceau run eastwards through the suburb of Pira'e before joining at Arue.

INFORMATION

The tourist office, main post office, the majority of the banks and the best bookshops are all clustered in Pape'ete.

Tourist Offices

The **Manava Visitors Bureau** (☎ 50 57 10, fax 43 16 78; e tahiti-manava@mail.micro tech.pf; Fare Manihini, Blvd Pomare; open 7.30am-5pm Mon-Fri, 8am-noon Sat & public holidays) is in the centre of Pape'ete in Place Vaiete. This tourist office has information about the whole of French Polynesia. Although Mo'orea and Bora Bora have helpful tourist offices, the more remote islands don't, so if you have any queries, make the most of this tourist office while you are in Pape'ete. There is also an information desk at the airport.

Money

There are banks (Banque Socredo, Banque de Tahiti and Banque de Polynésie) and ATMs scattered around Pape'ete and its suburbs. Banque Socredo and Banque de Polynésie have branches at Faa'a airport, where there's also an ATM. See Money in the Facts for the Visitor chapter for general information on banks and changing money.

Most banks in Pape'ete change money and travellers cheques; the ATMs accept Visa and MasterCard for cash advances and let you withdraw money from your home account.

The **Banque Socredo** (Blvd Pomare) in the Fare Tony shopping centre has a machine that changes foreign banknotes.

Post

Pape'ete's main **post office** (Blvd Pomare; open 7.30am-5pm Mon-Fri, 8.45am-10.45am Sat) is next to the Parc Bougainville. For stamps and general postal services go upstairs from the Blvd Pomare entrance; the post office also offers phone, fax and telegram services. Poste restante is downstairs. Stamp lovers can kick up their heels at the Centre Philatelique, next door.

There are also post offices in the surrounding suburbs and at Faa'a airport.

Email & Internet Access

The Internet is yet to take a firm grip of Pape'ete. There are a few places where you can check your email, but you certainly won't be tripping over Internet cafés.

Tiki Soft C@fé (☎ 88 93 98, 77 44 34; e tikisoft@mail.pf; w www.tikisoft.pf) is a funky place run by glamorous French women and frequented by a chic clientele. It charges 1000 CFP per hour.

Upstairs in **La Maison de la Presse** (Blvd Pomare) is a room of snazzy computers where you can check your email to the accompaniment of local music. It charges 1000 CFP for one-and-a-quarter hours.

The (Cnr Blvd Pomare & Av du Prince Hinoi) also has Internet access; it charges 1000 CFP per hour.

Bookshops & Newsagencies

Pape'ete has a few good bookshops, but the range in English is always poor compared to the French texts and newspapers on offer. You can find all the French newspapers (from *Le Monde* to *Libération*) and the French-language Tahitian newspapers and magazines, such as *Les Nouvelles de Tahiti* and *Tahiti Pacifique*. You'll easily find a novel (anyone for Patricia Cornwell or Tolkien *en français?*) or a reference guide of interest.

If you don't read French very well, there are a few English-language newspapers (always some days old) available at Pape'ete's better newsagencies. The only local English-language magazine is *Tahiti Beach Press*, which is aimed at tourists and not really up to much.

The best bookshop is the **Librarie du Vaima** (☎ 45 57 57; e *vaimalib@mail.pf; Vaima Centre; open 8.30am-6pm Mon-Fri, 8am-5pm Sat)*. **La Maison de la Presse** *(Blvd Pomare)* has a good selection of newspapers and magazines, and **Le Kiosque** *(Blvd Pomare)*, at the front of the Vaima Centre, is also good. **Librarie Archipels** (☎ 42 47 30; 68 *Rue des Remparts; open Mon-Sat)* is a good bookshop, but, again, there's very little in English. There is also a bookshop in the **Prince Hinoi Centre** *(Av du Prince Hinoi; open 7.30am-6pm Mon-Fri, 8am-5pm Sat)*.

Photo Developing
There are lots of photo-developing centres around Pape'ete but the costs are sky-high. You'll pay anywhere from 3400 to 4300 CFP to develop a 36-exposure film. Take your undeveloped films home with you to be developed there (also see Photography in the Facts for the Visitor chapter).

Laundry
Getting clothes washed on Tahiti is mighty pricey, although after returning from the outer islands you may appreciate just being able to find a Launderette. **Lavomatic** *(☎ 43 71 59; Rue Paul Gauguin; open 6.30am-noon & 1.30pm-5.30pm Mon-Sat)* charges 1600 CFP for a load to be washed and dried. **Lavex** *(Blvd Pomare; open Mon-Sat)* charges 1650 CFP to wash and dry a 7kg load; to get a shirt washed, dried and ironed costs 400 CFP.

Toilets
There are clean public toilets near the tourist office on the quay (there were even fresh flowers when we popped in); there are also loos in the tourist office. All cafés and restaurants have toilets, so if need be you can pop in and have a quick drink before availing yourself of the facilities.

Left Luggage
There's a **left-luggage department** *(open 6am-7pm Mon-Fri & 2hr before international flights)* opposite the domestic flights area in Faa'a airport. It costs 640 CFP a day for a suitcase or backpack, more for bigger items. You might try leaving your baggage with your hotel, although the cheaper places are often reluctant to let you do this.

Medical Services & Emergency
For police, phone ☎ 17; for an ambulance, phone ☎ 15. You can also call **SOS Médecins** *(☎ 42 34 56)* or **SOS Infirmières** *(☎ 43 56 00)*.

The **Mamao Hospital** *(☎ 46 62 62, 24hr emergencies ☎ 42 01 01; Av Georges Clémenceau)* is the biggest hospital in French Polynesia, with good facilities and a range of medical specialities.

There are two 24-hour private clinics: **Clinique Cardella** *(☎ 42 81 90; Rue Anne-Marie Javouhey)*, behind the cathedral, and **Clinique Paofai** *(☎ 46 18 18; Cnr Blvd Pomare & Rue du Lieutenant Varney)*, which are more expensive than the hospital. If in doubt, ask your hotel reception to recommend someone.

You can usually find a pharmacy open on Sunday morning, in addition to normal business hours.

WALKING TOUR
Central Pape'ete is compact, and lends itself to strolling. Ideally head off in the freshness of the early morning, or wait until the cool of the early evening. Most of the places described in the walking tour are also covered in more detail in the sections that follow.

Start a waterfront stroll from the west along the four-lane Blvd Pomare, which is shaded by overhanging trees and brightened by hibiscuses. The **Place To'ata**, which marks the westerly point of Pape'ete, has been nicely paved and generally jazzed up in recent times. During the Heiva this is where you'll see most dance and music performances, and the little restaurants and snack bars along here stay open late.

You can't miss Central Pape'ete's imposing pink church, the **Église Évangelique de Polynésie Française**; the missionaries would be rapt to see how busy the church is on a Sunday morning.

Across the road is a memorial to the great double-canoe *Hokule'a*, which sailed from Hawaii to Tahiti in 1967. As you walk east there are racing pirogues lined up under the trees like tadpoles. Local teams can be seen practising some afternoons and every Saturday morning.

TAHITI

On the inland side of the road is the **Parc Bougainville** (Bougainville Park), which was undergoing work at the time of writing but will hopefully again be a shady, green haven in among the dust and bustle.

Next up on the island side is the useful but rather drab **Vaima Centre**, with shops, a few restaurants and most of the airline offices.

Head down Rue Jeanne d'Arc to the **Cathédrale de l'Immaculée**, built in 1875. This is a lovely cool spot for a quiet moment or two.

Following Rue du Général de Gaulle, turn left into Rue du 22 Septembre to the **Marché de Pape'ete** (Pape'ete Market). Here you can buy almost any produce that is available in French Polynesia, and you get the feeling you might even see Jack buying some magic beans in a dark corner.

If you stroll back towards Blvd Pomare, on the harbour side is the Place Vaiete and the **Manava Visitors Bureau**, the very helpful tourist office. This area has been given a mighty facelift in recent times, and at night the **roulottes** (food vans or mobile diners) illuminate the area immediately to the east of the tourist office. There are plenty of public benches along here where you can sit and watch the world go by.

On the inland side of Blvd Pomare, the sometimes seedy but always noisy and energetic **entertainment district** starts just south of Av du Prince Hinoi and extends north past Av du Chef Vairaatoa.

Tourism and entertainment fades out further along the waterfront as the road continues through the docks and industrial zone of **Fare Ute** (which becomes Motu Uta after the bridge). This is the sweaty working part of the harbour where the copra boats unload their cargoes from the islands and the sweetish smell of coconuts hangs in the air. Pallets of everything, from building materials to crates of Hinano beer, drums and shiny new Taiwanese bicycles are loaded on ships bound for the outer islands.

MARCHÉ DE PAPE'ETE

Head straight for the Marché de Pape'ete (Pape'ete Market) and get your head around local produce on the ground floor and have your fill of gaudy fabrics and the like on the second floor. The prime time to visit is early Sunday morning, when local residents flock in from all around Pape'ete.

The market covers the whole block between Rue du 22 Septembre and Rue F Cardella, just one block back from Blvd Pomare. It has lived through a tumultuous 250 years of cyclone damage and rebuilding and was even destroyed by German cruisers in WWII. Today's airy structure was built in 1987.

Dotted among the fruit, vegetables, meat and fish downstairs are cake stalls, pizza places and little patisseries. Wander and munch, and then stroll upstairs to the clothes, jewellery and nick-nacks upstairs. Fish from other islands is on sale early in the day but the Tahitian catch does not appear until late afternoon.

CHURCHES & TEMPLES
Église Évangelique de Polynésie Française

Although the Catholic cathedral stands squarely in the town centre, Tahiti remains predominantly Protestant, a lasting legacy of the LMS missionaries. The large pink church makes a colourful scene on Sunday morning, when it is bursting at the seams with a devout congregation dressed in white and belting out rousing *himene* (hymns). This is the site of the first Protestant church in Pape'ete, which was built in 1818.

Cathédrale de l'Immaculée

Also known as the Cathédrale de Notre Dame, the Cathédrale de l'Immaculée Conception has pride of place in the centre of town. The cathedral's story began in 1856, when plans were hatched for it to be built of stone imported from Australia, with a doorway carved out of granite from Mangareva in the Gambier Archipelago. Construction began, but money soon ran out; the original edifice was demolished in 1867, and a smaller cathedral was completed in 1875.

Mission Quarter

From the cathedral, Av Monseigneur Tepano Jaussen leads into the Mission district, the site of Catholic colleges and Protestant schools. Jaussen, the Catholic bishop of Tahiti from 1848, acquired the mission lands in 1855 and turned them into a local **botanical garden**. He is buried in the mission's cemetery, beside Father Honoré Laval, the controversial apostle of the Gambier Archipelago. The road from the cathedral crosses the Papeava River on a small stone bridge and leads in to the gardens of the fine **bishop's palace** (1875). The gardens also contain a pretty Gothic-style chapel.

MUSÉE DE LA PERLE

In the Vaima Centre on the Rue Jeanne d'Arc side, the Musée de la Perle (Pearl Museum; ☎ 45 21 22; admission 600 CFP; open 8am-7pm Mon-Sat, 9am-7pm Sun) was created by pearl magnate Robert Wan. It's a small, modern and well-presented museum that covers all facets of the pearl cultivating business including its history, cultivation techniques, economics and art. There are explanations in English. Of course, at the end of the visit you magically find yourself in one of Monsieur Wan's pearl boutiques.

PARC BOUGAINVILLE

The Parc Bougainville (Bougainville Park) stretches from Blvd Pomare to Rue du Général de Gaulle and, not surprisingly, is fronted by a 1909 bust of the great French navigator.

ADMINISTRATIVE BUILDINGS

Named Place Tarahoi after Marae Tarahoi, the royal marae of the Pomare family, the **Territorial Assembly** and other government buildings occupy the former site of the Pomare palace. The termite-riddled 1883 palace was razed in 1960, but you can get an idea of what it looked like from the modern *mairie* (town hall), a few blocks east, which is built in a similar style. On Rue du Général de Gaulle the assembly building is fronted by a **statue** of Pouvana'a Oopa, the late pro-independence figure of heroic proportions (see the boxed text 'Pouvana'a a Oopa – A Tahitian Leader' in the Huahine chapter).

The **High Commissioner's Residence** that stands to one side of the assembly building replaced the 1843 Palace of the Governor (those pesky termites again). The earlier building arrived on Tahiti in pieces and was intended to be assembled on Nuku Hiva in the Marquesas, but was sidetracked to become the governor's residence! Behind and between the two buildings is the freshwater spring. The pool is still known as the Bain de la Reine (queen's bathing place), as the young Queen Pomare used to visit it. A more recent addition is the **Presidential Palace**, an imposing building used by the president.

To the west, along Av Bruat, is the brand-spanking-new **Ministère de la Culture** (☎ 50 15 01). There's an **exhibition space** (admission free; open 7.30am-noon, 1.30pm-5pm) in here that is well worth a peek. There were some amazing car tyres incised with traditional Polynesian tattoo markings when we visited.

Pape'ete's **mairie** (town hall) is two blocks back from Blvd Pomare and a block north of Marché de Pape'ete. It was completed in 1990, in vague imitation of the old queen's palace.

BAIN LOTI

From east of the centre, the Route de Fautaua runs 2.5km inland to Bain Loti (Loti's Bath). It was here in Pierre Loti's 1880 novel *Le Mariage de Loti* (The Marriage of Loti) that the beautiful Rarahu, a 14-year-old Polynesian girl, met Loti (Frenchman Julien Viaud's nom de plume). This pool once supplied the town with drinking water, but now it's led through a concrete channel and surrounded by development. Nevertheless, it remains a favourite meeting place and swimming hole for locals. A bust of Pierre Loti overlooks the scene.

See Fautaua Valley in the Outdoor Activities chapter for details of the walk that leads inland from Bain Loti.

TOMB OF POMARE V

On Point Outuaiai in Arue, on the water's edge, signposted and just a short detour off the coastal road, is the tomb of the last of the Pomare family (see History in the Facts about French Polynesia chapter for more about the Pomare family).

The Tomb of Pomare V looks like a stubby lighthouse made of coral boulders. It was actually built in 1879 for Queen Pomare, who died in 1877 after 50 years in power. Her ungrateful son, Pomare V, had her remains exhumed a few years later and when he died in 1891 it became his tomb. It's said that he drank himself to death and that the Grecian urn replica atop the structure should be a liquor bottle. Gauguin witnessed the funeral and described it in his book *Noa Noa*.

Other Pomares are buried (or may be buried – their tombs are unmarked) in the Cimetière Pomare at PK5.4. There's a board at the cemetery indicating where Pomare I, II, III and IV are apparently interred.

TAHITI

BEACHES

Tahiti is really not a beach destination, but if you just want to get in to the water there are a few places where you can do so within a reasonable distance of Pape'ete. Tahiti's beaches are black sand, which makes the sand particularly hot underfoot but rather beautiful under sunlight. Eight kilometres west of the centre, just beyond Faa'a airport, there's a bit of beach by the Sofitel Maeva Beach. The Outumaoro le truck stop is just across the main road from the hotel, so getting here is very easy.

On the other side of town, 3km to the east in Pira'e, there's a stretch of black-sand beach by Le Royal Tahitien hotel. There's also a nicer stretch of beach at PK7, and further along again at Point Vénus (PK10). Unhappily, beaches within Pape'ete's urban sprawl can be subject to the same problems as city beaches in many modern countries, such as pollution from badly treated (or even untreated) sewage and industrial waste, so ask around before diving in.

PLACES TO STAY

There's a cluster of mid-range places to stay right in the heart of Pape'ete, while most of the top-end and budget places tend to be on the edges of town. Although there's a fair range of places to choose from, bargains are rare and the price-to-quality ratio is dispiriting. You won't find stylish places with that mythical Polynesian feel unless you're paying an arm and a leg for it to be recreated by an international hotel chain.

It's wise to reserve ahead during the Heiva festivities in July, when many hotels are completely booked out. Most international flights arrive at ungodly hours of the night, so you may decide it's easier to book your first night before leaving for Pape'ete so as to avoid traipsing around with your luggage looking for somewhere to stay.

As elsewhere in French Polynesia, there is a hefty 11% TVA *(taxe sur la valeur ajoutée)* heaped upon the price of rooms at all 'certified' hotels, plus 150 CFP daily tax (per person per night). At hostels and *pensions* (guesthouses), TVA is 6% and daily tax is 50 CFP. See Money in the Facts for the Visitor chapter for the full story.

Even though you will be often quoted prices that do not include these weighty taxes, prices quoted here do include them.

When you get a quote, make sure you clarify exactly what little additions you should expect on your bill at the end of your stay.

Central Pape'ete

Budget The budget places in the centre of Pape'ete are possibly the worst spots to rest your weary limbs in French Polynesia, and you are unlikely to find yourself anywhere so decidedly average on the rest of your trip. The following places are rudimentary and have shared bathrooms only, but they'll do for a night or two. Location is their sole attraction.

Teamo Pension (☎ 42 00 35, 42 47 26, fax 43 56 95; Rue du Pont-Neuf; dorm beds 2000 CFP, doubles 4500 CFP) is the cheapest place to stay and is far from flash. Hot water is only available from 6pm to 9pm. There's a shared kitchen. Credit cards are accepted.

Mahina Tea (☎ 42 00 97; doubles 5000 CFP) is very low-key and friendly but is not scrupulously clean. Discounts kick in if you stay for three nights. Walk southeast past the Ministère de la Culture on Av Bruat and turn right at the *gendarmerie* (police station) along Route de Sainte Amélie – it's about 250m further.

Victoria Hotel (☎ 43 13 93, fax 43 27 28; 10 Rue Général de Gaulle; doubles 7100 CFP, twins 8100 CFP), just west of Av Bruat, is strictly a last resort. You may hear the Jane Fonda-esque shrieks of joy from the aerobics place a few doors up.

Mid-Range These hotels are all a bit uninspired, but they are fairly clean and very central. They all have private bathrooms and TVs, and they all accept credit cards.

Royal Papeete (☎ 42 01 29, fax 43 79 09; Blvd Pomare; doubles from 7900 CFP) is definitely past its use-by date. However, the staff speak English and are very helpful.

Kon Tiki Pacific (☎ 54 16 16, fax 42 11 66; 271 Blvd Pomare; singles/doubles 11,250/13,700 CFP) is a remarkably unremarkable hotel, but it has a certain seedy charm and terrific views from the rooms at the front.

Tiare Tahiti Hotel (☎ 50 01 00, fax 43 68 47; Blvd Pomare; doubles 14,600-20,100 CFP) overlooks the water in the hub of it but is afflicted by the noise of the traffic and late-night revellers. This is where many tour groups come. The staff are not particularly friendly.

Hotel Prince Hinoi (☎ 42 32 77, fax 42 33 66; Cnr Blvd Pomare & Av du Prince Hinoi; doubles around 15,000 CFP) is well positioned in the heart of the nightlife quarter. Management is sometimes willing to offer reduced rates. The rooms are comfortable but far from dazzling.

Hôtel Le Mandarin (☎ 50 33 50, fax 42 16 32; e chris.beaumont.pf; Rue Colette; singles/doubles from 14,000/16,250 CFP) is clean and quiet, and is possibly the best of this bunch. The rooms have great wooden furniture and the bathrooms are good.

Outer Pape'ete

Most places on the fringes of the city are on the west coast between Faa'a (the airport district) and Maeva Beach. The handy Pape'ete–Faa'a–Outumaoro le truck trundles along here all day and, unusually, well into the night.

Budget The following budget places do not accept credit cards. Unless otherwise mentioned, these places have shared bathrooms only.

Chez Fifi (☎ 82 63 30; dorm beds 2000 CFP, singles/doubles 3500/6000 CFP) is a good cheap option for late or early arrivals in Pape'ete. Take the small, steep road beside the Mea Ma laundry across from the airport car park (there's a sign); the guesthouse is 150m up that horrifically steep road on the left. The *pension* is impeccably clean, and rates include breakfast; other meals cost 2000 CFP. There's a communal kitchen. The airport and Mo'orea can be viewed from the lounge room.

Chez Myrna (☎/fax 42 64 11; e dam meyer.family@mail.pf; singles/doubles 4600/6400 CFP) is about 500m from Matavai Hotel along the Route de Tipaerui. Chez Myrna is clean and simple – a great budget option. Breakfast is included in the price; airport transfers cost 1000 CFP each way. There's no sign for the guesthouse.

Tahiti Airport Lodge (☎ 82 23 68, fax 82 25 00; singles 5000 CFP, doubles without/with bathroom 6000/8000 CFP) overlooks the airport, about 200m from the coast road. Breakfast and daytime airport transfers are included in the price (transfers at night cost 1000 CFP). This place is a tragedy: it's a lovely *pension* with clean rooms in a pretty garden, and is very handy for the airport, but the owner is one of the grumpiest people we've ever had occasion to meet. There's even an enticing little swimming pool that guests are *not* allowed to use!

Chez Lola (☎/fax 81 91 75; singles/doubles/triples 5000/6700/7000 CFP) is also near the airport but is on the inland side of the RDO, high up in the Saint-Hilaire district. Rates include breakfast and airport transfers during the day (at night they cost 1000 CFP). It's a quiet spot and the Saint-Hilaire le truck passes close by about every hour during the week (although it's easier to ask the owners to take you down to the main road).

Hotel Hei Tiare Inn (☎ 83 33 52, 82 77 53; PK4.3; doubles with/without air-con 8500/7500 CFP) is just a kilometre or so from the airport, towards the city, in a very sooty part of town. All rooms have bathroom and are spacious and tiled, but this is not the spot for a relaxed sleep-in – you'll be woken early by traffic and perpetual drilling. The busy little snack bar may also disturb your sleep. There's a communal kitchen.

Mid-Range At Maeva Beach, **Moana Surf Tours** (☎/fax 43 70 70; PK8.3; 12,000 CFP per person) is a surfers' haven. The price includes airport transfers, accommodation in a dorm, half-board and transport to the best surf spots of the moment. Run by Moana David, the brother of the famous local surfer Vetea David, this place is popular (you generally need to book well in advance).

Sofitel Maeva Beach (☎ 42 80 42, fax 43 84 70; Maeva Beach; doubles from 14,100 CFP, suites 25,400 CFP) is on one of the best beaches in this area, but is in dire need of a facelift (renovations are planned). The Outumaoro le truck stop is immediately beyond the roundabout, on the inland side of the road. Breakfast costs 2100 CFP, while half-board adds 6400 CFP. The hotel has two restaurants: Restaurant Bougainville and the Sakura.

Le Royal Tahitien (☎ 50 40 40, fax 50 40 41; doubles 20,900 CFP) is about 3km east of Pape'ete in Pira'e. This hotel is on a reasonable stretch of black-sand beach, and has clean, motel-like rooms and a pleasantly grassy setting. There's a waterfront restaurant with a deck looking out over the beach. Local musicians perform on Friday and Saturday evenings. A le truck stops less than 100m from the hotel.

TAHITI

Matavai Hotel (☎ 42 67 67, fax 42 36 90; e matavai@mail.pf; singles/doubles 16,200/ 21,400 CFP) is to the west of Pape'ete, on the Route de Tipaerui. It's a bit out of the way, but it has a swimming pool and spacious rooms. Airport transfers are free.

Top End Luxury reigns supreme at these hotels, which are all west of Pape'ete, positioned by the lagoon. You can pretend their small artificial beaches are real because they are quite authentic-looking. Most rooms have beautiful views of Mo'orea. Several times a week these hotels offer Polynesian dance performances by the best groups on the island, as well as *tamaaraa* (traditional-style feasts) at the weekend. These establishments accept all credit cards.

Sheraton Hotel Tahiti (☎ 86 48 48, fax 86 48 00; e reservations.tahiti@sheraton.pf; doubles from 17,900 CFP, suites from 30,700 CFP) is a lovely hotel that is still ironing out a few hitches (such as getting the bedroom doors to open with the security card).

Tahiti Beachcomber Intercontinental Resort (☎ 86 51 10, fax 86 51 30; e tahiti@ intercinti.com; doubles from 33,800 CFP, over-water bungalows from 52,900 CFP), just to the west of the airport, is luxury incarnate. If you want to treat yourself, this is the spot – you can sip cocktails and swim at the same time.

PLACES TO EAT
Oh to have a few more hours in the day to squeeze in more meals! Whatever you think of the capital, you are sure to have memorable eating experiences here. Cuisine-skip from French to Polynesian to Chinese and back again via Italian and Vietnamese – you couldn't possibly tire of dining in Pape'ete. On the whole, service is quick and friendly, and the food is fresh.

Sunday is the one day of the week you may go hungry in Pape'ete because so many places close. For breakfast you'll be able to find a snack bar in the centre where you can get an early coffee, baguette or pastry. A few of the cafés that double as bars (for example, Le Rétro) remain open on Sunday.

Central Pape'ete
The centre of Pape'ete yields most epicurean delights imaginable. There is often not much difference between the 'cheap' places (not very cheap by the rest of the world's standards!) and the really special restaurants, which could be an argument for throwing caution to the wind and worrying about the finances later. Unless otherwise mentioned, the following places all accept credit cards.

Polynesian & French Just down from the Tiki Soft C@fé is **Brasserie des Remparts** (☎ 42 80 00; Pont de l'Est; mains from 1800

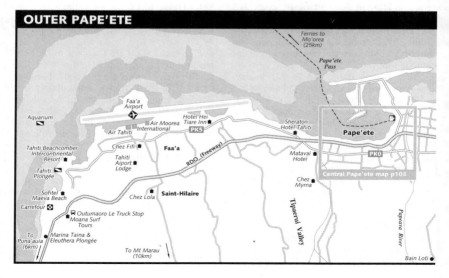

OUTER PAPE'ETE

CFP; open 6.30am-10pm Mon-Fri, 10am-2pm Sat), a relaxed place that is usually brimming with espresso-sipping, cigarette-smoking regulars. The service is very good and the food is reasonably priced.

Café Koké (☎ 50 22 44; Rue Paul Gauguin; appetizers 550-2450 CFP, mains 1250-2600 CFP; open lunch Mon-Fri, dinner Fri & Sat) is a sleek, modern restaurant with fabulous food. Try the hot and cold tuna with lime and sweet red-pepper sauce – sublime. The only criticism is that it's not open for dinner more often.

Le Manava Restaurant (☎ 42 02 91; Av Bruat; mains 1400-2200 CFP; open lunch Mon-Fri) has a seedy but charming bar, a covered outdoor dining area and a more formal dining area. The restaurant was about to close for renovations at the time of writing.

Le Gallieni (☎ 42 01 29; Blvd Pomare; appetizers 700-3000 CFP, mains 1400-2600 CFP; open dinner daily), in the Royal Papeete hotel, has a lovely antiquated setting.

Voo Doo Lounge Bar (☎ 48 08 48; Rue du Commandant Jean Gilbert; tapas 700-10,000 CFP, appetizers from 900 CFP, mains from 1900 CFP; open Tues-Sat) is on a narrow street leading from Blvd Pomare to Rue Albert Leboucher. This is a stylish, intimate spot to drink or dine on faux leopard print. The 'Asian style' marinated tuna dish is to die for. The food here is well worth the prices asked.

Morrison's Café (☎ 42 78 61; appetizers 900-2300 CFP, mains 1700-2700 CFP), atop the Vaima Centre, takes its name from Jim (not Van), which is abundantly clear as soon as you step inside. It's a cheesy but popular place with rooftop and open-air sections.

L'O à la Bouche (☎ 45 29 76; Passage Cardella; mains 1700-2900 CFP; open lunch Mon-Fri, dinner Mon-Sat) is an unpretentious restaurant where you will be treated like royalty. This is one of the best restaurants in this town of great restaurants, and le patron clearly revels in his customers' gastronomic delight. The 'salmon of the gods', with ginger and passion fruit, toes that delicate line between sweet and savoury. You could lose yourself in the gooey handmade chocolates that arrive at the end of the meal. There's a veggie platter (1660 CFP) for languishing vegetarians.

L'Excuse (☎ 53 13 25; Rue du Maréchal Foch; appetizers 1600-2600 CFP, mains 1700-2800 CFP; open lunch Mon, lunch & dinner Tues-Fri, dinner Sat) is a small establishment, near the junction with Rue Cardella, with a very French menu. This restaurant has changed hands in recent times, and some say it's not the place it once was.

Le Rubis (☎ 43 25 55; Rue Jeanne d'Arc; appetizers 900-2900 CFP, mains 2500-3600 CFP; open lunch Mon-Sat, dinner Tues-Sun) is an impeccable French restaurant right in

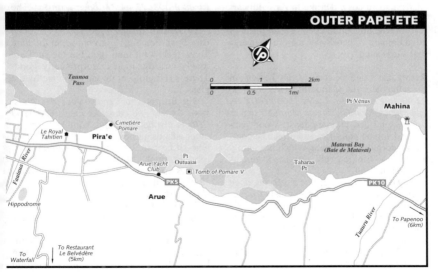

OUTER PAPE'ETE

the middle of it all, near the Vaima Centre. The menu is extensive, the service very professional and the clientele terribly glamorous. It looks expensive, but it's decent value for Pape'ete.

La Petite Auberge (☎ 42 86 13; appetizers 1250-1950 CFP, mains 2650-3650 CFP; open lunch & dinner Mon-Fri, dinner Sat), close to the Pont de l'Est roundabout, is one of the oldest restaurants in Pape'ete. It indulges French-cuisine enthusiasts with its very fine cooking. It's an intimate little restaurant, despite its busy location.

La Corbeille d'Eau (☎ 43 77 14; Blvd Pomare; appetizers 1700-3400 CFP, mains 2500-4600 CFP; open lunch & dinner Mon-Fri, dinner Sat) is a small, interesting restaurant with burnt-orange walls decked with modern art and crisp white tablecloths. It's a bit out of the way, but it's a good spot for a romantic meal.

Italian With hearty pizza and pasta dishes, **Lou Pescadou** (☎ 43 74 26; Rue Anne-Marie Javouhey; dishes 600-2700 CFP; open Mon-Sat) is a real Pape'ete institution.

La Squadra (☎ 41 32 14; Passage Cardella; pasta dishes 1400-1600 CFP; open lunch Mon-Sat, dinner Wed-Sun) has an interesting menu with rarities such as polenta (2050 CFP) and eggplant parmigiana (2050 CFP).

L'Api'zzeria (☎ 42 98 30; Blvd Pomare; dishes 770-2380 CFP; open 11.30am-10pm Mon-Sat) is a cosy, denlike haven with cars streaking by on either side (you can approach it from Rue du Commandant Destremeau or Blvd Pomare). There's also a more open area that's less snug.

Asian Just round the corner from the hotel of the same name, **Le Mandarin** (☎ 50 33 90, 50 33 50; Rue des Écoles; mains 1500-3600 CFP; open lunch Mon-Fri, dinner Mon-Sat) makes for a visual and culinary feast. Wood panelling, hanging tapestries and ornate lacquerwork adorn this restaurant, which has hardly acquired a wrinkle (well, very few) since its opening in 1964.

City d'Or (☎ 42 86 28; Rue des Écoles; open 11am-midnight daily) has extensive vegetarian options, including 'special monk's meat' (1350 CFP; your guess is as good as ours), as well as soups (from 1050 CFP) and seafood dishes (from 1650 CFP).

Le Dragon d'Or (☎ 42 96 12; Rue Colette; appetizers 900-2200 CFP, mains 1300-2300 CFP; open Tues-Sun), next to Hôtel Le Mandarin, is another classic Chinese restaurant. It's cool and dark – a total escape from the bustling Pape'ete of outside.

Restaurant Tehoa (☎ 42 99 27; Rue du Maréchal Foch; mains 1060-1920 CFP; open lunch Mon-Sat, dinner Wed-Sat) is pretty rough and ready, but it's popular with locals. The servings are large, the food is fresh and the prices are low.

Pitate Mamao (☎ 43 86 40, 42 86 94; Av Georges Clémenceau; mains 1100-2000 CFP; open Mon-Sat) is just after the Pont de l'Est roundabout. The menu is predominantly Chinese, but there are also French and Polynesian specialities.

Sushi Bar (plates 300-500 CFP; open lunch Mon-Thur, lunch & dinner Fri & Sat) is in the Vaima Centre, directly above Jack Lobster. It has great views, chic wooden interior and orange-clad waiters. What more could you want from a rotating sushi bar in the Pacific? Grab your meal before it passes you by.

La Restaurant Saïgonnaise (☎ 42 05 35; Av du Prince Hinoi; mains 1150-2700 CFP) has excellent Vietnamese food, despite its hideous location on the traffic-clogged Av du Prince Hinoi.

Cafés & Snack Bars A hip spot for a quick coffee or snack during the day, when you can also check your emails, is **Tiki Soft C@fé** (☎ 88 93 98, 77 44 34; open Mon-Sat).The fun doesn't stop at sundown.

Le Janoko (mains 1300-1800 CFP; open 6am-5pm Mon-Sat, Fri evenings), in the Fare Tony, feels a bit mall-like, but the staff are lovely and the food is surprisingly good. There's Hinano beer on tap and wine by the glass.

Big Burger (Au Rendez-Vous des Amis; ☎ 43 01 98; Rue Largarde; meals 600-2300 CFP) is always jumping. Women from the outer islands sit next to chic French expats, who sit next to local families with children running amok. Meals are generous: hefty burgers cost from 700 CFP, omelettes cost 1200 CFP and a tuna club sandwich with chips costs 1200 CFP.

Snack Hollywood (Rue Largarde; open daily) is just up from Big Burger, and is very similar.

Le Patachoux is a lovely little place sandwiched between Snack Hollywood and Big Burger. It has the usual sandwiches (600

Sunset, Mo'orea

Sunset, Tahiti

Surfing, Pa'ea, Tahiti

Marché de Pape'ete

Passengers on a le truck (local bus), Pape'ete

Fresh produce, Pape'ete

CFP) and good pastries (200 CFP), as well as delicious vegetarian quiche (400 CFP).

Le Festival des Glaces (☎ 42 40 01; Rue Largarde) also celebrates the festival of hamburgers (390 CFP), salads (700 CFP) and fresh juices (550 CFP).

Café de la Gare (☎ 42 75 95; Rue du Général de Gaulle; dishes 1400-2300 CFP) hovers between twee and chic – great service tips it firmly over to the latter. It's a *très français* spot for a glass of wine (600 CFP) over lunch, but it is a little pricey.

Right in the centre of town (in fact it defines the town centre), the Vaima Centre has a number of excellent cafés and cheap eats.

Le Rétro (☎ 42 86 83; Blvd Pomare; open daily), on the sea side of the Vaima Centre, is a good spot for a light meal, ice cream or a stiff drink, and always seems to be open (a godsend on bleak Sundays). A sign kindly informs customers that 'tips are not forbidden', in case you were wondering.

L'Oasis (☎ 45 45 01; mains from 1400 CFP; open Mon-Sat) is on the Rue du Général de Gaulle side of the Vaima Centre, facing the cathedral. It has excellent pastries to start the day, and also has terrific takeaway French-bread sandwiches (from 400 CFP) at lunch time. There's an air-con room upstairs, but it lacks atmosphere.

Jack Lobster (☎ 42 50 58; open lunch & dinner Mon-Fri, dinner Sat), on the Blvd Pomare side of the Vaima Centre, is a saloon-style place – an odd choice in decor for a restaurant on Tahiti. A Texas burger costs 1600 CFP, a veggie fajita costs 1600 CFP and a steak will set a cowboy back 1990 CFP.

Le Motu is a little stall with a great selection of sandwiches. There are tables where you can prop yourself up but there's nowhere to sit.

Aux Délices Chez Louisette (Passage Cardella; open 6am-5pm daily) is a genteel little nonsmoking patisserie with marble tables and little else in the way of decor, which is fine because the focus is on the food. Pastries cost about 200 CFP, mini quiches about 400 CFP.

Polyself Cafeteria (Rue Paul Gauguin; open lunch Mon-Fri) is a self-service café and is excellent value, although it's very cafeteria-esque.

L'Épi d'Or (☎ 43 07 13; snacks 300-1000 CFP; open Mon-Sat) has a takeaway window that is handy for a quick snack on the run;

there is also now a clean little restaurant attached (salads from 1400 CFP, mains from 1300 CFP).

There are a few little **stalls** on the ground floor on the Marché de Pape'ete where you can buy yourself a brightly coloured, artery-clogging cream cake, a piece of pizza or takeaway Chinese dishes. Upstairs is **La Cafeteria du Marché** (☎ 42 25 37; open 5am-4pm daily), which is big on the faux Polynesian decor but fairly short on quality. There's no table service (except on Sundays) and the whole operation feels a bit half-baked, which is a shame because it has a great setting overlooking the bustle of the market below.

Roulottes The famous roulottes (literally 'caravans' in French, these are food vans or mobile diners) will be a wondrous addition to your gastronomic pleasure in Pape'ete; meals here are also gentle on the wallet. These little stalls sizzle, fry and grill up a storm every evening from around 6pm; things don't quieten down until well in to the night (the public toilets stay open late, too). If you decide to eat elsewhere, consider sideling by for dessert or a spot of people-watching. The roulottes area, which has recently been paved and generally jazzed up, is just to the east of the tourist office – you can't miss it.

Hong Kong is one of the most popular roulottes. Squeeze in next to that guy devouring his steak and chips and that woman relishing her chow mein; **Pizza Napoli** has good thin-crust pizzas with appropriately delicious toppings; **Crêperie du Port** somehow manages to serve everything from hamburgers to crepes; and **Glacier du Port** whips up outrageous combinations such as Nutella-and-banana waffles.

Self-Catering Self-catering is a distinct possibility in Pape'ete. The **market** has wonderful fresh fish, fruit and vegies (you'll miss this on the islands, so make the most of it while you are on Tahiti), and Pape'ete has a few large, well-stocked supermarkets (generally open Monday to Saturday from 7am to 7.30pm or 8pm, and Sunday morning). If you are staying in the centre, the most handy supermarket is **Supermarché Champion** (Rue du Commandant Destremeau), close to the Paofai Church.

Outer Pape'ete

Restaurants & Cafés Perched 600m above the city in Pira'e, at the start of the walking track to the top of Mt Aorai, is **Restaurant Le Belvédère** (☎ 42 73 44; dishes 1650-3950 CFP; open lunch & dinner Wed-Sun). The views over Pape'ete are fantastic, particularly at sunset. Fondues are the speciality here. Le Belvédère provides free transport from some hotels in Pape'ete at 11.45am, 4.30pm and 7pm. If you drive, take the first right after the Hamuta Total fuel station. The 7km road to the restaurant is steep, winding and rugged towards the top.

Hilaire – Pâtissier, Confisseur, Glacier (☎ 43 65 85; Cnr Av du Commandant Chessé & Av Georges Clémenceau; open 5am-5.45pm Mon-Fri, 5am-noon & 3pm-5.45pm Sat, 5.30am-10am Sun) is a fabulous salon de thé just next to the Chinese temple. There's a huge and enticing range of pastries, whole cakes (2000 CFP), quiches (1700 CFP) and home-made chocolates (7500 CFP per kg), all of which more than make up for the characterless decor.

Pâtisserie-Salon de Thé Moutet (Cnr Av du Prince Hinoi & Av du Commandant Chessé; open breakfast & lunch Mon-Sat; pastries 100-200 CFP) is an impeccably clean, air-con patisserie that also has fresh bread, ice creams and sandwiches at moderate prices.

Snack Lagon Bleu (burgers 400-600 CFP, mains 900-1100 CFP), on the bypass road to Patutoa and 100m from the crossroads with Av du Commandant Chessé, struggles to compete with McDonald's but is certainly superior. Tourists are rare at this clean little snack bar, and the food is surprisingly good.

Self-Catering There are a few **Carrefour** supermarkets (including those at PK4.5 in Arue and in the Moana Nui Commercial Centre at PK8.3 in Puna'auia); there's **Hyper U** in Pira'e; and **Cash & Carry** at PK3 in Faa'a, between the airport and town.

ENTERTAINMENT

After a stay on other islands, where nightlife is, frankly, nonexistent, Pape'ete could almost pass for a city of wild abandon, though it only gets busy on weekends.

Bars

On a balmy tropical evening the first question is where to go for a cold Hinano or a well-poured maitai (local-style punch). Many of the places along Blvd Pomare, the noisy nightlife strip, look pretty seedy, but they are frequented by local women and families, and are generally safe for single female travellers (although you may be bothered by harmless suitors). The best thing about most of the places listed here is that they are filled with as many locals as tourists.

Le Rétro (☎ 42 86 83; Blvd Pomare; open daily) fits the bill for most things and it'll do for a watch-the-world-go-by cold beer as well.

Café de la Gare (☎ 42 75 95; Rue du Général de Gaulle) was only open during the day when we visited, but there were plans for evening revelry. Even during the day, this is a great, terribly French, spot for a drink.

Tiki Soft C@fé (☎ 88 93 98, 77 44 34; e tikisoft@mail.pf; w www.tikisoft.pf) is an interesting place that has DJs at the weekend. During the week it's a chilled spot to check out the chic while sipping a fresh fruit juice or a maitai.

Voo Doo Lounge Bar (☎ 48 08 48; Rue du Commandant Jean Gilbert) has great low-key music, a languid atmosphere and much more style than most Pape'ete watering holes (it used to be the Café des Négociants). A gin and tonic will set you back about 800 CFP (there's even Bombay Sapphire gin), and a glass of wine starts from 900 CFP.

Several places along the busy and noisy nightlife strip of Blvd Pomare are also good spots for a contemplative beer at any time, particularly the popular **3 Brasseurs** (Blvd Pomare; open daily). It has excellent boutique-brewery beer on tap for 400 CFP and a constant stream of locals and tourists wanting to sample it. Cover bands perform here at the weekend, when local hips swing to the beat.

Morrison's Café (☎ 42 78 61), upstairs in the Vaima Centre, is a popular spot to drink, and it has rock and blues groups playing several times a week.

The snazzy top-end hotels, such as the **Sheraton Hotel Tahiti** and the **Tahiti Beachcomber Intercontinental Resort**, all have bars where you can enjoy the ocean breezes and nibble the free peanuts; 'unchaperoned' women are much less likely to be under the spotlight in these bars.

Nightclubs & Discos

Blvd Pomare is the main drag for nightclubs and discos. From the Tahitian waltz to European electronic music, it's all here. Some establishments open only at the weekend, when you will need your elbows to force an entrance (although women tend to be more than welcome). They typically close around 3am or 4am.

Piano Bar *(admission 1500 CFP Fri & Sat; open Mon-Sat)*, a few steps back from the waterfront, has a reputation that precedes it: the Piano Bar isn't a place for prudes. The clientele ranges from lovelorn sailors to passing tourists – the whole world seems to come and go from the Piano Bar. The music (techno, dance, local) isn't as important as the general atmosphere. There's a drag show on Friday and Saturday nights around 1am. The weekend entry price includes a drink.

Le Paradise *(Blvd Pomare; admission men 2000 CFP Fri & Sat; open 10pm-3am daily)*, next to Kon Tiki Pacific, attracts a slightly older crowd.

La Cave *(Blvd Pomare; admission men 1500 CFP; open Fri & Sat)*, beside the Royal Papeete, is the place to head if you want a more *kaina* (local) atmosphere. The attraction is the music – the Royal Band has a local repertoire including the Tahitian waltz, zouk and foxtrot. It really gets going after midnight. The plain decor is there to remind you that dancing is first and foremost – the setting is secondary. The entry price includes a drink.

Royal Kikiriri *(Rue Colette; admission 1000 CFP Fri & Sat; open Wed-Sun)*, between Rue des Écoles and Av du Prince Hinoi, is home to the Trio Kikiriri, who ensure that you won't hear any techno here. The admission fee includes a drink at the weekend; entry is free other nights.

Club 106 *(admission men 2000 CFP; open Thur-Sat)* is on the waterfront, near Av Bruat. The crowd is mostly on the other side of 30. The admission price includes a drink.

Cinemas

There are a few very small cinemas in town, including **Concorde** *(☎ 42 63 60; Rue du Général de Gaulle)* in the Vaima Centre; **Hollywood** *(☎ 42 65 79; Rue Largarde)* in the Fare Tony; and **Liberty** *(☎ 42 08 20; Rue du Maréchal Foch)*. They tend to screen average Hollywood blockbusters and the occasional French film. *Version originale* (VO; original version) indicates that the film will be shown in its original language; sadly *version*

Française (VF; French version) tends to dominate, which means you'll have to put up with the dubbing of well-known actors – *quelle horreur!* Admission costs 950 CFP.

Dance Performances

Tahiti is a good island to tap your toes along to some of the best Polynesian dance and music groups, many of which appear several times a week in the big hotels. Those worried about cheesy, touristy performances can rest assured these groups are very professional and are enjoyed every bit as much by locals as by wide-eyed visitors. If you are in the region during the Heiva you'll be spoilt for choice (there are performances most nights), but, otherwise, don't miss these excellent performers in their extravagant costumes perform the *ote'a* (when dancers are arranged in a row) and the furious and sensual *aparima* (a dance with hand gestures; see the special section 'Tahitian Dance'). The performances generally last about 45 minutes – any longer and spectators and dancers alike would be exhausted! When held in the luxury hotels, these performances are often accompanied by a sumptuous buffet (which usually costs around 6000 CFP), although parking yourself at the bar and ordering a drink will sometimes suffice. Check with the hotel reception desks at the **Sheraton Hotel Tahiti**, the **Tahiti Beachcomber Intercontinental Resort** and the **Sofitel Maeva Beach** about their programmes and entrance policies.

SHOPPING

Although you didn't come to French Polynesia for the shopping, you may find yourself shopping anyway. In Pape'ete you can buy products from all over French Polynesia, including clothes, pearls and more pearls.

Handicrafts

Upstairs in the Marché de Pape'ete (Pape'ete Market) you can wander for ages among the handicrafts. If you are after reasonably priced gifts for jealous friends back home, start here. Wooden salad servers, fabric (it may look good in this context but think about how bright it will look when you get it home), the wonderful monoi (fragranced coconut oil), pareu, jewellery and even mother-of-pearl love-heart key rings can be purchased here. By the by, you can also get a quick tattoo done, as there are a few artists based upstairs (follow that buzzing on the Blvd Pomare side of the building).

There are heaps of craft and souvenir shops (of varying quality) along Blvd Pomare and Rue du Général de Gaulle and in the Fare Tony and Vaima Centre. **Horizons Lointains** (☎ 82 93 93; Rue Largarde) next to Air France has beautiful local, Chinese and Japanese bits and bobs.

Art

Pape'ete is home to a number of art galleries, including **Galerie des Tropiques** (☎ 41 05 00; Cnr Blvd Pomare & Rue Cook); **Olivier Creations** (☎ 48 29 36; Rue Paul Gauguin); and **Gallerie Winkle** (☎ 42 81 77; Rue Jeanne-d'Arc), which has an interesting mix of etchings, paintings and crockery.

Pearls

There are so many jewellery shops and pearl specialists in Pape'ete that you have to be careful not to trip over them. Look around before buying, and consider purchasing a pearl here and getting it set at home (this will probably work out cheaper and ensures you get exactly what you want). Depending on the quality, you can by a single pearl for around 15,000 CFP (cheaper if you don't mind imperfections); for a decent-quality ring you are looking at anywhere from an almighty 140,000 CFP. Also bear in mind that there are numerous pearl shops and pearl farms on the outer islands, so don't rush into purchasing a pearl.

Music

Music shops where you can find local and Western music are dotted around Pape'ete. Try **Tahiti Music**, diagonally opposite the cathedral, which has a decent selection of CDs by local artists for around 3200 CFP; you can listen before you buy.

GETTING THERE & AWAY
Air

Faa'a airport (pronounced fa-**ha**-ha) is the aviation centre of French Polynesia. All international flights arrive here, and Air Tahiti and Air Moorea flights to the other islands leave from here. Flights within each archipelago hop from one island to the next, but many connections between archipelagos are via Faa'a.

International check-in desks are at the east end of the terminal. Air Tahiti's domestic check-in is at the west end; Air Moorea is in a separate small terminal slightly to the east of the main terminal.

For international flights to/from Tahiti, see the Getting There & Away chapter; for general information about air travel within French Polynesia, see the Getting Around chapter; for connections to/from an island group or an individual island, see the relevant chapter or section.

Airlines In Pape'ete, **Air Tahiti** (☎ 86 42 42, fax 86 40 69 or ☎ 86 41 84 Sat afternoon & Sun; Rue du Maréchal Foch; open 7am-5pm Mon-Fri, 8am-11am Sat) is at the intersection with Rue Edouard Ahnne. There's also an Air Tahiti office in the domestic area of the airport (open 5am-5.30pm daily).

On Tahiti, **Air Moorea** (☎ 86 41 41) is based at Faa'a airport.

For international airline offices, see the Getting There & Away chapter near the beginning of this book.

The following charter operators and helicopter services are available on Tahiti and are based at Faa'a airport:

Air Archipels (☎ 81 30 30)
Héli Pacific (☎ 85 68 00)
Héli-Inter Polynésie (☎ 81 99 00)
Wan Air (☎ 80 05 59)

Sea

All boats to other islands moor at the ferry quay at the northern end of Blvd Pomare. Cruise ships and other interesting visitors moor at the Quai d'Honneur close to the tourist office and Capitainerie (harbour master's office). The numerous cargo ships to the different archipelagos work from the Motu Uta port zone, to the north of the city (le truck route 3 from the *mairie*).

See the Getting Around chapter for general information on inter-island ships, and the individual island chapters or sections for specific information on travel to/from those destinations.

GETTING AROUND
To/From the Airport

Given that most flights into Faa'a arrive at an ungodly hour of the morning, and le trucks tend to disappear after 10pm, Pape'ete joins that long list of places in the world that make travellers pay exorbitant fees to get from the airport into town.

Taxis are expensive everywhere in French Polynesia, so if your hotel offers to collect you from the airport, jump at the chance. Otherwise the short drive to central Pape'ete will set you back 1600 CFP during the day and 2500 CFP at night (8pm to 6am). That's US$15 to US$20! Officially the taxis also charge an extra 100 CFP for baggage, but this is sometimes waived. At least drivers don't expect to be tipped.

If you arrive at a reasonable time of the day, you will be able to catch any le truck going towards town from the airport (northeast bound or to your left as you leave the airport), which will take you straight to the centre of Pape'ete in about 15 minutes for a flat fare of 130 CFP during the day and 250 CFP after 6pm (children cost 65 CFP; it's an extra 100 CFP for your baggage). Walk straight across the car park outside the airport, up the steps to street level and across the road to hail a city-bound le truck. From Pape'ete, catch a le truck heading to Faa'a and Outumaoro – the destination will be clearly posted on the front – from along Rue du Général de Gaulle.

Le Truck

Sadly, le trucks are on their way to bus heaven and are being replaced by 'real' aircon buses that, in theory, will only stop at designated stops and will run to a timetable. The routes will remain the same, however, and there are plenty of locals who think this transition will take a long time, and that the new buses will continue to behave in a relaxed, 'le truck-like' fashion, stopping wherever people hail them. Given that the system is about to change, it's best to check at the tourist office for details and routes.

On weekdays le trucks operate roughly every 15 minutes (though this varies) from dawn until about 5.30pm except for the Pape'ete–Faa'a–Outumaoro line, which supposedly operates 24 hours but in reality gets very quiet after 10pm. At the weekend, particularly on Sunday, services are less frequent. Fares for the shortest trips, from Pape'ete to a little beyond the airport, for example, start from 130 CFP (65 CFP for children and students); this fare rises to 250 CFP after 6pm. Outside this area, the prices are less clear. Out to about 20km from Pape'ete

the fare will go up in stages to around 200 CFP; getting to the other side of the island might cost 450 CFP. Once the new system is up and running, these fares may well rise.

Tahiti's le trucks have their route number and the final destination clearly marked. Although there are official le truck stops, complete with blue signs, they are rather difficult to spot, and le trucks will still generally stop anywhere sensible for anybody who hails them. Just make sure you are on the correct side of the road for the direction you want to go!

There are basically three routes: greater Pape'ete, which is handy for the Pape'ete–Faa'a airport trip (catch this along Rue du Général de Gaulle); the east coast, which is also handy for Tahiti Iti (catch this along Blvd Pomare); and the west coast (catch this along Rue du Maréchal Foch and Rue du Général de Gaulle).

Car

Driving on Tahiti is quite straightforward and, although accident statistics are not encouraging, the traffic is fairly light once you get away from Pape'ete. Apart from on the RDO out of Pape'ete to the west, the traffic doesn't travel too fast. As always, beware of children wandering on the road, and prepare yourself for a rather casual approach to overtaking. Don't leave anything on view in your car, and even consider making it clear there's nothing to steal – leave the glove box open, for example.

Remember to check the car over carefully before accepting it. For the price you'll be paying, you may be unpleasantly surprised by the standard of the hire cars.

Many of the following car-rental companies on Tahiti also have desks at the bigger hotels:

Avis (☎ 54 10 10, fax 42 19 11) Cnr Rue des Remparts & Av Georges Clémenceau, Pape'ete; (☎ 43 88 99) Quai des Ferries, Pape'ete; (☎ 85 02 84) Faa'a airport
Centre Auto Paea (☎ 53 33 33) PK20.2, Pa'ea
Daniel Rent-a-Car (☎ 82 30 04, 81 96 32, fax 85 62 64) Faa'a airport
Europcar (☎ 45 24 24, fax 41 93 41) Cnr Av du Prince Hinoi & Rue des Remparts, Pape'ete; (☎ 86 60 61) Faa'a airport
Hertz (☎ 82 55 86) Faa'a airport
Robert Rent-a-Car (☎ 42 97 20, fax 42 63 00) Rue du Commandant Destremeau
Tahiti Rent-a-Car (☎ 81 94 00) Faa'a airport

Taxi

Taxis are so expensive that most visitors chose to ignore them (except when arriving at the airport late at night, when many people have no choice but to fork out the money for one). Apart from the official government-established flat fares from the airport to most hotels, taxis are metered. Any trip of a reasonable length will approximate a day's car rental, so if you want wheels you may as well rent them (see Car, following).

All the big hotels have taxi ranks, and there are plenty of taxis in central Pape'ete. To order a taxi, phone Faa'a airport (☎ 86 60 66), the Vaima Centre (☎ 42 60 77), or Marché de Pape'ete (☎ 43 19 62).

Hitching

Hitching (*auto-stop* in French) is not really a part of life on Tahiti in the way that it used to be (or in the way that it still is on the other islands). It is, however, still possible where le truck services are less frequent or nonexistent. Nonetheless, it's never an entirely safe means of travel, and women should never hitch alone. We don't recommend it.

Elsewhere on Tahiti Nui

Try to do a day trip around Tahiti Nui if you can. It's a great way to get a feel for life outside Pape'ete and to enjoy the island's wonderful lush vegetation. There are pockets of poverty, particularly in the valleys, where the water is not drinkable and unemployment is high – if you are finding French Polynesia financially crippling, imagine how difficult an unemployed local would find it. Nonetheless, you'll be hard pressed to find a long face, and you will find plenty of churches, kids on bikes and little stalls along the way.

COASTAL ROAD

The coastal road runs right around Tahiti Nui, the larger of Tahiti's double circles. The 114km circuit is marked by PK markers that start at 0 in Pape'ete and increase in both a clockwise and an anticlockwise direction. They meet at Taravao, the town at the isthmus that connects Tahiti Nui with Tahiti Iti. Taravao is 54km from Pape'ete clockwise (via the east coast) and 60km anticlockwise (via the west coast).

A circle around the island by car makes a lovely day trip, or you could extend the adventure and stay in an interesting little *pension* – there is a smattering of these around the more remote parts of the island.

The circuit that follows, heads around Tahiti Nui from Pape'ete in a clockwise direction. See the Tahiti Iti section later in this chapter for excursions beyond Taravao on to the smaller circle of Tahiti.

Taharaa Point (PK8.1)

Taharaa Point is the western boundary of Matavai Bay (Baie de Matavai; see Outer Pape'ete map), the favourite locale of early European explorers, who seemed enormously keen on renaming the point. Samuel Wallis named the point 'Skirmish Hill', but when Cook came along two years later he noted a solitary tree on the point and renamed it 'One Tree Hill'.

There are fine views back to Pape'ete from the viewpoint, but don't look straight down towards the beach – this is also an unofficial garbage dump.

Point Vénus & Baie de Matavai (PK10)

Part of Cook's mission on his three-month sojourn in 1769 was to record the transit of Venus across the face of the sun in an attempt to calculate the distance between the sun and the earth. Point Vénus, the promontory that marks the eastern end of Matavai Bay, was the site of Cook's observatory. Mahina marks the eastern end of Pape'ete's coastal sprawl.

Today Point Vénus is a popular beach excursion. There are shady trees, a stretch of lawn, a black-sand **beach**, a couple of souvenir shops and an impressive **lighthouse** (1867). There is no sign to Point Vénus from the main road; just turn off when you see shops and activity at the PK10 point. It's about a kilometre from the road to the car park near the end of the point.

There is a **memorial** to the first LMS Protestant missionaries, who made their landfall at Point Vénus on 4 March 1797.

Papenoo (PK17)

There's a popular **surf break** just before the headland that signals the start of the small village of Papenoo. A long bridge crosses the Papenoo River at the far end of the village, and the 4WD route up the Papenoo Valley, cutting through the ancient crater rim to Relais de la Maroto, starts up the west side of the river. See Inland later in this chapter for more information about this interesting route.

Arahoho Blowhole (PK22)

Appropriate swell conditions produce a geyser-like fountain of water from the *trou du souffleur* (blowhole) by the road just before Tiarei. If you're coming from Pape'ete, the blowhole is on the corner and there's a car park just beyond it; take care walking to the blowhole as there's a blind corner here. When the waves are right, the blow can be very dramatic – so dramatic that people have been swept right off the rock and out to the sea. Take care.

Just past the blowhole there's a fine sliver of black-sand **beach**, ideal for a picnic pause. There are sometimes vendors here with fruit for sale.

Faarumai Waterfalls (PK22.1)

About 100m past the blowhole, a signposted road leads just over a kilometre inland to the car park for the three Faarumai waterfalls. Bring a swimsuit if you want to stand under the cooling shower, and mosquito repellent if you simply want to stand still and enjoy the view in peace. It's a couple of hundred metres through a forest of *mape* (chestnut) trees to Vaimahutu, the first of the waterfalls. Another 20-minute stroll leads to the other two falls, Haamarere Iti and Haamarere Rahi, which stand almost side by side.

Hitiaa (PK38)

A plaque on the river bridge at the village of Hitiaa commemorates Bougainville's visit to Tahiti in April 1768. The small village of Hitiaa has a new **church** and a charming but fast-decaying old one, topped by a tower made of coral blocks.

Taravao (PK54)

Strategically situated at the narrow isthmus connecting Tahiti Nui with Tahiti Iti, the town of Taravao has been a military base on and off since 1844, when the first French fort was established. The original fort was intended to forestall Tahitian guerrilla forces opposed to

the French takeover from mounting operations against Tahiti Nui from Tahiti Iti.

From Taravao, roads run along the north and south coasts of Tahiti Iti. The central road into the Tahiti Iti highlands commences a short distance along the north-coast road. Although there is little of interest in the town, it does have shops, banks, petrol stations and a number of small restaurants, and so is a good place for a pit stop on a round-the-island circuit.

Jardin Botanique & Musée Gauguin (PK51.2)

Tahiti's Jardin Botanique (Botanical Gardens) and the interesting Musée Gauguin (Gauguin Museum) share an entrance road and car park.

The 137-hectare **Jardin Botanique** (*admission 500 CFP; open 9am-5pm daily*) has walking paths that wind their way through the garden past ponds, palms and a superb thicket of bamboo. The gardens were founded in 1919 by an American, Harrison Smith, who introduced many plants to Tahiti including the large, thick-skinned Southeast Asian citrus fruit known on Tahiti as *pamplemousse*, the French word for grapefruit. Unfortunately, Smith also introduced one or two botanical disasters that Tahiti could well have done without. Look out for the huge Galapagos tortoises. Mosquitoes in the gardens can be fierce.

The Restaurant du Jardin Botanique, near the entrance building to the gardens, is cheaper and less touristy than the Restaurant du Musée Gauguin, which is 500m further west (see Places to Eat later in this chapter).

The **Musée Gauguin** (*☎ 57 10 58; admission 600 CFP; open 9am-5pm daily*) is definitely worth a visit. Much of the well-written text about Gauguin and his particularly difficult life is in English, and although the museum is dimly lit and there is a conspicuous lack of original works by Gauguin, there's a lovely natural setting. The museum gardens are home to three superb tiki from Raivavae in the Australs. Tiki do not like to be moved, and there are colourful stories about what happened to the men that moved these tiki here (they apparently died 'mysteriously' within weeks of the move). The huge tiki figure beside the walkway stands 2.2m high and weighs 900kg; it's a baby compared with the figure towards the waterfront, which stands 2.7m high and weighs 2110kg. You'll find a third, smaller figure beside the giant.

It is possible to get to the gardens and museum from Pape'ete by le truck but the last return trip usually departs early in the afternoon. Check the departure times carefully or risk being stranded.

Bain de Vaima & Vaipahi Waterfall (PK49)

Beyond the botanical gardens there are more gardens along the mountain side of the road. Just past these gardens is the Bain de Vaima (Vaima Pool). The Vaipahi Waterfall is a few minutes' walk inland and drops from pool to pool through a stand of stately *mape* trees. There are great views from a small plateau beyond the falls and there are a number of short walks you can take from here. A one-hour walk brings you back to the road at PK50.2.

Mataiea

Between 1891 and 1893, Gauguin lived in Mataiea. Although he was sick and impoverished, this was a good period in his rather depressed life. He produced works including *Two Women on the Beach, Woman with a Mango* and *Ia Orana Maria – Hail Mary* during this time.

The **Church of St John the Baptist** (1857) is just outside the town. The curious Protestant **chapel** by the road in the village looks vaguely like a Hindu temple.

To the east of the Mataiea district is the golf course at Atimaono at PK42, the site of the 1860s Terre Eugénie cotton plantation. Chinese workers were shipped in to supplant unwilling Polynesians, and descendants of the Chinese immigrants still live on the island today. The cotton plantation and other land devoted to coffee and sugar production played an enormously important role in the Tahitian economy for some years.

To the east of Mataiea, at PK47.5, is the turn-off for the rough track up to Lake Vaihiria, the Relais de la Maroto hotel and the north coast.

Marae Mahaiatea (PK39.2)

Just east of the village of Papara, the Marae Mahaiatea was the most magnificent marae on Tahiti at the time of Cook's first visit (according to Cook it measured 80m by 27m at its base, rising in 11 great steps to a height of 13m). It was the marae of Obarea, an ancestor of the Pomare dynasty. Today the crumbling remains of the marae are still impressive for their sheer size – only as you clamber up the tree-covered 'hill' does it become clear that this is no natural feature.

Coming from Pape'ete, take the first turn towards the sea past the PK39 sign. Follow the road about half a kilometre all the way towards the coast. In the middle of the car park area, what looks like a densely vegetated hill is, on closer inspection, the massive remains of the stone marae.

Maraa Grotto (PK28.5)

Along the coastal road a manicured path runs through a garden past a series of overhung caverns, with crystal-clear pools and ferny grottoes. It's a popular stop on round-the-island circuits.

Pa'ea

In the Pa'ea district, **Marae Arahurahu** at PK22.5 is a tranquil and beautifully maintained marae, undoubtedly the best-looking one on the island. Beliefs in the powers of tiki aside, there is an amazing feel at this marae.

Marae Tataa at PK19 may have been quite important in its time. It was restored in 1973, but it's on private land and is now hard to get to.

The **Orofero River** at PK20, now a popular surfing site, was the spot where Pomare II fought the 1815 battle that reinstated him as ruler of Tahiti.

Musée de Tahiti et des Îles (PK15.1)

Only 15km from Pape'ete along the west coast, the excellent Musée de Tahiti et des Îles (*Museum of Tahiti & Its Islands;* ☎ 58 34 76; admission 600 CFP; open 9.30am-5.30pm Tues-Sun) is in Puna'auia. This is a great place to get your head around the geology and history of the area. The museum is divided in to four sections: geography and natural history; pre-European culture; the European era; and outdoor exhibits. It's in a large garden and if you get tired of history, culture and art, you can wander out to the water's edge to watch the surfers at one of Tahiti's most popular breaks.

The museum is on the coast, several hundred metres from the coastal road after the

Punaruu bridge. From Pape'ete, a Puna'auia le truck will drop you at the road junction. Check the time of the last return trip (generally about 4.30pm).

Puna'auia

There are some good **beaches** between PK15 and PK10, in and around Puna'auia. Puna'auia also has an excellent restaurant scene (see West Coast under Places to Eat, later in this chapter). The most expensive homes on Tahiti are found along this stretch of coast and are often set high above the coast to better enjoy the breathtaking views of Mo'orea.

On the hillside above the bridge at PK14.8 in Punaruu Valley is the site of a French fortification from the 1842–46 conflict, when France took control of Tahiti. It's now used as a TV relay station. A walking trail leads up to the Tamanu Plateau (600m), an area known for its wild **orange trees**, escapees from the citrus plantations that once grew here.

Lagoonarium (PK11)

Within Pape'ete's urban sprawl, the **Lagoonarium** (☎ 43 62 90; adults/children 500/300 CFP; open 9am-6pm daily) is a pleasant little tourist trap. A meshed-in area of lagoon with a very modest underwater viewing room is reached through a giant concrete shark's mouth. You can watch the small sharks and other creatures, although a snorkelling trip on one of the outer islands is far more interesting. The entrance to the Lagoonarium is part of the Captain Bligh Restaurant, a very popular stop for tour groups. If you eat at the Captain Bligh Restaurant, there's no charge to visit the Lagoonarium.

Organised Tours

You'll be swamped by brochures about the various organised tours offered on Tahiti every step of the way. Hotel activity desks, Pape'ete travel agencies and a number of independent operators offer island tours by minibus. Trips into the interior of the island require a 4WD and usually cost around 7500 CFP, including lunch (see Organised Tours under Inland later in this chapter). For hikes in the interior, see the Outdoor Activities chapter. For scenic helicopter flights, contact **Héli-Inter Polynésie** (☎ 81 99 00) or **Héli Pacific** (☎ 85 68 00).

Places to Stay

East Coast The **Fare Nana'o** (☎ 57 18 14, fax 57 76 10; e farenanao@mail.pf; PK52; bungalows with/without kitchen 11,000/7500 CFP) is unlike anywhere else you'll stay in French Polynesia. The bungalows border on the Gaudi-esque (not a straight line or a right angle in sight) and are simply stunning. Accommodation ranges from the famous tree house to two-storey, four-person bungalows. A sumptuous breakfast (no bleak mornings of bread and jam here) adds 1200 CFP; other meals cost 3000 CFP. If you stay here at the beginning of your trip to French Polynesia, all other places will pale in comparison: you've been warned.

South Coast On the lagoon side in Papara, **Hiti Moana Villa** (☎ 57 93 93, fax 57 94 44; e hitimoanavilla@mail.pf; PK32; bungalows with/without kitchen from 9500/8500 CFP) is a great option. Set around a well-tended garden, the bungalows here are impeccably clean. There is no beach, but there is a pontoon for swimming and a small swimming pool. Bicycles, pirogues and kayaks can be rented, and bus tours (5000 CFP per person) are offered. There's a supermarket and the Nuutere Restaurant is nearby. Airport transfers cost 1500 CFP per person each way. Travellers cheques and credit cards are both accepted.

Papara Village (☎ 57 41 41, fax 57 45 74; PK38.1; bungalows 10,000 CFP) is perched on the hillside in a garden 800m off the coastal road. The small Marae Tetaumatai is on the site, which has fantastic views of the lagoon and the mountains. There are two basic bungalows with kitchen, and there's a nice little swimming pool. Airport transfers cost 5000 CFP for two, round trip.

West Coast There are a number of places to stay along the west coast, particularly around Puna'auia. Compared with Pape'ete these places are tranquil, and they are close to some black-sand beaches. During the day there are regular le trucks into Pape'ete, but these dry up towards 4pm or 5pm.

Le Méridien (☎ 47 07 07, fax 47 07 08; e reservations@lemeridien-tahiti.pf; doubles 39,000 CFP, suites 53,400-111,200 CFP, over-water bungalows 53,400 CFP), in the town of Puna'auia, rivals the Tahiti Beachcomber in the luxury stakes. Le Méridien's over-water bungalows are equally divine and are definitely bigger than their Beachcomber counterparts. You get transported around in little golf buggies.

Pension de la Plage (☎ 45 56 12, fax 82 85 48; e laplage@mail.pf; PK15.4; singles/doubles from 6600/8500 CFP) is on the mountain side of the road, right across the road from the Toaroto beach in Puna'auia. This place is impeccably maintained (and is cleaned every day). Breakfast is available for 700 CFP, dinner for 1500 CFP.

Pension Armelle (☎ 58 42 43, fax 58 42 81; e armelle@mail.pf; PK15.5; singles/doubles/bungalow 6300/8100/9200 CFP) is on the lagoon side of the road in Puna'auia, just beyond the Musée de Tahiti and Le Méridien, and has a certain charm. The bungalow is worth the extra money. There's a very basic snack bar here. Credit cards are accepted.

Le Relais Fenua (☎/fax 45 01 98; e relais.familial@mail.pf; PK18.25; singles/doubles/quads 7000/8400/14,000 CFP), in Pa'ea, is a great place to stay. Clean, spacious rooms with TV, bathroom and air-con are set around a swimming pool. Airport transfers cost 2000 CFP and breakfast costs 1000 CFP per person; children under 12 can stay for free.

Pension Te Miti (☎/fax 58 48 61; PK18.6; dorm beds 2500 CFP, doubles 5500-7000 CFP) is on the mountain side of the main road in Pa'ea, about 200m from the shore. It has a friendly atmosphere and is deservedly popular with young travellers. It's run by a young French couple who are lovely and not out to separate you from your pennies. Prices include breakfast; there's also an equipped kitchen, and meals are available. There are a few bicycles for guests' use and a laundry service (500 CFP); airport transfers cost 1000 CFP per person. Credit cards are accepted.

Places to Eat

There are lots of little stalls set up along the road around Tahiti Nui, and restaurants dot the coastal road, particularly around Taravao.

East Coast Heading east out of Pape'ete, there are not many restaurants until you reach Taravao, although there are a number of excellent snack bars.

Fare Nana'o (☎ 57 18 14, fax 57 76 10; e farenanao@mail.pf; meals 3000 CFP) is an eccentric, endearing place to stay, but nonguests can also dine here, as long as they make a reservation. The food is reputedly very good.

L'Escale Restaurant (☎ 57 07 16; mains 1500-2700 CFP; open Tues-Sat), in Taravao, serves fine French cuisine in a classic setting. It also has Moroccan specialities such as couscous. Credit cards are accepted.

Te Hono (☎ 57 21 84; mains 800-1300 CFP; open Tues-Sun) is in the centre of Taravao, next to the Continent supermarket. The rotunda-shaped tiled room is antiseptic, but the Chinese food is reasonably priced and very good. Vegetarians can get stuck into the tofu, a rarely sighted treat on Tahiti. The restaurant is closed Sunday evening. Credit cards are accepted.

South Coast Right in the middle of Tahiti's two 'blobs' of land, **Restaurant Baie Phaeton** (☎ 57 08 96; mains 900-1600 CFP; open lunch Tues-Sun, dinner Tues-Sat) is a delightful place. A terrace table here affords views of both bits. The terrace is build out over the lagoon. Credit cards are accepted.

Restaurant du Jardin Botanique (appetizers 600-1950 CFP, mains 1700-3200 CFP) is a shady spot for a light meal. The poisson cru (raw fish) here is very good. You may have a few pleasant sprays of salt water with which to contend.

Restaurant du Musée Gauguin (☎ 57 13 80; PK50.5; appetizers 1500-2000 CFP, mains 1900-2500 CFP; open lunch daily) is firmly targeted at tourist groups visiting the museum, and is unfortunately rather closed in. The Sunday buffet costs 3200 CFP. Wander out onto the pier and look at the fish – you might see a shark or two.

Restaurant Nuutere (☎ 57 41 15; PK32.5; appetizers 1600-2400 CFP, mains 2300-3500 CFP; open Wed-Mon), in Papara, is a great little restaurant with an extravagantly painted facade. French specialities using local ingredients are served in an intimate and refined dining room and bar. The wine list is a sight to behold. Outside there's a garden with play equipment for children. Credit cards are accepted.

West Coast The chic suburb of Puna'auia, on the western edge of the Pape'ete coastal strip, has some great places to eat.

Restaurant L'Impérial (☎ 45 18 19; PK15; appetizers 1000-1200 CFP, mains 1300-3300

CFP; open lunch & dinner Tues-Sun), not far from Le Méridien, is a good Chinese restaurant (with the obligatory plastic flowers). The menu is huge. Credit cards are accepted.

Coco's Restaurant (☎ 58 21 08; PK13; appetizers 1800-3800 CFP, mains 2400-4100 CFP; open lunch & dinner daily) is romance incarnate. Tables are set around a neat lawn, with waves breaking on the shore, and, of course, there are some coconut trees framing the image.

La Fleur de Lotus (☎ 41 97 20; PK13; appetizers 1300-2300 CFP, mains 1300-4100 CFP; open Mon-Sat) is a popular Chinese restaurant. Locals bring big bowls to cart away their takeaway – if you are staying nearby and have wheels, consider following suit. There's a games area for kids, and live music on Saturday.

Venezia (☎ 41 30 56; PK12.7; appetizers 1500-1700 CFP, mains 1800-3000 CFP) is near La Fleur de Lotus and is a pleasant restaurant cooled by ceiling fans.

Captain Bligh Restaurant (☎ 43 62 90; PK11.4; appetizers 1300-2000 CFP, mains 1800-3400 CFP; open lunch Tues-Sun) is at the Lagoonarium. This is a touristy, cavernous place but is not at all unpleasant. The main attraction is the Friday and Saturday evening dance performance by O Tahiti E, one of the island's best dance groups.

L'Auberge du Pacifique (☎ 43 98 30; PK11.2; appetizers 2000-3400 CFP, mains 2600-3800 CFP; open lunch & dinner Mon-Sat), beside the lagoon, has been a Tahiti institution since its opening in 1974. It's not cheap, but Mo'orea smiles at you from across the water and the food is very good; the wine list is excellent. Le patron has a remarkably talented young son, whose artwork you can buy from the restaurant.

Casablanca (☎ 43 91 35; PK9; appetizers 1300-2500 CFP, mains 2400-3500 CFP; open lunch & dinner daily), at the Taina Marina, is a nice spot surrounded by yachts. There are plenty of outdoor tables, fresh flowers and superb views. Evening performances lift the tone on Thursday, Friday and Saturday evenings.

INLAND
Mt Marau
Directly across from Faa'a airport, a road signposted as Saint-Hilaire runs inland, under the RDO and up towards the summit of Mt Marau (1493m). It's possible to drive 10km to a height of 1441m, although the rough road requires a 4WD. The route passes through varied vegetation before emerging among the damp ferns above 800m. It reaches a belvédère (lookout) at 1241m. From the end of the road it is only a half-hour walk to the top of Mt Marau, from where there are superb views of the peaks around Tahiti Nui's central crater, the Tamanu Plateau to the south and the ridge-line running from Mt Marau to the Diadème (1321m), Mt Aorai (2066m) and Mt Orohena (2241m). The Fautaua River and its waterfalls, reached by the walk from Bain Loti, can be seen to the north. There are also walking paths up Mt Marau from Puna'auia that take about 3½ hours.

Papenoo to Papeari
Although there are a few tracks that climb some distance into the central highlands of Tahiti, there is only one route that extends right across the island. This 39km route is wonderful and rugged, and runs from Papenoo in the north to Papeari in the south, via the Relais de la Maroto hotel and Lake Vaihiria. The crossing makes a great day trip and presents a unique, 'lagoonless' view of Tahiti.

These central valleys once sheltered a dense population, and it was around here that the *Bounty* mutineers took refuge. When Christianity began to spread along the coastal regions, the Papenoo Valley became a last refuge for those faithful to the ancient Polynesian religion, and until 1846 it was also a shelter for the Tahitian rebel forces that opposed the French takeover. Archaeologist Kenneth Emory started the first systematic study of the valley's historic sites in 1925.

Some parts of the track are quite perilous, so don't attempt it on your own without a 4WD. Specialised operators do this route regularly and safely. From the Relais de la Maroto, there are heaps of walking tracks and the cross-island route is a fine two-day walk.

Papenoo to the Relais de la Maroto
The 18km route from Papenoo on the north coast to the Relais de la Maroto follows the wide Papenoo Valley, the only valley to cut right through the ancient crater. The Papenoo River is the largest on Tahiti. In Papenoo, the turn-off is just past PK17; the track has

its own PK markers. After an ugly garbage dump and signs warning of the dangers of the track, the **Topatari Waterfall** at PK5 cascades down to the river. A little further up the valley the **Vaiharuru Waterfall** comes down from the west side and, further, the **Puraha Waterfall** from the east. At PK16 the track passes the **Vaituoru Pool** (Bassin Vaituoru) before reaching the Relais de la Maroto just past PK18.

Papeari to the Relais de la Maroto

Coming from the west, the turn-off on the south coast is at PK47.5, just beyond the Seventh-Day Adventist church and just before the Tahiria River bridge and a settlement of modern, prefab-like buildings. Close to the ancient crater rim the rough track goes through a tunnel and then emerges inside the crater.

From the turn-off the road runs directly inland for about 200m before taking a signposted sharp-left turn. From there the track follows the Tahiria River upstream to a small catchment lake (6.7km, 145m) and **Marae Vaihiria I** (7.5km). The extensive remains of the marae include an artificial canal, used to carry water through the site, which stretches up the hillside. The marae was in use from the 16th to the 19th century, and there are several informative notice boards by the roadside and up the hill. Another marae is being restored further down the valley, about 4km from the start of the cross-island road.

Continuing uphill, there is a second small catchment lake (10km, 270m) before the road makes a very steep and winding (but paved) climb to Lake Vaihiria (11.3km, 450m), the 200m-long tunnel (14.9km, 770m) and finally the Relais de la Maroto (20.7km). The 4WD track runs up the west side of Lake Vaihiria to the tunnel, but there is a walking track that runs around the east shore of the lake and then climbs up to meet the vehicle track at the tunnel, just below the Urufau Pass.

Around the Relais de la Maroto

The Relais de la Maroto was originally built as accommodation quarters for workers on the hydroelectricity project that began in 1980. From the Relais de la Maroto, tracks fan out to the various hydropower dams, but you really need a guide to navigate these tracks, some of which are 4WD tracks and some of

which are walking tracks only. The restored **Marae Farehape** site is almost directly below the ridgeline on which the Relais de la Maroto perches; you can see an archery platform from where arrows were shot up the valley.

From the marae, a track climbs up to the Tahinu dam. A walking track skirts around the edge of the lake behind the dam to the **Marae Tahinu** archaeological sites, which are on both sides of the river. Another 4WD track starts from the dam and climbs up the Maroto Valley. A rough track turns off this route and leads to the top of the spectacular **Maroto Waterfall**. There are great swimming pools above and below the falls, but getting to the bottom of the falls entails an hour or so of rock-hopping up the river, starting from Marae Farehape.

The **Marae Anapua**, perched up above the Vainavenave dam, has been beautifully restored. The **Anapua Caves** are directly below the marae site, which can be reached on foot around the side of the dam or by the track around the valley side.

Organised Tours There are a few companies that specialise in 4WD island crossings. Try **Tahiti Safari Expedition** (☎ 42 14 15, fax 42 10 07), **Patrick Adventure** (☎ 83 29 29, 72 08 09) and **Natura Exploration** (☎ 43 03 83). You'll pay around 7000 CFP for a full day and around 5000 CFP for a half-day. In the high season it's wise to book several days in advance.

Places to Stay & Eat Smack in the lush heart of the island, **Relais de la Maroto** (☎ 57 90 29, fax 57 90 30; e maroto@mail.pf; singles/doubles 6500 CFP, bungalows from 9500 CFP) has renovated motel-style rooms and a few lovely bungalows to choose from. The wine cellar at the restaurant here is exceptional. Book ahead of time, particularly at the weekend.

Getting There & Away A few companies organise trips across the island (see Organised Tours, earlier), but you can also walk it in a couple of days or ride across on a mountain bike, if you've brought one with you. You can also rent 4WDs, but check out the conditions of the track and the dangers before you start out. In the rainy season this route can be truly perilous.

Tahiti Iti

The smaller loop of Tahiti's figure eight is known as Tahiti Iti (literally 'Small Tahiti') or the Presqu'île (Peninsula). You cannot drive around Tahiti Iti: the road only goes as far as Teahupoo to the south and Tautira in the north. The PK markers start at 0 at Taravao for both coastal roads. Although walking trails extend around the coast from both road ends, the sheer Te Pari Cliffs at the southeastern corner cut the trails off, and walking right around the coast is not easy. Nonetheless, there are some superb walks on Tahiti Iti, including a fine walk from Tautira to a series of marae and petroglyphs in the Vaiote River valley. See the Outdoor Activities chapter for details.

NORTH-COAST ROAD

The coastal road from Taravao runs through Pueu, past steep hills and numerous waterfalls, to Tautira. This stretch of coast has the highest rainfall on Tahiti. It's easy to walk beyond Tautira for a further 12km.

The north coast of Tahiti Iti has had some interesting European visitors. In 1772 the Spanish captain Boenechea anchored his ship *Aguilla* off the Aiurua River, about 10km beyond Tautira; Cook landed here in 1774; and many years later, in 1886, the writer Robert Louis Stevenson spent two months here. The landings of Catholic missionaries at Tautira eventually led to the French takeover of Tahiti and the end of the Protestant monopoly.

The sealed road ends at Tautira, but you can bump along for another kilometre or two before the road becomes impassable to vehicles. A good **walking track** leads round the coast for another 12km or so before reaching the **Te Pari Cliffs**, which make walking all the way to Teahupoo so difficult.

Near the Vaiote River are some interesting **petroglyphs** inscribed on coastal boulders and a series of marae inland in the valley. See the Outdoor Activities chapter for information about walking in the area.

Offshore is Motu Fenua Ino, a popular picnic spot.

INLAND

There are two routes that climb to an inland **lookout**. Both start from the north-coast road and can be combined to make a loop. In Afaahiti, at PK0.6, the first turn-off is signposted shortly before a school. The 7km road climbs through green fields, some home to very un-Tahitian-looking herds of cows, to the car park just before the lookout. The alternative route turns off the north-coast road at PK2.5 and is rougher and more potholed. It meets the first route just before the car park, from where it's a short walk to the viewpoint. There are superb vistas across the isthmus of Taravao to the towering bulk of Tahiti Nui. It's possible to walk for about an hour towards **Mt Teatara** (1197m).

SOUTH-COAST ROAD

The south-coast road runs by beaches and bays to Vairao and the small settlement of Teahupoo before abruptly stopping at the Tirahi River at PK18. From the end of the road it is possible to walk about another 10km before the steep Te Pari Cliffs cut off the path.

This area is described by Zane Grey, an American author who spent time here in the 1920s, in *Tales of Tahitian Waters*. The Tapuaeraha Pass through the reef is the widest and deepest around Tahiti, but because of its remote position it's rarely used.

A turn-off at PK9.5 leads a short distance inland to the scant remains of **Marae Nu-utere**, restored in 1994. There are three paved yards known as *tohua* (meeting places) with *ahu* (altars) at the end of them and large *turui* (seats) for priests or *ari'i* (chiefs). See the special section 'Civilisation & Archaeology' for more information on marae and traditional culture.

The south-coast road ends very decisively at Teahupoo, where the Tirahi River is crossed only by a footbridge. From here it is an easy 2½-hour walk to **Vaipoiri Cave**. See Te Pari in the Outdoor Activities chapter for details.

PLACES TO STAY & EAT

Chez Maïthé (☎/fax 57 18 24; *PK4.5; doubles 7000 CFP*) is on the north coast and has two small, simple rooms. No meals are available, but there's a kitchen for guests' use.

Punatea Village (☎/fax 57 71 00; **e** *puna tea_village@hotmail.com; PK4.7; doubles 6100 CFP, bungalows 9500 CFP*) is nicely situated by the sea. The five small rooms share a bathroom; the four bungalows are spacious

TAHITI

and well equipped, with private bathroom. Meals are available (breakfast 600 CFP, dinner 2500 CFP).

Pension Chayan (☎ 72 28 40; PK14; bungalows 10,800 CFP), on the mountain side of the road, is a fairly new place with four very comfortable bungalows. Excursions can be arranged, and there are kayaks for guests' use. Credit cards are accepted.

Pension Bonjouir (☎ 77 89 69; e bonjouir@ mail.pf; tent sites 1200 CFP, doubles 5000-6500 CFP, 2-person/family bungalows 8000/ 15,000 CFP) is just east of Te Pari Village and also has that Robinson Crusoe feeling. It's only accessible by boat. Isolated though it is, it's well known to surfers who come here for the nearby reef break. You can put your tent up (this is the only camp site on Tahiti), and there are also simple bungalows available. Luxurious it isn't, but the setting and ambience are lovely. There's a kitchen for guests' use, or you can choose half-board for 4000 CFP. Transfers from the airport to Teahupoo cost 3000 CFP per person return, and it costs 1400 CFP from the Teahupoo pier. There are kayaks and pirogues for guests' use, and surfers can be ferried out to the waves for 700 CFP to 900 CFP. Various other excursions are offered.

Te Pari Village (☎/fax 42 59 12; bungalows with full board per person 9500 CFP), 10 minutes by boat from the Teahupoo pier, is in the middle of a magnificent coconut grove beside the lagoon. It's a place for a complete escape. Various expeditions to the end of the island can be organised and daily excursions are included in the price.

Meherio Iti (☎/fax 52 17 50; PK11.9; singles/doubles 6000/8000 CFP), on the south coast beside the lagoon, has three well-equipped bungalows. Half-board is available. Various activities can be organised and airport transfers cost 1000 CFP per person.

Chez Jeannine (☎/fax 57 07 49; PK4; doubles 5000 CFP, bungalows 7900 CFP) is an isolated place on the plateau road with beautiful views of the isthmus. There's a well-kept main building with a few clean rooms, and four large, separate bungalows. There's a small swimming pool and the setting is green and pleasant. Bungalows are also available for rent by the month (45,000 CFP). Airport transfers are available. Credit cards are accepted.

Auberge Te Pari (☎ 57 13 44; mains 1800-3300 CFP; open lunch Sat-Thur) is in Teahupoo, at the end of the road and right beside the beach. There's a pleasant seaside terrace. Crustaceans are the house speciality – count on 8600 CFP for a seafood platter for two. The restaurant is open for dinner on demand. Credit cards are accepted.

Restaurant l'Eurasienne (open Fri-Wed), part of Chez Jeannine, serves Vietnamese, Chinese and French dishes, and is a clean, airy restaurant.

Mo'orea

pop 14,230

This is the island paradise you've been daydreaming about all winter: mountains that leap almost vertically out of the clear lagoon; lush vegetation; restaurants dripping in fresh fish; stylish accommodation; and a languid pace of life. When you have to leave you'll be kicking and screaming.

Transport from Tahiti is absurdly easy, so you've no excuse but to spend, at the very least, a day or two on this veritable gem of an island. If idling away the days ceases to do it for you, there are challenging walks, scuba diving, snorkelling, and interesting marae to keep you entertained.

The island remains seductive to artists, disenfranchised *popaa* (Westerners) and Tahitians, many of whom treat Mo'orea as a weekender *par excellence*. Although the island retains a palpable air of traditional Polynesia, and locals pride themselves on having avoided the jam-packed development of Bora Bora, the island is dominated by tourism. But you can still tuck a *tiare* (fragrant white flower) behind the ear and jump on a bicycle and head south, where hotels are rare and islanders eke out a quiet existence.

Live it up in style or visit on the cheap: the island has a healthy dash of deluxe hotels, but shoestringers can also find comfortable places to rest their weary limbs after a day of sunburnt fun.

History

The island's ancient name was Aimeho (sometimes spelt Eimeo). Some say that Mo'orea, which means 'golden lizard', was the name of one of the ruling families of the island, while others attribute this name to an image seen by a high priest while visiting the island.

Before the Europeans arrived on the island's idyllic doorstep, Mo'orea was heavily populated. Samuel Wallis was the first European to sight the island (1767), and he was soon followed by Louis-Antoine de Bougainville (1768) and James Cook (1769). The missionaries arrived on the scene in the early 1800s and made themselves at home, soon establishing their headquarters on the island (see Papetoai, later in this chapter). As elsewhere, European diseases,

Highlights

- Splashing around the shallows of the aqua lagoon
- Devouring sweet, juicy pineapples, fresh from the island's plantations
- Getting the blood pumping on a guided hike in the fecund interior
- Cycling around the magnificent Cook's and Opunohu Bays
- Exploring the remote southern coast of the island

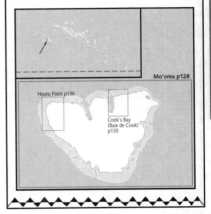

Mo'orea p128

Hauru Point p136

Cook's Bay (Baie de Cook) p135

and the introduction of weapons and alcohol, had a disastrous effect on the population of Mo'orea, which continued to decline during the 19th century.

Copra and vanilla have been important crops in the past; today Mo'orea is the pineapple-growing centre of French Polynesia, and tourism is the island's other major industry. Development on Mo'orea is an unstoppable beast, but the island has managed to maintain a tranquillity lacking in its more developed neighbours, Tahiti and Bora Bora.

Geography & Geology

Mo'orea is an extinct volcano. Cook's Bay (Baie de Cook) and Opunohu Bay (Baie d'Opunohu) mark the floor of the ancient crater, and if you follow the trail from the Opunohu Valley up to Three Coconut Trees Pass, you stand very clearly on the knife edge of the old crater rim.

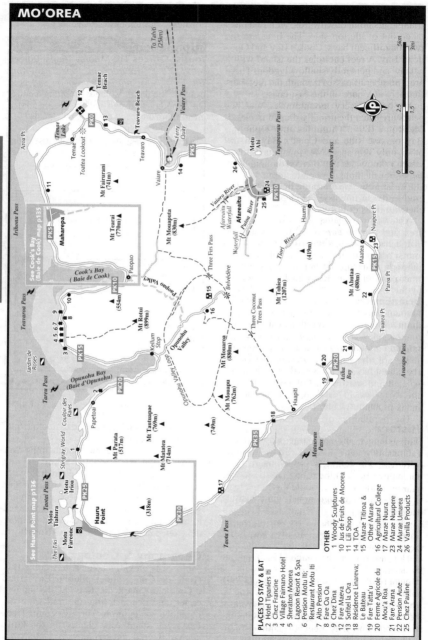

MO'OREA

PLACES TO STAY & EAT
2 Hotel Tipaniers Iti
3 Chez Francine
4 Village Faimano Hotel
5 Sheraton Moorea
   Lagoon Resort & Spa
6 Pension Motu Iti;
   Restaurant Motu Iti
7 Aito Pension
8 Fare Oa Oa
9 Chez Dina
12 Fare Maeva
13 Sofitel Ia Ora
18 Résidence Linareva;
   Le Bateau
19 Fare Tatta'u
20 Ferme Agricole du
   Mou'a Roa
21 Fare Arana
22 Pension Aute
25 Chez Pauline

OTHER
1 Woody Sculptures
10 Jus de Fruits de Moorea
11 Lili Shop
14 TOA
15 Marae Titiroa &
   Other Marae
16 Agricultural College
17 Marae Nuura
23 Marae Nuupere
24 Marae Umarea
26 Vanilla Products

The island is shaped like an equilateral triangle, its point downwards, with two bites taken out of the top side. The bites are the two magnificent bays, Cook's Bay and Opunohu Bay. A reef encircles the island with a narrow and generally shallow lagoon. There are a number of passes through the reef, particularly at Vaiare on the east coast.

Mo'orea is very mountainous, and her peaks are often theatrically draped in cloud. Mt Rotui (899m) tumbles into Opunohu Bay on one side and Cook's Bay on the other, only 3km apart. Mt Mouaputa (830m), which is known as the 'pierced mountain', is famed for the hole through its top.

The largely impenetrable interior is covered in dense forests of *mape*, the gigantic chestnut trees of Polynesia.

As on most French Polynesian islands, great beaches are rare; the only ones worthy of the name are at Hauru Point, the main tourist area, and at Temae, near the airport, although there are tempting little strips in other parts of the island, too.

Orientation

The coastal road that rings the island is about 60km right around. Depending on your energy and fitness level, the circuit can be made in one very sweaty day by bicycle (there are, thankfully, few hills to tackle). The southern coast of the island is far more isolated and sees much less traffic. If your hire car or bicycle is going to break down, this is probably where it will do it!

The population of Mo'orea is concentrated in the villages around the coast, including Paopao, Papetoai, Haapiti, Afareaitu, Vaiare and Maharepa. With its frenetic ferry quay, Vaiare is the busiest part of the island, but Afareaitu is the administrative headquarters.

Dense tourist development is in two strips: one from Maharepa down the eastern side of Cook's Bay to Paopao, the other around Hauru Point on the northwestern corner of the island.

The airport is at the northeastern corner of the island.

Adhering to French Polynesian logic, the *pointe kilométrique* (PK; kilometre point) markers start at 0 at the airport and go round the coast in both clockwise and anticlockwise directions; they meet at Haapiti (which is therefore at PK24 along the southern –

clockwise – route, and PK37 along the northern – anticlockwise – route).

Information

Tourist Offices The **Moorea Tourist Bureau** (☎ 56 29 09; Hauru Point; open 8am-4pm Tue-Thur, 8am-3pm Fri, 8am-noon Sat) is in front of Le Petit Village shopping centre. On Monday you can call ☎ 56 38 53 for information.

Money The Banque Socredo across from the quay at Vaiare has an automatic teller machine (ATM). There are banks (Banque Socredo, Banque de Tahiti and Banque de Polynésie) and ATMs clustered around the small shopping centre in Maharepa at PK6.3. In Le Petit Village (the Hauru Point shopping centre) there's a Banque de Polynésie and an ATM.

The rates are generally not as good here as on Tahiti, so consider changing or withdrawing money before you arrive.

Post & Communications There is a **post office** (open 7.30am-noon & 1.30pm-4pm Mon-Thur, 7.30am-3pm Fri, 7.30am-9.30am Sat) at the Maharepa shopping centre (see Cook's Bay map). Mo'orea's other post office is in Papetoai, just before Hauru Point.

Phone booths can be found all around the island, and often at hotels. As elsewhere in French Polynesia, phones do not accept coins; phonecards are available at some supermarkets, petrol stations and newsagencies, as well as at some hotels.

Internet has finally found its way to Mo'orea. **Maria@Tapas** (☎ 55 01 70; e maria tapas@mail.pf; PK5; open 8am-11pm Mon-Wed, 8am-1am Thur-Sat) in the Centre Kikipa has fast connections and friendly staff, and charges 500 CFP per half-hour.

A small **tabac** (café; open Mon-Sat until 5pm) in Paopao on the lagoon side has three computers with Internet access and charges 500 CFP per half-hour.

Le Petit Village in Hauru Point has two Internet places: **Tiki@Net** (☎ 56 39 42) is open until about 6pm daily; **Restaurant Iguane Rock Café** (☎ 56 17 16) is open until midnight daily.

Medical Services Your hotel should be your first point of call if you need medical assistance. There is only one hospital on the

MO'OREA

island, the **Moorea Hospital** (☎ 56 23 23, 56 24 24), which is in Afareaitu.

There's a **pharmacy** (☎ 56 10 51; PK6.5; open 7.30am-12pm & 2pm-6pm Mon-Fri, 8am-12pm & 3.30pm-6pm Sat, 8am-11am Sun & public holidays) in Maharepa (see Cook's Bay map), not far from the Centre Kikipa. There's another **pharmacy** (open Mon-Sat & Sun morning) at PK31.

AROUND THE ISLAND

The following circuit starts at the airport and moves in an anticlockwise direction, following the northern PK markers.

Temae (PK1)

This village, which is well inland from the coast – unusual in Polynesia – has long been famed for its dancers. If you manage to time your visit with the July *heiva* festivities, you may well see dancers from this village gyrating on Tahiti. See the special section 'Tahitian Dance'.

Maharepa (PK4 to PK5)

Technicolour pareu, floating in the breeze like an artist's washing line, announce the beginning of Maharepa village at the Lili Shop.

The early-20th-century **Maison Blanche** (PK5) is a fine example of a *fare vanira*, a plantation house from Mo'orea's vanilla-boom era. Just past the Moorea Pearl Resort, the Maison Blanche is now a souvenir shop with a fairly typical selection of pareu and Balinese wood carvings.

From 1860 to 1960, vanilla dominated the island's economy, but a vanilla-crop disease brought the trade to a sorry end. Today, hardly any vanilla is produced on Mo'orea. See the boxed text 'Taha'a – the Vanilla Island' in the Ra'iatea & Taha'a chapter.

Cook's Bay to Paopao (PK6 to PK9)

The spectacular Cook's Bay (Baie de Cook) is something of a misnomer because Cook actually anchored in Opunohu Bay (Baie d'Opunohu). With Mt Rotui as a backdrop, Cook's Bay is a lovely stretch of water; it is also one of Mo'orea's main tourist centres (the other being Hauru Point). There's no real centre to the Cook's Bay shops, restaurants and hotels, there's simply a handful of them dotted along the road. As you head east, Cook's Bay merges with Maharepa.

La Poterie de l'Aquarium – Teva Yrondi is an interesting jewellery and pottery shop and garden, and **Galerie van der Heyde** has a collection of oceanic art set around a pleasant garden.

At the base of Cook's Bay is the sleepy village of Paopao. This is where the *Ono-Ono* docks, and there's the former **fish market** and a few shops here. Even though the fish market is no more, you can still see the wall mural painted by Mo'orea-based artist François Ravello.

Just before the bridge in Paopao is an **entertainment area** that, come evening, is full of locals and tacky rides, particularly during the month of the *heiva* celebrations. There are small snack stalls, and it's quite a fun area to wander through.

Settlements are creeping up the Paopao Valley but the principal activity is still agriculture, with many hectares of pineapple plantations. The road leading inland from Paopao and Cook's Bay meets the Opunohu Valley road, just before the agricultural college and the walking track up to the Three Coconut Trees Pass (see Hiking in the Outdoor Activities chapter). A small *fare* at the agricultural college sells delicious ice creams in local flavours. The road then continues inland and up to the marae sites and finally to the *belvédère* (lookout), on the slopes of Mt Tohiea (1207m).

Jus de Fruits de Moorea (PK11)

About 300m inland from the coastal road, the Jus de Fruits de Moorea (Fruit Juices of Moorea; ☎ 56 11 33; admission free; open 8.30am-4.30pm Mon-Sat) makes for a welcome thirst-quenching stop, particularly if you have been riding a bike around the island. The various fruit liqueurs won't do you much good (although they are delicious), but a bottle of 100% pineapple juice (320 CFP) is the perfect tonic. This place is owned by the omnipotent Coca-Cola company.

Opunohu Bay (PK14 to PK18)

Even with the occasional truck thundering by, Opunohu Bay (Baie d'Opunohu) is definitely worth cycling around – it still feels wonderfully fresh and isolated. The coastal road rounds Mt Rotui, and at about PK14 turns inland along the eastern side of Opunohu Bay. There is less development along here than around Cook's Bay, and Opunohu

Bay is spectacularly beautiful. Most of the Polynesian scenes in the 1984 *Bounty* movie were shot on Opunohu Bay.

Kellum Stop (☎ *56 18 52; PK17.5*) is almost at the top of the bay; a small sign on the mountain side of the road indicates the turn-off. In 1925, Medford Kellum came to Polynesia with six scientists from the Bishop Museum in Hawaii, including Kenneth Emory (who subsequently spent over a year in the region studying ancient Polynesian marae). Kellum ended up buying land in the Opunohu Valley, which facilitated Emory's early archaeological investigations on Mo'orea. The Kellum's daughter Marimari still sometimes conducts personal tours around the gardens of her house, which are dense with local plants and flowers. Visitors are welcome, but try to call ahead; a stroll around the garden costs 500 CFP.

At PK18, right at the top of the bay, a road turns off inland along the Opunohu Valley to the valley marae, the *belvédère* and the walking route to Three Coconut Trees Pass.

Papetoai (PK22)
A busy little village with a post office and a number of restaurants, Papetoai was established as the Pacific headquarters of the London Missionary Society (LMS) in 1811. In the 1870s, the missionaries constructed an octagonal **church** at Papetoai; today this is the oldest-standing European building in the South Pacific. As was often the case, the missionaries deliberately built this church atop an old marae. A single spike-like stone is the sole reminder of the ancient Marae Taputapuatea, dedicated to the god 'Oro.

Hauru Point (PK25 to PK30)
The coastal road rounds Hauru Point, the northwestern corner of the island, between PK25 and PK30. This is one of the island's major tourist enclaves. Addresses can be a little confusing here as the area is often referred to as Haapiti, because it's in the Haapiti district, even though the village of Haapiti is well to the south. The tourist strip starts with the Moorea Beachcomber Intercontinental Resort at about PK25, and finishes at around PK31.

Hauru Point has one of the best **beaches** on the island, a narrow but sandy stretch that extends for about 5km. Finding your way to the beach is not easy because the area is so built-up along here. But all beaches are public property in French Polynesia and the hotel proprietors do not seem to mind if you walk through their grounds.

Immediately offshore are **Motu Tiahura** and **Motu Fareone**, attractive little islets so close to the shore you can easily swim out to them and enjoy fine snorkelling on the way. A little further east is the tiny **Motu Irioa**. Remember that the actual motu are private (although the littoral areas aren't).

Marae Nuurua (PK31.5)
Marae Nuurua is right on the water's edge, just past the end of a football field. There's an impressive wall of coral boulders at the water's edge, and a restored three-level structure. This is flanked by twin spike-like, upright stones with clear **petroglyphs**. Despite neglect and its relatively populated setting, it's a very evocative ruin, overgrown with vegetation and surrounded by coconut trees. Marae Nuurua was dedicated to the god Ta'aroa, popular before the 'Oro cult developed (see the special section 'Civilisation & Archaeology').

Haapiti to Atiha Bay (PK30 to PK20)
The largest village on the west coast, **Haapiti** boasts two **churches**. The small grey-trimmed church in the centre of the village is dwarfed by the huge twin-towered Catholic Église de la Sainte Famille, which is made of coral and lime. Haapiti's Matauvau Pass has a popular surf break.

Mo'orea's lazy west-coast atmosphere continues round to **Atiha Bay** (Baie d'Atiha), a quiet fishing village that also attracts surfers.

Marae Nuupere (PK14)
Nuupere Point is immediately southwest of Maatea village; Marae Nuupere stands just 100m or so south of the point. All that remains is a massive coastal cairn of coral boulders, and it stands on private property. The property owner is not enthusiastic about visitors, so permission must be obtained before entering the property (ask at the tourist office in Hauru Point).

Afareaitu (PK10)
Afareaitu is the administrative centre of the island, but don't blink or you'll miss it. Chez Pauline, the village's hotel, has a collection

of ancient stone tiki and other traditional artefacts. Only about 100m south of Chez Pauline is **Marae Umarea**, which is thought to date from about AD 900 and is the oldest marae on the island. Take the road that goes straight to the coast to see the marae, which is a long wall of coral boulders right along the waterfront.

Afareaitu's two **waterfalls** are a major island attraction (although they are but feeble trickles in winter). There are a few short walks available (see Hiking in the Outdoor Activities chapter for details).

Vaiare (PK4)

The constant toing and froing of ferry boats and high-speed catamarans at the ferry quay, the busy market scene, and cars, taxis and le trucks shuttling visitors around, renders the 100m or so near the dock area the busiest patch of real estate on Mo'orea.

Vaiare is the starting point for the interesting walk across the ridge to Paopao and Cook's Bay.

Teavaro & Temae Beaches (PK1 to PK0)

The best beaches on the east coast stretch from Teavaro round to the airport. The Sofitel Ia Ora hotel occupies **Teavaro Beach**, where there's good snorkelling in the shallow water. **Temae Beach** is close to the end of the airport runway and is a pleasant stretch of sand, but it is often blighted by litter. When the swells run from the south, the reef at the southern end of the runway can have the most powerful waves in French Polynesia.

A road on the lagoon side of the runway extends around **Temae Lake**, almost to Aroa Point, but the route is cut off by the swampy inlet so it is not possible to rejoin the main coastal road.

Paopao & Opunohu Valleys

From Mo'orea's two great bays, valleys sweep inland, meeting south of the coastal bulk of Mt Rotui. In the pre-European era the valleys were densely populated and the Opunohu Valley was dotted with marae, some of which have been restored and maintained. The great marae sites of Titiroa and Afareaito were extensively reconstructed by Dr Yoshihiko Shinoto in 1967. All marae seem to attract mosquitoes and these ones are no exception. Bring insect repellent or expect to

have difficulty withstanding their onslaught while you read the information boards!

Archaeological Sites The Opunohu Valley has the greatest number of marae in French Polynesia, and these archaeological sites are among the most important in French Polynesia. Unusually, you can walk to them along marked tracks and there are explanatory panels in French and English. The complex includes a range of partially restored remains including family and communal marae as well as dwellings, archery platforms and other structures.

It's believed the valley was continuously inhabited for six centuries, and the oldest surviving structures date from the 13th century. This agricultural community reached its apogee in the 17th and 18th centuries. The first excavations date from 1925. In 1960, Roger Green did the most complete research on the area, and 500 structures have been inventoried. See the special section 'Civilisation & Archaeology' for more information on marae.

Marae Titiroa & Other Marae Past the agricultural college, the valley road comes to a parking area beside the huge **Marae Titiroa**, on the edge of a dense forest of magnificent *mape* (chestnut) trees. From the marae a walking track leads to the *tohua* (council platform), and two smaller marae. From there the track continues to the **Marae Ahu-o-Mahine**, a more recent marae of individually hewn round stones with an imposing three-stepped *ahu* (altar). You can cross the small water course running down the valley to discover other more modest marae.

A short distance along the road from Marae Titiroa is **Marae Afareaito**. Although there is a walking path between these two, it is not easy to follow; the main road is an easier route. The large marae has a small, raised-terrace *ahu* and back rests that were used by the priests. The marae is flanked by two crescent-shaped archery platforms from which competing archers would shoot their arrows down a cleared range. Archery was strictly a pastime of the nobility and was a ritual sport: bows and arrows were not used in battle.

Belvédère Beyond Marae Afareaito the road continues to climb steeply, winding its way up to the *belvédère*. This lookout offers superb views of Mt Rotui, which splits the two bays, and back to the towering mountains that rise in the centre of the island and once formed the southern rim of the ancient crater.

ACTIVITIES

It is wise to book activities as soon as you arrive on the island; contact organisers directly or check with your hotel or guesthouse. Many of the bigger hotels, including **Sheraton Moorea Lagoon Resort & Spa** (☎ 55 10 19); **Moorea Beachcomber Intercontinental Resort** (☎ 55 19 19, ext 1903) and **Sofitel la Ora** (☎ 55 03 55), have activities desks.

Water Activities

Prepare yourself for soggy fingers and toes: you'll probably spend as much time in the water as out of it on Mo'orea. There are several beaches that are ideal for swimming, and you can even swim across to the two motu north of Hauru Point. For the best **snorkelling**, join an organised lagoon tour.

To the north of the island, there is some great **diving** for beginners and more experienced divers, both inside and outside the reef. The island has a number of dive centres. **Aqua Blue** (☎ 56 53 53, fax 56 42 51; e aquablue_pf@hotmail.com) in the Moorea Beachcomber Intercontinental Resort allows you to walk along the sea bed in the relatively shallow water at Papetoai's lagoon wearing a *scaphandre* (weighted helmet) into which air is pumped. A diving monitor accompanies you and, since you actually walk on the bottom, you don't even need to be able to swim. **Galaxsea** (☎/fax 56 58 55; e galaxsea@magicmoorea.com) offers a similar service.

Dolphin Quest (☎ 55 19 48) in the Moorea Beachcomber Intercontinental Resort has dolphins in an enclosed basin, where you can have a 'shallow water encounter'. Obviously this is a totally unnatural experience for the dolphins, and it doesn't come cheap for humans (adults/children 16,500/9900 CFP; snorkelling with the dolphins costs 18,700 CFP).

Dolphin & Whale Watching Expeditions (☎ 56 14 70) has a very different approach from Dolphin Quest. Several times a week, Dr Michael Poole takes people on a morning or afternoon boat trip to observe and research dolphins and whales around Mo'orea.

Mahana Tours (☎ 56 20 44, fax 56 38 66) offers boat tours to see dolphins and, in the right season, whales.

Cycling

Mo'orea is a great island to cycle around. Doing the 60km circuit in a day is possible (depending on the state of those thighs), although tiring, particularly given the rather sorry state of the bikes available.

Rando-Cycles (☎ 56 51 99; e randocycles@ mail.pf) has bikes for hire and also offers mountain-bike tours. Many of the hotels also have bikes for their guests to use. **Europcar** (☎ 56 34 00; e europcar-moorea@mail.pf) can also organise bike hire.

Hiking

Mt Rotui and Mt Mouaputa, the Afareaitu waterfalls, the Three Coconut Trees Pass and the Vaiare–Paopao route are exhilarating hikes, of varying difficulty, that tackle the lush inland areas. Some of the trails are not often used and are poorly marked, so it's wise to use a guide. See the Outdoor Activities chapter for information on hiking.

Horse Riding

Tiahura Ranch (☎ 56 28 55) at Hauru Point in front of the Moorea Village Hotel offers two-hour guided rides into the island's interior for 4500 CFP.

Moorea Beachcomber Intercontinental Resort (☎ 55 19 55, ext 1903) offers horse riding for 5800 CFP for two hours.

Other Activities

For **game fishing** aboard the *Tea Nui*, contact the Moorea Beachcomber Intercontinental Resort's **activities desk** (☎ 55 19 19, ext 1903). A half-day trip costs 15,400 CFP per person (minimum of four participants).

Go to the same activities desk for **parasailing**, which costs 6640 CFP per person for 10- to 15-minute flights.

Jet-ski tours can be organised by the Sofitel Ia Ora, Moorea Beachcomber Intercontinental Resort, Moorea Village Hotel and Club Bali Hai.

For helicopter flights over Mo'orea, contact **Héli Pacific** (☎ 85 68 00) or **Héli Inter Polynésie** (☎ 81 99 00).

To hire a boat, contact **Moorea Locaboat** (☎ 78 13 39; 2 hours 6000 CFP, 8 hours 10,000 CFP).

MO'OREA

ORGANISED TOURS
Lagoon Tours
The best way to discover Mo'orea's magnificent lagoon is by joining a lagoon excursion in a pirogue with outboard motor. Tours typically visit the two bays, stop to feed the sharks, swim with the rays and picnic and snorkel on Motu Fareone. The costs vary from operator to operator, so shop around a bit to see what's on offer. For a six-hour trip of shark and ray feeding, and a picnic on a motu, you'll pay around 6000 CFP; a four-hour tour of the island by boat costs 4000 CFP. Again, your first port of call should probably be your hotel or guesthouse.

4WD Tours
Several operators organise island tours aboard open 4WDs. There are complete tours of the island with visits to the archaeological sites in the Opunohu Valley, stops at the *belvédère* and the Afareaitu waterfalls and visits to pineapple and vanilla plantations and the fruit-juice factory. The three-hour tours cost around 4500 CFP per person and are good value if you're by yourself or don't want to rent a car. Check that you have a mutual language with the guide. Operators include **What to do on Moorea** (☎ 56 57 64; *wtdMoorea@mail.pf*), **Torea Nui Safari** (☎ 56 12 48, fax 56 15 05), **Inner Island Safari Tours** (☎ 56 20 09), **Ron's Adventure** (☎ 56 42 43), **Tefaarahi Safari Tours** (☎ 78 82 61) and **Albert Transport & Activities** (☎ 56 13 53, fax 56 40 58; e albert transport@mail.pf).

PLACES TO STAY
If you've just arrived from Tahiti, you'll be pleasantly surprised by accommodation on Mo'orea. You won't have the roaring traffic (though you will have roaring mosquitos – whip out that tropical-strength insect repellent), and even the budget places often have lovely garden settings.

Although there is accommodation scattered around the island, most is concentrated on the eastern side of Cook's Bay and around Hauru Point. Both these centres are very spread out; if you're staying at one end and want to eat at the other, it's not a case of just wandering a few steps along the road.

Mo'orea has superb over-water bungalows, but it also has the best selection of budget (by local standards, of course!) *pensions* (guesthouses) in French Polynesia. There are backpacker places with camp sites and dorm facilities; quaint and artistic little *pensions;* some cheaper hotels; and a host of local-style bungalow complexes that generally have a small kitchen.

Note that while most places will supply sheets and other bedding, towels are often not provided in the cheapest places. All top-end places and most of the mid-range places accept credit cards; most budget places don't. In the mid-range and top-end world of bungalows with garden, beach and overwater settings, the rule is that the closer you get to the water, the higher the rate soars.

As elsewhere in the book, we have included the government taxes in the prices cited. When in Polynesia, you will generally be quoted before-tax prices for accommodation (bear in the mind the *taxe de séjour* or accommodation tax is priced per person).

Cook's Bay
The magnificent Cook's Bay (Baie de Cook) does not have any beach, but is the quieter, less-touristy sister to Hauru Point.

Motel Albert (☎ 56 12 76, fax 56 58 58; *PK7; units for 3/4 people from 4300/8600 CFP*), on the mountain side of the road at Cook's Bay, is one of the best budget places on the island. The units here are spacious, have kitchen and bathroom with hot water, and are set in a lush garden full of roosters and kids. There's an extra charge of 1000 CFP if you stay just one night, but reductions are offered for stays of more than a few days. Staff are welcoming and speak English. If you're preparing your own food, there are several places to shop nearby, and there's free grapefruit on offer when it's in season.

Club Bali Hai (☎ 56 13 68, fax 56 13 27; e *reservations@clubbalihai.pf;* w *www.club balihai.com; doubles 15,700-17,900 CFP, bungalows 24,600-32,300 CFP*), just across from Motel Albert, is a stylish, breezy spot with views of Mt Rotui. There's a swimming pool and tennis court, and the restaurant, L'Ananas Bleu, is a great spot for breakfast or lunch (although it can get quite windy). This place is very popular with American travellers, and you can still have a drink with one of the American 'Bali Hai boys' for a sundowner and interesting chat about Mo'orea in the 1960s.

Kaveka Hotel (☎ 56 50 50, fax 56 52 63; e kaveka@mail.pf; bungalows 9800-22,000 CFP) has nice dark-wood bungalows set in a well-tended garden. Half-board, with meals at the hotel's pleasant restaurant, the Fisherman's Wharf (see Places to Eat, later), is an extra 4000 CFP per person; return transfers to the airport or ferry quay cost 1200 CFP.

Moorea Pearl Resort (☎ 50 84 52; doubles 26,800-31,200 CFP, garden/beach/over-water bungalows 36,800/54,500/65,600 CFP) has recently opened and occupies the site of the old Bali Hai Moorea. The end result is quite spectacular, although of course it lacks the history of the old Bali Hai. The bungalows are worth the extra money. There are plans afoot to have soirees twice a week, and every activity under the sun can be arranged.

Cook's Bay to Hauru Point

Doilies reign supreme at **Chez Dina** (☎ 56 10 39; PK12.5; bungalows for 2/4/5 people 6400/7100/8500 CFP), a delightful, homey place on the mountain side of the road.

Fare Oa Oa (☎ 56 25 17; e fareoaoa@ magicmoorea.com; singles/doubles 2600/3900 CFP, dorm bed 1800 CFP) is a charming, eccentric place on the mountain side on the road. There's not much privacy, but there's as much character and style as you could hope for. There are four rooms that all share a clean bathroom (with hot water) and lovely kitchen area. There's a public phone, and Hervé, le patron, will even do your washing if you stay a few days.

Aito Pension (☎/fax 56 45 52; Plage de Pihaena; doubles 5900-13,300 CFP) is delightfully dilapidated. Rooms have a distinct home-made feel about them, but the bigger room with a terrace and the two-storey room (with picturesque garden bathroom) are very comfortable.

Pension Motu Iti (☎ 55 05 20, fax 55 05 21; e pensionmotuiti@mail.pf; garden/beach bungalows 10,500/12,000 CFP) has not been open long but has already created a wonderful atmosphere; the restaurant here is also lovely. You couldn't punch the smile off the owners' face (not that we tried). Corners have not been cut: it's a great choice.

Sheraton Moorea Lagoon Resort & Spa (☎ 55 11 11, reservations 86 48 49; garden/beach/over-water bungalows 42,300/71,300/80,100 CFP) is every bit as deluxe as its sis-

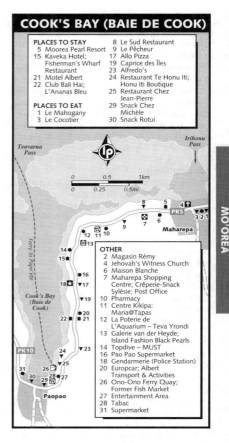

COOK'S BAY (BAIE DE COOK)

PLACES TO STAY		8	Le Sud Restaurant
5	Moorea Pearl Resort	9	Le Pêcheur
15	Kaveka Hotel;	17	Allo Pizza
	Fisherman's Wharf	19	Caprice des Îles
	Restaurant	23	Alfredo's
21	Motel Albert	24	Restaurant Te Honu Iti;
22	Club Bali Hai;		Honu Iti Boutique
	L'Ananas Bleu	25	Restaurant Chez
			Jean-Pierre
PLACES TO EAT		29	Snack Chez
1	Le Mahogany		Michèle
3	Le Cocotier	30	Snack Rotui

OTHER
2 Magasin Rémy
4 Jehovah's Witness Church
6 Maison Blanche
7 Maharepa Shopping Centre; Crêperie-Snack Sylésie; Post Office
10 Pharmacy
11 Centre Kikipa; Maria@Tapas
12 La Poterie de L'Aquarium – Teva Yrondi
13 Galerie van der Heyde; Island Fashion Black Pearls
14 Topdive – MUST
16 Pao Pao Supermarket
18 Gendarmerie (Police Station)
20 Europcar; Albert Transport & Activities
26 Ono-Ono Ferry Quay; Former Fish Market
27 Entertainment Area
28 Tabac
31 Supermarket

ters in Tahiti and Bora Bora (although you may think that the claw-toed baths here put it in first place). The resort is on one of the few bits of beach along this strip.

Village Faimano Hotel (☎ 56 10 20, fax 56 36 47; e faimanodenis@mail.pf; bungalows for 2/3/6 people from 9600/9200/13,600 CFP) has very comfortable bungalows, all with kitchen and bathroom. You are required to stay at least three nights; there are reductions on offer for longer stays. Credit cards are accepted.

Chez Francine (☎ 56 13 24; bungalows 12,500 CFP) is close to PK14 and has a big garden right by the lagoon. This place is so private you won't be able to find it alone; call ahead for directions. Rates drop dramatically after a week, and you'll find a barbecue and a pirogue available for guests' use. The owner will drive guests to the shops to stock up every other day.

Hotel Tipaniers Iti (☎ 56 12 67, fax 56 29 25; bungalows 9100 CFP) is the isolated little sister of Les Tipaniers Hotel Restaurant at Hauru Point. It's an impeccably clean and quiet spot; all the bungalows have kitchen, sitting area, bathroom and veranda. Guests can participate in the main hotels' activities, and a free shuttle runs to the Les Tipaniers restaurant in the evening.

Hauru Point

Unlike Cook's Bay, Hauru Point has a pleasant beach, although it's rather narrow and access is not easy, and the idyllic motu are just off shore. The downside is this strip can feel quite crowded.

Camping Chez Nelson (☎ 56 15 18; w www.camping-nelson.pf; PK27; tent sites per person 1100 CFP, dorm beds 1600 CFP, doubles 4300 CFP, bungalows 3400-4500 CFP), by the beach, is very popular with backpackers. Prices drop if you stay more than one night. This place is very basic, and the welcome is sometimes rather cool.

Moorea Camping (☎ 56 14 47, fax 56 30 22; PK27.5; tent sites per person 1000 CFP, dorm beds 1200 CFP, bungalows 4500-6000 CFP) is another place popular with shoestring travellers. However, the staff are remarkably unhelpful, the tents are crammed in next to one another, and the communal bathrooms are of dubious cleanliness. There are some decent, shady communal areas.

Fare Auti'rua (☎ 56 14 47; 2-/4-person bungalows 7000/10,000 CFP, 2 nights minimum) is the more upmarket section of Moorea Camping (and you may find the management is less than accommodating). There are comfortable and spacious bungalows with mezzanine, bathroom and equipped kitchen. There's a two-night minimum stay. Guests can access the beach via Moorea Camping. Credit cards are accepted.

Chez Billy Ruta (☎ 56 12 54; PK28; bungalows with/without kitchen 6800/5700 CFP) is right on the water, but the bungalows, which are lined up side by side along the beach, are very rudimentary.

Les Tipaniers Hotel Restaurant (☎ 56 12 67, fax 56 29 25; e tipaniersresa@mail.pf; bungalows with/without kitchen from 15,000/ 9000 CFP) is on the outskirts of the Hauru

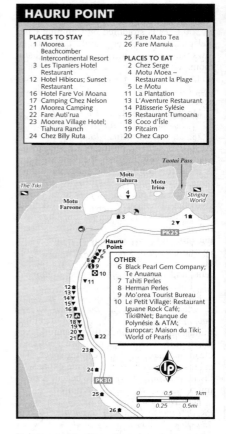

HAURU POINT

PLACES TO STAY	25 Fare Mato Tea
1 Moorea Beachcomber Intercontinental Resort	26 Fare Manuia
3 Les Tipaniers Hotel Restaurant	**PLACES TO EAT**
12 Hotel Hibiscus; Sunset Restaurant	2 Chez Serge
16 Hotel Fare Voi Moana	4 Motu Moea – Restaurant la Plage
17 Camping Chez Nelson	5 Le Motu
21 Moorea Camping	11 La Plantation
22 Fare Auti'rua	13 L'Aventure Restaurant
23 Moorea Village Hotel; Tiahura Ranch	14 Pâtisserie Sylésie
24 Chez Billy Ruta	15 Restaurant Tumoana
	18 Coco d'Île
	19 Pitcairn
	20 Chez Capo

OTHER
6 Black Pearl Gem Company; Te Anuanua
7 Tahiti Perles
8 Herman Perles
9 Mo'orea Tourist Bureau
10 Le Petit Village: Restaurant Iguane Rock Café; Tiki@Net; Banque de Polynésie & ATM; Europcar; Maison du Tiki; World of Pearls

Point area. Its bungalows are in a garden leading down to the beach, where there's a restaurant and bar and fine views of the motu (see Places to Eat, later). The thatched-roof bungalows have a veranda, small lounge area and bathroom; some have kitchen. Credit cards are accepted.

Hotel Hibiscus (☎ 56 12 20, fax 56 20 69; e hibiscus@mail.pf; PK27; garden/beach bungalows 14,800/17,200 CFP) has 29 very functional and slightly spartan thatched-roof bungalows in a pleasant garden. They all have three beds, attached hot-water bathroom, veranda and kitchen. The Sunset Restaurant on the beach is quite good (see Places to Eat, later) and there's a swimming pool. Half-/full board adds 5300/8300 CFP per person. Credit cards are accepted.

MO'OREA

Hotel Fare Vai Moana *(☎/fax 56 17 14; PK27.5; garden/beach bungalows 13,200/17,500 CFP)* is straddled by Camping Chez Nelson and has 13 very comfortable bungalows with refrigerator, mezzanine and bathroom with hot water; each accommodates up to four people. There's a restaurant here (see Places to Stay, later). Credit cards are accepted.

Moorea Village Hotel *(Fare Gendron; ☎ 56 10 02, fax 56 22 11; e mooreavillage@mail.pf; PK28; bungalows with/without kitchen from 20,300/10,700 FP)*, on the beach side of the road, has lovely English-speaking staff and is ideal for families. The fairly functional bungalows all have bathroom with hot water, fan and refrigerator; the more expensive ones also have kitchen. Half-/full board adds 4600/5800 CFP per person. The site is rather crowded but hedges and trees break the monotony. You'll find a tennis court, swimming pool, bar and restaurant; bicycles, pedal boats and kayaks are available to rent, and motu excursions are organised. The hotel accepts credit cards.

Fare Mato Tea *(☎ 54 14 36, fax 56 32 54; e mtt@mail.pf; PK28.7; bungalows for 4/6 people 9100/10,700 CFP)* is out of the hub of things, and feels wonderfully tranquil, even when full. The bungalows are spotlessly clean and have lots of sleeping space. The cabins are dotted around a wide expanse of lawn, sweeping down to the beach. A minimum stay of two nights is required.

Fare Manuia *(☎ 56 26 17, fax 56 10 30; PK30; bungalows for 4/6 people 10,200/13,000 CFP)* has a sunny stretch of beach. There are six bungalows spaced out around the grassy grounds of this kiddy-friendly place. All have bathroom with hot water, kitchen, TV and large veranda. You'll find a washing machine, a pirogue for free use and a kayak that can be rented. There's a two-night minimum stay.

Moorea Beachcomber Intercontinental Resort *(☎ 55 19 19, fax 55 19 55; e moorea@interconti.com; doubles 35,400 CFP, garden/beach/over-water bungalows 39,800/48,700/65,600 CFP)*, with its beautifully maintained grounds, is one of the most luxurious and expensive hotels on the island. There are two very civilised spots to eat here: Fare Nui is a fairly formal restaurant on the open terrace looking out at the lagoon; Fare Hana, beside the swimming pool, has a lighter menu. Every activity you could imagine is offered, as well as a few you probably couldn't imagine (such as walking along the sea bed with a weighted helmet).

Club Med is officially closed for renovations, although there is much doubt about it ever reopening.

Haapiti to Afareaitu

North of Haapiti village, near where the PK24 clockwise markers meet the PK35 anticlockwise ones, is **Résidence Linareva** *(☎ 55 05 65, fax 55 05 67; e linareva@mail.pf; w www.linareva.com; PK34.5; bungalows for 1/2/4 people from 8700/10,500/22,500 CFP)*. It has very pleasant and well-furnished bungalows in a well-kept garden by the beach. Bicycles, pirogues and snorkelling equipment are all provided free of charge. If you don't mind the somewhat isolated location, it's a great place to stay. The restaurant here, Le Bateau, has a good reputation (see Places to Eat, later).

Fare Tatta'u *(☎/fax 56 35 83; PK21.3; dorm beds 2700 CFP, bungalows 6400 CFP)* is well away from the tourist crush. There's a friendly, family atmosphere in a quiet and green location with four miniature cabins with two beds and bathroom (cold water only). Prices quoted are for more than one night. In the middle of the property is a superb *fare potee* (open dining area), which is used as a kitchen. Purotu, one of the best tattooists on Mo'orea, did much of the decoration. This place is popular with surfers because of its proximity to Haapiti's Matauvau Pass; boat rides out to the break are available.

Ferme Agricole du Mou'a Roa *(☎ 56 58 62, fax 56 40 47; e ferme.mouaroa@mail.pf; PK 21; dorm beds 2500 CFP)* is a great, ecofriendly place for those looking for calm but who are not fussed about privacy. A clean and simple colonial-style house has eight rooms with four to six beds in each. Camping is possible, and three little bungalows were in the pipeline at the time of writing. Half-board adds 3700 CFP per person. Call ahead to be picked up, as you need a 4WD to access the farm.

Fare Arana *(☎ 56 44 03; e patcoucuret@mail.pf; PK 19.5; bungalows 11,400 CFP)* is a stylish, well-equipped place on the mountain side of the road. It has a swimming pool, magnificent views and friendly staff.

MO'OREA

Pension Aute (☎/fax 56 45 19; PK 16.2; bungalows 11,400 CFP) has an amazing position on the rather wild southern side of the island. There are only two bungalows here, and the stretching horizon...

Chez Pauline (☎ 56 11 26; doubles 6000 CFP) is all by itself in the village of Afareaitu, 5km south of the Vaiare ferry quay. Opened by owner Pauline Teariki's mother in 1918, it was for many years the only hotel on the island. Although it most definitely lacks the comforts of a modern hotel, it has a historic (albeit dilapidated and dark) charm and offers a real opportunity to sample local life. There are seven rooms, sharing two bathrooms with cold water; breakfast is included in the price. The restaurant specialises in Tahitian cuisine. Credit cards are not accepted.

Temae

Looking across to Tahiti from Temae Beach, just 2km south of Mo'orea's airport, **Sofitel Ia Ora** (☎ 55 03 55, fax 56 12 91; beach/garden/over-water bungalows from 18,200/20,700/42,200 CFP) sits pretty on one of the island's best beaches. It has two restaurants: one in the garden looking across a pretty pool of lilies, and another next to the swimming pool (both are of a very high standard). All the activities you could dream of are offered, and there are three Polynesian dance performances a week.

Fare Maeva (☎/fax 56 18 10; bungalows 8100 CFP) is a charming, isolated place that is dominated by bushes, coconut trees and coral debris, giving it an atoll flavour; unfortunately it is also dominated by the arrivals and departures at the airport. All bungalows have bathroom and kitchen. There is a food store nearby. Finding this place is quite a feat – follow the signs to the Golden Nugget; Fare Maeva is about 150m further on.

PLACES TO EAT

Although Mo'orea is not quite the epicurean delight that Tahiti is, you will certainly eat well here. Cook's Bay and Hauru Point are the dining epicentres.

Most places close towards 9pm Monday to Saturday, and on Sunday the options can be surprisingly bleak. Menus are generally translated into English and some establishments will collect you from your accommodation and return you after your meal.

Restaurants & Cafés

Maharepa & Cook's Bay In the Maharepa shopping centre, **Crêperie-Snack Sylésie** (open 6am-6pm) is an ideal place for breakfast, a crepe or a modestly priced snack, but the setting is nothing special.

Le Sud Restaurant (☎ 56 42 95; e lesud .Moorea@mail.pf; mains 1100-2500 CFP; open lunch & dinner Tue-Sat, lunch Sun) is very Provençal and calm, with good food.

Le Mahogany (☎ 56 39 73; starters 600-1200 CFP, mains 1550-2450 CFP) is just past PK4 in Maharepa, and exhibits work by local artists. The menu is French with a sprinkling of Chinese. And yes, there's mahogany. Transport is offered between the Moorea Pearl Resort and Club Bali Hai. Credit cards are accepted.

Le Cocotier (☎ 56 12 10; daily specials 2050 CFP; open lunch & dinner daily), in Maharepa, specialises in French cuisine. Transport is offered anywhere between the restaurant and Sofitel Ia Ora and Cook's Bay. Credit cards are accepted.

Le Pêcheur (☎ 56 36 12; open lunch & dinner daily) specialises – surprise, surprise – in seafood. It's on the 'wrong' (ie, mountain) side of the road, but the water is just over there, and wafts of salty air mingle with the great food. The restaurant offers transport between the Moorea Pearl Resort and Village Faimano hotel.

Fisherman's Wharf Restaurant in the Kaveka Hotel (☎ 56 50 50; see Places to Stay under Cook's Bay, earlier) juts out over the lagoon and has tables arranged around a hole in the floor. The menu has a vegetarian section, a rare sight in French Polynesia.

Allo Pizza (☎ 56 18 22; pizzas 900-1500 CFP; open lunch Wed-Sun, dinner Tue-Sun) is just opposite the gendarmerie (police station), and offers about 30 different pizzas. It will even deliver in this area.

Caprice des Îles (☎ 56 44 24), in Cook's Bay, just before the Club Bali Hai, was closed 'for hollydays' when we popped in. The restaurant looks like an enormous Polynesian fare. Everything is made of coconut, including the tables, chairs and flooring. The food is French, Chinese and Tahitian. Credit cards are accepted.

L'Ananas Bleu (open breakfast & lunch daily), on the water in the Club Bali Hai, has great snacks and light lunches. The fishburger (1100 CFP) is delicious.

Alfredo's (☎ 56 17 71; mains 1450-2950 CFP; open Mon-Sat) is a popular little Italian restaurant. Rest assured that the obligatory red-and-white tablecloths are in place. Transport is offered from as far as the Moorea Pearl Resort. Credit cards are accepted.

Restaurant Te Honu Iti (☎ 56 19 84; appetizers around 1300 CFP, mains around 2600 CFP; open lunch & dinner daily), next to the Honu Iti Boutique, has excellent French food. The terrace juts over the water, and at night the water is lit up so you can watch rays and fish pottering about below you – so much entertainment you could almost neglect the stylish food. It's in a lovely building that is lit up like a Christmas tree at night.

Restaurant Chez Jean-Pierre (☎ 56 18 51; appetizers from 1050 CFP, mains from 1350 CFP; open lunch Mon, lunch & dinner Tues, Thur, Fri & Sun, dinner Sat) is in a featureless building at the very top of the bay and offers decent Chinese food. This restaurant is popular with locals and is recommended for those tiring of raw-fish dishes. Credit cards are accepted.

Snack Chez Michèle (salads 1350 CFP, mains from 1600 CFP; open lunch & dinner daily) is great little place in Paopao, just next to the bridge. The food is great and the prices are reasonable. The prawn curry (1850 CFP) is delicious.

Just near Snack Chez Michèle is **Snack Rotui**, a small snack bar.

Restaurant Motu Iti (☎ 55 05 20) in the Pension Motu Iti (see Place to Stay under Cook's Bay to Hauru Point) has great pizzas (1050 CFP) as well as Chinese and Polynesian dishes.

Hauru Point The strip along Hauru Point is teeming with places to eat.

Chez Serge (☎ 56 13 17; PK25; open lunch & dinner daily), where prices are reasonable and the welcome is friendly, has retained its focus on the home-grown, the local and the very delicious. This is one of the rare establishments where you can try *fafaru*, a delicious dessert of *poe* bananas baked in coconut milk. Credit cards are accepted.

Les Tipaniers Hotel Restaurant (☎ 56 12 67), at the hotel of the same name, combines French-Italian food with a Tahitian flavour and has a great reputation. It's a movable feast, with breakfast and lunch served at the beach, while dinner is served

up near the main road. Transport from the Beachcomber area can be arranged for 400 CFP. Credit cards are accepted.

La Plantation (☎ 56 45 10; appetizers 1650 CFP, pizzas 1400 CFP; open lunch & dinner Wed-Mon), just south of Le Petit Village, is in a nice building but has a fairly undesirable position along this busy stretch of road. Credit cards are accepted.

Sunset Restaurant (☎ 56 12 20; open lunch & dinner daily), the beachfront restaurant at the Hotel Hibiscus, looks out over the lagoon to the two motu and is an ideal place to catch the brief Pacific sunset over drinks or dinner. Credit cards are accepted.

L'Aventure Restaurant (☎ 56 53 59) is a low-key Chinese restaurant next to the Hotel Hibiscus.

Restaurant Tumoana (☎ 56 37 60; mains 1100-2300 CFP; open lunch & dinner Mon-Sat) is set back from the road and serves Chinese and Polynesian dishes (a small bottle of French wine is cheaper than a pineapple juice). Dull decor is compensated for by beautiful views from the terrace. Credit cards are accepted.

Fare Vai Moana (☎ 56 17 14; mains 1500-2900 CFP) is in the Hotel Fare Vai Moana and has a great beachside setting; the deck, decked out with stylish local wood, offers front-row seats for the sunset. There is sometimes live music.

Moorea Village Hotel (☎ 56 10 02) has a restaurant next to the swimming pool, in a beautiful room in local style, facing the motu. There is a barbecue on Saturday evening and a traditional Polynesian feast on Sunday afternoon. Prices are very reasonable and there's often music with dinner.

Le Motu (open 9am-9pm Tues-Sat, morning Sun), in a small shopping centre, is a rather ordinary place serving light meals, salads, pizzas, crepes and a lion's choice of burgers.

Pâtisserie Sylésie (open 6am-5pm daily) has a dull roadside setting. You can get light lunches (from 500 CFP), sweet or savoury crepes (400-900 CFP), ice creams and the like; this is a good place for a breakfast of pastries and coffee.

Coco d'Îsle (☎ 56 59 07; open 6.30am-10pm daily) is a good little place with good grub. The daily specials cost around 1200 CFP. This is a pretty dusty spot, but the restaurant is pleasant nonetheless. Prices drop if you order takeaway.

Pitcairn (☎ 56 55 46; appetizers 1500 CFP, mains from 1900 CFP; open breakfast & lunch daily) is more upmarket than Coco d'Îsle; it's also more protected from the road.

Chez Capo (☎ 56 54 89; appetizers 1300 CFP, mains 1500 CFP; open lunch Sun-Fri, dinner Sat-Thur) is set back from the road, and is an agreeable, shady place for a light lunch. The mahi mahi burger with chips costs 1000 CFP.

Motu Tiahura A fairly new edition to Mo'orea's ever-growing list of places to eat, **Motu Moea – Restaurant la Plage** (☎ 74 96 96) has an idyllic setting on Motu Tiahura (also known as Motu Moea). The food is simple, fresh and reasonably priced. Take a dip once you've digested your meal – this is the life! You can get a boat over to the motu from Les Tipaniers Hotel Restaurant (500 CFP).

Haapiti In Résidence Linareva, **Le Bateau** (☎ 55 05 65; mains 1650-3750 CFP; open lunch & dinner daily) is an excellent floating restaurant in a boat at the end of the quay. The food is essentially French but with many a local twist. There are cocktails at the bar, and transport from Hauru Point can be arranged for 500 CFP. Reservations are recommended. Credit cards are accepted.

Self-Catering

It's not a bad idea to consider self-catering while on Mo'orea. As is typical of French Polynesia, restaurants are expensive, and many places to stay have little kitchens where you can whip up your own storms. There are quite a few supermarkets and smaller shops around the island where you can buy wonderful fresh baguettes, cool drinks, canned food, cereal, milk and the like (be prepared for high prices). However, it's not as easy as you'd hope to find fresh produce on Mo'orea: there are pineapples, limes and *pamplemousses* (grapefruits) aplenty, but a dinner out of these three would take a *chef extraordinaire*.

TOA (open 8am-8pm Mon-Sat, morning Sun) is the biggest supermarket and is about 500m south of the quay in Vaiare. **Pao Pao Supermarché** in Cook's Bay and **Magasin Rémy**, near Le Cocotier restaurant, just east of PK5, are other supermarkets. Just over the bridge in Paopao is another supermarket.

There's a little fish shop next to the old **fish market** in Paopao, but you may be better off buying fresh fish from along the road in the afternoons (make sure it's that day's catch, not yesterday's that's dressed up to look fresh).

ENTERTAINMENT
Bars

Mo'orea is more the place to pay off that sleep-debt than kick up your heels. A boozy dinner and a dance performance is about as lively as things get. The big hotels have bars where all are welcome to whet their palates with a predinner drink, and many of the restaurants listed earlier, such as **Le Cocotier**, **Les Tipaniers** and **Sunset Restaurant**, are good spots to glimpse those split-second tropical sunsets.

Maria@Tapas (☎ 55 01 70; PK5; e maria tapas@mail.pf; open 8am-11pm Mon-Wed, 8am-1am Thur-Sat) in the Centre Kikipa is a great, hip place for a drink in the evening; you can also eat here. Staff will pick you up if you are eating.

The Linareva's floating restaurant, **Le Bateau** (PK34.5) is another great place to watch the sunset with a cocktail in hand.

Dance Performances

A couple of times a week (usually Wednesday and Saturday evenings) the bigger hotels organise Polynesian music and dance performances by local groups. These performances tend to be of a very high standard, so it's worth trying to catch one. Try **Moorea Village Hotel**, **Sofitel la Ora**, **Moorea Beachcomber Intercontinental Resort**, **Club Bali Hai** and **Moorea Pearl Resort** (see Places to Stay earlier in this chapter for hotel details). Call the hotels for dates and times.

If you manage to time your visit with the July *heiva* celebrations, chat to the tourist office or your hotel about what is happening on Mo'orea.

SHOPPING

There are two small shopping centres on the island. The shopping centre in Maharepa has a few shops and banks and the **Librarie Kina Maharepa**, which has a decent selection of magazines and one or two English-language newspapers (usually the *Herald Tribune*, always few days old). Le Petit Village has various shops and souvenir outlets, a bank, a supermarket and a bookshop/newsagency.

Retail therapy cannot always be administered on Sunday, as many boutiques and jewellery shops close.

Souvenirs & Crafts

Not far from the Galerie van der Heyde, **La Poterie de L'Aquarium – Teva Yrondi** (☎/fax 56 30 00; open 9.30am-12pm & 2.30pm-5.30pm Wed-Sun), has a fascinating range of jewellery that is pottery, pearls that are jewellery and pottery that is (thankfully) pottery. There's a garden to wander through, where you'll find yet more pottery.

The coastal road is littered with places selling pareu (some of them hand painted), T-shirts, the Balinese wood carvings that have become worldwide tropical souvenirs, and other curios. At the eastern end of the Cook's Bay strip, **Maison Blanche**, easily recognised by its colonial architecture, has a fairly typical selection including shells, mother-of-pearl and wood sculptures. Look for the colourful roadside display of hand-painted pareu at the **Lili Shop**, between the airport and Cook's Bay.

At Hauru Point, **Te Anuanua** is a T-shirt and pareu emporium, and **Sable Blanc** is another pareu and T-shirt specialist. In Le Petit Village, the **Maison du Tiki** offers sculptures and Polynesian art including tapa, mother-of-pearl work, Marquesan sculptures, prints and watercolours.

In Cook's Bay, there are **Honu Iti Boutique** and the boutique in the Club Bali Hai.

You will find all things vanilla at **Vanilla Products** (PK6.7), in Afareaitu.

Art Galleries

At Cook's Bay, **Galerie van der Hyde** displays the Dutch owner's art around the inside wall of the compound. Close to the Kaveka Hotel, **La Poterie de L'Aquarium – Teva Yrondi** displays Teva's pottery.

Woody Sculptures (☎ 56 37 00; Papetoai), just before the Hauru Point enclave, has interesting wood carvings.

There are also a number of places dotted around the island where artists display their work. Keep an eye out for signs along the coastal road.

Black Pearls

Although there are no pearl farms on Mo'orea, a number of places around Mo'orea specialise in black pearls. They include the major Tahitian pearl specialists whose pearls come from the Leeward Islands and the Tuamotus. Some of them will even provide free transport to their shops.

At Hauru Point, in Le Petit Village and around, there are several jewellery shops, including **World of Pearls, Pai Moana Pearls, Herman Perles, Tahiti Perles** and the **Black Pearl Gem Company**. At Cook's Bay you'll find **Heiva Black Pearl**, in front of the Club Bali Hai, and **Island Fashion Black Pearls**, next to Galerie van der Heyde. The **boutiques** of the Sofitel Ia Ora and Beachcomber Intercontinental also display pearls.

GETTING THERE & AWAY

There's less than 20km of blue Pacific between Tahiti and Mo'orea, and getting from one island to the other is simplicity itself. You can stroll down to the quay in Pape'ete, hop on one of the high-speed ferries, and be on Mo'orea in less than half an hour. Or you can go out to the airport, get an Air Moorea flight and be there in less than 10 minutes.

Air

Conveniently, **Air Moorea** (☎ 86 41 41 on Tahiti, ☎ 56 10 34 on Mo'orea) flies from Faa'a airport on Tahiti to Mo'orea (adult/child 3200/1600 CFP one-way) at least every half-hour. If you're not in a hurry, there's no need to book – just turn up. If there's an oversupply of passengers, Air Moorea puts on more flights. At Faa'a airport, Air Moorea is in a separate small terminal, a short stroll to the east of the main terminal.

Air Tahiti (☎ 86 42 42, 86 41 84 weekends) also flies to Mo'orea but is chiefly for passengers making onward connections to other islands in the Society group. There are usually only one to three flights a day.

Boat

Competition is fierce across the 'Sea of the Moon', between Tahiti and Mo'orea. First departures in the morning are usually around 6am; the last trips are in the afternoon around 4.30pm or 5.30pm.

Aremiti 4 (☎ 42 88 88 in Pape'ete, 56 31 10 on Mo'orea; one-way/return 1060/2120 CFP) has four crossings daily; the **Aremiti Ferry** (☎ 42 85 85 in Pape'ete, 56 31 10 on Mo'orea) has a very similar schedule. The **Moorea Ferry** (☎ 45 00 30; one-way 850 CFP) runs daily. The **Ono-Ono** (☎ 45 35 35 *in Pape'ete, 56 12 60 on Mo'orea; one-way/ return 1050/2200 CFP)* also has at least four crossings daily; it docks at Cook's Bay, which is handy if you are staying nearby.

From Pape'ete, departures take place from the ferry quay, about 300m northeast of the tourist office and the Vaima Centre.

Because the ferries are so frequent and are rarely filled to capacity, even in high season, it's not necessary to make a reservation, except perhaps if you are taking a car over during a busy period. You can buy tickets at the ticket counter on the quay just a few minutes before departure.

GETTING AROUND

Getting around Mo'orea without a car or bicycle is not all that easy. Distances are not particularly great but are often just a bit too great to walk. Bear in mind that many of the restaurants and quite a few pearl shops will pick you up for free or for a nominal fee if you call them.

To/From the Airport & Quay

The Cook's Bay hotels and *pensions* are 5km to 9km from the airport; the Hauru Point establishments are 25km to 30km away. It's a further 5km from the Vaiare quay. A shuttle bus meets 'some' of the boat arrivals and departures. If you happen upon this bus, it's only 200/100 CFP for adults/children or from any of the Cook's Bay or Hauru Point hotels. Mo'orea's taxis are notoriously expensive: from the airport to the Beachcomber Intercontinental, at the very start of Hauru Point, will cost about 3500 CFP. However, you may be able to find a shared taxi willing to take you from the quay to Cook's Bay, for example, for around 2000 CFP.

Most hotels, even the budget places, offer airport transfers. Air Moorea offers a 500 CFP minibus service to any of the island's hotels after each flight.

Car

If you're not on an organised tour, this is an island where having your own wheels is very useful. Car-rental operators can be found at the Vaiare ferry quay, at the airport, at some of the major hotels and dotted around the Cook's Bay and Hauru Point tourist centres. Four-, eight- and 24-hour rates, are quoted as well as cheaper rates after two or three days. Generally, you'll pay from around 7000/5500

CFP a day/half-day for a little Fiat, including liability insurance and unlimited mileage.

Europcar *(☎ 56 34 00, fax 56 35 05)* has its main office at Le Petit Village. You can also find it at the ferry quay at Vaiare (☎ 56 28 64), at the Sofitel Ia Ora (☎ 56 42 30), in front of Club Bali Hai (☎ 56 46 84) and at the Beachcomber Intercontinental Resort (☎ 56 19 50). **Avis** *(☎ 56 32 61, 56 32 68, fax 56 32 62)* is at the ferry quay at Vaiare, at the airport and in the Club Bali Hai. **Albert Transport & Activities** *(☎ 56 19 28, 56 33 75)* is a local operator found around the island, including in front of Club Bali Hai. Its prices are generally lower than the international companies.

There are petrol stations near the Vaiare ferry quay, close to the airport, beside Cook's Bay and at Le Petit Village on Hauru Point.

Taxi

There's no doubt that taxis are horribly expensive on Mo'orea, even by French Polynesian standards. It's not much more expensive to rent a car than to take a taxi from the airport or ferry quay to a hotel at Hauru Point. If you have to take a **taxi** *(☎ 56 10 18)*, you can find one at the airport from 6am to 6pm.

Scooter, Fun Car & Bicycle

Tehotu Location *(☎ 56 52 96, 78 42 48)* at the Vaiare ferry quay rents scooters for around 5000 CFP a day; **Europcar** *(☎ 56 34 00)* rents scooters for 4500/5000 CFP for a half-/full day. Europcar rents out those funny little 'fun cars' (4300 CFP for a half-day), which are not a bad idea if you've never ridden a scooter before (or don't want to do so without protective gear) but don't want to hire a car (but beware: local kids may giggle at the sight of you).

Rando Cycles *(☎ 56 51 99; e randocycles@ mail.pf)* rents mountain bikes for 1500 CFP a day and organises guided rides for 5000 CFP per person (minimum of five participants). It has bicycles at Hotel Hibiscus at Hauru Point. Les Tipaniers Hotel Restaurant, the Moorea Village Hotel and the Beachcomber Intercontinental Resort also have bicycles for rent.

Boat

Moorea Loca Boat *(☎ 78 13 39)*, at Hibiscus and Tipaniers hotels, rents out boats – this is an ideal way to explore the lagoon and the small motu. They cost 6000/8000/10,000 CFP for two/four/eight hours, including fuel.

Other Windward Islands

Tahiti and Mo'orea are the major islands in the Windward group. However, the group also includes two small high islands (Maiao, to the west of Mo'orea, and uninhabited Mehetia, well to the east of Tahiti) and a single atoll, Tetiaroa, north of Tahiti.

TETIAROA
pop 50 • area 6 sq km

A dozen or so sandy motu dotted around a lagoon 7km in diameter, 55km in circumference and 30m deep – that's Tetiaroa. It's a postcard-perfect atoll: beautiful beaches, lovely clear water and a population mainly comprising migratory birds. The whole show is owned by actor Marlon Brando. Nowhere does Tetiaroa rise more than 3m above sea level. The atoll was known as Teturoa in the pre-European period.

The first European known to have visited the atoll was none other than William Bligh, who went there in search of three deserters in January 1789. Later he probably wished he hadn't found them, as they all joined the mutineers on the *Bounty*.

The island was once a Pomare family playground, an escape from its kingdom on Tahiti. In 1904 the Pomare family presented Dr Williams, Tahiti's only dentist, with the atoll, perhaps as payment for its dental bills. Williams was the British consul for French Polynesia from 1916 to 1935. He turned Tetiaroa into a copra plantation. Tetiaroa had its next significant change of ownership in 1965 when Brando, fresh from making *Mutiny on the Bounty* (see the boxed text 'Mutiny in the Cinema' in the Facts for the Visitor chapter), acquired the island on a 99-year lease. He added the airstrip and the low-key hotel on Motu Onetahi.

Motu Rimatuu was the Pomare family residence. There are **marae** ruins on the island and a number of gigantic *tuu* trees (their dark, hard, grained wood is greatly valued by sculptors). Motu Tahuna Rahi (also known as Île aux Oiseaux or Bird Island) is the **nesting island**, a reserve used by countless migratory sea birds to lay their eggs and hatch their young. Frigates, gannets, petrels, black terns, brown boobies, red-footed boobies and long-tailed tropical birds all nest on Tetiaroa.

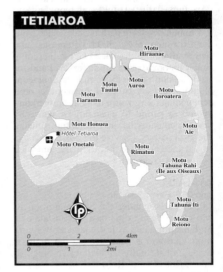

TETIAROA

Motu Hiraanae
Motu Tauini
Motu Auroa
Motu Horoatera
Motu Tiaraunu
Motu Honuea
Motu Aie
Hôtel Tetiaroa
Motu Onetahi
Motu Rimatuu
Motu Tahuna Rahi (Île aux Oiseaux)
Motu Tahuna Iti
Motu Reiono

Bring along a mask and snorkel, and thongs or waterproof sandals to protect your feet. Also bring a hat and sunscreen.

Places to Stay
Tetiaroa's hotel, indeed the only habitation, is on Motu Onetahi, where the airstrip is.

Hôtel Tetiaroa (*☎ 82 63 02, 82 63 03, fax 85 00 51; 2 days accommodation & return flight per person 38,300 CFP*) is a small complex with 14 local-style beach bungalows with private bathroom. Five of them were recently built, while the others are a bit older. You can book directly with the hotel, or, in Pape'ete, go to the Hôtel Tetiaroa counter at the Air Mo'orea terminal at Faa'a airport (facing the airport, it is to the right of the main building).

Getting There & Away
Tetiaroa is 40km north of Tahiti and is accessible by air and sea.

Air Mo'orea operates regular 20-minute flights from Tahiti. The return fare, including lunch at Hôtel Tetiaroa and an excursion to Motu Tahuna Rahi, is 24,900 CFP; you leave at 8.15am and return at 4pm. Contact the Hôtel Tetiaroa counter at the Air Mo'orea terminal for details.

Jet France (*☎/fax 56 15 62)* has catamaran crossings three times weekly from Pape'ete. The fare is 11,000 CFP but you have to bring your own lunch. The trip takes about 2½ hours.

L'Escapade (*☎ 72 85 31*) offers the same trip by monohull for 11,000 CFP, including lunch on board. The trip takes 4¼ hours.

Boats don't enter the lagoon; a Zodiac inflatable takes visitors in across the reef. Bring something warm to wear on the boat; if you're prone to seasickness you may want to consider taking medication. During the high season it's wise to book some days in advance but note that trips are cancelled if the seas are rough.

MAIAO
pop 250 • area 9 sq km

Maiao comes under the administration of Mo'orea, 75km to the east. It consists of a high island, rising to 154m, and a low-lying motu that wraps itself around the high island, almost totally enclosing two brackish lakes, Roto Iti and Roto Rahi.

The island was sighted by Samuel Wallis in 1767, a postscript to his 'discovery' of Tahiti, but until 1809, when a pair of London Missionary Society (LMS) missionaries were forced to stop here, no Europeans are known to have visited the island. During the late 1920s and early 30s, an Englishman named Eric Trower tried to take over the island so that he could exploit the guano deposits he thought were there. His actions resulted in the islanders developing a strong mistrust of foreign influence, and for many years Europeans and Chinese were forbidden to live on the island. Even today the small population prizes its isolation and has vigorously resisted the construction of an airstrip.

Some copra is produced on Maiao but the island is famed for the exceptional quality of its pandanus leaves, used for traditional Tahitian roof thatching. Today houses on Maiao are roofed with tin; although not traditional and less picturesque, this is infinitely better for collecting rainwater on an island where freshwater supplies are scarce.

There are no organised trips to Maiao. The only way to get there is by chartered yacht – see Bareboat Charters & Cruises in the Outdoor Activities chapter for more in-

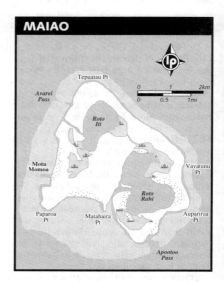

formation. Avarei Pass on the northwest side has been widened to allow small boats to enter; Apootoo Pass to the southeast is the only other pass.

MEHETIA
area 3 sq km

Geologically the youngest island in the Society group, Mehetia is situated 100km east of Tahiti. It is 1.5km across and rises steeply from the sea to its highest point of 435m. The island is uninhabited and has no lagoon; landing on the uninviting shoreline is, to say the very least, difficult. Only in one place does the rocky shoreline form a small pebbly beach. Yet when Wallis chanced upon Mehetia in 1767, the population is said to have been 1500. It seems scarcely possible that the population could have been that large, but the **marae** ruins on the island confirm that it certainly was populated. The fierce piratical warriors of Anaa Atoll (Tuamotus) drove the population off Mehetia in 1806, and it was used briefly in 1835 as a penal colony. The island has freshwater springs, and coconut and *uru* (breadfruit) trees grow there. The surrounding waters are rich with fish and other marine life. The island is now privately owned, and Tahitians occasionally visit to gather copra.

LINDA MUSICK

MANFRED GOTTSCHALK

PETER HENDRIE

PAUL KENNEDY

Mo'orea

Traditional tattoos

TATTOOING

Since the early 1980s, tattooing has enjoyed a strong revival, becoming one of the most expressive and vibrant vehicles of traditional Polynesian culture.

With encouragement from the great Samoan masters, young Tahitians and Marquesans have delved into their ancient traditions and have brought this ancestral form of bodily adornment, with its undisputed artistic qualities, completely up to date. Today many Polynesian men and women sport magnificent tattoos as symbols of their identity.

The word 'tattoo' comes from the Tahitian *tatau*, which refers to the practice of carving indelible marks onto the skin. This practice is well known in a number of cultures, but within the Polynesian triangle (Hawaii–Marquesas–New Zealand) it took its most consummate and spectacular form.

Eighteenth-century European navigators were the first Westerners to give an account of the practice, which was unknown at the time in Europe. When the missionaries settled in Polynesia, tattooing suffered the same fate as the rest of Polynesian culture: considered pagan, it was banned.

Tattooing was significant in many ways. Firstly it was a symbol of community or clan membership, a form of social recognition. It was also an initiation rite: in the Marquesas, the onset of adulthood was marked by a ceremony during which young men would display their tattoos as symbols of their bravery. Social status also was expressed through tattooing: as people progressed through different stages of life, they covered their bodies with more tattoos. This aesthetic adornment played a part in the seduction process as well. Finally, tattooing served to intimidate: in the Marquesas, warriors tattooed their faces with thick horizontal stripes to make themselves look terrifying to enemies. Both women and men were tattooed, although women tended to have fewer tattoos.

The techniques and designs used followed strict conventions. The art of tattooing was the prerogative of a guild of master-tattooists who underwent a long apprenticeship before they could practise their art. They used pieces of bone that were sharpened to a point and joined together in the shape of a sort of comb. The comb was then fixed onto a wooden stem. The tattooist soaked the comb in a black pigment made from a mixture of soot and water or vegetable matter, and struck the stem with a small mallet to cause the pigment to penetrate the skin. Designs consisted mainly of abstract geometrical shapes or of highly stylised animal or plant motifs.

Polynesians are going back to their roots and rediscovering this form of bodily decoration. Women tend to wear discreet motifs around the ears or navel, and around the wrists or ankles. Men are usually distinguished by magnificent adornments covering the shoulders, torso, thighs or calves.

Polynesian Tattoos, by ex-fashion photographer Gian Paolo Barbieri, features photos of the tattoos and physiques of beautiful young Polynesian men.

Inset: Traditional tattoo (Photograph by Jean-Bernard Carillet)

Tattoo Artists

In French Polynesia there are between 20 and 30 professional and semiprofessional tattooists. All the professional tattooists have tattooing machines and sterile needles. Dozens of amateurs work with electric razors that they have adapted, in a makeshift way, to hold a needle, but the reliability of this technique is limited and the results can be disappointing. It is far better to pay more and deal with a tattoo artist who has a solid reputation and uses professional equipment.

It's worth taking your time when choosing a tattooist. Make an appointment to see the artist and ask to see a portfolio to get an idea of their style and work. Talk to the artist: is the level of communication good, and is the artist listening to your wishes? A minimal amount of tacit understanding between you is essential. Also, get a feel for the atmosphere in the studio: is it congenial and does it inspire confidence? How clean is everything?

The following list of tattooists is by no means exhaustive.

Pape'ete

Efraima Huuti (☎ 79 64 71) This Marquesan tattooist has a good reputation. The studio is upstairs in the Marché de Pape'ete, next to a shop selling pareu. Efraima Huuti specialises in Marquesan designs and offers good prices.

Polynesian Tattoo (☎ 78 06 73) Three Tahitian tattooists work out of this studio on Blvd Pomare. All styles of tattoo are available (local, Celtic, tribal, colour), as well as custom-created pieces; the artists work both freehand and with tracings.

Varii Huuti (☎ 78 52 82) This excellent Marquesan tattooist is based at Faa'a.

Tahiti Iti Tatoo (☎ 78 58 14) At Taravao on Tahiti Iti, Marcel specialises in Polynesian designs (Maori, Tahitian and Marquesan).

Mo'orea

The greatest masters practise their art on Mo'orea. They work freehand and only do traditional designs. Considering their skill and reputation, prices are very reasonable (about 10,000 to 15,000 CFP for a bracelet around the arm).

Chimé Tattoo This tattooist works out of his house at PK14 between Opunohu and Cook's Bays. One of the pioneers of the revival of this art form, he worked for several years in Spain and posed for photographer Gian Paolo Barbieri for the book *Polynesian Tattoos*.

Roonui Tattoo (☎ 56 37 53) Roonui, who is almost completely tattooed, was also a model for *Polynesian Tattoos*. His studio is at Hauru Point.

Taniera Tattoo (☎ 56 16 98; PK 27.3) At Hauru Point, opposite the Pitcairn restaurant, this studio offers Tahitian and tribal-style tattoos

Here Tatau (☎ 56 48 71, 56 42 43) This studio-*fare* is opposite the beach at PK 38. Herenui does fine work.

Purotu Tattoo (☎ 77 57 59, 56 22 92) This studio is opposite the Banque de Tahiti at Maharepa. Purotu is one of the rare artists offering tattooing using a comb, in the Polynesian tradition.

Tiki Village (☎ 56 18 97) Three tattooists work here at PK 31, including Tavita, the best known, who is entirely tattooed.

Huahine

Tihoti Tatau (☎/fax 68 77 27) This tattooist is based at Fare. He offers traditional Marquesan tattooing and Tahitian- and Hawaiian-style tattoos, as well as creative, stylised designs.

Ra'iatea

Isidore Haiti (☎ 66 15 97) This artist based at PK 13.5 specialises in Marquesan tattooing, with some tribal influences.

Bora Bora

Marama (☎ 67 66 73) This studio is on Matira Point, after Bungalows Temanuata; it's open from 9am to 5pm Monday to Friday. The artist, who offers traditional Polynesian tattoos, has a good reputation. A small design costs about 5000 CFP and a bracelet on the arm costs about 15,000 CFP.

Fati (☎ 71 54 84) This studio is at Matira. This Marquesan artist recently began working on Bora Bora. A small design costs about 5000 CFP.

The Marquesas

Teiki Barsinas (☎ 92 92 67) This artist, based at Tahuata, has an excellent reputation.

Fii Brothers (☎ 92 93 04) Also at Tahuata, these artists are well respected.

Choosing a Tattoo

Choosing a tattoo is a difficult task, especially since you'll have the tattoo for the rest of your life. It is preferable to select a traditional design, since it is the type of image that is authentic and executed best. Study the tattooist's portfolio and be clear about what you want. Any self-respecting tattooist will not reproduce an exact copy of a pre-existing design but will display creative ability in tailoring the design you have chosen to suit your own requirements.

You should also take into account the symbolism of the design; the tattoo artist will explain it to you. Think about where you wish to be tattooed and the size of the design. If you care for something both aesthetically pleasing and discreet, Marquesan bracelets around the ankles and arms are particularly popular. Or you might prefer a complex tattoo covering the shoulder, pectorals, thigh or calf.

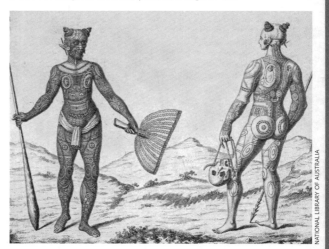

Right: Marquesan warriors with intricate 'clothing' of tattoos (engraving 1810)

NATIONAL LIBRARY OF AUSTRALIA

You should also agree on a price. There is no official price list. The relevant factors are the size, intricacy and originality of the design, as well as the reputation of the artist, and the facilities. Some artists work for a flat fee, and others at an hourly rate. For a small bracelet around the ankle or arm, expect to pay between 10,000 and 15,000 CFP.

A Tattoo Session

Once you've agreed on a design with the tattoo artist, the work can start. You sit on a mattress or armchair and your skin is cleaned and disinfected. Some artists work freehand, which means they draw the design directly onto the skin. Others create the design on paper and trace it onto the skin. With a tattooing machine, the artist inks in the outlines, and uses a set of several needles to fill in the design.

As for pain, it all depends on where you want the tattoo. The most sensitive areas are those where the skin is the most delicate (eg, the inside of the thigh) and those directly next to a bone (such as the shin or spine). According to people who have been tattooed, the pain is definitely bearable. It is unwise to take aspirin, since it has the effect of thinning the blood.

The length of sessions can vary considerably. A small design might be completed in half an hour, but some require three hours or even a whole day, including breaks.

Once the tattoo is finished, you have to apply a coating of oily cream for several days. A scab will form and scarring will not be complete for a week or two. During that time you must not go swimming in the sea or expose the tattooed area to sunlight – so it's wise to leave your tattooing until the end of your stay.

Huahine

pop 5411 • area 75 sq km

Huahine (hoo-ah-hee-nay) is actually two islands of fairly similar size: Huahine Nui (Big Huahine) to the north and Huahine Iti (Little Huahine) to the south. The islands are only barely separated and at low tide you can wade from one to the other; a road bridge spans the narrow gap. According to a Polynesian legend, the split came about when the god Hiro ploughed his mighty canoe into the island, creating Bourayne Bay to the west and Maroe Bay to the east. Huahine Nui is more developed and is home to the main tourist and administrative facilities, while Huahine Iti is wilder in character. Agriculture and fishing are the mainstays of the island economy.

Huahine is lush and beautiful and its easy-going atmosphere entices visitors to kick back and watch the world go by. It has some fine beaches to the south, easily accessible motu, fantastic snorkelling and scuba diving, popular surf breaks and, in the village of Maeva, the most extensive complex of pre-European marae in French Polynesia. Each year in October or November, Huahine is the starting point for the annual Hawaiki Nui pirogue (outrigger canoe) race. See the boxed text 'Hawaiki Nui Canoe Race' in the Facts for the Visitor chapter.

History

North of Fare, archaeological excavations have revealed some of the earliest traces of settlement in the Society Islands. Huahine maintained a degree of independence during the era when powerful chiefs of Bora Bora were extending their power to the east and west.

In 1769 James Cook was the first European to visit Huahine and, although he did not receive a warm welcome, he returned in 1774 and 1777. A group of London Missionary Society (LMS) missionaries moved to Huahine in 1808 to escape the turmoil on Tahiti, but they remained for only a year. They did, however, return in 1818.

Huahine supported Pomare in the struggle against the French, which resulted in a number of clashes between 1846 and 1888, when French rule was eventually accepted. Although the French kicked the Protestant

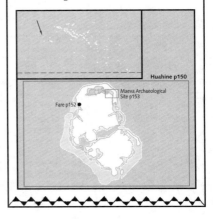

English missionaries out, the island remains predominantly Protestant.

Orientation

A road follows the coast most of the way around both islands. Between Faie and the Hôtel Bellevue on Huahine Nui, and on the brief Parea–Tefarerii section on Huahine Iti, the road is unsealed.

A series of motu stretches along the east coast of the two islands, while around the north coast is Lake Fauna Nui, which is actually an inlet from the sea. It almost cuts off the motu-like northern peninsula, where the airport is, from the rest of Huahine Nui. The reef fringes the north coast and there are only a few beaches.

Fare, the port and administrative centre, is on the west coast of Huahine Nui, 2.5km south of the airport. Faie and Maeva, on the east coast, and Fitii, on the west, are the other main settlements on Huahine Nui.

HUAHINE

PLACES TO STAY
1 Pension Fetia
2 Pension Fare Maeva;
   Restaurant Tehina
3 Vaihonu Océan
4 Pension Mama Roro
5 Motel Vanille; Restaurnat
   Vanille
6 Chez Ella
7 La Petite Ferme
8 Sofitel Heiva; Omai
9 Pension Te Nahe Toetoe
11 Pension Poetaina
12 Chez Henriette
13 Huahine Vacances
14 Villas Bougainville
15 Hôtel Bellevue
16 Pension Tupuna
18 Te Tiare Beach Resort
19 Pension Mauarii;Maraamu
   Sailing; Restaurant Mauarii
20 Relais Mahana; Restaurant
   Tenahe
21 Ariiura Camping Écologie

OTHER
9 Huahine Nui Pearls&
  Pottery
17 Eden Parc
22 Marae Anini

Manua Pt
Motu Ovarei
Fa'a Miti
Lake Fauna Nui
See Maeva Archaeological Site map p153
Maeva
Avamoa Pass
Avamoa Pass
Fare
Vaipunuu River
Mt Tapu (429m)
See Fare map p152
La Cité de Corail
Motu Mahare
Tiare Pass
The Canyon
Tevaipoopoo River (271m)
Avapeihi Pass (Fitii Pass)
Cook Bay
(280m)
Mt Turi (669m)
Huahine Nui
Vaiumete River
Faie Bay
Faie
Motu Vavaratea
Huimoo Pt
Fitii
Mt Paeo (440m)
Belvédère
(347m)
Vaitoa River
Villas Bougainville
Farerea Pass
Motu Topati
Motu Murimahora
Vaitou Bay
(261m)
Puravai Bay
Maroe Bay
(180m)
Teavaava Bay
Faauoo Bay
Faauoo Bay
(198m)
Maroe
Huahine Iti
Tefarerii
Bourayne Bay
(186m)
Motu Taiahu
Motu Vaiorea
Tiapaa Bay
Haapu Bay
Haapu
(409m)
Mt Pohue Rahi (462m)
Mahuti River
Mahuti Bay
(322m)
Parea
Safari Aquarium
Avea Bay
Motu Araara
Araara Pass
Parea Pass

0 1 2km
0 0.5 1mi

Pouvana'a a Oopa – A Tahitian Leader

French Polynesia's most famous politician came from Huahine. Born in 1895, Pouvana'a a Oopa founded the Rassemblement Démocratique des Populations Tahitiennes (RDPT; Democratic Assembly of Tahitian Populations) in 1949. For nearly 10 years he was at the forefront of local politics, opposing French colonial rule, denouncing capitalism and pushing for local employment in government and administrative posts. A man of the people and a devout Protestant, this charismatic leader was strongly supported by Polynesians, who considered him a *metua* (father) figure.

It all fell apart in 1958 when a 'yes' vote in the referendum to remain linked to France destabilised the party. Pouvana'a a Oopa was blamed for the riots that shook Pape'ete on 10 and 11 October 1958 and he was exiled to France. Split by internal dissension, the RDPT was unable to mobilise itself against the nuclear-testing programme in 1963, and was dissolved. Pouvana'a a Oopa was allowed to return to the Pacific in 1968 and until his death in 1977 he struggled tirelessly, but unsuccessfully, for his rehabilitation. Today he remains the pre-eminent Polynesian father figure, a man who made the all-powerful colonial structure tremble.

There are four villages on Huahine Iti: Haapu, Parea, Tefarerii and Maroe. Mt Turi (669m) is the highest peak on Huahine Nui, and Mt Pohue Rahi (462m) is the highest on Huahine Iti.

Information

The **tourist office** (*☎/fax 68 78 81; open 7.30am-11.30am Mon-Sat)* is on the main street in Fare.

In Fare, **Banque de Tahiti** *(open Mon-Fri)* is opposite the quay and **Banque Socredo** *(open Mon-Fri)* is on the bypass road. Both have ATMs.

The **post office** *(open 7am-3pm Mon-Thur, 7am-2pm Fri)* is to the north of the town towards the airport. Internet access is available at **Ao Api New World** (*☎ 68 70 99; open 8.30am-5pm Mon-Fri)*, upstairs in the same building as the tourist office (enter from the rear). It charges 30 CFP per minute. On Huahine Iti, you can log on at **Pension Mauarii** (see Huahine Iti under Places to Stay, later) for 40 CFP per minute.

There are two private **medical centres** (*☎ 68 82 20, 68 84 93)* in Fare on the bypass road. There's also a **clinic** and a **pharmacy** opposite the quay.

Visiting yachties can obtain water from Pacific Blue Adventure, on the quay. The *capitainerie* (harbour master's office) is also on the quay.

AROUND HUAHINE NUI

This 60km circuit of the larger island starts with Fare and goes around the island in a clockwise direction.

Fare

The town of Fare is the image of a sleepy South Seas port, where people sit on the quay waiting for boats to arrive while children splash and tumble in the water. There's a colourful little waterside **market**, roulottes (food vans), shops, nice restaurants and a selection of hotels and pensions (guesthouses). Throw in banks, a post office, car- and bike-rental facilities and a dive shop and it's easy to see why many visitors find Fare the ideal place to relax for a few days.

Fare looks out over **Haamene Bay**, which has two passes out to the sea. The northern Avamoa Pass is the main entry point for inter-island shipping, while the Avapeihi Pass (Fitii Pass) is to the south. The town came into existence with the arrival of the missionaries in 1818 and within a few years it was a bustling little port. Whalers started to call in at Fare from the 1830s and the French protectorate brought an influx of island merchants and traders. The wooden shops and buildings along the main street came with the Chinese shopkeepers who settled here in the 1920s.

Old Hotel Bali Hai Archaeological Site

The site of the old Hotel Bali Hai, damaged in a cyclone in 1998, is only a few minutes' walk along the beach north of Fare. The ponds winding around the site were a swamp until they were dredged out during the hotel's construction in 1972. When pre-European artefacts were found, archaeologists were notified and work started on the site in 1973.

HUAHINE

The swampy ground preserved wooden objects including house foundations, canoe planks and water bailers, and a variety of tools and weapons. It is estimated that the area was inhabited from around AD 850 to 1100. Also found here were *patu*, flattened club-like weapons made of wood or whalebone that were used for striking and thrusting under the ribs. Such weapons had never been found outside New Zealand; their discovery here supports theories of ancient voyages between Tahiti and New Zealand.

Lake Fauna Nui & Fish Traps

The shallow expanse of Lake Fauna Nui (also known as Lake Maeva) is in fact an inlet from the sea. The land to the north is known as Motu Ovarei.

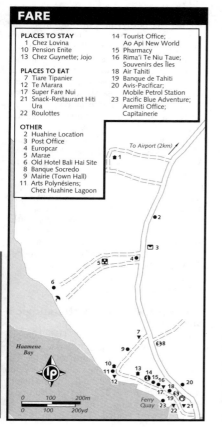

FARE

PLACES TO STAY
1 Chez Lovina
10 Pension Enite
13 Chez Guynette; Jojo

PLACES TO EAT
7 Tiare Tipanier
12 Te Marara
17 Super Fare Nui
21 Snack-Restaurant Hiti
  Ura
22 Roulottes

OTHER
2 Huahine Location
3 Post Office
4 Europcar
5 Marae
6 Old Hotel Bali Hai Site
8 Banque Socredo
9 Mairie (Town Hall)
11 Arts Polynésiens;
  Chez Huahine Lagoon

14 Tourist Office;
  Ao Api New World
15 Pharmacy
16 Rima'i Te Niu Taue;
  Souvenirs des Îles
18 Air Tahiti
19 Banque de Tahiti
20 Avis-Pacificar;
  Mobile Petrol Station
23 Pacific Blue Adventure;
  Aremiti Office;
  Capitainerie

To Airport (2km)

Haamene
Bay

Ferry
Quay

0   100   200m
0   100   200yd

About 2km north of Fare, the main sealed road runs along the inland side of Lake Fauna Nui. It's also possible to turn off to the airport and take the unsealed road on the ocean side of the lake and then return to the main part of the island by the bridge at Maeva village. At this end the lake narrows down to a channel, extending for 3km to Faie Bay.

Beside the bridge are a number of V-shaped fish traps, made from coral blocks. They have been here for centuries and some are still in use. The tips of the Vs point towards the ocean, the long stone arms emerging above the water level. The fish, as they are pulled towards the sea by an ebb tide, are trapped in the circular basin at the point of the V, where they are easily caught, usually by net or harpoon.

Maeva

Prior to European influence, Maeva was the seat of royal power on the island, and marae (traditional temples) are still found along the shoreline, scattered among the modern buildings of the village, and up the slopes of Matairea (Pleasant Wind) Hill. Excavations and restoration of the site commenced in 1923 and nearly 30 marae have been located, more than half of which have been restored. The exceptional density of marae on the hillside has led to a theory that it was entirely inhabited by families of the chiefs and nobility.

Maeva village is about 7km from Fare. The walk around the site, along the water's edge and up Matairea Hill, takes around two hours and can be hot work, so take some drinking water, as well as insect repellent. A brochure with a map of the site is available from the museum (see Fare Potee, following).

For more information on marae see the special section 'Civilisation & Archaeology'.

Fare Potee On the water's edge on the Fare side of Maeva, the *fare potee* houses a small **archaeological museum** (*admission 300 CFP; open 9am-4pm Mon-Fri*). The original *fare potee* was destroyed in the 1998 cyclone and rebuilt in 2001 using traditional materials. Around the site are 10 or more marae, some of which may date back to the 16th century. Flagstones cover a wide expanse of land along the shoreline.

HUAHINE

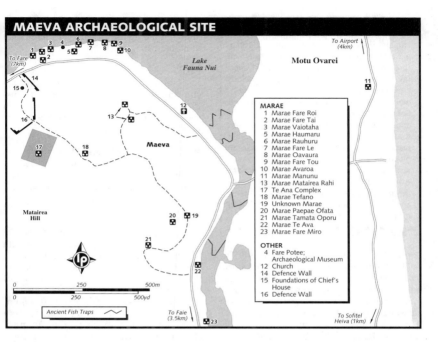

MAEVA ARCHAEOLOGICAL SITE

To Airport (4km)

To Fare (7km)

Lake Fauna Nui

Motu Ovarei

Maeva

Matairea Hill

Ancient Fish Traps

0   250   500m
0   250   500yd

To Faie (3.5km)

To Sofitel Heiva (1km)

MARAE
1 Marae Fare Roi
2 Marae Fare Tai
3 Marae Vaiotaha
5 Marae Haumaru
6 Marae Rauhuru
7 Marae Fare Le
8 Marae Oavaura
9 Marae Fare Tou
10 Marae Avaroa
11 Marae Manunu
13 Marae Matairea Rahi
17 Te Ana Complex
18 Marae Tefano
19 Unknown Marae
20 Marae Paepae Ofata
21 Marae Tamata Oporu
22 Marae Te Ava
23 Marae Fare Miro

OTHER
4 Fare Potee;
   Archaeological Museum
12 Church
14 Defence Wall
15 Foundations of Chief's
   House
16 Defence Wall

Marae Walk It is easiest to start the walk at the **defence wall** on the Fare side of Maeva. It is thought that the wall was constructed in 1846, when French marines mounted an assault on resistance forces. Look for the trail going uphill; it soon enters dense forest and passes through patches of vanilla plantations, then crosses through another **fortification wall**. This second, older wall was built during the pre-European era, probably as protection against the warlike Bora Bora tribes.

A side path leads off to the big multitiered complex of **Te Ana**, or Matairea Huiarii, draped up the hillside. This area includes marae, houses, agricultural terraces and other signs of habitation dating from around AD 1300 to 1800, plus signs of an earlier settlement dating from around AD 900.

The side path winds through the forest to **Marae Tefano**, with a massive banyan tree overwhelming one end of the *ahu* (altar).

Further on, a trail branches off to the left and runs slightly downhill to **Marae Matairea Rahi**. Once the principal marae at Maeva, where the most important island chief sat on his throne at major ceremonies,

it was superseded by Marae Manunu, on the motu below. Also surviving are the foundations of a *fare atua* or 'god house', where images of gods were guarded day and night.

Nearby is the small **Marae Matairea**. You can continue down this way, as the trail eventually emerges behind a house in the middle of the village. Retrace your steps to the main trail and continue to the turn-off to **Marae Paepae Ofata**, a steep climb above the main trail. It's worth the effort: the marae is like a large platform perched on the edge of the hill, with fine views down the hillside and across Motu Papiti to the outer lagoon, and down to the mouth of Lake Fauna Nui.

Retrace the route to the main path, which winds around the hillside to **Marae Tamata Uporu**, before dropping steeply down to the road.

The path emerges just south of **Marae Te Ava**. A short walk east leads to **Marae Fare Miro**, which has some particularly neat stonework and a fine setting.

A final marae, **Marae Manunu**, stands on the motu, across the bridge from the main Maeva complex. Manunu means 'eye of the north', and this massive structure, standing

HUAHINE

Island Agriculture

Huahine has a busy agricultural workforce, with plantations of vanilla, grapefruit, *uru* (breadfruit), taro and pineapples on local *faapu* (agricultural allotments). On the motu, melons and *pastèques* (watermelons) are grown, many of which are sold in Pape'ete's market. Some village plantations look remarkably wild and neglected, but don't think for a moment that somebody doesn't own every single plant. Casually gathering fruit, in particular the much-prized pineapples, may result in an enraged villager emerging from the undergrowth with a sharp machete. Mangoes are one of the few exceptions: they fall from the trees, and, delicious though they may be, are left to rot on the ground.

2m high, measures 40m long by nearly 7m wide. It replaced Marae Matairea Rahi as the community marae of Huahine Nui and features a two-stepped *ahu* platform. (The only other such platform in the Leeward Islands is at Marae Anini, the community marae of Huahine Iti.) This marae was primarily dedicated to Tane, Huahine's own god of war and fishing.

Faie

The coast road turns inland beside narrow Faie Bay to the village of Faie. Huahine's famous **blue-eyed eels** can be seen in the river immediately downstream of the bridge.

Inland from Faie it's a steep climb to the *belvédère* (lookout) on the slopes of Mt Turi. From this high point, the road drops even more steeply to the shores of Maroe Bay. A heavily loaded small rental car can have real difficulty getting up this road; if it's wet it may be impossible.

Eden Parc

Near the Hôtel Bellevue, this farm (☎ 68 86 58; admission 500 CFP; open 9am-4pm Mon-Sat, closed mid-Dec–Jan) is about 1.5km off the main coast road. It produces organically grown tropical fruit and coffee as well as jams, preserves and dried fruit. The entry charge is waived if you buy something, such as a glass of excellent fruit juice.

It's possible to visit the farm and its orchards, have lunch in the restaurant (see Around the Island under Places to Eat, later)

and climb up to the panoramic viewpoint, although the 800m walk to get there is not very interesting.

Fitii

Just before completing the Huahine Nui circuit, the road passes through the Fitii district. This is an important agricultural area in the shadow of Mt Paeo (440m), where taro, vanilla and other crops are grown.

AROUND HUAHINE ITI

The smaller southern island is reached by the bridge that separates the two bays, Maroe and Bourayne. This route circles the island in a clockwise direction.

East Coast

The village of **Maroe** stands on the southern side of Maroe Bay, an area dotted with reminders of the god Hiro's splitting of the island in two with his canoe. You can spot the marks left by his paddle, the imprint of his finger, and even his rocky phallus. The coast road skirts across the mouth of a number of shallow inlets, looking across to Motu Murimahora, before coming to **Tefarerii** (House of the Kings). A century ago, this small village was the centre of Huahine's most powerful family. Today the inhabitants devote their time to fishing and growing watermelons and other produce on the nearby motu.

Marae Anini

Right at the southern tip of Huahine Iti is the Marae Anini, which was a community marae. Made of massive coral blocks, this comparatively recent construction was dedicated to 'Oro (the god of war) and Hiro (the god of thieves and sailors). The 'Oro cult, with its human sacrifices, was virtually the last gasp for the old religion, which soon collapsed before the growing influence of Christianity.

Despite its beautiful lagoonside setting and its historical importance, the area is liberally sprinkled with garbage and many of the marae stones have been disfigured with feeble graffiti. One almost wishes for some modern human sacrifices. There's no signpost from the coast road but the site is about 600m after the now-closed Huahine Beach Club, at an exit near a wide bend and on the left when coming from Tefarerii.

West Coast

Some of the best **beaches** around Huahine are found on the southern peninsula and along its western shore around Avea Bay. The road comes to a junction where a left turn leads to the little village of **Haapu**. Turning right, the road soon brings you back to the bridge and the completion of the island circuit.

ACTIVITIES
Water Activities

Huahine has one dive centre, offering magnificent **dives** for all levels of experience. See the special section 'Diving' earlier in this book.

Fare has a pretty, sandy **beach** by the site of the old Hotel Bali Hai, just north of the town. The lagoon here is very wide, but further north the fringing reef means there is no beach or place to swim until you get right around to the Sofitel Heiva. Near the visitor car park at the Sofitel there's **La Cité de Corail**, offering superb **snorkelling** among coral pinnacles and rich marine life just a few metres from the shore. **Motu Topati**, at the entrance to Maroe Bay, is a magnificent site accessible by boat.

Around the hotel and guesthouse area of southwestern Huahine Iti there's a beautiful white-sand beach that's good for **swimming**. The lagoon here is very wide, and Relais Mahana and Ariiura Camping Écologie have fine beaches. Unfortunately, the same cannot be said of rubbish-strewn Anini Beach, at the southern tip.

Huahine has some of the best and most consistent **surf** in French Polynesia. Local surfers can be very possessive. There are reef breaks, both left and right, best tackled by experienced surfers. See Surfing in the Outdoor Activities chapter for details.

The lagoon around Huahine is superb and includes many untouched motu accessible only by boat. You can rent a **boat** with outboard motor to explore the lagoon and visit the motu by yourself. **Huahine Lagoon** (☎ 68 70 00), at the end of the main street in Fare, charges 3000/5000/8000 CFP for two/four/eight hours. Nautical maps and scuba equipment are provided but you have to pay for fuel.

On Huahine Iti, contact **Maraamu Sailing** (☎ 68 77 10) at Pension Mauarii, where a boat costs 10,000 CFP for half a day, including fuel and fishing gear.

Hiking

Opportunities for walking on the island are very limited. There are no clearly marked trails and the occasional paths in the interior grow over quickly if they're not maintained. The **marae walk** at Maeva (see Maeva under Around Huahine Nui, earlier) will work up a sweat for most people. Another interesting walk is the **3km trail** which starts midway along the road between Fitii and the Hôtel Bellevue and goes across to the mountainous inland section of the main road, not far from the *belvédère*. It's possible to climb Mt Turi from Fare but you certainly need a guide.

On Huahine Iti, a short **circuit walk**, easily done in an hour, goes from Parea, taking the fork towards the interior just before the bridge. Enjoy the fruity and floral fragrances as you cross a number of *faapu* before arriving back at Parea on the other side of the bridge.

ORGANISED TOURS
Lagoon Tours

Various lagoon tours are offered, with stops for snorkelling, swimming, feeding the fish and a picnic on a motu. Departures are at around 9am or 10am, returning towards 4pm. A minimum number of participants is required, so book ahead.

Poetania Cruises (☎ 68 89 49) offers lagoon tours for 7500 CFP per person, including a picnic, while **Huahine Nautique** (☎ 68 83 15) has tours for 6500 CFP with picnic lunch (4000 CFP without picnic).

Island Tours

There are numerous tours by 4WD or minibus which provide a quick view of the island. They typically start in the morning or early afternoon and take three hours. Reserve ahead because a minimum number of participants, usually two, may be required. The tours cover the principal places of interest including villages, archaeological sites, viewpoints, plantations, pearl farms, fish parks, and handicraft outlets.

Tours with **Huahine Land** (☎ 68 89 21) cost 4000 CFP per person. **Huahine Explorer** (☎ 68 87 33), based at Vaihonu Océan, charges 3850 CFP, while **Félix Tours** (☎ 68 81 69) charges 3500 CFP. When you book make sure you check whether the guide speaks English.

HUAHINE

La Petite Ferme (☎ 68 82 98), on the main road between Fare and the airport, offers guided horse-riding trips; its 15 Marquesan horses are suitable for beginners and children as well as more experienced riders. For 4500 CFP you can take a two-hour ride along the beach, through the coconut plantations and along the shore of Lake Fauna Nui. Longer excursions include an all-day ride for 9800 CFP, which includes a visit to a vanilla plantation, a picnic lunch and a stop at the Sofitel Heiva before returning to Fare via the motu.

PLACES TO STAY

Most of Huahine's accommodation is concentrated in and around Fare but there are a few places further afield and three places on the southern point of Huahine Iti. Prices here include the 11% TVA in certified hotels (6% in hostels and *pensions*), plus the 150 CFP daily tax (50 CFP in hostels and *pensions*).

Fare

There are two places to stay right in Fare; several are north of Fare towards the airport and two others are just south of the town. Although some places are by the lagoon, the fringing reef means that there isn't a good beach.

Chez Guynette (☎/fax 68 83 75; e chez guynette@mail.pf; dorm beds 1600 CFP, singles/doubles/triples 4200/5100/6200 CFP) is one of the most popular backpacker centres in French Polynesia. It's right on the main street opposite the beach, about a minute's walk from the quay. The seven simple but reasonably comfortable rooms, with fan, are named after French Polynesian islands. The shared bathroom has cold water. If you only stay one night there's an extra charge of 200/300 CFP per person/ room. Airport transfers are 500 CFP. There is a large kitchen and laundry area (1000 CFP for a load). Breakfast (800 CFP), lunch and refreshments are served on the shady open terrace at the front (see Fare under Places to Eat, later). There's an excellent notice board at the entrance. Book ahead – this place is often full.

Pension Enite (☎/fax 68 82 37; rooms per person 8000 CFP), set back across the road from Chez Guynette, has eight well-kept rooms with fan and shared bathroom (with hot water). There's also a small TV lounge. Rates are for half-board (bed, breakfast and either lunch or evening meal) and a two-night minimum stay. It has an excellent restaurant (see Fare under Places to Eat, later). Airport transfers are 1200 CFP return.

North of Fare

There are a few places between Fare and the airport, 2km to the north. Several are by the sea, although there is not much of a beach, while others are set slightly back.

Chez Lovina (☎/fax 68 88 06; camping per person 1000 CFP, dorm beds 1600 CFP) will mainly appeal to budget travellers. Surfers will appreciate the nearby breaks. Bathroom facilities are shared and there's a big, well-equipped kitchen. *Fare* and bungalows are also available, but they are overpriced and not well maintained.

La Petite Ferme (☎ 68 82 98; e lapetite ferme@mail.pf; dorm beds 1900 CFP, singles/ doubles 3300/4500 CFP, single/double bungalows 5300/8000 CFP), is a popular horse-riding centre that also offers accommodation. There's a simple six-bed dorm and a small double room. There is an additional 500 CFP charge for a one-night stay. The small bungalow has a private bathroom (cold water only); a minimum stay of two nights is required. Prices include breakfast; dinner costs 1800 CFP. Transfers to the airport or the quay in Fare are free.

Pension Fare Maeva (☎ 68 75 53, fax 68 70 68; e faremaeva@mail.pf; bungalows 9100 CFP), by the ocean, is accessible by a track off the coast road just south of La Petite Ferme. There are 10 well-kept bungalows sleeping one or two people, with kitchen, private bathroom (with hot water) and mosquito screens on the windows. Airport transfers are included. In association with Europcar, there is a room-plus-car deal at 12,000 CFP (plus taxes) per day for two people. **Restaurant Tehina** (see North of Fare under Places to Eat, later) is here.

Vaihonu Océan (☎ 68 87 33, fax 68 77 57; e vaihonu@mail.pf; camping per person 1000 CFP, dorm beds 1600 CFP, 2-person fare 6700 CFP, single/double cabins 3000/ 4300 CFP), 150m from Pension Fare Maeva, by the water, provides a good blend of price and quality. Étienne, the friendly owner, speaks perfect English. The clean six-bed dorm is tiled and has mosquito screens.

Cabins come with fan and shared bathroom. The *fare* is fully equipped. Bicycles are available for guests' use and airport transfers are free.

Chez Ella (☎ *68 73 07, 77 92 78; rooms from 7600 CFP)*, at the intersection of the coast road and the turn-off to the airport, has two houses with two bedrooms each and a chalet with mezzanine. They're comfortable and have a lounge area, TV, washing machine, refrigerator, kitchen and bathroom (with hot water).

Motel Vanille (☎/fax *68 71 77;* e *yves motelvani@hotmail.com; rooms 5000 CFP, bungalows 9500 CFP)* is off the airport road, 50m from the intersection with the coast road. This pretty guesthouse has five local-style bungalows with bathroom (with hot water) and small veranda, set around a swimming pool. Bicycles are available for guests' use. Half-board is an additional 2900 CFP per person. The restaurant here is good (see North of Fare under Places to Eat, later).

Pension Mama Roro (☎/fax *68 84 82; fare from 7100 CFP)* is 100m from Vaihonu Océan, on the other side of the track. There are two fully equipped *fare* with bathroom (with hot water), TV and kitchen area. This tidy, functional place may appeal to families (1500 CFP per extra person). Airport transfers are free.

Pension Fetia (☎ *72 09 50; bungalows for 2/4 people 6700/8700 CFP)*, in an isolated spot in the northeast corner of the island, has simple, clean local-style bungalows with bathroom, kitchen and mosquito net. Dinner (2000 CFP) is available.

South of Fare

About 1km south of town, on the inland side of the road at the turn-off just past the bridge, is **Pension Poetaina** (☎/fax *68 89 49;* e *pensionpoetaina@mail.pf; doubles with/ without bathroom 10,200/8000 CFP)*. This huge place is immaculately kept and has a well-equipped kitchen, a lounge and a small swimming pool. Prices include breakfast.

Chez Henriette (☎/fax *68 83 71; small/ large bungalows 4700/6700 CFP)* is only 500m away from Pension Poetaina, beside the lagoon. The bungalows all have a small kitchen area, refrigerator, mosquito net, fan and bathroom (with cold water). The large bungalows can accommodate up to four people. Airport transfers are 200 CFP.

Maeva Area

At the southern tip of Motu Papiti, 8km from Fare, is the **Sofitel Heiva** (☎ *60 61 60, fax 68 85 25; bungalows from 33,100 CFP)*. It's the biggest hotel on the island and is beautifully situated, with a sandy beach and shallow water separating it from Motu Mahare. There's magnificent snorkelling at La Cité de Corail, and there's a popular surf break just off the reef edge. There are garden bungalows, beach bungalows and overwater bungalows. Add another 7100 CFP per person for half-board. There's a swimming pool, a bar and a restaurant.

Faie

Near the marina is **Pension Te Nahe Toetoe** (☎ *68 71 43, 78 13 53; singles/doubles 3100/ 4300 CFP)*. This Polynesian-style place is constructed using local materials. You stay in the owner's house in one of three small mezzanine rooms reached by a ladder. Although basic and somewhat lacking in privacy, it offers an original and pleasant immersion in the Polynesian world. The shared bathroom has hot water and you can use the kitchen or order a meal (1500 CFP). A pirogue and bicycles are available for guests' use and airport transfers are free.

South of Huahine Nui

Rather a long way from anywhere is **Hôtel Bellevue** (☎ *68 82 76, 68 81 70, fax 68 85 35; singles/doubles 4000/5300 CFP, bungalows from 6800 CFP)*. It's 5km south of Fare and 7km from the airport. The main building has eight rooms with bathroom (cold water only) and 12 bungalows with bathroom (with hot water), mosquito screens and veranda. Although the hotel has seen better days, the quiet setting and views over Maroe Bay are superb. There's a restaurant (Chinese and Polynesian dishes cost 1500 CFP), and a swimming pool. Add 3200 CFP for half-board. Airport transfers are 800 CFP per person one way.

Pension Tupuna (☎ *68 70 21, fax 68 70 36; 2-person bungalows 6100 CFP)* is in an isolated spot near Bourayne Bay, in a coconut plantation by the lagoon. It has three simple local-style bungalows with shared bathroom. Meals (2000 CFP) are served in a *fare potee* and airport transfers are free.

Te Tiare Beach Resort (☎ *60 60 50, fax 60 60 51;* e *tetiarebeach@mail.pf; bungalows*

35,700-77,900 CFP) is at the southwestern corner of Huahine Nui, a good location for a complete getaway. Accessible only by sea, this appealing complex has 41 traditional-style but luxurious bungalows, 16 of them over water. The restaurant has fine food at reasonable prices and there's a full range of activities. Airport transfers cost 5500 CFP return.

Villas Bougainville (☎/fax 68 81 59; villas 16,600-23,600 CFP), in a verdant setting on the north shore of Maroe Bay, comprises three fully equipped villas accommodating up to five people. Rates include the use of a car and a boat, ideal for visiting idyllic Motu Topati. The car and boat are guaranteed to be in good condition, but it's a good idea to check this. Airport transfers are included.

Huahine Vacances (☎/fax 68 73 63; e hua hinevacances@hotmail.com; villas 23,600-26,000 CFP), next to Villas Bougainville, has three fully equipped villas, situated in a garden and overlooking the bay. The spacious, modern villas can accommodate up to seven people. A car and boat are available for guests' use. Airport transfers are free.

Huahine Iti

The (marginally) smaller island has several ideally situated places, the most beautiful beaches and the widest lagoon. If you're fixing your own food, however, it's a long way to any shops, and there's no public transport to speak of.

Ariiura Camping Écologie (☎ 68 85 20; camping per person 1300 CFP, singles/doubles in camping fare 2900/3900 CFP) is right on the beach, south of Relais Mahana. It's a good place for people on a budget looking for a relaxed atmosphere and Polynesian setting. It's also close to prime surfing. The 'camping fare' are small, simple cabins on the sand with a bed and mosquito net. The cabins don't lock and even the toilet facilities are local-style! A small thatched fare beside the beach offers meals if you don't wish to use the communal kitchen. Le trucks (300 CFP) leave for Fare at around 7.30am and return at 11am . There's also a pirogue available for guests' use and you can rent snorkelling equipment for 300 CFP per day.

Pension Mauarii (☎/fax 68 86 49; e vetea @mail.pf; singles 6900 CFP, doubles from 8100 CFP, bungalows from 10,600 CFP) is about 3km from Parea in a beautiful seafront

garden. It's full of style and character, with four impeccable garden bungalows with bathroom (with hot water). There are two comfortable local-style beach bungalows. Close to the beach, a traditional fare has two rooms on the ground floor. The adjoining lagoonside restaurant is well known; see Around the Island under Places to Eat, later. Half-board costs an additional 3000 CFP per person. Return airport transfers are 2000 CFP. You can do your washing for 1500 CFP.

Relais Mahana (☎ 68 81 54, fax 68 85 08; e relaismahana@mail.pf; bungalows from 20,100 CFP; open mid-Dec–mid-Nov), 1km south of Pension Mauarii, almost at the southern point of Huahine Iti, has beach and garden bungalows. It's on a beautiful shady beach with coconut palms and is owned by popaa (Westerners). Meals are served in a lagoonside restaurant fare. Breakfast starts at 1120 CFP and à la carte dining is available. There's a small laundrette (1100 CFP a load), a swimming pool and a variety of sporting equipment available free for guests' use. Airport transfers are 1300 CFP one-way.

PLACES TO EAT
Fare

For cheap eats and late eats, the quayside **roulottes** are Huahine's best bargain. They operate from early morning until late at night. Fish, chicken, burgers, steaks and chips are the order of the day, and a meal typically costs around 800 CFP to 1200 CFP. Your meal could be followed by crepes, gaufres (waffles) or a slice of pastèque (watermelon). Plan to eat early, as after 9pm most places start to close their doors.

There are a number of places to eat along the main street. **Chez Guynette** (breakfast 850 CFP, lunch 1000-1500 CFP; open daily) offers light lunches in a pleasant open-air area.

Te Marara (☎ 68 70 81; dishes 1000-1700 CFP; open Mon-Fri, closed Fri night, Sat & Sun), at the end of the main street and pleasantly situated by the lagoon, offers local specialities at reasonable prices. Grilled mahi mahi (dorado) is 1500 CFP; other dishes include raw fish, sashimi, tuna tartare, freshwater shrimps, and lobster.

Pension Enite (☎ 68 82 37; meals 2800 CFP; open Mon-Sat dinner only) has a charming restaurant in a fare by the water. Local specialities are served and the food has an excellent reputation. Bookings are essential. Seafood meals cost 3800 CFP.

Tiare Tipanier (☎ *68 80 52; dishes 1100-2000 CFP; closed Sun & Mon lunch)* is very popular, offering an excellent blend of price and quality. The small menu features fish dishes such as mahi mahi with banana and vanilla sauce (1700 CFP), pizzas starting at 1200 CFP and some meat dishes. There's also a 2200 CFP set menu including wine or beer.

Snack-Restaurant Hiti Ura *(dishes 1000-1500 CFP; open Tues-Fri lunch & dinner, Sat & Sun dinner)* is a local snack bar in the centre of Fare, opposite the quay. It serves simple, reasonably priced dishes, such as grilled mahi mahi and raw fish in coconut milk.

If you're preparing your own meals, fruit, vegetables and fish are available from the impromptu quayside **marketplace**. Fare has several well-stocked food shops, including **Super Fare Nui**, opposite the waterfront, and **Taahitini**, immediately south of the town centre, both open Monday to Saturday and Sunday morning.

North of Fare
Facing the sea, **Restaurant Tehina** (☎ *68 75 53; dishes 1400-2600 CFP, lunch 600-1400 CFP; closed Sun lunch)* is the restaurant at Pension Fare Maeva (see Places to Stay). The varied menu includes fried tuna (1400 CFP), tuna carpaccio, baked papaya and simple sandwiches.

Restaurant Vanille (☎ *68 71 77; dishes 1200-2200; closed Mon)*, at Motel Vanille (see North of Fare under Places to Stay, earlier), is a good choice. The menu includes tasty Polynesian-style tuna *chaud froid* (cold jellied tuna), tuna tartare with local honey (1700 CFP) and fish steaks.

Around the Island
Once you've left Fare there aren't too many places to eat, apart from the hotels. You can try the pleasant **Omai** at the Sofitel Heiva (see Maeve Area under Places to Stay, earlier), where there's a varied menu including an evening buffet.

Eden Parc (☎ *68 86 58; set menus 1000-2500 CFP; open Mon-Sat, lunch only)*, in the southwestern corner of Huahine Nui, is a local fruit farm and orchard. In addition to the delicious fruit juices starting at 300 CFP, you can choose between four set menus made with organic produce.

Restaurant Mauarii (☎ *68 86 49; dishes 1500-4300 CFP; open daily lunch & dinner)*, at Pension Mauarii on Huahine Iti, has some of the best food on the island. For a real feast, try the traditional Polynesian meal, which includes chicken *fafa* (chicken with taro leaves), braised *pua* (pork) with cabbage, raw fish, taro, *fei* (a type of banana), *uru* (breadfruit), and *poe* (crushed fruit wrapped in a banana leaf and then baked in the oven with a vanilla bean) for dessert, all for a bargain 2650 CFP. Shark curry (2300 CFP), swordfish or mahi mahi gratin and various seafood dishes are also available.

Restaurant Tenahe (☎ *68 81 54; dishes 1100-2700 CFP, set menu 3000 CFP; open daily lunch & dinner)*, at Relais Mahana (see Places to Stay), gets favourable word-of-mouth reviews. The setting is a light-filled room by the lagoon, and the menu features well-presented local specialities with a welcome twist of originality. A simple snack menu is available at lunch time.

There are a few small **food shops** with variable opening hours at Maeva and Fitii on Huahine Nui, and at Haapu and Parea on Huahine Iti.

ENTERTAINMENT
Entertainment on Huahine is very limited. **Sofitel Heiva** has twice-weekly buffet dinners with good-quality traditional dance performances for 5000 CFP to 6000 CFP.

SHOPPING
Plenty of places sell souvenirs and local crafts in and around Fare. Opposite the quay, on the main street, **Rima'i Te Niu Taue** sells pottery, jewellery and colourful pareu (sarong-type garments). **Souvenirs des Îles**, next door, also has a pretty good selection. You can buy postcards and other souvenirs at the bright and energetic **Jojo**. At the end of the main street, **Arts Polynésiens** has good-quality local crafts, including paintings and pottery.

In Faie, don't miss a visit to **Huahine Nui Pearls & Pottery**. Peter Owen, the owner, is a potter as well as a pearl farmer, and his work is shown in Pape'ete galleries. His studio is on his pearl farm on the lagoon. From Faie a ferry operates at 10am and 3pm daily except Sunday (1000 CFP). Credit cards are accepted at the shop.

HUAHINE

At Maeva, several families grow and sell vanilla, including **Chez Michèle**, 800m before the *fare potee* if you're coming from Fare, on the inland side. Next to Marae Manunu is **Atiho Peinture**, a small studio where you can find pareu and engraved pearl shells.

GETTING THERE & AWAY

Westbound from Tahiti it's 170km to Huahine, the first of the Leeward Islands. The twin islands of Ra'iatea and Taha'a lie a further 35km to the west.

Air

Huahine's airport is 2.5km from Fare. Air Tahiti has flights from Pape'ete three to five times daily, taking 35 minutes (a bit longer via Mo'orea). Onward flights continue to Ra'iatea and/or Bora Bora. The short hop over to Ra'iatea takes barely 15 minutes. For Maupiti you have to change aircraft at Ra'iatea. One-way adult fares to/from Huahine are: Bora Bora 7300 CFP, Maupiti 7700 CFP, Mo'orea 11,500 CFP, Pape'ete 9200 CFP and Ra'iatea 4600 CFP. **Air Tahiti** (☎ 68 77 02, 60 62 60; open 7.30am-11.45am & 1.30pm-4.30pm Mon-Fri, 7.30am-11.30am Sat) is on the main street in Fare, opposite the quay.

Boat

The *Aremiti 3* links Pape'ete, Huahine and Ra'iatea twice a week, on Monday and Wednesday. It departs Pape'ete at 7am and arrives at Huahine at 10.45am. From Pape'ete to Huahine costs 4770/2385 CFP adult/child; from Huahine to Ra'iatea costs 1760/880 CFP adult/child. The **Aremiti 3 office** (open 9am-12.30 & 1.30pm-3pm) is on the quay in the centre of Fare. Call ☎ 74 39 40, 73 52 73 or 68 75 16 for information.

Inter-island cargo ships are another option, although less reliable. The *Vaeanu*, *Taporo VII* and *Hawaiki Nui* depart from Pape'ete and stop at Huahine. (See Ferry & Cargo Ship in the Getting Around chapter for more information.)

GETTING AROUND
To/From the Airport

You could walk into town if you were really intent on saving money, but *pensions* and hotels in Fare will arrange taxi transfers, (sometimes included in their tariffs). It costs 600 CFP to go to Fare and 1100 CFP to go to the south of the island.

Le Truck & Taxi

The extreme shortage of public transport is Huahine's biggest drawback. Le trucks belonging to each district shuttle in to Fare early each morning and return to the various villages later in the morning for 300 CFP. **Pension Enite** (☎ 68 82 37) and **Félix Tours** (☎ 68 81 69) can organise taxis.

Car

There are three car-rental operators in Huahine. They will deliver directly to the airport or to your hotel. It's wise to book ahead for long weekends, school vacations, Christmas and peak tourist seasons. Rental periods of four, eight, 24 and 48 hours are offered, with or without unlimited mileage. If you intend to drive all the way around the island, unlimited mileage will probably be cheaper. It's worth asking if there are any discounts. Credit cards are accepted.

The main agency of **Europcar** (☎ 68 82 59, 68 88 03, fax 68 80 59; open 7am-6pm daily) is north of the centre of Fare, near the post office. It also has counters at the airport, Sofitel Heiva and Relais Mahana. A Citroën Saxo costs 8400 CFP for 24 hours with unlimited mileage.

The main agency of **Avis-Pacificar** (☎ 68 73 34, fax 68 73 35; open 7am-6pm daily) is next to the Mobil petrol station in Fare and also has a counter at the airport. A Citroën Saxo or Peugeot 106 costs 8300 CFP for 24 hours with unlimited mileage.

Huahine Location (☎/fax 68 78 85; open 7am-6pm daily), about 100m from the post office towards the airport, charges 8220 CFP for 24 hours with unlimited mileage for similar models to those already mentioned.

There are two petrol stations in Fare; one or the other will be open Sunday morning and afternoon.

Scooter & Bicycle

You can rent bicycles from Europcar and Huahine Location (see Car, earlier, for details) for 2000 CFP a day. **Chez Huahine Lagoon** (☎ 68 70 00, 68 87 57), on the waterfront at the northern end of the main street in Fare, charges 1500 CFP a day for a mountain bike in excellent shape.

For scooters, check with Europcar, which charges 5900 CFP for 24 hours, or Huahine Location, which charges 6700 CFP with free delivery.

LINDA CHING

JEAN-BERNARD CARILLET

JEAN-BERNARD CARILLET

Dancers and costume details

Traditional dancers

TAHITIAN DANCE

Tahitian dance has enormous cultural and symbolic significance. Much more than a tourist attraction, it is one of the most vibrant forms of expression underlying Maohi (Polynesian) culture, and it plays a major part in spreading the influence of Tahitian culture abroad. Behind every performance lies months of rehearsals, rigorously standardised choreography and an important piece of legend that is consummately acted out with its own hierarchical structure and meaning. In this land of oral traditions, dance is not merely an aesthetic medium but also a way to preserve the memory of the past. It is also a discipline in a constant state of evolution and a social mirror that reflects the frictions in current Tahitian society, which is torn between tradition and modernity.

The luxury hotels offer top-quality dance shows around twice a week. On Tahiti and Mo'orea they are performed by the very best semiprofessional groups. On other islands, the companies are rather more amateur but, in any event, it will not be a typically touristy show, and no matter where you are you will see rehearsals and 'coaching sessions'. These shows come with a buffet (around 7000 CFP), open to all. If you only wish to attend the show, inquire about the hotel's policy. Some ask for an entrance fee or insist you have the buffet, while others require you to buy a drink at the bar (about 1000 CFP). The performances last about 45 minutes, and comprise several sequences of *otea* and *aparima* and, sometimes, a fire dance.

History

Little is known about Polynesian dance before the arrival of the Europeans. What we do know, from the accounts of the first explorers and missionaries, is that entertainment, and especially dancing, held an important place in the society of that period. Dancing accompanied group rituals and ceremonies on the *marae* (traditional temples). It also had sacred overtones that were embodied by the *ario'i*, the actor-dancer-troubadours who performed in various clans. Many different *heiva* (celebrations) in the life of the community incorporated dancing, singing and mime. Dancing was accompanied by *pahu* (drums) and *vivo* (nasal flute).

After the arrival of the missionaries, dancing suffered the same fate as tattooing and the traditional places of worship. Deemed to be both pagan and lewd, dancing was forbidden by the Code of Pomare of 1819. The practice was carried on in secret. From 1895, a number of tightly controlled dance performances were allowed to take place to celebrate the festival of 14 July (Bastille Day) called Tiurai (and now known as the Heiva).

From 1956 onwards, traditional dancing was modernised by a former primary school teacher by the name of Madeleine Moua and was given a new image free of demonic overtones. She created Heiva, the first professional dance group, perfected the costumes and made choreography more straightforward, while still drawing on the rich Maohi cultural heritage. Since then other dance companies have appeared on the scene, and Tahitian dance has become vibrant once again, even though the dancing we see today probably has little to do with the spectacles of former times.

Inset: A Traditional Marquesas dance group (Photograph by Jean-Bernard Carillet)

Types of Dance

There are five types of dance. They are seldom performed on their own but instead are usually integrated into a programme where each is performed in turn. Beware the *tamure*, a term of recent origin referring to a popularised form of Tahitian dance that has absolutely no traditional cultural basis.

The Otea Impressive and highly physical, the *otea* is a very distinctive group dance: the accompanying music is provided entirely by percussion instruments. Originally this was a male-only war dance. Nowadays dancers are more likely to be both male and female, but the 'manly' character is still preserved in the body language, the rhythm and the sudden loud cries of the dancers.

The men's steps are radically different from the women's. The men mainly use their legs to perform a very specific and highly spectacular movement known as *paoti*: with knees bent and heels together but slightly raised, they alternately open and close their knees with a scissor-like movement that can be fast or slow, depending on the tempo set by the percussion. The basic female movement is a swaying of the hips caused by intensive bending and straightening of the knees with the feet kept level on the ground. The men should not move their hips in the slightest and the women should keep their chests and shoulders completely still.

There is an extensive repertoire of steps in the *otea*, especially for the men. The *tu'e* (forward kick), the *ui* (a movement towards the side or the front while at the same time performing a *chassé* with one leg), the *patia* (a piston-like movement with the leg) and the *horo* (another, lesser movement) are the most frequent steps after the *paoti*.

The movements in which arms and hands are directed in a rather sharp and angular fashion towards the upper part of the body are equally common to men and women. On stage the dancers are placed in a geometric formation, in men-only or women-only rows.

The *otea* occasionally includes a solo performance: the group sits or kneels while a single performer or a couple stands up and dances, each in turn.

The choreography is governed by a number of underlying themes, such as volcanoes, sharks, historical events or legends, all of which may be suggested by the use of props. Since it is so gruelling, an *otea* sequence lasts only a few minutes.

The Aparima The *aparima* is free flowing and graceful, and beguiles and soothes the spectator. In very rough terms, the *aparima* is a mixed-gender dance that tells a story using hand movement and song. The story may be a legend, a love song or a scene from everyday life. In contrast to the *otea*, the hand and arm movements are predominant. There is a great deal of expressiveness and realism: the dancers mime each scene very effectively (eg, paddling, opening a coconut), using props where necessary.

The musical accompaniment is provided by guitar and ukulele. Percussion is less important and simply there to set the tempo. The dancers follow every hand movement with their eyes and faces.

There are two variants of the *aparima*: the *aparima himene*, sung by the orchestra and the dancers, and the *aparima vava*, which is instrumental, the story told entirely by means of gesture. An *aparima* sequence lasts only a few minutes.

The Hivinau The *hivinau* mimics the body language of English sailors hoisting the anchor to the shouts of 'heave now'.

Men and women form a double circle surrounding the orchestra (drums only) and a male vocal soloist, known as the *ra'atira hivinau*. The soloist recites a few words and the dancers, playing the part of the choir, reply with a chorus. The two groups of dancers cross and turn in opposite directions or both groups go in a clockwise direction. During the chorus, the dancers in each circle turn and face a partner and dance as a couple. The steps are the same as those of the *otea* but less complicated. The drums merely keep time.

The predominant aspect of the *hivinau* is the interplay between the vocals of the soloist and the responses from the choir. Performance of the *hivinau* is becoming something of a rare occurrence since it requires such a large number of participants.

The Paoa The *paoa* is said to have its origins in the manufacture of *tapa* (bark cloth). The women, sitting in a circle, would sing for motivation as they pounded the bark. One of them would get the group going by singing the words and the others would respond. Every so often a woman would get up to dance a few steps.

A male and female choir seated on the ground forms a semicircle, in the centre of which a male vocal soloist recites a few words, often based on legend. The members of the choir respond and keep time by slapping their thighs with both hands. The orchestra (drums only) maintains a position next to the soloist. One couple then comes into the centre and improvises a dance using the simplified steps of the *otea*, interspersed with shouts of 'hi' and 'ha' that have strong erotic overtones. As in the *hivinau*, it is the dialogue between the leader and the choir that is the key element of the *paoa*.

The Fire Dance This dance, which is thought to have originated in Samoa, is frequently put on as part of shows in hotels because it is so impressive. The performer, always a man, juggles a flaming torch alight at both ends, against a background of drums.

Marquesan Dance The Marquesans, who have their own distinctive cultural identity, have developed types of dance that are very different from the *ori Tahiti* (Tahitian dances). These dances are performed on the Marquesas for specifically Marquesan festivals. The most famous of these is the Haku Manu, modelled on the movements of a bird. The Dance of the Pig, very impressive on account of its physicality, mimics the symbolic phases of the animal's life. The action is punctuated by loud husky shouts of 'hi' and 'ha'. Percussion instruments alone are used. The enormous drums can be up to 1.5m high. Usually Marquesan costumes are plainer than Tahitian ones, being simply loincloths made out of plant fibres.

Instruments

Dancers and musicians must display perfect harmony and synchronisation. The musicians usually stand at the front of the stage and to one side so as to maintain visual contact with the group.

Percussion is used for the *otea*, *hivinau*, *aparima vava*, *paoa* and fire dance. Stringed instruments accompany the *aparima himene*. The orchestra is considered a male preserve, and this is true particularly of percussion. Very much all-rounders, the musicians play both percussion and stringed instruments and also sing.

Drums are the Maohi instruments *par excellence*. Three types are used. The *toere* is a drum with no skin that is carved out of a piece of wood. It is cylindrical in shape, and hollowed out with a narrow slit down the whole of its length, and it is this that produces resonance. The orchestra comprises different sizes of *toere*, each of which produces a distinct sound. *Toere* are played in two ways: when placed vertically, the drummer holds the upper end with one hand and with the other hits the split side with a stick; when supported horizontally on trestles, two sticks are used to hit it. The drummers may be either seated or kneeling. Usually an orchestra comprises between one and five *toere*.

The *faatete* is a drum with a single skin. It is played with two sticks, and rests on a support aimed at raising the height of the resonance chamber.

The *pahu*, or *tari parau*, is a drum with two skins, rather like a bass drum. The musician plays from a seated position and strikes the drum, held on his side, with a special beater to produce a more muffled sound.

String instruments are of European origin, though the ukulele, a mini-guitar with four strings, comes by way of Hawaii. Guitars are also now an integral part of the orchestra.

Costumes

Costumes, made from plant matter, are a key component of Tahitian dance and the glamour surrounding it. A distinction is made between two types of costume, one for the *otea* and the other for the *aparima*.

For the *otea*, the outfit covers the dancers' bodies from head to foot. Dancers wear a crown of fresh flowers (frangipani, *tiare* or gardenia, and bougainvillea) or a huge and elaborate headdress, as well as garlands of flowers and seashells. Women wear a bikini top made of two halves of a coconut, polished and dyed black, and held together with a piece of string. Dancers of both sexes wear a *more* (skirt) made of *purau* (hibiscus) bark cut into very thin strips, sewn together and dyed red or yellow. Men's *more* hang down slightly below the knees and are attached to the waist; women's are knotted around the hips and hang down as far as the ankles.

A decorative belt of flowers, mother-of-pearl, pieces of polished coconut and seashells is worn over the *more*. The inner part of the belt is fitted with pendants made of vegetable fibres and seashells, which emphasise the swaying movements of the hips as the women dance. Men wear *purau* fibres around their calves, and dancers of both sexes sport plumes that they wave in their hands to emphasise movement of the upper limbs

The outfit for the *aparima* is simpler and usually consists of a pareu (sarong-type garment) worn as a loincloth for the men, or tied like a skirt or dress for the women. Garlands of flowers or seashells are used as hats.

The costumes are designed by the group leader to suit the theme, which is reinforced by frequent use of props (eg, paddles). Usually the dancers have to produce their own outfits.

Dance Groups

A dance company might well perform with as many as 150 participants on important occasions but, as a rule, there is a core of about 20 dancers.

There is no truly professional group. The best-known groups are semiprofessional. Their members perform in hotels two or three times a week but the group fees are not sufficient to allow the performers to make a living out of their activities.

Usually between 15 and 35 years of age, the dancers are from very different social and ethnic backgrounds. The *demis* (mixed race, of Polynesian and European heritage) are in the majority, but you also find Maohi, Chinese and even *popaa* (Westerners). The criteria for employment are motivation and a love of bodily expression rather than a beautiful physique but, given the sheer physical energy required and the bodily exposure, dancers' bodies tend to be very impressive. Three to five months' rehearsing is necessary before a dancer can hope to perform in public.

On Tahiti, O Tahiti E, Les Grands Ballets de Tahiti, Te Maeva and Heikura Nui are the groups that you will find performing in hotels most frequently. Every company has its own style and personality, depending largely upon the choreographer's charisma, as well as on the group's charisma.

Companies are highly structured. The *ra'atira* (leader) is choreographer and conductor, directing rehearsals, choosing costumes, selecting themes and deciding on the exact positions of performers on stage. During major performances the *ra'atira* encourages the dancers by circulating among the spectators and shouting out recommendations. The *'orero* (orator) announces the theme to the public. The most experienced dancers, male and female, are called *pupahu* and are placed at the front of the stage.

The musicians are an integral part of the group. They are highly versatile, singing, playing percussion and strings. They are always men.

The Heiva

The Heiva is the high point in the celebration of Maohi culture. Every year for a month, from late June to late July, islanders from all the archipelagos join together for a full programme of festivities in Pape'ete and on some of the other islands. The emphasis is on traditional dance contests and singing competitions, but there are numerous other activities on offer, from craft demonstrations to Maohi sports and events such as walking over fire. For the tourist, this is a unique opportunity to discover first-hand the rich Maohi cultural heritage.

Prior to 1985, the Heiva was known as Tiurai (July). The first Heiva took place in 1882, when the object of the event was to celebrate 14 July (Bastille Day). Dancing was at first banned but was slowly introduced. Gradually the festival's republican overtones disappeared and the Tiurai became a festival of Polynesian culture.

The Heiva is organised by Tahiti Nui 2000 (☎ 50 31 00). Reservations for the evening dance contests can be made from May onwards at the kiosk at Place Toata. You can also inquire at the tourist office. The evening will set you back between 1000 and 2500 CFP. Dance performances take place next to the cultural centre.

Events The star events of the Heiva are the **dance** contests. Over a period of several evenings about twenty groups from different islands compete with each other before a jury for a number of different prizes including Best Group, Best Orchestra, Best Costume, Best Couple, and Best Piece of Music. A strict set of rules governs the performances. The jury pays great attention to synchronisation, thematic interpretation, costumes and choreography.

There are two categories: freestyle and traditional. In the traditional category, each group must perform a classical dance based on a theme inspired by Polynesian history or legend. In the freestyle category, innovations in choreography and body language are the order of the day.

Although **singing** competitions are less prestigious than dancing, they are part of the Heiva, and various competing choirs are held in high esteem. Unfortunately, they are more or less impenetrable to the novice, owing to the complexity of the polyphonic structures of songs such as the *himene ruau*, *himene tarava tahiti*, *himene tarava raromatai* and *ute paripari*. The choirs are mixed, both male and female, and comprise up to ten voices. The themes are suggestive of Maohi legend.

In ancient times, the *'orero* acted as the 'memory' of Maohi culture. His role was to recite ancestries and to pass on cultural heritage. This new competitive category, the **'orero contest**, launched at the 1998 Heiva, aims to revive and preserve the tradition. Each *'orero* recites a text lasting five to 10 minutes, either based on legend or on a theme particular to the group he belongs to.

The national sport of **canoeing** is in great favour at every Heiva. The finest rowers in Polynesia, in crews of one, three, six or 16 men and women, compete in several races over a distance of 2600m or 3500m in the Tahiti lagoon or out at sea. One race goes all the way round Mo'orea (84km) but changes of crew are allowed.

Amoraa ofae (rock lifting), which originated in the Australs, is truly spectacular and calls for great strength and skill. Competitors are dressed in pareu and are required to lift a smooth rock weighing between 90 and 145 kilos, which they must hoist on to their shoulders.

The ancestral sport of **patia fa** (javelin throwing) from the Tuamotus truly comes to life at the Heiva. The object is to hit a coconut tied to the top of a 7.5m pole from a distance of 22m. Individuals or two-person teams can compete in this event.

Coconut shelling, which is still widespread on the Tuamotus and the Marquesas, has been turned into a competition for the Heiva. Each team of three competitors has to split open and scoop out the insides of between 150 and 200 coconuts in the shortest possible time and place the meat in a hessian sack. The tools used are an axe and a *pana* (curved knife).

In ancient times, Polynesian fruit bearers would hang the fruit they had picked from both ends of a stick, which they carried on their shoulders. There are two **fruit-bearing races** over a distance of about 2km. The first is run with a burden of 30kg and the second with a load of 50kg.

The marae come back to life in a number of **historical reconstructions**. The most usual scenes you will encounter are of ceremonies investing kings with royal powers, and princely marriages. The sites selected for these events are usually the marae at Pae'a (Arahurahu) or those in the Papenoo Valley.

Other features of the Heiva include demonstrations of *niau*-making (woven coconut-palm leaves), *tifaifai*-making (appliqué) and *tapa*-making, as well as a stone-carving competition, a procession of floral floats, voting for Miss Heiva and Mr Heiva, a funfair, firework displays, fire walking and tattoo displays.

Ra'iatea & Taha'a

Between Huahine and Bora Bora, the twin islands of Ra'iatea (rah-ee-ah-tay-ah) and Taha'a (ta-hah-ah) are separated by a narrow 3km channel and share a common lagoon. Less touristy than their neighbours, these islands offer an opportunity to enjoy a more relaxed Polynesian lifestyle. The airport is on Ra'iatea and most inter-island ships dock at Uturoa, so visitors to either island will usually come to Ra'iatea first.

The Hawaiki Nui canoe race, which starts on Huahine, continues to Ra'iatea and Taha'a before finishing on Bora Bora (see the boxed text 'Hawaiki Nui Canoe Race' in the Facts for the Visitor chapter).

Ra'iatea

pop 10,057 • area 170 sq km
The largest of the Leeward Islands and second largest in the Society group after Tahiti, Ra'iatea has no beaches. This may account for its comparatively untouristed flavour, although there are fine beaches on its many motu, and its yachting marinas make it the sailing centre of French Polynesia. The lagoon is ideal for diving courses and pirogue tours, while the mountainous interior is the place for walks and horse rides.

Often referred to as 'sacred Ra'iatea', the island had an important role in ancient Polynesian religious beliefs. It is home to Marae Taputapuatea, the most important marae (traditional temple) in French Polynesia.

Ra'iatea's Faaroa River, which feeds into Faaroa Bay, is the only navigable river in French Polynesia. Polynesian oral history relates that it was from this river that the great migration voyages to Hawaii and New Zealand commenced.

History
Ra'iatea, known as Havai'i in ancient times, is the cultural, religious and historic centre of the Society Islands. According to legend, Ra'iatea and Taha'a were the first islands to be settled, probably by people from Samoa far to the northwest. It is said that Ra'iatea's first king was the legendary Hiro, who with his companions built the great canoes that sailed to Rarotonga and New Zealand.

Highlights

- Visiting Marae Taputapuatea, the Leeward Islands' most famous archaeological site
- Discovering the lagoon and its motu in a pirogue with an outboard motor
- Taking a guided hike to Mt Temehani to look for the rare *tiare apetahi* flower
- Diving at Teavapiti Pass
- Visiting a pearl farm and a vanilla plantation
- Walking the Taha'a cross-island track from Haamene to Patio

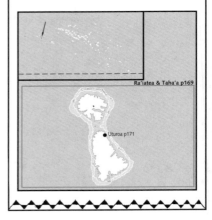

Ra'iatea & Taha'a p169

Uturoa p171

Later, Ra'iatea was a centre for the 'Oro (god of war) cult, which was in the process of replacing the earlier Ta'aroa (god of creation) cult when Europeans turned up and disrupted the entire Polynesian religious structure. At the time of James Cook's first Polynesian visit, Ra'iatea was probably under Bora Bora's control and its chiefs were scattered far and wide.

Cook first came to the island on the *Endeavour* in 1769, when he anchored off Opoa. He returned in 1774 during his second Pacific voyage. In 1777 he made a prolonged visit before sailing to Hawaii.

The English missionary John Williams came to Ra'iatea in 1818 and the island remained under British missionary influence long after Tahiti came under French control.

RA'IATEA & TAHA'A

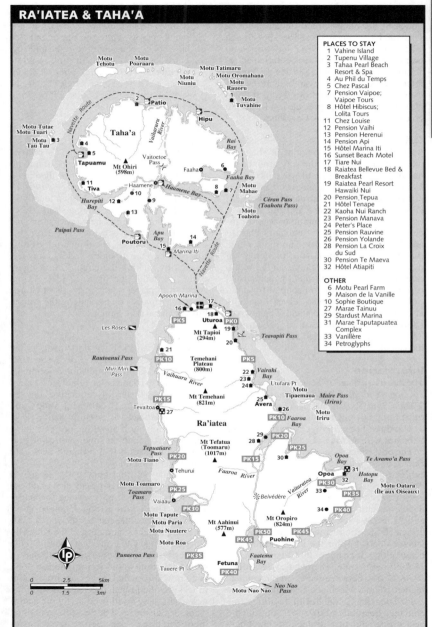

PLACES TO STAY
1 Vahine Island
2 Tupenu Village
3 Tahaa Pearl Beach Resort & Spa
4 Au Phil du Temps
5 Chez Pascal
7 Pension Vaipoe; Vaipoe Tours
8 Hôtel Hibiscus; Lolita Tours
11 Chez Louise
12 Pension Vaihi
13 Pension Herenui
14 Pension Api
15 Hôtel Marina Iti
16 Sunset Beach Motel
17 Tiare Nui
18 Raiatea Bellevue Bed & Breakfast
19 Raiatea Pearl Resort Hawaiki Nui
20 Pension Tepua
21 Hôtel Tenape
22 Kaoha Nui Ranch
23 Pension Manava
24 Peter's Place
25 Pension Rauvine
26 Pension Yolande
28 Pension La Croix du Sud
30 Pension Te Maeva
32 Hôtel Atiapiti

OTHER
6 Motu Pearl Farm
9 Maison de la Vanille
10 Sophie Boutique
27 Marae Tainuu
29 Stardust Marina
31 Marae Taputapuatea Complex
33 Vanillère
34 Petroglyphs

It was from Ra'iatea that missionaries continued to Rarotonga in the Cook Islands in 1823 and to Samoa in 1830. The French takeover of Tahiti in 1842 led to a long period of instability and fierce Ra'iatean resistance. It was not until 1888 that the French attempted a real takeover and 1897 that troops were sent to put down the final Polynesian rebellion. Teraupoo, the last Ra'iatean chief, was exiled to New Caledonia.

Orientation

Ra'iatea is vaguely triangular in shape. A road hugs the coast all the way around; it's not all sealed, but is suitable for cars. *Pointe kilométrique* (PK) distances are not signposted, but start in Uturoa near the *gendarmerie* (police station) and run south to Faatemu Bay. The mountainous interior includes the 800m-high Temehani Plateau and Mt Tefatua (1017m). The main range runs north–south for most of the length of the island, with smaller ranges in the south, separated by a valley through which a road runs from Faaroa Bay to Faatemu Bay.

The airport, which also serves Taha'a, is at the northern tip of the island. The town of Uturoa extends southeast of the airport. Small villages are scattered across the rest of the island.

Information

The **tourist office** (☎ 60 07 77, fax 60 07 76; open 8am-4pm Mon-Fri, 8am-3pm Sat, 9.30am-3pm Sun) is in the *gare maritime* (boat terminal) in Uturoa.

The three French Polynesian banks have branches with **ATMs** in Uturoa.

The **post office** (open 7am-3pm Mon-Thur, 7am-2pm Fri, 8am-10am Sat) is north of the centre of Uturoa towards the airport. **Le Phénix** (☎/fax 66 20 66; open 8am-12pm & 2pm-5pm Mon-Fri, 8am-12pm Sat), between the marina and the airport, offers internet access; it's set back from the road on the ground floor of an isolated building on the lagoon side (look for the parrot painted on the window). It charges 900 CFP per hour or 15 CFP per minute. There's also **Techniîles** (☎ 66 12 00), between the Champion supermarket and the Moemoea snack bar.

Ra'iatea has good health facilities, including a **hospital** (☎ 60 02 01), opposite the post office, and several doctors. The **pharmacy** (open daily) is on the main street.

The **Bleu des Îles laundry** (open 7.30am-11.30am & 2pm-6.30pm Mon-Fri) in the Tahina shopping centre, on the inland side of the airport road, charges 1500 CFP per load for washing and drying. **Laverie Jacqueline** (☎ 66 28 36; open 8.30am-11.30am & 1pm-4.30pm Mon-Fri), at the Apooiti Marina, charges 300 CFP per kilogram for washing and drying.

AROUND THE ISLAND

The 98km circuit of Ra'iatea provides an opportunity to enjoy the island's relaxed atmosphere and splendid views of mountains and motu. Just over half of the circuit is on roads of crushed coral – *soupe de corail* (coral soup), as it's known locally.

In the south of the island, a short stretch of fine mountain road between Faaroa and Faatemu Bays takes you away from the coast and past an excellent lookout. Adding this road into the itinerary – adding it twice, in fact, by making the circuit into a figure eight – extends the drive to just 111km. Apart from places on the outskirts of Uturoa there is virtually nowhere along the way to buy lunch, so take a picnic.

Uturoa

Uturoa, Ra'iatea's busy port town, is the largest town in French Polynesia after Pape'ete and is the administrative centre of the Leeward Islands. Its jumble of varied buildings is not terribly attractive, but the main street, with its colourful **shops** and busy **marketplace**, is certainly active. Restoration and modernisation projects have been undertaken in the town centre and port district. One result is the superb new **gare maritime** on the quay.

The quay is often busy with the arrival and departure of inter-island boats and the regular *navette* (shuttle) service to nearby Taha'a. There is a strong Chinese community here, evidenced by the many Chinese shops and restaurants and the Kuo Min Tang building. The Protestant church on the northern side of the town centre has a **memorial stone** to pioneer missionary John Williams. Queen Pomare, exiled from Tahiti in 1844 by the French takeover, took refuge in Vairahi, now swallowed up by the southward expansion of Uturoa. She remained there for three years before returning to Tahiti. **Mt Tapioi** (294m) overlooks Uturoa.

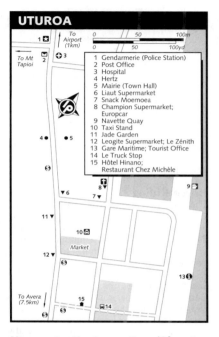

UTUROA

To Airport (1km)

To Mt Tapioi

To Avera (7.5km)

Market

0   50   100m
0   50   100yd

1 Gendarmerie (Police Station)
2 Post Office
3 Hospital
4 Hertz
5 Mairie (Town Hall)
6 Liaut Supermarket
7 Snack Moemoea
8 Champion Supermarket;
  Europcar
9 Navette Quay
10 Taxi Stand
11 Jade Garden
12 Leogite Supermarket; Le Zénith
13 Gare Maritime; Tourist Office
14 Le Truck Stop
15 Hôtel Hinano;
   Restaurant Chez Michèle

Uturoa to Faatemu Bay (0km to 22.5km)

Bustling Uturoa blends seamlessly into **Avera**, site of the final battle between the French and local rebels, before following the contours of the narrow and magnificent **Faaroa Bay**. At 12.5km the road passes Stardust Marina, one of two major yacht-charter operations. Soon after, you reach the turn-off to the south coast. The Faaroa River leads inland from the bay.

From the turn-off the road runs to a **belvédère** (lookout) with great views of Faaroa Bay, the coast and the surrounding mountains, then drops down to the south-coast road.

Faatemu Bay to Marae Taputapuatea (22.5km to 42km)

Turn left at the coast; the bottom half of the figure-eight circuit will take you around the coast anticlockwise.

In places near the village of **Puohine** (25km) the road runs on embankments, cutting off shallow ponds used for farming oysters and mussels. There's a long stretch past the village where the steep green mountain-

sides are streaked with **waterfalls** during the wetter months of the year. Along this part of the road many king-sized **crabs** scuttle across the road; not all of them make it, although traffic is light. Just before reaching Ra'iatea's sacred marae you come to the outskirts of the village of **Opoa** (41km).

Marae Taputapuatea, the most important marae in French Polynesia, looks out to the Te Avamo'a Pass. Dedicated to 'Oro, the god of war who dominated 18th-century Polynesian religious beliefs, the marae sprawls extensively across Cape Matahira. It dates from the 17th century, when it replaced nearby Marae Vaearai, which was dedicated to Ta'aroa, the god of creation.

Despite its relatively short history, this marae assumed great importance in the Polynesian religion. Any marae constructed on another island had to incorporate one of Taputapuatea's stones as a symbol of allegiance and spiritual lineage. When the first Europeans arrived, this was the centre of spiritual power in Polynesia. Its influence was international: *ari'i* (chiefs) from all over the Maohi world, including the Australs, the Cook Islands and New Zealand, came here for important ceremonies.

The site encompasses an international, a district and a domestic marae. The main part of the marae is a large paved platform with a long *ahu* (the equivalent of an altar) stretching down one side. At the very end of the cape is the smaller **Marae Tauraa**, a *tapu* (taboo) enclosure with a tall 'stone of investiture', where young *ari'i* were enthroned. The lagoonside **Marae Hauviri** also has an upright stone. The whole site is made of pieces of coral. The huge double canoes of royal pilgrims used to sail through the Te Avamo'a (Sacred) Pass en route to the marae.

The well-restored marae is imposing, but unfortunately there is little explanation for visitors. It's well worth taking a guide who can explain the site's cultural significance – see Island Tours under Organised Tours later in this chapter and the special section 'Civilisation & Archaeology' for more information on marae.

Marae Taputapuatea to Tevaitoa (42km to 95km)

There's 10km of unsealed road winding around bays and inlets before the surface improves along the southern side of Faaroa Bay. At 57.5km you again turn off the coast road and repeat the short mountain stretch back to the south coast.

The road follows the coast, sometimes running over causeways cutting off shallow, stagnant inlets, to the village of **Fetuna** (68km). During WWII, when the US military occupied Bora Bora, a landing strip was constructed here. **Motu Nao Nao**, just across from Fetuna, has a pleasant beach. The road passes the unremarkable villages of **Vaiaau** (85.5km) and **Tehurui** (88.5km).

In the middle of the village of **Tevaitoa** (95km) stands the island's oldest Protestant church, an architectural curiosity built (in one of those heart-warming examples of Christian respect for other beliefs) smack on top of the magnificent **Marae Tainuu**. Behind the church the walls of the marae stretch for just over 50m, some of the massive upright stones standing over 4m high.

Tevaitoa to Uturoa (95km to 111km)

To Apooiti Marina (107km), the road follows the coastline, with turn-offs leading to the **Temehani Plateau**. Apooiti was the last centre for fire walking on Ra'iatea. The mega-bucks **Apooiti Marina** has shops, a restaurant, a bar and a diving centre. From the marina the road passes by the airport and returns to Uturoa.

ACTIVITIES
Water Activities

There are two **diving** centres for beginners and experienced divers. One is at Apooiti Marina (it also has a base at Raiatea Pearl Resort Hawaiki Nui; see Uturoa under Places to Stay, later) and the other is at the marina at Uturoa. There are about 10 dive sites along the east and west coasts and around Taha'a. A highlight is the superb Teavapiti Pass. See the special section 'Diving' for more information.

Ra'iatea has no beaches – a hotel or guesthouse pontoon is the most you can expect – but some of the reef motu are splendid, and perfect for **swimming** or **snorkelling**. Ask at your accommodation about renting a boat or joining a lagoon tour.

Ra'iatea is the principal nautical centre in the Leeward Islands and is the departure point for numerous **cruises**. For more infor-

Ra'iatea's Emblem

Ra'iatea has one of the world's rarest flowers, the *tiare apetahi*. This endemic species is found only on Mt Temehani. The white flower is shaped like a half-corolla and opens dramatically at dawn. You should be able to see it while hiking on the mountain – but note that it is strictly protected, so no picking.

mation, see Sailing in the Outdoor Activities chapter and Lagoon Tours under Organised Tours later in this chapter.

Horse Riding

The respected **Kaoha Nui Ranch** (☎/fax 66 25 46) is 6km south of Uturoa. It offers 1½-hour rides for 3700 CFP per person and half-day rides for 5300 CFP (minimum of two people). The routes generally follow ridgelines or valley bottoms.

Game Fishing

Game-fishing trips, costing 70,000 CFP to 80,000 CFP per day for up to four people, can be organised on board the **Sakario** (☎ 66 35 54, 66 33 53, 66 34 94) and the **Tevaite** (☎ 66 20 10).

Hiking

There are some good, although largely underutilised, walking opportunities on Ra'iatea. There's the walk up to Temehani Plateau (for which you'll need a guide); the easier climb up Mt Tapioi; and the Three Waterfalls walk in the valley behind Kaoha Nui Ranch. See the Outdoor Activities chapter for more information.

ORGANISED TOURS
Lagoon Tours

Several companies offer lagoon tours in pirogues, with a picnic on a motu and snorkelling and swimming stops. Reserve ahead, as a minimum number of participants is required.

Raiatea Discovery (☎ 66 24 16) offers a half-day tour of Ra'iatea for 5000 CFP, while **Tumatahi Tours** (☎ 66 25 17) offers tours of Ra'iatea and Taha'a for 5500 CFP. **André Topspots** (☎ 60 05 20, 79 22 03) offers half- and full-day tours of both islands; prices for full-day tours range from 6000 CFP to 8000 CFP.

Tane Charter (☎ 66 16 87) offers full-day catamaran tours for 7500 CFP per person.

Manava Tours (☎ 66 28 26) and **Kaoha Nui Ranch** (☎/fax 66 25 46) offer boat trips to Taha'a for 5500 CFP and 7000 CFP respectively. **Hôtel Atiapiti** (☎ 66 16 65) offers motu trips for 2000 CFP to 2500 CFP per person, as well as tours of Taha'a for 6000 CFP to 9000 CFP per person.

Island Tours
If you're alone or don't want to rent a car, 4WD island tours to Marae Taputapuatea, fruit plantations, Faaroa Bay and other sites can be a good alternative. For island tours, contact **Raiatea Discovery** (☎ 66 24 16, 78 33 25), **Rauvine Safari Tours** (☎ 66 25 50), **Jeep Safari Raiatea** (☎ 66 15 73) or **Hinerani Tours** (☎ 66 25 75). Tariffs vary between 4000 CFP and 5000 CFP per person and you should book as soon as you arrive.

PLACES TO STAY
Places to stay on Ra'iatea are generally in or close to Uturoa. None are on a beach, although some have pontoons anchored in the lagoon. There are three places where you can camp. Prices here include the 11% TVA in certified hotels (6% in hostels and *pensions*), plus the 150 CFP daily tax (50 CFP in hostels and *pensions*).

Uturoa
The only place right in the centre of Uturoa is **Hôtel Hinano** (☎ 66 13 13, fax 66 14 14; singles/doubles 6100/7100 CFP, with air-con 7100/8100 CFP). It's only 100m from the docks and has modern, spacious, although somewhat overpriced motel-style rooms around a patio, with bathrooms (with hot water). **Restaurant Chez Michèle** is on the ground floor (see Uturoa under Places to Eat, later). Airport transfers are included.

Raiatea Pearl Resort Hawaiki Nui (☎ 60 05 00, fax 66 20 20; e info@spmhotels.pf; w www.pearlresorts.com; PK2; singles & doubles 16,700 CFP, bungalows 24,500-46,700 CFP) is just south of the centre of Uturoa. It has over-water, lagoonside and garden bungalows as well as rooms overlooking a magnificent flower bed. All rooms are spacious and comfortable and have a bathroom (with hot water), telephone, TV, refrigerator, fan and terrace. There's a restaurant (see East Coast under Places to

Eat, later), bar and boutique. Transfers to a motu cost 1000 CFP return.

Pension Tepua (☎ 66 33 00, fax 66 32 00; e pension-tepua@mail.pf; PK2.5; dorm beds 1600 CFP, singles/doubles 3800/6000 CFP, bungalows from 9100 CFP) is half a kilometre further along the road. This small lagoonside hotel has options for all budgets: a dorm with bunk beds, simple rooms with fan and shared hot-water bathroom, and bungalows with hot-water bathroom, mezzanine and fan. It also has a communal kitchen, a small pool, washing machines and a bar-restaurant. Airport transfers are 1000 CFP per person. You can be dropped on a motu for the day for 1000 CFP return or rent a bicycle for 1000 CFP a day.

Raiatea Bellevue Bed & Breakfast (☎/fax 66 15 15; singles/doubles 7100/8000 CFP), a quiet and relaxing place perched high above the northern side of Uturoa, has extraordinary views. Its five small but tidy rooms have a bathroom (with hot water), TV, refrigerator and fan and open onto a terrace beside a small swimming pool; rates include breakfast. Airport transfers cost 1400 CFP per person return. To get here, take the first sealed road on the left after PK1 and follow it for 800m.

Tiare Nui (☎ 66 34 06, fax 66 16 06; PK1; single/double bungalows 5400/6000 CFP) is in the Europcar compound, shortly before the airport. Small, neat bungalows come with bathroom (with hot water), fan, TV and refrigerator. The location is rather noisy but there is a very competitive package including a car or boat with outboard motor for 10,500/11,000 CFP a single/double. Transfers are included.

East Coast
At Avera, south of Uturoa, between PK6 and PK10, you have the choice of five establishments. There are also several places between Faaroa Bay and Opoa.

Kaoha Nui Ranch (☎/fax 66 25 46; e kaoha .nui@mail.pf; PK6; singles/doubles 1900/3500 CFP, bungalows from 6400 CFP) has four simple, impeccably neat rooms, each with two single beds and shared bathroom (with hot water). The dividing walls don't reach the ceiling, so privacy is somewhat lacking. A separate double room has a hot-water bathroom and fan. There's also a comfortable bungalow. Prices are for a two-night minimum stay (add 20% for a one-night stay).

There's a fully equipped kitchen and bicycle hire costs 800/1200 CFP a half/full day. Breakfast costs 700 CFP, lunch 2300 CFP. Airport and dock transfers are free.

Pension Manava (☎ 66 28 26, fax 66 16 66; e manava@free.fr; PK6; singles & doubles 4200 CFP, bungalows from 5600 CFP) is a friendly place with two rooms in a *fare* with shared bathroom (with hot water) and equipped kitchen. Tidy, spacious bungalows in the leafy garden all have bathrooms (with hot water). Two have equipped kitchens. There's an additional 20% charge for one-night stays; breakfast is an additional 600 CFP to 900 CFP. Free transfers are provided. Trips to Marae Taputapuatea (3300 CFP) and lagoon pirogue trips are also offered, or you can be dropped on a motu for the day for 1000 CFP per person (minimum four people).

Peter's Place (☎ 66 20 01; PK6.5; camping/rooms per person 900/1400 CFP), just beyond Pension Manava, offers spartan rooms or spots on the lawn where you can pitch your tent. There's a shared kitchen area, showers and toilets, all fairly rustic. As simple as this place is, economy-minded backpackers may find that its Polynesian ambience hits the spot. Return transfers are 1000 CFP per person.

Pension Rauvine (☎/fax 66 25 50; e pensionrauvine@mail.pf; PK8.5; single/double bungalows 5000 CFP) has eight simple but accessibly priced bungalows with kitchenette and bathroom (cold water); prices include transfers. There are various activities, including half-day island tours for 4000 CFP.

Pension Yolande (☎/fax 66 35 28; singles/doubles 5100/6100 CFP, half-board 8600/13,100 CFP), right on the water near PK10, has four functional rooms with kitchen facilities and bathroom (with hot water). Although the walls are paper thin, the *pension* is clean and well kept. Meals are available in a small *fare* facing the sea. Transfers cost 1500 CFP.

Pension La Croix du Sud (Southern Cross; ☎/fax 66 27 55; singles/doubles 7300/8000 CFP, half-board 9000/13,600 CFP) is opposite the entry to the Stardust Marina on the northern side of Faaroa Bay, 12km from the centre of Uturoa. The hillside setting offers fantastic views. There are three rooms, two in the same *fare*, with bathroom (with hot water). Prices include breakfast. Meals are served on a pleasant terrace looking out over the bay.

The *pension* is rather isolated, but there's free use of bicycles for getting around. Airport transfers cost 1500 CFP per carload.

Pension Te Maeva (☎/fax 66 37 28; e te maeva@mail.pf; PK24.7; camping for 1/2 people 1700/2300 CFP, single/double bungalows 6100/7300 CFP, half-board 7300/9800 CFP) is a tranquil place 7km north of Marae Taputapuatea. There are two comfortable bungalows perched on the mountain flank, with hot-water bathroom, fan, fridge and terrace. Prices include breakfast and transfers. A shower and toilet are reserved for campers. There are no kitchen facilities, but you can buy fresh supplies from the vans that pass twice daily and meals can be provided for 2000 CFP. Bicycles are available for guests and you can also do your washing for 500 CFP.

Hôtel Atiapiti (☎/fax 66 16 65; e atiapiti@mail.pf; beach bungalows from 9600 CFP, garden bungalows from 12,600 CFP), next to Marae Taputapuatea, is a relaxing place beside the lagoon and a small beach. Spacious, comfortable beach bungalows come with bathroom (with hot water), fan, lounge area and terrace. There's also a garden bungalow that can accommodate one to two people. Breakfast costs 1100 CFP; add 4000 CFP for half-board. Motu drop-offs cost 2000 CFP to 2500 CFP per person. Airport transfers are 2200 CFP per person return.

West Coast

Right on the waterfront, on an extensive coconut plantation, **Sunset Beach Motel** (☎ 66 33 47, fax 66 33 08; e sunsetbeach@mail.pf; PK5; camping per person 1100 CFP, single/double/triple bungalows 7700/8800/10,000 CFP) has 22 large, comfortable bungalows, all with hot-water bathroom, kitchen and TV. There's a 1000 CFP extra charge per bungalow for one-night stays. You can also camp and there are excellent kitchen facilities and bathrooms. Breakfast costs 1000 CFP. Pirogues and pedal boats are available. Transfers to/from the airport are free.

Hôtel Tenape (☎ 60 01 00, fax 60 01 01; e hoteltenape@mail.pf; PK8.8; rooms/suites 20,700/29,600 CFP), 4km from the airport, is a two-storey colonial-style place. From its mountainside location there are great views of the lagoon and across to Bora Bora. There are comfortable air-con rooms with terrace, and one suite. There's a good restaurant (see West Coast under Places to Eat, following), a bar and a swimming pool. Add 5300 CFP for half-board and 1500 CFP for return airport transfers.

PLACES TO EAT
Uturoa
On the waterfront, **Snack Moemoea** (☎ 66 39 84; dishes 800-2800 CFP; open 6am-5pm Mon-Sat) is a pleasant, busy little café with an open terrace and straightforward dishes at modest prices.

Restaurant Chez Michèle (☎ 66 14 66; dishes 800-2000 CFP; open Mon-Fri & Sat lunch), in Hôtel Hinano, offers Chinese, Tahitian and French dishes, including pork with taro (1500 CFP) and Chinese beef (1000 CFP). Breakfast is also available.

Jade Garden (☎ 66 34 40; dishes 1400-3000 CFP; open Wed-Fri lunch & dinner, Sat dinner) is a good Chinese restaurant on the main street. Try the chicken with ginger, the eggplant and salted fish or the duck with taro (around 1600 CFP).

Quai des Pêcheurs (☎ 66 43 19; dishes 1200-2400 CFP; open daily lunch & dinner) is in the gare maritime. The setting is functional and impersonal, although there's an attractive terrace. The menu features fish and meat dishes.

Sea Horse (☎ 66 16 34; dishes 900-1800 CFP; closed Sun night), also in the gare maritime, serves excellent Chinese food, such as taro with chicken (1500 CFP), roast pork with coconut milk (1800 CFP) and sea cucumber soup (900 CFP).

Uturoa has several well-stocked supermarkets, which are open Monday to Saturday, some on Sunday morning. They include **Champion** on the seafront and **Leogite** and **Liaut** on the main street.

Around Uturoa
There are several options towards the airport and Apooiti Marina.

Napoli (☎ 66 10 77; dishes 900-1600 CFP, set menu 1800 CFP; closed Sat lunch, Sun lunch & Mon) is a pizzeria near the Europcar agency, offering a good range of Italian dishes including pasta, wood-fired pizzas starting at 900 CFP, and meat and fish dishes.

Club House (☎ 66 11 66; dishes 1100-3400 CFP; closed Mon & Tues lunch) is in Apooiti Marina. The setting is striking – a large airy room overlooking the marina –

but its Franco-Polynesian cuisine doesn't quite live up to its inventive and stylish ambitions. Patrons can be picked up and dropped off for free as far as Sunset Beach Motel and Pension Manava.

La Voile D'Or (☎ 66 12 97; dishes 750-1900 CFP; set menu 2900 CFP; closed Sun dinner & Mon lunch), at the end of Apooiti Marina, is an average seafood place.

East Coast
Bring a picnic if you're travelling around the island, as there are not many places to get a meal, although some places to stay offer food.

Raiatea Pearl Resort Hawaiki Nui (☎ 60 05 00; PK2; dishes 1000-2500 CFP) has an attractively situated restaurant, but the food is ordinary. The bar serves good cocktails for about 800 CFP.

Pension La Croix du Sud (☎ 66 27 55; set menu 2900 CFP; open daily) – see East Coast under Places to Stay, earlier – has good, inventive food; meals are served on a terrace with an unbeatable view over Faaroa Bay. Bookings are required.

If you're a little peckish after visiting Marae Taputapuatea, head for the nearby restaurant at **Hôtel Atiapiti** (☎ 66 16 65; dishes 1000-2000 CFP; open daily lunch). The setting, facing the lagoon, is calm and pleasant. Stand-out dishes include sea crabs and shrimps in curry or saffron sauce.

West Coast
Hôtel Tenape (☎ 60 01 00; PK8.8; dishes 1600-2900 CFP; open daily lunch & dinner), on the west coast towards Tevaitoa, is a tablecloths-and-starched-napkins sort of a place offering classic French specialities at reasonable prices. You can get foie gras and other pâtés, fish and meat dishes. There's a good wine list.

ENTERTAINMENT
It's difficult to find a reason for a late night on Ra'iatea. A sunset drink at the Apooiti Marina **Club House** is mandatory. There's also the bar at **Ra'iatea Pearl Resort Hawaiki Nui**, which has weekly Polynesian dance performances.

On weekends Restaurant Moana, above Leogite in Uturoa, metamorphoses into the disco **Le Zénith** (admission female/male free/1000 CFP).

SHOPPING

Uturoa has several well-stocked souvenir outlets. **Arii Création**, on the main street facing the market, specialises in Polynesian *tapa* (nonwoven bark cloth). For Tahitian black pearls, head for **La Palme d'Or**, also on the main street. Next door is **Anuanua**, a gallery with works by island craftspeople, including sculptures, pottery, paintings and mother-of-pearl objects. **Te Fare**, in the Banque Socredo building, sells fabrics, paintings, jewellery, basketwork and sculptures. Next to the *gare maritime*, women sell their crafts, particularly shellwork, woodwork and pareu (sarong-type garments).

You can buy silver and mother-of-pearl jewellery at **Atelier du Margouïa** (open Tues-Sun), near Peter's Place. **Art-Expo** (☎ 66 11 83), at Apooiti Marina, sells jewellery, clothes, decorative trinkets and handicrafts. For vanilla products, head to **Vanillère** (☎ 66 15 61; PK33.5) at Hotopu Bay.

GETTING THERE & AWAY

Ra'iatea is 220km northwest of Tahiti and 40km southeast of Bora Bora.

Air

Air Tahiti flies to Ra'iatea three to eight times daily from Tahiti, directly (40 minutes) or via Mo'orea and/or Huahine. There are also daily connections with Bora Bora and Huahine, and three-times-weekly connections with Maupiti. One-way fares to/from Ra'iatea include: Bora Bora 5800 CFP; Huahine 4600 CFP; Maupiti 6400 CFP; and Pape'ete 10,500 CFP. **Air Tahiti** (☎ 60 04 44, 60 04 40; open 7.30am-noon & 2pm-5.15pm Mon-Fri, 7.30am-11.15am Sat, 2.30pm-5.15pm Sun) has an office at the airport.

Boat

Ra'iatea is separated from Taha'a by a 3km-wide channel.

Taha'a There are two *navette* services between Uturoa and various stops on Taha'a – Marina Iti, Poutoru, Tapuamu, Patio, Tiva, Hipu and Haamene – operated by **Enota Transport** (☎ 65 67 10, 66 13 33). You can buy tickets on board. Services operate Monday to noon on Saturday; there is no service on Saturday afternoon or Sunday. It takes less than 15 minutes from Uturoa to Apu Marina, the closest stop on Taha'a. The one-

way fare is 500 CFP and there are one to two services a day, depending on the destination.

There is also a **taxi-boat service** (☎ 65 65 29) between the two islands, which operates daily between 6am and 6pm. It costs 1500 CFP to go to southern Taha'a and 3500 CFP to go to northern Taha'a (prices are per person, with a minimum of two people). You can be picked up at the airport or any of the accessible pontoons. Advance booking (24 hours) is required.

The **Tamarii Taha'a** (☎ 65 65 29) goes to the west coast of Taha'a twice daily from the Uturoa *navette* quay, at around 10.30am and 4.30pm. It operates Monday to Friday and Saturday morning. The one-hour trip to Patio costs 850 CFP.

Other Islands The **Aremiti 3** (☎ 74 39 40, 74 39 41) departs from Pape'ete stopping at Huahine and Ra'iatea on Monday and Friday. It departs Pape'ete at 7am and arrives at Ra'iatea towards noon; from Ra'iatea it departs at 12.30pm and arrives at Pape'ete at 6pm. From Pape'ete to Ra'iatea costs 5500/2750 CFP adult/child; from Huahine to Ra'iatea costs 1760/880 CFP adult/child.

The **Maupiti Express** (☎ 67 66 69) travels between Bora Bora, Taha'a and Ra'iatea. On Monday, Wednesday and Friday it leaves Vaitape (Bora Bora) at 7am, arrives at Taha'a at 8.15am and at Uturoa at 8.45am. The same days it leaves Uturoa at 4pm, stops at Taha'a and arrives back at Bora Bora at 5.45pm. The one-way/return fare is 2500/3500 CFP; it costs 500 CFP to go from 'Ra'iatea to Taha'a.

The cargo ships *Vaeanu*, *Taporo*, *Hawaiki Nui* and *Maupiti Tou Ai'a* also make a stop at Ra'iatea. See the Getting Around chapter for details.

GETTING AROUND

The options for getting around are to rent a car or hitchhike. Hitchhiking appears to be fairly accepted on Ra'iatea as a result of the low-key tourism and lack of public transport. However, remember that there are always dangers associated with hitching.

To/From the Airport

There are taxis at the airport; the 3km-trip into Uturoa costs 1000 CFP. Most island accommodation will pick you up if you have booked (although there may be a charge).

Le Truck

Don't count on le trucks. They're so infrequent that they're useless for visitors. They operate mainly in the morning, between outlying districts and Uturoa, then return in the early afternoon. They are colour coded; the blue ones go to Opoa near Marae Taputapuatea, and the turquoise ones go to Fetuna on the south coast. The le truck terminus is in Uturoa near the *gare maritime*. Check that there will be a return trip if you don't want to get stuck at your destination.

Car

The head office of **Europcar** (☎ *66 34 06, fax 66 16 06;* e *europcar-loc@mail.pf)* is on the edge of Uturoa towards the airport; it also has desks at the airport, in Uturoa and in the Raiatea Pearl Resort Hawaiki Nui. A Citroën Saxo costs 9000 CFP for a day. **Avis** (☎ *66 20 00)* has a desk at the airport and charges 8800 CFP for a similar model. **Te Maire** (☎ *60 00 95, 71 74 26, fax 60 00 96),* opposite the Mobil petrol station in Uturoa, charges 11,200 CFP for 24 hours. **Hertz** (☎ *66 44 88, fax 66 44 89)* opposite the town hall in Uturoa, charges 8600 CFP for 24 hours. Cars can be delivered to the airport.

Bicycle & Scooter

Europcar rents scooters for 5500 CFP for 24 hours. Some hotels and guesthouses rent bicycles.

Taxi

There's a **taxi stand** (☎ *66 20 60)* by the market and taxis can also be found at the airport. All taxis are very expensive.

Boat

Europcar rents boats with outboards for 8800/9900 CFP for eight/24 hours; they're the perfect way to explore the lagoon.

Taha'a

pop 4470 • area 90 sq km

Taha'a is even quieter than Ra'iatea. The island is an undiscovered jewel, little known by tourist operators and accessible only by boat. It has a village atmosphere but also some good places to stay. There are no beaches to speak of on the main island and the tourist facilities are even more basic, although with the opening of the Tahaa Pearl Beach Resort & Spa in 2002, luxury accommodation has come to the island. A coast road encircles most of the island but traffic is very light and there is no public transport. Vanilla cultivation and pearl farming dominate the island's economy. The main tourist attraction is the string of beautiful motu along the northern reef edge. Taha'a's easily navigable lagoon and safe yacht anchorages make it a favourite for visiting yachties.

History

Taha'a was once known as Kuporu (or Uporu), a name which pops up in other Polynesian centres, perhaps indicating a migratory connection. Taha'a lived in the shadow of Ra'iatea, its larger, stronger and more important neighbour, and was at times a pawn in the struggles between Ra'iatea and the rulers of Bora Bora.

The first missionaries arrived from neighbouring Ra'iatea in 1822 and the island came under French control at the same time as Ra'iatea. Taha'a was once a centre for firewalking ceremonies, but this practice has died out.

Orientation

The northern coastline is fairly continuous, while the south of the island is punctuated by deep and impressive bays. A 70km road winds around the coast; the northern part is sealed, while the southern part is mostly crushed coral. The road is in reasonable condition and there are sealed sections through the main towns and where the road leaves the coast and climbs over the hills, particularly the nicely sweeping road up and over the centre from Haamene to Tiva.

The population is concentrated in eight villages on the coast. Tapuamu has the main quay, Patio is the main town and Haamene is where the roads round the southern and northern parts of the island meet, forming a figure eight. Apu Bay to the south, Haamene Bay to the east and Hurepiti Bay to the west offer sheltered anchorages.

Information

There is no tourist office on Taha'a, but you can get information from the tourist office on Ra'iatea. Taha'a's only bank branch is the **Banque Socredo** (open *8am-12pm & 2pm-3.30pm Mon-Fri)* in Patio.

Taha'a – The Vanilla Island

Taha'a is accurately nicknamed 'the vanilla island', since three-quarters of French Polynesian production (about 25 tons annually) of vanilla comes from here. This is a far cry from the 150 to 200 tons produced a century ago, when vanilla cultivation flourished in the Society Islands.

Several vanilla farms are open to the public and at these small family-run operations you can buy vanilla pods at reasonable prices, about 1000 CFP a dozen. You can also find out about the technique of 'marrying' the vanilla, a delicate operation in which the flowers are fertilised by hand because the insects that do the job in other regions are not found in French Polynesia. Nine months later the pods are put out to dry, and turn brown over four to five months. They are then sorted and boxed in sachets or bamboo tubes before being sold in Pape'ete or exported.

AROUND THE ISLAND

The 70km circuit of the island is quite possible as a bicycle day-trip, although most of the route is unsealed crushed coral and there are some steep sections. PK markers start at Haamene and go up clockwise around the northern half of the island, terminating at Patio at around PK25.

Starting from the Marina Iti (the first *navette* stop if you're coming from Ra'iatea, and the best place to rent bicycles), the road follows the coast around Apu Bay. At the top of the bay there's a turn-off south to Poutoru, where the road ends. The main road leaves the coast and climbs up and over to the larger village of **Haamene**.

On the right of the road into Haamene is the **Maison de la Vanille** (☎ 65 67 27), a small family-run operation where you can see vanilla-drying and preparation processes and buy vanilla pods. You will be asked for a small contribution. A little further along, a right turn leads to the red-and-green house of another vanilla producer, **Alfred** (☎ 65 61 16). See the boxed text 'Taha'a – The Vanilla Island' for information about vanilla cultivation.

The road climbs again, making a long sweeping ascent and descent down to pretty Hurepiti Bay and the village of **Tiva**, where there are several **pearl farms** by the coast.

Bora Bora comes into view as you round the end of the bay; it looks surprisingly close beyond the lagoon edge.

Tapuamu is the site of the island's main quay. From here the chain of motu that fringes the northern coast of the island comes into view. **Patio** is the administrative centre of the island, with offices, a post office, a bank, shops and a small artisans' centre. Beyond Patio more of the 60-odd motu around the north of the island are visible as the road winds along the coast. Continuing around the coast, the road passes copra plantations, before reaching **Faaha** and Faaha Bay. On the northern side of the bay you can visit **Motu Pearl Farm** (☎ 65 66 67), which has a small shop.

From the bay the road climbs over a headland and drops down to Haamene Bay. Alternatively, a rougher track turns off the coast road just beyond Patio and takes a direct route over the hills and down to **Haamene**. This track starts shortly after the village but although the first part is driveable, the second section needs a 4WD. It's really better as a walk or mountain-bike ride.

Where the coast road meets Haamene Bay, turn east to Hôtel Hibiscus, where the **Foundation Hibiscus** (☎ 65 61 06) is dedicated to saving turtles that have become entangled in local fishers' nets. The hotel owner Léo buys turtles from the fishers. They are kept in pens beside the hotel's pier and fed every morning until they've grown large enough to be released. By early 2002 around 1000 endangered turtles had been saved.

From Hôtel Hibiscus the coast road goes around the northern side of the bay to Haamene, passing the pearl farms of **Pension Vaipoe** (☎ 65 60 83; admission 100 CFP) and Rooverta Ebbs' **Poerani** (☎ 65 60 25; admission 100 CFP), where you can watch pearl grafting. Mounted and unmounted pearls and mother-of-pearl are sold, as well as vanilla pods. The road then continues along the southern side of the bay and, on the final long stretch back to the starting point, winds in and out of small bays before coming back to the Marina Iti.

ACTIVITIES
Water Activities

Apart from the dive centre at Tahaa Pearl Beach Resort & Spa, there's no dive centre on Taha'a. The dive centres on Ra'iatea regularly use the **dive sites** to the east of the island by Céran Pass and will collect you from hotels in the south of the Taha'a. See the special section 'Diving' for more details.

Like Ra'iatea, there are no beaches on Taha'a and you have to go to the motu for **swimming** and **snorkelling**. Some guesthouses will drop you on a motu for the day or you can join an organised pirogue tour.

Fishing

Both **Hôtel Marina Iti** (☎ 65 61 01) and **Hôtel Hibiscus** (☎ 65 61 06) organise fishing trips.

Hiking

You can take the little-used 7km track across the centre of the island from Patio to Haamene, but otherwise there are very few trails into the island's interior. There are dazzling views of Haamene Bay from **Vaitoetoe Pass.**

ORGANISED TOURS
Lagoon Tours

The various tour operators offer more or less the same thing: swimming and snorkelling stops on a motu and visits to a pearl farm and a vanilla plantation. Prices vary between 5500 CFP and 8000 CFP per person for a full day with picnic.

Contact **Tahaa Pearl Tours** (☎ 66 10 90), **Vaipoe Tours** (☎ 65 60 83) at Pension Vaipoe, **Manava Excursions** (☎ 66 28 26), **Tumatahi Tours** (☎ 66 25 17), **André Topspots** (☎ 60 05 20, 79 22 03) and **Kaoha Nui Ranch** (☎/fax 66 25 46), based at Ra'iatea.

Island Tours

Half-day island tours by 4WD or minibus visit pearl farms, craft shops, vanilla plantations and possibly take the track from Patio to Haamene, costing between 3500 CFP and 5000 CFP per person. A minimum number of people, usually four, is required, so book ahead.

Vanilla Tours (☎ 65 62 46), charges 4500 CFP per person and has a good reputation. Pearl-farm visits cost an extra 500 CFP. Its office is at Hurepiti Bay, near the Sophie Boutique.

Tahaa Tour Excursion (☎ 65 62 18, 79 27 56) also has a good reputation, offering full-day 4WD tours with a picnic on a motu for 5500 CFP. Transfers to Uturoa are included.

Stone-Fishing Festival

The annual stone-fishing festival takes place in the last week of October. Events include singing and dancing, agricultural and craft displays, local sporting events (including fruit-carrying races!), fishing contests and canoe races. A fire-walking ceremony is a highlight of the festivities before the final event, when flower-bedecked pirogues fan out across the lagoon and the surface of the water is beaten with stones to herd the fish into an enclosure.

Other tour operators include **Lolita Tours** (☎ 65 61 06) at Hôtel Hibiscus, **Poerani Tours** (☎ 65 60 25), **Hainanui Tours** (☎ 65 61 90) and **Vaipoe Tours** (☎ 65 60 83) at Pension Vaipoe.

PLACES TO STAY

Taha'a's places to stay are dotted around the coast. It's wise to make reservations so you'll be collected from the appropriate village quay, or even the airport on Ra'iatea.

The Island

On Toamaro Point, **Hôtel Marina Iti** (☎ 65 61 01, fax 65 63 87; [e] marinaiti@mail.pf; VHF 68; bungalows from 12,300 CFP) is the busiest place on the island. Right on the waterfront looking across to Ra'iatea, it has a tiny beach. There are pleasant lagoon and garden bungalows, with mosquito net, bathroom (with hot water) and veranda. Half-board costs 5300 CFP extra. It has a good restaurant (see Places to Eat, later) and bar by the pier. Cars and bicycles can be rented and a variety of tours are offered. Return transfers from the airport on Ra'iatea cost 3600 CFP per person.

Pension Api (☎/fax 65 69 88; [e] jjwatlp@ mail.pf; bungalows from 6100 CFP), is 1.5km from Hôtel Marina Iti, by the sea. It offers two comfortable, well-maintained bungalow-style rooms. Each has a private bathroom, mosquito net and a terrace. Breakfast is available for 600 CFP; add 3500 CFP for half-board. To get there, take a navette or taxi-boat to the quay at Hôtel Marina Iti and call the owners, who will come and pick you up. Free kayaks and bicycles are available for guests' use.

Pension Herenui (☎ 65 62 60, fax 65 64 17; bungalows from 8100 CFP), just beyond Poutoru, on the inland side of the road, rents three charming bungalows with bathroom (with hot water); add 3500 CFP per person for half-board. There is a swimming pool and the lagoon is across the road. Airport transfers cost 1500 CFP per person one way. The owner is an agent for Europcar (see Car & Bicycle under Getting Around later in this chapter). You can also hire a boat for 7000 CFP per half day.

Pension Vaihi (*☎ 65 62 02; single & double bungalows 6400 CFP*), on the southern side of Hurepiti Bay, provides isolation and tranquillity. There are three bungalows with bathrooms beside the lagoon. Half-/full board adds 3000/4500 CFP per person. To get there, ask the *navette* to drop you at the quay at Tiva, where the owners will pick you up. Bicycles can be hired for 1500 CFP.

Chez Louise (*☎ 65 66 88, fax 65 69 33; dorm beds with breakfast/half-board 1500/ 3500 CFP*) is the place to stay if you're really penniless. It has beds in a basic dorm opposite the restaurant of the same name (see Places to Eat, later). Kayaks and bikes are available for hire and you can be dropped off on Motu Tau Tau. Several bungalows are planned for the site.

Chez Pascal (*☎ 65 60 42; bungalows per person 2600 CFP, with breakfast/half-board 3100/5100 CFP*) is the cheapest place on the island. Past Tapuamu, after the bridge, take the first turn-off inland. It's spartan but clean and there's a typically Polynesian family atmosphere. Small bungalows have shared toilet and shower. Bicycles cost 1500 CFP and motu excursions are 4000 CFP. Transfers to/from the quay at Tapuamu are free.

Au Phil du Temps (*☎/fax 65 64 19; e mout te.junior@mail.pf; bungalows with breakfast/ half-board/full board per person 5100/9100/ 12,100 CFP*) is on the outskirts of Tapuamu, going towards Patio, on the inland side. It has two simple, well-kept, local-style bungalows a few metres from the lagoon, with TV, mosquito net and private outside bathroom. Transfers to the airport cost 2000 CFP per person one way.

Tupenu Village (*☎ 65 62 01; doubles 6100 CFP*), by the lagoon about 1.5km west of Patio, is the only place on the north shore of the island. There's a big two-level *fare* with five rooms sharing two bathrooms (with hot water). Breakfast is 600 CFP and lunch or dinner is 1800 CFP; cheaper meals are also

available. Motu drop-offs cost 2500 CFP per person with picnic. Transfers to/from Patio are free.

There are two places on the north shore of Haamene Bay:

Hôtel Hibiscus (*☎ 65 61 06, fax 65 65 65; e hibiscus@tahaa-tahiti.com; VHF 68; bungalows from 9500 CFP*) has bungalows with bathroom (with hot water), terrace, mezzanine, fan and refrigerator. There are also bungalows with shared bathroom (cold water only). Add 4200 CFP per person for half-board. It's on the inland side of the road but just across from the water. Transfers from Ra'iatea depart from Snack Moemoea and cost 1400 CFP per person each way. Island tours, traditional fishing trips, motu picnics and even a motu wedding can be organised. Bicycle rental costs 1000 CFP per day.

Pension Vaipoe (*Chez Patricia et Daniel; ☎/fax 65 60 83; e v.p@mail.pf; single & double bungalows 8100 CFP*) is a popular place just east of Hôtel Hibiscus. On the inland side of the road, with access to the lagoon, its bungalows have bathroom (with hot water), kitchenette and terrace; add 3500 CFP for half-board. Activities include a motu picnic and swimming stop (1000 CFP), island tours (3500 CFP) and game fishing. Airport transfers cost 3000 CFP per person return.

The Motu

Occupying a motu to the north of Taha'a is **Vahine Island** (*☎ 65 67 38, fax 65 67 70; e vahine.island@usa.net; VHF 70; beach bungalows 33,500 CFP, over-water bungalows 54,500 CFP*). This small resort has just nine bungalows, but competes very effectively with the luxury resorts on other islands. There's a white-sand beach and clear water. Add 7000 CFP per person per day for half-board. Pirogues and snorkelling equipment are available for free, lagoon tours and mountain-bike trips are organised, and there are pedal boats and outboard-motor boats for lagoon exploration. Transfers from the airport on Ra'iatea cost 6000 CFP per person return.

Tahaa Pearl Beach Resort & Spa (*☎ 50 84 52, fax 43 17 86; e info@spmhotels.pf; w www.pearlresorts.com; bungalows from 77,900 CFP*) is really sumptuous. The setting on Motu Tau Tau, to the west of the island, is exceptional. There are 12 beach suites (each with private pool!) and 48 over-water bungalows. Bars, restaurants, a spa and activities ensure a dream stay.

PLACES TO EAT
There are **shops** in each village but the dining options are very limited.

Hôtel Marina Iti (☎ 65 60 87; dishes 950-2400 CFP; open daily lunch & dinner) has a well-known restaurant that features French specialities with a local twist. Dishes include sautéed veal with vanilla and mahi mahi (dorado) with shrimps (each costs 1900 CFP).

Hôtel Hibiscus (☎ 65 61 06; dishes 1200-3100 CFP; open daily lunch & dinner) has a good restaurant offering dishes such as mahi mahi with seafood sauce (1700 CFP) and crab with green lemon (3100 CFP).

Chez Louise (☎ 65 66 68; dishes 1100-5700 CFP; open daily lunch & dinner), at Tiva, is the place for something more local. This small domestic establishment enjoys an excellent reputation. The 3700 CFP 'marina menu' is a true feast, with a half-lobster, curried shrimps, raw fish and rice.

ENTERTAINMENT
Taha'a is not the island for night owls. There are really just the bars at the **Marina Iti** and **Hôtel Hibiscus**. A group of dancers and musicians performs on Saturday night at the Hibiscus.

SHOPPING
Black pearls and vanilla are directly available from some producers. See Island Tours under Organised Tours earlier in this section for details.

Sophie Boutique (☎ 65 62 56), on the southern side of Hurepiti Bay, sells paintings, pottery, pareu and jewellery.

The owner of **Au Phil du Temps** (☎ 65 64 19) – see The Island under Places to Stay, earlier – has a small workshop where she sells bamboo objects.

GETTING THERE & AWAY
There is no airport on Taha'a. The airport on Ra'iatea is only 15 minutes across the lagoon and some hotels will pick up guests from the airport or from the ferry quay at Uturoa on Ra'iatea.

See Getting There & Away in the Ra'iatea section earlier in this chapter for information on the *navette* service between Ra'iatea and Taha'a.

The **Maupiti Express** (☎ 67 66 99) operates Monday, Wednesday and Friday between Bora Bora, Taha'a and Ra'iatea. See Getting There & Away in the Ra'iatea section earlier in this chapter.

Inter-island ships stop at Tapuamu on Taha'a en route from Ra'iatea to Bora Bora, but not on every voyage. If your trip doesn't stop at Taha'a it's easy enough to disembark at Uturoa and take the *navette* across.

GETTING AROUND
There is no public transport on Taha'a. If you're contemplating hitching remember that traffic is very light. Renting a car or a mountain bike are the only ways to see the island independently. The coast road, not all of which is sealed, is quite OK. If you decide to tackle it by bicycle keep in mind that there are some steep stretches on the south of the island.

Car & Bicycle
Hôtel Marina Iti (☎ 65 61 01) rents Fiat Pandas for 9640 CFP for eight hours including insurance, petrol and 100km – enough to do the island circuit. Bicycles are 1000/1500 CFP for a half/full day.

Monique Locations (☎/fax 65 62 48), near the church in Haamene, rents Citroën Saxos for 9000/10,500 CFP for eight/24 hours plus 1200 CFP for petrol, and bicycles for 1500 CFP for 24 hours. **Europcar** (☎ 65 67 00, fax 65 68 08), at the Total petrol station at Tapuamu, has Fiat Pandas for 8200 CFP for 24 hours, including unlimited mileage and insurance but not petrol. At Poutoru, the **rental agency** (☎ 65 62 60; closed Sun) run by Pension Herenui charges 10,000 CFP for 24 hours, including petrol.

You can rent a scooter on Ra'iatea and bring it across on the *navette*. There are petrol stations in Patio and Tapuamu, open Monday to Saturday.

Bora Bora

pop 7300

Bora Bora is where postcards of aqua lagoons come to life, the rich and famous come to play, and hotel chains come to open resorts. This makes for an island of contradictions: breathtaking volcanic peaks, lush vegetation and expanses of turquoise water juxtaposed with perpetual development largely of the five-star variety.

Spend the days snorkelling, working on that tan and paddling in the shallows; at night, grab yourself a cocktail at a bar, wave to James Bond (or Pierce Brosnan, as his friends call him) and enjoy a Polynesian dance performance. Worry about your credit-card bill when you get home.

History

In ancient times, the island was known as Vava'u, perhaps supporting the theory that it was colonised by inhabitants from the Tongan island of the same name. 'Bora Bora' roughly translates as 'first born', indicating that this may have been the most important island after Ra'iatea to the southeast. According to local myths, the legendary Hiro, the first king of Ra'iatea, sent his son Ohatatama to rule Bora Bora.

Due to the shortage of level ground on Bora Bora, land pressures created an unusually defensive population of fierce warriors. Only Huahine managed to resist the warriors of Bora Bora at their most expansive.

James Cook sighted Bora Bora in 1769, on his first voyage; a London Missionary Society (LMS) base was established on the island in 1820. Bora Bora supported Pomare in his push for supreme power over Tahiti, but resisted a French protectorate (established over Tahiti in 1842) until the island was annexed in 1888.

During WWII, a US supply base was established on Bora Bora, prompted by the bombing of Pearl Harbor in 1941. From early 1942 to mid-1946 Operation Bobcat transformed the island and, at its peak, up to 6000 men were stationed on Bora Bora. Today, the runway on Motu Mute is the clearest (and most useful) reminder of those frenetic days. Until Faa'a airport on Tahiti opened in 1961, this was French Polynesia's international airport. Eight massive

Highlights

- Admiring the lush scenery, lagoon and idyllic motu on a boat tour
- Ogling the fish on a snorkelling trip
- Working up a sweat on an island tour by bicycle
- Feasting on traditional food on a remote motu and then digesting it in the shade of a coconut tree
- Sipping heavenly cocktails as you enjoy a traditional dance performance

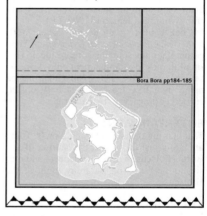

Bora Bora pp184-185

7-inch naval cannons were installed around the island during the war; all but one are still in place.

In 2001 reports of a discoloured lagoon and bleached coral, the result of El Niño, spread like Chinese whispers. Although the entire Pacific was affected, Bora Bora was particularly vulnerable as it has only one pass into its lagoon. The water is once again a sparkling aqua, but the damage to the coral is irreversible.

There has been a general effort to clean up Bora Bora in recent years, and local children on cleaning bees are a fairly common sight. But you'll still see and smell more rubbish than you'd hope to, particularly in the remote northern parts of the island. It's a fragile situation: an island dependent on tourism but at risk of deterring visitors as a result of overdevelopment, while at the same time the island's major drawcard – marine life – is seriously under threat. Let's hope the juggling act can be managed, because this is a truly beautiful part of the world.

Geography & Orientation

Bora Bora was created by volcanic action around three or four million years ago. The rim of the ancient volcano can be easily traced; the sea has broken into the crater to form Povai Bay, and Motu Toopua and Motu Toopua Iti are fragments of the old crater rim. Bora Bora is spectacularly mountainous, rising to Mt Hue (619m), Mt Pahia (661m) and Mt Otemanu (727m).

The main island stretches about 9km from north to south and is about 4km in width at the widest point. A 32km road runs around the coast.

A wide, sheltered and navigable lagoon encircles the island, with sandy motu edging most of the outer reef. The Teavanui Pass on the western side is the only pass into the lagoon.

Dusty Vaitape on the western side of the island is the main town, but Matira Point is the anchor for tourists. The quay for inter-island ships is at Farepiti, between Vaitape and Faanui. The airport is on Motu Mute at the northern extremity of the outer-reef edge.

INFORMATION
Tourist Offices

The **Bora Bora Visitors Bureau** (℡/fax 67 76 36; open 7.30am-4pm Mon-Fri) has an office on the quay at Vaitape. You won't find anyone here between noon and 1.30pm, but the office remains open to pamphlet hunters.

Money

There are branches of **Banque de Tahiti**, **Banque de Polynésie** and **Banque Socredo** in Vaitape. They all seem to keep slightly different hours but the approximate opening hours are 7.30am to 4pm or 4.30pm, with one or $1\frac{1}{2}$ hours off for lunch. All three banks have **ATMs** that accept Visa and MasterCard.

Post & Communications

The **post office** (℡ 67 70 74; open 8am-3pm Mon, 7.30am-3pm Tues-Fri, 8am-10am Sat) is in the middle of Vaitape.

There are public telephones all around the island; phonecards can be bought at a number of shops, hotels and supermarkets.

L'Appetisserie (℡ 67 78 88; Centre Le Pahia; open 9am-1pm & 4pm-6pm Mon-Fri, 9am-1pm Sat) in Vaitape offers Internet access. Only two computers were available when we visited, but you can hardly be fussy about Internet on Bora Bora. It charges a hefty 2500 CFP an hour.

Medical Services

If you need medical assistance, it's a good idea to inquire first at your hotel. There's a **medical centre** (℡ 67 70 77) in Vaitape, or you can contact **Dr Juen** (℡ 67 70 62), **Dr Roussanaly** or **Dr Boutry** (℡ 67 77 95). There's a **pharmacy** (℡ 67 70 30; open 8am-12pm & 3.30pm-6pm Mon-Fri, 8am-12pm & 5pm-6pm Sat, 9am-9.30am Sun) in Vaitape just near Le Cocotier restaurant.

AROUND THE ISLAND

Bora Bora's 32km coast road hugs the shoreline almost all the way around the island and rarely rises above sea level. The road is still not sealed the entire way around. It's a great island for a challenging days' bike ride (mere mortals may find themselves walking their bike up the hill around Fitiiu Point), although scooters and cars can also be rented. The tour that follows starts in Vaitape and goes anticlockwise around the island.

Vaitape

If you arrive by air, you'll be transported from the Motu Mute airport to Vaitape, which is the island's main settlement. It's not the most evocative little town, but most of the tourist services are here – offices, banks and the island's only Internet café are clustered around here. Vaitape is busy during the day but takes on a fairly sleepy aspect by late afternoon, when *pétanque* (boules) players take centre stage.

At Vaitape quay stands a **monument** to Alain Gerbault, who in 1923 was the first yachtsman to do a nonstop solo crossing of the Atlantic. He lived on Bora Bora in the 1930s.

Overland Road

Past the last houses south of Vaitape the road curves around Povai Bay. One hundred metres before Galerie Alain et Linda there's a small road that shortcuts across the island (it's easy to miss, so you may

BORA BORA

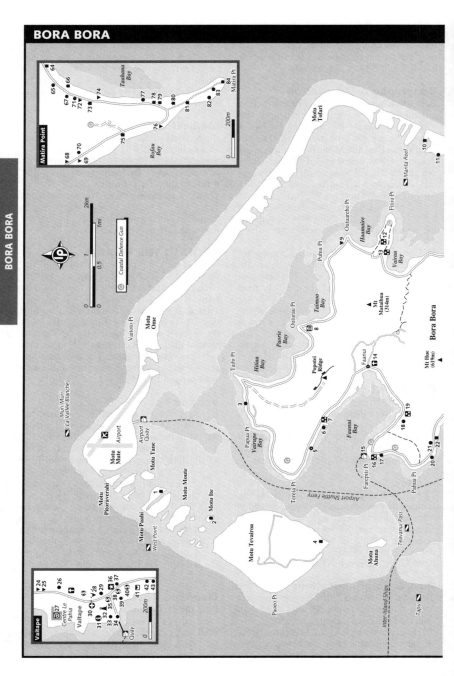

BORA BORA

Matira Point

64
65
66
67
71
72
74
73
77
78
79
80
81
83
84
68
70
69
75
76
82

Taahana Bay
Matira Pt
Rofau Bay

200m
0

Bora Bora

2km
1mi
0.5
1
0

Coastal Defence Gun

Muri Muri
(La Vallée Blanche)

Vaitoto Pt

Motu Ome

Airport
Motu Mute
Airport Quay

Motu Tane

Motu Piti Aau

Motu Moute

Motu Ite

Motu Paahi
West Point

Motu Tevairoa

Paopao Pt

Motu Ahuna

Tapu

Inter-Island Ships

Teavanui Pass

Airport Shuttle ferry

Terei'a Pt

Farepiti Pt

Pahua Pt

Faanui
Faanui Bay

Mt Hue
(619m)

Mt Mataihua
(314m)

Popote Ridge

Vairape Bay
Papua Pt

Taihi Pt

Hitiaa Bay
Paurie Bay
Outurui Pt
Taimoo Bay

Puhia Pt

Outuaveho Pt

Haamaire Bay
Fitiiu Pt

Vairau Bay
Manta Reef

1
2
3
4
5
6
7
8
9
10
11
12
13
14
15
16
17
18
19
20
21

Vaitape

24
25
26
27
28
29
30
31
32
33
34
35
36
37
38
39
40
41
42
43

Centre Le Pahia
Vaitape
Quay

200m
0

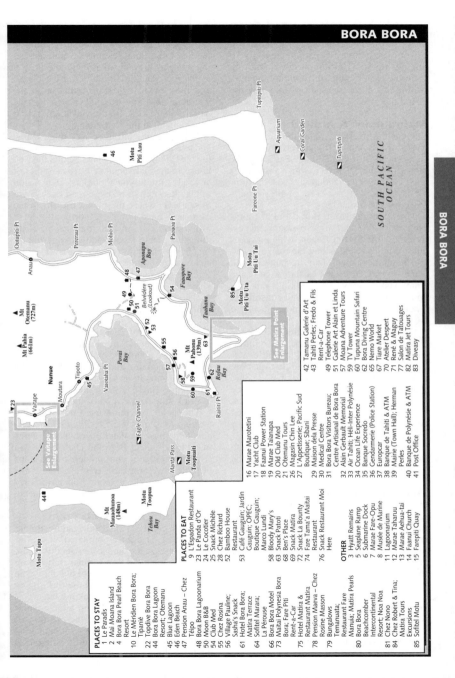

BORA BORA

PLACES TO STAY
1 Le Paradis
2 Mai Moana Island
4 Bora Bora Pearl Beach Resort
10 Le Méridien Bora Bora; Tipanié
22 Topdive Bora Bora
44 Bora Bora Lagoon Resort; Otemanu
45 Blue Lagoon
46 Eden Beach
47 Pension Anau – Chez Teipo
48 Bora Bora Lagoonarium
50 Moon B&B
54 Club Med
55 Chez Rosina
56 Village Pauline; Sasha's Snack
61 Hotel Bora Bora; Matira Terrace
64 Sofitel Marara; La Pérouse
66 Bora Bora Motel
73 Maitai Polynesia Bora Bora; Fare Pîti
75 Hotel Matira & Restaurant Matira
78 Pension Maeva – Chez Rosine Masson
79 Bungalows Temanuata; Restaurant Fare Manuia; Matira Pearls
80 Bora Bora Beachcomber Intercontinental Resort; Noa Noa
81 Chez Nono
84 Chez Robert & Tina; Matira Tours Excursions
85 Sofitel Motu

PLACES TO EAT
9 L'Espadon Restaurant
23 Le Panda d'Or
24 Le Cocotier
25 Snack Michèle
28 Chez Richard
52 Bamboo House Restaurant
53 Café Gauguin; Jardin Gauguin; OPEC; Boutique Gauguin; Marco Lundi
58 Bloody Mary's
63 Snack Patoti
68 Ben's Place
69 Snack Matira
72 Snack La Bounty
74 Fare Tama'a Maitai Restaurant
76 Snack Restaurant Moi Here

OTHER
3 Hyatt Remains
5 Seaplane Ramp
6 Submarine Dock
7 Marae Fare-Opu
8 Musée de Marine
11 Lagoonarium
12 Marae Taharuu
13 Marae Aehua-tai
14 Faanui Church
15 Farepiti Quay
16 Marae Marotetini
17 Yacht Club
18 Faanui Power Station
19 Marae Taianapa
20 Old Club Med
21 Otemanu Tours
26 Magasin Chin Lee
27 L'Appétisserie; Pacific Sud Boutique; Sibani
29 Maison dela Presse
30 Medical Centre
31 Bora Bora Visitors Bureau; Centre Artisanal de Bora Bora
32 Alain Gerbault Memorial
33 Air Tahiti; Héli-Inter Polynésie
34 Ocean Life Experience
35 Banque Socredo
36 Gendarmerie (Police Station)
37 Europcar
38 Banque de Tahiti & ATM
39 Mairie (Town Hall); Herman Perles
40 Banque de Polynésie & ATM
41 Post Office
42 Tamanu Galerie d'Art
43 Tahiti Perles; Fredo & Fils Rent-a-Car
49 Telephone Tower
51 Galerie Art Alain et Linda
57 Moana Adventure Tours
59 TV Tower
60 Tupuna Mountain Safari
62 Bora Diving Centre
65 Nemo World
67 Tiare Market
70 Atelier Despert
71 René & Maguy
77 Salon de Tatouages
82 Matira Jet Tours
83 Diveasy

need to ask around) and offers great views of the profiles of Taha'a and Ra'iatea. You can only go partway by car. It takes only 10 minutes up and 10 minutes down (starting from the eastern side, the path commences behind the truck workshop) to cross the island this way.

Matira Point & Around

Beyond the overland road, the coast road passes the Bamboo House Restaurant and some shops. Just after Village Pauline is the turn-off to the **TV tower**, which provides a good view over the lagoon. Just past the turn-off is Bloody Mary's, one of the island's most popular restaurants.

The luxurious Hotel Bora Bora at Raititi Point marks the start of the pleasant and easily accessible **Matira Beach**, which sweeps out to Matira Point. Along the road are several boutiques, snack bars, restaurants and places to stay. From the eastern edge of the Hotel Matira property, a walking trail runs up the hill to a battery of **WWII coastal defence guns**. It's only a 10-minute hike up to the emplacement.

On the eastern side of Matira Point is the classy Bora Bora Beachcomber Intercontinental Resort. The hotel and a few little *pensions* are down the small road that runs out to Matira Point; the public **beach** along here is great. The annual Hawaiki Nui canoe race finishes the final leg, Taha'a to Bora Bora, right on the beach (see the boxed text 'Hawaiki Nui Canoe Race' in the Facts for the Visitor chapter).

The point takes its name from the British ship *Mathilda*, which was wrecked in the Tuamotus in 1792.

Matira Point to Anau

From Matira Point, the coast road passes a busy little collection of shops, restaurants and hotels. The road rounds the point and passes Club Med, which has its own bay and its own *belvédère* (lookout) atop the ridge above the bay. The road climbs as it passes Club Med, and then drops back down to the coast just before the fishing village of Anau, a rather strung-out affair. The short and steep pathway to the telephone tower and down to the other side of the island starts from beside the truck workshop; ask around for directions as this path is very difficult to find.

Fitiiu Point

A finger-like peninsula extending out into the lagoon, Fitiiu Point features several interesting sites, but they are all difficult to find. Just as the road starts to climb, a track peels off and runs down to **Marae Aehua-tai** at the water's edge. There are good views across the bay from the marae (traditional temple), with Mt Otemanu in the background.

Further up the hill there's a natural marae and two more **WWII coastal guns**. The walking trail along the ridge starts behind the first house, at the sharp bend in the road. If there's anybody around you should ask permission to take the trail, or take the road back down to sea level where the track turns off to the right and runs along the northern side of Fitiiu Point. The track terminates at, of all things, a scenic lagoonside garbage dump! Just before the dump a steep path runs uphill and emerges on the top of the ridge just before the gun site. From the site there are fine views out over the lagoon to the motu.

Backtrack along the ridge-top footpath to **Marae Taharuu**, a natural rock pinnacle.

Haamaire Bay & Taimoo Bay

The road beyond Fitiiu Point traverses the most lightly populated stretch of coast as it rounds Haamaire and Taimoo Bays. The middle-of-nowhere L'Espadon Restaurant on Taimoo Bay is a good place for a lunch or drink stop on a circuit of the island.

The small, private **Musée de la Marine** (Marine Museum; ☎ 67 75 24; admission by donation) has a collection of model ships made by architect Bertrand Darasse. If you are interested in seeing models of the ships of the early European explorers, this is the place for you. The opening hours are fairly haphazard, so you might like to call ahead.

Taihi Point to Farepiti Point

The north coast of the island, leading around Taihi Point, is lightly populated. Just after the point, a steep and often muddy track climbs up to an old WWII radar station atop Popotei Ridge and on to a **lookout** above the village of Faanui. Nearby is the forlorn site of the abandoned Hyatt hotel project.

At the end of Tereia Point, a rectangular concrete water tank marks the position of another **coastal gun**. There's no path; just clamber for a couple of minutes straight up the hill behind the tank.

Marae Fare-Opu is squeezed between the roadside and water's edge. Two of the slabs are clearly marked with the turtle **petroglyphs** seen incised into stones at numerous other sites in the Society Islands.

Faanui Bay was the site of the main US military base during WWII. From the picturesque **church** at the head of the bay a road runs inland. Where the sealed road bends to the right, take the unsealed fork to the left. The road climbs up towards the ridge; continue to bear left at each fork. The track often deteriorates into a muddy morass, but eventually it drops down the other side to Vairau Bay.

Set on the edge of a coconut plantation, back off the mountain side of the road, **Marae Taianapa** is on private property. You've overshot the marae by about 100m if you get as far as the Hinano Beer and Coca-Cola depot.

Farepiti Point to Pahua Point

Inter-island ships dock at the rather drab Farepiti quay, which was built during WWII and is at the western end of Faanui Bay.

A hundred metres southwest along the shoreline is **Marae Marotetini**, which is unfortunately on an appallingly littered stretch of beach. This is the second royal marae on the island and was restored in 1968.

Along the road from Farepiti Point to Pahua Point, one of the WWII defence guns can be seen silhouetted against the skyline. The road rounds the point and arrives at the remains of the old Club Med, rotting in the tropical air. Two **coastal defence guns** overlook the point. They're a short walk up from the road, and as usual, the route is not marked. These guns were placed here to overlook the Teavanui Pass, the shipping route into the lagoon.

ACTIVITIES

Bora Bora's activities focus on the wonderful lagoon, although there are also plenty of opportunities in the mountainous interior for those who don't like to get their feet wet.

Although Bora Bora has clear, aqua water and a brochure-esque appeal, the beaches are not her strong point. Even the best bits of beach are fairly narrow. For a day of working on the tan and paddling in the warm water, you can either get dropped off on a motu, which feels wonderfully secluded even in high season, or head to Matira Point. One of the best spots along Matira Point is opposite

the Bora Bora Beachcomber Intercontinental Resort. There are public toilets, showers, shady areas and plenty of local kids and their footballs (don't worry, they tend to stick to the grassy area away from the beach).

Many of the motu remain untouched and idyllic, but it's important to remember that these little paradise islands belong to local families or have been bought buy the luxury hotels: don't treat the land as yours to explore without permission. If the motu is owned by a hotel, visitors are usually welcome if they buy a drink at the bar or a meal at the restaurant, and there are free shuttle boats that will take you back and forth.

Water Activities

Bora Bora's most popular activity is probably **diving**. Sharks, rays and other marine life abound, and can be seen in quite shallow waters in the lagoon or outside the reef. Check the special section 'Diving' for details about dive centres.

Swimming and **snorkelling** will probably feature prominently during your stay on Bora Bora. The water is shallow and warm and makes splashing around with children or your snorkelling gear very appealing and safe. The snorkelling is particularly good around Hotel Bora Bora, where fishing is banned and the currents are ideal.

Try to do a **lagoon tour** at some stage during your stay, allowing you to view the island in a different way, and to snorkel and splash your way around. Or, if you can get a group together, hire a boat and do it your own way.

You can even stroll along the bottom of the sea bed, accompanied by a dive expert, with **Underseawalk** (☎ 67 77 42) for about 6000 CFP.

Hiking

There are beautiful walks on Bora Bora, including the Mt Pahia ascent, but a guide is recommended as the paths are notoriously difficult to follow. See the Hiking section in the Outdoor Activities chapter for details.

Horse Riding

Horse riding on Motu Piti Aau is available for all levels of experience at **Ranch Reva Reva** (☎ 67 63 63). A ride, which lasts about an hour, costs 6500 CFP; 2½-hour moonlight rides cost 8500 CFP, including transfers from your accommodation.

BORA BORA

Parasailing

Solo or two-person parasails are offered at **Parasail** (☎ 67 70 34, fax 67 61 73); it charges 10,000 CFP per person or 17,000 CFP for two.

ORGANISED TOURS
Lagoon Tours

Boat tours have become a standard part of the Bora Bora experience. There are half-day and full-day tours to some of the most beautiful spots around the lagoon, often with a stop to feed the sharks, a barbecue lunch on a motu, a swimming and snorkelling stop at the Coral Garden, a swim with the rays and a walk on the outer reef. Of course there's no chance of playing Robinson Crusoe when your motu has 10 or 20 other tourists on it, but this is a pleasant and easy way to see the marine life and get to otherwise inaccessible sites. Bring waterproof sandals, a hat and sunscreen.

It costs about 5000 CFP for half-day trips and 7500 CFP for day trips, which typically go from 9am to 4pm and include lunch. As well as the regular operators, many hotels and guesthouses offer these lagoon tours. Try **Matira Tours Excursions** (☎ 67 70 97), **Lagoonarium** (☎ 67 71 34), **Teremoana Tours** (☎ 67 71 38) at Chez Nono, **Ocean Life Experience** (☎ 74 51 11), **Chez Robert & Tina** (☎ 67 72 92), or **Moana Adventure Tours** (☎ 67 61 41), which also does trips in glass-bottomed boats.

4WD Tours

Four-wheel-drive tours are run by **Tupuna Mountain Safari** (☎/fax 67 75 06). The tours include visits to American WWII sites and archaeological sites, with discussion of the island's flora and a fruit-tasting along the way. Half-day trips cost about 5500 CFP per person. **Otemanu Tours** (☎ 67 70 49) does two-hour tours by minibus or truck for 2200 CFP per person.

Catamaran & Deep-Sea Fishing

Half-day lagoon trips with swimming and snorkelling stops are organised by **Taaroa** (☎/fax 67 61 55) for 6500 CFP; sunset cruises for at least four people are 3800 CFP. All trips take place on the *Taaroa*, a 12m catamaran. **Taravana** (☎ 67 77 79, fax 67 77 78) hires out the 15.3m catamaran *Taravana* for 90,000/120,000/220,000 CFP for a half-

day/full day/24 hours, and also operates deep-sea fishing trips. **Jessie L** (☎/fax 67 75 22) and **Moana Adventure Tours** (☎ 67 61 41) organise deep-sea fishing as well; count on at least 35,200 CFP for four hours for up to four people.

Helicopter Tours

Next door to Air Tahiti in Vaitape, **Héli-Inter Polynésie** (☎ 67 62 59; e helico-tahiti@ mail.pf) offers 15-minute flights for 15,000 CFP per person. You'll do a quick loop of the lagoon and fly over Matira Point, the Coral Garden, Mt Otemanu, Faanui Bay, the airport on Motu Mute, Teavanui Pass, Motu Tapu and Motu Toopua. There are commentaries in English.

PLACES TO STAY

You could easily whittle away your life savings on deluxe hotels on Bora Bora, which are as sumptuous as the hype leads you to believe. But you can also benefit from the cheaper little *pensions* (guesthouses) that have sprung up over the past few years, and there are even a few camp sites, which is fairly rare in French Polynesia.

Although places to stay can be found all around the island and on the motu, the majority are concentrated along the southern coast.

All the top-end and mid-range places accept credit cards, but many of the budget places do not. Prices cited here include the myriad taxes that apply. Remember that it is the norm to quote accommodation prices before tax, so do check before booking in.

There were two new hotels planned at the time of writing: construction for a **Paladien** had begun, and **Hotel Bora Bora Nui Resort** (☎ 86 48 48; e reservation.Tahiti@sheraton .pf; w sheratonsintahiti.com) was due to open in 2003.

West Coast

There are a few nice places to stay dotted along the west coast.

Topdive Bora Bora (☎ 60 50 50, fax 60 50 51; e info@topdive.com; w www.topdive.com; garden/over-water bungalows 28,500/38,500 CFP) is to the north of Vaitape, just after the Total petrol station. The cathedral ceilings in the bungalows and communal areas set this place apart. There's no beach, but it's right by the lagoon and there is a lovely swimming pool. The restaurant here (see Places to

Eat, later in this chapter) has a very good reputation. This place is a great location for divers. Breakfast is included in the price. Credit cards are accepted.

Blue Lagoon (*☎/fax 67 65 64; rooms per person 2200 CFP*), about 20 minutes on foot south of Vaitape, should be at the end of your list of budget places to try. There are five very basic rooms with shared bathroom; half-board adds another 2200 CFP.

Moon B&B (*☎/fax 67 74 36;* e *moonbun galow@netcourrier.com; single/double bunga-lows with bathroom 7500/8500 CFP*) has lovely little bungalows. There's a shared kitchen area, and breakfast is included in the price. Fresh pineapple juice (300 CFP) is sometimes available.

Chez Rosina (*☎/fax 67 70 91;* e *adesaint pierre@mail.pf; singles/doubles 5400/6500 CFP, with bathroom 5900/7500 CFP, bunga-lows 13,800 CFP*), on the mountain side of the road, 4.5km from Vaitape, has a warm and friendly atmosphere. The two new bun-galows have their own kitchen; occupants of the other rooms share the lounge, dining room and kitchen facilities.

Village Pauline (*☎ 67 72 16, fax 67 78 14;* e *vpauline@38mail.pf; camping per person 2500 CFP, dorm beds 3200 CFP, bungalows 7400-12,800 CFP*) is right after Chez Rosina towards Matira Point, on the inland side of the road. This welcoming place runs like a well-oiled machine and is a good option for the budget-minded traveller. The accommo-dation is beautifully maintained and is set in a Polynesian-style village with a tropical garden. There's one new bungalow, which rivals the top hotels but is a fraction of the price and has the added bonus of a kitchen. Transfers from the Farepiti quay cost 500 CFP; transfers from Vaitape quay cost 300 CFP. There are bicycles for rent, and this is certainly the place to come if you are serious about kayaking. The staff speak English. Credit cards are accepted.

Matira Point & Around

Matira Point, the southern toe of Bora Bora, is packed with places to stay. If you stay in the area, you'll benefit from the great beach along here.

Budget They may lack the luxury of the top hotels, but there are a number of little *pen-sions* around Matira Point that lay claim to the best sweep of beach on the main island. Most of the following places have cold water only; unusually for budget places, they all accept credit cards.

Chez Nono (*☎ 67 71 38, fax 67 74 27; singles/doubles 5900/7000 CFP, bungalows 9100-12,200 CFP*), near the Beachcomber Intercontinental, has six rooms in a quaint two-storey house (facilities are shared); some have verandas and a couple even have lagoon views, although the walls are thin and the rooms can get very hot. There are also two small bungalows with double bed, and two larger family bungalows, all with bathroom.

Chez Robert & Tina (*☎ 67 63 55, 67 72 92; singles/doubles 5400/6600 CFP*), right at the end of the point, has rooms in simple, fan-cooled houses, all with shared bathroom and kitchen. Rates drop dramatically on subse-quent nights. Full-day boat tours of the island cost 7200 CFP per person, including picnic lunch on a motu, or you can be dropped off on a motu for the day for 1700 CFP. Transfers from Vaitape cost 500 CFP.

Pension Maeva – Chez Rosine Masson (*☎/fax 67 72 04; dorm beds/doubles 3500/6900 CFP*), right on the water's edge, has loads of charm and character, as does Rosine herself. The house creaks and the walls are paper thin, but this place is full of the late Jean Masson's paintings and the lagoonside setting is a delight. There are two rooms downstairs for one or two people, and three upstairs (two with sea views). A dorm-style room with three single beds is pleasant but obviously doesn't offer much privacy. There's a shared lounge room, kitchen and two bathrooms (one with hot water). Trans-fers cost 500 CFP.

Mid-Range As you saunter into the mid-range category, you can safely expect pri-vate bathrooms with hot water; credit cards are accepted at all mid-range places.

Hotel Matira (*☎ 67 78 58, 67 70 51, fax 67 77 02;* e *hotel.matira@mail.pf;* w *www .hotelmatira.com; bungalows 21,300-38,400 CFP*), right on Matira Beach, has a restau-rant on the lagoon side of the road and 20 simple, thatched-roof bungalows. The bun-galows are tastefully done, and some also have kitchen. Half-board adds 4800 CFP per person, full board (all meals) adds 8000 CFP. Return transfers from Vaitape cost

1300 CFP. Reception, the restaurant and four of the bungalows are in one spot; the rest of the bungalows are just up the road to the north.

Bungalows Temanuata (☎ 67 75 61, fax 67 62 48; family bungalows from 18,100 CFP, garden/beach bungalows 12,800/16,000 CFP), just after the Matira Point turn-off and the Beachcomber Intercontinental, is behind the Restaurant Fare Manuia. This is a great mid-range choice and is often heavily booked.

Bora Bora Motel (☎ 67 78 21, fax 67 77 57; w www.boraboramotel.pf; double/triple bungalows 14,600/21,100 CFP) is a smaller, beachfront place right across the road from the Tiare Market supermarket. The site is a little cramped, but this is a good stretch of beach.

Top End On Raititi Point, about 7km from Vaitape, **Hotel Bora Bora** (☎ 60 44 60, 60 44 11, fax 60 44 66; e hotelborabora@amanresorts.com; garden/beach/over-water bungalows from 67,000/83,600/107,000 CFP) has the best location on the island and is unashamedly the domain of the rich and famous. Island gossip has it that John Travolta stayed here and Pierce Brosnan is a regular. The hotel has a restaurant overlooking the lagoon and a bar and restaurant down towards the beach; the restaurant is reputedly one of the best places to eat on the island. Because the hotel owners have made efforts to protect the fish around the point, this is one of the island's better snorkelling sites. The hotel has a boutique and tour desk and hires out cars, scooters and bicycles. The buffet and dance performance here costs 7000 CFP.

Bora Bora Beachcomber Intercontinental Resort (☎ 60 49 00, fax 60 49 99; e reservations_borabora@interconti.com; w www.borabora.interconti.com; beach/over-water bungalows from 65,600/82,300 CFP) is on the eastern side of Matira Point. The over-water bungalows come complete with the trademark glass coffee tables for lagoon viewing. A pier is being constructed so that guests can be brought directly here from the airport motu. Dinner and dance performances (from around 6400 CFP) are regular events.

Maitai Polynesia Bora Bora (☎ 60 30 00, fax 67 66 03; e maitaibo@mail.pf; w www.hotelmaitai.com; doubles/units 28,000/37,900 CFP, beach/over-water bungalows 45,700/

54,500 CFP) sprawls across both sides of the road, just beyond the Matira Point turn-off. Although this hotel is not as isolated or glamorous as its more luxurious competitors, the prices are a tad lower and it's nicely designed. Unfortunately the pleasant bar and restaurant are not right on the lagoon (although Fare Tama'a Maitai, the hotel's other restaurant just to the south, is on the lagoon side). There's a Polynesian dance performance once a week.

Sofitel Marara (☎ 60 55 00, fax 67 74 03; garden/beach/over-water bungalows from 42,900/56,800/61,200 CFP) was originally built by film-maker Dino de Laurentis. Although the hotel still has a certain style, it doesn't quite match up to its fiercest competitors. You'd probably be better off paying the extra to be on the Sofitel's offshoot, Sofitel Motu, on the idyllic and exclusive Motu Piti Uu Uta (see The Motu, later). There's a beachfront restaurant and bar, a swimming pool, a tennis court and the usual sporting and shopping facilities. Performances are organised three times a week.

East Coast
The east coast is less built-up than the rest of the island, and there are only a few places to choose from along here.

Bora Bora Lagoonarium (☎ 67 71 34, fax 67 60 29; camping per person 1600 CFP, dorm beds 2500 CFP, doubles 6400 CFP, 2-person bungalows 8600 CFP) is seemingly made of cardboard, but it's clean and in a quiet area. There's a communal kitchen, bicycles can be rented and boat trips across to the Lagoonarium are offered.

Pension Anau – Chez Téipo (☎ 67 78 17, fax 67 73 24; single/double/quad bungalows 7000/8000/11,000 CFP), near Club Med, is one of the best budget places on the island. The bungalows are well equipped, the trees are laden with bananas, and breakfast is included in the price. Free transfers from the Vaitape quay are offered, and bikes are available. There's no beach here, but there's a nice decked area. Credit cards are accepted.

Club Med (☎ 60 46 04, fax 60 46 10; e cmbora@mail.pf; singles 31,000-37,200 CFP, doubles per person 25,800-31,000 CFP) is painted in a rather odd choice of pastels and is a veritable steal by Bora Bora standards, but nowadays it lacks the finesse of the other big hotels on the island. Any activity offered on the island can be arranged through Club Med, and there's a private stretch of beach on Motu Piti Aau. The Club Med pirogue shuttles back and forth to the motu opposite. Club Med visitors generally book through a travel agent, but if there is space, casual visitors are accepted here.

The Motu
Staying on a motu ensures unrivalled tranquillity, a complete escape and great views of Bora Bora. The following motu hotels are listed clockwise around the island.

Le Méridien Bora Bora (☎ 60 51 51, fax 60 61 52; e sales@lemeridien-tahiti.com; beach/ over-water bungalows from 66,800/77,900 CFP), on the long motu on the eastern side of the lagoon, almost defies description. The architecture is fantastic and at times eccentric and the view of Mt Otemanu on Bora Bora is unique to this site; the vast glass floors in the over-water bungalows are mesmerising. There's a shuttle boat to and from Anau on the main island from 8am to midnight. This place is sometimes booked out by large and revelling groups, when access is denied to mere mortals. Le Méridien is now involved in sea-turtle protection work, so guests have the added bonus of watching the rehabilitating turtles as they potter about.

Eden Beach (☎ 74 24 62, fax 67 69 76; e info@spmhotels.pf; garden/beach bungalows 27,900/33,500 CFP) may not be quite as luxurious as some motu hotels, but it's still a divine and very stylish place to relax, and it is certainly more environmentally friendly than other places. It's very intimate and, what is more, is largely solar-powered. There are only 12 bungalows, so you are ensured a peaceful stay. Bora Bora needs more green hotels like Eden Beach if it is to survive. If you can afford it, and have booked in time, this is the number-one place to stay on Bora Bora.

Sofitel Motu (☎ 60 56 00, fax 60 56 66; beach/over-water bungalows 66,800/83,400 CFP), on the tiny Motu Piti Uu Uta, is five glorious minutes by boat from the main island. The bungalows are perched on a hillside, scattered among the coconut trees. Polynesian architecture hides the air-con, satellite TV and computer modems. There's a restaurant with a panoramic view, a sunset bar and regular shuttle boats from Sofitel Marara. Ahh!

Bora Bora Lagoon Resort (☎ 60 40 00, fax 60 40 01; e bblr@mail.pf; garden/beach/ over-water bungalows from 55,100/66,800/ 91,700 CFP) is on Motu Toopua, looking across the lagoon to Vaitape. You name it, this place has got it: swimming pool, tennis courts, gymnasium, boutiques, canoes and pedal boats, restaurants and bars. A shuttle shuttles between the resort and the main island (from just in front of the tourist office) every half-hour from 8am to midnight.

Bora Bora Pearl Beach Resort (☎ 60 52 00, fax 60 52 22; e info@SPMhotels.pf; bungalows 53,400-80,100 CFP), on Motu Tevairoa, has luxurious bungalows constructed from natural materials. It's an extra 7500/10,000 CFP for half-/full board. There's a magnificent swimming pool and an over-water restaurant. Traditional dance performances are generally held three times weekly. There's a shuttle every 45 minutes between 8.15am and 10pm.

Mai Moana Island (☎ 67 62 45, fax 67 62 39; bungalows 27,000 CFP), on Motu Ite, also has a dreamlike setting. Run by a retired Polish film-maker (who speaks French and English), it has three big bungalows on the motu. Airport transfers cost 1000 CFP for two, breakfast costs 1320 CFP, lunch 2600 CFP and dinner 4000 CFP. You can hire the entire motu for 45,000 CFP. Credit cards are accepted.

Le Paradis (☎/fax 67 75 53; single/double/ triple bungalows 10,700/16,000/18,200 CFP), on Motu Paahi, is a perfectly affordable motu pension with a relaxed atmosphere. There are five simple bungalows in a lagoonside coconut plantation. Bathroom facilities are generally shared (there are two bungalows with private bathroom). Airport transfers are free; transport to Vaitape costs 1000 CFP per person. Credit cards are not accepted.

PLACES TO EAT
The tourist influx aside, Bora Bora goes to bed early. Most restaurants firmly shut the door at 9pm, so don't wait until then or you may go hungry. A number of restaurants, including Bloody Mary's, Bamboo House Restaurant, L'Espadon Restaurant and Snack La Bounty, offer free transport to and from your hotel.

All of the luxury hotels have dance performances with buffet dinners several times a week. Expect to pay around 6500 CFP to 7000 CFP.

BORA BORA

West Coast

North of Vaitape, **Topdive Bora Bora** (☎ 60 50 50; see West Coast under Places to Stay, earlier; appetizers 1900-2000 CFP, mains 3300-3600 CFP; open daily breakfast, lunch & dinner) has a restaurant with fabulous cathedral ceilings and stylish decor.

Vaitape is no culinary capital, but there are a few good places for breakfast, a snack or a cheap meal. There's a string of **stalls** (open daily) along the main road that sell sandwiches and cool drinks; you can also get a beer and play lotto, should you so fancy. In the evening several **roulottes** (food vans or mobile diners; dishes around 1000 CFP) take up position along the main road and serve simple dishes.

Le Panda d'Or (☎ 67 62 10; open Mon-Sat lunch & dinner) is an impersonal but reasonably priced restaurant just to the north of Vaitape that has Cantonese specialties.

Le Cocotier (appetizers 550-1500 CFP, mains 1200-2100 CFP; open 6.30am-8.30pm Mon-Sat), on the northern side of Vaitape, is a very basic but good Chinese restaurant.

L'Appetisserie (☎ 67 78 88; pastries 130-400 CFP, toasted sandwiches 480-880 CFP; open Mon-Sat) is a very pleasant little snack bar and patisserie in Centre Le Pahia, near the quay. It's certainly the most sophisticated place in town for breakfast or a snack, and the coffee is excellent. This is also the place to check your email, although note this is not possible over lunch time (see Post & Communications under Information earlier in this chapter).

Chez Richard (☎ 67 69 69; takeaway meals 1000-1500 CFP), a simple place on the inland side of the road facing the medical centre in Vaitape, specialises in Chinese takeaway food. You'll see all the old favourites, including lemon chicken, fried wontons and spring rolls.

Blue Lagoon (see West Coast under Places to Stay, earlier; appetizers 600-2500 CFP, mains 1200-2500 CFP), about 1km south of Vaitape, is no longer particularly cheap. You may find the menu doesn't reflect what is actually available (this place always seems to have run out of everything). Free transfers are offered at any time and delivery to your accommodation is possible. Credit cards are not accepted.

Bamboo House Restaurant (☎/fax 67 76 24; appetizers 1200-1600 CFP, mains 2500-5500 CFP; open lunch & dinner Tues-Sun) is an unpretentious but fairly upmarket little bamboo-dominated restaurant. There is also a very reasonably priced snack menu at lunch time. The restaurant provides free transport, and credit cards are accepted.

Café Gauguin (sandwiches 1200 CFP; open 8am-4pm Mon-Sat) is a special little spot for lunch or a cool drink. Sasha, who also masterminds the restaurant at Village Pauline, is at the helm, and you can satisfy most urges here: there's an art shop (Jardin Gauguin), a painter's studio (Marco Lundi) and a rare-pearls shop (OPEC) all in together.

Sasha's Snack in Village Pauline (see West Coast under Places to Stay, earlier) has a very Polynesian restaurant with great, simple food. Try to go to one of Sasha's buffet nights; locals and expats alike swear by them.

Bloody Mary's (☎ 67 72 86; appetizers 1200-1500 CFP, mains 2500-2800 CFP; open Mon-Sat) is quite the place to be seen dining on coconut-tree stools. Although this restaurant is pretty pricey, and is inordinately proud of the celebrities who have dined here, it does have a wonderful festive atmosphere. You hand-pick your piece of fish or meat before you take a seat (vegetarians will be nibbling the tree stumps with hunger – try calling ahead). Unfortunately, our wonderfully fresh fish was overcooked. Free transport is provided from anywhere between Vaitape and Club Med. Credit cards are accepted.

Magasin Chin Lee is a supermarket in Vaitape. There are also a few bigger supermarkets just north of Vaitape on the mountain side of the road.

Matira Point & Around

Restaurants You'll find excellent food in a romantic open-air setting at **Matira Terrace** (☎ 60 44 60). It's at the Hotel Bora Bora (see Matira Point & Around under Places to Stay, earlier). The prices are not unreasonable for the standard.

Restaurant Matira (☎ 67 70 51; appetizers 1050-1250 CFP, mains 1250-1550 CFP), part of Hotel Matira (see Matira Point & Around under Places to Stay, earlier), has a magnificent location and great, reasonably priced food. The lights are a bit too bright in the evening, but this dims in importance as you enjoy the great service and delicious food. The cuisine is largely Chinese, though there are also some Polynesian dishes such as the

Bora Bora

Black pearls, the Tuamotus

Black-tipped sharks, the Tuamotus

Pearl farm, the Tuamotus

Lagoon, Rangiroa

delicious mahi mahi (dorado) with vanilla (1550 CFP). Free transport is offered anywhere between Hotel Bora Bora and Anau.

Noa Noa (☎ 60 49 00) at the Bora Bora Beachcomber Intercontinental Resort (see Matira Point & Around under Places to Stay, earlier) has an especially attractive setting right on the beach. Among the various fish dishes is mahi mahi cooked in papaya butter; there's a lighter lunch-time menu. The Beachcomber's buffet and dance performance (around 6500 CFP) has a fine reputation.

Restaurant Fare Manuia (☎ 67 68 06; appetizers 1500-2600 CFP, 3-course set menu 3950 CFP; open lunch & dinner daily), part of Bungalows Temanuata (see Matira Point & Around under Places to Stay, earlier), is an intimate restaurant with bright tablecloths and plenty of greenery. The tuna tartare with wasabi and lime (1900 CFP) makes for a decadent but healthy lunch. Free transport is offered anywhere between Vaitape and Anau.

Fare Tama'a Maitai Restaurant (open lunch & dinner daily) is part of the Maitai Polynesia (see Matira Point & Around under Places to Stay, earlier), but is a bit further along this strip, after all the bungalows. The parrotfish 'breadcrumbed' in coconut (2000 CFP) is the house speciality.

Snack La Bounty (☎ 67 70 43; mains 1100-2100 CFP; open lunch & dinner Tues-Sun) is hardly chic, but is a popular place that has fish specialities such as delicious mahi mahi with vanilla sauce and raspberry vinegar; there are also some interesting pizzas (around 1450 CFP) on offer. Credit cards are accepted.

La Pérouse (☎ 67 70 46) at the Sofitel Marara (see Matira Point & Around under Places to Stay, earlier) has a lunch-time snack menu with sandwiches, burgers and several hot dishes. In the evening the menu is more elaborate.

Cafés & Snack Bars A popular vegetation-fringed café, **Ben's Place** has a straightforward menu, though there are also Mexican dishes, such as fajitas. Opening hours are variable. Credit cards are accepted.

Snack Matira (☎ 67 77 32; burgers 450-600 CFP, mains 800-1400 CFP; open 10am-6pm Tues-Sun), beside the lagoon and diagonally opposite Ben's Place, has pleasantly low prices and very decent food. The grilled mahi mahi (1100 CFP) is wonderfully garlicky. Takeaway food is available.

Snack Restaurant Moi Here (☎ 67 68 41; burgers from 550 CFP, steaks 1200 CFP; open 6.30am-9pm daily) has great wooden tables, a good menu and lapping water, but the service is not particularly gracious. The poisson cru (raw fish; 1250 CFP) is delicious.

Snack Patoti (☎ 67 61 99; breakfast 1000 CFP, snacks 800-1300 CFP, mains 1300-1500 CFP; open 8am-2pm & 7pm-9pm Mon-Sat) has a good mix of Polynesian dishes (including prawn curry for 1500 CFP) and Chinese dishes (such as chow mein for 1300 CFP). It's in a lovely raised position that catches the breeze.

Self-Catering Across from the Bora Bora Motel, **Tiare Market** (open 6.30am-1.30pm & 3pm-7pm Mon-Sat, 6.30am-1pm & 3pm-6.30pm Sun) is well stocked with all the necessities, from wine and fresh bread to sunscreen and toothpaste.

East Coast

The east coast remains relatively underdeveloped, so you certainly won't be tripping over places to eat (in fact, there's currently only one place to choose from), although there are often little **stalls** along the road where you can get a light snack.

L'Espadon Restaurant (☎ 67 71 67; appetizers 1200-2480 CFP, mains 1500-2690 CFP) is seemingly in the middle of nowhere. Even the flies and ants on the tables don't detract from the very good food here. This was originally part of the old Revatua Club, which is no longer open to the public. There's a cheaper lunch-time menu (snacks 500 CFP to 1500 CFP). Credit cards are accepted and transport can be arranged.

The Motu

Free shuttles, which generally operate until midnight, allow you to enjoy the restaurants at the luxury hotels on the motu around Bora Bora. Like their competitors on the main island, they offer evening performances with dinner buffets several times a week. Reservations are advisable, and you may not be allowed over if the hotel is fully booked. See The Motu under Places to Stay, earlier in this chapter, for details of these hotels.

BORA BORA

Tipanié (☎ 60 51 51) in Le Méridien Bora Bora is a superb surfboard-shaped restaurant right by the lagoon. Every evening there's a different set menu or you can order à la carte. There's a smaller restaurant beside the swimming pool. The shuttle operates from the Anau quay.

Otemanu (☎ 60 40 02), in the Bora Bora Lagoon Resort, defies superlatives. You can enjoy a wonderful candlelit dinner as you watch the sunset. Of course, the prices are as heady as the romantic atmosphere. There are shuttles from the Vaitape quay.

There are two restaurants at the **Bora Bora Pearl Beach Resort**. One is beside the magnificent swimming pool and serves snacks until mid-afternoon; the other is a more formal restaurant on stilts over the lagoon, with a fancier menu and Polynesia and seafood buffets (6200 CFP and 6900 CFP respectively). A shuttle leaves from the yacht club, to the north of Vaitape.

ENTERTAINMENT

You'll feel like a pumpkin if you find yourself out after 10pm on Bora Bora. Despite its glamorous reputation, nightlife on Bora Bora is as restrained as it is on the other islands of French Polynesia. Dinner and a show in one of the big hotels is about the sum of things, but you'll find you wake up so early here that you'll be yawning in unison with the bartender who wants to close at 9pm.

Bars

You can waltz into most of the luxury hotels for a cold beer or cocktail; some even have happy hours. The motu hotels offer free shuttle services, usually until about midnight. There's usually a rather appealing snack menu around, too. The bar at the **Bora Bora Beachcomber Intercontinental Resort** is particularly relaxed and welcoming. A gin and tonic will set you back only 470 CFP (and the mahi mahi burger with chips or salad for 2000 CFP, or a delicious *poisson cru* for 1800 CFP, makes for a feast).

Bloody Mary's (see West Coast under Places to Eat, earlier) has a very popular bar, where you'll find all nationalities pleasantly inebriated and enjoying themselves.

Blue Lagoon, on the edge of Vaitape heading towards Matira Point, is pretty rough and ready, but it has a terrace and very reasonably priced beer.

Dance Performances

Don't miss a traditional dance performance by a local group in one of the luxury hotels. The men often look a bit clumsy alongside the remarkably nimble women, who seem to have a few extra joints to achieve the mesmerising gyrations required. You can usually get in for the price of a drink at the bar, or for around 6000 CFP to 7000 CFP you can also feast on a sumptuous buffet dinner. There are performances two or three times weekly; ask at the reception desks about the schedule and entry policy. When we visited, some hotels were charging up to 2000 CFP for entry to their soirees (and then you'll find yourself paying at least 1500 CFP for a cocktail at the bar), so the days of simply buying a drink to see the performances may be numbered.

SHOPPING

Shopping on Bora Bora tends to mean hopping from the many galleries that are scattered around the island, buying (or dreaming about buying) pearls, or wrapping yourself in various brightly coloured pareu (sarongs). Unless you fancy a tattoo?

Arts & Crafts

This is by no means an exhaustive list of the galleries and craft shops on Bora Bora. You'll enjoy finding others along the coastal road.

Atelier Despert (☎ 689 60 48 15; ⓔ *despertbora@aol.com;* ⓦ *www.despert.com)* is a lovely art studio where you'll find Alain and Karen at work. Alain only does originals (no prints), so it's worth visiting if you are interested in buying paintings.

Jardin Gauguin (☎ 67 76 23), behind Café Gauguin, specialises in art and crafts from the Marquesas. You won't find your usual souvenir numbers here – this is beautiful *objets d'art* only. **Marco Lundi** (☎/fax 67 52 04; open 9am-5pm Mon-Sat), a painter, has his studio behind Jardin Gauguin, in this 'garden' of culture and food. The price of paintings ranges from around 25,000 CFP to 900,000 CFP. **Boutique Gauguin** (☎ 67 76 67), next door, sells pareu, clothes, crafts and sculptures.

Galerie Alain et Linda (☎ 67 70 32), about halfway between Vaitape and Matira Point, has a little bit of everything, including a mix of art, books and pottery.

Tamanu Galerie d'Art (☎/fax 67 66 89) is just next to the post office in Vaitape. It's another pretty special gallery with Polynesian art.

Centre Artisanal de Bora Bora in the tourist office by the Vaitape quay has lots of stalls selling pareu, basketwork and other crafts produced by island women. In Le Centre Pahia, **Pacific Sud Boutique** is a good place to find T-shirts and other clothing.

Pearls

You'll find pearl shops all around Bora Bora. The owners invariably speak some English.

Office Polynésien d'Expertise et de Commercialisation (OPEC; ☎/fax 67 61 62), an impeccably run rare-pearl company, is the only place that can put your pearl in a machine so you can see its quality. If you're serious about your pearl-buying, this is the place to come, even if it's only for a quick lesson on cultured pearls. You can't get the pearls you've bought elsewhere assessed here; it's just a guarantee of the pearls you buy from OPEC.

The **Sibani** black pearl specialists have jewellery shops in Le Centre Pahia in Vaitape and at several hotels. Other companies, including **Tahiti Perles**, **Herman Perles** and **Matira Pearls**, also have a vast assortment of mounted and unmounted black pearls.

Tattoos

You'll see so many stretches of beautiful tanned skin adorned with traditional tattoos that you may start feeling bare without one yourself. If you are interested in returning home with your very own example of Polynesian art, **Salon de Tatouages** (☎ 67 66 73, 72 03 75) in Matira Point is a popular, sterile and reliable place to start your research.

GETTING THERE & AWAY

Bora Bora is 270km northwest of Tahiti and can be reached by air or boat from the capital.

Air

At least six times daily **Air Tahiti** (☎ 67 70 35, 67 70 85; open 7.30am-11.30am & 1.30pm-4.30pm Mon-Fri, 8am-11am Sat) flies between Bora Bora and Tahiti (13,600 CFP one-way). These flights are sometimes direct (about 45 minutes), other times via Mo'orea, Huahine, Ra'iatea or a combination of those islands. Flying into Bora

Bora, the left side of the aircraft offers the best views of the spectacular scenery.

One-way fares to or from Bora Bora to surrounding islands include: Huahine 7300 CFP, Mo'orea 17,500 CFP and Ra'iatea 5800 CFP. See the Getting Around chapter near the beginning of this book for other fares.

Air Tahiti also has direct flights from Bora Bora to the Tuamotus, with a very handy flight to Rangiroa (22,500 CFP, 80 minutes) and an onward connection to Manihi (25,400 CFP). Flights operate to Rangiroa five times a week, but only twice a week in the reverse direction.

The Air Tahiti office is on the quay at Vaitape.

Boat

Inter-island boats dock at the Farepiti quay, 3km north of Vaitape.

The cargo ship **Vaeanu** (☎ 41 25 35, fax 41 24 34) makes three trips a week between Pape'ete and Bora Bora (via Huahine, Ra'iatea and Taha'a), leaving Pape'ete on Monday, Wednesday and Friday at 5pm; it leaves Bora Bora on Tuesday, Thursday and Sunday.

The **Maupiti Express** (☎ 67 66 69) makes regular trips between Bora Bora, Maupiti, Taha'a and Ra'iatea. The boat departs the Vaitape quay at 8.30am Tuesday, Thursday and Saturday (the trip takes about 1½ hours and costs 2500/3500 CFP one-way/return); the return trip leaves Maupiti at 4pm the same day. It's quite possible to visit Maupiti as a day trip from Bora Bora.

Hawaiki Nui (☎ 45 23 24) also does the Society Islands circuit.

GETTING AROUND
To/From the Airport

Arriving on Bora Bora is quite dramatic. The airport is on a motu, Motu Mute, at the northern edge of the lagoon; transfers are then offered to and from the Vaitape quay on two large catamaran ferries (the price of this trip is included in the cost of your ticket). This makes for a wonderful free tour of the western side of the island! There's a regular bus service from the quay to the hotels at Matira Point (500 CFP).

When leaving by air, you need to be at the quay at least 1¼ hours before the flight. The top hotels transfer their visitors directly to and from the airport; everyone else is picked up at the quay by the catamaran ferries (the cost of this is included in the ticket).

Le Truck

Officially, there's no public transport on Bora Bora. Nonetheless, there sometimes seems to be a le truck going somewhere at the appropriate time, particularly for flight and boat departures. It's more common, and reliable, to organise transport to and from the quay through your hotel or guesthouse.

Car, Scooter & Bicycle

Cars, scooters and bikes can be rented for two-, four-, eight- and 24-hour periods.

Europcar (*☎ 67 70 15, 67 70 03, fax 67 79 95; car hire 2/4/8 hrs 6700/7300/8500 CFP; open 8am-6pm*) has its main office in the centre of Vaitape, as well as desks in several of the main hotels; **Fredo & Fils Rent-a-Car** (*☎ 67 70 31, fax 67 62 07; car hire 2/4/8 hrs 4800/6200/7200 CFP*) is also in Vaitape and at several hotels; and **Fare Piti Rent-a-Car** (*☎ 67 65 28, fax 67 65 28; car hire 2/4 hrs 4800/5800 CFP; open Mon-Sat*) is in the Maitai Polynesia Bora Bora.

Fare Piti has scooters for hire (2/4 hours 3800/4350 CFP). You will find bicycles for rent at Europcar (2/4/8 hours 1300/1400/1800 CFP) and Fare Piti (2/4/8 hour 850/1000/1300 CFP), and many of the hotels have bikes that their guests can use.

There's a Total petrol station (open Monday to Friday) north of Vaitape, just before Topdive Bora Bora.

Boat, Kayak & Jet Ski

Renting a boat is a heavenly way to explore the lagoon, and if you can get a few of you together, this is a cheaper option than the organised tours available. **René & Maguy** (*☎ 67 60 61, fax 67 61 01*), next to Snack La Bounty, rents outboard-powered boats for 8200 CFP for a half-day and 11,550 CFP for the full day. The boats can seat up to four passengers, and snorkelling equipment is included.

Village Pauline has kayaks for rent.

Miki Miki Jet Ski (*☎ 67 76 44*) is shortly before the Maitai Polynesia Bora Bora, coming from Vaitape, and rents out jet skis for 14,000 CFP for two hours.

Maupiti

pop 1127 • area 11 sq km

The smallest and most isolated of the Society high islands, Maupiti is a miniature version of Bora Bora, boasting impressive soaring rocky peaks with tumbling slopes cloaked in coconut plantations. Like Bora Bora it has a shimmering, shallow lagoon edged by a string of motu flaunting luxurious beaches.

Maupiti is like Bora Bora once was – it's still quite traditionally Polynesian and much more low key, perhaps too low key for some. Apart from *pensions* (guesthouses), Maupiti has hardly any tourist infrastructure – cars have yet to supplant scooters and bicycles. Visit Maupiti for quiet, tranquillity and isolation. Agricultural work on the motu, fishing on the lagoon, working on the pearl farms, and church services set the pace of life. Although TV has taken its toll on village life, the homes still have a traditional touch.

Easily accessible from Bora Bora, Tahiti and Ra'iatea, Maupiti offers a different facet of Polynesia, well off the beaten track.

History

Like Ra'iatea, Maupiti enjoyed great cultural importance and chiefs from other islands used to come here for ceremonial purposes. Archaeological investigations on Motu Paeao, at the northern end of the lagoon, have revealed fish hooks and other items dating back to around AD 850. Their similarity to objects discovered in New Zealand has been factored into the theories on Polynesian migration. This is one of the oldest archaeological sites in the Society Islands.

The European 'discovery' of Maupiti is credited to the Dutch explorer Roggeveen in 1722, nearly 50 years before Wallis, Bougainville and Cook made their important landfalls on Tahiti. Early in the 19th century the island came under the influence of Bora Bora. European missionaries brought another power struggle, eventually installing Protestantism as the major religion. Later in the century another struggle blew up with Bora Bora over control of the remote Scilly atoll. French influence first touched the island during this period but

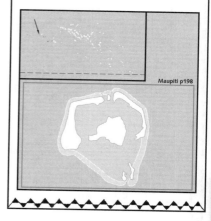

Highlights

- Touring the magnificent lagoon by boat
- Lazing on Tereia Beach
- Escaping to a motu for a day
- Climbing Mt Teurafaatiu for the view over the lagoon

Maupiti p198

missionaries and local chiefs continued to wield power until after WWII.

Maupiti has remained remarkably untouched by mass tourism. The tricky Onoiau Pass, site of a number of shipwrecks over the years, is frequently suggested as one of the reasons for Maupiti's lack of tourist development, but perhaps the islanders simply aren't too keen on being overrun.

Growing watermelons on the motu is a major source of income for the islanders. Copra production, heavily subsidised by the government, remains important but recently much energy has gone into producing pearl oysters on the atoll of Mopelia.

The devastating cyclone Oséa ravaged the island in late 1997 and many houses have been replaced by new buildings, which, although dull to look at, have the virtue of being built to withstand winds of 200km/h.

Orientation

A 10km road encircles the island, only deviating from the coastline for a short stretch, where it climbs over the ridgeline near

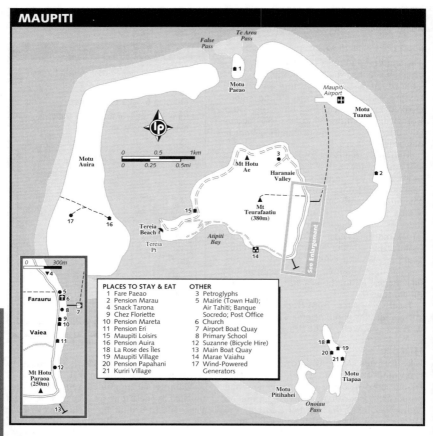

MAUPITI

PLACES TO STAY & EAT
1 Fare Paeao
2 Pension Marau
4 Snack Tarona
9 Chez Floriette
10 Pension Mareta
11 Pension Eri
15 Maupiti Loisirs
16 Pension Auira
18 La Rose des Îles
19 Maupiti Village
20 Pension Papahani
21 Kuriri Village

OTHER
3 Petroglyphs
5 Mairie (Town Hall);
   Air Tahiti; Banque
   Socredo; Post Office
6 Church
7 Airport Boat Quay
8 Primary School
12 Suzanne (Bicycle Hire)
13 Main Boat Quay
14 Marae Vaiahu
17 Wind-Powered
   Generators

Tereia Point. On the east coast there are technically two villages, Farauru to the north and Vaiea to the south, but in practice the island's single real village is just one long main street. The main shipping quay is at the southeastern corner of the island. The small airport quay is halfway up the eastern side of the island, south of the church.

Inland the terrain climbs steeply to the summit of Mt Teurafaatiu (380m), also known as Mt Nuupure, but the most conspicuous feature is the sharp ridgeline running north-south, overlooking the village. The high island mass is encircled by a wide but shallow lagoon. The motu that fringe the lagoon equal the main island's area. To the north are Motu Auira and Motu Tuanai, where the airport is located. To the south, the

smaller Motu Tiapaa and Motu Pitihahei flank Maupiti's single accessible pass. The island's only beach is at Tereia Point, but the motu have fine white-sand beaches.

Information
To the north of the village centre the *mairie* (town hall), **post office** *(open 7.30am-12.30pm Mon & Wed-Fri, 7.30am-12.30pm & 1.30pm-3pm Tues)*, Air Tahiti office and Banque Socredo are grouped together. The bank is open only when a representative comes to the island, so don't plan to change money here; bring enough cash with you.

AROUND THE ISLAND
You can walk around the island in a couple of hours. The road is paved only for a kilo-

metre or so through the village. Neat houses, brightened with hibiscus, are strung along the road and often have *uru* (breadfruit) trees shading the family tombs that front many of them. The following tour starts in the village and proceeds around the island in an anticlockwise direction.

Petroglyphs

Leave the village towards the north, round the point and pass the basketball court near the church. You're now in the Haranaie Valley; on the mountainside and just after a green house is a track heading inland. Follow it for 200m to a small pumping station, and then follow the rocky riverbed, which may have water in it during the wet season. After only 100m, on the left, you'll find boulders in the stream cut with petroglyphs. The biggest and most impressive is a turtle image on a flat boulder just to the right of the stream.

Tereia Beach

At the western end of the island is the only beach on the island, Tereia Beach. It's easy to walk right across the lagoon to **Motu Auira**, particularly at low tide (you'll be waist-deep in water at high tide). Beware of rays lying in the sand, although they usually shoot away when they sense your approach.

Continuing around the island, the coast road climbs up over the low ridgeline running down to the point, then drops down to Atipiti Bay on the south side of the island.

Marae Vaiahu

Northwest of the main quay is the area known as **Tefarearii** (House of the Kings), where the island's nobility once lived. Marae Vaiahu, Maupiti's most important marae, is a large coastal site covered with flagstones, featuring a 'fish box'. Made of four coral blocks set edgewise in the form of a rectangle, with a fifth serving as a lid, the box was used for ceremonial purposes to ensure successful fishing. Four fish kings were represented on the sides of the box. Traditionally, the marae guards would put a stone fish in the box to invoke the god of fishing before the canoes set out on fishing expeditions.

Just beyond the marae a sheer rockface rises up beside the road, overlooking the shipping quay. There are traces of a *pa* (fortification) atop this imposing outcrop.

THE MOTU

Many of the island *pensions* organise picnic trips to Maupiti's idyllic motu.

Motu Paeao, at the northern end of the lagoon, is the site of an important archaeological discovery – a series of thousand-year-old burial sites. False Pass, to the west, and Te Area (Hiro's) Pass, to the east, are both unnavigable. Legend has it that the god Hiro tried to create this pass one night, using his canoe to plough through the reef. He had already divided Huahine in two by the same method. A warrior who discovered his plan hid nearby with his well-trained rooster. At the warrior's signal the cock crowed and Hiro, thinking dawn was about to break, sailed away.

HIKING

Two walks offer an opportunity to explore the mountains and discover unbeatable views of the island and surroundings.

Mt Hotu Paraoa

The impressive rocky wall that is Mt Hotu Paraoa (250m) looms above the village. It takes about one hour to walk up it. The climb is relatively easy, except for a steep section requiring the use of your hands to clamber up, and nearly all of the route is shaded. Although some dangerous sections mean that you can't walk completely to the end of the rocky ridge, your efforts will be rewarded by the beautiful panorama over the village and lagoon. When the weather is good you can see Bora Bora to the east and, beyond, Ra'iatea and Taha'a. The path begins near Pension Eri. As the trail is not marked, it's essential to take a guide (about 2000 CFP per person). Ask at your *pension* or contact **Auguste Taurua** (☎ 67 81 83).

Mt Teurafaatiu

It's a superb climb to the 380m summit of Mt Teurafaatiu. Allow three hours for the return trip and bring plenty of drinking water. You need to be fit to do this walk and there are some particularly steep parts that are more like rock climbing than walking. Don't go in bad weather, as the rocks are very slippery and some areas become unstable. It's essential to take a guide as the trail is often indistinct (a dot of red paint on the rock or the trees). Ask at your *pension* or contact **Auguste Taurua** (☎ 67 81 83).

MAUPITI

The track starts virtually opposite Snack Tarona. Fortunately the climb is shaded for most of the way. The most difficult part is towards the end, with a climb up steep rock required to get up to the ridge. At the summit there's a small platform from which you can enjoy a unique 360-degree panorama encompassing all the motu of the lagoon and, in good weather, Bora Bora, Taha'a and Ra'iatea.

It's also possible to make the ascent from the west side of the island.

WATER ACTIVITIES
Maupiti has a magnificent lagoon with many coral pinnacles and dense fish populations, particularly around the Onoiau Pass. There are superb **snorkelling** sites and beautiful **beaches** for picnics. The *pensions* will arrange excursions and organise lagoon tours with snorkelling stops for around 2000 to 5000 CFP.

PLACES TO STAY
There are no 'hotels' on Maupiti – everything is family-style, although the motu resorts are a little more sophisticated. Most visitors opt for *demi-pension* (half-board – a room plus breakfast and dinner), or *pension complète* (full board – all meals). Hot water is not available and credit cards haven't arrived at Maupiti either – make sure you have enough cash. Prices quoted here include the 6% TVA in hostels and *pensions*, plus the 50 CFP daily tax.

The Island
None of the village guesthouses has any signage, but anybody from the village will point them out. They're all either right on the lagoon or very close to it.

Pension Mareta (Chez Manu; ☎ 67 82 32; rooms with breakfast/half-/full board per person 2600/4600/5600 CFP), south of the primary school, is the cheapest place on the island. There are three very basic rooms sharing a bathroom. Add 200 CFP to use the fan and 300 CFP to use the communal kitchen. A two-person kayak can be hired for 1000 CFP per person. Island tours with picnic are 5000 CFP.

Chez Floriette (☎ 67 80 85; rooms with half-/full board per person 6100/7100 CFP), next to Pension Mareta, has two basic bungalows with fan and shared bathroom.

Prices include airport transfers. Motu excursions with a picnic lunch are 1000 CFP per person.

Pension Eri (☎ 67 81 29; rooms with half-board per person 5100 CFP), 200m south and also on the lagoon side of the road, is a well-run place with three small rooms with fan and shared bathroom. Trips cost 1000 CFP to Motu Tiapaa and 2500 CFP to Motu Auira, while tours of the island cost 4000 CFP.

Maupiti Loisirs (☎ 67 80 95; camping 2000 CFP, rooms with half-board per person 5400 CFP) is a pleasant place close to Tereia Beach, with two rooms with shared bathroom. Although a bit cramped, the rooms are clean and equipped with fan and mosquito nets. The food here is very good. Bicycle hire is 1000 CFP per day.

The Motu
Exchange the low-key bustle of village life for the pleasures of isolated white-sand beaches on the motu. If you want to return to 'civilisation', transfers to the main island are easily arranged, but be aware the range of facilities and activities here is very limited.

Pension Auira (Chez Edna; ☎/fax 67 80 26; camping 1500 CFP, beach/garden bungalows with half-board 9100/10,100 CFP) is on the eastern side of Motu Auira. At low tide you can wade across to the mainland, as the deepest water is about waist high. The three pleasant beach bungalows with bathroom, mezzanine, fan, terrace and mosquito screens are more modern and a better option than the two very small, basic garden bungalows (also with bathroom, fan and mosquito screens). For campers, there are bathroom facilities, a kitchen and a fridge, and meals are available for 2500 CFP. Airport transfers cost 2000 CFP, lagoon tours 5000 CFP.

Pension Papahani (Chez Vilna; ☎ 67 81 58; bungalows with full board from 9600 CFP), at the northern end of Motu Tiapaa, is right on a pretty beach. It has three new, functional and well-equipped bungalows with fan, bay window and small terrace. There are also two older bungalows out the back; although cheaper they're not very good value compared with the newer ones. Prices include airport transfers; village transfers cost 1000 CFP return. Island tours by boat cost 2000 CFP and there are kayaks for use.

Maupiti Village (☎/fax 67 80 08; dorm beds/rooms/bungalows with full board 5600/

6600/8100 CFP) is a beautiful property on the ocean side of Motu Tiapaa. It's a good-value option for budget travellers. You can choose from two small, basic bungalows with bathroom; three matchbox-sized rooms in the main house with a shared outside bathroom; and a six-bed dorm. There are no fans or mosquito nets. It's basic but adequate and the food is very good. A kayak and pirogue are available for use. Airport/village transfers are 1800/1300 CFP per person return.

La Rose des Îles (☎/fax 67 82 00; rooms with half-board per person 6600 CFP) is in a tranquil location on the lagoon side of Motu Tiapaa near Pension Papahani. There's just one well-priced, local-style, attractively decorated bungalow with a private outside bathroom. The outdoor setting features small tables, outdoor showers, hammocks and a profusion of plants and trees. Kayaks are available for use. Prices include airport transfers.

Kuriri Village (☎/fax 67 82 23, 74 54 54; e kuriri@bigfoot.com; half-/full board per person 11,500/14,100 CFP) is on the ocean side of Motu Tiapaa. It is the only place on Maupiti aiming much above the budget-accommodation bracket. Five bungalows with private bathroom are situated in a tropical garden, at either end of which is a beach (one lagoonside, one oceanside). The food here has an excellent reputation. Lagoon tours cost 4000 CFP per person and airport transfers 1000 CFP.

Fare Paeao (Chez Jeanine; ☎ 76 81 01; ☎/fax 67 81 92; double/triple bungalows 10,600/12,100 CFP) is in an exceptional location to the north of Motu Paeao. There are six clean, comfortable, new bungalows with fan, electric anti-mosquito devices, bathroom and terrace. There are free kayaks. Airport transfers are 1100 CFP per person return.

Pension Marau (☎ 76 81 19, fax 67 82 46) is on Motu Tuanai, facing the village. At the time of research seven bungalows were under construction.

PLACES TO EAT
Most visitors opt for the half-board or full board option with their accommodation. In the village, several small **shops** sell basic supplies and soft drinks.

Snack Tarona (☎ 67 82 46; dishes 900-1200 CFP; open lunch & dinner Mon-Sat), to

A Ship in Port

The arrival of a ship at Maupiti is a major event. Late one afternoon the small Maupiti Tou Ai'a zipped in through the pass, bustled importantly up to the quay and was fallen upon by what looked like half the island's population. The other half sat down to watch the frenetic activity. Is there a Polynesian dockers' union? If so they were on holiday – everybody seemed to pitch in and most goods appeared to go straight into the hands of their intended owners. Bicycles were handed down off the stern while 3000-odd bottles of beer in cases of 20 went from hand to hand and into the back of a pick-up. An equal or even greater supply of soft drink followed a parallel route. Drums of fuel were rolled off the ship, across the dock and straight into waiting dinghies. Furniture was carried off on strong shoulders.

The working party was nearly equally divided between male and female. In between this confusing melee children ran back and forth while overhead the ship's crane nonchalantly swung bags of cement, bundles of water pipes, stacks of roofing iron and pallets of cement blocks. An hour or two later the activity was over and the docks were deserted once again.

the north of the village, serves simple dishes such as raw fish, tuna sashimi, pork with taro, and braised beef.

Fare Paeao (see Places to Stay; breakfast 1000 CFP, lunch & dinner 1600-2600 CFP) has a dining room facing the beach.

GETTING THERE & AWAY
Maupiti is 320km west of Tahiti and 40km west of Bora Bora.

Air
Air Tahiti has three to five flights a week between Pape'ete and Maupiti, most via Ra'iatea. One-way fares from Maupiti are Ra'iatea 6400 CFP and Pape'ete 14,000 CFP. The **Air Tahiti office** (☎ 67 80 20, 67 81 24; open 8am-11am Mon-Thur, 9.30am-11am Fri) is in the village beside the mairie.

Boat
The narrow Onoiau Pass is the only entry point to the Maupiti lagoon. Strong currents and a tricky sand bar mean that it can be

MAUPITI

navigated only by smaller ships, which are often forced to wait for appropriate tidal conditions.

The **Maupiti Express** (☎ 67 66 69) travels to Maupiti on Tuesday, Thursday and Saturday for 2500/3500 CFP one way/return. Departing Vaitape (Bora Bora) at 8.30am, it arrives at Maupiti at 10.15am, then departs for the return trip at 4pm and arrives at Bora Bora at 5.45pm. The schedule allows enough time to have a good look around Maupiti and return to Bora Bora on the same day, although the crossing can be quite rough at times.

The rustic little *Maupiti Tou Ai'a* makes a once-weekly Pape'ete–Maupiti trip, occasionally via Ra'iatea. It departs Wednesday evening and arrives on Thursday morning, returning on Friday. A berth on the deck costs 2400 CFP; bring bedding. See the Getting Around chapter for details.

GETTING AROUND

If you've booked accommodation you'll probably be met at the airport. The return trip typically costs 1000 to 2000 CFP. Otherwise, there's a boat that takes Air Tahiti staff and any hangers-on to the main island after the flight has departed. The one-way fare for the 15-minute trip is 400 CFP (children 200 CFP). The Air Tahiti boat also goes out to the airport motu for departing flights. Boat departure times, usually one to 1½ hours prior to flights, are posted at the Air Tahiti office.

For bicycle hire, ask at your accommodation or contact Maupiti Loisirs (see Places to Stay) or Suzanne, near the quay. The average cost is 1000 CFP per day.

It's relatively simple to arrange a boat out to the motu from the village and vice versa. It costs between 500 and 1000 CFP to go from the main island to the motu and between 2000 and 5000 CFP for a lagoon excursion.

Other Leeward Islands

There are four other Leeward Islands in the Society group, all of them atolls. Three of these are far to the west of the high islands of the Leeward group. All are important breeding grounds for green turtles, which lay eggs on the beaches from November each year.

Immediately north of Bora Bora is Tupai, which is very much under Bora Bora's influence. The other three islands come under the aegis of Maupiti. Wallis, the first European to come upon Tahiti, sighted Mopelia and Scilly in 1767 as he continued west, but he did not pause to investigate them further. Mopelia is the only one of these Leeward atolls with a pass allowing ships to enter its lagoon.

TUPAI

Ancient Polynesian beliefs held that the souls of the dead had to pass through Tupai on their way to the afterworld. Also known as Motu Iti, the 11-sq-km atoll is only 16km north of Bora Bora and has a double lagoon. An outer reef encompasses a narrow lagoon, inside of which is the circular atoll. Cloaked in coconut palms, the atoll's motu are used by Bora Bora as copra plantations. There is an airstrip on the island but no pass big enough to allow ships to enter the lagoon.

MOPELIA

The atoll Mopelia (also known as Maupihaa) is considered a quasi-possession of Maupiti, 160km to the southeast. The atoll is roughly circular, with a diameter of about 8km and an area of about 4 sq km.

In 1917 the German raider *Seeadler* (Sea Eagle) was wrecked on Mopelia when it attempted to stop for repairs. The ship's commander, Count Felix von Luckner, wrote an account of his Pacific adventure, *The Sea Devil*, which became a postwar bestseller. One of the *Seeadler*'s cannons can be seen in Parc Bougainville in the centre of Pape'ete.

Mopelia has a population of almost 100 people, stationed there purely to harvest pearl oysters, which are taken to Maupiti and then sold to pearl farmers. They, in turn, fly them to the Tuamotus, where they are implanted with seed pearls. This isolated island is home to many bird species and abundant turtles.

The atoll's tricky pass is just wide enough for small ships to enter. The *Maupiti Tou Ai'a* sails from Maupiti to Mopelia every two weeks; it's an overnight trip. See the Getting Around chapter for details.

There is no formal accommodation on Mopelia so potential visitors must arrange to stay with one of the residents. This is usually organised through a friend or relation on Maupiti. The options are to stay two days, while the ship is in port, or two weeks, until the next visit. Yachts occasionally call into Mopelia.

SCILLY

Like Mopelia, the even more remote Scilly atoll (also known as Manuae) is home to green turtles and oyster beds. Scilly is about 60km northwest of Mopelia and is covered in coconut palms. Although the atoll is about 15km in diameter, it has a land area of only about 4 sq km. In 1855 the three-mast *Julie Ann* was wrecked here and the crew and passengers, including 24 women and children, were marooned for two months before they managed to build a small boat and sail to Ra'iatea.

BELLINGHAUSEN

Bellinghausen (also known as Motu One) was 'discovered' in 1824 by the Russian explorer of that name. Four low-lying islands, with a total area of about 3 sq km, encircle the reef, but there is no pass providing entry to the lagoon.

OTHER LEEWARD ISLANDS

The Tuamotus

In the heart of French Polynesia, the Tuamotus (too-ah-moh-toos) are a world apart. The 77 atolls stretch 1500km northwest to southeast and 500km east to west. The closest islands are about 300km from Tahiti. These rings of coral are the posthumous witnesses to intense volcanic eruptions that left them scattered like confetti on an ocean of ink.

The Tuamotus are very different from the Society Islands and the Marquesas. The atolls, a coral crown not reaching more than a few metres above the water, surround a central lagoon. Each atoll has its own distinct features. For 30 islands, the outer ring is cut by passes or channels, as at Fakarava and Rangiroa, while others are completely enclosed, such as Takapoto and Anaa. Some are huge (Rangiroa is 75km long), while others are minute (Nukutepipi is no more than 4km across). Their shapes are equally variable: circular, square or rectangular. In some cases the lagoons are so shallow they are almost filled in, while Makatea is a high island, not an atoll at all.

The total land area of the Tuamotus is only about 700 sq km but the narrow chains of low-lying motu that make up the islands encircle about 6000 sq km of sheltered lagoons, more than 1000 sq km in the vast Rangiroa lagoon alone.

The atolls are fragile and vulnerable places. Their lack of height means that there is no protection against cyclones, and the poor soil and lack of fresh water make agriculture difficult. The Paumotu, the inhabitants of the archipelago, required great ingenuity to cope with this hostile environment.

The Tuamotus have always been a dangerous place for navigators and they long remained in the shadow of the Society Islands. That has changed thanks to pearl cultivation, which has become a central pillar of the Polynesian economy. The growth of pearl cultivation has reversed the outward migration of the population, which has grown from 12,500 to 15,500 people over the last two censuses. There are 45 inhabited islands, ranging from those with a mere handful of often transient occupants to Rangiroa, with a total population of 1900. In a parallel development, infrastructure has been dramatically improved.

Highlights

- Exploring the lagoon of Rangiroa (or Tikehau) and almost untouched parts of the atoll

- Diving or snorkelling in the passes at Rangiroa, Manihi, Tikehau or Fakarava

- Visiting a pearl farm at Manihi, Fakarava, Takapoto or Takaroa

- Enjoying the beaches of Takapoto and Mataiva

- Living like Robinson Crusoe on Fakarava

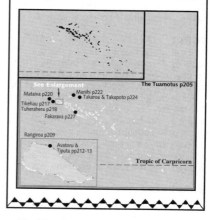

The big winners in this modernisation are the north and the west of the archipelago – places such as Rangiroa, Arutua and Manihi, which placed their bets on pearls and tourism. Others, such as Hereheretue and Tematangi, remain connected to the outside world only by infrequent cargo ships.

Life in the idyllic Tuamotus is simple and distractions are rare. The rhythm of life encompasses fishing and pearl culture, work in the coconut groves, the arrival and departures of planes and ships, and weekly church services.

History

The history of the Tuamotus is a mystery; stories from the early European navigators, archaeological remains and information contained in island traditions are the only historical sources.

THE TUAMOTUS

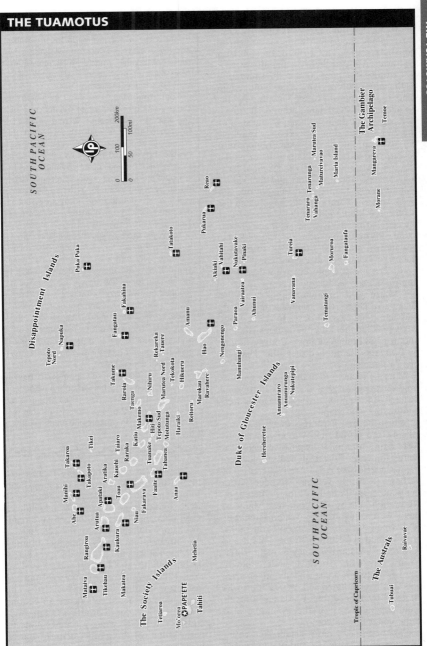

SOUTH PACIFIC OCEAN

200km
100mi
100
50
0
0

Disappointment Islands

The Gambier Archipelago

Temoe

Mangareva

Morane

Maria Island

Matureivavao

Marutea Sud

Tenaruga

Tenararo

Vahanga

Reao

Pakarua

Tureia

Moruroa

Fangataufa

Pukapuka

Tatakoto

Akiaki

Vahitahi

Nukutavake

Pinaki

Paraoa

Vairaatea

Ahunui

Vanavana

Tematangi

Tepoto Nord

Napuka

Fangatau

Fakahina

Amanu

Rekareka

Tauere

Tekokota

Hikueru

Hao

Nengonengo

Manuhangi

Takume

Raroia

Taenga

Nihiru

Marutea Nord

Haraiki

Marokau

Ravahere

Reitoru

Motutunga

Tahanea

Tuanake

Hiti

Tepoto Sud

Makemo

Katiu

Tikei

Takaroa

Takapoto

Aratika

Manihi

Taiaro

Kauehi

Raraka

Ahe

Apataki

Toau

Arutua

Fakarava

Niau

Kaukura

Rangiroa

Mataiva

Tikehau

Makatea

Anaa

Mehetia

Duke of Gloucester Islands

Herehetetue

Anuanuraro

Anuanurunga

Nukutepipi

SOUTH PACIFIC OCEAN

The Society Islands

Tetiaroa

Mo'orea

PAPE'ETE

Tahiti

SOUTH PACIFIC OCEAN

Tropic of Capricorn

The Australs

Raivavae

Tubuai

One theory is that the Paumotu, the people of the archipelago, fled from the Leeward Islands and the Marquesas following conflicts during the 14th, 15th and 16th centuries. Another theory is that the eastern Tuamotus were populated at the same time as the major Polynesian diaspora moved on from the Marquesas to the Gambier Archipelago and Easter Island, around 1000 AD.

A survey of dialects in use at the start of the 20th century, together with archaeological excavations, divided the region into seven sociopolitical and linguistic areas: the Mihiroa (Makatea, Mataiva, Tikehau, Arutua, Apataki and Kaukura) and the Vahitu (Manihi, Ahe, Takaroa and Takapoto) to the northwest, the Parata and the Tapuhoe in the centre, the Manrangai to the southeast and the Napuka and the Fangatau to the northeast.

The Portuguese explorer Ferdinand Magellan was the first European to chance upon the Tuamotus, at Puka Puka in 1521. Later European explorers were less than complimentary about the group – in 1616 Le Maire and Schouten spoke of the 'Islands of Dogs', the 'Islands without End' and the 'Islands of Flies'. In 1722 Roggeveen called them the 'Pernicious Islands' and in 1768 French explorer Louis-Antoine de Bougainville dubbed them the 'Dangerous Archipelago'.

Thus the reputation of the group as an uninviting place was sealed and the Europeans turned their attention towards the more welcoming Society Islands.

When the first explorers touched on the islands, the central and western Tuamotus were being torn apart by intense wars. Towards the end of the 18th century, the ferocious warriors of Anaa Atoll spread terror across the whole region. Islanders from many other atolls fled to Tahiti, where they were sheltered by the Pomares. Many of them were converted by the missionaries who were establishing themselves on Tahiti, and when they returned to the Vahitu and Mihiroa islands in 1817 they brought Christianity with them. In 1821, under Pomare III, war between Anaa and its adversaries was finally concluded and, when Tahiti was annexed by France, the Tuamotus, considered dependencies of the Pomares, also came under French control.

Christian missionaries established copra production in the 1870s and planted coco-

From Coconut to Copra

Copra is found everywhere in the Tuamotus and Marquesas, and you can recognise it by the unmistakable, rancid smell emanating from coconut plantations, rack dryers and warehouses near the wharves.

Copra (from the Tamil word *kopparah*) is the dry residue of the white substance lining the inside of the coconut. Rich in vegetable fat (palmitin), it is regularly collected by schooners and taken to Pape'ete. Crushed, heated, pressed and refined as oil, it is then sold to the food and cosmetics industries.

Copra production is relatively recent. Introduced by the missionaries in the 1870s, it has continued to develop and is still an essential economic activity on numerous islands and atolls in French Polynesia.

The copra producers gather the fallen coconuts from the coconut plantations. The coconuts are split with a blow from a machete. The half-nuts are then turned over and left in the sun for a few days. The coconut is scooped out with a *pana* (an implement with a short handle and a curved, narrow metal blade) to separate the dried kernel from the shell. The shavings are then placed on copra dryers (like raised racks topped with a movable roof to protect them from rain) until completely desiccated.

They are then packed in hessian bags, weighed and put in a hangar until a schooner arrives to collect them. The copra producer is paid directly by the inspector at the time of weighing, or by the supercargo when loading the ship.

nut plantations. In 1900 copra represented 40% of the total exports of the colony. Pearl diving and mother-of-pearl production enjoyed a golden age from 1850, and Chilean, Australian and American traders were regular visitors to the lagoons of the Tuamotus.

From 1911 until 1966, phosphate mining on Makatea was the principal export activity not only for the Tuamotus but for all of French Polynesia, but this was an unusual exception to the slow pace of life. The population of the islands began to decline dramatically as copra production fell away and, in the 1960s, when plastic buttons finally killed off the mother-of-pearl button business.

In the 1970s, when airstrips were built on many of the islands, the population decline was slowed and the group's economic prospects began to brighten. Regular flights from Tahiti brought tourists to the archipelago. The flights back to Tahiti carried not only suntanned tourists but loads of fresh reef fish for the busy markets of Pape'ete. At the same time new techniques of pearl grafting led to the establishment of pearl farms and the production of the black pearls that have become synonymous with French Polynesia.

The 1970s brought another far less congenial employment prospect to the Tuamotus when France's Centre d'Expérimentation du Pacifique (CEP) took over the central atoll of Hao and began to test nuclear weapons on the western atolls of Moruroa and Fangataufa.

The early 1980s brought a series of disastrous cyclones that wreaked havoc on a number of the atolls, particularly during the short period from December 1982 to April 1983.

Population & People

The traditional local culture varies only slightly from Tahitian culture. In the east of the archipelago, the people still speak a Paumotu dialect that is a variant of Tahitian. Because of the scarcity of natural resources, crafts and artwork are less developed than on other archipelagos. The Paumotu had the same beliefs as other Polynesians but their marae differed in that they were constructed with huge slabs of coral.

The islanders' use of their limited land was quite exceptional. To overcome the lack of water, they dug pits, sometimes stretching for hundreds of metres, down to the water table. They were then filled in with vegetable matter. This improvised compost enabled the cultivation of taro, which guaranteed regular nutrition. The development of coconut plantations and direct supplies from Tahiti by schooners eventually made these ingenious systems obsolete. Fish traps made of coral blocks provided animal protein and have survived to the present day.

Activities

You don't go to the Tuamotus for monuments, museums or food – activities in the lagoons are the attraction. Scuba diving is the number-one activity. Rangiroa, Tikehau, Manihi, Fakarava, Ahe and Makemo have dive centres (see the special section 'Diving'). Dive cruises are another way to dive the Tuamotus – see the Outdoor Activities chapter.

Pearl farming is a major economic activity and you can visit pearl farms where you may see the grafting operation. Many accommodation operators also have pearl farms.

Fishing is also important, both spear- and line-fishing. You can also see fish parks, snorkel, explore archaeological sites and visit bird reserves on remote motu. Definitely bring a mask and snorkel.

There are many tourist operators on the islands, although hotels and *pensions* often organise trips for guests. The best beaches are often on remote motu. Operators will take you on picnic trips to these motu, or arrange to leave you there and collect you later. Try not to leave yourself at the mercy of one hotel, *pension* or operator. If you ask around you'll find many other possibilities.

Getting There & Away

The archipelago is accessible by plane; 27 atolls have airstrips and are served by Air Tahiti. Most of the traffic is to and from Pape'ete, but there are also connections with Bora Bora, the Marquesas and the Gambier Archipelago. Within the archipelago, Rangiroa and Hao are the principal flight hubs. If you're visiting an island, always give the Air Tahiti representative a contact address or phone number, as schedules are subject to change.

The *Dory*, *Corbia*, *Mareva Nui*, *Taporo V and VI*, *Saint-Xavier Maris-Stella*, *Kura Ora II* and *III*, *Hotu Maru*, *Vai-Aito*, *Nuku Hau* and *Aranui* all serve the archipelago from Pape'ete and most take passengers. See the Getting Around chapter for details. On those islands without quays, loading and unloading of cargo and passengers is done by *bonitier* (whaleboat).

See Sailing in the Outdoor Activities chapter for information on cruising yachts.

Getting Around

Road networks are often just crushed-coral or sand tracks, perhaps a few kilometres long, linking the village to the airport or to the areas where copra is produced. Apart from le trucks doing the school run, public transport usually does not exist. Ask at your hotel or *pension* about transport.

Airports are sometimes near the villages, sometimes on remote motu on the other side of the lagoon. If you have booked accommodation, your hosts will come and meet you but transfers are not necessarily free. If there is a charge it will depend on the distance travelled and the means of transport. Hitching (by car or boat) is possible as many islanders go to the airports for arrivals and departures, although there may not be room for you by the time all the freight is loaded!

It's usually easy to get across the lagoons by local outboard-motor boats. On atolls with a road or relatively long track there may be a handful of cars but traffic is usually nonexistent. Bicycles and scooters are often used in the villages; some *pensions* rent them out or they can be hired from islanders.

Rangiroa

pop 2330 • lagoon area 1640 sq km

Rangiroa (pronounced rung-ee-roh-ah) takes a silver medal for being the second-biggest atoll in the world, but comes in with a gold medal as a wonderfully languorous, remote place to explore – a far cry from the glamour and pace of Bora Bora and Mo'orea in the Society Islands.

The devastating effects of El Niño have taken their toll here as elsewhere in the region, and much of the coral has died in recent years. But other marine life prospers, and wading through warm aqua water on an excursion around the idyllic lagoon has a dream-like quality.

Rangiroa (from 'Rairoa', literally 'long sky') is home to more than 10% of the total population of the Tuamotus.

HISTORY

Historically, Rangiroa has had to contend with two equally destructive threats: pirates and cyclones. Rangiroa's inhabitants sought refuge close to Motu Taeoo (the Lagon Bleu) on the southwestern side of the atoll, until a cataclysm, probably a tsunami, destroyed these settlements in around 1560.

Two centuries later, the population was settled mainly around the three passes – Tivaru, Avatoru and Tiputa – and strong relations were established with the inhabitants of the other atolls of the northern Tuamotus. Anaa warriors pillaged Rangiroa at the end of the

1770s; survivors were forced into exile on Tikehau and Tahiti. They were able to return to Rangiroa in the early 1820s and repopulated the atoll.

Although sighted in April 1616 by Le Maire, a Dutchman, Rangiroa didn't receive its first European settlers – Christian missionaries – until 1851.

Copra production played a vital economic role until it was overtaken by fishing, which remains an important industry; cultured-pearl production is also a highly lucrative industry. The opening of the airport in 1965 boosted tourism, which has been big business since the 1980s. But the tourist industry is dependent on Rangiroa's marine life to draw crowds, and the warming of the Pacific, related to the phenomenon known as El Niño, has resulted in the bleaching of much of the coral in this area. This, coupled with the impact of French nuclear testing in the region, makes for a vulnerable ecosystem.

Life on Rangiroa still retains a parochial, village-like feel: word travels fast, and your business is everybody else's.

ORIENTATION

Rangiroa measures 75km from east to west and 25km from north to south. From the edge of the lagoon, it is impossible to see the opposite bank. The atoll's coral belt is no more than 300m wide, but the long circuit of islands, motu and *hoa* (channels) stretches for more than 200km. The lagoon opens to the ocean via three passes: Tivaru, Avatoru and Tiputa. The Tivaru Pass is narrow and shallow; the Avatoru and Tiputa Passes are each more than 200m wide. About 10km separates the Avatoru and Tiputa Passes.

Rangiroa has two sleepy villages: Avatoru and Tiputa. Avatoru is to the west of a string of islets that are separated by a number of *hoa* which are usually dry. At the eastern end, beyond the Tiputa Pass, is the village of Tiputa. Most places to stay and eat are dotted along the string of islets east of Avatoru.

INFORMATION
Money

In Avatoru, there's a **Banque Socredo** (☎ 96 85 63; open 7am-3.30pm Mon-Thur, 7.30am-2.30pm Fri) and ATM next to the post office, and a **Banque de Tahiti** (☎ 96 85 52; open 8am-11am & 2pm-4pm Mon, Wed & Fri,

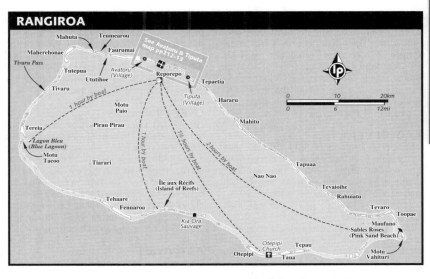

RANGIROA

8am-11.30am Tue & Thur) a few doors down. You can exchange currency and travellers cheques or withdraw cash with your credit card at either bank.

In Tiputa, there's a **Banque Socredo** (☎ 96 75 57; open 1.30pm-4pm Mon & Thur) in the *mairie* (town hall), but the hours are hopeless, and although you can change currency – with advance warning to the Avatoru branch – you can't withdraw cash with your credit card.

Post & Communications

There are **post offices** in Avatoru (open 7am-noon & 1pm-3pm Mon-Thur, 7am-noon & 1pm-2pm Fri) and Tiputa (open 7am-12.30pm Mon-Thur, 7am-11.30am Fri).

There are phone-card telephone booths – which use the same cards as elsewhere in French Polynesia – in and east of Avatoru (next to the post office; at the airport; not far from the secondary school; and at the quay in front of Chez Glorine) and in Tiputa. You can buy phone cards at the post offices, at some supermarkets and at Boutique Paréo Carole.

The only place with Internet access in the Tuamotus is **Taaroa Web** (☎ 96 03 04; e fet ia@taaroa-bijoux.com; open 8am-8pm daily), where you can surf the Net and also peek at some local pearls. It charges 500 CFP per half-hour.

Medical Services & Emergency

The **Centre Médical Avatoru** (☎ 96 03 75) is 2km east of Avatoru. The **Centre Médical Rai Roa** (☎ 96 04 44, 96 04 43), just east of Boutique Paréo Carole, has a private clinic operated by Dr Thirouard. There is no pharmacy on Rangiroa, but the doctor has medicinal supplies, and Boutique Paréo Carole also has some medicines.

The **gendarmerie** (police station; ☎ 96 73 61) is towards the eastern end of the Avatoru islets, not far from Hotel Kia Ora.

AVATORU

Around the middle of the day, you could pretty safely fire a gun along the main street in Avatoru and not hit anyone. Avatoru has a post office, a few banks and a supermarket with hopeless opening hours (but a decent selection of groceries by Tuamotu standards). There are two churches, one Catholic and one Mormon, and a few little places to eat.

TIPUTA

Avatoru may be somniferous, but Tiputa, on the edge of the pass and the lagoon, is even quieter. It's a charming little village, and there are fewer *popaa* (Westerners) here; getting a boat across the Tiputa pass adds to the whole experience. Believe it or not, Tiputa is the administrative centre serving

Rangiroa, Makatea, Tikehau and Mataiva. It has a *gendarmerie* with authority over several atolls. The village is also home to the Centre d'Études des Techniques Adaptées au Développement (Cetad), which trains young people for catering and hotel jobs.

After leaving the village the track continues east through coconut plantations until it's halted by the next pass.

LAGON VERT
The Green Lagoon is only five minutes away from Avatoru by boat. It's a small area, but attracts fewer visitors than its blue counterpart (see next section), and so can make for a less-touristy adventure.

LAGON BLEU
Blue Lagoon is a popular spot about an hour away by boat on the western edge of the atoll, close to Motu Taeoo. A string of motu and coral reefs have formed a natural pool on the edge of the main reef, creating a lagoon within a lagoon. The fact that visitors tend to go in fairly large groups only slightly detracts from the sparkling white sand, ruffled coconut trees, and water the colour of lapis lazuli. The lagoon is not deep and offers safe **snorkelling** among the myriad little fish, but don't expect much from the coral. Feasting on freshly barbecued fish and feeding the sharks are usually on the itinerary.

SABLES ROSES
Sables Roses (Pink Sand Beach), on the southeastern edge of the lagoon near Motu Vahituri, is about two hours from Avatoru by boat. The sands contain foraminifera deposits and various coral residues that glow with reflected pink light when the sun is shining. Magnificent! It's rarely visited, and trips tend to be fairly expensive, so save up and try to organise your excursion as soon as you arrive on Rangiroa.

ÎLE AUX RECIFS
South of the atoll, an hour by boat from Avatoru, Île aux Recifs (Island of Reefs), also known as Motu Ai Ai, lies in water dotted with raised *feo* (coral outcrops), weathered shapes chiselled by erosion into strange petrified silhouettes. Because they're on the ocean side you don't immediately see them when arriving by boat. They stretch for several hundred metres, with basins and channels that make superb natural swimming pools. There's also a good *hoa* for swimming and a picturesque coconut grove by the beach that is an ideal picnic spot. This is a great day trip, although even in high season it can be hard to get a big enough group together (minimum four people).

OTEPIPI
Otepipi is a motu on the southeastern side of the atoll, about 1½ hours away from Avatoru by boat. It once had a village, but some say a contagious illness forced the inhabitants to leave; others maintain that cyclones and the demands of copra production caused the inhabitants to abandon the area and regroup closer to Avatoru and Tiputa. Only a church remains; religious retreats and pilgrimages are still made to the church periodically.

ACTIVITIES
Diving is the main activity on Rangiroa and, for the brave, sharks are the big attraction. The dive centres can provide equipment, and are generally happy to have two of you share a 10-dive pass; you'll pay around 6000/53,000 CFP for one/10 dives. See the special section 'Diving' for details.

All Aboard

There are sharks aplenty in this region, and they are an obvious tourist attraction. You can stand in the shallows of the Lagon Bleu and throw food to the harmless but impressive sharks that flock to eat; you can also get closer than that when tour operators haul sharks on board so that visitors can see that the sharks are friendly and get a quick snap to show the folks back home.

The feeding of sharks and rays, which is a feature of the tourist industry across French Polynesia, is itself causing concern because it disrupts the delicate balance of the food chain (and creates an association between people and a meal!). But to be literally dragging a shark aboard for a closer look, before chucking the poor brute back into the ocean, is disruptive to say the least.

Expressing your distaste for this practice is the only way to curb it: as long as visitors are interested in stroking jaws, there'll be operators willing to facilitate this.

Snorkelling through the Tiputa Pass, accompanied by a guide who knows it and its currents, has become a popular activity, although you can also just grab a snorkel and splash around near your hotel or guesthouse (many of which provide snorkelling gear for guests). You'll generally pay around 4500 CFP for a three-hour snorkelling trip through the passes.

ORGANISED TOURS

The huge Rangiroa atoll contains sights well worth a day's excursion by boat. Organised tours tend to be the easiest and cheapest way of exploring the area and, if you happen upon a nice group, make for a wonderful day. Ask other travellers about their experiences, and ask at your *pension* or hotel for operators, as prices and trips offered tend to change rapidly on Rangiroa. Most tours are to the opposite side of the lagoon from Avatoru, which takes at least an hour to cross; uncomfortable if you don't have sea legs and the sea is rough. Usually a minimum of four to six people is required, but in July–August it can be so busy that you're either in an uncomfortably large group or have trouble getting a place at all.

Obviously, the tours rely on the state of the lagoon and weather conditions. In the event of *maraamu* (southeasterly winds), tours may be cancelled. Bring waterproof sandals, sunscreen, sunglasses, a swimsuit and a change of clothes; snorkelling gear can be arranged, although you may have to pay for this. Full-day tours generally depart at 8.30am and return at 4pm and include a picnic or barbecue. It's worth trying to bargain for a reduced price for the kids, although many operators will not budge on this.

A half-day trip to the Lagon Vert costs around 1500 CFP; the full-day version, including picnic, costs around 3500 CFP per person.

Trips to the Lagon Bleu and Île aux Recifs cost around 7500 CFP, including a picnic lunch. An excursion to Sables Roses usually costs a rather hefty 10,000 CFP.

Try **Atoll Excursion** (☎ 96 02 88), which does boat trips to the Lagon Bleu, Île aux Recifs and, less frequently, Sables Roses; **Tane Excursion** (☎ 96 84 68), at Chez Henriette *pension*, which specialises in excursions to the Lagon Bleu; **Ariitini Excursions** (☎ 96 04 41); and **Punua Excursions** (☎ 96 84 73),

which does trips to the Lagon Vert, just 10 minutes from Avatoru.

Matahi Excursions (☎ 96 84 48) has a glass-bottomed boat and does 1½-hour trips to Motu Nuhi Nuhi, to the south of the Tiputa Pass.

For tours of pearl farms, see Shopping, later in this section.

PLACES TO STAY

Rangiroa is riddled with little family-run *pensions*, which are generally rather quaint and quite comfortable, although luxurious they ain't. There are a few more sumptuous places on offer, but they tend to be less personal and more in the Bora Bora mould. Staying in a *pension* will be more enjoyable if you speak a little French, which tends to work as the lingua franca of budget travellers; it also allows you to communicate with locals (assuming you haven't mastered Tahitian, which would be even better!).

Prices quoted here include all the relevant taxes; bear in mind these taxes seem to rise fairly regularly, and many hotels and *pensions* quote their prices *hors taxe* (not including tax), so if pennies are tight, clarify exactly what the price (including all taxes) is when you book.

Budget

There's plenty of charm among the *pensions* scattered along the edge of the lagoon, on the Avatoru string of islets. Bungalows usually accommodate two people, but a mattress or single bed can be added for a nominal fee and there's generally at least one family bungalow available. Accommodation with half-board is the norm; prices are usually calculated per person and often drop after a few days. Most of these places do not take credit cards. Budget places rarely have hot water, so brace yourself for refreshing showers at the end of the day. Except where noted, prices here are per person.

Avatoru Popular with people who appreciate simplicity, authenticity and home-made coconut bread, **Chez Henriette** (☎ 96 84 68, fax 96 82 85; half-board 5400 CFP) has fairly rudimentary bungalows with bathroom that are ideal for families.

Chez Punua & Moana (☎/fax 96 84 73; half-board 5900 CFP) has simple bungalows with bathroom. Punua and Moana also have

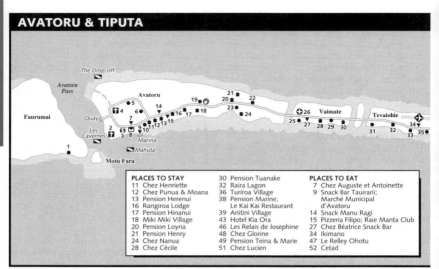

AVATORU & TIPUTA

PLACES TO STAY	30 Pension Tuanake	PLACES TO EAT
11 Chez Henriette	32 Raira Lagon	7 Chez Auguste et Antoinette
12 Chez Punua & Moana	36 Turiroa Village	9 Snack Bar Tauirarii;
13 Pension Herenui	38 Pension Marine;	Marché Municipal
16 Rangiroa Lodge	Le Kai Kai Restaurant	d'Avatoru
17 Pension Hinanui	39 Ariitini Village	14 Snack Manu Ragi
18 Miki Miki Village	43 Hotel Kia Ora	15 Pizzeria Filipo; Raie Manta Club
20 Pension Loyna	46 Les Relais de Josephine	27 Chez Béatrice Snack Bar
21 Pension Henry	48 Chez Glorine	34 Ikimano
24 Chez Nanua	49 Pension Teina & Marie	47 Le Relley Ohotu
28 Chez Cécile	51 Chez Lucien	52 Cetad

a *pension* at the Lagon Vert, 10 minutes away by boat, with three bungalows with communal facilities and the possibility of camping.

Pension Herenui (*☎ 96 84 71; half-board 6400-7500 CFP*) has two small bungalows for two or three people, and one bigger family bungalow with a mezzanine area and a huge shower. It's all very simple but clean and comfortable.

Rangiroa Lodge (*☎ 96 82 13; dorm beds 1900 CFP, doubles with/without bathroom 5400/4300 CFP*) has small, dull rooms, though there's a nice eating area on the pebble beach. Meals are not available, but there is a communal kitchen.

Pension Hinanui (*☎ 96 84 61; singles/ doubles with half-board 6300/9000 CFP*) has three comfortable and well-designed bungalows with mezzanine, small veranda and bathroom. Credit cards are accepted.

Pension Loyna (*☎/fax 96 82 09; half-board 5900-7000 CFP*) is a lovely, clean *pension*, oozing homeliness. There are cheaper rooms in the owner's home (shared bathroom), as well as three rooms with bathroom and one two-bedroom family bungalow with bathroom out the back. The ocean is 300m away, but the warm welcome and high standards make up for everything.

Pension Henri (*☎/fax 96 82 67; half-board 7000 CFP*) has three airy and spacious local-style bungalows (others are in the making)

with bathroom, small veranda and the roar of the ocean. Meals are served in a large *fare*.

Chez Nanua (*☎ 96 83 88; half-board 4500-5100 CFP*) is set back from Boutique Paréo Carole and is a very cheap, relaxed place. Accommodation is very simple, dogs potter around and granddad sits by the road. Don't expect any luxuries, but the atmosphere is typical of the islands. The more expensive bungalows have a bathroom. Simple meals are taken with the family.

Chez Cécile (*☎ 96 05 06; singles/doubles with half-board 6900/8500 CFP*) is a deservedly popular place and is famous for Cecile's simple but wonderful cooking. The fish-based meals are taken in a *fare potee* (open dining area) in a garden setting. There are some recently built bungalows (more are planned) that are very spacious, many with lagoon views and all with bathroom. Prices drop for longer stays. Credit cards are accepted.

Turiroa Village (*☎/fax 96 04 27; bungalows with/without bathroom 8500/6400 CFP, half-board 2500 CFP per person*) is about 1km west of the airport behind the Ocean Passion boutique. The family bungalows sleep four people, and there's one bungalow for two, with bathroom nearby. Olga, who keeps the place shipshape, is a delight. Meals can be taken on the charming raised area overlooking the water. The owners

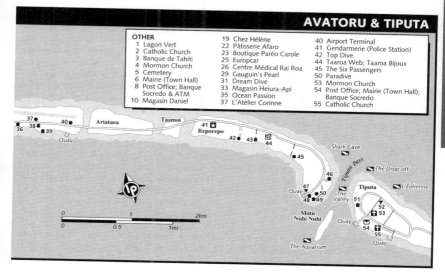

AVATORU & TIPUTA

OTHER
1 Lagon Vert
2 Catholic Church
3 Banque de Tahiti
4 Mormon Church
5 Cemetery
6 Mairie (Town Hall)
8 Post Office; Banque
　Socredo & ATM
10 Magasin Daniel

19 Chez Hélène
22 Pâtisserie Afaro
23 Boutique Paréo Carole
25 Europcar
26 Centre Médical Rai Roa
29 Gauguin's Pearl
31 Dream Dive
33 Magasin Heiura-Api
35 Ocean Passion
37 L'Atelier Corinne

40 Airport Terminal
41 Gendarmerie (Police Station)
42 Top Dive
44 Taaroa Web; Taaroa Bijoux
45 The Six Passengers
50 Paradive
53 Mormon Church
54 Post Office; Mairie (Town Hall);
　Banque Socredo
55 Catholic Church

have a pearl farm and the transplants are made just next door.

Pension Martine (☎ 96 02 53, fax 96 02 51; half-board 7500 CFP), about 600m west of the airport, has four pleasant bungalows for two to four people, with bathroom. Renovations on the communal areas had begun at the time of writing. Credit cards are accepted.

Ariitini Village (☎ 96 04 41; half-board 8000 CFP), next door to Pension Martine, has nine comfortable bungalows with thatched roofs. The *pension* is set back from the road.

Pension Teina & Marie (☎ 96 03 94, fax 96 84 44; half-board 6400 CFP), at the end of the Avatoru string of islets and on the edge of Tiputa Pass, is a simple place that is popular with divers (it's near Paradive). Meals are taken in a large *fare* opposite the lagoon. The two bungalows with verandas facing the lagoon are your best bet.

Chez Glorine (☎ 96 04 05, 96 03 58, fax 96 03 58; half-board 7500 CFP) bungalows are at the end of the Avatoru string of islets, next to the quay. Lovers of fine food will enjoy the cooking here (Glorine has made a name as an adept chef, and can often be seen wielding a knife and some freshly caught fish). Fried *taro* and *uru* (breadfruit) chips, and Glorine's pancakes and banana cake, have long tempted visitors. The meals are taken in a *fare potee* (open dining area) on the edge of the lagoon.

Tiputa All on its own in Tiputa, **Chez Lucien** (☎ 96 73 55; BP 69, Tiputa; half-board 6000 CFP) is a well-maintained guesthouse that is sure to please. There are three spacious bungalows, one accommodating up to seven people, with mezzanine and bathroom. Return transfers to the airport cost 1000 CFP per person. If you stay for a minimum of three nights, Lucien will take you for a free picnic on a motu.

Mid-Range

You can safely pay with a credit card in the mid-range bracket.

Miki Miki Village (☎ 96 83 83, fax 96 82 90; singles/doubles with half-board 11,700/ 19,200 CFP) has charming, nicely furnished bungalows. There's a bar/restaurant over the lagoon. Prices drop after three nights.

Pension Tuanake (☎ 96 04 45, fax 96 03 29; singles/doubles with half-board 10,700/ 16,000 CFP), between the airport and Avatoru, has two small bungalows with room for three people; two bungalows for six people; and two new bungalows being built. It's extremely clean and is set in a coconut plantation near the lagoon. There's a separate shower *fare* with hot water. The food here is very good.

Raira Lagon (☎ 96 04 23, fax 96 05 86; e rairalag@mail.pf; half-board per person 10,700 CFP), about 1km west of the airport,

THE TUAMOTUS

has 10 fan-cooled bungalows with bathroom. The bungalows are certainly more luxurious than the cheaper *pensions*, but Raira Lagoon lacks the warmth and charm of the *pensions* in the area. The restaurant balcony faces the lagoon and the chef serves tempting fish dishes.

Les Relais de Josephine (*☎/fax 96 02 00; bungalows with half-board per person 14,000 CFP*) is so immaculate and luxurious that it could just about squeeze into the top-end listings, except that it's so much cheaper. Les Relais is a very French interpretation of the Polynesian *pension*, and is excellent value for money by local standards. The restaurant here (see Place to Eat, later) is equally special.

Top End
If you are in search of luxury, look no further than **Hotel Kia Ora** (*☎ 96 03 84, fax 96 04 93; e resa@hotelkiaora.pf; w www.hotel kiaora.com; garden/beach/over-water bungalows 31,200/46,800/64,500 CFP*), which is the only Bora Bora-esque hotel in the Tuamotus. Bungalows are dotted around a magnificent coconut plantation on the edge of the lagoon. There's a white-sand beach, a restaurant and bar on stilts and a few little boutiques and craft stalls. Any activity available on the island can be arranged.

Kia Ora Sauvage (*bungalows with full board per person 46,300 CFP*) is Hotel Kia Ora's 'savage' sister, situated on Motu Avearahi, which is about an hour away by boat. The setting of this hotel will delight you. The price includes return boat transfers and full board, which is compulsory; there's a minimum stay of two nights.

PLACES TO EAT
Given the lack of restaurants on Rangiroa, most visitors opt for half-board at their *pension*. These meals are invariably based around freshly caught fish, so those who don't eat fish should come prepared to look after themselves! The food is generally very good, but is, of course, limited to what is either found locally or can be imported. A standard evening meal at a *pension* would normally begin with *poisson cru* (raw fish), usually served with carrot, cucumber and onion, and fresh bread; this is followed by more fish, probably grilled and served with white rice, and the meal is finished off with

a yoghurt or light cake, or fresh fruit if it's available. Breakfast tends to be French-style, with fresh bread, butter and jam and a bowl of coffee or hot chocolate as the dipping agent.

Even when the food is very good it can quickly become monotonous when you're eating at the same place with the same people everyday; full board is even more constrictive.

Some guesthouses are renowned for their excellent cooking and accept casual diners, provided there is space and you have booked in advance. However, transport is not always available, which may render the whole thing impossible (the streets are not lit at night, so even the smallest distances can be unmanageable). This is true for Chez Glorine, Pension Teina & Marie, Raira Lagon, Pension Tuanake, Miki Miki Village and Chez Lucien. Most *pensions* charge 2500 CFP for a set menu of fish, rice, bread and a light dessert, without drinks.

Restaurants
You can feast on anything from pizza to grilled fish at **Ikimano** (*☎ 96 05 96; appetizers 900-1300 CFP, mains 1300-2800 CFP*), which is a very good restaurant. There were a number of loitering dogs when we visited, but they were harmless and are admittedly a part of life on Rangiroa.

Les Relais de Josephine (*☎/fax 96 02 00; see Places to Stay; set lunch 1200 CFP, set dinner 3500 CFP*) should be top of your list for an evening of indulgence. The setting is idyllic, the decor wonderfully French and the food divine. The set meals are always based around fish dishes, so, if you don't eat seafood, alert the staff when you make a reservation (which you must do).

Hotel Kia Ora (*☎ 96 03 84; see Places to Stay; appetizers 850-1400 CFP, mains 2500-4000 CFP*) is about as fancy as Rangiroan cuisine gets. There's a lovely over-water restaurant and bar, and the lunch menu (appetizers 1300-1600 CFP, mains 1400-2400 CFP) is much cheaper than the evening version. On Wednesday and Sunday there's a buffet and Polynesian dance performance (5000 CFP).

Cafés & Snack Bars
Each village has a few snack bars where you can eat in or order a takeaway meal. There's

also a café at the airport that opens before every flight.

Chez Auguste et Antoinette (☎ 96 85 01; *sandwiches 300-450 CFP, mains 900-1200 CFP; open lunch & dinner Mon-Sat)* doesn't have the most glamorous of settings, but it does have great, fresh food. The *poisson cru* is prepared in the Chinese style with lots of lime and a vinegar dressing, and it is delicious; the other Chinese dishes, such as chow mein (vegetarian on request), are also very good.

Snack Bar Tauirarii (☎ 96 83 33) is a lovely cheap little place opposite the marina in Avatoru, not far from Magasin Daniel.

Snack Manu Ragi *(open lunch & dinner daily)*, a popular place in Avatoru, is a simply but pleasantly decorated little spot for a meal. It's owned by Moana of the adjacent Chez Punua & Moana and specialises in fish.

Chez Béatrice Snack Bar (☎ 96 04 12) is usually open for lunch and dinner and specialises in Chinese food.

Pizzeria Filipo (☎ 73 76 20; *appetizers 650-1200 CFP, pizzas 1000-1500 CFP; open lunch & dinner Thur-Tues)* is a great little place that has not been open long. The food is delicious (try the tuna capaccio with ginger for 800 CFP); the large pizzas are huge, and come served on wonderful plates.

Le Kai Kai Restaurant (☎ 96 03 39; *appetizers 700-1400 CFP, mains 1200-2000 CFP; open lunch & dinner daily)* is a nice restaurant in front of Pension Martine. Unfortunately it's right by the road, but Rangiroa doesn't see enough traffic for this to be a big problem.

Le Relley Ohotu *(burgers 400-800 CFP, mains 800-1100 CFP)* is a buzzing snack place opposite Chez Glorine, overlooking the water. The servings are generous.

Cetad (☎ 96 72 96, 96 02 68; *open lunch Tues & Thur)*, the hospitality school in Tiputa, has a restaurant where students prepare and serve lunch twice a week. The school closes in July and August, when most visitors come to French Polynesia, but if you're here when the school is open, give the food a shot. You can get a boat transfer from the quay next to Chez Glorine.

Self-Catering
Self-catering on Rangiroa is quite possible, although if you try to buy fish people will tell you to get your fishing rod out, and good luck to anyone trying to track down substantial quantities of fresh fruit and vegies (the range is remarkably limited). Avatoru has a few supermarkets, including the **Magasin Heiura-Api** and the better **Magasin Daniel**, which is near the post office. There are a few little grocery stores in sleepy Tiputa where you can buy provisions. Supermarkets are generally open Monday to Saturday, and close for lunch (Magasin Daniel closes at 11.45am and reopens at 2.30pm).

Finding **Pâtisserie Afaro** (☎ 96 04 91; *open Tues-Sun)* is a real feat. It's a wholesale bakery, although the public can put in big orders a day in advance (this is not the place to go for one croissant). Follow the fabulous wafts of buttery deliciousness: look for the old Magasin Rochette sign, and take the road about 10m after this; it's 100m back from the road in a private home.

ENTERTAINMENT
The roosters might make a racket all night long, but most people are well and truly slumbering by 10.30pm.

Unless you count chatting to locals over an early, simple dinner, the only island entertainment is the twice-weekly buffet (held on Wednesday and Sunday evenings; 5000 CFP) with traditional dance organised by **Hotel Kia Ora**. It's possible to skip the buffet and just have a drink in the bar if you want to catch the entertainment. The bar here, **Bar Te Miki Miki**, closes at 11pm.

SHOPPING
Boutique Paréo Carole, about 1.5km east of the village, sells clothes, souvenirs, pharmacy items and French magazines and papers. **Ocean Passion**, near Turiroa Village, has hand-painted pareu. There are handicraft shops in the Hotel Kia Ora.

If you fancy a pearl purchase, Rangiroa is not a bad place to start. You'll find pearl farms and boutiques dotted along the main road, and most places organise tours of pearl farms, which makes the whole experience more meaningful.

Gauguin's Pearl (☎/*fax 96 05 39; open 9am-12pm & 1.30pm-5pm Mon-Fri, 9am-12pm Sat)* does free tours of a pearl farm at 8.30am and 2pm.

A smaller farm belongs to the family who owns Pension Martine. Direct sales take place at the small shop **L'Atelier Corinne**

(☎ 96 03 13), opposite the guesthouse on the ocean side. Pearls are available mounted and unmounted, and visits to the pearl farm can be arranged.

Heipoe Ura (☎ 96 04 35) is another family business where you can buy mounted and unmounted pearls, *keshi* (pure mother-of-pearl) and *mabe* (hollow cultured pearls).

The owners of the Turiroa Village guesthouse also have a small pearl farm and make direct sales (the farm is just next to the *pension*).

GETTING THERE & AWAY
Air
The airport is smack in between Avatoru (to the west) and Tiputa (to the east). **Air Tahiti** (☎ 96 03 41, 96 05 03; open Mon-Fri) has an office inside the airport *fare*. Tickets can be purchased (with credit cards) and flights can be reconfirmed here (but don't expect to find anyone here over lunch).

Rangiroa is an important link for air and sea communication and is connected by air to Tahiti, Bora Bora, the Marquesas and other atolls in the Tuamotus. There are several flights daily between Pape'ete and Rangiroa (one hour). There's a weekly flight from Rangiroa to Nuku Hiva (Marquesas).

One-way fares include Pape'ete– Rangiroa 15,000 CFP, Bora Bora–Rangiroa 22,500 CFP, Rangiroa–Tikehau 5100 CFP, Rangiroa–Manihi 9800 CFP (see the Getting Around chapter for more details).

Boat
The *Dory*, *Mareva Nui*, *Vai-Aito*, *Saint-Xavier Maris-Stella* and *Rairoa Nui* all serve Rangiroa; the *Aranui* stops on Rangiroa on its way back from the Marquesas.

For details, see the Getting Around chapter.

GETTING AROUND
Getting around Rangiroa is a fairly haphazard affair. There's no public transport, and there's not really enough traffic to rely on hitchhiking (which is never entirely safe, although you'd be very unlikely to run into problems on Rangiroa).

A sealed road runs the 10km from Avatoru village at the western end of the string of islets to the Tiputa Pass at the eastern extremity. The road is not lit at night, which makes getting around without a car in the evenings virtually impossible. Hire a bicycle

or a scooter (it's hardly worth getting a car) for getting around during the day, or resign yourself to not moving much!

There are regular boats (1000 CFP return) that cross the pass separating the Avatoru islets from Tiputa village; taking a bicycle over costs 500 CFP extra.

To/From the Airport
If you have booked accommodation, your hosts will be at the airport to welcome you. If your *pension* is near the hotel, transfers will probably be free; places further away tend to charge (ask when you book). Your only other option is to hitch, which is always harder when you are weighed down with baggage.

Car, Fun Car, Scooter & Bicycle
Locally known as Rangi Location, **Europcar** (☎ 96 03 28) is east of Avatoru and rents cars from 6300/7350 CFP for a half-/full day; fun cars, those curious little three-wheeler devices, rent for 5500/6500 CFP; and scooters cost 4350/5350 CFP. Credit cards are accepted. Several guesthouses work with Europcar and have bicycles and scooters at the same rates.

Chez Hélène (☎ 96 82 84) rents out bicycles for 600/1200 CFP a half-/full day; prices drop to 900 CFP a day after the first day.

Arenahio at Boutique Paréo Carole (☎ 96 82 45; open 7.30am-6pm Mon-Sat), about 800m east of Avatoru village, hires out cars for 6200/8400 CFP for a half-/full day; scooters are 3800/5200 CFP and bicycles 700/1300 CFP. Credit cards are accepted.

Hotel Kia Ora also rents out bicycles and scooters.

Northern Tuamotus

Though Rangiroa is the main tourist destination in the Tuamotus, other atolls in the north of the archipelago are also equipped for tourism.

The northern group includes Makatea, southwest of Rangiroa; Tikehau and Mataiva in the west; and Manihi and Ahe in the northeast. Only the atolls of Tikehau, Mataiva and Manihi and Ahe have airports and accommodation for travellers.

To the east, Takaroa and Takapoto, both accessible by air, also have accommodation facilities. Arutua and Kaukura are less well

The Rise & Fall of Makatea

It's difficult to imagine an island in the Tuamotus covered in mining installations with more than 1000 workers, but for 50 years Makatea made French Polynesia an industrial centre.

The presence of phosphate was noted at the end of the 19th century and the Compagnie Française des Phosphates d'Océanie (CFPO) was created in 1908 to exploit the deposit. Infrastructure appeared from nowhere: industrial equipment (including a rail network), houses, schools, a cinema, places of worship and shops. Until the early 1950s labour came largely from Asia.

With 3071 inhabitants in 1962, Makatea was the most populated island in the Tuamotus. Vaitepaua mushroomed like a boom town in a gold rush. Makatea phosphate became the core of the French Polynesian economy. From 12,000 tonnes in 1911, the extraction rate rose to 251,000 tonnes in 1929 and 400,000 tonnes in 1960, a record year. Until WWII, exports were mainly to Japan, New Zealand and Australia.

By 1966, when the reserves were depleted, nearly 11 million tonnes of phosphate had been torn from the island. In the space of a few weeks, the workers packed everything up and Vaitepaua became a ghost town. Today only a few people live in Moumu, making their living from copra production and the sale of *kaveu* (coconut crabs) to passing tuna boats.

known. To the southeast, the giant Fakarava competes in size with Rangiroa. Anaa is a small atoll further south.

MAKATEA
pop 84 • area 30 sq km
The only high island in the Tuamotus, Makatea is a bean-shaped plateau with 80m-high cliffs forming its outer edge. These cliffs used to be a barrier reef and the plateau was once the basin of a lagoon, where vast amounts of phosphate accumulated (see the boxed text 'Makatea Phosphate'). The atoll may have emerged as an indirect consequence of the uplifting of Tahiti. It was 'discovered' by the Dutch navigator Roggeveen in 1722.

TIKEHAU
pop 400 • lagoon area 461 sq km
Tikehau, 14km west of Rangiroa, was 'discovered' in 1816 by the Russian navigator Kotzebue. The roughly oval-shaped atoll is 26km on its longest axis. It's cut by Tuheiava Pass in the west and by more than 100 *hoa*. A number of motu dot the lagoon.

The islanders are grouped in the village of Tuherahera, in the southwest of the atoll. Their livelihood is copra production and fishing (the variety and quantity of fish are exceptional). Frequent connections by plane and boat to Tahiti allow the transport of fresh fish to the markets of Pape'ete. The enchanting landscape of the motu and the quietness of Tuherahera, attractions disappearing on Rangiroa, mean that more and more Tahitians and tourists are choosing Tikehau as a holiday destination.

Information
There is no bank on Tikehau. The **post office** has fax facilities and sells phonecards. There is a card-operated telephone booth in front of the post office. The infirmary adjoins the *mairie* (town hall).

Things to See & Do
Tuherahera is a pretty and prosperous village, made colourful by rows of *uru* (breadfruit) and coconut trees, bougainvillea and

hibiscus. The village has several places of worship including Catholic, Sanito, Seventh-Day Adventist and Protestant churches.

Lagoon excursions allow visitors to explore a number of picturesque sites. The scattered motu are populated by several species of ground-nesting birds. Brown noddies and *uaau* (red-footed boobies) are the most common species. *Pensions* generally organise trips to **Motu Puarua** (Île aux Oiseaux or Bird Island), to the northeast, charging 4000 to 7000 CFP per person.

Tuheiava Pass, to the west of the atoll, about 30 minutes by boat from the village, is another popular excursion. Fishers regularly come to the fish parks here. Ask at your *pension* about trips, which cost 3000 to 4000 CFP. *Pensions* also offer motu picnic trips.

Scuba diving in the magnificent Tuheiava Pass is a great reason for a visit to Tikehau. Rangiroa's Raie Manta Club has an offshoot at Tikehau Village (see Places to Stay). There are also dive centres in the village and at Tikehau Pearl Beach Resort. See the special section 'Diving' for details.

Places to Stay

There are a few moderately priced, good-quality *pensions* and you can choose between bungalows and rooms. The places in the village are not directly beside the lagoon, unlike those near the airport. Prices quoted are per person per day and include transfers to the airport as well as taxes.

Aito Motel Colette (*☎/fax 96 22 47, 96 23 07; rooms 3800 CFP, bungalows with half-/full board 8300/10,200 CFP)* has five rooms in a house in the village with shared bathroom and equipped kitchen, and five bungalows by the beach, in an enchanting spot between the village and the airport. Kayaks can be rented for 1500 CFP per day. Note that the electricity cuts out at 10pm.

Pension Hélène (*☎/fax 96 22 52; half-board 5900 CFP)* is at the village entrance on the left track coming from the airport. Hélène from the post office offers four clean rooms for two or three people with fan and shared bathroom.

Tikehau Village (*☎ 96 22 86; singles/doubles with half-board 8500/6900 CFP)* is between the village and the airport. There are nine two-person bungalows with bathroom, fan and mosquito net. Two of the beachside bungalows were built recently;

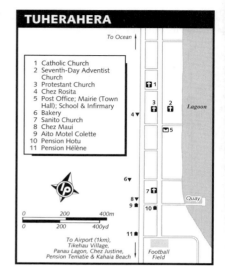

TUHERAHERA

To Ocean

1 Catholic Church
2 Seventh-Day Adventist Church
3 Protestant Church
4 Chez Rosita
5 Post Office; Mairie (Town Hall); School & Infirmary
6 Bakery
7 Sanito Church
8 Chez Maui
9 Aito Motel Colette
10 Pension Hotu
11 Pension Hélène

Lagoon

Quay

Football Field

To Airport (1km),
Tikehau Village,
Panau Lagon, Chez Justine,
Pension Tematie & Kahaia Beach

the older ones are more rustic and basic. Meals featuring local specialities are served in a large *fare potee* with a bar. There are bicycles and kayaks for guests' use. This is the only place that accepts credit cards.

Pension Tematie (*☎/fax 96 22 65; half-/full board 7500/9100 CFP)*, nearby, is a very popular place. There are three bungalows only metres from the crystal-clear waters of the lagoon, with bathroom, mosquito net and fan. Bicycle/kayak hire costs 500/1000 CFP per day.

Panau Lagon (*☎/fax 96 22 99; half-/full board 6900/8000 CFP)*, 250m on the right coming from the airport, on the edge of the lagoon, has six simple, rustic bungalows for two people, with bathroom, fan and mosquito net. Pirogue hire costs 1000 CFP for a half-day.

Chez Justine (*☎ 96 22 87; camping per person with breakfast 1300 CFP, bungalows with half-/full board 6400/8000 CFP)*, on the edge of the lagoon, is 1.5km from the village entrance and 500m on the right coming from the airport. It has five bungalows with bathroom, mosquito screens, fan and terrace. There is no communal kitchen for campers, but you can order meals for 1500 to 2000 CFP.

Pension Hotu (*Chez Isidore et Nini; ☎/fax 96 22 89; half-/full board 5900/8000 CFP)* is a family-run place offering three spacious and clean bungalows (with a fourth under construction), all with bathroom, fan and thatched roof. It's near a very attractive beach.

Kahaia Beach (☎ 96 22 77; half-/full board 6100/7600 CFP), the most remote option, is on a motu to the northeast of the airport. There are five lagoonside bungalows with bathrooms (some outside); the level of comfort is very basic.

Tikehau Pearl Beach Resort (☎ 96 23 00, fax 96 23 01; e info@spmhotels.pf; w www .pearlresorts.com; bungalows 42,200-66,700 CFP) is on Motu Aua, a perfect place for a luxury version of Robinson Crusoe, with white-sand beaches, coconut palms, hammocks and crystal-clear waters. The hotel, well integrated into the environment, has 16 over-water bungalows and 14 beach bungalows. A small pool, a restaurant and a bar complete the picture. There are shuttle boats to the village.

Places to Eat
Chez Maui and **Chez Rosita** are shops selling general supplies, and on certain days of the week you can get coconut pastries from the village's only bakery. The restaurant at **Tikehau Village** (see Places to Stay) sometimes accepts nonguests; you must book.

Getting There & Away
The airport is about 1km east of the village entrance. **Air Tahiti** (☎ 96 22 66) has ten flights a week between Pape'ete and Tikehau, direct or via Rangiroa. There are also several flights between Bora Bora and Tikehau, direct or via Rangiroa. Pape'ete–Tikehau costs 14,200 CFP, Tikehau–Rangiroa 4600 CFP and Bora Bora–Tikehau 21,500 CFP.

The *Mareva Nui*, *Saint-Xavier Maris-Stella*, *Dory* and *Vai-Aito* stop at Tikehau.

Getting Around
A 10km track goes around the motu on which Tuherahera is situated, and passes by the airport. Bicycles can be borrowed or hired (about 500 to 700 CFP a day) from your hosts.

MATAIVA
pop 227 • lagoon area 25 sq km
The first European to land on Mataiva was Bellingshausen, in 1820. The atoll's appearance may change dramatically in coming years, as there are plans to mine the lagoon

substratum, which contains about 70 separate phosphate deposits. The accessible part is estimated to contain 12 million tonnes, enough for 10 to 15 years of mining. Large-scale industrial activity in such a restricted space will undoubtedly cause ecological problems. For the 200 inhabitants of the peaceful village of Pahua, the prospect of the phosphate-mining project is like the sword of Damocles.

Pahua is divided by a pass a few metres wide and no deeper than 1.5m, suitable only for very small boats. A bridge spans the pass and links the two parts of the village. Nine *hoa*, thin trickles of water, provide small links between the lagoon and the ocean. Mataiva (literally 'nine eyes') is named after these channels. Ill fortune struck the village in 1998 when a huge wave partially destroyed it. Most people live off fishing and copra production.

The structure of the Mataiva lagoon gives it a particular appearance: the coral constructions at the surface of the water create dividing walls 50m to 300m wide, forming about 70 basins with a maximum depth of 10m. Seen from a plane, the play of light on this underwater tessellation forms a mosaic of green.

Despite the limited tourist infrastructure, the atoll provides a delightful escape. There are superb and easily accessible beaches, numerous snorkelling spots, lots of fish and one of the few noteworthy archaeological sites in the Tuamotus. Air Tahiti flights make it possible to spend a pleasant weekend here.

Information
There is no bank on the atoll. Pahua has two **shops** and a post office, south of the bridge. The **post office** has a fax service and sells phonecards. There are card-operated telephone booths next to the post office and at the airport.

Things to See & Do
Ofai Tau Noa (Rocher de la Tortue or Turtle Rock) is a remnant of an uplifted coral reef *feo*, shaped like a splayed mushroom. Legend says that if a cloud of the same shape as the rock appears above the pass, a change in the weather is on the way and the turtles will come to the surface. It will then be time to hunt them. To get there, take the track that starts at the bridge on the northern side of

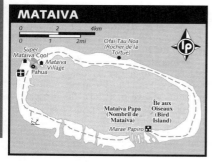

MATAIVA

the pass and follow it for 4.7km. Then take the side track on the left, which crosses the coconut plantation to the ocean.

Stuck right in the middle of a coconut plantation, a rusted **shipwreck**, of which only a part of the bow remains, is a symbol of nature's violence. According to elders, this ship sank in the 1906 cyclone and was carried to the coconut plantation by cyclones in later years. To get there, follow the track south from Pahua for about 3km, and then take the side track that turns right towards the ocean. After 450m, you will come to a fork, where you can catch a glimpse of the ocean. Don't head towards the ocean, but follow the track to the left for 250m to reach the wreck.

Marae Papiro is a well-kept marae on the edge of a *hoa*, about 14km from the village, southeast of the atoll at the end of the track. In the centre of this marae, you can see the stone seat from which, according to legend, the giant Tu guarded the pass against invasion. In case of attack from enemy tribes, he needed to take no more than three steps to push the assailants off the island and crush them. Tu is one of the gods in the Tahitian pantheon. It is also the name of a fierce warrior king from Anaa Atoll, an ancestor of the Pomares, who conquered the surrounding atolls as far as Fakarava. The throne is surrounded by rectangular marae and bordered by little blocks of coral limestone driven into the ground. In the centre of each marae, two larger stones stand on their sides.

In the south, along the edge of the lagoon, there are many fine **beaches**. Take your mask and fins along.

Île aux Oiseaux (Bird Island), to the east of the lagoon, is a crescent-shaped coral spit

covered in small shrubs. It is a favourite nesting place for *oio*, *tara* and red-footed boobies.

According to legend, a rock on the surface of the lagoon, next to Île aux Oiseaux, called **Mataiva Papa** (Nombril de Mataiva or Navel of Mataiva), is the place where Tu took his first step. Tradition has it that a foreigner reaching Mataiva should put a foot on this rock.

Don't miss the chance to accompany the fishers on their way to trap fish in one of the numerous **fish parks** around the lagoon and the pass. A first fisher jumps into the water carrying fencing wire that is closed at one end in the form of a hoop net, while the other fisher splashes at the surface. The frightened fish rush into the trap. All the fishers have to do is empty them into the boat and repeat the routine. The few big fish that escape the trap are harpooned. Sorted, scaled and gutted, they are sold in the village.

Places to Stay & Eat

The people of Pahua hope that an increasing number of tourists will dissuade the government from setting up drilling sites on the lagoon. The two *pensions* are very similar; only the locations differ. Prices are per person per day and include taxes and airport transfers.

Mataiva Village (☎ 96 32 33; camping 1000 CFP, bungalows with half-/full board 5600/7100 CFP) is north of the pass, 150m from the bridge and by the lagoon. There are five clean and comfortable two-person bungalows with bathroom (cold water only). Crayfish are a speciality in the large dining room on stilts. This is one of the few places in the Tuamotus where you can camp; there are bathroom facilities for campers.

Super Mataiva Cool (☎ 96 32 53; singles with half-/full board 5500/7000 CFP, doubles with half-/full board 10,000/13,000 CFP), south of the bridge and on the edge of the pass, is run by the Huri family. There are four basic but decent units with bathroom (cold water only).

Apart from the *pensions* there's really nowhere to eat, although there are several small **shops** with basic food supplies.

Getting There & Away

Mataiva is 350km northeast of Tahiti and 100km west of Rangiroa.

Black Pearl, Jewel of the Tuamotus

The trump card of the Polynesian economy, the *poe rava* (black pearl) is the result of natural phenomena and complex human intervention. The main centres of production are on the Tuamotus and in the Gambier Archipelago.

The shells of *Pinctada margaritifera*, an oyster found in abundance in Polynesian lagoons, were used in ancient times to make ceremonial jewellery, fish hooks and lures, and were once much sought-after by the European button industry. The overexploitation of natural beds and the decline of the button industry sounded the death knell in the 1960s, and the culture of oysters for pearl production took over, initially on Manihi.

The formation of a pearl results from the accidental or artificial introduction of a foreign body inside the oyster. In response to this intrusion, the epithelial cells of the mantle (the secretory organ) produce material to isolate the foreign body. The nucleus is gradually covered in nacre (mother-of-pearl). If the foreign body (eg, a grain of sand or coral) is introduced by natural means, the result is an extremely rare natural pearl, known as a fine pearl.

The pearl farmer must reproduce this natural process. The oysters are methodically reared. At certain times of the year, they release sexual substances that are fertilised in the water. After swimming around for several weeks, the young oysters (seed oysters) attach themselves to the coral. The pearl farmer catches the seed oysters in collectors sunk in the lagoon and then attaches them to underwater rearing lines.

The first stage consists of sacrificing a perfectly healthy mature oyster, known as the donor oyster. A fragment of its mantle is removed and divided into about 50 minute particles, called grafts. The second stage is the grafting, which takes just a few seconds. The recipient oyster is fixed to a support and held open with forceps. Using a scalpel, the grafter firstly incises the back of the gonad (reproductive organ) and inserts the graft. A perfectly spherical bead (the nucleus), about 6mm in diameter, is introduced into the gonad so that it is in contact with the graft. The graft cells develop around the nucleus to form the pearl sack which, once closed, secretes the nacreous material. The grafted oysters are placed inside metal baskets and lowered back into the lagoon. They are then regularly inspected and cleaned.

Layer upon layer, the mother-of-pearl thickens around the nucleus at the rate of 1mm a year. Eighteen months later, the first harvest is gathered. A second nucleus may be implanted to obtain a second, larger (15mm to 20mm) pearl 15 months later.

Grafting entails risks inherent to all surgical operations: of 100 grafted oysters, 25 to 30 do not survive the shock of the operation and another 25 to 30 reject the nucleus. When the time comes to harvest them, only five of the remaining 40 (just 2%) will have produced perfect pearls. When a second graft is performed, the success rate increases to just under 10%.

Until recently, the only grafters were Japanese, but they are gradually being replaced by Polynesians who have allegedly discovered the 'secret' of the technique. A training centre for the pearl-shell and pearl-culture professions has been established on Rangiroa. Nonetheless, the act of grafting is still partially veiled in mystery.

The pearls are mainly used for rings and pendants. Several factors determine their value: the diameter, shape, quality (absence of flaws or marks) and colour. 'Black pearl' is in fact an inaccurate term. The pearls produced by *Pinctada margaritifera* range in colour from pearly white to black, and include deep purple, champagne and grey. The orient (the pearl's iridescent reflection) and lustre (mirror effect) also enter into the equation. Jewellers generally classify pearls by using two letters followed by a figure: a pearl classed as RB 12 is perfectly round (R), has a few pits or surface flaws, has a correct orient (B) and measures 12mm in diameter.

Less well known are *keshi* and *mabe*. *Keshi* is pure mother-of-pearl, a pearl without a nucleus. In some cases the nucleus is rejected but the secreting graft continues to produce mother-of-pearl. *Mabe*, by contrast, is the result of deliberate manipulation. The technician sticks a plastic mould on the inner surface of the shell. The mould is gradually covered in layers of mother-of-pearl. After a few months, the mother-of-pearl is cut off with a diamond disk and the mould is removed. The result is a pure, hollow *mabe*, which is filled with epoxy resin before a small mother-of-pearl plate is welded on to form the base. *Mabe* is used for making pendants, brooches, earrings and cufflinks.

The proprietor of the Mataiva Village *pension* is the local representative of **Air Tahiti** (☎ 96 32 48). There are two Pape'ete–Mataiva flights (14,200 CFP one-way) a week, usually on Thursday and Sunday. Return flights depart on the same days.

Mataiva is on the routes of the *Mareva Nui* and *Saint-Xavier Maris-Stella*.

Getting Around

A track goes almost all the way around the island, in the middle of the coconut plantation. The northern track finishes at Marae Papiro, about 14km away. The southern track is about 10km long.

Cycling is an excellent way of getting to Ofai Tau, Marae Papiro and the shipwreck. The *pensions* rent bicycles for about 1000 CFP per day.

The *pensions* organise trips to the various sites by motor boat and by car, costing about 3000 CFP for the day, including a picnic.

MANIHI

pop 769 • lagoon area 192 sq km

Some 175km northeast of Rangiroa, Manihi has acquired an international reputation for pearl production. The big names in this business chose to set up here, and the lagoon is now scattered with family-run and industrial pearl farms.

Shaped like an ellipse, the atoll is 28km long and 8km wide, with only one opening, the Tairapa Pass in the southwest. The exhilarating beauty of the lagoon and the riches of its underwater world were quickly recognised and an international hotel was built in 1977. Tourism and pearl production provide work for most of the inhabitants; fishing and copra production provide a supplementary income.

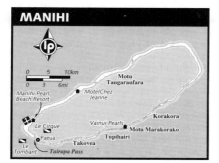

Information

There is no bank on the atoll, but the **Manihi Pearl Beach Resort** (see Places to Stay) may be able to change money in emergencies. The **post office** is in Paeua village opposite the marina. There are card-operated telephone booths on the ground floor of the post office building, at the airport and at the Manihi Pearl Beach Resort. The village also has a hospital.

Things to See & Do

The charmless, almost neglected village of **Paeua** is in striking contrast to villages on other atolls and will not entice you to stay. The pace of life is set to the rhythm of the pearl farms, where most of the inhabitants work.

Visiting a **pearl farm** is a must. The first pearl farm was set up on Manihi in 1968 and the atoll has steadily established itself as a principal centre for black pearls in the South Pacific. See the boxed text 'Black Pearl, Jewel of the Tuamotus' earlier in this chapter. It is interesting to visit a small family-run farm and a larger industrial farm. Avoid holiday periods, particularly Christmas, when the workers are away.

The **Manihi Pearl Beach Resort** (see Places to Stay) is the main organiser of pearl-farm visits, usually combined with a picnic and village excursion; there are tours three times weekly (2500 CFP). It has a well-stocked shop selling mounted and unmounted black pearls directly from the farm. Credit cards are accepted.

Vainui Pearls (☎ 96 42 89) is a farm run by the Buniet family, who also own a *pension* on Motu Marakorako. They specialise in *mabe* (hollow mother-of-pearl) and also make direct sales of pearls. Again, credit cards are accepted.

Nothing stops you from contacting the small firms directly. All you have to do is go to the village and ask; you may even find the pearl of your dreams at a very reasonable price.

There are a number of magnificent **diving** sites near the pass. A dive centre operates from the Manihi Pearl Beach Resort. See the special section 'Diving' for details.

Places to Stay

Reasonably priced accommodation is difficult to find on Manihi and the facilities are scattered over the atoll.

Motel Chez Jeanne (☎ 96 42 90, fax 96 42 91; beach/over-water bungalows per person 9600/13,900 CFP) is on the lagoonside on Motu Taugaraufara, about 9km northeast of the airport. It has two well-equipped bungalows with bathroom. Meals are not provided, but there is a small shop on the premises. Prices include airport transfers and credit cards are accepted. Lagoon tours are organised through the Manihi Pearl Beach Resort (6000 CFP).

Vainui Pearls (☎ 96 42 89, fax 96 43 30; full board per person 8900 CFP) is on Motu Marakorako, east of the village and about half an hour by boat from the airport. It has eight rooms with shared bathroom (which, according to some readers, compromises privacy), with rates including airport transfers and fishing and picnic excursions. The owners have a small pearl farm and sell mabe, keshi and pearls. If they are going to the village or airport they'll take you to the diving centre at Manihi Pearl Beach Resort for free; otherwise it costs 4500 CFP return. Credit cards are accepted.

Manihi Pearl Beach Resort (☎ 96 42 73, fax 96 42 72, in Pape'ete ☎ 43 16 10, fax 43 17 86; beach/over-water bungalows 30,300/49,700 CFP), two minutes from the airport, at the southwestern end of the lagoon, is a top-end establishment with 22 bungalows on the beach and 10 over-water bungalows. The development is harmoniously integrated into the idyllic natural setting, which includes airy coconut groves, white-sand beaches, a sea-water swimming pool and the magnificent lagoon. The restaurant (see Places to Eat) has a beachfront terrace and there is a bar overlooking the pool, the lagoon and the beach. Credit cards are accepted.

Places to Eat

Apart from the pensions and hotels, there are hardly any places to eat. In Paeua, there is a well-stocked **shop** near the marina.

At Manihi Pearl Beach Resort, the **Poe Rava Restaurant** (appetizers 800-2000 CFP, mains 1300-2500 CFP, desserts around 900 CFP) has extremely reasonable prices, especially for lunch. The setting by the swimming pool and lagoon is delightful.

Getting There & Away

The office of the representative of **Air Tahiti** (☎ 96 43 34, 96 42 71 on flight days) is in Paeua. On flight days the representative goes to the airport. There are almost daily flights between Pape'ete and Manihi, direct or via Ahe or Rangiroa. Pape'ete–Manihi costs 17,200 CFP and Rangiroa–Manihi 9800 CFP. Manihi is also linked to Bora Bora, via Rangiroa; there are four flights weekly from Bora Bora to Manihi and two flights weekly from Manihi to Bora Bora (24,300 CFP).

The Mareva Nui, Saint-Xavier Maris-Stella, Dory and Vai-Aito service Manihi. Loading and unloading takes place at the Paeua quay in the pass.

Getting Around

The only track on Manihi links Motu Taugaraufara to the airport – covering a total distance of only about 9km. Getting around the atoll requires some ingenuity! The Manihi Pearl Beach Resort rents bicycles for around 900 CFP per day.

The airport is at the southwestern end of the atoll, two minutes away from Manihi Pearl Beach Resort. To get to the village you have no choice but to hitch a boat ride from the quay, right next to the airport fare.

To get to the dive centre from the village, you can use the Manihi Pearl Beach Resort staff shuttle boat, which generally leaves the Paeua marina at about 6am and returns around 4pm. It'll take you for free. If they're going to the airport or the village, resort owners will generally take you across to the dive centre. For other points around the atoll, talk to boat owners in the village.

AHE

pop 377 • lagoon area 170 sq km

Until recently, Ahe, 15km west of Manihi, was only known to pearl farmers and to yachties, who often pull in when sailing from the Marquesas. In 2001 an upmarket pension opened, followed in 2002 by a dive centre. Those who want to head off the beaten track will appreciate this atoll's quietness, idyllic scenery and gentle pace of life.

Ahe was 'discovered' by Wilkes in 1839. The atoll is 20km long by 10km wide and is entered by the Tiareroa (or Reianui) Pass in the west. The village of Tenukupara is on the southwestern side.

There are new adventures to be had for keen divers with the opening of the **Ahe Plongée** dive centre. Run by an experienced dive master from Rangiroa, the centre is at Coco Perles *pension*. For more information see the special section 'Diving'.

Places to Stay & Eat

Coco Perles (*☎/fax 96 44 08; singles with half-/full board from 10,000/12,200 CFP, doubles with half-/full board from 17,700/ 22,100 CFP*) is isolated on a motu. In a coconut plantation facing the lagoon there are six charming, well-designed bungalows made with local materials and attractively decorated, with bathroom (cold water only), fan and mosquito screens. Meals are served in a *fare* by the lagoon. You can visit the owners' pearl farm; mounted or unmounted pearls can be purchased. Activities include diving, snorkelling (there are three beautiful coral pinnacles opposite) and kayaking. Village transfers cost 1500 CFP and motu excursions 1000 CFP.

Getting There & Away

Air Tahiti flies to Ahe four times weekly, departing from Pape'ete; flights are direct or via Manihi. From Pape'ete to Ahe costs 17,200 CFP.

The *Saint-Xavier Maris-Stella*, *Mareva Nui*, *Dory* and *Vai-Aito* service Ahe.

TAKAROA

pop 488 ● lagoon area 113 sq km
First seen by European eyes in 1616 by Le Maire, Takaroa (literally, Long Chin) and its close neighbour, Takapoto, form a pair. Marine maps have persisted in calling them the King George Islands, ever since Byron's visit in 1765.

Takaroa is, along with Manihi and Tepoto, one of the northernmost islands in the Tuamotus. The atoll is 27km long by 6km wide and has only one pass, Teauonae, in the southwest. The only village, Teavaroa, is on the edge of the pass. Takaroa's most singular feature is that the population is 90% Mormon; consequently alcohol is prohibited. The inhabitants live off pearl production and, to a lesser extent, fishing and copra production.

Information

There is no bank on Takaroa. The **post office**, near the bridge at the end of the village and next to the hospital, has fax facilities and phonecards. There's a card-operated public

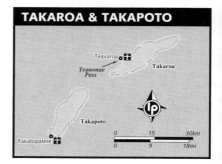

telephone in front of the *mairie* and a first-aid room beside the post office.

Things to See & Do

Sleepy quietness emanates from the village of **Teavaroa**. Life takes a gently monotonous course, punctuated by fishing, copra production and work at the pearl farms. In the evening, young Paumotu gather near the pass and fish with long wooden rods to the sound of *kaina* (Polynesian) music. A meteorological station, the largest in the northern Tuamotus, is near the *mairie*.

There is an imposing **shipwreck**, a four-masted vessel that ran into the coral reef at the beginning of the twentieth century – an indication of how difficult sailing is in the Tuamotus and how violent the cyclones can be. From the airport *fare*, it is 6km along the track, heading north from the village.

Several major pearl producers have **pearl farms** on Takaroa; there is also a host of small family businesses. Your hosts will probably be delighted to show you their own pearl-grafting operation or will direct you towards other operators.

Takaroa's lagoon has numerous coral formations near the beach that are wonderful for **snorkelling**. Ask village kids about accompanying them when they go **spear fishing**.

Places to Stay & Eat

Pension Poe Rangi (*☎ 98 23 82, 98 23 09; full board 9600-10,700 CFP*) literally means 'pearls of heaven' and guests may think it's a good description. It's on the south side of the pass, 10 minutes by boat from the village. There are three bungalows with bathroom (cold water only), one with a kitchenette. Rates include airport transfers. Meals including local specialities (*maa paumotu* or

Paumotu food) and Caribbean dishes are served in the *fare potee*, where there's also a bar. Various activities are offered, including kayaking (free), snorkelling, fishing trips, visits to pearl farms and various excursions on the atoll (3000 to 5000 CFP).

Apart from the **pension** there's really nowhere to eat. You will have to make do with basic supplies and canned food from the **shop** in the village.

Getting There & Away
Takaroa is 575km northeast of Pape'ete and less than 100km east of Manihi.

The airport is 2.5km northeast of the village. The office of the Air Tahiti representative is in the village. There are at least four weekly flights from Pape'ete to Takaroa (18,800 CFP); the trip takes just over 1½ hours.

The *Mareva Nui* and *Saint-Xavier Maris-Stella* stop at the atoll, drawing up to the quay in the pass.

Getting Around
The only track goes from the village to Paul Yu's pearl farm, through the airport – about 10km.

TAKAPOTO
pop 612 • lagoon area 102 sq km

Takapoto (literally, Short Chin) Atoll, 9km south of Takaroa, was 'discovered' in 1616 by Le Maire. It's 20km long and 6km across at its widest point and doesn't have a pass. This atoll has been the subject of multi-disciplinary studies since 1974 under the auspices of Unesco's Man & Biosphere (MAB) programme.

The second pearl farm in the Tuamotus was built on this atoll in the late 1960s. As this activity flourished in the beginning of the 1970s, the characteristic huts on stilts mushroomed along the shore. Apart from pearl production, the traditional practice of collecting young oysters in the protected lagoon continues. Copra production and fishing are a further source of income. With its pearl farms, beaches and archaeological remains, Takapoto could one day become a popular tourist attraction.

Information
There is no bank on the atoll. The **post office**, next to the *mairie*, offers fax facilities and phonecards. There is a card-operated telephone in front of the *mairie*. The community clinic is also next to the post office.

Things to See & Do
The little village of **Fakatopatere**, on the southwest of the atoll and next to the airport, has a surprising appearance; it spreads across the entire width of the reef crown, and its streets (sand tracks, in fact) create a criss-cross pattern, with a Catholic church in the middle.

Pearl farm visits enable you to see the whole process of pearl production. You'll have to make an appointment with the pearl producers, from whom you can also buy pearls directly.

Takapoto has many idyllic and unspoiled spots, including quite a few white-sand **beaches** around the lagoon, which are easily accessible via the track. In the village itself, there is a small beach close to Takapoto Village (see Places to Stay). During their stopover in Takapoto, tourists from the *Aranui* usually picnic on a beach 2km east of the village. Follow the track through the coconut grove until you come to the white building on the left, less than 1.5km from the village. Continue for 700m and turn off at the path on the left that crosses the coconut grove towards the lagoon. You'll find several fishers' *fare* and the beach of your dreams.

Marae Takai is worth the long walk. It consists of three small marae surrounded by vertical coral slabs. According to the owner of the land it could be a funeral site containing bones. Northwest of Fakatopatere, the marae is well hidden behind bushy vegetation. Follow the track that goes past the cemetery at the village exit for 15km. You will see a *hoa*, spanned by a stone bridge. Cross this bridge and immediately on the right walk 60m along the *hoa* towards the lagoon. Turn left for about 30m, clearing your way through bushes and coconut trees and you will come upon the three marae in a little clearing. The walk will take you through magnificent coconut plantations. The lagoon shore is festooned with pearl farms and white-sand beaches.

To get to **Teavatika**, a fish park built of coral blocks in a *hoa*, follow the northeastern track to the end, about 9km. This public park is a rare example of its kind.

Places to Stay & Eat

Takapoto Village (☎ 98 65 44; half-/full board 6800/8300 CFP) is on a small beach beside the lagoon, southeast of the village. There are two well-kept bungalows for two people with bathroom (cold water only). Mr Toti, the owner, is mayor of Takapoto and has a thorough knowledge of the history of the Tuamotus and can tell you stories about the frightening raids of the Anaa warriors.

Apart from this *pension*, the options for food are limited to some modest **shops**.

Getting There & Away

Takapoto is 560km northeast of Pape'ete and less than 100km east of Manihi.

The airfield is just a stone's throw to the southeast of the village. Air Tahiti has three weekly flights, connecting Pape'ete, Takaroa and Takapoto. The Pape'ete–Takapoto flight costs 17,200 CFP and takes 1½ hours.

The *Saint-Xavier Maris-Stella* and *Mareva Nui* stop at Takapoto. *Taporo IV* and *Aranui*, en route to the Marquesas, also stop here. Transfers of passengers and freight by *bonitier* take place at the landing stage next to the shop Nadine.

Getting Around

There are two tracks from the village. The first one goes in a northeasterly direction for about 9km, to the fish park. The other goes in a northwesterly direction. It's fine as far as Marae Takai, 15km out, but then reaches a few *hoa* that are impossible to cross.

The ideal way to explore the atoll is by bicycle (500 CFP per day). Picnics on deserted motu, reached by speedboat, cost about 2000 CFP; ask at the *pension*.

ARUTUA

pop 520 • lagoon area 570 sq km

This almost circular atoll is nearly 25km in diameter. The lagoon waters meet the ocean through the small Porofai Pass in the east, near the village of **Rautini**. The village is on a motu south of the airport, half an hour away by boat.

The village, which was devastated by cyclones in 1983, has been entirely rebuilt. Arutua's lagoon has a reputation for being rich in fish and crayfish. Fishing, copra production and, most importantly, cultured pearls are the main economic activities on the atoll.

Places to Stay

Chez Neri (☎ 96 52 55; full board 6100 CFP) in Rautini is the only place to stay. There are two rooms in a house with shared bathroom (cold water only). The owners also have a pearl farm and will take you to visit fish parks on the lagoon. Airport transfers cost 3000 CFP per person return.

Getting There & Away

Arutua is about 375km northeast of Tahiti. To the west, only 30km separates it from the eastern extremity of Rangiroa.

There are three flights weekly between Pape'ete and Arutua (14,600 CFP). Getting to Rautini from the airport, at the west of Motu Tenihinihi, takes half an hour by boat.

The *Saint-Xavier Maris-Stella*, *Rairoa Nui*, *Mareva Nui*, *Dory* and *Corbia* stop at Arutua.

KAUKURA

pop 379 • lagoon area 546 sq km

Kaukura was first reached by a European (Roggeveen) in 1722. Oval shaped, it measures 50km by 14km at its widest point. Kaukura, together with Tikehau, is the Tuamotus' biggest provider of fish to the markets in Pape'ete. Transport to the atoll is by cargo boat and plane. The inhabitants live in **Raitahiti** village, on the northwestern side of the lagoon.

Places to Stay

Pension Rekareka (☎ 96 62 40, 96 62 39; rooms/bungalows with full board per person 5100/6100 CFP), run by the Parker family in Raitahiti, is a house with six two-person rooms with shared bathroom. There are also five bungalows for two people with a shared external bathroom on Motu Tahunapona, 15 minutes by boat from the village. Transfers from the airport are included. Excursions to fish parks and fishing trips can be organised.

Getting There & Away

Kaukura Atoll is 55km southeast of Rangiroa and 340km northeast of Tahiti.

The airport is 2km from the village. Air Tahiti flies Pape'ete–Kaukura twice weekly via Rangiroa for 14,600 CFP. The trip takes 1 hour and 40 minutes.

The *Saint-Xavier Maris-Stella*, *Mareva Nui*, *Corbia*, *Rairoa Nui* and *Dory* stop at Kaukura.

FAKARAVA

pop 467 • lagoon area 1121 sq km

Fakarava is the second largest atoll in the Tuamotus. Roughly rectangular in shape, its lagoon is 60km long and 25km wide. The lagoon waters merge with the ocean through Garuae Pass in the north and Tumakohua Pass in the south. The opening of a permanent airstrip in 1995, near the northern pass, has helped to open up this magnificent atoll. One day it could be a second Rangiroa but in the meantime its huge tourist potential is seriously underexploited. Visits to **pearl farms** and picnics on idyllic motu are the order of the day. Fakarava has amazing **diving** in the Garuae Pass (see the special section 'Diving') and it's also on the programme for several dive-cruise operators.

Most of the population is gathered in **Rotoava** village at the northeastern end, 4km east of the airport. A handful of inhabitants also live in Tetamanu village, on the edge of the southern pass. On the eastern edge, an uninterrupted reef strip stretches for 40km. The western side, on the other hand, has a few scattered motu. Copra and cultured-pearl production and fishing are the main industries.

Places to Stay

The prices quoted here are inclusive of tax.

Relais Marama (☎ 98 42 51; camping 1400 CFP, single/double/triple rooms 3600/4600/5600 CFP, single/double/triple bungalow 4400/5400/6400 CFP) on the ocean side of the motu at Rotoava, behind the *mairie* has four functional rooms with fan and two bungalows with shared bathroom (cold water only). All prices include breakfast; there's no full-board option, but half-board is available for an extra 1800 CFP or you can use the communal kitchen. There are bikes for guests' use and airport transfers are free.

Pension Havaiki (☎/fax 98 42 16; e havaiki@mail.pf; bungalows with breakfast/full board per person 5000/9000 CFP), 1km from the village centre, offers four bungalows on a small but magnificent beach. Each decorated bungalow has a double and single bed with mosquito nets. The food is tasty and plentiful. Masks, snorkels and bikes are available for guests' use. Airport transfers are free.

Veke Veke Village (☎ 98 42 80; 2- or 4-person bungalows with full board per person 8500 CFP), 3km south of Rotoava has four comfortable bungalows with bathroom (cold water only) by the lagoon. Kayaks and bicycles are available for hire. Airport transfers are free.

Pension Paparara (☎/fax 98 42 66; full board 7500 CFP) is about 5km south of the village, beside the lagoon. There are three bungalows with mosquito nets and shared bathroom (cold water only). Bicycles are available for guests' use. Airport transfers are 1000 CFP per person return.

Hôtel Maitai Dream Fakarava (☎ 43 08 83, fax 43 08 93; e maitaifa@mail.pf) should be open by the time you read this. It will be in the top-end category, with 30 bungalows, a restaurant and numerous activities on offer.

At the other end of Fakarava, near Tumakohua Pass, is the village of Tetamanu, with two options that will appeal to lovers of isolation and tranquility.

Motu Aito Paradise (☎/fax 41 29 00; e motu-aito@mail.pf; w www.fakarava.org; full board per person 10,000 CFP), on a superb motu, has six pretty bungalows constructed using local materials, with bathroom (cold water only). Prices are for a three-night minimum stay; free excursions are organised and airport transfers are included.

Tetamanu Village (☎ 43 92 40, fax 42 77 70; e tetamanuvillage@mail.pf; 3/4/5 days with full board per person 47,500/58,000/61,000 CFP) is beside the Tumakohua Pass. There are six two-person bungalows with bathroom (cold water only). Prices are for a three-night minimum stay and include airport transfers. Meals are served in an overwater restaurant. Diving is one of the activities on offer (three nights' accommodation and four dives costs 52,500 CFP, or you can pay 5000 CFP for a single dive). We've received mixed reports from readers about this place.

Getting There & Away
The atoll is 488km east-northeast of Tahiti and southeast of Rangiroa.

The airport is about 4km west of Rotoava. **Air Tahiti** (☎ 67 70 35, 67 70 85; e reservation@airtahiti.pf; w www.airtahiti.pf) flies Pape'ete–Fakarava every day except Thursday for 17,400 CFP one-way, Rangiroa–Fakarava every Wednesday for 5500 CFP and Fakarava–Kauehi every Wednesday for 5500 CFP.

The *Saint-Xavier Maris-Stella, Vai-Aito* and *Mareva Nui* stop at Fakarava.

Getting Around
From Rotoava, a track goes to the southwest of the atoll for about 40km.

ANAA
pop 411 • lagoon area 184 sq km
Anaa Atoll is just 28km long and 5km wide. It's made up of 11 motu scattered on the reef circumference and it doesn't have a pass. Anaa, which used to be densely populated, became known for the ferocity of its inhabitants, who extended their domination over the northern part of the archipelago, pillaging the atolls they conquered.

Cyclones have cost Anaa dearly. Tukuhora village, razed by a tidal wave in 1906 that left 100 people dead, was devastated again in the 1982–83 cyclone season. The inhabitants live off fishing and copra production.

Places to Stay
Pension Maui Nui (☎ 98 32 75; half-board per person 5100 CFP), in the village, has two bungalows with shared bathroom, and two rooms, also with shared bathroom. Prices include airport transfers.

Pension Toku Kaiga (☎ 98 32 69; half-board 5100 CFP), also in the village, offers a choice between a bungalow and a fully equipped 'chalet'. Excursions on the atoll cost about 4000 CFP. Bicycles are available for use and airport transfers are included.

Chez Louise (☎ 98 32 69; full board 5100 CFP), in the village near the lagoon, offers two rooms with shared bathroom.

Getting There & Away
Anaa is 450km east of Pape'ete. There are Pape'ete–Anaa flights once or twice a week (15,600 CFP, 1¼ hours). It's also on the shipping routes of the *Auura'Nui 3, Kura Ora II* and *Kura Ora III*.

Southern & Eastern Tuamotus

If not for the presence of the infamous Centre d'Expérimentation du Pacifique (CEP) conducting nuclear-testing operations, this totally isolated region would have remained forgotten.

Cultured-pearl and copra production and fishing are the major industries of these islands. Hao is the regional centre. The smallest atolls in the archipelago are in this region; some, such as Nukutavake, Pinaki and Akiaki, are barely 5 sq km. Tourist facilities are rare and so are visitors.

NUKUTAVAKE
pop 190 • lagoon area 5.5 sq km
Situated 1125km southeast of Tahiti, Nukutavake is the only inhabited atoll where the lagoon has been completely filled in by sand and limestone particles from the external reef. It is entirely covered by a coconut plantation.

Pension Afou (☎ 98 72 53; full board 7100 CFP), in the village of Tavananui, 1km from the airport, has three local-style bungalows with shared bathroom. Airport transfers cost 1500 CFP.

Hao serves as a hub for Air Tahiti flights to other far-flung atolls, including Nukutavake. Contact Air Tahiti for details.

HAO
pop 1317 • lagoon area 609 sq km
The Spaniard Quirós was the first European to set foot on this atoll in the centre of the Tua-

motus in 1606. Hao experienced great demographic growth from the 1960s onwards as an administrative and transit centre for the CEP. Its state-of-the-art infrastructure includes a 3300m runway built to handle the military transport planes carrying highly sensitive material destined for Moruroa. When atmospheric tests were conducted, there were up to 5000 people busy on the atoll. With the switch to underground testing, most of the military staff were moved to Moruroa and Fangataufa. The end of nuclear testing in 1996 resulted in further major changes to the situation on the atoll. Hao has a college and a medical centre and most inhabitants earn their living from cultured-pearl production in Otepa, a village in the northeast.

Chez Amélie *(☎ 97 03 42, fax 97 02 41; rooms without/with air-con per person 5600/ 6600 CFP)* is in Otepa. Amélie Danzer, the Air Tahiti representative, has four rooms, two of which have air-con, in a house with attached bathroom (with hot water).

Air Tahiti flies Pape'ete–Hao three or four times a week via Anaa or Makemo. The Pape'ete–Hao trip takes about 2½ hours and costs 23,000 CFP. There are also connections from Hao to Takume, Fangataufa, Fakahina, Takakoto, Tureia, Vahitahi, Nuku-tavake, Pukarua and Reao. Inquire at Air Tahiti about flight schedules.

The *Auura'Nui 3*, *Nuku Hau*, *Kura Ora II* and *Kura Ora III* stop at Hao.

MORUROA
pop 20 • lagoon area 324 sq km
Often mistakenly spelt 'Mururoa', this atoll, 1250km southeast of Tahiti, will forever be synonymous with nuclear tests (see the boxed text 'French Nuclear Testing' in the Facts about French Polynesia chapter). 'Discovered' in 1792 by the Englishman Weatherhead, it is 28km long and 11km wide, and has only one pass.

The atoll was chosen for the tests because of its isolation from inhabited zones and its suitability for the necessary infrastructure. It was equipped with ultramodern electricity-production installations, a desalinisation plant and an airport for large aircraft. Entertainment facilities and an internal radio and TV channel were established for military staff. The atoll was ceded to the French state in 1964. With the final tests, jurisdiction was returned to the French Polynesian government and the installations were dismantled. Today there's just a small contingent of French legionnaires.

The Marquesas

Te Henua Enana (Land of Men) is the Marquesans' name for their archipelago. These bewitching islands of legend boast a wealth of archaeological remains, many of which are still to be catalogued.

Four thousand kilometres south of Hawaii, 500km from the closest of the Tuamotus and 1400km northeast of Pape'ete, this is the most northerly archipelago of French Polynesia. The 15 islands stretch diagonally about 350km from northwest to southeast. The islands are divided into two groups: northern and southern.

These unprotected blocks of lava rise abruptly from the vastness of the Pacific Ocean, their rugged contours the result of erosion caused by sea and wind. There are no sheltering reefs or lagoons to soften the harsh assault of the waves. As a result, necks, needles and peaks towering more than 1000m stand side by side with high plateaus bordered by steep cliffs. This dramatic, sharp relief is ridged with deep valleys covered with luxuriant tropical plants and flowers.

Partly sunken calderas (volcano craters) have formed vast amphitheatres. In these more sheltered areas the Marquesans chose to build their homes.

The archipelago is not affected by cyclones. Rainfall is very variable, but is generally evenly spread throughout the year, with greatest precipitation between June and August. Torrential downpours are often followed by lengthy droughts. Temperatures can be vastly different between one valley and another, and are slightly higher than those in Pape'ete.

The islands' flora and fauna differ little from those of the other archipelagos. The *nono*, a minute black or white fly with a painful bite, is endemic. The islands are also home to wild horses and goats, introduced by Europeans.

The six inhabited islands have a total of about 8000 inhabitants. Copra cultivation is a major activity in the agricultural sector. More recently, *noni*, a fruit with therapeutic properties, has become a major export to the USA. The public service (health, education, administrative services) is also an important source of employment.

Highlights

- Inspecting the giant tiki at Iipona (Hiva Oa)
- Riding a horse on 'Ua Huka
- Meeting artists on all the islands
- Succumbing to the charms of the peaceful villages of Hatiheu and Anaho (Nuku Hiva)
- Diving with Electra dolphins at Nuku Hiva

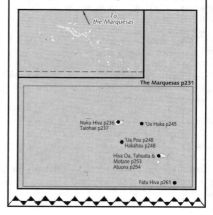

To the Marquesas

The Marquesas p231

Nuku Hiva p236 • • 'Ua Huka p245
Taiohae p237

• 'Ua Pou p248
Hakahau p248

Hiva Oa, Tahuata & •
Motane p253
Atuona p254

Fatu Hiva p261 •

Notoriously underdeveloped until the early 1980s, the Marquesas are beginning to catch up. There are projects aimed at reducing the islands' isolation and dependence on Tahiti, including the development of fishing and agricultural resources, construction of new schools, improvement of roads and inter-island transport, more frequent flight connections and the promotion of tourism.

Ecotourism and the discovery of the islands' cultural, historic and natural heritage offer great potential. The small numbers of visitors who do come here are privileged to experience the mysterious ambience and warm welcome of a place that has to be experienced to be understood.

History

The Marquesas were among the first islands to be settled by the Polynesians during their great South Pacific migrations. They served as a dispersal point for the whole Polynesian triangle, from Hawaii to Easter Island and New Zealand. The exact date of the islands' initial colonisation has not been established; estimates vary from prehistory to between AD 300 and 600.

This initial period of settlement is characterised by the affirmation of a distinct cultural identity, evidenced by the numerous archaeological remains that have survived to modern times, including *tohua* (meeting places), *me'ae* (the Marquesan equivalent of marae), *pae pae* (paved floors or platforms) and *ti'i* (stone carvings, known elsewhere as tiki). See the special section 'Civilisation & Archaeology' for information on traditional Marquesan culture.

The Marquesas' isolation was broken in 1595 when Spanish navigator Alvaro de Mendaña y Neira sighted Fatu Hiva by pure chance. His expedition had left Peru a month earlier with the aim of discovering the hypothetical Terra Australis Incognita. This initial, unexpected contact ended in the death of several islanders. Mendaña's fleet then sailed along past Motane and Hiva Oa and anchored for around 10 days in Vaitahu Bay at Tahuata. Mendaña christened these four islands Las Marquesas de Mendoza in honour of his sponsor the viceroy of Peru, García Hurtado de Mendoza, Marquis of Cañete.

In 1774 Captain Cook lingered for four days on Tahuata during his second voyage. He formed a more cordial relationship with the islanders. Ingraham, the American commander of the *Hope*, 'discovered' the northern group of the Marquesas in 1791, arriving

THE MARQUESAS

slightly ahead of Frenchman Étienne Marchand, whose merchant vessel took on fresh supplies on Tahuata and then landed on 'Ua Pou. In 1797 a young Protestant pastor with the London Missionary Society (LMS), William Crook, landed at Tahuata. Although his attempts at evangelism were unsuccessful, he recorded some irreplaceable impressions of Marquesan society. A Russian geographical and commercial mission took Admiral Krusenstern to Nuku Hiva in 1804. Scientists and artists aboard the vessel published their observations when they returned to Europe.

Haakakai O Te Henua Enana: The Legend of the Land of Men

This creation legend, which likens the birth of the archipelago to the construction of a *ha'e* (house), is one of the most important Marquesan myths.

At the dawn of humanity, two deities, Oatea and Atuana, ruled over the vastness of the ocean. One day Atuana expressed the wish to live in a house. Oatea, her husband, decided to draw upon his divine powers and promised the house would be built by dawn the following day.

He devoted himself to incantations and chose a site on the ocean. He put up two posts and exclaimed, 'This is 'Ua Pou!' He then took a roof beam and placed it on the two posts. After tying it with coconut-fibre rope he cried, 'This is Hiva Oa!' When fitting the rafters he said, 'This is Nuku Hiva!' He made the roof from nine coconut-palms and cried, 'This is Fatu Hiva!' To bury the leftover vegetation strewn over the ground, he dug a hole.

Atuana saw the glimmer of dawn on the horizon. 'This is Tahuata!', Oatea shouted. When Atuana added impatiently, 'I can hear the morning birdsong!', Oatea replied, 'This is Motane!' He quickly threw the scraps into the hole and said, 'This is 'Ua Huka!' He felt his divine powers leaving him with the sunrise and with his last breath he murmured, 'This is Eiao!'

Marquesan Handicrafts

Marquesan handicrafts enjoy an excellent reputation, particularly sculpture. *Ti'i*, pestles, *umete* (bowls), adzes, spears, clubs, fishhooks and other items are carved from *miro* (rosewood), *tou* (a dark, hard-grained wood), bone or volcanic stone. You will also find necklaces and *umu hei*. This is an assortment of gently fragrant plant material such as ylang-ylang, vanilla, pieces of pineapple covered in sandalwood powder, and various other fruits and plants, held together with a plant fibre, which you can use to perfume a room or tie in your hair. Fatu Hiva prides itself on being the only island in French Polynesia to have perpetuated the manufacture of *tapa*, cloth made from beaten bark and decorated with traditional designs.

In most villages there is a small *fare artisanal* (craft centre) with items for exhibition and sale. It may open only when requested or when the *Aranui* is in port. It's also well worth approaching crafts-people directly. Ask around for suggestions. With a little luck you may see the craftspeople work-ing in their studios but be aware that the amount of stock that they carry is variable. Twice a year, usually in June and November, they participate in Marquesan craft exhibitions in Pape'ete and it takes some time to replenish their stocks. Some work is done to order only, so if you stay several days on an island it's worth making a visit as soon as you arrive.

Bring enough cash because you cannot pay by credit card. Prices may be relatively high but they're still lower than in Pape'ete. Expect to pay at least 1500 to 2000 CFP for a small *tapa* piece (up to 10,000 CFP for a piece 1m long), 3000 CFP for a small 15cm-high *ti'i* (perhaps 20,000 CFP for a large one), 5000 CFP for a *umete* or an adze of about 50cm. It's possible to bargain a little, but re-member that this is not a Pacific tradition so don't expect to beat the prices down very much.

From the early 19th century onwards, sea traffic in this area increased. A triangular trading route was established between the Marquesas, China and Australia; during this time the islands' precious sandalwood trees were plundered. Then the Marquesas acted as a supply base for whalers.

In 1813 Nuku Hiva was requisitioned as a US naval base by Captain Porter during the conflicts between the USA and Britain. The US presence was short lived, as Porter's territorial designs were not supported by his government.

French interest in the region grew as a means of countering English expansion in the Pacific. After a reconnaissance voyage in 1838, Rear Admiral Abel Dupetit-Thouars took possession of Tahuata in 1842 in the name of King Louis-Philippe. The Marque-san chieftains, who didn't realise the rami-fications of the act, did nothing to oppose this transfer of sovereignty. Only Iotete, a chieftain from Tahuata, rebelled some months later, but his opposition was in vain.

The Marquesas were quickly margin-alised in favour of Pape'ete for geograph-ical, economic and strategic reasons. Only the Catholic missionaries, who had been ac-tive since their arrival on Tahuata in 1838,

persevered. Their evangelising endeavours were more fruitful than those of their Protes-tant rivals and Catholicism became firmly entrenched in the Marquesas.

Upon contact with Western influences, the foundations of Marquesan society col-lapsed. Whaling crews brought alcohol, firearms and syphilis. The colonial admin-istration and missionaries paid little attention to the ancestral values of the Marquesan people. The stunning decline in population reflects the steady process of disintegration: from an estimated 18,000 in 1842, the popu-lation fell to 5264 in 1887 and 2096 in 1926.

Thanks to the efforts of Louis Rollin, the doctor appointed to the Marquesas from 1923 to 1930, the decline in population was stemmed. Vaccinations, sanitary measures and assistance for new arrivals also helped boost the population.

In the 20th century, the painter Paul Gau-guin and singer Jacques Brel, who both took up residence at Atuona on Hiva Oa, drew world attention to the Marquesas. More recently, the development of local infra-structure has helped lessen the archipelago's isolation, while archaeological discoveries have underlined the significance of Marque-san civilisation.

Getting There & Away

Air There are direct flights between Pape'ete and the Marquesas (three hours) and, once weekly, a direct flight from Rangiroa in the Tuamotus to Nuku Hiva. There are airports at Nuku Hiva, Hiva Oa, 'Ua Huka and 'Ua Pou. The Nuku Ataha (or Terre Déserte) airport on Nuku Hiva gets the most traffic. There are three weekly flights from Nuku Hiva to 'Ua Pou, and one to 'Ua Huka.

High airfares have been a major obstacle to the development of tourism in the Marquesas and, although they have dropped, the costs are still very high. There are Air Tahiti representatives on each of the major islands. Don't forget that the Marquesas are a half-hour ahead of Tahiti time.

Sea The *Taporo IV* and *Aranui* service the Marquesas, departing from Pape'ete and travelling via the Tuamotus (Takapoto and/or Rangiroa). The *Aranui* does about 15 trips a year while the *Taporo IV* departs every two weeks. Taiohae, Hakahau and Atuona are the only places with quays where the ships can dock; at other ports unloading is done with whaleboats. See the Getting Around chapter and the boxed text 'The Aranui'.

Getting Around

Getting around the Marquesas is difficult. The valleys are isolated, making it virtually impossible to do island tours by road, and only the main towns and villages have sealed roads. Some villages have no landing stage and rough seas make landings difficult. The introduction of helicopter shuttles within the northern and southern groups has improved inter-island transport.

Between Islands Visitors should be prepared for a certain amount of uncertainty and definitely should not expect things to go strictly to schedule.

There are various means of transport including Air Tahiti, helicopters, *bonitiers* (old whaleboats, from the term 'Boston whalers') and the cargo ships *Taporo IV* and *Aranui*.

Between the south and north Marquesas there are regular links between Hiva Oa in the southern group and Nuku Hiva in the northern. It's impossible to travel directly from Tahuata or Fatu Hiva in the south to 'Ua Pou or 'Ua Huka in the north without a transit stop on Nuku Hiva or Hiva Oa.

Traffic demands or mechanical breakdowns can complicate the situation. Travel between Nuku Hiva and 'Ua Pou in the northern group is generally fairly easy because these two islands are linked several times a week by plane, helicopter or *bonitier*. Nor is there a problem between Hiva Oa and Tahuata in the southern group. However, there is only one weekly service between Nuku Hiva and 'Ua Huka. Fatu Hiva, in the southern group, is virtually isolated; a *bonitier* stops at the island only once a week.

Nuku Hiva is the main island in terms of transport infrastructure. It's linked to Hiva Oa, 'Ua Pou and 'Ua Huka. It's also the headquarters for Héli Inter Marquises, which provides helicopter services between different centres on the island as well as between 'Ua Pou and the town of Taiohae.

On the Islands Transport around an island is generally very difficult. The roads are rough and the terrain spectacularly steep and divided by numerous valleys, requiring a 4WD. There's no public transport and, as surprising as it may sound, on Nuku Hiva helicopters are the main means of getting around the island.

By sea, *bonitiers* and speedboats usually link the villages more rapidly than 4WDs. When there's not even a track these may be the only means of transport. At villages where there is no jetty, it's necessary to land on the beach.

Helicopter Based at Taiohae (Nuku Hiva), Héli Inter Marquises has been operating in the northern group since 1994. From Taiohae there are three flights a week to 'Ua Pou (the trip takes only a few minutes) and there are flights to 'Ua Huka on demand. It's a convenient but costly service.

Car The 4WD is the most common means of transport. With two exceptions (Atuona and Taiohae), 4WDs are hired with the services of a driver. Self-drive rental has been abandoned because most visitors are not used to the road conditions and inevitably damage the vehicles.

Enforced passenger status does have its advantages. Driving in such conditions is exhausting and dangerous. Distances are measured in hours, not kilometres, and drivers proceed with infinite caution at an average of

THE MARQUESAS

The Aranui

Exploring the Marquesas aboard the *Aranui* (Big Road) is one of the most popular Polynesian adventures. For nearly 20 years, the *Aranui* has been the umbilical cord between Tahiti and the Marquesas, an integral part of life in the archipelago. A real favourite with tourists, this 104m cargo-and-passenger vessel does 15 trips annually. Its 16-day voyage, departing from Pape'ete, takes it to Takapoto in the Tuamotus and the six inhabited islands of the Marquesas (some of them twice) before returning via Rangiroa in the Tuamotus. At the end of 2002, the *Aranui 3* was put into service; it's essentially the same as its predecessor but a bit more comfortable.

The *Aranui* is a real cargo vessel; it has been supplying the remote islands of the Marquesas since 1984 and that is still its primary mission. Unless you're on a yacht, there's simply no other way to visit so many islands in the Marquesas (along with two Tuamotu atolls thrown in as a bonus). Furthermore the prices aren't excessive. Of course, 15 days to visit six islands and two atolls without a whole day (often only a half-day) on any of them can seem rushed, but it does give visitors enough time to get a feel for the archipelago. However, it's worth noting that this is an organised journey. If you don't like to be tied to a schedule or forced to live with a group, then it may not be for you.

The front half of the *Aranui* looks just like any other cargo boat of its size, with two cranes, and holds for all types of goods. The back, however, is more like a cruise ship, with cabins, several decks, a mini-swimming pool, sundeck, dining room, bar, small lounge and library and a video room. There's nothing luxurious about it – everything is simple and functional. Foreign currency and travellers cheques can be changed and credit-card advances made, with appropriate commissions of course. There's a doctor permanently on board and an infirmary but no telephone service.

There are four classes of accommodation. The suites are large cabins with balcony, double bed and bathroom; A-deluxe cabins have double beds and bathroom with bath; A-standard cabins have two single beds and bathroom with shower; and the C-class accommodation is 30 dorm-style beds in groups of two with a locker, a curtain for some privacy and shared bathroom facilities. All the accommodation has air-con, towels are provided and there's a laundry service twice a week. In the restaurant there's a buffet breakfast and a set lunch and dinner with French and Polynesian dishes in copious quantities and, since this is *French* Polynesia, lots of wine.

There's also a rather spartan deck class used by islanders, for whom the ship is their local transport.

The stops are tied up with the loading and unloading of freight, a major event on the islands. You can watch the unceasing ballet of cranes offloading pallets of cement, crates of beer, children's bicycles, drums of fuel, loads of timber and even cars and motorcycles. Locals will be waiting with their 4WDs to load the goods ordered from Pape'ete the previous month. In turn copra, sacks of citrus fruit and *noni*, the new wonder fruit, are loaded aboard.

10km/h to 15km/h. They can also introduce you to local communities and guide you to hard-to-find archaeological sites.

The rental rates are for the vehicle rather than per person, and are astronomical if you're by yourself, so try to get a group together or ask about excursion programmes. Bookings for 4WD tours are essential. Your hotel or *pension* will do this for you but it's wise to meet your driver and check if there will be any communication difficulties. Tours often take a full day so check that the vehicle isn't too crowded.

Hitching Although the traffic volume is very small, hitching is possible and for some solo travellers this is the only way to avoid the high cost of renting a 4WD. Position yourself at the edge of the road or approach 4WD or commercial-vehicle owners directly outside premises such as shops, the post office or *mairie* (town hall). Alternatively, you can try your luck with the valley dwellers, who come into the main towns on a regular basis. All the usual cautions apply.

Boat Speedboats and *bonitiers* are faster than 4WDs and can reach the entrances to all the valleys. Ask at your hotel or *pension* or go directly to the boat owners and inquire about finding other visitors to share the costs. *Bonitiers* can take up to 15 people.

The Aranui

There are no nights ashore; all the shore visits last just a day or half-day and include multilingual guides. There are only three places – Nuku Hiva, 'Ua Pou and Hiva Oa – where the *Aranui* can tie up at a wharf. Elsewhere it has to transfer passengers and freight to *bonitiers* (whaleboats), hefty open boats which can carry about 30 people. Getting on the whaleboats can be tricky if the seas are rough but the crew are strong, efficient and well practised. The longest period at sea without a stop is three days.

While the ship is unloading and loading, passengers make excursions ashore, which may vary from one trip to the next but typically include picnics, visits to pearl farms, scuba diving, snorkelling, glass-bottom boat excursions, 4WD trips to archaeological sites and remote villages and horse-riding excursions. Stops are made at craft centres where you can meet craftspeople and make purchases. Bring cash – nobody will accept credit cards. There is a demonstration of *tapa*-making on Fatu Hiva. Passengers also get to make culinary visits and participate in a gargantuan *kaikai enana*, a traditional Marquesan meal with 10 or more dishes.

European and North American art-history experts, archaeologists and ethnologists are invited on the cruise and bring some cultural insights.

The prices following are for an adult, including all meals and taxes, for a 15- or 16-day trip ex-Pape'ete. Cabins are usually for two people; there are additional costs for solo occupancy.

A suite costs US$4795. An A-deluxe cabin costs US$4145, an A-standard cabin costs US$3535, and a bed in C class costs US$1995. Children aged three to 15 sharing a cabin with adults pay US$975 while children under 12 in C class pay US$1080. It is possible to join the *Aranui* on Nuku Hiva just for eight days in the Marquesas: deck class costs US$1390, A-standard costs US$2395, A-deluxe costs US$2790 and a suite costs US$3210. Tourists are dissuaded from using deck class, but if you are just going from one island to the next and there's room, there shouldn't be a problem. Contact the tour guides at the stopovers and count on about 3000 CFP from one island in the Marquesas to another. Meals are included but are not taken in the dining room with the other passengers. Excursions are not included. Only a mattress is provided, so bring a sleeping bag.

Bookings are essential and peak periods (July-August and December) are booked out months in advance. Contact your travel agency or go directly to the shipowner, the **Compagnie Polynésienne de Transport Maritime** (CPTM; ☎ 42 62 40, 43 76 60, fax 43 48 89; e reservations@aranui.com; w www.aranui.com; BP 220, Pape'ete; open 7.30am-11.30am & 1.30pm-5pm Mon-Fri). CPTM's Pape'ete office is at the entrance to the Motu Uta port.

In France, contact **Quotidien Voyages** (☎ 01 53 63 84 50, fax 01 53 63 84 55; e quotidien voyages@wanadoo.fr). In the USA, contact **CPTM** (☎ 650-574 2575, 1-800 972 7268; e cptm@aranui.com; 2028 El Camino Real S, Suite B, San Mateo, CA 94403).

Tahuata has a communal *bonitier* that runs a twice-weekly ferry service to Hiva Oa.

Hitching a boat ride is possible; ask boat owners in the marinas or passing yachts. Another possibility is to hitch a ride with the medical or administrative personnel who regularly do a one-day round of the remote valleys by speedboat or 4WD.

The route of the *Kaoha Nui*, a fairly large vessel that provides inter-island transport for sports tournaments, religious celebrations and school outings, is totally unpredictable. If it should happen to moor, jump on. Cargo ships pass at more or less regular intervals and may let you make a few short hops. Ask about arrival dates of the *Aranui* or *Taporo IV*.

The Northern Group

The northern group consists of three main inhabited islands – Nuku Hiva, 'Ua Huka and 'Ua Pou; and the deserted *motu* (islets) further to the north – Hatu Iti (Motu Iti), Eiao, Hatutu (Hatutaa), Motu One (Sand Island) and the Clark Sandbank.

NUKU HIVA
pop 2372 • area 340 sq km

The main island of the northern group, and the largest in the archipelago, Nuku Hiva is the administrative and economic capital of the Marquesas.

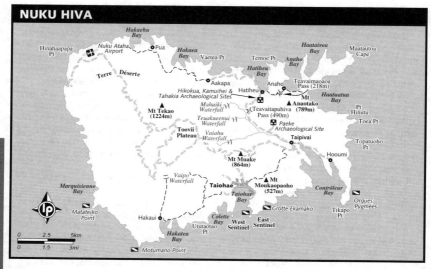

NUKU HIVA

Nuku Hiva has the largest population of the Marquesas but one of the lowest population densities. Settlement is concentrated in Taiohae on the south coast, Hatiheu on the north coast and Taipivai in the east. Hamlets such as Anaho, Hooumi, Aakapa and Pua are home to only a handful of people.

Nuku Hiva was formed from two volcanoes, stacked one on top of the other to form two concentric calderas. The top of the main caldera forms a jagged framework that surrounds the Toovii Plateau; the broken-mouthed caldera of the secondary volcano reaches its highest point at Mt Muake (864m) and outlines a huge natural amphitheatre. At its foot is a vast harbour, around which curls Taiohae, the main town. Deep bays cut into the south and east coasts. On the north coast, erosion by wind and rain has shaped impressive basalt *aiguilles* (needles).

In 1791 the American Captain Ingraham was the first Westerner to see Nuku Hiva. In the first half of the 19th century, sandalwood merchants and whalers put into port in Taiohae Bay. A fortress was built on Nuku Hiva in 1813 by the American Captain Porter in a fleeting attempt at annexation of the island. Catholic missionaries reached the island in 1839 and the religion took hold when the archipelago was seized by the French in 1842. During the second half of the 19th century the island was ravaged by disease.

There are frequent flight connections to Nuku Hiva from Pape'ete. The island offers magnificent landscapes, varied accommodation, high-quality handicrafts (particularly sculpture), interesting archaeological heritage and activities such as diving, walking and horse riding.

Information

The **tourist office** (☎/fax 92 03 73; e *marquises@mail.pf; open 7.30am-11.30am Mon-Fri*) is in the *mairie* building in Taiohae. Deborah Kimitete at the tourist office speaks English and can provide you with information. Some free brochures are also available.

The **Banque Socredo** (☎ 92 03 63; open 7.30am-11.30am & 1.30pm-4pm Mon-Fri) is on the Taiohae seafront, on the corner of the street that leads to Vallée des Français. It handles exchange and credit-card withdrawals and also has an ATM inside.

The **post office** (open 7am-3pm Mon-Thur, 7am-2pm Fri) is on the eastern side of the bay, opposite the *gendarmerie* (police station). Phonecard telephone booths can be found at the marina, in front of the post office, at the cargo-ship quay, near the Kovivi restaurant, at the airport, in Taipivai and in Hatiheu.

Several doctors, surgeons and dentists are based at the **hospital** (☎ 91 20 00), 100m from the post office in Taiohae. Each village has an infirmary or first-aid post.

Taiohae

The economic and administrative capital of the archipelago, Taiohae has about 1700 inhabitants. The town hugs Taiohae Bay for nearly 3.5km, from the cargo-ship quay in the east to the Nuku Hiva Keikahanui Pearl Lodge in the west. Nearly all the town's hotels, restaurants, shops and services are clustered together on the seashore.

Three roads run back from the seafront and climb up into valleys, one of them crossing the Pakiu Valley and continuing to Taipivai. The entrance to the bay is flanked by two islets, the East Sentinel and the West Sentinel.

Climbing the Meau Valley for less than 1km you reach a restored **me'ae**, with a small contemporary *ti'i*. An enormous banyan dominates the site. To the west of the town, between the cemetery and the nautical club, stands the **Herman Melville Memorial**, a magnificent wooden sculpture by Kahee Taupotini.

Approaching the centre, 700m further along, is the **Piki Vehine Pae Pae**, also known as Temehea. Rebuilt for the 1989 Marquesas Festival, this open-air museum in the form of a *ha'e* (traditional house) contains modern sculptures and a dozen magnificent *ti'i* made by the island's sculptors and by artisans from Easter Island. In front of the *ha'e*, a sculpture representing a trad-itional Marquesan house is decorated with scenes symbolising unity. Other images include a double-hulled war canoe containing an eel (an animal that featured in many legends), a man-bird, an egg with a *ti'i* head and a *moai* (Easter Island *ti'i*) head.

About a hundred metres east stands a stone cross at a crossroad, marking the commencement of the Catholic mission. Take the road that turns left to **Notre-Dame Cathedral of the Marquesas Islands**, built on the Tohua Mauia, a sacred place venerated by the ancient Marquesans. The stone used in the construction of the church comes from the archipelago's six inhabited islands.

On the seafront, opposite the Kamake shop, is the **Monument to the Dead**, an obelisk bearing a commemorative plaque in honour of Étienne Marchand. This is a popular area for Sunday pastimes; the men play *pétanque* while the women play bingo in the *fare* beside the shipping quay.

The **Tohua Koueva** is 1.5km up the Pakiu Valley on the road to Taipivai. It takes about 15 minutes to reach by walking up to the machine that crushes stones for road-building, crossing the stream and walking along the small track. Restoration began in 1998 and it was opened during the 1999–2000 Marquesas Festival. It's believed this communal site, with its paved esplanade, belonged to the war chief Pakoko. During a confrontation

THE MARQUESAS

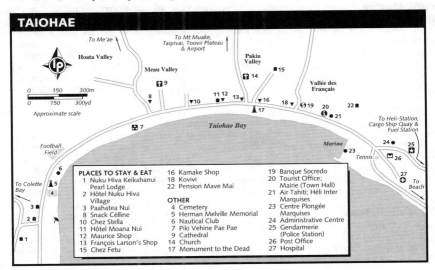

TAIOHAE

To Me'ae
To Mt Muake, Taipivai, Toovii Plateau & Airport
Hoata Valley
Pakiu Valley
Meau Valley
14
15
9
Vallée des Français
8
11 12
13
16
18
19
20
22
10
17
21
Approximate scale
0 150 300m
0 150 300yd
7
Taiohae Bay
To Heli-Station, Cargo Ship Quay & Fuel Station
Football Field
Marina
24
25
23
Tennis
26
6
27
To Colette Bay
5
To Beach
4
3
2
1

PLACES TO STAY & EAT
1 Nuku Hiva Keikahanui Pearl Lodge
2 Hôtel Nuku Hiva Village
3 Paahatea Nui
8 Snack Célline
10 Chez Stella
11 Hôtel Moana Nui
12 Maurice Shop
13 François Larson's Shop
15 Chez Fetu

16 Kamake Shop
18 Kovivi
22 Pension Mave Mai

OTHER
4 Cemetery
5 Herman Melville Memorial
6 Nautical Club
7 Piki Vehine Pae Pae
9 Cathedral
14 Church
17 Monument to the Dead

19 Banque Socredo
20 Tourist Office; Mairie (Town Hall)
21 Air Tahiti; Héli Inter Marquises
23 Centre Plongée Marquises
24 Administrative Centre
25 Gendarmerie (Police Station)
26 Post Office
27 Hospital

THE MARQUESAS

with the French in 1845 he killed five soldiers on this *tohua* and was subsequently executed by the French.

Colette Bay

Colette Bay, a small cove beyond the western spur of Taiohae Bay, is also called Haaotupa, a derivative of Haeotupa (House of Tupa). According to legend, Tupa was a great builder, a sort of Marquesan Hercules. The enormous diamond-shaped rock on the hill between the bay and Taiohae is said to be his unfinished house. Tupa wanted his house to reach right up to heaven and, as he was afraid of the gods, he worked by night. Unfortunately, his sister, who was supposed to warn him at the first light of dawn, was misled by the crowing of the cockerel and so the house remained earthbound.

Colette Bay is 3.5km from the centre of Taiohae, and can be reached on foot, on horseback, by speedboat or by 4WD. To get there, take the track that goes up to the Nuku Hiva Keikahanui Pearl Lodge, at the western side of the bay. Instead of branching left to go to the hotel, keep right and continue for about 2km. The track climbs along the western side of the cove and then descends to the beach at Colette Bay. It's an ideal place for a picnic, but take something to protect yourself from the *nono* (sand midge).

Mt Muake

The grey mass of Mt Muake (864m) forms the backdrop to Taiohae Bay and affords spectacular views. It is used as a launch site for hang-gliders.

Mt Muake can be reached on foot or by 4WD along a picturesque track. From the seafront at Taiohae, near François Larson's shop, take the road that goes up towards Pakiu Valley. Continue for nearly 7km to the first fork, go left, and continue 4km until you reach another fork. Turn left again into the forest (if you go straight you're heading towards Toovii and the airport) and continue for about 2km to the radio relay station. At the summit, be particularly careful because the rock is crumbly and the face vertical.

Toovii Plateau

Toovii Plateau, crossed by the Taiohae-Terre Déserte (airport) track, has an average altitude of 800m. Partly surrounded by a chain of mountains, a welcome coolness can be enjoyed here, in marked contrast to the sweltering heat of the bay areas. With its plantations of conifers and resinous trees and vast pastures where cattle graze, it looks surprisingly like the mountains of Bavaria. Toovii supplies the whole archipelago with meat, dairy produce and timber. There is a *ferme-auberge* (a farm offering accommodation) here (see Places to Stay later in the Nuku Hiva section).

Hakaui Valley

About 8km west of Taiohae as the crow flies, the Hakaui Valley is one of the most imposing sights on Nuku Hiva. On either side of the river, vertical walls rise to nearly 800m and **Vaipo Waterfall**, one of the highest in the world at 350m, flows vertically into a basin through a narrow gutter. It's a fine natural swimming pool but during prolonged droughts it can be reduced to a mere trickle.

Numerous remains attest to ancient human occupation; the valley was once the fiefdom of King Te Moana and Queen Vaekehu. A paved road, which was an ancient royal road, goes up the valley following the river past **pae pae**, **tohua** and **ti'i** hidden behind a tangle of vegetation.

From Taiohae, the valley can be reached by speedboat (about 20 minutes), and on foot or on horseback by a 12km bridleway. Take a picnic, some waterproof sandals, bathers, mosquito repellent and a waterproof bag for your camera. From the bay where the boat anchors, allow two hours to reach the waterfall on foot. This path, which is not particularly difficult except for a few fords, follows the river and includes stretches of the ancient paved royal road. At Hakaui Bay, walk 100m east to the magnificent **Hakatea Bay**.

Hatiheu

Scottish writer Robert Louis Stevenson succumbed to the charm of this village on the north of the island. Its focal point is a wooden **church** with a yellow facade and twin symmetrical red steeples. To the rear, the cemetery encroaches on the hill behind the church. The **seafront** is planted with lawns and coconut palms and decorated with *ti'i*, the recent work of local sculptors. On one of the peaks to the west, at a height of 300m, is a white **statue** of the Virgin Mary, erected in 1872.

The tiny *mairie* on the seafront houses a small **museum** with a collection of traditional Marquesan artefacts. Yvonne Katupa, mayor of the village and owner of the village's only *pension*, actively promotes Marquesan cultural heritage.

From Taipivai, follow the main road inland and west. The track deteriorates as it climbs to the impressive **Teavaitapuhiva Pass** (490m), 7.5km from Taipivai, from which there are magnificent views. Four kilometres further on and shortly before Hatiheu, **me'ae** are concealed under the vegetation to the right and left.

Taipivai

The ancient fiefdom of the Taipi tribes, Taipivai lies northeast of Taiohae. The town carpets the floor of a river valley and its single street follows the river's course for nearly 2km. At the eastern end of the village the river rushes into Contrôleur Bay.

The majority of Taipivai's inhabitants are farmers and the village is filled with the subtle perfume of vanilla, the cultivation of which is well suited to this fertile alluvial plain. Pods can be purchased when stocks are available (1000 CFP to 1500 CFP for 100g); ask in the village. The production of copra is another important activity in Taipivai.

In the early 19th century, the people of Taipivai fiercely resisted the incursions of the American Captain Porter, who tried to annex the island in 1813. His soldiers used cannons to massacre the population.

Literature has also made Taipivai well known. In July 1842 the American whaler *Acushnet* put in at Taiohae and on board was Herman Melville, future author of *Moby Dick* and *Billy Budd*. Melville jumped ship and spent three weeks at Taipivai. He wrote of his unusual experiences in *Typee*, which was published in 1846.

Allow 1½ hours by 4WD to reach Taipivai from Taiohae; take the road at right angles to the seafront in front of François Larson's shop.

Hooumi

Once inhabited by the fierce Teavaaki, this charming hamlet is about 4km east of Taipivai. The track from Taipivai, initially going along the cliff top road, affords marvellous views over Contrôleur Bay. On the left hand side of the track through the village, there is a row of **pae pae** on which houses have now been built, and the usual copra-drying sheds. The village also has a picturesque small timber **church**. The track ends at a stunning white-sand **beach**. Unfortunately the beach is plagued by *nono* and mosquitoes.

Anaho

In 1888 Robert Louis Stevenson moored in Anaho Bay while he was cruising the Pacific on the *Casco*. The setting inspired him to write many pages eulogising the unsettling beauty of the place.

A few families live in this peaceful hamlet. The long white-sand **beach**, infested with *nono*, stretches for nearly 1km and the bay is perfectly sheltered from the wind and the swell, contrasting sharply with the coves on the other Marquesas. It's a popular anchorage for visiting yachts. The only **coral reef** on the Marquesas is found here, creating a lagoon-like effect. Along the shore are copra-drying sheds, a magnificent **coconut plantation** and a tiny chapel.

Anaho is less than 10 minutes by speedboat from Hatiheu, or can be reached by foot along a picturesque track. Wear walking shoes and take water and mosquito repellent. At the crossroad 100m east of the Hinakonui restaurant, take the sealed road up to the right. About 500m further on, there's a small clearing; if you have a vehicle it's best to leave it here. The start of the path is on the left, beyond the little bridge, 100m uphill from the white house built on a *pae pae*. It's about a 45-minute walk to Anaho Beach.

From the **Teavaimaoaoa Pass** (218m) there's an unbroken view over Anaho Bay, and the descent, right through the middle of a huge coconut plantation, is quite steep.

Aakapa

On the north coast, this village is in a superb setting characterised by peaks forming a sharp-edged wall. Aakapa can be reached by the path from Hatiheu or by speedboat.

Beaches

Nuku Hiva has several beautiful white-and black-sand beaches. **Taiohae** has two beaches, one to the west, which is not particularly attractive, and another to the east (close to the tennis courts, below the hospital). The beach at **Colette Bay** is remote and wild, like the one at **Hakaui Bay**.

THE MARQUESAS

Nono a Gogo

Prepare to face a (nearly) invisible but (sort of) deadly enemy in the Marquesas: the *nono*. The bites of this tiny endemic sand midge are itchy and can easily become infected. White *nono* live on beaches, while black ones inhabit vegetation. The only prevention is to make liberal use of *monoi* (fragrant oil), or insect repellent, and to cover up well.

▲▲▲▲▲▲▲▲▲▲▲▲▲▲▲

The most beautiful beaches on the island are, without doubt, the ones to the north at **Anaho** and in the adjacent bay at **Haatuatua**. Unfortunately *nono* will give you a hard time, so bring mosquito repellent.

Archaeological Sites

Hikokua One of the most attractive archaeological sites in the Marquesas, Hikokua was discovered by the archaeologist R Suggs in 1957 and restored by Hatiheu locals from 1987. It dates from around AD 1250 and was in use until the 1800s. Once a place of ceremony and human sacrifice, today ancient sculptures stand alongside modern works.

The **tohua**, a vast, central, rectangular esplanade, stretches north-south and was used for dance performances at community festivals. It's flanked by tiers of small flat basalt blocks that were used as steps for the spectators.

On the terrace stand two modern **sculptures** by Uki Haiti, and a flat rock that was used for various purposes, including solo dances and rituals associated with puberty.

To the southeast of the esplanade are nine **Christian tombs**. They probably date from the time of the first missionaries' arrival, after the abandonment of the site.

The platform at the bottom, on the northern side of the esplanade towards the ocean, was the **tuu**, or ceremonial activity centre. It's flanked with *keetu* (volcanic rock) tiles and to the front are three **ti'i**, one of which is relatively well preserved. It was on this *tuu* that sacrifices and display of the victims' bodies took place. The chief's residence stood at the northeast corner of the esplanade.

On the platform immediately to the left, at the entrance to the site, is a metre-long **ti'i** phallus. Nearby is an **ua ma** (food pit).

Today the site is regularly used for traditional dances, particularly the impressive Dance of the Pig (see the special section 'Tahitian Dance').

Coming from Taipivai, this site is about 1km from the Chez Yvonne *pension*, on the right and set back. You can get there along a small track suitable for vehicles. Ask at the *pension* for Alphonse Puhetini (also known as Rua) to accompany you, as he has worked with the archaeologists in this valley.

Kamuihei & Tahakia About 300m towards Taipivai from the Hikokua site, this vast site spreads across both sides of the track. A team led by the archaeologist Pierre Ottino began restoration in 1998.

It's thought the Puhioho clan lived here. The site was built around a stream and assembled numerous tribal architectural elements: there are vestiges of *pae pae*, *tohua*, *me'ae*, petroglyphs, *ua ma* and sacred banyans. The importance and sheer number of these structures testifies to the dense population this valley once sheltered. The site is spectacular, its air of mystery emphasised by the large moss-covered basalt rocks and the enormous banyans. It has not been dated.

Beside the track a **ha'e** has been rebuilt on the largest of the *pae pae*. Further along a **me'ae** stands at the foot of an immense banyan, along with a pit, presumably dug for the remains of sacrifices or for taboo objects that it was necessary to avoid contact with. Other pits are scattered about the site; these *ua ma* may have stocked *popoi*, the dough fermented from *uru* (breadfruit), as a provision during times of scarcity. A little higher are two large rocks about 2.5m high by 3m wide and decorated with **petroglyphs**. There are clearly visible representations of turtles, fish, and the eyes of a *ti'i*, and human figures that could be representations of ancestors or divinities. It's estimated that the valley contains more than 500 such images.

On the other side of the track is the restored Tahakia **tohua**, one of the biggest in the Marquesas, and some *pae pae*. This was the site of the warrior Keikahanui's clan.

It is difficult for the nonexpert to understand the significance of the site, so it's best to get a guide who can explain it to you (contact Yvonne Katupa at Chez Yvonne *pension* in Hatiheu).

Paeke This site features two well-maintained me'ae, flanked by a set of brick-coloured ti'i. Massive and squat, with well-developed lower limbs, they radiate a forbidding power that makes them look like petrified Cerberuses. The me'ae further up the hill has a pit into which human remains were thrown.

To get to the site from the little bridge in the centre of Taipivai, take the Hatiheu road (uphill) for about 1.5km until you leave the village. At the blue house on the right, follow the path to the right, which goes up through the coconut plantation. It's a 20- or 30-minute steep walk uphill, so take some mosquito repellent, a hat and sunscreen.

Activities

There are a dozen magnificent **diving** sites, which are very different to those of the Society group or the Tuamotus. There's a diving centre at Taiohae, and diving with Electra dolphins at Nuku Hiva is a highlight of the region. See the special section 'Diving' for more details.

There are good **walking** tracks all over the island, including the hikes to the Hakaui waterfall, to Colette Bay and from Hatiheu to Anaho.

There are good opportunities for **horse riding** on Nuku Hiva. From Taiohae, it is easy to reach Colette Bay on horseback. Other popular rides are to the Hakaui waterfall, along the track between Hatiheu and Aakapa and on the Taiohae ridgeline.

In Taiohae ask at your hotel or contact Patrice Tamarii at **Le Ranch** (☎ 92 06 35; one-hour guided rides adult/child 2000/1000 CFP, day rides 8000 CFP). He has docile and very well-trained horses with leather saddles. There are rides for all levels, from one-hour rides in the Taiohae Valley, to day trips to the Taiohae ridge or the southwest coast, and outings lasting several days.

In Hatiheu contact Yvonne Katupa at **Chez Yvonne** (☎ 92 02 97; guided rides 5000 CFP per day).

The only **parasailing club** (☎ 92 05 29, 92 05 30) in the Marquesas is in Taiohae. There's a takeoff platform at the top of Mt Muake. Experienced parasailers leap off the sheer cliff with its absolutely vertical drop. Beginners can take their first steps on the slopes of the hills above the town. At the time of writing there was no parasailing (parapente) instructor at Taiohae, so only experienced members of the club could participate in this activity; a three-month membership costs 1500 CFP. It costs 3000 CFP to rent a parasail for one flight.

Héli Inter Marquises (☎ 92 02 17, fax 92 08 40; e helico-nuku@mail.pf) operates scenic 20-minute **helicopter flights** for a minimum of four people at 16,500 CFP each. The circuit makes a loop from Taiohae over the Hakaui Valley towards the Toovii Plateau, then north to the needles of Aakapa and the village of Hatiheu, passing Anaho Bay and the beach at Haatuatua, before turning south towards the Taipivai Valley and Mt Muake. Inquire as early as possible so a group can be organised. It's often possible to join a group from the Aranui when it is in port.

Organised Tours

Pua Excursions (☎ 92 02 94, 92 06 12, fax 92 01 35) offers three-day tours. The itinerary includes Toovii, Taiohae, Taipivai, Hatiheu and Anaho. The price of 42,000 CFP (for two people) includes accommodation and meals.

Places to Stay

Nuku Hiva has accommodation ranging from a room in a pension to traditional bungalows and good-quality hotels.

Taiohae A note-worthy option in the budget category, located in the centre of Taiohae, is **Chez Fetu** (☎ 92 03 66; rooms per person 2200 CFP). Chez Fetu has a fully equipped bungalow for three people with kitchen and bathroom (cold water only). The atmosphere is simple and homely. To get there, follow the small path that starts at the west side of the Kamake shop for 200m.

Paahatea Nui (Chez Justin et Julienne; ☎ 92 00 97, fax 92 00 97; rooms/bungalows per person 2700/4300 CFP), next to Hôtel Nuku Hiva Village, has six rooms with shared bathroom and two bungalows with their own bathroom. Apart from breakfast (700 CFP) no meals are available at this pension, but you can use the kitchen.

Hôtel Moana Nui (☎ 92 03 30, fax 92 00 02; singles/doubles with breakfast 7400/8000 CFP, with half-board 9600/13,500 CFP, with full board 12,900/17,400 CFP), a more upmarket option, is ideally situated right in the centre of Taiohae on the seafront. The seven

THE MARQUESAS

spotless rooms have fans and bathrooms (with hot water). Meals are served in the ground floor restaurant, credit cards are accepted and there's a laundry service.

Pension Mave Mai (*☎/fax 92 08 10; e pension-mavemai@mail.pf; singles/doubles 6200/7300 CFP, with half-board 8900/12,600 CFP*) is a quality *pension* that has a good reputation. It is to the east of Taiohae, near the marina. It has six rooms with bathroom, fan and terrace or balcony. Excursions to the main sights are offered, as well as dolphin-watching trips. Credit cards are accepted.

Hôtel Nuku Hiva Village (*☎ 92 01 94, fax 92 05 97; singles/doubles 7000/8000 CFP*), a lush green property facing the beach at the western end of Taiohae Bay, has six local-style *fare*, which sleep two to three people and have a bathroom (with hot water), fan and small veranda. Add 3800 CFP per person for half-board. Meals are served in the large restaurant *fare*.

Nuku Hiva Keikahanui Pearl Lodge (*☎ 92 07 10, fax 92 07 11; w www.pearlresorts.com; bungalows 29,000 CFP*) is the most luxurious establishment in the northern Marquesas. Overlooking the western extremity of Taiohae Bay, it has 20 air-con bungalows. Add 6000 CFP per person for half-board. All sorts of activities are offered and there's a swimming pool.

Hatiheu The excellent *pension* **Chez Yvonne** (*☎ 92 02 97, fax 92 01 28; e hinakonui@mail.pf; bungalows per person with breakfast/half-board/full board 4800/8500/11,700 CFP*) comprises four clean, although rather cramped, local-style bungalows for two people and one family bungalow with bathroom (cold water only). They are situated opposite the seafront, at the entrance to the village as you come from Taipivai. Meals are served in the Hinakonui restaurant a little further on. Airport transfers are 4000 CFP per person one-way. Travellers cheques are accepted.

Toovii Plateau For something out of the ordinary there's **Ferme-auberge de Toovii** (*☎ 92 07 50, fax 92 00 04; e ferme-auberge@mail.pf; singles/doubles 5400/7500 CFP, with half-board 7500/11,700 CFP, with full board 9600/16,000 CFP*). At 800m altitude, this *ferme-auberge* (farm-inn), in the heart of the island's main crater, is completely

isolated. There are five clean bungalows with bathroom and terrace, and there is a dining room and a bar. Meals are prepared using meat from animals raised on the farm and vegetables from the farm's market garden.

Anaho There are two *pensions* at Anaho, where the quietness of a coconut plantation, the magical setting of Anaho Bay and the sea only metres away await you. However, it's only accessible by foot (about 45 minutes from Hatiheu) or by speedboat (also from Hatiheu). Coming by foot along the track from Hatiheu, follow the path down to the beach and head north for a couple of hundred metres.

Te Pua Hinako (*☎ 92 04 14; rooms with breakfast/half-board/full board per person 2800/4400/6000 CFP*) is a favourite weekend getaway for people from Taiohae. There are two clean though rather impersonal rooms, which can sleep three people, with shared bathroom (cold water only) and an equipped kitchen.

Kaoti Ae (*☎ 92 00 08; bungalows per person 2700 CFP*) is a few metres away, offering small bungalows with bathroom and terrace. Prices include breakfast and you can order meals.

Places to Eat

Taiohae On the waterfront, 200m west of Hôtel Moana Nui, **Chez Stella** (*dishes 850 CFP; open lunch & dinner Mon-Fri, until noon Sat*) is a permanently stationed roulotte attached to a small *fare*. It offers dishes such as chow mein or chicken curry for lunch (750 CFP) to eat in or take away, snacks for 300 to 700 CFP, refreshments and some desserts. Crepes are served on Friday and Saturday.

Kovivi (*☎ 92 00 14; set lunch 1400 CFP, dishes 1500-3500 CFP, desserts 500-1000 CFP; closed Sun & Mon evening*) is hidden by lush vegetation beside Banque Socredo. The restaurant has an excellent reputation, offering classic French cuisine with tropical influences. There's a good set lunch or you can order à la carte. The chef's speciality is smoked lobster for 3500 CFP. Wine by the bottle starts at 2200 CFP; half-litre carafes cost 550 CFP. There's a children's menu for 1100 CFP. Kovivi closes during July.

The hotel restaurants are also worth exploring.

The restaurant at **Hôtel Moana Nui** (☎ 92 03 30; dishes 1200-2400 CFP; open lunch & dinner Mon-Sat) offers traditional cuisine at reasonable prices in a pleasant setting. The lunchtime dish of the day is 1300 CFP. You can also choose from salads, pizzas (1400 CFP), a generous serving of sashimi (1200 CFP), fish and meat dishes (from 1200 to 2400 CFP) and snacks such as a Moana Nui burger (1200 CFP). Credit cards are accepted.

The restaurant at **Hotel Nuku Hiva Village** (☎ 92 01 94; dishes 800-1500 CFP; open lunch & dinner daily), to the west of the bay and right by the beach, is in an airy, local-style *fare* with a thatched roof supported by columns carved with *ti'i*. Credit cards are accepted.

There's also a restaurant at the **Nuku Hiva Keikahanui Pearl Lodge**.

In the centre of Taiohae **Kamake**, **François Larson** and **Maurice** are three well-stocked shops on the waterfront selling everything from food to hardware. They are open 7.30am to 11.30am and 2.30pm to 5.30pm Monday to Saturday, and on Sunday morning after mass. Kamake also serves as a bakery from 5.30am; the entrance is at the side. There's another **bakery** on the waterfront, about 200m west of Hôtel Moana Nui but there's no sign. It sells some pastries also (120 CFP for a *firifiri* or sweet fritter). **Snack Céline**, on the waterfront and very close to the river, is also a grocery store.

Toovii Plateau At **Ferme-auberge de Toovii** (☎ 92 07 50; set menus 2000-4000 CFP; open daily) you can enjoy meals made with organic produce, with almost all ingredients being grown on the farm itself.

Hatiheu At the *pension* Chez Yvonne, **Restaurant Hinakonui** (☎ 92 02 97; dishes 1600-2500 CFP) has a deservedly good reputation. Its magnificent terrace opens directly onto the seafront, 50m from the church. The menu includes *poisson cru* (raw fish), lobster and shrimp. To have the chance to try the excellent Marquesan oven (pork and fish wrapped in foil, placed in an oven hollowed out of the ground, covered with earth and baked), you need at least 12 people, so contact Chez Yvonne to see if the *Aranui* or some other group will be visiting. There's also a popular bar here. Reservations are essential.

Getting There & Away

Air The **Air Tahiti** office (☎ 92 03 41; open 8am-noon & 2pm-4pm Mon-Fri) is on the eastern side of the cove at Tahiohae, on the seafront. These opening hours are somewhat theoretical as the company's representative is also on duty at the **Nuku Ataha airport** (☎ 92 01 45) on days when there is a flight. On those days there's a note on the office door. Credit cards are accepted.

There are six to seven flights a week between Pape'ete and Nuku Hiva in each direction (26,500 CFP one-way, three hours). One of these flights stops at Rangiroa in the Tuamotus.

Within the Marquesas there are flights from Nuku Hiva to Atuona (Hiva Oa; 9800 CFP one-way), 'Ua Huka and 'Ua Pou (both cost 5800 CFP one-way). Depending on the season, there are four or five return Nuku Hiva–Atuona flights weekly. There is one Nuku Hiva–'Ua Huka return flight a week on Thursday, and there are three Nuku Hiva – 'Ua Pou return flights weekly; these flights connect with services from/to Pape'ete and cost 29,800 CFP through to Pape'ete.

Héli Inter Marquises (☎ 92 02 17, fax 92 08 40; e helico-nuku@mail.pf; open 8.30am-noon & 1.30pm-4pm Mon-Thurs, 8.30am-noon & 1.30pm-3pm Fri) is next to Air Tahiti on the seafront at Taiohae.

There are regular helicopter shuttle services to Hakahau ('Ua Pou; 12,500 CFP one-way, 15 minutes) on Wednesday, Friday and Sunday. The heliport, at the eastern end of Taiohae Bay, overhangs the cargo-ship quay. Credit cards are accepted.

Boat It is possible to charter a *bonitier* to go to 'Ua Pou or 'Ua Huka (about 50,000 CFP for the crossing). Contact **Laurent (Teiki) Falchetto** (☎ 92 05 78) or **Xavier Curvat** (☎ 92 00 88), the director of the dive centre.

The *Aranui* and the *Taporo IV* stop at Nuku Hiva and dock at the end of the bay in Taiohae. The *Aranui* goes to Taipivai and Hatiheu as well as Taiohae.

Getting Around
A network of tracks links the airport, Taiohae, Taipivai, Hooumi, Hatiheu and Aakapa.

To/From the Airport It takes at least two hours to reach the airport from Taiohae along a bumpy, winding track, longer if it has rained and the ground is muddy – and it's only 18km as the crow flies!

Approved 4WD taxis that carry four to six people generally wait for each flight. It is nevertheless wise to book, either through your hotel or *pension*, or directly by contacting the taxi drivers: **Nuku Hiva Transports** (☎ 92 06 08), **Rose Marie Tours** (☎ 92 05 96) or **Huku Tours** (☎ 92 04 89). It's also possible to hitch.

Héli Inter Marquises provides a helicopter shuttle service coinciding with each Pape'ete–Nuku Hiva flight, going to Taiohae, Hatiheu and Taipivai. The trip costs 7000 CFP per person (half-fare for children under 11) and takes eight minutes. Reservations are necessary for flights going to the airport, but not from it.

4WD You can rent 4WDs with or without a driver. Taiohae has several 4WD operators who make excursions to the various tourist sites and villages. Your accommodation can make arrangements or you can book directly (see To/From the Airport earlier in the Getting Around section for phone numbers).

From Taiohae, for the whole vehicle (which will take four passengers), expect to pay 3000 to 5000 CFP to Mt Muake, 15,000 CFP to Taipivai, 20,000 CFP to Hatiheu and 25,000 CFP to Aakapa. The hotels in Taiohae will try to group their customers. It costs about 6000 CFP between Hatiheu and Aakapa.

Charles Monbaerts (*Hôtel Moana Nui*) has a four-seater Suzuki for 11,000 CFP for 24 hours including insurance and unlimited mileage. This is good value if you are alone, but for two or more people it's cheaper and less stressful to get a vehicle with driver. There's a fuel station on the cargo-ship quay.

'UA HUKA

pop 571 • area 83 sq km
'Ua Huka lies 50km east of Nuku Hiva and 56km northeast of 'Ua Pou. 'Ua Huka's topography is quite different from these nearby islands, yet it rarely features in the itinerary of travellers, who tend to concentrate on its two neighbours.

The island consists of two volcanoes stacked on top of one another. The caldera of the main volcano forms an amphitheatre facing southwest to southeast, while the secondary volcano occupies only the southeastern part of the large caldera. Vaikivi Plateau, covered with impenetrable clumps of vegetation, occupies the northern edge of the island, while the island's three villages – Vaipaee, Hane and Hokatu – nestle around the edges of steep-sided valleys on the south coast.

'Ua Huka, the driest island in all of French Polynesia, features almost desertlike plains in the south. Between Hane and Vaipaee there are some wonderfully chaotic landscapes, accentuated by free-ranging herds of semi-wild horses (hence the nickname 'Island of Horses'). Goats also roam free and several offshore islets are home to thousands of nesting birds.

The island boasts archaeological treasures such as the Hane *ti'i* and the Vaikivi petroglyphs, and the Marquesas' first museum devoted entirely to archaeology. Each of the three villages has a *fare artisanal* (craft centre) and, surprisingly perhaps, a first-rate arboretum is the pride of the island.

Information

There is no bank on 'Ua Huka. The **post office** (*open 7.30am-11.30am & 1pm-2.30pm Mon-Fri; also open when the Aranui calls in*) is in Vaipaee, next to the museum. Each village has phonecard telephone booths and an infirmary or first-aid post.

Vaipaee

The island's main town is at the end of a very deep, narrow inlet, which measures about 1km and is rightly named Invisible Bay. When the *Aranui* comes in, it manoeuvres in a space the size of a handkerchief and ties up to the rock face with hawsers.

The village stretches along the valley with the church, the museum, the post office and *mairie* constituting the centre. The rest of the township is in the adjacent valley to the east, while there is an incongruous housing development a few kilometres away towards Hane.

The **museum** (*admission free*), in the centre of Vaipaee, opened in 1987. Its size may be modest, but it has great symbolic value for the heritage-proud Marquesans.

The collection includes pestles, *ti'i*, finely carved sculptures, *pahu* (drums), jewellery and period photos as well as a *ha'e*. There are also scale reproductions of ancient sites and objects such as paddles, spears and clubs. Donations are appreciated.

'UA HUKA

The **arboretum**, created in 1974, is well worth a short visit. It is beside the road, halfway between Vaipaee and Hane and includes dozens of species from around the world. There is a striking contrast between this wealth of plants and the relative aridity of the island. The fact that so many species have adapted to the dry Marquesan soil opens up great possibilities for local agriculture. The species best adapted to the climate are used for reforestation where the vegetation has been destroyed by wild goats and horses.

Hane
Experts believe that the first Polynesian settlement on the Marquesas was here, tucked away in a bay protected on the east by the impressive Motu Hane. The local personality is sculptor Joseph Vaatete, whose **workshop** is 200m from the beach.

The white house on the seafront contains the **craft centre** as well as a little **marine museum**, which opened in 1995 and contains some traditional pirogues and hooks used for shark fishing. Ask Joseph Vaatete for the key.

Hokatu
This peaceful village lies about 3km east of Hane in a sheltered bay. The main street leads to the **fare artisanal** and the black-pebble **beach**.

Grotte aux Pas (Footstep Cave)
Tupapau (ghosts) are said to haunt this cave, slightly west of Point Tekeho, between Vaipaee and Haavei Bay.

According to legend, a fisherman took refuge in the cave during a storm. He awoke to note large footprints on the sand. A few

days later, although the tide should have washed them away, the footprints were still there. Today, people swear they are still there.

The cave can be reached at low tide when there is not much swell. If you visit with a guide, the boat will stop about 30m from the crevice and you will have to swim to the edge, taking care not to be swept onto the reefs by the undertow. Take waterproof sandals and ask your guide to bring a torch (flashlight).

Motu Teuaua & Hemeni
Thousands of *kaveka* (sooty terns) have taken up residence on the islets of **Hemeni** and **Teuaua**, near the southwestern point of 'Ua Huka. They lay thousands of eggs daily, which the islanders regularly gather.

Access to Hemeni is prohibited in order to protect the species. Teuaua, the neighbouring islet (also known as Île aux Oiseaux or Bird Island), is accessible by speedboat, but the boat isn't able to come in too close because of the swell. It's necessary to jump on to a rocky ledge and clamber up the rock using a length of permanently fixed rope, a rather perilous exercise.

There's a final test: the nauseating smell emanating from the thousands of birds. Their eggs, whitish and speckled with brown or black marks, are not all fit for eating and only an expert eye can spot which ones are suitable. As you approach, the *kaveka* become infuriated and their cries are deafening. The more reckless among them swoop over your head and you will soon be reliving a scene from Alfred Hitchcock's *The Birds*.

If, despite all this, the experience still attracts you, wear a hat.

Beaches
'Ua Huka has the most beautiful beaches in the Marquesas, although the *nono* spoil the pleasure. Bring insect repellent. Accessible by speedboat or 4WD, **Manihina Beach**, between Vaipaee and the airport, is fringed with fine white sand. There are excellent opportunities for snorkelling, as the beach is sheltered by a bay. **Hatuana Beach** is in the west of the island; there are petroglyphs nearby. **Haavei Beach** is a lovely inlet that belongs to the Lichtlé family. Ask the family, who live on the coconut plantation, for permission before you plunge in.

THE MARQUESAS

Motu Papa

This island, ideal for picnicking and snorkelling, is just offshore from the airport. It is a large block of volcanic rock that, at low tide, reveals a fairly wide rocky ledge where you can sit. As the speedboat cannot come alongside, you have to swim about 50m to the edge of the rock. Food and various items of equipment are loaded in a large floating bin and all you have to do is swim with it to the rock. Take sunscreen (there are few shady spots) and waterproof sandals, as the rock is very slippery.

Archaeological Sites

Meiaute Less than 30 minutes' walk from Hane, this site is one of the major attractions on 'Ua Huka. It includes three, 1m-high, red-tuff *ti'i* that watch over a group of stone structures, *pae pae* and *me'ae*, which have not yet been restored and are partly overgrown. Two of these *ti'i* have projecting ears. One has legs and a phallus, while the other two have only a head and trunk. The clearing forms a natural **lookout** with magnificent views of Hane Bay on one side and the caldera on the other.

To get there, follow the track for about 200m from the Auberge Hitikau (see Places to Stay later in the 'Ua Huka section) at the edge of Hane village; head in the direction of the mountain. At the crossroad continue straight ahead; after about 20 minutes you will come to a cement stairway on your right, 30m after a sharp bend. Leave the main track at this point and climb the steep hill to the *pae pae*. A little higher up, in a clearing, you will find the *ti'i*. From the stairway, arrows on trees indicate the path, but you need to look carefully.

Vaikivi Petroglyphs This little-visited archaeological site on the Vaikivi Plateau is worth the detour, if only for the walk or horse ride to get there (see next). The well-restored petroglyphs are engraved on a grey stone. They represent an octopus and a human face and there are other petroglyphs nearby.

Activities

It's a beautiful three-hour **walk** inland to the Vaikivi petroglyphs. Take a guide because it's a long way and the trail is not marked. You can depart from Vaipaee or Hane.

From Hane follow the main road to the edge of the village on the mountainside and then take the track that branches to the left before the last house. A little further on, there's a small path; at this point the walk becomes harder. The path climbs the steep volcano caldera (one to 1½ hours). From the clearing at the ridge there are wonderful views over Hane Bay, with Motu Hane visible to the west and the village a speckled ribbon of red and white. When it's clear you can see Fatu Huku to the southeast.

The track continues inland and begins to descend gently, as the thick vegetation gives way to tree ferns. The contrast with the coastal scenery is striking. After about 30 or 45 minutes, branch left and hack your way through a forest of pandanus and other vegetation. Just over half an hour later you reach the petroglyphs.

Wear good shoes and take sufficient food and water. A guide will cost 3000 to 5000 CFP; ask at your *pension* or contact Léonard Teatiu or Napoléon at the *mairie* at Vaipaee, Gilles Brown at Vaipaee or Patrick Teiki at Hokatu.

The coastal route between Haavei to the west and Hokatu to the east offers spectacular views and is also worth doing.

Horse riding is a popular activity on 'Ua Huka. The most popular ride is from Vaipaee to Hane, passing the arboretum, airport and wind-swept arid plateaus before reaching the coastal road, which plunges down towards Hane. If the weather cooperates, this ride will certainly be one of the highlights of your stay on the Marquesas.

Ask at your *pension* about where to find horse owners. A ride typically costs 6000 CFP, including a guide. Wooden saddles are still quite commonly used, but fortunately padding is provided to relieve the discomfort.

Places to Stay

Considering the small number of visitors, 'Ua Huka has a surprising number of *pensions*. Prices include airport transfers. Excursions by boat, 4WD and horse are often organised. Credit cards are not accepted.

Vaipaee In a blue house beside the main road, on the right as you come from the quay, is **Chez Alexis Scallamera** (*☎/fax 92 60 19; rooms per person 2000 CFP, with half-board 4700 CFP*). The pension has four quiet, well-kept doubles with shared bathroom (cold water only). Guests can use the kitchen facilities.

Chez Christelle (☎ 92 60 85, 92 60 04; *rooms per person 2200 CFP, with half-board 5000 CFP)* has four sparkling-clean rooms with shared bathroom (cold water only). The proprietor, Christelle Fournier, is the Air Tahiti representative.

Mana Tupuna Village (☎/fax 92 60 08, ☎ 92 61 01; half-board 7000 CFP), at the exit from the village towards Hane, is perched on the side of a hill. There are three local-style bungalows on stilts, elegantly arranged with covered veranda, mezzanine and bathroom (with hot water). There are beautiful views over the valley below. One of the bungalows is used as a restaurant.

Hane There is a very good restaurant at **Auberge Hitikau** (☎/fax 92 61 74; *rooms per person 2200 CFP, with half-board 5500 CFP)*. It has four simple but clean double rooms with shared bathroom (cold water only). To get to the guesthouse, go up the main street towards the mountain; it's 300m past the church, on the large, ranch-like property.

Hokatu The first house on the left as you enter the village from Hane is the excellent **Chez Maurice & Delphine** (☎/fax 92 60 55; *rooms per person 2200 CFP, with half-board 4500 CFP; bungalows per person 3200 CFP, with half-board 5600 CFP)*. In the owners' house there are two clean and welcoming double rooms with shared bathroom (with hot water), one with a fan. From the terrace, there's a beautiful view over the village and the bay. For more privacy and wonderful views of Motu Hane, there are three bungalows with verandas perched above the edge of town. One has a bathroom (cold water only) and a fridge and will accommodate six people. The two others are smaller and have a small kitchen.

If you stay several days you will have the opportunity to enjoy a traditional meal from a Marquesan oven. Owner Maurice is also one of the best sculptors on the island. There's a small shop in the house's garage.

Places to Eat
Apart from several small snack bars and food shops, the choice is limited on 'Ua Huka. Fortunately, the food offered by the

*pension*s is good and includes Marquesan specialities. Try a *kaveka*-egg omelette, the undisputed speciality of the island.

Auberge Hitikau *(set meal 2000 CFP)*, in Hane, is the only real restaurant. Local specialities have pride of place: goat, pork, fish in coconut milk, *kaveka*-egg omelettes and delicious cakes. Bookings are essential.

Getting There & Away
On Thursday a 20-seat plane flies from Nuku Hiva to 'Ua Huka (5800 CFP one-way) and return, connecting with the Pape'ete–Nuku Hiva flight (29,800 CFP Pape'ete to 'Ua Huka one-way). Contact the Air Tahiti representative (☎ 92 60 85) in Vaipaee.

In Hokatu, **Maurice Rootuehine** (☎/fax 92 60 55) and **Paul Teatiu** (☎ 92 60 88) do crossings to 'Ua Pou (50,000 CFP) or Nuku Hiva (60,000 CFP). The *Aranui* and the *Taporo IV* stop at 'Ua Huka.

Getting Around
A 13km track links Vaipaee to Hokatu via Hane; the stretch from Vaipaee to Hane is surfaced. Haavei is also accessible by the track from Vaipaee.

'Ua Huka's airport is situated on an arid plateau midway between Vaipaee and Hane. Airport transfers are usually included in the *pension*s' prices.

The *pension* owners have 4WDs and can take you to visit the villages of the island (about 10,000 CFP per day).

'UA POU
pop 2013 • area 125 sq km
Lying 45km south of Nuku Hiva, 'Ua Pou was the site of a settlement estimated to have been established around 150 BC. Frenchman Étienne Marchand landed on the island in June 1791 and, believing that he was the first to discover it, claimed it on behalf of France; in fact Ingraham, the American captain of the *Hope*, had noted its existence two months earlier.

'Ua Pou is geologically the youngest island in the archipelago, with its sharp contours and 12 pointy pinnacles, like obelisks or columns of basalt, often shrouded by cloud cover.

Hakahau, the island's main settlement, is home to most of the population. A few villages nestled in the steep-sided valleys are dotted along the east and west coasts.

'UA POU

'Ua Pou is noted for its culture and arts. It was the birthplace of the Motu Haka Association and the revival of Marquesan identity. It is a breeding ground for talent: the singer Rataro, the Kanahau Trio musical group and most of the well-known Marquesan dance groups are from 'Ua Pou. Its sculptors, who work in wood and stone, have also brought fame to the island.

Fascinating archaeological remains can be seen in the Hakamoui and Hohoi valleys.

Information

For tourist information, contact the director of the **tourist office** (☎ 92 54 20) or **Rosita Teikitutoua** (☎ 92 53 36), the head of the tourism committee.

There's a branch of **Banque Socredo** (☎ 92 53 63; open 7.30am-noon & 1pm-3pm Mon-Fri) in a wing of the *mairie* (town hall) in Hakahau, not far from the post office. You can change currency and travellers cheques or get a cash advance with your credit card.

The **post office** (open 7am-3pm Mon-Thur, 7am-2pm Fri) is near the bank. There are phonecard telephone booths beside the post office, on the quay and opposite the Air Tahiti office.

Contact the **Restaurant-Pension Pukuéé** (☎/fax 92 50 83) to get laundry done; a machine load, washed and dried, costs 1500 CFP.

In Hakahau, a small **medical centre** with a doctor and dentist is in the south of the village, halfway between the church and the museum. Every village has an infirmary or first-aid post.

Hakahau

The town stretches from the cargo-ship quay in the east right around the bay, with four sealed streets running north-south. The Cetad (technical school) and the secondary school, decorated with frescoes representing *ti'i*, face the black-sand **beach**, which is frequented by young surfers fresh from school. Further west, the **market** livens up each Sunday after mass.

Inaugurated for the 1995 Marquesas Festival, the **Museum of Hakahau** (*admission free*) faces the esplanade. Locals were encouraged to lend objects representative of Marquesan culture to be displayed; unfortunately, the museum's display cabinets remain somewhat empty.

As part of the festival, a team from the archaeological department of the Museum of Tahiti & Its Islands travelled to Hakahau to restore the **Pae Pae Tenei** right in the middle

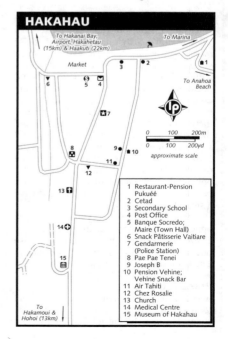

HAKAHAU

1 Restaurant-Pension Pukuéé
2 Cetad
3 Secondary School
4 Post Office
5 Banque Socredo; Maire (Town Hall)
6 Snack Pâtisserie Vaitiare
7 Gendarmerie (Police Station)
8 Pae Pae Tenei
9 Joseph B
10 Pension Vehine; Vehine Snack Bar
11 Air Tahiti
12 Chez Rosalie
13 Church
14 Medical Centre
15 Museum of Hakahau

of the village. This site is representative of the structure of traditional dwellings.

The recently built Catholic church, to the south of the village on the Hohoi road, houses some very noteworthy **sculptures** by local artisans. The pulpit representing the bows of a boat balancing on a net full of fish is particularly interesting.

For a beautiful view of **Hakahau Bay** head east from Restaurant-Pension Pukuéé along a track until you reach a small pass. At the pass, take the right fork and climb steeply for five to 10 minutes until you reach a small flight of steps leading to a white cross, which you can see from the quay. The view is magnificent: In addition to the jagged profile of Nuku Hiva to the north, you can also see Anahoa Bay and its white border of sand to the east. In clear weather you can see 'Ua Huka to the northeast.

Hohoi

This picturesque little village on the southeast of the island is accessible from Hakahau. A 12km track passes through varied luxuriant vegetation, which contrasts strikingly with the aridity of the plateaus in the northwest of the island. There are some good views over the sea, particularly of Haakaunui Bay.

Time seems to stand still in Hohoi. You may pass locals returning to the village leading horses laden with bunches of bananas or bags of coconuts. As you enter the village, 100m before the blue-roofed *mairie* on the left, you will spot two **pae pae**. On the corner beehives are lined up on a stone platform. The curious pagoda shape of the **church** is also noteworthy.

On the beach there are a few thatched fishers' huts. It's here that Hohoi's famous **galets fleuris** (flowering pebbles) can be found. These are pieces of phonolite that have crystallised to form amber-coloured flower shapes.

Hakamaii

This one-street village, stretching along the Kahioa River, is only accessible by boat. Landing is a delicate operation. The *bonitier* is anchored in the bay and you get into a small pirogue. The person paddling has to catch a wave at just the right moment so that the pirogue is gently propelled rather than dumped onto the shore.

The façade of the town's stone **church**, facing the ocean, has unusual yellow, blue and red painted wooden panels that replicate stained-glass windows. Seen from the ocean, the illusion is almost perfect.

You can walk along the path along the river at the far end of the village; take some mosquito repellent.

Haakuti

The tiny village of Haakuti is the provisional terminus of the 22km track from Hakahau, which will one day be extended further down the west coast to Hakatao. Meanwhile, Haakuti feels deliciously like the end of the world. Its one street links the stone **church**, built on a *pae pae* at the top of the village, with the tiny sea-swept quay some 600m below. At nightfall, don't miss the return of the **fishers**. Good-sized bonito and tuna form a large part of the catch.

Hakahetau

This charming village, noted for the red **bell-tower** of its church, near the waterfront, was the residence of Monsignor Le Cleac'h, known for his translation of the Bible into Marquesan. Hakahetau's inhabitants live off copra production, fishing, and arts and crafts.

A 15km track snakes between the bare plateaus of the island's northwest and, along the section between Hakahau and Aneou airport, you will see **wild horses and goats**. In the background, due south, the slender profile of **Mt Oave** (1203m) appears, while in the north you can make out the contours of Nuku Hiva.

Motu Oa

South of the island, this motu is home to colonies of thousands of **sea birds**.

Beaches

Twenty-five minutes' walk east of Hakahau, **Anahoa Beach** fringes Anahoa Cove, contrasting with the wildness of the neighbouring volcanic scenery. Go there on foot or by horseback to enjoy the panoramic view going down towards the bay. From the Hakahau quay, follow the direction indicated by the sign for Restaurant-Pension Pukuéé and continue along the track beyond the restaurant. After about 10 minutes' climb to the pass, there's a hill with a superb view of Hakahau Bay and its peaks.

Shortly after the airport at Aneou, 11km from Hakahau below the track leading to Hakahetau, is **Hakanai Bay**. It's a popular local picnic spot. It's been named Plage aux Requins (Shark Beach) because of the many sharks seen in the cove.

The black-sand **Puamau Beach** is popular with young surfers. Wherever you go it's imperative to have mosquito repellent to cope with the horrible *nono*.

Archaeological Sites

Hakamoui Valley This valley, also known as the Valley of the Kings, is now deserted. Formerly inhabited by the dominant Atipapa tribe from which the island's chieftain came, it was one of the main centres of population on the island.

The valley is easily accessible from Hakahau. Follow the road to Hohoi for about 3km and take the left fork, which descends eastward towards the ocean. One kilometre further on, on the right and set back from the track, is a *pae pae* that was used as the platform for a recent dwelling but now lies abandoned. You can see a clear bas-relief and hollowed-out carvings, one on the northern side and the other on a stone slab placed edgeways on the eastern side, both slightly hidden by vegetation. Both are representations of human features with round staring eyes and disproportionate rectangular mouths. Not far away is a well-preserved *ti'i*. This site, called **Mataautea**, was restricted to the chief of the Atipapa tribe, who reigned over the whole island.

Two hundred metres further on is the imposing **Temenaha Pae Pae**, built by Chief Puheputoka. If you get up onto the platform, you will see a series of carvings on the stone.

If you continue for just over 1km, you will reach a pretty coconut plantation fringing a black-pebble beach.

Hakaohoka Valley The Hakaohoka Valley, in the southeast of the island, opens onto Hohoi Bay. From the pebbly shore the site extends more than 2km inland. This area, once very populous, has been studied by archaeologist Pierre Ottino.

According to a legend told by Jacques Dordillon, who owns the land, Heato, the last king of 'Ua Pou, wanted to marry the daughter of the chief of the Kaavahopeoa tribe who had taken up residence in Hakaohoka Valley. He was given a categorical refusal. Mad with rage, he instructed his warriors to capture the young woman and to massacre the Kaavahopeoa. The latter fled aboard huge bamboo rafts, which they constructed in one night with the help of the gods. At dawn, as their aggressors were preparing to make their assault, the fugitives were already in view of Tahuata. Due to the hostility of that island's inhabitants, they were unable to land and continued on to Napuka (in the Tuamotus), where they settled.

The valley was deserted in the 1860s as the result of a smallpox epidemic and the dwellings became ossified. For a stretch of 70m on each side of the main river bed there are sandstone structures, the remains of ancient human occupation, consisting of *pae pae*, paving and low walls. Start your visit with **Chief Hamipohue's pae pae**, which is protected from run-off water and the sun by a corrugated-iron roof. At one end, you can see the chief's back-rest. At right angles to the terrace are some rough stone carvings. The whole area is full of more *pae pae*, *tohua* and *me'ae*. The ghostly silhouette of the banyans, sacred trees, reinforces the mystical atmosphere of this place.

The Hakaohoka site is 13km from Hakahau along the track. At Hohoi head to the pebbly beach and follow it along the track bordered with *miro* and *tou* trees. After the first fishers' shelter, you will see a sign with a map of the site. Take the track up and walk for 15 minutes until you see the *pae pae* on the right under the plant cover. At Hohoi, don't forget to give 1000 CFP to the custodian, Willy Hikutini, who can also act as your guide. This money is used to finance the upkeep of the track and restoration of the site.

Activities

There are many opportunities for **walking**, including simply following the tracks from one village to another. If you intend to leave the tracks it's advisable to take a guide.

For **horse riding**, contact **Tony Tereino** (*☎ 92 51 68; 6000 CFP per day*) at Pension Leydj in Hakahetau.

Places to Stay

Restaurant-Pension Pukuéé (*☎/fax 92 50 83; singles/doubles 3200/5900 CFP*) is well known to the yachties who anchor in the bay below. It's ideally located away from the rest of the village of Hakahau, by the track that leads to Anahoa Beach. The building, on a hillside, looks like a chalet and has fine views over the bay. Rooms come with shared bathroom (with hot water). The owners have a restaurant, organise excursions and can arrange to do laundry for 500 CFP.

Pension Vehine (☎ 92 50 63, fax 92 53 21; singles/doubles 2200/3200 CFP) is next to the Vehine snack bar and 500m from the seafront in Hakahau. The functional building has two rooms, a lounge area, hot water and a veranda.

Chez Dora (☎ 92 53 69; rooms with breakfast/half-board/full board per person 3200/5400/7500 CFP) is in the centre of Hakahau, about 1km from the quay. Chez Dora offers three rooms, one of which has a bathroom.

Pension Leydj (☎ 92 51 68; rooms with breakfast/half-board per person 3800/5900 CFP), near the quay in Hakahetau, has four rooms with two shared bathrooms. Various excursions can be organised.

Places to Eat
The only real eating places are in Hakahau; there are also a few snack bars and grocery shops in the village centre where you can stock up. In the other villages, you can go to a *pension* or make do with a few provisions from the grocers'.

Snack-Pâtisserie Vaitiare (☎ 92 50 95; dishes 1200 CFP; open daily lunch & dinner) is on the airport road, past the *mairie*. It's the place to go if you are dying for a pastry; light meals are also served. It has a pleasant little terrace with a view over the coconut plantation by the sea.

Chez Rosalie (☎ 92 51 77; Marquesan meal 2500 CFP) only opens when the *Aranui* is in port. Don't hesitate to join in for a feast.

Vehine (☎ 92 53 21; dishes from 750 CFP, set menu 2000 CFP; open lunch Mon-Sat), opposite Joseph B, has cheap eats. Hamburgers with chips cost 700 CFP, steak and chips 850 CFP and *poisson cru* 750 CFP. On request only, you can have a full set menu. It's open on demand in the evening.

Restaurant-Pension Pukuéé (☎ 92 50 83; meals 2500 CFP) flies the flag for Marquesan cuisine and excels at cooking lobster and shrimp. The restaurant is in a terrace looking out over the seafront and the quay.

Getting There & Away
Air Tahiti (☎ 92 53 41; open 9am-noon Mon & Tues, 2pm-4pm Wed, 9am-noon & 3pm-4pm Fri) is in Hakahau. There's another **branch** (☎ 92 51 08) at the airport.

There are flights to the island every Wednesday, Thursday and Friday on a 20-seater plane, which does the Nuku Hiva–'Ua Pou (5800 CFP one-way) run and connects with the Pape'ete–Nuku Hiva flight (29,800 CFP one-way Pape'ete–'Ua Pou). There are also two weekly Atuona–'Ua Pou flights via Nuku Hiva (9800 CFP one-way).

Based on Nuku Hiva, **Héli Inter Marquises** (☎ 92 02 17) has regular services between Taiohae and Hakahau on Wednesday, Friday and Sunday (12,500 CFP one-way, 15 minutes).

Boat The *Aranui* and *Taporo IV* stop at Hakahau; the *Aranui* also stops at Hakahetau.

Getting Around
On the east coast, a track connects Hakahau with Hohoi and continues to Hakatao. On the west coast, Hakahau is connected to Hakahetau, Haakuti and Hakamaii.

The airport is at Aneou, about 10km west of Hakahau, on the Hakahetau track. Your hosts will come to collect you if you have booked accommodation; it costs 2000 CFP per person return for the transfer.

Ask at your *pension* about transport by car. Expect to pay 10,000 CFP to go to Hakamoui and Hohoi on the east coast, and 15,000 CFP to go to Hakahetau and Haakuti on the west coast.

The Southern Group

The Marquesas' southern group comprises three inhabited islands – Hiva Oa, Tahuata and Fatu Hiva – and the four deserted islands of Motane (Mohotani), Fatu Huku, Terihi and Thomasset Rock.

HIVA OA
pop 1829 • area 320 sq km
Formerly the administrative capital of the Marquesas, Hiva Oa, in the southeast of the archipelago, is now overshadowed by Nuku Hiva in the northern group. However, it maintains its pre-eminence within the southern group.

THE MARQUESAS

The first European to see Hiva Oa, in July 1595, was the Spanish navigator Mendaña. He contented himself with sailing along its coast and christened it Dominica because it was a Sunday.

Stretching 40km west to east and about 10km north to south, this hook-shaped island's distorted relief is evidence of former volcanic activity. A ridge forms a spine across the length of the island and has an average height of 800m. Steep ridges at right angles to this backbone separate each valley, making access difficult.

The slopes of Mt Temetiu (1276m) and Mt Feani (1126m) form a vast, impressive amphitheatre, at the base of which is Atuona, the island's capital. Atuona proudly cultivates the memory of its two distinguished guests: the painter Paul Gauguin and the Belgian singer-poet Jacques Brel, who both chose this small town as the last stop on their wanderings.

On the northeast coast, Puamau, ringed by mountains more than 700m high, features the most important archaeological remains discovered to date on the Marquesas. The site at Taaoa, in the southwest, is also an archaeological treasure. The lush valleys of Hanaiapa, Hanapaaoa and Nahoe in the north, where the pace of life is set by the

Gauguin: The Wild & the Primitive

The evocative paintings of Paul Gauguin are largely responsible for Polynesia's enduring reputation as a paradise lost.

Born in 1848, Gauguin began to paint in his mid-20s. After a childhood in Peru he prepared for naval college, joined up as an officer cadet and, from 1868 to 1871, roamed the seas. He then worked as a stockbroker in Paris and began to paint his first landscapes. Having come to the notice of Camille Pissarro, he exhibited with the Impressionists in 1879. Gauguin gained the friendship of Edgar Degas, who supported him by buying his pictures. The collapse of the stock market in 1882 put an end to Gauguin's business career and, leaving his wife and children, he devoted himself exclusively to painting. Condemned to solitude by poverty, he took refuge in Pont-Aven, a small town in Finistère, before voyaging to Martinique and returning to Paris, where he met Vincent van Gogh.

Gauguin's second stay in Pont-Aven, in 1888, was artistically decisive. Influenced by Japanese prints, he adopted a new, simplified style, characterised by large flat areas of colour with clearly defined outlines: 'Pure colour, everything must be sacrificed to it!'.

After a two-month stay in Arles with van Gogh – it was during this period that van Gogh mutilated his ear – Gauguin painted a series of masterpieces (Yellow Christ, Beautiful Angel), but could think only of escape. In a letter to the painter Odilon Redon in 1890, he wrote: 'I am going to Tahiti and hope to finish my life there. I consider that my art…is just a seed and I hope to cultivate it there for myself, in its primitive and wild state'.

In Mataiea on Tahiti, where the Gauguin museum now stands, he concentrated on capturing images of daily life and, in 1892 and 1893, experienced an intensely productive period, painting Te Nave Nave Fenua (Delicious Land), Manao Tupapau (Spirit of the Dead Watching) and Arearea (Amusements). Exuberant settings and flamboyant colours, with yellow, red and blue predominating, increasingly pervaded the artist's painting.

Gauguin sold few canvases and was again impoverished. He sailed for France in 1893 and in November of that year a large exhibition devoted solely to his work opened in Paris. He took up ceramics and embarked on writing a narrative, Noa Noa, inspired by his Tahitian period and designed to make the public understand his work. But the time was not ripe for his talent to be recognised and he set off for the South Seas again in 1895.

His most powerful compositions, Te Arii Vahine (The Royal Woman; 1896), Nevermore (1897) and Where Do We Come From? What Are We? Where Are We Going? (1897), date from this second and final stay in Polynesia, which was marked by illness and distress. After a failed suicide attempt, he took refuge on the island of Hiva Oa in the Marquesas, where he defended the inhabitants against the colonial administration and the all-powerful Catholic mission. Although weakened, he did not stop writing, drawing, sculpting and painting, and it was during this period that he produced one of his most beautiful nudes, Barbaric Tales (1902). Gauguin died in May 1903.

HIVA OA, TAHUATA & MOTANE

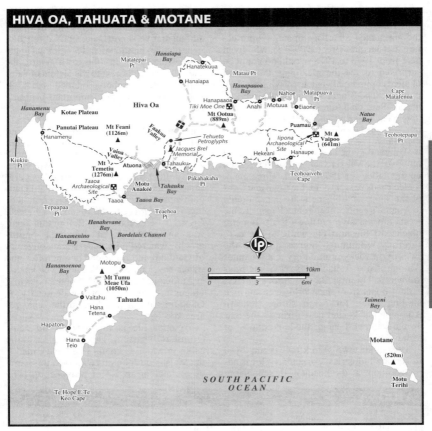

ccoming and going of the cargo ships, safe-
guard the traditional Marquesan way of life.

Information

Atuona's **tourism committee** *(open 7.30am-
11.30am 'Mon-Fri)* is in the *fare artisanal* behind the museum, in the centre of the
village.

The **Banque Socredo** *(☎ 92 73 54; open
7.30am-11.30am & 1.30pm-4pm Mon-Fri)* is
next to the Air Tahiti office, opposite Tohua
Pepeu, right in the centre of Atuona. You
can change currency and travellers cheques
and make credit-card withdrawals. There is
an ATM inside the bank accessible during
opening hours.

In Atuona, the **post office** *(open 7.30am-
11.30am & 1.30pm-4.30pm Mon-Thur, 7.30am-*

*11.30am & 1.30pm-3.30pm Fri, 7.30am-
8.30am Sat)* is next to the *mairie*, 50m east
of the *gendarmerie*. It has a fax service and
sells phonecards.

Phonecard telephone booths are in front
of the post office and near the school in
Atuona and at the harbour in Tahauku. There
is another **post office** in Puamau. Some villages have phonecard telephone booths; if
not, a telephone service can be provided by
a private individual.

The Atuona snack bar **Snack Kaupe** (see
Places to Eat later in the Hiva Oa section)
has two computers with Internet access.

In Atuona, the **hospital** *(☎ 92 73 75)* and
the **dental surgery** *(☎ 92 73 58)* are behind
the *mairie* buildings. There is an infirmary
or first-aid post in each village.

Atuona

This trim, tidy town of 1300 residents has the antiquated air of a tropical subprefecture, but Jacques Brel (1929–78), who lived here from 1975 to 1978, would no doubt be surprised to see the gleaming 4WDs and opulent commercial vehicles driving through it today. The singer's shadow, as well as that of Paul Gauguin, still hovers over the town. The museum and the Calvaire Cemetery are great places of pilgrimage for their fans.

Atuona is at the north of Taaoa Bay, at the mouth of the Vaioa River, and stretches back up the valley for about 1.5km. Three main, sealed roads pass through the town and most of the shops and business are concentrated in Atuona's centre, near Tohua Pepeu. To the west, the massive outline of Mt Temetiu blocks off the horizon, while to the east, carefully maintained houses cling to the sides of the rocky promontory that separates Atuona from Tahauku Bay. Sometimes known as Traitors' Bay, this cove attracts sailing boats from the world over and is a landing stage for cargo ships. Beneath Atuona a black-sand beach fringes the bay. To the southwest stands the lookout post of Motu Anakée.

Most of the town's workforce is employed in service industries, particularly local administration, at the hospital, in schools, at the Service Militaire Adapté (SMA) garrison or in small businesses. The medical and administrative services are housed together in attractive traditional-style buildings in the east of the town. In the town centre, the Catholic church is next to **the Sisters of Saint Joseph of Cluny** school, founded in 1843. It is now one of the most important boarding schools in French Polynesia.

Museum Don't expect to see anything extraordinary in Atuona's small museum (☎ 92 75 10; adult/child 400/200 CFP; open 7.30am-11.30am Mon-Fri), in the town centre. The collection has been revised several times. When we visited copies of Paul Gauguin's paintings by a French forger, including Sur la Plage, La Sieste and La Femme Éventail were on display. Before this, there was an exhibition of drawings, photographs, watercolours, letters and souvenirs of Gauguin and his friend and admirer, the writer-physician Victor Ségalen, who landed at Atuona in August 1903. Some books and videos are on sale. For the centenary of Gauguin's death in 2003, further changes are expected.

To one side is the **Maison du Jouir** (House of Pleasure). This is a replica of the cabin in which Gauguin lived. He called it the Maison du Jouir and engraved this name on a lintel in an act of provocation. The

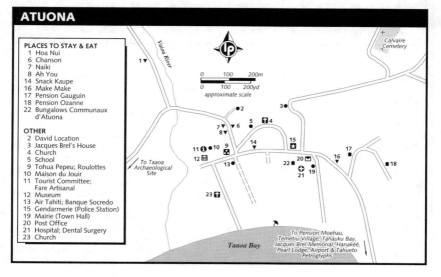

ATUONA

PLACES TO STAY & EAT
1 Hoa Nui
6 Chanson
7 Naiki
8 Ah You
14 Snack Kaupe
16 Make Make
17 Pension Gauguin
18 Pension Ozanne
22 Bungalows Communaux d'Atuona

OTHER
2 David Location
3 Jacques Brel's House
4 Church
5 School
9 Tohua Pepeu; Roulottes
10 Maison du Jouir
11 Tourist Committee; Fare Artisanal
12 Museum
13 Air Tahiti; Banque Socredo
15 Gendarmerie (Police Station)
19 Mairie (Town Hall)
20 Post Office
21 Hospital; Dental Surgery
23 Church

Vaioa River

Calvaire Cemetery

0   100   200m
0   100   200yd
approximate scale

To Taaoa Archaeological Site

Taaoa Bay

To Pension Moehau, Temetiu Village, Tahauku Bay, Jacques Brel Memorial, Hanakéé, Pearl Lodge, Airport & Tahueto Petroglyphs replica's main facade has been decorated with copies of the carved wooden panels fashioned by Gauguin. Carved in wood are the maxims the painter passed down to posterity: 'Be mysterious' and, 'Be in love and you will be happy'. The inside of the building has been stripped bare and at best you may find some work by craftspeople on display. There is talk of moving the Ségalen-Gauguin collection here.

Calvaire Cemetery Jacques Brel and Paul Gauguin were laid to rest a few dozen metres from each other in the small, well-maintained Calvaire Cemetery.

Jacques Brel's grave is in the lower part of the cemetery, near the access steps, on the left. The gravestone, partly hidden by vegetation, is adorned with a medallion depicting him with his companion, Madly.

Two rows further up, at the right-hand edge of the cemetery, is **Paul Gauguin's tomb**, with a replica of the statue *Oviri* (literally, 'wild') standing guard. Gauguin identified with the violent symbolism of this statue and chose it for his last resting place.

Head north on the road just east of the *gendarmerie*; *a*fter 200m you'll see Jacques Brel's house on the left by the first bend in the road. Continue for another 400m until you reach a fork in the road: follow the direction indicated on the sign to the cemetery 100m further on. It takes about 10 to 15 minutes on foot.

Tohua Pepeu Restored for the 1991 Marquesas Festival, this *tohua* faces Banque Socredo in the centre of town. It includes a reconstructed *ha'e*.

Jacques Brel Memorial This memorial to the Belgian singer was erected in 1993 at the place where he wished to build his house, some kilometres east of Atuona, not far from the airport. His illness prematurely ended the project. The site, a narrow spit of land accessible by track, is magnificent and wild, with a superb view of Atuona Bay.

The memorial is a black marble plaque set into a large rock. Beside a portrait of the artist is the famous line from his song *Les Marquises*: *'Veux-tu que je te dise, gémir n'est pas de mise...aux Marquises'* (Do you want me to tell you, moaning is not acceptable...in the Marquesas).

There are two possible routes here. From Tahauku snack bar, follow the track that goes up to the airport. Pass the small access road to the Hanakéé Pearl Lodge, which goes off to the left, and go straight for 400m. You will then see a track on your left leading to a private property. Go up here, past the front of the house (beware of the dogs!) and continue for about 200m. You will then come out at a small piece of open ground overlooking the Hanakéé Pearl Lodge. The path leading to the memorial bends to the left and goes 2km uphill to the hillside site.

Another possibility, considerably longer, is to follow the track leading to the airport and, 300m before the Rural Development Department buildings, turn left and continue along the path for approximately 2.5km.

THE MARQUESAS

The Last Song of Jacques Brel

A fighter against hypocrisy and proudly iconoclastic, Belgian-born singer-songwriter Jacques Brel derided the flaws of society and left masterpieces such as 'Dans le Port d'Amsterdam' (In the Port of Amsterdam), 'Le Plat Pays' (The Flat Country) and 'Les Bigotes' (The Bigots).

Wishing to escape media pressure, he set out to sail around the world on the *Askoy*, his private ketch, accompanied by his companion, Madly, from Guadeloupe. In November 1975 they arrived at Atuona and, seduced by its serenity, Brel never left. In 1976 he and Madly set up a small home on the hillside above the village. He equipped himself with *Jojo*, a Beechcraft aeroplane in which he travelled between the islands of the northern group and as far as Pape'ete.

Jacques Brel and Madly became involved in village life and were well liked by the locals. From time to time the artist would perform medical evacuations to Pape'ete in his plane.

Jacques Brel died of cancer in October 1978 at the age of 48. His last song, 'Les Marquises' (The Marquesas), resounds as a vibrant homage to this generous place. At Calvaire Cemetery, where he rests near Paulo (as he called Gauguin), Brel's tomb is lovingly decorated with flowers.

It's better to walk to the site than try to get here by 4WD; the tracks are very narrow and some sections are in terrible condition.

Puamau

The village of Puamau is a 2½ hour drive from Atuona, in the northeast of the island. It occupies a coastal plain, bordered by a vast ring of mountains. To enjoy the **view** over the whole bay, follow the track to the Iipona archaeological site and continue as far as the pass. The elegant seafront is lined with ironwood trees and a black-sand **beach**. The village has the most beautiful archaeological site in the Marquesas, if not all of French Polynesia. See Archaeological Sites later in this section for more information.

Hanapaaoa & Surrounding Hamlets

This tiny village of 40 people is on the north coast of the island between Hanaiapa and Puamau. Far from the 'bustle' of Atuona, goat hunting, fishing and catching lobsters, and copra and *noni* production set the rhythms of daily life.

The area surrounding Hanapaaoa has a wild beauty. The secondary **track** that links Hanapaaoa to **Anahi** and **Nahoe**, a few kilometres to the east, winds through valleys covered in fruit trees. The track, which goes partly along the cliff top, also affords superb views over Fatu Huku and the north coast. Wild goats abound, scarcely frightened away by your approach, and dozens of **pae pae** are covered by the vegetation.

It's a two-hour journey by 4WD to Hanapaaoa from Atuona. The track, which is accessible to motor vehicles, passes the airport and shortly after it splits; the first turn-off goes to Hanaiapa, and the second leads to Hanapaaoa. Take a guide or arm yourself with a map and ask at the Atuona tourism committee for further information. From Hanapaaoa to Anahi and Nahoe, the track is narrow, winding and steep. Great care is needed to prevent your vehicle veering off the road and into the ocean.

Hanaiapa

It is not difficult to succumb to the charm of this flower-bedecked village in the north of the island, accessible by a track from Atuona and Puamau. The village stretches for more than 1km along a single street, which follows the course of the Teheitahi River. Traditional copra-drying sheds are scattered here and there.

In the centre of the village, opposite the reconstructed Marquesan hut, a remarkably well-maintained **pae pae** has pride of place. One of its pavements has three cup-shaped structures, which are thought to have been designed to contain the substances used in tattooing. At the back of the *pae pae*, slabs of the island's red tuff indicate that the site was the abode of a chieftain or priest.

Beaches

Hiva Oa's beaches include the black-sand stretches at **Atuona** and **Puamau**. Those of **Hanamenu** and **Hanatekuua** can be reached by pirogue. As everywhere in the Marquesas, bring mosquito repellent because the *nono* are terrible.

Archaeological Sites

Tehueto Petroglyphs The Tehueto site is in the Faakua Valley, near Atuona and features stylised, horizontal human figures, their arms in the air, which have been carved into an enormous basalt block.

The site is a good walk from Atuona. Take the road towards Tahauku Bay; by the Tahauku snack bar go 100m along the unsealed road leading to the airport. You will then see a secondary track and a sign indicating the Tehueto site on the left. After about 1.4km, turn left at the fork. The petroglyphs are 800m away, in a clearing. The track is narrow and includes a small ford.

Taaoa This site, 7km southwest of Atuona, has more than 1000 **pae pae**. It has been partially restored; the remainder lies buried under a tangle of vegetation.

Firstly, you will find yourself facing a vast **tohua** built on several levels. Continue for 100m and, on the right, is a well-preserved **ti'i** more than a metre in height sitting on a platform. From a distance it looks like a plain block of basalt, but as you get closer you can clearly pick out the contours of the eyes and mouth. The shoulders and arms are truncated, compared with the large head.

To get to the site from the Atuona *gendarmerie*, follow the sealed road as far as Banque Socredo, turn right and continue for about 7km. Turn right at the telephone booth at the entrance to Taaoa village, 200m before the stone church, and go up this secondary track for 1.4km; it's accessible by 4WD. You will then reach a clearing; the *tohua* is set back on the left.

Iipona (Oipona) Known to ethnologists and archaeologists in the 1800s, the Iipona site, near Puamau, is one of the most important testimonies to precontact Marquesan civilisation. The site has been extensively restored under the leadership of French archaeologists Pierre and Marie-Noëlle Ottino.

Iipona is an exceptional collection of impressive and varied paving, platforms and stone sculptures. It is a *me'ae* arranged on two large main terraces covering 5000 sq m; various trees form a shady fringe.

The area's topography played a key role in the establishment of the *me'ae* and its layout. Orientated along a north-south axis, the site is bordered on the west by **Toea peak**, a remarkable grey mass that pierces the tangle of vegetation. Until the 19th century it sheltered skulls and a funeral cave. To the east, the *me'ae* is bounded by the Ahonu stream. Between the peak and the stream, the site measures 120m in width and 150m in length.

It is said that the valley was inhabited by the Naiki tribe, led by three nobles who captured and sacrificed a Hanapaaoa chieftain. To avenge his death, clans joined forces against the Naiki and drove them out. The victors transformed the residence of the three nobles into a *me'ae* and erected the large *ti'i*. Archaeologists date these events to the 18th century.

The site's main attraction is its five monumental **ti'i**. As you advance towards the first platform, your attention will be caught by the reclining **Maki Taua Pepe**, representing a woman lying on her stomach, her head stretched out and arms pointing to the sky. Experts believe she represents a woman giving birth. The petroglyphs on the pedestal represent dogs but their meaning is unknown.

A few metres further on, the **Manuiotaa ti'i** is in complete contrast with the others: less massive, its proportions are harmonious and balanced. The hands are clearly recognisable, as is its female sex. It was decapitated but its head has been replaced by archaeologists.

Takaii, the site's emblematic *ti'i*, is named after a warrior chief renowned for his strength. Measuring 2.67m above the soil, it is the largest *ti'i* in French Polynesia. It is the archetype of strength, balance and beauty.

The **Te Tovae E Noho ti'i** is set to the left of Takaii, on a lower platform. Less finely worked than the others, its upper torso is hard to make out and the head has disappeared. Note that its hands each have six fingers. Further back stands the **Fau Poe ti'i**. Measuring about 1.8m, it is sitting with its legs stretched out, a position typical of women when they work in the fields. Experts believe it to be Takaii's wife.

To reach the site from Puamau, follow the track directly back from the seafront, next to the football ground, and continue for about 1.5km. You will need to pay 200 CFP to the person who maintains and guards the site.

Tohua Pehe Kua In Puamau, on the property of the Chez Marie-Antoinette *pension*, shortly before the Iipona site, is the tomb of the valley's last chief and his partner, who died early in the 20th century. They were buried according to Christian rituals, although some pagan elements are present. One of the four tombs at the site is flanked by two **ti'i** and to one side is an imposing **pae pae**.

Ti'i Moe One About 15 minutes' walk southeast of Hanapaaoa stands one of the strangest *ti'i* in the Marquesas, the *ti'i* Moe One, about 1m in height. The statue's head is adorned with a carved crown of flowers. According to legend, the inhabitants used to take the *ti'i* down to the beach every year where they bathed it and coated it with *monoi* (fragrant oil) before putting it back in place. It is believed to be endowed with strong *mana* (supernatural power). Nearby, some human bones and a *pu* (conch shell) are concealed at the foot of an enormous banyan. The sacred character of this place is almost palpable. It is almost impossible to find this *ti'i* on your own; ask some of the village children to take you there.

Activities

The island's 4WD tracks are good for **walking**, but don't venture off them without a guide. Around Atuona there are easy walks to the Tehueto petroglyphs and to the Jacques Brel Memorial.

If you are interested in **horse riding**, ask at your *pension* or contact **Maui Ranch**

THE MARQUESAS

Tahauku (☎ 92 74 92), which organises rides to the Jacques Brel Memorial or the Tehueto petroglyphs.

For **deep-sea fishing**, contact **Ozanne Rohi** (☎ 92 73 43), **Médéric Kaimuko** (☎ 92 74 48) or **Gaby Heitaa** (☎ 92 73 02), who can take you fishing for tuna, *mahi mahi* (dorado), marlin or tazar aboard their *bonitiers* for 15,000 CFP a day (flat rate), tackle included.

Places to Stay

Accommodation is mainly concentrated in Atuona and its surrounding area, with the exception of one *pension* in Puamau.

Atuona Next to the administrative centre, the **Bungalows Communaux d'Atuona** (☎ 92 73 32 at the mairie 7.30am-11.30am & 1.30pm to 4.30pm Mon-Fri, fax 92 74 95; beds 2700 CFP) has seven bungalows *(fares)* with bathroom (cold water only), small equipped kitchen, refrigerator, fan and shower. Although reserved for administrative officials, they can be let to tourists depending on availability. Prices are per person; add 500 CFP for each additional person. Booking is recommended.

Pension Ozanne (☎/fax 92 73 43; singles/ doubles 4300/5400 CFP), on a hillside to the east of Atuona, is a wonderfully peaceful place. There are three fully equipped bungalows with an outstanding view over the black-sand beach below. Each has bathroom, kitchenette, TV and two balconies. Meals are available. To get there, follow the road towards Pension Gauguin, walk about 100m and take the first road on the right. Continue for 150m; the *pension* is set back on the left, partly concealed behind an enormous avocado tree.

Pension Gauguin (☎/fax 92 73 51; e pens .gauguin@mail.pf; singles/doubles with half-board 7000/12,800 CFP), in the village's east near the Make Make snack bar, is a very popular address with travellers. Nestling in luxuriant vegetation, this elegant, two-storey building comprises six spotlessly clean rooms, four of which have their own bathroom (with hot water) outside the room. A spacious terrace opens onto the bay and the food served here is stimulating and varied. The *pension* also organises excursions to Hiva Oa and Tahuata, particularly to the Hanahevane Valley. Credit cards are accepted.

Pension Moehau (☎ 92 72 69, fax 92 77 62; e moehaupension@mail.pf; half-board 9500 CFP) is the newest place on the island. It's on a hillside near the outskirts of Atuona going towards Tahauku Bay and has views over Atuona Bay and the beach below. There are eight modern, functional rooms of a superior standard with bathroom, television and fan. There are dining facilities on the ground floor. Credit cards are accepted.

Temetiu Village (Chez Gaby; ☎ 91 70 60, fax 91 70 61; e heitaagabyfeli@mail.pf; singles/ doubles 5400/6400 CFP, with half-board 8900/ 13,400 CFP), a 20-minute walk from Atuona, on the Tahauku Bay side, is the other popular choice for travellers. There are six pleasant, well-designed bungalows with bathroom (with hot water). They look directly out over Tahauku Bay. Excursions to Tahuata are offered. From the centre of Atuona take the road towards Tahauku Bay for a little over 1km and then take the first left after the SMA building (which flies the French flag). The road climbs for 400m to the *pension*. Credit cards are accepted.

Hanakéé Pearl Lodge (☎ 92 75 87, fax 92 75 95; w www.pearlresorts.com; bungalows from 29,000 CFP) is the only luxury accommodation on the island. It's perched on the hillside above the cargo-ship quay at Tahauku Bay. It has 20 air-con bungalows, an unforgettable view of the bay and a swimming pool. Various activities can be organised. Add 2900 CFP for lunch and 4600 CFP for dinner. Credit cards are accepted.

Puamau The only option outside Atuona is **Chez Marie-Antoinette** (☎ 92 72 27; half-/full board 6100/7500 CFP). It has two bare but clean double rooms with shared bathroom (cold water only). Lunch, featuring local specialities, costs 2000 CFP. There's an archaeological site with several tombs and *ti'i* on the *pension*'s land (see Tohua Pehe Kua under Archaeological Sites earlier in the Hiva Oa section).

To get there, follow the road that is at right angles to the track along the seafront, beside the football ground, for 700m. The house is on the corner where the road branches off to the right.

Places to Eat

In Atuona, you will find well-stocked food shops such as **Naiki**, **Ah You** and **Chanson**.

Ah You and Chanson are also bakeries. There are two small **grocery shops** in Puamau.

Atuona & Around On school days (in the morning) and on Sunday morning after mass, one or two **roulottes** take up position near the Tohua Pepeu and sell sandwiches, banana or coconut turnovers, chocolate cakes and simple meals at modest prices.

Make Make (☎ 92 74 26; dishes 850-1400 CFP; open lunch Mon-Fri), 100m from the administrative centre, on the inland side of the road, sells scrumptious·snacks such as poisson cru in coconut milk, lemon chicken and shrimps with vegetables or curry, at very reasonable prices. You can eat in or take away. A bottle of mineral water is an exorbitant 300 CFP, a beer 400 CFP. The opening hours are variable.

Snack Kaupe (☎ 92 70 62; dishes from 1000 CFP; open lunch Tues-Sun), in the centre of the town, is run by a couple of popaa (Westerners) and offers pizzas, fish dishes and some specialties from Réunion. You can eat in or take away.

Hoa Nui (☎ 92 73 63; meals 2500 CFP; open lunch & dinner every day) is concealed in vegetation to the left of the road that goes along the Vaioa River, to the north of the village. This restaurant specialises in Marquesan cuisine. In the large, airy dining room, you can try pork, fish or seafood dishes. The atmosphere heats up when it puts on a feast for Aranui passengers. You must book.

Temetiu Village (☎ 91 70 60; meals 2600 CFP; open lunch & dinner daily) has a restaurant with a terrace with views over Tahauku and Taaoa bays. Enjoy local specialities such as poisson cru or goat in coconut milk. Bookings are essential and credit cards are accepted.

Hanakéé Pearl Lodge (☎ 92 72 27; set menu 2000 CFP), overlooking Tahauku Bay, is another tasty but more expensive option.

Puamau Tourists staying in Atuona who spend the day at Puamau tend to have lunch at **Chez Marie-Antoinette** (set menu 2000 CFP). The menu features Marquesan specialities such as uru, poe (pieces of crushed banana mixed with starch, wrapped in a banana leaf, baked with a vanilla bean and sprinkled with coconut milk), poisson cru, wild pig, and goat or beef in coconut milk.

Getting There & Away

Air There are flights from Atuona to Pape'ete, Nuku Hiva, 'Ua Pou (via Nuku Hiva) and Ua Hika (via Nuku Hiva). Pape'ete-Atuona return flights go five to six times a week, nearly always via Nuku Hiva (28,800 CFP one-way). There are five Atuona–Nuku Hiva return flights a week (9800 CFP one-way). There are one or two Atuona–'Ua Pou return flights a week (9800 CFP one-way) and one 'Ua Huka–Atuona return flight per week (9800 CFP).

Air Tahiti (☎ 92 73 41; open 8.30am-11.30am & 2pm-4pm Mon-Fri) is in Atuona next to Banque Socredo, opposite the Tohua Pepeu, and a **branch** (☎ 92 72 31) is at the airport. Credit cards are accepted.

Boat The Aranui and Taporo IV stop at Hiva Oa. The Aranui stops at Atuona, Puamau, Hanaiapa and, less frequently, Hanapaaoa.

Ozanne Rohi (☎/fax 92 73 43) and **Médéric Kaimuko** (☎ 92 74 48), 200m behind Atuona's Banque Socredo towards the beach, have bonitiers that can be chartered. It costs 20,000 to 25,000 CFP for an Atuona–Vaitahu/Hapatoni (Tahuata) roundtrip, about 15,000 CFP for the Atuona–Motopu (Tahuata) round-trip and 55,000 CFP for an Atuona–Hanavave (Fatu Hiva) round-trip. Find out which charters are being organised during your stay.

The Fatu Hiva communal bonitier connects Atuona with Fatu Hiva once a week, usually on Monday (4000 CFP).

Getting Around

To/From the Airport The airport is 13km from Atuona. If you have booked your accommodation, your host will come and collect you for about 1900 CFP; the journey takes about 25 minutes. It's also possible to hitch a ride.

Car Excursions by 4WD cost about 10,000 to Taaoa, 12,000 CFP to Hanaiapa, 15,000 to 20,000 CFP to Hanapaaoa and 15,000 to 21,000 CFP to Puamau. For information, contact pension owners or **Ida Clark** (☎ 92 71 33). In Puamau, ask for **Étienne Heitaa** (☎ 92 75 28).

An exception to the seemingly fixed rule of hiring a 4WD with a driver is offered by **David Location** (☎ 92 72 87), in a small street a stone's throw from the Chanson, Ah You and Naiki shops. There's one Suzuki for hire at 15,000 CFP a day, with unlimited kilometres and insurance included. **Atuona Rent-a-Car** *(☎ 92 76 07, 72 17 17)* offers the same rates. Read the contract carefully, particularly the clauses regarding responsibility in the case of an accident. The owner can come to you at the airport. There's a petrol station at the cargo-ship quay at Tahauku Bay.

TAHUATA
pop 637 • area 70 sq km
Separated from Hiva Oa by the 4km-wide Bordelais Channel, Tahuata is the smallest inhabited island in the archipelago. Orientated along a north-south ridgeline, it has numerous inlets, two of which shelter the island's main villages, Hapatoni and Vaitahu.

Vaitahu Bay was the scene of several important episodes in Marquesan history. In 1595 the Spanish navigator Mendaña dropped anchor, naming the bay Madre de Dios and the island Santa Cristina. In 1774 explorer Captain James Cook visited the bay and named it Resolution Bay. In 1791 the Frenchman Étienne Marchand anchored off Hapatoni.

The pastors of the LMS and the Congregation of Picpus (also known as the Picpus Fathers) established a foothold in Vaitahu between 1797 and 1838 and the island became a bridgehead for the evangelisation of the Marquesas.

The year 1842 was a turning point in the island's history: Dupetit-Thouars forced his former ally, Chief Iotete of Tahuata, to sign the treaty of annexation by France. Realising that he had been duped, Iotete later opposed the transfer, but his rebellion was crushed by the French. It was also during this period that the island's reserves of sandalwood were plundered.

Tahuata lives in the shadow of its powerful neighbour, Hiva Oa and its economy is based on copra production and high-quality arts and crafts. Several commemorative monuments, well worth visiting, attest to the island's tumultuous past. The dreamlike scenery is another good reason to come here. Enchanting Hanamoenoa Bay is a favourite anchorage for yachts from March to August.

Information
For tourist information, contact the **mairie** *(☎ 92 92 19)* in Vaitahu.

Bring cash, as there is no bank on Tahuata. The **post office** *(open 7.30am-11.30am Mon-Fri)* is in Vaitahu, as is the phonecard telephone booth and infirmary.

Vaitahu
This tiny village, built against the steep slopes of the central ridge, retains a few vestiges of its stormy past. On the seafront stands a modest **memorial** topped by a rusty anchor, recalling the first meeting between Admiral Dupetit-Thouars and Chief Iotete in 1838. It was unveiled in November 1988 to commemorate the 150th anniversary of their meeting.

Next to the post office, you can read an **epitaph** to Halley, a French lieutenant commander who perished at Tahuata in 1842 during the revolt by Iotete and his warriors.

On the hill that dominates the village to the south are a few remains of a building known as the **French Fort**, in an advanced state of decay.

The monumental stone **Catholic church** is opposite the seafront. Financed by the Vatican and opened with great pomp and ceremony in 1988, it recalls the importance of Tahuata in the evangelisation of the archipelago. The church has beautiful stained-glass windows, which diffuse an atmospheric halo above the altar. Outside, have a look at the imposing wooden **statue** *Virgin with Child*, nearly 4m in height, by Damien Haturau of Nuku Hiva. It reflects both Marquesan culture and Catholic archetypes. The child is not curled up in his mother's lap but is held out in both hands, an attitude reminiscent of the posture of *ti'i*; he is also holding an *uru* as an offering, a symbol of the Marquesas.

There is a small Polynesian art and history **museum** in the *mairie* on the seafront.

Vaitahu is a good place to have a wander. Copra-drying sheds are dotted here and there, and brightly coloured traditional *vaka* (outrigger canoes) line the shore. Some toprate Marquesan sculptors work in Vaitahu.

Hapatoni
Hapatoni curves around a wide bay and is accessible from Vaitahu, several kilometres north, by boat in less than 15 minutes or by the bridleway.

The **royal road** is the village's main attraction. Built on a dike on the orders of Queen

Vaekehu II in the 19th century, this paved road, lined with 100-year-old tamanu trees, extends along the shore. At the promontory a path leads up to a **lookout**, marked by a cross, with a magnificent view of the bay.

On the seafront, a **memorial** commemorates the peaceful visit of Étienne Marchand; it was erected for the bicentennial of the event. In the middle of the village, a magnificent **me'ae** has been restored.

Moputu
This village, to the north, has a few dozen inhabitants and is accessible by 4WD by the vehicle track that crosses the island's interior.

Horse Riding
The track which joins Vaitahu and Motopu in the northeast, a distance of about 17km, is ideal for horse riding. Ask the locals about hiring a horse.

Places to Stay & Eat
Pension Amatea (☎ 92 92 84; rooms per person 3800 CFP, with half-board 6400 CFP) is in Vaitahu. This *pension* has five rooms with shared bathroom.

Every village has one or two small **shops**.

Getting There & Away
Tahuata is not accessible by air as it has no landing strip.

The **Te Pua O Mioi** (☎ 92 92 19), the communal *bonitier*, runs a Vaitahu-Atuona ferry service on Tuesday and Thursday (1000 CFP return, one hour). It departs at about 6.30am and usually returns at around noon.

For private *bonitier* **charters** in Vaitahu, ask for **Yves-Bertrand Barsinas** (☎ 92 92 40) or **Louis Timau** (☎ 92 92 71). See the Hiva Oa Getting There & Away section for information on *bonitier* charters between Tahuata and Hiva Oa. It costs between 20,000 CFP and 25,000 CFP to charter a boat between Vaitahu or Hapatoni and Atuona.

The *Aranui* and *Taporo IV* stop at Tahuata.

Getting Around
A 17km track, accessible to 4WD vehicles, crosses the island's interior to link Vaitahu with Motopu. It costs 15,000 CFP for one day's hire with driver.

Hapatoni is less than 15 minutes from Vaitahu by speedboat. It costs about 6000 CFP to hire a boat between Vaitahu and Hapatoni return, and 7000 to 10,000 CFP between Vaitahu and Hanahevane Bay.

UNINHABITED ISLANDS
The uninhabited island of **Motane** (Mohotani) lies southeast of Hiva Oa and east of Tahuata. With an area of 15 sq km and highest altitude of 520m, this inhospitable island is now home to only wild goats, but it was once occupied by humans. The islet **Terihi** is south of Motane.

Fatu Huku is to the north of Hiva Oa and **Thomasset Rock** lies east of Fatu Hiva. The waters of Fatu Huku and Motane are occasionally visited by fishing vessels.

FATU HIVA
pop 631 • area 80 sq km
Fatu Hiva is the island of superlatives: the most remote, the farthest south, the wettest, the lushest and the most authentic. It was also the first in the archipelago to be seen by the Spanish navigator Mendaña, in 1595. He christened it Santa Magdalena after the saint whose day it was.

About 75km south of Hiva Oa, Fatu Hiva consists of two craters stacked one on top of the other, forming arcs open to the west. Between the flanks of the calderas are two valleys, in which nestle the only villages on the island: Hanavave in the north and Omoa in the south, 5km apart as the crow flies.

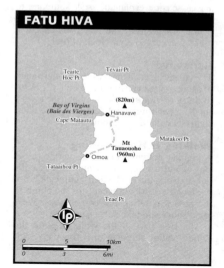

FATU HIVA

Teaite Hoe Pt · Tevaii Pt · (820m) · Bay of Virgins (Baie des Vierges) · Hanavave · Cape Matautu · Mt Tauaouoho (960m) · Matakoo Pt · Omoa · Tataaihoa Pt · Teae Pt

0 · 5 · 10km
0 · 3 · 6mi

THE MARQUESAS

With no landing strip and only poorly serviced by the *bonitiers*, Fatu Hiva's gentle atmosphere of untouched paradise remains intact. Thanks to its plentiful rainfall, mango, banana, grapefruit, *uru*, orange and lemon trees thrive on the steep slopes of the island.

The jagged relief of the island has created some curiously shaped outcrops. The phallic protuberances of Hanavave Bay caused it to be named Baie des Verges (Bay of Penises). Outraged, the missionaries hastened to add a redeeming 'i' to make the name Baie des Vierges (Bay of Virgins). At sunset, it is drenched in purple and the surrounding peaks give off bronze reflections, forming an entrancing spectacle that has intoxicated hundreds of international yachties.

Fatu Hiva prides itself on its top-quality art and crafts, whose reputation has spread far beyond the Marquesas.

Information
There is a **post office** in Omoa and an **infirmary** or first-aid post in both villages. There is no bank on the island.

Omoa
In the south of the island, Omoa is dominated by a **church** with a red roof, white façade and slender spire. Facing the shore, which is partly obscured by a string of multicoloured canoes, the football ground forms a vast seaside esplanade. Ask someone to take you to the giant **petroglyph** at the edge of the village, near the river: it's an enormous fish carved on a block of rock.

Hanavave
The village is set on the seashore, at the mouth of a steep-sided valley leading onto the beautiful **Bay of Virgins**. Near the shore, the town's small, sober **church**, white with a blue door, contrasts with the church in Omoa.

Walking & Horse Riding
A popular activity is to walk or ride to the Bay of Virgins from Omoa along the island's only existing track. The four-hour walk is not particularly difficult except for the climb to the pass separating the two valleys. Wear good shoes and take sufficient water.

The first part of the walk goes up the **Omoa Valley** along a cliff-top path with beautiful views over the village below. The trail then crosses through the interior of the island; the **caldera** is clearly visible and very impressive. It's a steep descent to Hanavave and there's not much shade along the way.

This route can be followed by horse or by 4WD if it's not too muddy.

Places to Stay & Eat
The following *pension*s are all in Omoa.

Pension Heimata *(☎/fax 92 80 58; half-/full board 4300/5900 CFP)* has two well-kept rooms with shared bathroom (with cold water).

Chez Norma *(☎ 92 80 13; doubles 3800 CFP, half-board per person 5400 CFP)* is near the beach. The six double rooms come with shared bathroom (with hot water). You will be served *kaikai enana* (traditional Marquesan dishes) featuring *poe*, *fei* (plantain bananas), goat in coconut milk and *poisson cru*.

Chez Lionel Cantois *(☎/fax 92 80 80; single/double bungalows 3200/5400 CFP, half-board per person 5400 CFP)* is the last house in the village, about 1.5km from the quay. It's beside the river, in the middle of a beautiful tropical garden. A well-equipped bungalow with bathroom is available.

Apart from the *pension*s, eating options on Fatu Hiva are limited to a few small grocers' **shops**.

Getting There & Away
Fatu Hiva is the most difficult island to get to in the Marquesas. Theoretically, there's a communal *bonitier* between Omoa and Atuona (Hiva Oa) on Tuesday (4000 CFP per trip). Otherwise try the *Aranui* and the *Taporo IV* or a chartered private *bonitier*.

Getting Around
The only road, of beaten earth, is 17km long and links Hanavave with Omoa. As it is impassable in wet weather, journeys between villages are often by motorised pirogue.

Ask at your *pension* about renting a 4WD; expect to pay 10,000 CFP a day with driver.

On Fatu Hiva, speedboats have not yet ousted the traditional outrigger canoes, which take three to four people. The only concession to modernity is the low-powered outboard motors. Expect to pay 5000 to 6000 CFP between Omoa and Hanavave; ask your *pension* for information.

The Australs

Well to the south of the Society Islands and Tahiti, the Australs are effectively an extension of the range of submerged peaks making up the southern Cook Islands. There are five inhabited islands in the Australs: Rimatara, Rurutu, Tubuai, Raivavae and remote Rapa. There are also two uninhabited islands: Maria Island to the northwest, and Marotiri, also known as the Bass Rocks, to the southeast. The chain extends 1300km from end to end.

The islands lie along the Tropic of Capricorn and the climate is much cooler than on the Society Islands, although only Rapa is far enough south to qualify as temperate. The islands are not lush and fertile like the Society Islands; their appearance is altogether more spartan. The population of the entire Austral group is just over 6000.

The Australs are remarkably varied and their features of interest include limestone caverns and ancient marae on Rurutu, reminders of the powerful artwork and massive stone tiki (sacred statues) of Raivavae and the *pa* (hilltop fortresses) of Rapa. Tourism is little developed but there are *pensions* (guesthouses) on the inhabited islands.

History
The Australs were the last of the Polynesian islands to be settled. It is believed the first arrivals came from Tahiti between AD 1000 and 1300. European sightings of the chain were a drawn-out affair. Cook first saw Rurutu in 1769, Gayangos and Varela 'found' Raivavae in 1775, Cook was back to make the first landing on Tubuai in 1777 and Vancouver 'found' Rapa in 1791. It wasn't until Captain Samuel Pinder Henry chanced upon Rimatara in 1811 that the last of the islands came to European attention.

Apart from a colourful chapter in the *Bounty* saga, when the mutineers unsuccessfully tried to establish themselves on Tubuai, contact with Europeans and the Western world was limited until the 20th century. In 1889 the French established a protectorate over all the islands, and in 1901 the last of them were formally annexed. This long period during which English missionaries, or more frequently their native representatives, held sway has ensured that Protestantism remains strong to this day.

Highlights

- Exploring the marae of Rurutu and Raivavae and marvelling at Raivavae's last great tiki
- Visiting the caves and caverns of Rurutu
- Watching the whales during Rurutu's humpback-whale season
- Motu-hopping in the beautiful Raivavae lagoon
- Climbing to the ancient *pa* on Rapa Iti

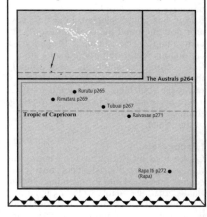

The Australs p264

Rurutu p265
Rimatara p269
Tubuai p267
Raivavae p271

Tropic of Capricorn

Rapa Iti p272
(Rapa)

Getting There & Away
Rurutu and Tubuai are about 600km south of Tahiti, Raivavae about 650km. You can get there easily by regular Air Tahiti flights. Rimatara can be reached by cargo ship. Getting to Rapa, over 1000km south of Tahiti, is a real adventure.

Only Rurutu, Raivavae and Tubuai have airports. Air Tahiti flies to Rurutu and Tubuai about four times weekly in the low season and five times weekly in the high season. The routes of the flights alternates: one travels a Tahiti–Rurutu–Tubuai route while the next travels Tahiti–Tubuai–Rurutu–Tahiti. One-way fares are Tahiti–Rurutu 18,100 CFP, Tahiti–Tubuai 20,200 CFP and Rurutu–Tubuai 9300 CFP.

The cargo ship *Tuhaa Pae II* does three trips a month to the Australs and accepts passengers. See the Getting Around chapter for details.

THE AUSTRALS

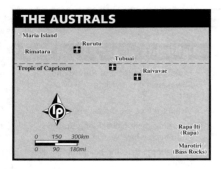

THE AUSTRALS

Maria Island
Rimatara   Rururu
Tubuai
Tropic of Capricorn
Raivavae
Rapa Iti (Rapa)
Marotiri (Bass Rocks)

0   150   300km
0   90   180mi

RURUTU

pop 2015 • area 36 sq km

Rururu has a high plateau, limestone caverns dotted around the coast and some ancient marae. The island is fringed by a continuous reef, rarely more than a stone's throw from the shoreline. Occasionally there are small pools between the shore and reef edge, but there's no lagoon as such. There are some good beaches, particularly south of Arei Point and at the southern end of the island.

History

Cook sailed by Rururu in 1769 during his first voyage, but the islanders' hostile reception prevented him from landing. Joseph Banks noted the quality of their canoes and weapons. There was little contact with Europeans until well into the 19th century, when the London Missionary Society (LMS) sent native teachers to establish a mission. Christianity quickly took hold. European diseases arrived at much the same time and the result was disastrous.

Rururu has the most extensive marae site in the Australs. The statue of the Rururu ancestor god A'a on display in London at the British Museum is one of the most important surviving Polynesian works of art.

Orientation & Information

Rururu is about 10km long and averages about 5km wide. The population is concentrated in three main villages on the coast. Moerai is the largest, with the island's only dock, a post office, a bank and several shops. A sealed road runs about a third of the way round the island, linking the airport with Moerai and Hauti (also spelled Auti). Another sealed road climbs over the centre of the island to link Moerai with Avera, the third village.

There is an ATM inside the **Banque Socredo** *(open 7.30am-11.30am & 1.30pm-4.30pm Mon-Fri)* branch in Moerai.

The **post office** *(open 7am-3pm Mon-Thur, 7am-2pm Fri)* has a computer with an Internet connection (220 CFP for 15 minutes).

Around the Island

It's 36km around Rururu, about the same distance as around Bora Bora. Unless you're a seasoned cyclist, don't even think about pedalling it though. Apart from the Moerai to Marae Vitaria section, which is practically flat, the route is very hilly, with short and steep rises that will discourage even those with the best of intentions.

The road runs through a variety of plantations, passes beautiful stretches of coast and skirts rocky headlands. The southern part of the island is particularly quiet.

Moerai The island's main town is about 4km southeast of the airport. Tauraatua Pass leads directly into the town's small artificial harbour. The picturesque little Protestant **church**, just back from the harbour, dates from 1865–72. The island's most famous resident, the French administrator Éric de Bisschop, who dedicated himself to making perilous voyages between South America and Polynesia in unsuitable craft, is remembered by a simple gravestone. His **grave** is in the cemetery to the south of the village.

Makatea

Rururu is the Austral island geologically most like the southern Cook Islands – it is a textbook example of *makatea*. Long ago, a sudden upthrust raised the whole island above sea level. The sheer, rocky cliff faces around much of the island were once the outer face of the island's fringing coral reef. The valley, along which the road from Hauti to Toataratara Point runs, was once the lagoon between the island and its outer reef. That reef is now the ridgeline falling sheer into the sea along the southeast coast of the island. Rururu is riddled with limestone caverns, another reminder of the cataclysmic upheaval that raised what were once underwater caves to their new location.

Moerai to Hauti The road continues from Moerai along the coast to Arei Point, one of Rurutu's impressive elevated reef cliffs. Just before the point, a short path leads up to a large cliff-face cavern with stalactites and stalagmites, **Tane Uapoto**. Nearby there's a whale-watching platform.

From Arei Point the road runs south along the coast until it reaches the Te Vaipa River, running into the sea beside Mauo Point, where there is another cavern in the cliff face, **Tiana Taupee**. From here the road climbs inland and skirts around the point before dropping down to Hauti.

Hauti to Avera Once out of Hauti the road (now unsealed) climbs, drops back almost to sea level, then climbs again to over 100m before dropping steeply down to the coast near the southern tip of the island, **Toataratara Point**. This road runs along what was once the lagoon bottom. This part of the coast, about 500m east of the road, ends in steep cliffs, dropping 50m into the sea, which were once the reef (see the boxed text 'Makatea').

At the south end of the island, near Toataratara Point, is the small **Marae Poreopi**, with the spike-like vertical stones characteristic of Austral marae. A series of beautiful little **beaches** runs to the east of the point.

The road rounds the point and heads north. Leaving the coast, it climbs steeply, passing through pine forests and a coffee plantation. Then it's down again, with superb views over the coast and, to the north, over Avera to the three peaks of Teape, Taatioe and Manureva. Avera is a small village beside a pretty beach.

Avera to Moerai The road climbs round the edge of the headland then drops down to the coast just beyond Parari Point. Behind Pension Teautamatea and in the middle of a coconut plantation are the remains of **Marae Vitaria**, the marae of the last Rurutu royal family. Said at one time to have stretched for 1km, it's still an extensive site, punctuated by many vertical stones. About 500m north, to the right, is **Tapuara Pito**, an ancient sacred site where women who had just given birth came to cut the umbilical cord of the newborn on a rock.

Another 500m farther, a little track going to the right leads to the huge **Ana Aeo Cave**.

RURUTU

With its abundant stalactites and stalagmites, it evokes the interior of a baroque cathedral.

The coast road continues past the Hôtel Rurutu Village, then, a little further on the right, past **Are Taofe**, a coffee house where you can taste and buy the distinctive coffee of the Australs.

The airport runway comes rapidly into view. Just before Moerai there's a whale-watching platform by the roadside.

Activities
Whale watching is a popular activity. See the boxed text 'Rurutu, Island of Whales'.

The interior of the island, with its gentle variations in altitude, is perfect for **walking**. To the north are the three highest peaks: Taatioe (389m), Manureva (385m) and Teape (359m). A network of walking tracks crisscrosses the fertile Tetuanui Plateau (200m), leading to these summits. Towards the south of the island is Mt Erai (289m). It is difficult to get lost as you can always see the sea. Ask someone to show you the way or, on the cross-island road between Moerai and Avera, take one of two tracks signposted at the side of the road (one says 'Manureva';

Rurutu, Island of Whales

HUGH D'ANDRADE

Rurutu is often nicknamed Island of Whales, due to the presence of these marine mammals from July to October. They come here to reproduce before heading back to the icy waters of the Antarctic. It's an ideal place for whale watching because the absence of a lagoon means that the whales come close to the shore, and several observation platforms have been built by the side of the road.

The Raie Manta Club organises whale-watching trips, open to all, during which you can swim with the whales (see the special section 'Diving' for more information).

the other says 'Pito' and leads to Mt Erai). There are panoramas over the bays and the vegetation is diverse, including coffee trees, mandarin trees, guava trees, ferns, pines, *mape* (Polynesian 'chestnut' tree) *purau* (hibiscus) and lemon trees.

For **horse riding**, contact Viriamu at Pension Teautamatea (see Places to Stay & Eat). Superb trips, suitable for all levels, follow trails in the interior of the island, particularly around Tetuanui Plateau and Mt Taatioe (5000 CFP for a half-day).

Places to Stay

The following places provide free airport transfers for their guests.

Hôtel Rurutu Village, about 1km from the airport, has long been Rurutu's best-known place to stay but was in search of a new owner when we visited. It will probably reopen; inquire when you arrive.

Pension Ariana (☎ 94 06 69; *singles/doubles 4100/5100 CFP, with half-board 7300/11,500 CFP, single/double bungalows 4600/5600 CFP, with half-board 7800/12,000 CFP*), near Hôtel Rurutu Village, has two rooms in its main building with shared bathroom, and seven simple, colourful bungalows with private bathroom.

Pension Temarama (☎/fax 94 02 17; **e** *pensiontemarama@mail.pf; singles/doubles 3600/4600 CFP, half-/full board per person 7600/*

9600 CFP), near the airport, has six rooms with bathrooms in a big white house. Although the setting is nothing special and the building is not particularly Polynesian, it's spotlessly clean, the welcome is warm and the food has a good reputation.

Pension Teautamatea (☎/fax 94 02 42; **e** *pension.teautamatea@free.fr; singles/doubles with breakfast 4600/6600 CFP, with half-board 7100/11,600 CFP, with full board 9100/15,600 CFP*) is an excellent pension. There are six extremely clean rooms, four with bathroom. The setting is enchanting: a coconut plantation (in which Marae Vitaria is located) stretches behind the building and you only have to cross a track to get to the beach.

Manôtel (☎/fax 94 06 99; **e** *manotel@mail.pf; bungalows from 6100 CFP*) is in the Peva area on the east coast, near Moerai. There are four clean, well-designed bungalows with bathroom, close to the sea. Add 3200 CFP per person for half-board.

Shopping

Rurutu is known for its hats made with pandanus, and *tifaifai* (colourful patchwork). Try the **shop** at the airport, which is open to coincide with flights, and **Pu Rimai Vaipurura**, a workshop at Moerai. The owners of Pension Ariana and Pension Teautamatea also have small shops. You can choose from hats, *peue* (mats), baskets and bags. Men's hats have a higher top and narrower brim, while women's hats are flatter on top and have a wider brim. Cheaper hats cost 1000 to 2000 CFP and mid-range ones 2500 to 4000 CFP, but the really fine hats are 10,000 CFP and more. A special type of pandanus, *paeore*, is used for hat making; it is grown on shaded hillsides and bleached before use.

Getting There & Away

Rurutu, about 600km south of Tahiti, is the most accessible of the Australs, served by regular flights and shipping services. **Air Tahiti** (☎ 94 03 57) has an office at the airport which is open before and after each flight. Cargo ships dock at Moerai. See Getting There & Away at the start of this chapter for details.

Getting Around

The airport is about 4km from Moerai. If you have booked accommodation you will be picked up at the airport. Most pensions offer 4WD island tours for around 4000 to 4500 CFP per person and rent out bicycles for about 1000 to 1500 CFP a day. Pension Temarama also rents out cars for a prohibitive 11,000 CFP per day, and scooters for 5300 CFP per day.

TUBUAI
pop 2049 • area 45 sq km

It's the largest of the Austral islands and their administrative centre, but Tubuai does not have the interesting geology, varied geography or ancient marae of Rurutu. Virtually the only unusual thing about Tubuai is that, unlike on other Polynesian islands, the pirogues (outrigger canoes) have their outriggers on the right. The *Bounty* mutineers tried, unsuccessfully, to establish themselves on Tubuai, far from the long reach of British naval justice, but there's barely any trace of that visit.

History

Captain Cook landed at Tubuai in 1777 en route to Tahiti on his third voyage. Some theories hold that it was only settled a few generations earlier, but the locals were certainly fiercely protective of their island, as the *Bounty* mutineers discovered when they attempted to settle there in 1789. Ships bound for Australia stopped on Tubuai from early in the 19th century and the LMS dispatched native teachers to the island in 1822.

At about this time European diseases started to afflict the islanders and, in the few years to 1828, the population reportedly plummeted from 3000 to less than 300. It was to fall further still before it began to recover. When Pomare II visited the Australs in 1819, the island chiefs ceded power to him, so when Tahiti came under France's wing in 1842, Tubuai followed. The island was formally annexed by France in 1880.

Orientation & Information

The coast of Tubuai lacks the dramatic peninsulas and bays of the Society Islands. The 25km coast road only leaves the water's edge as it passes the airport. There are two mountain ranges sloping down to flat plains by the sea, separated by an equally low-lying central region. A *route traversière* (cross-island road) between Mataura and Mahu bisects the

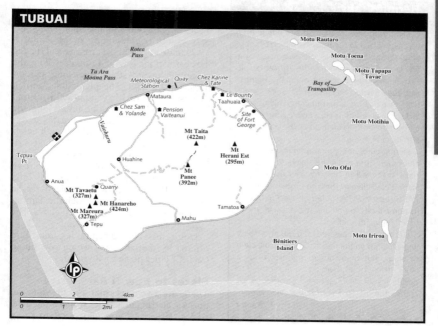

TUBUAI

Motu Rautaro
Motu Toena
Rotea Pass
Motu Tapapa Tavae
Ta Ara Moana Pass
Meteorological Station   Quay   Chez Karine & Tate
Bay of Tranquility
Mataura   Le-Bounty
Taahuaia
Chez Sam & Yolande   Pension Vaiteanui
Site of Fort George
Vaiakuru
Motu Motihia
Mt Taita (422m)
Tepuu Pt
Mt Herani Est (295m)
Huahine
Motu Ofai
Anua   Quarry
Mt Panee (392m)
Mt Tavaetu (327m)
Mt Hanareho (424m)
Mt Mareura (327m)
Tamatoa
Tepu   Mahu
Motu Iriroa
Bénitiers Island

0   2   4km
0   1   2mi

THE AUSTRALS

island. Mt Taita (422m) is the highest point on the island. The island is surrounded by a wide, very shallow lagoon with an outer reef dotted by a handful of motu (popular for beach excursions) at its eastern end.

Mataura, about 4km from the airport, is the main village and has a **post office**, a **Banque Socredo** *(open 7am-11.30am & 1.30pm-4pm Mon-Fri)* with an ATM inside and a couple of reasonably sized **stores**. A few smaller **stores** are dotted round the island.

The owner of **Pension Vaiteanui** (☎ 95 04 19) is head of the small local committee for tourism.

Around the Island

One quick circuit of Tubuai and you've pretty much done it. From the centre of Mataura, proceeding clockwise, the coast road runs past the Météo France meteorological station, the shipping wharf and through **Taahuaia**, the island's second village. Just past the village, an empty patch of green is the site of the *Bounty* mutineers' **Fort George**. There's no sign or memorial drawing attention to the site's history.

Hermit Crabs

Cycling round the coast road late one night I was astonished to see hefty hermit crabs scuttling across the road, all of them occupying the large brown shells of the African snails that have become a pest on many islands. Had they evicted the snails from their shells? It's a nice picture, a hermit crab hauling a reluctant snail out of its shell and leaving it shivering in the undergrowth while the crab settles into its new home.

Hermit crabs are common on many islands, and range from miniature things to medium-sized snail-shell inhabitants and even larger. Hermit crabs live in shells to protect their fragile carapace. When a hermit crab outgrows its home it has to find and make a swift move to a new larger shell.

Hermit-crab races are a popular activity with children on the beach. Gather a collection of crabs, put them down together, draw a large circle around them and wait for them to decide it's all clear, emerge from their shells and scuttle off. First outside the circle wins.

Tony Wheeler

The three larger motu are visible at the edge of the lagoon as you round the island's eastern end. The village of **Mahu** marks the southern end of the cross-island road, and at the end of the village Nöel Ilari's self-made **tomb** stands in front of his home. Born in 1897, Ilari was a larger-than-life Frenchman who married a Tubuaian woman and became president of the French Polynesian Territorial Assembly in 1954. His squabbles with the French government led to a self-inflicted exile on Tubuai. He never forgave the government and the inscription recounts his indignation. Convinced his death was imminent, Ilari constructed the tomb in the 1970s, and then lived until 1985!

From Mahu the road makes a sharp right turn at the island's southwest corner, another sharp right at the airport and quickly ends up back in Mataura. The best **beaches** and **swimming** are along this stretch; the beach at the Ta Ara Moana Pass, just west of Mataura, is excellent and the water is deep.

The Mormons have a major presence on Tubuai. Their modern, functional churches, each with a floodlit basketball court, are sprinkled around the island's coast road.

Activities

There is one good **walking** opportunity, the easy climb to the summit of Mt Taita. A 4WD track begins at the cross-island road in the centre of the island. It runs east along the ridgeline towards the peaks then switchbacks up through pine plantations until it rounds the top of Mt Panee (392m). From here the 4WD track continues along the ridgeline until it finally terminates and a much more attractive walking path takes over. This pushes through small thickets of guava trees (watch out for wasps' nests) and patches of ferns until you eventually arrive at the tumble of boulders that tops Mt Taita (422m). It's a bit of a scramble over the moss-covered boulders to reach the summit but you're rewarded with superb views. The return journey takes three hours.

Don't miss the **pirogue lagoon tours** offered by the pensions, which cost about 6000 CFP per person with picnic.

Places to Stay & Eat

There are two **supermarkets** in Mataura, plus a scattering of smaller **stores** around the island. However, you may want to bring supplies with you. Come prepared for mosquitoes as well. Don't count on using credit cards on Tubuai. Airport transfers are free.

Pension Vaiteanui (*☎/fax 95 04 19;* e *bod inm@mail.pf; singles/doubles 3400/5400 CFP)* is about 1km from Mataura on the Mataura–Mahu road and has five rooms with bathroom. Add 3400 CFP per person for halfboard. Activities can be organised including motu picnics (5500 CFP) and island tours by boat (6100 CFP) or 4WD (4450 CFP).

Chez Sam & Yolande (*☎/fax 95 05 52; halfboard from 6100 CFP)* is right by the sea about 1.5km from the Mataura mairie, towards the airport. It has six well-kept rooms with bathroom in a modern and functional house; the welcome is warm and the food is good.

Chez Karine & Tale (*☎ 95 04 52; singles/doubles 5100/8100 CFP)*, about 1km west of the quay at Mataura, offers two equipped and spacious bungalows, which are clean and well maintained, set back from the road.

Le Bounty (*☎ 95 03 32, fax 95 05 58; fare singles/doubles 3600/5600 CFP)*, in Taahuaia, is a clean, functional and fully-equipped *fare* attached to the college.

Getting There & Away
Tubuai is 600km south of Tahiti and about midway between Rurutu to the northwest and Raivavae to the southeast. It can be reached by plane or cargo ship. **Air Tahiti** (*☎ 95 04 76)* has an office at the airport. Cargo ships enter through the large passes on the northwestern edge of the reef and dock at Mataura. See Getting There & Away at the start of this chapter for details.

Getting Around
If you book your accommodation ahead you will be collected from the airport or dock. **Pension Vaiteanui** and **Chez Sam & Yolande** have bicycles and a car for the use of their clients (rates negotiable).

Other Australs

Rurutu and Tubuai are the most developed and accessible of the Australs. Raivavae, having been opened up to air transport in 2002, will probably take off more as a destination. The other islands in the group, only accessible by sea, are rarely visited and remain on the margins of organised tourist activity. Moving down the chain from the northwest, these less-frequented islands start with Maria Island.

MARIA ISLAND
Uninhabited Maria Island is an atoll with four motu on a triangular-shaped reef. It is about 200km northwest of Rimatara and 400km east of the Cook Islands. The name comes from the whaler *Maria*, whose crew sighted the island in 1824; it's also known as Hull Island. The *Tuhaa Pae II* makes occasional stops at Maria Island for the harvest of copra. The low-lying island has a very shallow lagoon and abundant **birdlife**.

RIMATARA
pop 929 • area 8 sq km
The tiny island of Rimatara is a rough circle 4km in diameter, rising to Mt Uahu (or Vahu; 83m) in the centre. Around this low mountain are the three villages of **Anapoto**, **Amaru** and **Mutua Ura**, linked by a road running inland from the coast.

Like Rurutu, the island is circled by a fringing reef, and the narrow Hiava Pass lets small boats in to land on the beach in front of Amaru or Anapoto. The waterfront cemetery is the first thing visitors see on landing at Amaru. Traditionally, arriving visitors would pass through the smoke of a purifying fire as they stepped ashore.

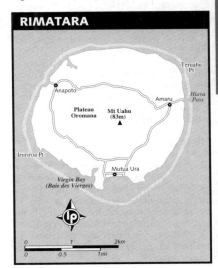

Rimatara is the most densely populated Austral island. Pandanus work and shell necklaces, plus the plantations, support the islanders, who have preserved their own distinct dialect.

Rimatara was the last of the Austral to be 'discovered', in 1811. The first native missionary teachers came to the island in 1821 and within two years the entire population of 300 had been converted to Christianity.

There are no hotels or pensions as such, but you won't have any difficulty negotiating directly with the locals for accommodation. It's a good idea to bring some supplies, as there are no grocery stores.

Getting There & Away

Rimatara is about 600km southwest of Tahiti and 150km west of Rurutu. Interisland cargo ships stop at the island about every three weeks (see Getting Around at the start of this chapter). Only small boats can enter Hiava Pass so goods are transferred to shore on *bonitiers* (whaleboats) that land right on the beach.

RAIVAVAE

pop 1049 • area 16 sq km

Often cited as one of the most beautiful islands in the Pacific, Raivavae (rye-vie-vie) is encircled by a motu-dotted reef. The island has five villages and its mountainous interior is dominated by Mt Hiro (437m). Raivavae's main shipping quay is at Rairua, but Mahanatoa is the largest of the villages.

A small revolution occurred in 2002, one which promises to unsettle the island's equilibrium: the construction of a runway allowing Air Tahiti planes to land. Without doubt, with its stunning lagoon and exceptional environment, Raivavae will attract visitors searching for tranquillity somewhere a bit different.

History

Raivavae was once noted for massive stone tiki that stood in the island marae. There is only one great tiki left today, at the site of the principal marae, near Mahanatoa. It emanates great *mana* (supernatural power). Its impressive relations are now standing in the gardens of the Gauguin Museum on Tahiti. The Raivavae islanders also made unusual sculpted drums, which have also become museum pieces.

Captain Thomas Gayangos of Spain was the first European to land on Raivavae when he stopped there in 1775 en route to Peru. Like Tubuai, the island was ceded to Pomare II of Tahiti in 1819, and then became a French protectorate in 1842 before being annexed by France in 1880.

At the time of the first European contact, Raivavae was a crowded island with around 3000 inhabitants who had a highly developed social order and were unparalleled seafarers. They regularly visited the Society Islands and even voyaged as far as New Zealand. In 1826 the same European fever that had devastated the island of Tubuai reached Raivavae and killed almost the entire population. Only about 100 people survived, and the island's cultural and seafaring traditions were wiped out.

Today a little fishing is done, but agriculture is the main activity. The cool climate and fertile soil are perfect for growing cabbages, carrots, potatoes, coffee and oranges.

Archaeological Sites

Raivavae's famous **tiki** is nearly 2m high and stands neglected and overgrown a short stroll off the coast road, just to the west of Mahanatoa. At the other end of the island, inland from the road along the south coast, is the better-maintained **Marae Maunauto** (Marae of the Sad Hero). Huge vertical slabs, many of them 2m high, surround the site, while a nearby grave is said to be that of a princess.

Places to Stay

Pension Ataha (☎ 95 43 69; room only/half-board/full board per person 3100/5600/7100 CFP) is at Rairua, by the sea, about 1.5km from the quay. There are two rooms with shared bathroom.

Pension Rau'uru (☎ 95 42 88; singles/doubles 2600/4100 CFP; half-/full board per person 5000/7000 CFP), in Mahanatoa, is an equipped house with bathroom, about 2km from the quay.

Pension Moana (☎/fax 95 42 66; singles/doubles 2600/4100 CFP), also in Mahanatoa, offers three rooms with shared bathroom.

Getting There & Away

Raivavae is about 650km southeast of Tahiti and 200km southeast of Tubuai. It has an airport served by Air Tahiti. The ship *Tuhaa Pae II* comes by about twice a month.

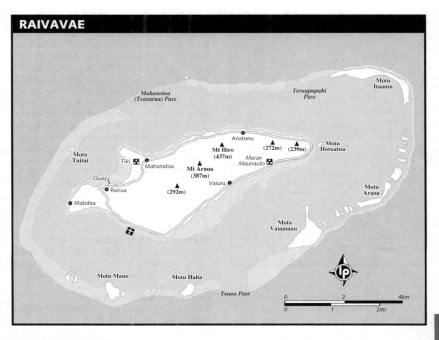

RAIVAVAE

RAPA ITI (RAPA)
pop 521 ● area 22 sq km

Rapa is the most remote and isolated island of French Polynesia – its nearest inhabited neighbour, Raivavae, is over 500km away. This far south, there are no coral reefs and no coconut palms, and the temperature can drop as low as 5°C in winter.

Of its soaring and jagged-edged peaks, six reach over 400m, the highest being Mt Perau (650m). The island is the remains of a gigantic volcano cone: a breach having formed in the eastern side of the cone, the ancient crater is now the wide expanse of Haurei Bay.

The island is known as Rapa Iti (Little Rapa) to distinguish it from Rapa Nui (Big Rapa), the Polynesian name for Easter Island. The population is concentrated in the villages of Haurei and Area, which are on opposite sides of Haurei Bay. They are generally linked by boat as there is only a rough road around the bay.

History

Rapa Iti is believed to have been settled by Polynesians around AD 1000 to 1300. It was once quite densely populated – at its peak about a dozen villages were scattered across the island – and divided into warring kingdoms whose *pa* (hilltop fortresses) were closely related to those of the warrior Maori of New Zealand. It is believed that pressures caused by overpopulation were the cause of this perpetual warfare.

The island's first European visitor was George Vancouver, in 1791. Vancouver had already accompanied Cook to the Pacific on his second and third voyages. It was not until 1816 that another European visited Rapa Iti, marking the start of a series of disastrous epidemics. From a crowded 2000 at the first contact, the population had plummeted to 500 by 1838 and a mere 150 people in 1864.

The final blow came when Peruvian slaving ships raided the islands and carried many people off to work on guano islands off the Peruvian coast. The men of Rapa Iti seized one of the ships, sailed it to Tahiti and demanded that the French take action. The Peruvians attempted to return over 300 of the Polynesians they had enslaved, but the vast majority died en route; the handful of

THE AUSTRALS

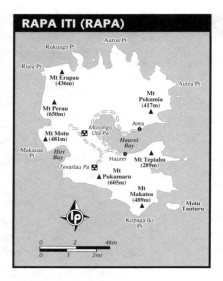

RAPA ITI (RAPA)

Rukuaga Pt
Auroa Pt
Ruea Pt
Mt Erapau
(436m)
Autea Pt
Mt
Pukumia
(417m)
Mt Perau
(650m)
Area
Morongo
Uta Pa
Mt Motu
(481m)
Haurei
Bay
Makauae
Pt
Hiri
Bay
Haurei
Mt Tepiahu
(289m)
Tevaitau Pa
Mt
Pukumaru
(605m)
Mt
Makatea
(489m)
Motu
Tauturu
Kopaga Iki
Pt

0   2   4km
0   1   2mi

survivors who landed on Rapa Iti brought a smallpox epidemic which decimated the rest of the population.

When steamships began to operate across the Pacific, a coaling station was established on Rapa Iti for ships crossing the Pacific Ocean to Australia and New Zealand. In an attempt to combat the English influence in Polynesia, the French annexed Rapa Iti. The waters around the island are rich in fish, and the island possesses an abundant population of goats. Taro is the principal crop but some fine coffee and excellent oranges are also grown.

Archaeological Sites

Morongo Uta, between Haurei and Hiri Bays, is the best preserved of Rapa Iti's ancient *pa*. It was restored by Norwegian archaeologists led by Thor Heyerdahl, and by New Zealand archaeologist and anthropologist William Mulloy in 1956. Heyerdahl wrote about their work on Rapa Iti in his book *Aku-Aku*. The great *pa* has terraces separated by deep moats around the central fortress, which has a perimeter of over 300m and is overlooked by a double-pyramid watchtower. Directly overlooking Haurei is the **Tevaitau Pa**, restored in 1960. Other *pa* can be found along the mountain ridge and at the passes from one valley to another. They typically have flat terraces and a lookout tower.

Places to Stay & Eat

Chez Titaua (*☎ 95 72 59, fax 95 72 60; at the mairie; full board per person 4600 CFP*), near the quay in Haurei, is the only pension.

Getting There & Away

Rapa Iti is more than 1000km southeast of Tahiti and more than 500km beyond Raivavae. The *Tuhaa Pae II* calls at Rapa Iti about once a month.

MAROTIRI

Also known as Bass Rocks, the uninhabited rocky spires of Marotiri rise from the sea about 70km southeast of Rapa Iti. Although even landing on the rocks is difficult, the largest one has a saddle between its two pinnacles – which is defended by a miniature *pa*!

THE AUSTRALS

The Gambier Archipelago

pop 1087 • area 27 sq km

The most remote of the French Polynesian island groups, the Gambier Archipelago lies at the extreme southeastern end of the long arc of the Tuamotus. On a map the islands appear to number among the many Tuamotu atolls, but in fact they are high islands and quite distinct from the neighbouring group. Well to the south, the islands' climate is relatively mild and in winter it can actually get cool. The archipelago is half an hour ahead of Tahiti.

The Gambier consists of high islands and motu within an encircling reef plus Temoe (or Timoe), a separate island to the southeast. Mangareva, which means 'floating mountain' in Polynesian, is the largest of the group; nearly all of the archipelago's population lives on this island. Mangareva was the centre for the obsessive missionary activities of Father Honoré Laval between 1834 and 1871.

History

The islands were populated in three waves from the 10th to the 13th century. There is much speculation that they may have been an important stopping point on the Polynesian migration routes to New Zealand or Easter Island.

The group was named in 1797 by James Wilson, captain of the *Duff*, who brought the pioneering London Missionary Society (LMS) missionaries to Tahiti in that year. He named the archipelago after Gambier, an English admiral who had supported the mission's activities. The islands' highest mountain is named after Wilson's ship. It wasn't until 1826 that FW Beechey, another Englishman, set foot on the islands and made contact with the islanders. The islands soon became an important port for ships replenishing their supplies, and a trade centre for the abundant mother-of-pearl from the lagoon.

The first Catholic mission in French Polynesia, the Sacred Heart Congregation, was established here in 1834 and quickly converted the entire population. Father Honoré Laval, leader of the mission, and his assistant François Caret became virtual rulers of the archipelago. Until persistent complaints about his behaviour led to his exile on Tahiti

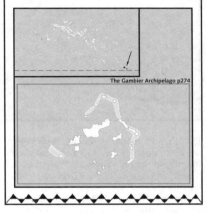

The Gambier Archipelago p274

in 1871, Laval ran the islands like his own personal fiefdom.

Laval transformed the islands, building wide roads, a huge cathedral, nine churches and chapels, monuments, lookout towers, quays and numerous buildings, including a prison. Unfortunately, at the same time, the people of the Gambier Archipelago simply died out. When Laval arrived the population may have been 5000 to 6000, spread across the four main islands, but it quickly went into a free fall. In 1887, when the first official census was conducted, the population was 463 and only recently has it once again passed 1000.

What role Laval played in this disaster is an open question. One view is that European diseases, imported by whalers and trading ships, caused the annihilation of the population, and that Laval was merely an observer. The opposite view is that Laval was a single-minded bigot who wiped out native culture and then worked the islanders to death constructing a collection of absurdly over-ambitious monuments to his beliefs.

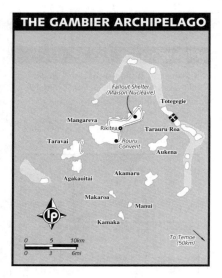

THE GAMBIER ARCHIPELAGO

Fallout Shelter
(Maison Nucléaire)

Totegegie

Mangareva
Rikitea
Tarauru Roa
Taravai
Rouru
Convent
Aukena

Agakauitai
Akamaru

Makaroa
Manui

Kamaka

To Temoe
(50km)

0   5   10km
0   3   6mi

largest of them, is populated. Mangareva is 8km long but only 1.5km across at its narrowest point. The highest points are Mt Duff (441m) and Mt Mokoto (423m). The three other larger islands are Aukena, Akamaru and Taravai. About 50km southeast is the small island of Temoe.

Getting There & Away
The Gambier Archipelago is about 1700km southeast of Tahiti.

Air Tahiti flies to the Gambier Archipelago about once a week. The flight takes about 3½ hours and sometimes goes via Hao; a return flight costs 55,500 CFP. Check with Air Tahiti as this schedule is subject to change.

From Tahiti, the cargo ships *Nuku Hau* and *Taporo V* sail via the eastern Tuamotus to the Gambier Archipelago about every three weeks. See the Getting Around chapter for details.

Getting Around
The airport is on the largest motu, Totegegie, on the northeastern side of the lagoon. Local boats from Mangareva meet every flight; the journey takes 45 minutes.

Pension owners can organise island tours by boat and visits to the major sites. On Mangareva there is a small network of walking tracks.

MANGAREVA
In the dry season the grass-covered hills of Mangareva have a sombre brown appearance, but **Rikitea**, the island's sole village, is a green, pleasant and quiet little place. At the upper part of the town stands the **Cathedral of St Michael**, built between 1839 and 1848, the ultimate symbol of Laval's single-minded obsession. It can accommodate 1200 people – more than the population of the island today! It has twin blue-trimmed towers and is 54m long. The altar is decorated with mother-of-pearl and the woodwork is also inlaid with pearl shell.

Various other Laval constructions can be found in the village, including the coastal watchtowers and the turret, which are all that remain of the 'palace' Laval built for the island's last king. This king, Maputeao, changed his name to Gregoria Stanislas at the instigation of Laval. There is a memorial to him in **St Peter's Cemetery**. The **Rouru Convent** once housed 60 nuns, and it's said

Laval's own memoirs recount with delight the destruction of the idols and symbols belonging to the old religion. Robert Lee Eskridge's *Manga Reva: the Forgotten Islands* tells the story of the missionary period.

Remarkably, Laval and Caret found time, soon after their arrival in the archipelago, to pop over to Tahiti and attempt to carry Catholicism to that bastion of Protestant missionary activity. Their subsequent clash with Queen Pomare IV and English missionaries was used as an excuse for the French takeover of Tahiti. Although France established a protectorate over the Gambier Archipelago in 1844, it continued as a semi-independent entity and was not formally annexed until 1881.

Today Mangareva is more or less self-sufficient, raising livestock and growing fruit, root crops and a little coffee. The Gambier Archipelago is also an important centre for the production of black pearls.

Geography
The wide polygon-shaped lagoon is protected by a 90km coral barrier. There are 25 motu dotted along the northern half of the reef. The southern half of the reef is partly submerged.

Within the lagoon there are 10 volcanic high islands. Apart from a handful of people on other islands, only Mangareva, the

Laval would hide the entire female population of the island in the convent when whaling ships paid a visit. An overgrown path leads up to the convent, passing a hollowed-out rock pool known as the **Queen's Bath** on the way and finally entering the nunnery through a triumphal arch. Only the empty shells of the convent buildings remain.

A much more recent construction stands beside the coast road on the northern side of the island – the **maison nucléaire**. Moruroa lies just 400km northwest of Mangareva and during the period from 1966 to 1974, when above-ground nuclear tests were conducted, the entire population of the island was herded into this ugly metal-walled fallout shelter if winds threatened to blow fallout towards the Gambier. Older island residents remember being squeezed into this windowless tomb for up to three days at a time. It's no wonder *faaore te atomi*, or 'no nuclear testing', is painted on Mangarevan walls.

Places to Stay & Eat

Chez Pierre & Mariette *(☎ 97 82 87; half-/full board per person 7000/8500 CFP)* is just 100m from the quay in Mangareva. The house has three bedrooms, a living room, a bathroom (cold water only) and kitchen.

Chez Bianca & Benoît *(☎/fax 97 83 76; half-/full board per person 6600/9400 CFP)* is 1km from the quay and offers fine views across the bay to Aukena from its hillside location. There are three rooms with shared bathroom (with hot water).

Chez Jojo *(☎/fax 97 82 61; half-/full board per person 6400/8000 CFP)* is by the water, 5km from the quay, and has three rooms with shared bathroom (with hot water).

Tara Etu Kura *(☎ 97 83 25; bungalow 4800 CFP)*, near the football field, has one bungalow for one or two people. Breakfast costs 500 CFP and lunch or dinner 2000 CFP.

There are some modest food shops in the village.

TARAVAI & AUKENA

When the missionaries arrived, Taravai had a population of 2000. Today only a handful of people live on the island, and the 1868 **Church of St Gabriel**, with its conch-shell decoration, is abandoned. There are other buildings in **Agokono**, the island's all-but-empty village.

Aukena also has reminders of the missionary period, including the 1839 **Church of St Raphaël** and the hexagonal **lookout tower**, still used as a landmark, on the south-western tip of the island.

AKAMARU & TEMOE

Akamaru is the island where Laval first landed and his 1841 **Our Lady of Peace Church** still stands on the utterly deserted island. Occasional groups come over from Mangareva to maintain the church or to pick oranges in season.

The remote island of Temoe, 50km southeast of Akamaru, has a **marae** with some Marquesan features, leading to theories that Marquesans may have paused here en route to Easter Island. Temoe was populated until 1838, when the missionaries shifted the inhabitants to Mangareva. Bishop Museum archaeologist Kenneth Emory carried out investigations here and on Mangareva in 1934, and in that same year James Norman Hall, coauthor of *Mutiny on the Bounty*, was shipwrecked on the island.

Language

Tahitian and French are the official languages of French Polynesia, but Tahitian is spoken more than it is written. Although French dominates, many of those working in the tourist industry can speak some English; once you venture to the more remote and less touristy islands where the Tahitian dialects are spoken, it's definitely useful to know some French. The Polynesians have given their French a wonderful island lilt. Fortunately, bad French is readily accepted in French Polynesia – wheel out that old school French and see how you go. For more extensive Tahitian-language tips, pick up a copy of Lonely Planet's *South Pacific phrasebook*.

TAHITIAN

Tahitian (also known as Maohi) belongs to the group of Polynesian languages which includes Samoan, Maori, Hawaiian, Rarotongan and Tongan. There are several dialects of Tahitian, including the Tuamotan or Paumotan dialect of the Tuamotus, the Marquesan dialect of the Marquesas and the Mangarevan dialect of the Gambier Archipelago. It was the spread of Christianity through French Polynesia that helped to make Tahitian, the dialect spoken on Tahiti, the most widespread dialect.

Few Tahitian words have managed to make their way into English or any other languages. The two familiar exceptions are 'tattoo' from the Tahitian *tatau* and 'taboo' from the Tahitian *tabu* (or *tapu*).

An interesting characteristic of Tahitian is the formation of words by agglutination. For 'helicopter', you say *manu tautau na te reva*, literally 'bird suspended in space'; 'television' is *afata teata*, literally 'theatre box', while 'refrigerator' is *afata fa'ato'e-to'eraa ma'a* or 'box for cooling food'. For more information on Tahitian, pick up a copy of Lonely Planet's *South Pacific phrasebook*, which also includes a useful section on Pacific French.

Tahitian grammar is pleasantly uncomplicated. There are no genders, declensions, conjugations or auxiliaries, and plural forms are denoted solely by the article: the definite article (the) is *te* in the singular and *te mau* in the plural. The notions of past, present and future are expressed by using prefixes or suffixes with the verb. A single word in Tahitian can be a verb, adjective or noun, eg, *inu* can mean 'to drink', 'a drink' or 'drinkable', according to the context.

Pronunciation

Tahitian isn't a difficult language for English speakers to pronounce, as most Tahitian sounds are also found in English. Likewise, the Tahitian alphabet, devised in the 19th century, is fairly simple to use.

Vowels

As with all other Polynesian languages, there are five vowels, pronounced much as they are in Italian and Spanish:

a	as in 'father'
e	between the 'e' in 'bet' and the 'ay' in 'bay'
i	as in 'marine'
o	as the 'o' in 'more'
u	as the 'oo' in 'zoo'

Tahitian and most other Pacific languages have a second series of long vowels. The 'shape' of these is the same as their shorter counterparts, but they are held for approximately twice as long. You can get an idea of this concept by comparing the pronunciation of English 'icy' and 'I see' – both are distinguished only by the length of the final vowel.

Long vowels are indicated in this language guide by a macron over the vowel (ā, ē, ī, ō and ū).

Consonants

Consonants are pronounced much as they are in English, with a few modifications.

h	as in 'house' or as the 'sh' in 'shoe' when preceded by i and followed by o, eg, *iho* (only/just)
p	as in 'sponge', not as the 'p' in 'path' (ie, not followed by a puff of breath)
r	often rolled as in Scottish or Spanish
t	as in 'stand', not as the 't' in 'talk' (ie, not followed by a puff of breath)

' glottal stop. This sound occurs between two vowels and is like the sound you hear between the words 'uh-oh'. In Tahitian, this sound isn't indicated in the normal spelling (with a few minor exceptions), since native speakers know where they occur. Foreigners, however, aren't so lucky – the glottal stop is indicated by the apostrophe (') in this language guide.

FRENCH

All French nouns are either masculine or feminine, and adjectives change their form to agree with the noun. In the following list of words and phrases, only the singular version of nouns and adjectives is given.

Basic French vowels are pronounced as they are in Tahitian, but there are a few other rules of pronunciation worth remembering:

ai	as the 'e' in 'pet'. Any following single consonant is usually silent.
eau/ au	as the 'au' in 'caught' but shorter
ll	as 'y', eg, *billet* (ticket), pronounced 'bee-yeh'
ch	always pronounced as 'sh'
qu	as 'k'
r	pronounced from the back of the throat

There is a distinction between **u** (as in *tu*) and **ou** (as in *tout*). For both sounds, the lips are rounded and pushed forward, but for the 'u' sound try to say 'ee' while keeping the lips pursed. The 'ou' sound is pronounced as the 'oo' in 'cook'.

For nasal vowels the breath escapes partly through the nose. They occur where a syllable ends in a single **n** or **m**; the **n** or **m** is silent but indicates the nasalisation of the preceding vowel.

USEFUL WORDS & PHRASES

English

French	Tahitian
Hello/Good morning.	
Bonjour.	*Ia ora na, nana.*
Goodbye.	
Au revoir.	*Pārahi, nana.*
Welcome.	
Bienvenue.	*Maeva, mānava.*

English

French	Tahitian
How are you?	
Ça va?	*E aha te huru?*
My name is ...	
Je m'appelle ...	*To'u i'oa 'o ...*
Thank you.	
Merci.	*Māuruuru roa.*
Pardon?	
Comment?	*E aha?*
Excuse me/Sorry.	
Pardon.	*E'e, aue ho'i e.*
No problem/ Don't worry.	
Pas de problème.	*Aita pe'ape'a.*
Yes.	
Oui.	*E, 'oia.*
No.	
Non.	*Aita.*
Good luck!	
Bon courage!	*Fa'aitoito!*
I don't understand.	
Je ne comprends pas.	*Aita i ta'a ia'u.*
How much?	
Combien?	*E hia moni?*
How many?	
Combien?	*E hia?*
Where is ...?	
Où est ...?	*Tei hea ...?*
When?	
Quand?	*Afea?*
What time is it?	
Quelle heure est-il?	*E aha te hora i teie nei?*
Cheers! (for drinking)	
Santé!	*Manuia!*
I'm ill.	
Je suis malade.	*E ma'i to'u.*

In the following nouns, the French definite article ('the' in English) is included for reference purposes.

address		
l'adresse		*vahi nohoraa*
bank		
la banque		*fare moni*
bathroom		
la salle de bain		*piha pape*
beach		
la plage		*tahatai*
bed		
le lit		*ro'i*

English		
French	**Tahitian**	
beer		
la bière	*pia*	
bicycle		
le vélo	*pereo'o tāta'ahi*	
boat		
le bateau	*poti*	
breakfast		
le petit déjeuner	*tafe poipoi*	
bus		
l'autobus	*pereo'o mata'eina'a*	
car		
la voiture	*pereo'o uira*	
chemist/pharmacy		
la pharmacie	*fare ra'au*	
coffee		
le café	*taofe*	
country		
le pays	*fenua*	
day		
le jour	*ao*	
embassy		
l'ambassade	*fare tonitera rahi*	
film (camera)		
la pellicule	*firimu*	
food		
la nourriture	*ma'a*	
map		
le plan	*hoho'a fenua*	
menu		
la carte	*tāpura mā'a*	
money		
l'argent	*moni*	
now		
maintenant	*i teie nei*	
parents (extended family)		
les parents	*fēti'i*	
plantation		
la plantation	*fa'a'apu*	

English		
French	**Tahitian**	
police station		
la gendarmerie	*fare mūto'i*	
restaurant		
le restaurant	*fare tāmā'ara'a*	
room		
la chambre	*piha*	
shop		
le magasin	*fare toa*	
telephone		
le téléphone	*niuniu paraparau*	
that		
cela	*terā*	
today		
aujourd'hui	*j teie nei mahana*	
tomorrow		
demain	*ānānahi*	
tonight		
ce soir	*i teie pō*	
water		
l'eau	*pape*	

1	*un*	*hō'ē/tahi*
2	*deux*	*piti*
3	*trois*	*toru*
4	*quatre*	*māha*
5	*cinq*	*pae*
6	*six*	*ono*
7	*sept*	*hitu*
8	*huit*	*va'u*
9	*neuf*	*iva*
10	*dix*	*hō'ē 'ahuru*
20	*vingt*	*piti 'ahuru*
100	*cent*	*hō'ē hānere*
500	*cinq cents*	*pae hānere*
1000	*mille*	*hō'ē tauatini*
5000	*cinq mille*	*pae tauatini*
10,000	*dix mille*	*hō'ē 'ahuru tauatini*

one million		
un million	*hō'ē mirioni*	

Glossary

ahi – sandalwood

ahima'a – underground oven used for cooking traditional Polynesian food

ahu – altar in a *marae*; in the marae of French Polynesia the ahu was generally a pyramid shape

aito – flame tree

anuhe – fern

aparima – dance with hand gestures

ari'i – high chief of the ancient Polynesian aristocracy; literally, 'king'

ario'i – priest caste or religious society of the pre-European Society Islands

Assemblée de Polynésie Française – Assembly of French Polynesia

atoll – type of low island created by *coral* rising above sea level as an island gradually sinks; postcard atolls consist of a chain of small islands and reef enclosing a *lagoon*; see also *low island*

atua – god or gods

aute – hibiscus; plant with strongly scented flowers of varying colours, usually orange-yellow

autostop – hitching

barrier reef – *coral* reef forming a barrier between the shoreline and the open sea but separated from the land by a *lagoon*

belvédère – lookout

bonitier – whaleboat; used for fishing and for transferring passengers and cargo from ship to shore on islands that have no wharf or quay

boules – see *pétanque*

BP – boîte postale; post-office box

breadfruit – see *uru*

bringue – local festival or party, generally accompanied by lots of beer

capitainerie – harbour master's office

caldera – volcano crater

CEP – Centre d'Expérimentation du Pacifique; the French nuclear-testing program

CESC – Conseil Économique, Social et Culturel (Economic and Social Committee)

CETAD – Centre d'Études des Techniques Adaptés au Développement; technical and vocational college

CFP – Cour de Franc Pacifique, usually known as 'franc cour pacifique'; currency of French Polynesia

ciguatera – malady caused by eating infected reef-fish

CMAS – Confédération Mondiale des Activités Subaquatiques; scuba-diving qualification; the Francophile equivalent of *PADI*

copra – dried coconut meat, used to make an oil

coral – animal of the coelenterate group which, given the right conditions of water clarity, depth and temperature, grows to form a reef

croque-madame – toasted ham-and-cheese sandwich with a fried egg on top; also known as croque-vahine

croque-monsieur – toasted ham-and-cheese sandwich

cyclone – tropical storm rotating around a low-pressure 'eye'; 'typhoon' in the Pacific, 'hurricane' in the Caribbean

demi-pension – see *half-board*

demi – person of Polynesian-European or Polynesian-Chinese descent

DOM-TOM – Départements et Territoires d'Outre-Mer; French overseas departments and territories

EFO – Établissements Français d'Océanie; official acronym for French Polynesia from 1903 to 1946

emergence – geological activity that pushes land up above sea level

ÉVAAM – Établissement pour la Valorisation des Activités Aquacoles et Maritimes; marine-research organisation

faapu – small cultivated field

fafa piti – ray

fara – pandanus; tree with strong leaves that are dried to make traditional roofing, wickerwork and woven articles

fare – traditional Polynesian house; hotel bungalow

fare atua – house for the gods on *marae*; actually a small chest in the form of a statue

fare potee – chief's house or community meeting place; open dining-room of a restaurant or hotel

fare tamoa – dining house

fare tupapau – shelter where dead bodies were laid out to decompose in pre-European Polynesia

fei – a type of banana
fenua – country or region of origin
feo – coral outcrop
fetii – extended family
fetue – pencil urchin
flamboyant – majestic, umbrella-shaped plant with vivid crimson flowers
fringing reef – *coral* reef immediately alongside the shoreline, not separated from the shore by a lagoon as with a *barrier reef*
full board – bed and all meals (French: *pension complète*); see also *half-board*

gaufres – waffles
gendarmerie – police station
goélette – cargo ship or schooner

ha'e – traditional Marquesan house
hakaiki – chief
half-board – bed, breakfast and lunch or dinner (French: *demi-pension*); see also *full board*
heiva – celebration or festival; the Heiva is a huge festival of Polynesian culture (mainly dance) that takes place on Tahiti in July
high island – island created by volcanic action or geological upheaval; see also *low island*
himene – Tahitian-language hymn
Hiro – god of thieves who features in many Polynesian legends
hoa – shallow channel across the outer reef of an atoll, normally carrying water into or out of the central lagoon only at unusually high tides or when large swells are running; see also *pass*
honu – turtle
huaka – clan
hupe – pleasant morning breeze

kaina – Polynesian; Polynesian person; local; see also *popaa*
kaikai enana – Marquesan food; see also *maa*
kava – traditional mildly intoxicating drink made from the root of *Piper methysticum* (the pepper plant)
kaveka – sooty tern
kaveu – coconut crab
keetu – characteristic red volcanic stone of the Marquesas
keshi – Japanese term for pearl formed from pure *nacre* (mother-of-pearl), when the *nucleus* has been expelled from the oyster

lagoon – calm waters enclosed by a reef; may be an enclosed area encircled by a *barrier reef* (eg, Rangiroa and Tetiaroa) with or without *motu*, or may surround a *high island* (eg Bora Bora and Tahiti)
lagoon side – on the lagoon side of the coast road (not necessarily right by the lagoon); see also *mountain side*
LDS – Mormon; follower of the Church of Jesus Christ of the Latter-Day Saints
leeward – downwind; sheltered from the prevailing winds; see also *windward*
le truck – public 'bus'; a truck with bench seats that operates a bus-like service
LMS – London Missionary Society; pioneering Protestant missionary organisation in Polynesia
low island – island created by the growth and erosion of *coral* or by the complete erosion of a *high island*; see also *atoll*

maa – food
maa tahiti – Tahitian or Polynesian food; Tahitian buffet
maa tinito – Chinese food
mabe – hollow cultured pearl
mahi mahi – dorado; one of the most popular eating fish in French Polynesia
mahu – transvestite or female impersonator; see also *rae rae*
mairie – town hall
maitai – local cocktail made with rum, pineapple, grenadine and lime juices, coconut liqueur and, sometimes, Grand Marnier or Cointreau
maito – surgeonfish
makatea – *coral* island that has been thrust above sea level by a geological disturbance (eg, Rurutu, and Makatea in the Tuamotus)
mana – spiritual or supernatural power
manahune – peasant class or common people of pre-European Polynesia
ma'o – shark (French: *requin*)
Maohi – Polynesian
manu – bird
mape – Polynesian 'chestnut' tree
maraamu – southeast trade wind that blows from June to August
marae – traditional Polynesian sacred site generally constructed with an *ahu* at one end; see also *me'ae*
marae tupuna – ancestor or family *marae*
maro ura – feather belt worn by a chief as a symbol of his dynasty

me'ae – Marquesan word for *marae*
meia – banana
meie – common people
Melanesia – islands of the western Pacific; Papua New Guinea, the Solomons, Vanuatu, New Caledonia and Fiji
Micronesia – islands of the northwest Pacific including the Mariana, Caroline and Marshall groups, Kiribati and Nauru
miro – *Thespesia populnea*; rosewood
monoi – coconut oil perfumed with the *tiare* flower and/or other substances
motoi – ylang-ylang; plant with strongly scented flowers
motu – small islet in a lagoon, either along the outer reef of an *atoll* or on a reef around a *high island*
mountain side – on the mountain side of the coast road (not neccessarily up in the mountains); see also *lagoon side*
mupe – skirt made from natural fibres and used in traditional dances

nacre – mother-of-pearl; iridescent substance secreted by pearl oysters to form the inner layer of the shell; shell of a pearl oyster
navette – shuttle boat
niau – sheets of plaited coconut-palm leaves, used for roof thatching
noni – yellowish fruit with therapeutic properties, grown in the Marquesas and popular in the USA; also known as nono
nono – very annoying biting gnat found on some beaches and particularly prevalent in the Marquesas
nucleus – small sphere, made from shells found in the Mississippi River in the USA, which is introduced into the gonads of the pearl oyster to produce a cultured pearl

ono – barracuda
ora – banyan; sacred tree often seen near religious buildings
'orero – orator
'Oro – god of war; the cult that was superseding the Ta'aroa cult when the first Europeans arrived

pa – hilltop fortress
PADI – Professional Association of Dive Instructors; the most popular international scuba-diving qualification
pae pae – paved floor of a pre-European house; traditional meeting platform

pahu – drum
pahua – giant clam
pamplemousse – grapefruit
pandanus – palm tree with aerial roots; the leaves are used for weaving hats, mats and bags
pareu – traditional sarong-like garment
pass – channel allowing passage into the lagoon through the outer reef of an atoll or the barrier reef around a high island; see also *hoa*
pastèque – watermelon
Paumoto – the Tuamotus; people from the Tuamotus
pension – guesthouse
pension complète – see *full board*
pétanque – French game in which metal balls are thrown to land as near as possible to a target ball; also known as *boules*
petroglyph – carving on a stone or rock
peue – mat; braided palm used for basketwork
phonolite – type of volcanic rock
pirogue – outrigger canoe (Tahitian: *va'a*)
pitate – jasmine
PK – pointe kilométrique; distance markers found along the roads of some French Polynesian islands
plat du jour – daily special; literally 'plate of the day'
poe – pieces of crushed banana or papaya mixed with starch, wrapped in a banana leaf, baked with a vanilla bean and sprinkled with coconut milk
poisson cru popular raw-fish dish
Polynesia – islands of the central and southeastern Pacific, including French Polynesia, Samoa, Tonga, New Zealand and the Cook Islands
popaa – European or Westerner; see also *kaina*
poti marara – motorboat; used for fishing in the *lagoon*
pu – conch shell
purau – hibiscus

ra'atira – middle rank of pre-European Polynesian society, above the lower class but below the *arii*
rae rae – *mahu*; sometimes applied to mahu who are transexual or homosexual, rather than just cross-dressers
RDPT – Rassemblement Démocratique des Populations Tahitiennes (Democratic Assembly of Tahitian Populations)

requin – shark (Tahitian: *ma'o*)
roi – groper
roulotte – mobile diner; a food van operating as a snack bar

Sanito – branch of the Mormon religion
scaphandre – weighted dive helmet
seamount – underwater volcano that rises more than 1000m above the ocean floor but does not break the surface
seaward – side of an *atoll*, island or *motu* that faces the sea rather than the *lagoon*
sennit – string or material woven from coconut-husk fibre
snack – snack bar

tahua – faith healer
tamaaraa – family meal
Ta'aroa – supreme Polynesian god whose cult was being superseded by worship of 'Oro, god of war, at the time of the European arrival
tabu – alternative spelling of *tapu*
tahua – priest of the ancient Polynesian religion
tamaaraa – traditional-style feast
tamure – hip-jiggling version of traditional Polynesian dance
tane – man
tapa – cloth made from beaten bark and decorated with traditional designs; worn by the people of pre-European Polynesia
tapu – sacred or forbidden; the English word 'taboo' comes from *tapu* or *tabu*
taro – root vegetable; a Polynesian staple food
tatau – tattoo; although tattoos were also known in Japan, it was on Tahiti that European sailors first discovered them and added the word to European vocabularies
tavana – mayor
taxe de séjour – accommodation tax
tiare – fragrant white gardenia endemic to the Pacific; the flower has become symbolic of Tahiti
tifaifai – colourful appliquéd or patchwork material used as blankets, bedspreads or cushion covers
ti'i – Society Islands term for the Marquesan word *tiki*

tiki – human-like sacred sculpture usually made of wood or stone and sometimes standing more than 2m high; once found on many *marae*
Tinito – Chinese
tipanie – frangipani; a plant with strongly scented flowers used to make crowns and flower lei (wreaths)
tiputa – *tapa* poncho; traditional attire in pre-European Polynesia
toa – chief warrior
toerau – north-northeast wind
tohua – meeting place or a place for festival gathering in pre-European Polynesia but especially in the Marquesas
tou – Cordia subcordata; tree, common in the Marquesas, that produces a dark, hard, grained wood popular with carvers
tuff – volcanic rock of Polynesia
tupa – land crab
tupapau – irritating spirit ghosts of the ancient Polynesian religion, still much feared

TVA – taxe sur la valeur ajoutée; a tax added to accommodation rates
tuu – ceremonial activities centre in the Marquesas

uaau – red-footed boobie
ua ma – Marquesan food pit
ume – unicornfish
umete – traditional Tahitian wooden dish or bowl
umu hei – Marquesan *monoi*; packet of fragrant natural vegetable essences
uru – breadfruit; starchy staple food of Polynesia that grows on a tree as a football-sized fruit (French: arbre à pain)
uruti – scad, a type of fish

va'a –outrigger canoe (French: *pirogue*)
vahine – woman
vana – sea urchin
vanira – vanilla
varua ino – malevolent spirit
vivo – nasal flute
VTT – vélo à tout terrain; mountain bike

windward – facing prevailing winds; see also *leeward*

Index

Text

Bold indicates maps.